D1560057

FIFTY YEARS OF JUSTICE

UNIVERSITY PRESS OF FLORIDA

Florida A&M University, Tallahassee
Florida Atlantic University, Boca Raton
Florida Gulf Coast University, Ft. Myers
Florida International University, Miami
Florida State University, Tallahassee
New College of Florida, Sarasota
University of Central Florida, Orlando
University of Florida, Gainesville
University of North Florida, Jacksonville
University of South Florida, Tampa
University of West Florida, Pensacola

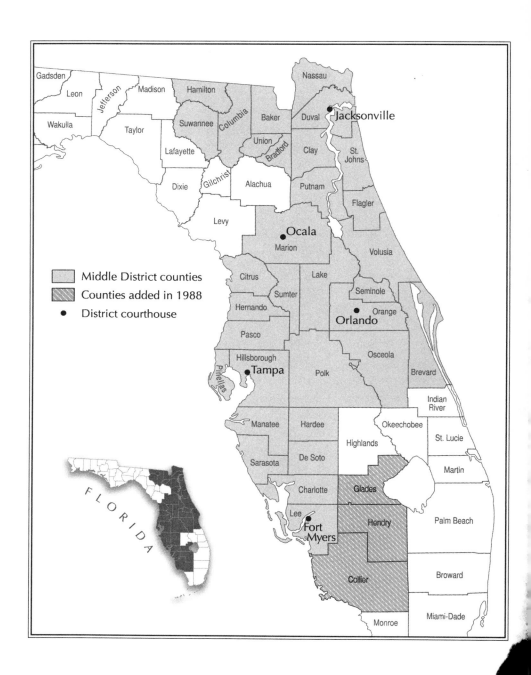

FIFTY YEARS
OF JUSTICE

A History of the U.S. District Court for
the Middle District of Florida

JAMES M. DENHAM

University Press of Florida
Gainesville · Tallahassee · Tampa · Boca Raton
Pensacola · Orlando · Miami · Jacksonville · Ft. Myers · Sarasota

A Florida Quincentennial Book

Copyright 2015 by The Historical Society of United States District Court for the Middle District of Florida, Inc.

This book may be available in an electronic edition.

20 19 18 17 16 15   6 5 4 3 2 1

Library of Congress Cataloging-in-Publication Data
Denham, James M., author.
Fifty years of justice : a history of the U.S. District Court for the Middle District of Florida / James M. Denham.
pages cm
Includes bibliographical references and index.
ISBN 978-0-8130-6049-1
1. United States. District Court (Florida : Middle District)—History. 2. Justice, Administration of—Florida—History. 3. District courts—Florida—History. I. Title.
KF8755.F56D46 2015
347.73'22097592—dc23
2014043924

University Press of Florida
15 Northwest 15th Street
Gainesville, FL 32611-2079
http://www.upf.com

Contents

Acknowledgments

I want to thank many people who assisted me in the writing of this book. First, I want to thank judges George C. Young and William Terrell Hodges for their support of this project and for sharing their time and memories with me. I also want to thank the History, Education, and Public Outreach Sub-Committee of the Middle District of Florida Historical Committee, whose membership is composed of judges and practicing attorneys. The publication of a history of the district is only one of the many initiatives that the committee has undertaken since its inception. The committee organized the Historical Society of the United States District Court for the Middle District of Florida, which has the mission to enhance historical awareness, to engage in community outreach, and to facilitate a greater understanding of the courts and the constitutional and judicial processes within which the federal courts operate. The society is currently engaged in teacher education programs, community outreach, and the construction of historical exhibits in Orlando, Tampa, Jacksonville, Fort Myers, and Ocala courthouses.

I want to thank U.S. Bankruptcy Judge Karen S. Jennemann and U.S. District Judge Harvey E. Schlesinger, cochairs of the History, Education and Public Outreach Sub-Committee when this project was first undertaken, as well as their successors, U.S. Bankruptcy Judge Catherine Peek McEwen and U.S. Magistrate Judge Anthony Porcelli. I also want to thank Chief Judge Anne Conway and the many other judges, attorneys, and staff who served on the history committee: U.S. District Judges Susan C. Bucklew, John Antoon, Howell Melton, Virginia M. Hernandez Covington, Marcia Morales Howard, William J. Castagna, William Terrell Hodges; and U.S. Magistrate Judges Elizabeth Jenkins and Douglas Frazier. Working closely with me and with the history committee were skilled federal practitioners, Michael V. Elsberry and Richard S. Dellinger, who frequently advised me on any number of issues.

I want to thank the dedicated and kind staff who assisted me in my research at courthouses in Orlando, Jacksonville, and Tampa. In Orlando, Judge Karen Jennemann and her secretary, Cindy Courtney, were always eager to assist me, cheerfully answering questions, kindly providing me work space, and opening doors that by necessity are closely guarded. Sheryl L. Loesch, clerk of the U.S. Middle District of Florida, and her staff were extremely helpful. Her staff assisted my research visits to courthouses. In Orlando, Elizabeth Warren was always available to assist me in various ways. In Tampa, Alycia H. Marshall arranged my interviews with U.S. District Judges James S. Moody Jr., Steven Douglas Merryday, William J. Castagna, Susan C. Bucklew, and Elizabeth Kovachevich, and with U.S. Magistrate Judges Elizabeth Jenkins, Thomas Wilson, and Mark Pizzo. During an active week in Jacksonville in summer 2010, U.S. District Judge Harvey E. Schlesinger cordially hosted me. Sandy Wallen in the clerk's office set up interviews with Eleventh Circuit Court of Appeals Judges Gerald Bard Tjoflat and Susan Black, U.S. District Judges Howell W. Melton and Henry Lee Adams, U.S. Magistrate Judge James Klindt, and Bankruptcy Judge Jerry Funk.

I also want to thank other judges and lawyers who offered important information and insights on any number of subjects relevant to this book: Judges E. J. Salcines, Susan Roberts, and Mary Catherine Green; lawyers Dan Warren, Don M. Stichter, Arnold D. Levine, Richard A. Hirsch, Robert H. Mackenzie, Walter Manley, Kent Lilly, Steven Senn, William Ellsworth, Don Wilson, Terrance Smiljanich, Robert J. Trogolo, Dorothy Trogolo, Howardine Garrett, Austin Maslanik, David Henderson, Robert Norgard, Andrea Norgard, Peter Mayer, Charles Mayer, Charles Carlton, Geraldyne Carlton, Michael Wood, Richard Nail, Dale Jacobs, Robert Puterbaugh, Mac Midyette, Sam Crosby, John DeVault, Buddy Schulz, Leonard Gilbert, William J. Sheppard, J. Tom Smoot, Kristina Szurkus, Andy Combs, and Joe Tessitore.

I want to thank professional archivists at numerous research facilities that assisted me, including Jim McSweeney, Robert G. Richards, and Guy Hall at the National Archives Records Center in Morrow, Georgia. I also want to thank Bruce Ragsdale and his staff at the history section of the Federal Judicial Center in Washington D.C., especially Jake Kobrick, Matt Sarago, and Deena Smith. Also I want to thank Jim Cusick, Carl Van Ness, and Florence Turcotte at the P. K. Yonge Library of Florida History at the University of Florida. Thanks also go to Paul Ortiz and his staff at the Samuel Proctor Oral History Center for making numerous oral histories available to me before they were completely processed. I also want to thank Middle District archivist Katie Marra, who saved me many trips to Orlando by cheerfully forwarding illustrations and other materials to me in the final stages of this project.

Writing is a lonely, solitary affair, yet every writer owes a debt of gratitude to friends and colleagues who read and offer comment on drafts. I want to thank the learned panel of lawyers who read and commented on this work, thus assisting this nonlawyer greatly: Hon. James S. Moody Jr., Phillip Buhler, Richard Dellinger, Tom Elligett, Michael V. Elsberry, George B. Howell III, Marilyn Moran, and Thomas Michael Woods. Martin Dyckman and Canter Brown also read the entire manuscript and offered many helpful suggestions. They are in no way responsible for any of the mistakes in this book.

Two of my main concerns when I undertook this project were whether I would be granted access to judges and, more important, that I would be writing about judges and other court personnel who were still alive. The first concern was easily swept away within the first few months after I began the work. The second concern, I must confess, is still with me. I can only hope that the accounts and incidents that occur in these pages are not only accurate but fair. That was my goal throughout. But, of course, that is for others to judge.

Introduction

This book aims to tell the history of the U.S. Middle District Court of Florida, which stretches from the Georgia border, down the peninsula to the Gulf Coast. Created in 1962, the district includes thirty-five of Florida's sixty-seven counties and incorporates the huge population centers of Jacksonville, Orlando, Tampa, and Fort Myers. It contains roughly half of Florida's population of nearly 19 million. The Middle District is one of the busiest in the nation. Throughout its fifty-year history the district has been the scene of many important cases and legal developments in judicial history. Cases involving organized crime, civil rights, desegregation, redistricting, the First Amendment, employment discrimination, voters rights, kidnapping, the environment, death penalty, abortion rights, the right to die, terrorism, arms trafficking, espionage, and a whole host of other types of cases have been litigated in its courtrooms.

Middle District courtrooms were the stage for numerous scenes of drama: In 1963 in Jacksonville Judge Bryan Simpson considered Martin Luther King Jr.'s, Andrew Young's and the NAACP's right to march in St. Augustine and subsequently ordered Gov. C. Farris Bryant into his courtroom to show cause why he shouldn't be held in contempt. In 1970 in Tampa Judge Ben Krentzman ordered Gov. Claude Kirk Jr. fined $10,000 for every day he failed to comply with a court order mandating the desegregation of the Manatee County Public Schools. Less dramatic, but perhaps more important, the Middle District served as the place where individual counties trod their long, often tedious path toward desegregation. From its inception in 1962 Middle District judges adjudicated the individual facts, circumstances, and conditions of each county within the context of circuit court and Supreme Court decisions. Prominent civil rights lawyers such as Thurgood Marshall, Constance Baker Motley, William Kunstler, Drew S. Days, Tobias Simon, and William Sheppard practiced their craft in Middle District courtrooms.

In the early 1970s Middle District judges presided over cases involving corruption allegations of a U.S. senator, and in 1973 the court was one of the first to arraign an operative in the unfolding Watergate saga. In the 1980s Florida became ground zero for the nation's war on drugs. Some of the first successful drug prosecutions came through the Middle District of Florida. Carlos Lehder was only the most notorious of these. Mobsters like Santo Trafficante and Harlan Blackburn were prosecuted in Middle Florida courtrooms, as were members of the gang known as the "Goodfellas." Even before the Supreme Court voided over six hundred death sentence convictions in its landmark case *Furman v. Georgia* (1972), one Middle District judge in 1967 had issued a moratorium on Florida executions on many of the same grounds—a ruling thought to be the first of its kind in the United States. After the restoration of the death penalty as a result of a 1982 case originating in its own courts, the district would eventually become one of the nation's leaders in handling postconviction *habeas corpus* petitions of death row inmates. Not all important activities took place in courtrooms. In the 1980s, for example, during a quiet lunch, an overly zealous, newly appointed U.S. attorney, who acquired the nickname "Mad Dog," audaciously tried to extract a promise from two district judges to sentence convicted defendants to maximums allowed by law.

The Middle District of Florida was also the scene of some of the nation's first successful racketeer and fraud prosecutions: Glenn Turner, the McCorkles, and the Bank of Credit & Commerce International prosecutions are cases in point. Finally, names and subjects as diverse as Manuel Noriega, Denny McLain, Wesley Snipes, Ted Bundy, Terri Schiavo, Sami Al-Arian, hanging chads, and Baby Sabrina immediately bring to mind important if not sensational incidents in the Middle District's, as well as America's, recent history.

The Middle District has also been the scene of some of the most important commercial litigation in the United States. From the rising commercial centers of Jacksonville, Tampa, Orlando, and Fort Myers, many complicated disputes emerged. The district's courts also adjudicated numerous disputes arising from army and naval bases in Jacksonville, Orlando, and Tampa, as well as the Kennedy Space Center at Cape Canaveral. Economists have noted that Florida is often at the extreme ends of boom and bust cycles of the U.S. economy. The district's bankruptcy docket became one of the most crowded in the nation, and its bankruptcy bench is recognized as one of the most distinguished in the nation. One of its judges, the late Alexander Paskay, it can be argued, did more to shape the laws and practice of bankruptcy than any other individual in the United States. But Judge Paskay was as dedicated to upholding his duties as a judge as he was to writing, lecturing, and teaching on the subject. In one instance, during a particularly critical time, Judge Paskay held court in his hospital room, signing documents and delivering last-minute instructions to law clerks ten minutes before he was wheeled into surgery.

Thus, over its fifty years Middle District judges have made many important decisions that shaped the law and affected thousands of lives in fundamental ways. Any number of these important cases could provide interesting popular or academic studies in the future. Perhaps this book may contribute to that effort.

For those who spend any time with members of the federal court establishment, the phrase "court family" is often heard. Members of the family are not only judges; they are the clerks, and numerous agents, staff, attorneys, and other officers who are essential for the courts to function properly. Middle District Judge Elizabeth Kovachevich often uses the word "teamwork" and is quick to acknowledge how critical staff is to the operation of judicial business. On one occasion she notes of her law clerks, office manager, court reporters, judicial assistants, and bailiff, "I couldn't be doing this job without their dedication. There was no such thing as the hours of the day, seven days a week. . . . You can't get the job done without the team."[1] Judge Kovachevich's comments on the importance of teamwork ring true for nearly every division, bureau, or department within the Middle District of Florida.

I am not a lawyer but a historian of Florida and southern history whose previous work has touched upon such subjects as crime and punishment, the courts, and law enforcement. This book, while certainly informative to legal scholars, is not intended as an academic legal treatise.

This book will address in narrative fashion these dramatic personages and will also shed light on lesser known but equally important subjects and individuals. The lives, times, and work of the district judges, magistrates, and bankruptcy judges are included in these pages. So are prosecutors, marshals, attorneys, and the many other dedicated professionals who made the Middle District of Florida function from its inception in 1962 to the present. Their collective story is the subject of this book.

Perhaps an obvious question is why is a study of one individual U.S. district court pertinent? What can be gained from pursuing such a study? One answer is that such a study can offer us a window into the political, social, economic, and legal history of a district over time. It can tell us how federal governmental disputes were adjudicated. But more than that, as legal scholar Kevin Lyles tells us, U.S. District Courts are unique in the federal judiciary apparatus. They are the "key determinants in deciding 'who gets what, when and how' from federal judicial policymaking." Lyles called district courts the

> workhorses of the federal judiciary. . . . They are the only courts in the federal system where the litigants meet in open combat, where witnesses are heard, where the "facts are determined," and where juries are used. District courts not only interpret and apply Supreme Court decisions to the large numbers of cases that the Supreme Court cannot possibly address, but also implement the decisions made by the higher Court. In addition, given the broad formulations and resulting ambiguity that characterize most higher court rulings, especially those of the Supreme Court, the more numerous district court judges are given considerable leeway and opportunity to interpret and apply higher court decisions to many cases, most of which are disposed of in these lower courts.[2]

Thus the power of the judges and the federal courts are enormous. According to one authority, "cases they hear involve the violation of federal laws, suits in which the U.S. is a party, or issues where there is a federal constitutional question. . . . In many ways a district judge, as a trial judge, is more powerful than the appellate courts above him—the Circuit Courts of Appeals and the Supreme Court. With few exceptions, the higher courts can only pass on questions that a district judge has already ruled on; and the overwhelming majority of District Court decisions are not appealed." Moreover, district judges "through their rulings . . . establish policy on a vast range of legal and social issues. They operate in a zone of tension between traditional legal standards and changing public values," especially when a "vital question finds its way to a federal court."[3]

Anyone who steps into a federal courtroom immediately notices a difference. "There's a cleanness about it," according to one commentator, "a sense of fairness. . . . There's an atmosphere of trust and dignity." As one person who frequently visited the federal court in Jacksonville during the 1960s noted, "you immediately realize that you are in the presence of the majestic dignity of the United States, whether it is to witness the naturalization of new Americans or observe a contest between a defendant at the bar and the law enforcement arm of the government."[4] U.S. District Judge Howell W. Melton, after more than two generations on both the state and federal benches, has observed that lawyers treat one another more civilly and generally behave better in federal court than in state court.

> I find that in the federal court, I don't know the reason why, but having been a state judge and a federal judge, I find that the attorneys are much more civil to each other in the federal court than they were in state court. For some reason, the attorneys have always been more impressed with being in federal court than in state court. For what reason, I don't know, but there has been that feeling. I think there has been a little more feeling of awe to be in federal court than in state court; although there shouldn't because we have a fine state court system.[5]

While U.S. district judges of the Middle District of Florida have been appointed by every president since John Kennedy, the district enjoys a particularly good reputation for the impartiality of its judges. As U.S. District Judge Richard Lazzara explained,

> I always find it interesting when people are talking about a particular case and the judge hearing the case, and they always say, well, this judge was a Bush appointee or a Clinton appointee or an Obama appointee, etcetera. . . . As if to say, that tells you how this judge is going to decide the case. . . . I'm always puzzled by that. . . . The facts are the facts and the law is the law, and that's the way you're going to have to decide it. I don't care whether you're an Independent, whether you belong to the Tea Party, whether you're conservative, liberal, Republican, Democrat, I don't care who you are. Once you put on that robe, the facts are the facts, the law is the law; and that's how you decide it, whether you like the law or not. . . . . The judges on this court were appointed by presidents who range the political spectrum, if you will, from conservative, to middle-of-the-road, to liberal. But I don't see any difference in our judicial philosophy. . . . I don't know of any judge who's decided a case based on by whom they were appointed, by whether they were appointed by a Republican or Democrat.[6]

I have consulted many of the original cases that are contained within these pages. Original Middle District case files are housed in the National Archives Record Center and comprise nearly five thousand cubic feet. It would take a lifetime to examine each individual case. All of the important cases originating in the Middle District of Florida are available online on Westlaw, LexisNexis, and other databases. The major sources used are oral histories, public documents, numerous secondary sources, and particularly newspapers. Fortunately, for the years of this study, Florida's major newspapers assigned skilled reporters to cover the federal courts' inner workings as well as important cases. And also fortunately, much of this fine reporting is available in online newspaper databases. I am indebted to many reporters who systematically covered cases and issues concerning the courts; where available, their bylines are included in the notes.

1

From the Southern to the U.S. Middle District
of Florida, 1950s–1962

The U.S. Middle District of Florida, created in 1962, was carved out of the Southern District of Florida, a huge district that spanned the entire peninsula from the Georgia border to the Florida Keys. The new Middle District resembled a crossways slash of territory running from the Georgia border east of the Suwannee River and then south along the Gulf of Mexico. On the Atlantic coast the district took in all the counties as far south as Brevard County and then the boundary swung west, along the southern limits of Brevard, Osceola, and Polk counties, then south down the peninsula taking in Hardee, DeSoto, Charlotte, and Lee counties. The new Southern District continued down the Atlantic coast through the high-density population centers of the Gold Coast to the Keys. It also included Glades, Hendry, and Collier counties west of Lake Okeechobee. The new Middle District contained thirty-three counties, and the new Southern District contained thirteen.[1]

At the time of the Middle District's creation, Florida's federal courts had functioned for more than one hundred years. During Florida's territorial days (1821–45) its superior courts enjoyed federal jurisdiction and also handled matters that traditionally fell under the perusal of state courts. Superior court judges held presidential appointments and rode circuit within the Western, Middle, Eastern, Southern, and the Apalachicola judicial districts. In 1845, when Florida became a state, Congress created only one federal district, but two years later a Southern and a Northern Judicial District were created, embracing the more populous part of the new state above Charlotte Harbor and Lake Okeechobee. The Southern District of Florida handled principally admiralty and salvage claims arising from the substantial maritime and wrecking activity at Key West.[2]

Florida's growth and demographic changes in the late nineteenth century necessitated alteration of boundaries between the Northern and the Southern districts. In 1879 Congress pushed the Southern District's boundary north, bringing Hernando, Hillsborough, and Polk counties within its limits. Then, in 1894, Congress transferred most of the counties east of the Suwannee River from the Northern to the Southern District of Florida.[3] Throughout the nineteenth century, federal courts heard cases in Pensacola, Tallahassee, Apalachicola, Jacksonville, and Tampa. Tampa first heard federal cases in 1879. After 1905 trials were held in Tampa's large four-story federal building. Court sessions also were heard for the first time in Ocala (1900), Fernandina (1905), and Miami (1906). By 1931 Miami had a huge federal building that housed the court, post office, and other federal agencies. Jacksonville followed with its own new courthouse in 1933. Also that year the first federal court was held in Orlando, and by 1941 the town had a new federal building to accommodate trials. A session of federal court was added in Fort Pierce in 1935. By that time Congress authorized three judgeships for the Southern District of Florida. In 1954 a fourth was authorized. In 1949 Congress created a "roving judge" position, and that official held court in selected locations in both the Northern and the Southern districts as needs arose. In 1952 sessions of the federal court in the Southern District were established in West Palm Beach and Fort Myers.[4]

In the nineteenth century, and for much of the twentieth, the jurisdiction of the federal courts was limited to matters in which the federal government was a party, such as land claims and maritime commerce. Federal courts also heard cases in violation of federal laws such as piracy, mail robbery, smuggling, and counterfeiting.[5] The criminal jurisdiction of the federal courts expanded over time, especially as developments in communication and transportation facilitated criminal activity across state lines. By the 1920s federal courts were hearing cases involving the illegal manufacture and sale of alcohol and income tax evasion. In 1932 Congress created the Federal Bureau of Investigation to combat bank robbery, kidnapping, and interstate racketeering, and these cases found their way into federal courts. Similarly, by the 1950s increased public awareness of organized crime and espionage during the Cold War necessitated a more robust federal response to the growing complexity of law breaking, and these matters contributed to growing jurisdiction of the federal courts.[6]

The Middle District of Florida was the first federal district created by Congress since 1928, and Florida's burgeoning population growth had caused the move. As early as 1953 a federal grand jury for the Southern

District of Florida had called for a new district to ease the overwhelming caseload.[7] By 1960 the Southern District's caseload had reached crisis levels. As one source noted, during 1959 the district had the largest number of criminal cases filed per judge of all the federal districts in the nation. Only the Southern District of New York exceeded the Southern District of Florida in the number of civil cases filed per judgeship. The district had only five judges who heard an average of 526 cases each, whereas the national average was 219 cases per judge at that time.[8]

The population in the Southern District grew faster than any other district in the country. With slightly less than three million inhabitants in 1950 to nearly five million in 1960, Florida could claim the fastest population growth rate of any state. Most of the growth was centered in Dade, Broward, Hillsborough, Pinellas, Orange, and Duval counties. Miami jumped to honors as the state's largest city by 1950, with a quarter million inhabitants. By mid-decade that figure had tripled. Formerly small communities emerged as thriving cities, among them Fort Lauderdale, Miami Beach, Orlando, West Palm Beach, St. Petersburg, and Daytona Beach.

Florida's rapid growth during the Eisenhower years (1952–60) stemmed from many causes. Many World War II veterans had received training in the Sunshine State and returned to enjoy the Florida lifestyle that they had experienced. Others used the GI Bill to pursue educational opportunities at the rapidly expanding University of Florida and the newly transformed Florida State University (formerly Florida State College for Women), and Florida A&M, still the only state school alternative for blacks. Enrollments at the University of Miami, Rollins College, Florida Southern College, Stetson University, University of Tampa, and Bethune-Cookman College also grew. Federal Housing Administration loans spurred housing developments and infused millions of dollars into the Florida economy. Mosquito control and air-conditioning made Florida's torrid heat livable for newcomers and retirees seeking respite from snow and icy winters in the north. Tourism also boosted Florida's economy, and large industries like insurance and military contractors such as Martin Marietta in Orlando were drawn to the Sunshine State. In 1959 Cuba's revolution sent thousands of refugees to Florida. The tide continued in spurts throughout the 1960s. The influx of Cubans into Florida was closely related to the Cold War, and the Eisenhower years saw Florida's U.S. Army, Navy, and Air Force bases in Jacksonville, Tampa, and Orlando expand. Military expenditures and payrolls that came with it boosted Florida's economy. Criminal and civil matters occurring on these federal military bases would be adjudicated in the federal courts.

Florida's growth also was spurred by the Space Race. In 1958 at Cape Canaveral, one year following the successful launching of the Soviet rocket *Sputnik*, America's first earth satellite, *Explorer I*, was launched. Within three years, answering President John F. Kennedy's call for sending a man to the moon, Congress authorized the massive expansion of the Cape Canaveral site. Nearly 140,000 additional acres were eventually acquired from property owners for the federal site. The acquisition of land from private property owners in the area for the new space center proved a windfall for some property owners. Yet numerous disputes arose regarding the value of the land, and these disputes would be settled in federal court.

Most trials in the Southern District of Florida took place in Jacksonville, Tampa, and Miami, but there was also some federal activity in Fort Myers and Orlando. Most of the actions in the latter two locations involved work completed by U.S. commissioners (the precursor of modern-day U.S. magistrate judges) who performed essential duties in the federal courts. According to former magistrate judge Paul Game, who was appointed in Tampa in 1962, U.S. commissioners could issue warrants, set bail, hold probable cause hearings, and perform important tasks. They usually held part-time positions and had no salary, but they were paid on a fee basis.[9]

Morison Buck, who preceded Game as commissioner, remembered that he often took his portable typewriter to the "old Tampa Courthouse for duty matters. On the third floor, a small room was used for criminal first appearances. He did all the paperwork himself, and swore the defendant, who either sat in a chair or stood before him."[10] The job was part-time and supplemented income from his limited law practice. Buck recalled that he never earned more than $3,000 per year for his duties.

George T. Swartz graduated from Washington University School of Law in 1958 and moved to Fort Myers shortly thereafter. After taking a job with the firm of Allen and Knudsen, Swartz became a part-time U.S. commissioner. Swartz described his duties in those early years as "more of an administrative type position. It was not actually considered a judicial position. . . . All you did as a commissioner was handle bonds and initial hearings." But because of Fort Myers's isolated position, he often handled various other matters as needs arose. "If somebody was arrested by any type of federal agency and it was in our area," he recalled, "they would bring it to me."[11]

In the years immediately preceding the Middle District's creation, judges

William Barker, George Whitehurst, Bryan Simpson, and Joseph P. Lieb held appointments to the Southern District of Florida. Barker was born on June 25, 1886, in Marietta, Georgia, but his family relocated to Tallahassee where Barker attended high school at West Florida Seminary, a precursor to Florida State University. After a brief career in business in Jacksonville, Barker pursued his legal studies at the University of Florida where one of his classmates was future governor and U.S. senator Spessard Holland. Returning to Jacksonville, he practiced in a large firm and served as assistant city attorney and city councilman from 1916 to 1925. After serving as a Florida circuit judge from 1925 to 1939, President Franklin D. Roosevelt appointed him district judge of the U.S. Southern District of Florida.[12]

According to Ted Mack, who was Barker's court reporter and joined him once he moved to the federal bench, there was an "interesting, possibly apocryphal, fable about his appointment to the effect that the two Senators, [Charles] Andrews and [Claude] Pepper, were unable to agree on a successor to Judge Alexander Akerman. As a sales ploy some friends of Barker arranged a hunting trip at which both Senators and Barker would be present. Barker was both a highly regarded circuit judge and a redoubtable outdoorsman, and both Senators immediately decided, 'He's our man.'" Mack thought that the trip may have been arranged by U.S. Marshal Chester S. "Ches" Dishong, a close friend of Claude Pepper. Mack remembered Dishong as a "great guy" who always reminded him of "one of those roistering characters in the Old West."[13]

If the anecdote on Barker's appointment seems quaint, it reflected a simpler time. Indeed, another ritual that Mack remembered in the Tampa federal establishment at that time would strike modern-day readers as unbelievable. Mack recalled in his early years reporting for Judge Barker that nearly every month or so the whole "Federal Gang" would meet at Commissioner Pinkerton's lake place on Saddleback Lake for a steak cookout and "beer bash to which all law-enforcement related personnel were invited. Nothing could have been more of a stimulus to good fellowship. . . . Judge Barker never missed one," Mack recalled, "and in fact he usually acted as Bar Tender."[14]

Whitehurst was appointed in 1950 by President Harry Truman after a long dispute between Sens. Claude Pepper and Spessard Holland over their recommended nominee. Whitehurst retired from the federal bench in 1962, but, like Barker, he continued to fill in as needs arose, especially in Fort Myers and Tampa. An avid outdoorsman, Whitehurst had a famous hunting camp in Lee County where he entertained friends, including Judge

Barker. He maintained a close relationship to southwest Florida and Fort Myers. Swartz recalled "every once in the while he would come down just to keep the place active and hold a series of cases down there, and that was as a senior judge."[15] One lawyer who practiced before Judge Whitehurst recalled that he was "stern" and "was a very keen observer. . . . He used to talk to you with his eyes. He would penetrate his eyes into a lawyer trying to figure out, 'Is this lawyer telling me the truth, is he telling me half-truths, how much of what he's telling me can I believe, can I rely on?' We always had a high opinion of the old man who was tough."[16] Another impressive trait that the lawyer remembered was Judge Whitehurst's ability to give instructions to the jury from memory and completely without notes. "We were always in awe of these old men and how they were able to instruct the jury on reasonable doubt and how to define circumstantial evidence . . . and the law of accomplice and the law of a co-conspirator and it would just flow naturally, and that is not found today."[17]

Another lawyer who practiced before Judge Whitehurst remembered him as a "wonderful gentleman" and a "big man physically, very fit, huge hands, an avid outdoorsman. . . . He did have one idiosyncrasy I remember," the lawyer noted.

> He would listen to your argument and with his huge hand he would point his index finger toward the ceiling at the end of the argument and begin to sum up the pros and cons of what he had heard. . . . Thinking out loud with his finger up like this, pointing toward the ceiling about shoulder height. Then his finger would start arching down toward the top of the table. Whatever he was saying at the moment would be it because once that finger reached the top of the table. Lord help the lawyer that wanted to interrupt him or begin to argue with him at that point, because he had decided. But in the instant before that finger touched the table, if you didn't like what he was saying, if you interrupted him, got his attention somehow and suggested to him that you weren't sure that you had made the argument the best way you could and stated it again, you might get that finger to come back, which I saw happen once or twice. But once that finger hit the table it was done, it was over.[18]

Two other Southern District judges who eventually joined the Middle District of Florida were Bryan Simpson and Joseph P. Lieb. Simpson graduated from the University of Florida in 1926, just as the Florida Banking Crash occurred, which sent the real estate boom tumbling. One person described

Judge Bryan Simpson on the occasion of his swearing in, October 6, 1950. *Left to right*: William Barker, George Whitehurst, Louis Strum, Bryan Simpson, and Dozier DeVane. John Milton Bryan Simpson was born in Kissimmee, Florida, on May 30, 1903. Simpson had two distinguished uncles on his mother's side. Both Nathan P. Bryan and William Bryan served in the U.S. Senate, and William was also a federal judge. Simpson entered private practice in Jacksonville in 1926. From 1933 to 1937 he served as assistant state attorney for the Fourth Judicial District and judge of the Duval County Criminal Court beginning in 1939. In 1943 Bryan entered the U.S. Army, serving in Europe in World War II. Simpson was serving as Duval County Circuit Judge at the time of his appointment to the federal bench by Harry Truman. William Terrell Hodges Photo Collection, Middle District of Florida Archives, George C. Young Courthouse, Orlando, Florida.

Simpson as a "rangy young man" of twenty-three "who came to the big city [of Jacksonville] fresh from Florida's cow country to practice law." He was a man "equipped not only to bulldoze a legal opponent," he could also "play a credible game of poker."[19] Upon his appointment in 1950, a newspaper asserted that Judge Simpson's "conduct, demeanor, ability and competence on the bench of both the Criminal Court of Record and the Fourth Judicial Circuit have won him the highest esteem within the ranks of his profession. He quickly achieved a reputation as one of the finest trial judges ever to sit on this circuit, showing courage, industry, and integrity, as well as a keen grasp of the law in his conduct of his court."[20]

Judge Simpson's investiture ceremony, held in Jacksonville on October 6, 1950, was attended by former governor John Martin, Northern District of Florida judge Dozier DeVane, judges Barker and Whitehurst, and Simpson's predecessor, Louis Strum, who had just been elevated to the Fifth Circuit Court of Appeals. The mood was festive. Yet off-color remarks by some of the participants reflected the time and place and would no doubt be unsettling if not shocking to modern ears, especially so because in later years Judge Simpson would later make important rulings in Jacksonville critical to advancing the civil rights movement. Much was made of Simpson's grandfather, who had served in the Confederacy. Herbert J. Phillips, U.S. attorney for the Southern District of Florida, told an off-color joke while referencing the fact that Strum had "just slipped off to Atlanta and took the oath quietly. It kind of makes me think of the story of the old negro" and his wife who asked the judge to perform a marriage ceremony for them, he quipped. The judge was perplexed because he saw the couples' "picanannies" all around. But as Phillips relayed to the receptive audience, the black man solemnly told the judge that "'we's had the 'matrimony now we's ready for the ceremony,'" which brought laughter all around. Jacksonville lawyer Hal P. Adair, also in jocular fashion, made humorous references to the ongoing and impending conflicts between the state and the federal courts. "For the Southern District of Florida," noted Adair, "where things are moving so fast that a judge must know not only his federal law, but must remember his Florida law, because the Supreme Court of the United States has decided—to some extent at least—that the States are still sovereign—[laughter]—and are entitled to have obedience to their laws, even from the Federal Judiciary."[21]

At the time Adair made his comments, racial segregation and black inequality seemed as normal and unchangeable to the vast majority of white Southerners as any institution could be. Enforced in law and custom, the separation of the races was unquestioned and based on the notion of black inferiority. Jacksonville native George Proctor, who would eventually occupy the bankruptcy bench in his hometown, recalled that as a youngster growing up in the 1930s, he faced discrimination as a Jew, but that was nothing compared to the prejudice that blacks endured. "After all, we were white. We may have had a different religion but we were white. Blacks were looked on by the white people as inferiors. I remember my dad saying to me, you know, you're going to want to talk to blacks on your same level, and it's all right to do that. In fact, it's commendable. But you have to know that you're going to offend somebody else by doing that." When Proctor began practicing law in the 1950s, he found that treating blacks in the courtroom on an equal footing caused the rest of the people to take offense. We did not shake hands with a black lawyer. We did not call a black lawyer Mr. Smith. We would use the term, Lawyer Smith or Attorney Smith, but we never said Mr. Smith. . . . And when the witness was on the stand and you were interrogating, you didn't call that person Mrs. Jones. You used the first name. You would call her Mary, you would call him John. The judges enforced that; they were the law. If you had done that . . . they would have run you out of the courtroom. . . . They were just so strong on that type of thing. It was a big deal.[22]

But it would turn out that Judge Bryan Simpson was cut from a different cloth. Simpson grew to manhood in a region of Florida less dominated by the sights, sounds, and smells of the Old South. Nicknamed "Cowboy" because of his roots in Osceola County on Florida's cattle frontier, Judge Simpson was an impressive figure in the courtroom. In 1960 he was fifty-seven years old and stood nearly six foot two, and his bronze complexion was set off by a thatch of white hair. John Crews, a frequent observer of Simpson's courtroom demeanor, noted that when he "stands to his full height on the raised bench, any attorney who draws his wrath is bound to feel mighty small below him." One of Simpson's habits was whittling in the courtroom. But the practice did not divert him from the important matters at hand. "He shows an impressive capacity for recalling testimony and evidence offered during the trial," Crews noted.[23]

Another Southern District judge who eventually served on the Middle District Court of Florida was Joseph Patrick Lieb, appointed by President Dwight Eisenhower in 1955. Lieb became known to Eisenhower in a number of ways. For one, he was a well-respected Republican in a state dominated by Democrats. Lieb's brother John had been a classmate of Eisenhower's at West Point. And Lieb's wife, Helen Bowman Lieb, had been active in state and national Republican politics for years. In 1961, after sitting on the bench in Miami for five years, Lieb was transferred to Tampa to fill the vacancy left by retiring judge George Whitehurst.[24]

Judge Lieb was a large, imposing figure, known for his calm, easygoing demeanor in the courtroom. According to one lawyer who practiced before him in the early 1960s, he was a "perfect gentleman in the courtroom, always welcoming you. When two lawyers would get a bit loud," the lawyer continued,

he would try to calm them down, and if not, he would say, "Look, Mr. Marshal, the court is going to take a brief recess." And then he would look at the lawyers and say, "Gentleman, why don't you join me in my chambers for a cup of coffee?" Well, when he got us in the chambers, he would quickly tell us, "Look, I know that you're fighting for your case and so forth, but you need to settle down, you need to calm down, you're beginning to get out of hand." And that's how he controlled his courtroom in a very nice manner. The public never knew it because he had that civility, natural civility.[25]

Thomas Wilson, who clerked for Lieb from 1964 to 1965 after finishing Duke University School of Law and then practiced before the judge as assistant U.S. attorney, agreed with the previous assessment. Wilson also observed that the judge still bore scars from the football field, and he looked like he had his nose broken a few times. But most of all his courtroom temperament was superb. "He had extraordinary patience," Wilson remembered. "He used the golden rule with lawyers. He had a great sense of humor. He was an outstanding trial judge—not a legal scholar—[but he] applied the law with great common sense."[26] A lawyer who practiced before him the early 1960s remembered Lieb as a "gentleman's gentleman. I never knew him to be discourteous to anybody. He was not an active participant from the bench, he didn't ask a lot of questions or interrogate witnesses but he would listen and make his ruling or take it under submission and that was that."[27]

One of Lieb's clerks in Miami was Alexander Paskay, a Hungarian war refugee. Born in Mohács, Hungary, in 1922, the son of a prominent attorney, Paskay attended "humanistic" gymnasium and eventually graduated from the University of Budapest College of Law in June 1944. Paskay was working for an anti-Nazi newspaper when Germans occupied the country in October 1944. Along with other Hungarian men in Budapest, he found himself conscripted into work gangs. He was transported to Vienna, Linz, Prague, and was on the Dutch border building defenses when German resistance collapsed. Picked up by a squad of British soldiers, he served briefly as an aide to a British officer who interrogated German soldiers. As a "displaced person" he worked in Baden-Baden in the French occupation zone of Germany until immigrating to the United States. After arriving in September 1949 at New Orleans, he went to Miami and lived with an aunt and uncle. He worked in various odd jobs until he was able to enter the University of Miami School of Law, graduating in 1958. He clerked for Judge Lieb in Miami for five and half years. During this time Paskay began reviewing bankruptcy cases for Lieb and Judge Emmett Choate. As Paskay himself later explained, "All bankruptcy at that time was called, not an appeal, but a review of the decisions of the referees, and it had to be reviewed by a district judge. The review material presented for the judge was so terrible that the judge told me that you straighten this business out because we have no idea what was the reasoning, because we can't rule on this thing. So I handled all the appeals at that time called the reviews." Paskay told Judge Lieb that if there was an opening, he wanted the job. The judges eventually selected Paskay to replace an older bankruptcy referee, and he was officially sworn in at Tampa on July 1, 1963.[28]

Tampa lawyer Leonard Gilbert recalled that "judges sort of tolerated bankruptcy in those days." Before the creation of the Middle District, bankruptcy proceedings were not even held in the regular courthouse. But even when proceedings were moved to the courthouse, "you would go over there and stand in the hall because there was only room in the hearing room for the judge and he had two clerks with him and they would call your case." Once called, the lawyer and perhaps a witness would go into the hearing room and testify before the judge. Eventually, once the district was created, Judge Paskay was given a hearing room on the fourth floor of the courthouse.[29]

Attorney Dan Warren practiced in the Jacksonville Court even before the creation of the Middle District. He remembered a far simpler time.

> You know at that time, going back to the '60s, there was a different atmosphere that prevailed among lawyers and judges. It wasn't unusual if you were in Jacksonville to walk into one of the judge's chambers and tell the secretary who you were and you'd just like to pay your respects to the judge. And you would be ushered into his office and you would sit down and chat with him. No business but just paying your respects. And we used to do that quite often. "Judge, I'm just up here on some other matters and I thought I'd come by and say hello and see how you were doing." But you can't do that anymore.[30]

While the foregoing is primarily a discussion of the years immediately preceding the Middle District's creation, it now becomes necessary to briefly describe the legal milieu under which the federal courts operated in the 1950s and 1960s. The rulings of the "Earl Warren Court" transformed jurisprudence in America from 1954 through 1968 in the areas of the right of the accused, school desegregation, legislative redistricting, and civil and voting rights. According to legal scholar Paul Finkelman, the Warren Court is "remembered for modernizing and rationalizing criminal procedure, striking down almost all forms of racial discrimination, strengthening the wall of separation between church and state, and expanding individual liberty in such areas as privacy, speech, and political expression."[31] Warren Court rulings facilitated a rapid rise in public law litigation, which had the effect of expanding the role of the federal courts in American life. Moreover, judges in the Middle District as elsewhere often found themselves in continuing involvement in administration and even reconstruction of public institutions to bring them into line with constitutional standards, or as one scholar has noted, employ "equitable tools . . . to reform constitutionally flawed institutions."[32] The rulings of the Warren Court were controversial, and nowhere more so than in the south. In Florida the winds of change blew forcefully and rapidly, conflicting with and undermining traditional legal precepts and customs. Federal judges in Florida and elsewhere girded themselves for the storm, and often found themselves in the maelstrom.

In 1954 most, but not all, white Floridians greeted the Warren Court's ruling in *Brown v. Board of Education, Topeka, Kansas*, that segregated schools were unconstitutional, with a mixture of shock, disbelief, and outrage. Unfortunately, another ruling the next year ordering that all schools be desegregated with "all deliberate speed" provided hardliners with excuses for foot-dragging because of the court's failure to provide a specific timetable for action. In 1956 a "Declaration of 96 Southern Congressmen" denounced the decision as a clear violation of the Constitution and a dangerous intrusion upon the rights of the states by the federal government. The next year the Little Rock crisis galvanized public attention when President Eisenhower called out U.S. troops to forcibly integrate Central High School. Some Florida politicians, like those in other southern states, called for "Massive Resistance." It is certainly within reason to state that the majority of Florida's white citizens, lawyers, and judges deplored the *Brown* decision. Glenn Terrell, justice of the Florida Supreme Court, denounced the decision in no uncertain terms. Former governor Millard F. Caldwell (and an eventual member of Florida's highest court) labeled members of the U.S. Supreme Court "Communists." LeRoy Collins was elected governor the same year that the *Brown* decision came down. The Tallahassean was a moderate who pledged to maintain segregation by all lawful means. Even so, Collins attempted to calm the public reaction to the *Brown* decision, but there were any number of local and state politicians who were eager to fan the flames, and the heat grew hotter as the years progressed.[33]

Florida's federal judges took these dire omens into account while understanding that these matters would eventually find their way into their courts. In 1958, while addressing a bar function at Stetson University College of Law in its new Gulfport, Florida, campus, Judge Simpson warned his hearers that there were "deeply held and widely divergent views in regard to integration in public schools, and the problem's solution will 'tax to the utmost the wisdom of both races.'" The issue could not be swept under the rug. "'It's going to stay with us and not go away because we wish it to,'" he declared.[34]

The pressure on Judge Simpson and his brethren mounted as time went on. One commentator noted in December 1960 that Judge Simpson, "like all federal judges in the South today . . . is occupying the hot seat." At that moment Simpson was hearing two desegregation suits—one for Duval County and another for Volusia County. A week earlier he had ruled against the City of Jacksonville in its attempt to restrict the use of recreational facilities along racial lines. Simpson understood it was his responsibility to interpret the law in line with rulings of the Supreme Court, but his decision made him unpopular. While his life tenure as an Article III federal judge protected Simpson's job, it did not shield him from the abuse that he and his brethren received for their unpopular rulings. By 1960 Simpson was already receiving angry phone calls and letters. He accepted the fact that it was the people's right to criticize him, but he was concerned about the long-term effect of criticizing the court as an institution. "I grant anybody the privilege to criticize this Court, the Supreme Court or any other Court," he said. "If a person doesn't like the way we're doing the job, he has the right to complain," but some of the criticism, he thought, was "of the sort tending to bring the courts into ill repute."[35]

The Warren Court's rulings were also crucial for protecting the rights of the accused. *Mapp v. Ohio* (1961) excluded evidence seized without a warrant. *Gideon v. Wainwright* (1963), a case originating in Florida, guaranteed the right to counsel in criminal cases. *Escobedo v. Illinois* (1964) and *Miranda v. Arizona* (1966) set out principles of how police should treat suspects after their arrests, enjoining the police to read each person their rights after their arrest. While laudable to modern ears, it must be remembered that many of the Warren Court's rulings were unpopular, especially among law enforcement personnel. One leading national law enforcement authority complained in 1965 that he could not recall one single Supreme Court decision in the previous decade that benefited the interests of law enforcement. Moreover, another commentator noted that the "Supreme Court's movement into the field of law enforcement violated traditional American attitudes toward state predominance in enforcement of criminal law and represented a substantial increase in federal judicial power."[36] This discomfort was true especially in the south—and Florida. As Fred P. Graham, a southerner who covered the court in the 1960s, noted, "It was 'as painful as turning around in a briar patch.'"[37]

Warren Court rulings also made significant strides in democratizing the voting process. *Gomillion v. Lightfoot* (1957) declared that racial gerrymandering violated voting rights guaranteed by the 15th Amendment. *Baker v. Carr* (1962) paved the way for "one man, one vote," and in *Reynolds v. Sims* (1964) Chief Justice Earl Warren "articulated the need for legislative districts based on population size. He noted that 'Legislatures represent people, not trees or acres. Legislators are elected by voters, not farms or cities or economic interests.' He declared that the right to be represented equally in a legislature was the 'bedrock of our political system.'"[38] The question of civil and voting rights for African Americans would be taken up by Congress in the early 1960s, and during the first years of the Middle District's operation, pivotal cases on these subjects would be heard in the various courts in the district.

When Middle District judges made controversial rulings, they could expect to get fair hearings on appeal. The Fifth Circuit Court of Appeals based in New Orleans heard appeals from Florida's and other Deep South District Courts. According to one source, the Fifth Circuit Court of Appeals functioned like an "institutional equivalent of the civil rights movement." That appeals court made crucial rulings that "established precedent-setting legal doctrines that helped implement the *Brown* decision in the classroom, in politics, and in the jury room. . . . The court . . . devised the legal basis for forcing schools to take steps to end segregation speedily, for overcoming past discrimination through affirmative action, for making reapportionment more equitable, and for making it more likely that defendants would be tried before a jury of peers. The impact of the court extended from jury boxes to schools to local governments, state legislatures, and congressional districts."[39] Among those judges who sat on that panel in the 1950s and 1960s were Elbert P. Tuttle, John Minor Wisdom, John R. Brown, Richard Taylor Rives, Griffin Bell, and eventually Frank Johnson. In 1966 Bryan Simpson himself was promoted to that distinguished panel.

As the decade came to a close, Americans and Floridians looked to the upcoming presidential election of 1960 with great anticipation. The two candidates, John F. Kennedy (Dem.) and Richard Nixon (Rep.), while nearly the same age, bore striking contrasts. Nixon, Eisenhower's sitting vice president, seemed a tired holdover from a previous generation—a candidate committed to staying the course—while Kennedy exuded youth, confidence, idealism, and the need to change. The candidates contrasted strikingly on television. As a Harvard-educated war hero, Kennedy captured the imagination of many Americans and his vigorous campaign promised to "get the country moving again." Great changes were in the offing. Kennedy's running mate, Lyndon Johnson, also inspired confidence, and his Texas drawl was more reassuring to Floridians even if Kennedy's Boston twang was not.

Kennedy was particularly impressive to Burke Kibler, one of Florida's leading lawyers, who eventually became chairman of the Holland and Knight law firm. Of Kennedy, he remembered, "He was just absolutely a magnificent speaker with an extra-ordinary memory. . . . He had that incredible vitality about him and charisma."[40] In the end, Florida went for Nixon as it had for Eisenhower in 1952 and 1956, but Kennedy won the national election by a razor-thin majority. The Kennedy–Johnson era began officially in January 1961, the day that Kennedy announced in his inaugural address that the "torch had been passed to a new generation of Americans."

Kennedy's election was crucial for the courts because circumstances would permit him to make many appointments, and thus the federal judiciary would bear Kennedy's imprint for years to come. In the selection of his brother Robert Kennedy as attorney general, the Kennedy administration would vigorously enforce federal laws in the civil rights area. Another of the new attorney general's passions would be a vigorous attack against organized crime. Both of these interests would have great relevance to Florida. Of course, in the selection of judges, "senatorial courtesy" played a crucial role and both of Florida's senators, Spessard Holland and George Smathers, were Democrats—albeit conservative ones. Spessard Holland had been in the U.S. Senate since 1946, winning his seat only one year after he left the governor's chair. The fact that the Bartow native had signed the "Declaration" opposing the *Brown* decision did little to diminish his popularity. Holland had worked hard to ban the poll tax in the Florida legislature, and banning the institution by constitutional amendment became his *cause célèbre* in the Senate. Yet he vigorously opposed civil rights measures as a blatant violation of state's rights.

By 1960 George Smathers had been Florida's junior senator for ten years. Raised in Miami the son of a prominent lawyer, Smathers was successful in nearly everything he attempted. A basketball star at the University of Florida, Smathers excelled in debate and attained nearly every accolade and leadership position at the university. Graduating in 1936, he immediately entered the law school and his circle of influential friends expanded. Smathers' good looks and winning personality destined him for a life in politics. During his first year in law school he met U.S. senator Claude Pepper and eventually ran the senator's reelection campaign in Alachua County. After law school Smathers returned to Miami and worked in his father's law firm. In 1940 he took a job as assistant U.S. attorney in the Southern District of Florida. Based in Miami, he soon gained the reputation as a tough prosecutor. Because of the relative isolation of Miami to other areas of the Southern District, Smathers was afforded much autonomy to pursue cases. According to one historian, Smathers "was blessed with a series of cases that propelled his name onto the front page. His cases fascinated the public, usually featuring sex, greed, and attractive women."[41]

After Pearl Harbor, Smathers volunteered and served in the Marines in the Pacific theater. In 1946 Smathers was elected to the U.S. House of Representatives. Joining Smathers in the House that year were two other young veterans elected that same year: Richard M. Nixon and John F. Kennedy. Smathers made friends rapidly in the House of Representatives, and among his closest was John F. Kennedy. They made quite a pair. It didn't take long for the ambitious Smathers to begin eying greater opportunities, and Pepper's Senate seat became the target. While other Democrats contemplated deserting Harry Truman in 1948, Smathers held true and reaped the benefits two years later when the President supported the congressman's goal of challenging Pepper. Smathers hammered Pepper's New Deal liberalism and charged that his soft stance on communism was out of touch with Florida voters, and it was. In one of the nastiest political campaigns in Florida history, and a bellwether for the nation, Smathers prevailed. That same year in the California senatorial race, mirroring Smathers' tactics, Richard Nixon bested Helen Gahagan Douglas. Smathers' labeled his opponent "Red Pepper," while Nixon dubbed Douglas the "Pink Lady" (that is, "pink right down to her underwear"). Two years later John Kennedy, also a rising star, entered the U.S. Senate.

While Smathers and Kennedy were close personal friends and members of the Democratic Party, their views on important issues often diverged. Both were "cold warriors" but Smathers understood that questions regarding state's rights and civil rights had to be in line with the majority of white voters in Florida. But these matters were not immediately of concern to Smathers in 1960. For the moment he could revel in Kennedy's election and feel sorry for his old friend Richard Nixon. As a Florida senator, even as the junior one, Smathers was ready to play an important role in Kennedy's

Judge William A. McRae on the occasion of his swearing in, March 20, 1961. *Left to right*: George W. Whitehurst, McRae, Bryan Simpson, and Julian Blake. Born in 1909 in Marianna, Florida, McRae graduated from the University of Florida in 1932, and from its law school one year later. McRae won a Rhodes scholarship and continued his legal and literature studies at Christ College of Oxford. Returning to the United States, McRae practiced law in Jacksonville from 1936 to 1940 and was on the law faculty at the University of Florida when World War II broke out. He joined the U.S. Army Air Corps., attained the rank of colonel, and served on Gen. "Hap" Arnold's staff. After the war McRae served as an advisor to the First General Assembly in the United Nations and as senior consultant to the Atomic Energy Commission. In 1946 McRae joined Sen. Spessard Holland's law firm in Bartow, Florida, adding his name to the firm: Bevis, Holland, and McRae. In 1952 McRae became president of the Florida Bar. William Terrell Hodges Photo Collection, Middle District of Florida Archives, George C. Young Courthouse, Orlando, Florida.

appointments to the court. And that involvement would come quickly, when Congress soon after the election authorized a large expansion of the federal judiciary.

The Omnibus Judgeship Act (1960) created 71 new judgeships. Plus there were many vacancies that had not been filled. In less than two years, Kennedy appointed 147 persons to the federal bench. As one writer has concluded, "in one slam-bang stretch of 47 days, from August 11 through September 27, 1961, 69 judges were nominated or appointed, an average of almost eleven per week. By mid-summer 1962 almost 40 percent of federal judges were Kennedy appointees."[42]

On February 20, 1961, William A. McRae became President John Kennedy's first nomination for a federal judgeship. A Bartow, Florida, attorney at the time of his nomination, McRae was practicing in Sen. Spessard Holland's law firm, Holland, Bevis, McRae, and Smith, the precursor of modern-day Holland and Knight. Under the leadership of Chesterfield Smith, the firm at that time was poised to become one of Florida's and the nation's "power law firms." The fifty-one-year-old lawyer had one of the most distinguished backgrounds of any Florida lawyer.[43] One young lawyer who witnessed McRae in a trial in Bartow recalled that the future judge was an imposing figure in the courtroom, a "substantial man in size," and eventually became a "no-nonsense judge."[44] With Holland's support as well as the nominee's sterling credentials, McRae's confirmation was a foregone conclusion. McRae lived in Lake Wales at the time of his appointment, and most assumed that he would choose to reside in Tampa. Instead McRae chose Jacksonville, a move that was disappointing to Kennedy's next appointee to the federal bench.

George C. Young grew up in Daytona Beach and attended Rollins College and then the University of Florida, where he became president both of Sigma Alpha Epsilon fraternity and the Blue Key. Young also headed the university debating club where he and his fraternity brother George Smathers excelled. Both men attended law school together. Young graduated in 1940 and worked briefly as assistant city attorney of Winter Haven. After Pearl Harbor, Young entered the Navy as communications officer, serving in Key West, Miami, Grand Cayman, and Nassau. At the close of the European war, Young was sent to Manila, Philippines, and became a communications officer in what was one of the busiest ports in the Pacific at that time.[45]

After the war Young took classes in taxation and administrative law at Harvard University. In 1947 he joined George Smathers' father's law firm until he became chief of staff to the congressman. Young worked in Washington for Smathers until resuming his law career in Jacksonville in 1952. Young's legal career flourished. After a brief stint as an assistant U.S. attorney, he practiced privately, became president of the Jacksonville Bar Association, and was a member of the Board of Governors of the Florida Bar. Young's nomination to the federal bench came as no surprise. With Smathers and Holland each literally at his side before the Senate Judiciary committee, his hearing, as he recalled, "consisted of the senators asking me my name, and was it true that I went to Harvard." Surrounded by friends and well-wishers in Jacksonville, Young took the oath of office before Judge Bryan Simpson.[46]

Judge George C. Young on the occasion of his swearing in, September 1961. *Front row, left to right*: Julian A. Blake, Young; *back row, left to right*: William A. McRae, Joseph P. Lieb, George W. Whitehurst, Bryan Simpson, two unidentified, and Dozier DeVane. George C. Young was born 1916 in Cincinnati, Ohio, and moved with his family to Daytona Beach during the Florida Boom in the 1920s. He attended the University of Florida where he excelled and earned his law degree. Young graduated in 1940 and worked briefly as assistant city attorney of Winter Haven. Young served in World War II and was in private practice in Jacksonville at the time of his appointment. William Terrell Hodges Photo Collection, Middle District of Florida Archives, George C. Young Courthouse, Orlando, Florida.

Young expected to be assigned to Jacksonville but instead was designated a "roving judge" for both the Southern and Northern Districts.[47] Young was a "floater" for several years until he became permanently located in Orlando. It was hard duty, and he was often away from home for extended periods of time hearing cases in Tallahassee, Jacksonville, Tampa, Orlando, and Miami.[48]

President Kennedy made two more important federal appointments. The same year that he appointed McRae and Young, Kennedy appointed Edward Boardman U.S. attorney and John E. Maguire U.S. marshal for the Southern District of Florida. Maguire was a native of Dobbs Ferry, New York, and forty-four years old when his old Navy friend John F. Kennedy appointed him U.S. marshal of the Southern District of Florida. Maguire had served with the new president aboard PT 109 in the Pacific. With his official tie clasp commemorating his service in the Navy, Maguire cut an impressive figure when in the courtroom or when performing official duties. Persons around the court referred to him as "109 Maguire."[49] As U.S. marshal, Maguire was responsible for maintaining the security of courtrooms and federal proceedings. He was also responsible for the personal protections of judges, jurors, witnesses, prosecutors, and officers of the court.

Within a year after McRae, Young, Boardman, and Maguire joined the U.S. Southern District of Florida, Congress, at Senators Holland and Smathers' urging, created a U.S. Middle District of Florida. The legislation had been a long time in coming. The growth of South Florida and the distances involved necessitated the move. As Judge Young explained, "the people in Miami wanted to have their own clerk and their own marshal and their own U.S. attorney, which they did not have up until that time mainly because the district was in Jacksonville. That's where the clerk was. The U.S. attorney, prior to the creation of the Middle District, was in Tampa. After the district was created, Miami had their own people that they wanted to have."[50]

2

The U.S. Middle District of Florida, First Years, 1962–1968

The act that created the U.S. Middle District of Florida took effect on October 30, 1962, and the first sessions of the court met soon thereafter. The legislation that created the new district contained no authorization for new judges, so the district inherited three judges from the Southern District. Judges Bryan Simpson, Joseph P. Lieb, and William A. McRae were permanently transferred to the Middle District. Judge Lieb and his bankruptcy assistant, Alexander Paskay, were assigned to Tampa. Judges Simpson and McRae remained in Jacksonville. Judge George C. Young continued as a "roving judge" for all three districts until 1964, when he was assigned to Orlando as a permanent member of the Middle District of Florida.[1] Judges George Whitehurst and William Barker, though retired, maintained chambers in Tampa and would often fill in as needed. The district also made use of visiting judges to handle heavy caseloads.

By most accounts the transition from the Southern to the Middle District of Florida was not difficult. If not exactly seamless, it moved forward with little disruption. In most cases the administrative personnel were simply retained in their old jobs at the various courthouses and federal buildings where they had labored before. The Southern District's clerk at the time was Julian A. Blake, who had been with the office in Jacksonville for forty-one years by the time of the new district's creation. The transition was a smooth one for Blake as he simply remained in place. All that was necessary was to strike the word "Southern" and add the word "Middle" to his stationery and office window.

In 1962, when the first sessions of the Middle District Court of Florida were held in Tampa, Jacksonville, and Orlando, federal jurisdiction in criminal cases was far more limited than it is today. Judge Young later recalled that when he first came on the bench, there were three types of cases:

Julian A. Blake served the clerk's office in the federal court in Jacksonville from 1922 to 1965. He was already clerk of the Southern District of Florida in 1962 when the Middle District was established and he became that district's first clerk. He retired in 1965. William Terrell Hodges Photo Collection, Middle District of Florida Archives, George C. Young Courthouse, Orlando, Florida.

"moonshine prosecutions, violations of the Mann Act for taking girls across state lines for immoral purposes, and a lot of bolita [gambling] cases."[2]

In addition to adjudicating criminal cases, the Middle District Court provided citizens a place of recourse when their civil rights were violated. The passage of the Civil Rights Act (1964) banned segregation in public places and prohibited owners of private businesses from discrimination or excluding persons from their facilities based on race. The Voting Rights Act, passed the next year, guaranteed blacks voting rights and included within it vigorous enforcement measures. Those excluded from enjoying the rights guaranteed under these federal laws sought recourse in the federal courts. Middle District judges also heard the complaints of individuals and groups such as the National Association for the Advancement of Colored People (NAACP) who demanded school integration. The U.S. Justice Department was often a party to these suits against county school systems.

And of course each county faced its own set of circumstances. Litigation in some counties lasted more than a generation, included many different plaintiffs, and stretched over decades. Court orders in several counties would not be lifted even as the first decade of the Twenty-first Century came to a close. Judges in the Middle District labored to adjudicate these cases in light of relevant federal law, appeals, and Supreme Court decisions.

Legal scholars have noted the trend beginning in the 1960s for work in the federal courts to shift from adjudication to administration. Thus, as Steven Harmon Wilson has noted, federal district judges since the 1960s have been "forced to become by necessity managers—of their growing courts, burgeoning dockets, and proliferating personnel—as well as to continue acting as the umpires of legal disputes."[3] This trend of shifting from adjudication toward administration was certainly visible in the Middle District as time went on, and as judges increasingly oversaw the work of school board members, superintendents, and their lawyers to ensure that local conditions were in line with higher court rulings.

In the fall of 1963 President Kennedy was gearing up for a tough reelection campaign. The embarrassment of the Bay of Pigs fiasco and his poor showing in his first meeting with Soviet premier Nikita Khrushchev was only partially redeemed by his skilled handling of the Cuban missile crisis. Most important, Kennedy's civil rights policies were alienating large swaths of the South's white, traditionally Democratic voters. He was losing close votes in Congress because of this. Even his friend George Smathers, it seemed, had deserted him. On November 18 Kennedy visited Tampa where he addressed Cuba and civil rights.[4] E. J. Salcines, a young lawyer, who was sworn in as assistant state attorney that day, remembered that nearly the entire court establishment shut down because everyone was slipping off to see the president.[5] Four days later the president lay dead, the victim of Lee Harvey Oswald's bullets fired from the sixth floor of the Dallas school book depository. Lyndon Johnson was sworn in as president by newly appointed U.S. District judge Sarah T. Hughes on the airplane carrying the former president's corpse and Mrs. Kennedy back to Washington. Federal court personnel, like the rest of the nation, were in shock. In the days following the assassination, Oswald himself was gunned down; the president was laid to rest in Arlington National Cemetery; and President Lyndon Johnson appeared before Congress in a nationally televised address. The theme of his message was to mourn America's fallen president and to issue the call of "Let Us Continue." Skillfully using the martyred president's legacy, Lyndon Johnson expanded the New Frontier far beyond what Kennedy had ever envisioned. Johnson's "Great Society," according to one authority "consti-tuted the most important expansion of the American state since the New Deal."[6]

After Johnson's election in 1964, the Great Society, including the presi-dent's "War on Poverty" moved forward rapidly. What followed was a diz-zying array of legislation that expanded the role of the federal government into people's lives as never before. Federal aid to education, Medicare, Med-icaid, and the creation of the agencies of Housing and Urban Development and the Department of Transportation—all were new and transformed government's role in revolutionary fashion. In 1964 Congress passed the Economic Opportunity Act, which created the Office of Economic Op-portunity (OEO) to oversee a variety of community-based antipoverty programs. Johnson selected Sargent Shriver to head the OEO, and one of its many initiatives was to develop legal aid programs for the poor. This new array of programs was unsettling to many Americans. Some openly opposed this new legislation, calling it unconstitutional—and these com-plaints would ultimately be heard in the federal courts.

For example, in one such instance, when it was learned that the OEO was preparing a legal aid service for the poor in Orange County, Orlando lawyer Russell Troutman became incensed and brought suit in the federal court against Shriver. The suit challenged the constitutionality of the law. Once he had settled permanently in Orlando, Judge Young regularly at-tended Orange County Bar meetings and was there the day that members discussed the program. Several lawyers in the room became agitated at the proposal and moved that the local bar association join Troutman's suit as coplaintiffs. Angry discussion ensued, and Judge Young, understanding that he might have to rule in the case, quietly "took his leave . . . and his departure was accompanied by a good-natured round of applause."[7]

This brief incident illustrates the controversial nature of Johnson's War on Poverty programs. It also demonstrates Young's determination as a judge to remain aloof from political controversies. In this instance and throughout his long career on the bench, Young shunned publicity and the limelight. He agreed with Judge Bryan Simpson, who declared at one point, "I feel very strongly by and large that the way a judge can be heard is in legal opinions. He shouldn't expound his views at bar meetings and luncheon meetings."[8] Young gained a reputation as a "modest, no-nonsense man with a booming voice" who had prodigious work habits. Laboring day after day from early morning until well into the night, he did not take a vacation between 1961 (when he came on the court) and 1971.[9]

Dan Warren had known Young as a practicing lawyer in Jacksonville. "He was a delightful person," remembered Warren. "And he was so down to earth. And this didn't change once he was appointed to the bench. Warren, who practiced frequently at the federal post office building in Orlando, remembered seeing Young often at the little cafeteria there. "I would go down there and get coffee or have lunch or something like that, and Judge Young would come in and get in the line just like everybody else and have his lunch and whatever."[10] Another lawyer who appeared before Young often in those years as an assistant U.S. attorney was particularly impressed by Young's courtroom demeanor and scrupulous attention to detail. Judge Young "demanded exactness and correctness. So we had to literally carry . . . ten or twelve law books into the courtroom" to verify our assertions; "you'd have to go to your statute to make sure and you would read it and then you would read that to him. . . . So George Young worked you hard but whoever was tried in front of George Young had had a very thorough proceeding."[11] Mark Horwitz, another lawyer who often practiced before Young, thought that Young was the most "intelligent trial judge I've been in front of. He looked down from the bench with those half-glasses, you felt he knew everything."[12]

In the 1960s Tampa's four-story federal building on Florida Avenue between Twiggs and Zack Street hummed with activity. The sixty-year-old structure would soon be air-conditioned. The post office remained on the first floor, but other parts of the building accommodated an enlarged federal district court presence. The second floor housed offices for the U.S. marshal and postal inspectors. Also on the second floor was the civil evidence vault. The third floor of the building was dedicated to the federal court employees, including the clerk's office, judges' chambers, and two large courtrooms. Judge Joseph P. Lieb and retired judges George Whitehurst and William Barker had their chambers there. Also on the third floor was the vault for criminal evidence. Adjacent to their chambers and court rooms, each judge had offices for his own court reporter and law clerk. The U.S. attorney, his assistants, and their supporting secretarial staff occupied the fourth floor of the federal building, as did bankruptcy referee Alexander Paskay and the room reserved for the grand jury.[13]

When the Middle District was created, Eddie Boardman chose to leave Miami and become the Middle District's first U.S. attorney. In 1962 Boardman had fewer than ten assistants and was responsible for prosecuting cases in Jacksonville, Orlando, and other locations as well as Tampa. Among his assistants in those early years were Thomas Wilson, Joe Mount,

Donald Stichter, Robert McGowan, Arnold Levine, Kendall Wherry (based in Orlando), Bill Hamilton (based in Jacksonville), and Charles Carriere. West Tampa native E. J. Salcines joined Boardman's office in 1964, after a brief stint in the state's attorney's office. The son of Spanish immigrant parents, Salcines grew up in West Tampa, attended Florida Southern College, and graduated from law school in 1963. On his first day of work Salcines remembered Boardman taking him down to the "south courtroom on the third floor, where U.S. District Judge George C. Young was presiding in a major trial. . . . They interrupted the proceeding and George C. Young administered the oath to me in that beautiful courtroom."[14]

By 1966 Boardman had nine assistants and fourteen secretaries. Boardman claimed his time was divided equally between criminal, civil, and administrative matters. He claimed to have collected nearly $3.50 for every dollar appropriated for the office. But the prosecutorial duties of his office were expanding. A 1965 statute gave the office the task of handing Federal Housing Administration and Veterans Administration mortgage foreclosures. That year his office handled 272 of them.[15] The Middle District ranked

Tampa Federal Courthouse, ca. 1918. Completed in 1905, the U.S. District Court for the Southern District of Florida and the Middle District of Florida met here until 2001. National Archives and Records Administration, Record Group 121.

Edward Francis "Eddie" Boardman was born in New York City in 1912 but relocated as a child with his family to Miami, Florida. After earning a law degree from the University of Florida in 1938, Boardman returned to Miami and formed the firm of Boardman & Bolles. In Miami he also served in numerous public positions such as municipal judge, Dade County School Board attorney, and city attorney for North Miami. Appointed by John Kennedy in 1961, Boardman served as U.S. attorney until resigning in 1969. E. J. Salcines Collection.

first in the nation in handling Veterans Administration mortgage foreclosures, seventh in overall civil cases, and tenth in the nation for criminal cases filed during the 1965–66 fiscal year. Boardman's assistants averaged approximately 415 cases a year. In 1965 the office brought in $222,000, and the amount more than doubled the next year. In 1966 Boardman's lawyers filed 1,702 cases (966 civil and 736 criminal).[16]

Boardman handled many cases himself, particularly ones in Orlando, to give his assistants time with their families. He also handled appeals in New Orleans and prepared an endless number of briefs. He tried to be familiar with every case. Yet, as he explained, "I have extreme confidence in my assistants and give them great latitude of decisions."[17] Boardman's chief secretary, Pam Lindquist, found her job exciting. "Every case is different and it doesn't seem like working," she said upon receiving a Justice Department award for outstanding service. "Sometimes I get the opportunity to meet the actual defendants and famous attorneys. . . . It's exciting to get involved and sometimes I would love to get in the courtroom and fight." According to a newspaper account, Lindquist makes "even the unglamorous jobs of civil docketing and the tedious job of handling government loan defaults seem exciting."[18]

U.S. Attorney Eddie Boardman confers with several of his assistants. *Left to right*: Robert McGowan, E. J. Salcines, Edward F. Boardman, and Bruce Fraser. E. J. Salcines Collection.

In 1966 Boardman's office hired the first African American assistant U.S. attorney in the Middle District and the entire south. Born in 1932 in Clearwater and a graduate of Florida A&M and Howard University School of Law, Joseph W. Hatchett passed the bar exam in 1959 and joined only twenty-five other black lawyers licensed to practice in the state. Hatchett practiced in Daytona Beach in the early 1960s before joining Boardman's staff. Serving for four years both under Boardman and later John Briggs, Hatchett specialized in prosecuting criminal cases. He was eventually promoted to first assistant U.S. attorney and supervised the Jacksonville office. Also in the Jacksonville office was the district's first woman prosecutor, Virginia Q. Beverly.[19]

In 1967 Boardman added two other assistant U.S. attorneys to the Tampa Division. Richard Hirsch (twenty-six), a graduate of George Washington University and Stetson University College of Law, had worked as an aide to Rep. Charles Bennett and had taught at Plant High School. Robert Mackenzie (twenty-seven) was a Tampa native and played football at Georgia Tech where he earned an engineering degree. After law school at the University of Florida, Mackenzie briefly entered private practice before joining Boardman's staff. The source announcing Hirsch and Mackenzie's hiring also added that E. J. Salcines would head the criminal prosecution division of the Tampa and the Orlando offices.[20]

Hatchett recalled good relations in the Jacksonville office between the U.S. Attorney's office and the FBI. Hatchett organized a basketball league and the U.S. Attorney's office in Jacksonville and the FBI played each other on Wednesday afternoons and evenings. Hatchett admitted they seldom defeated the FBI. "We had a lot of fun," he remembered. "The teams changed all the time, because two guys were off on a special assignment and one of us is out trying a new case. But it was something to do and it helped bind us together. We had to work together."[21]

Another important practitioner in the Middle District at the time was Robert Evans, the federal probation officer. Evans had headed the office in the Southern District of Florida since 1953, serving in Tampa the entire time. When the new district was created, he remained in Tampa and became the first federal chief probation officer for the Middle District. Longtime court reporter Edward (Ted) Mack noted that Evans was one of the most popular staff members in federal court service.[22]

In Orlando, sessions of court were held in the federal post office building on East Robinson Street. Judge Young remembered that when he permanently located there, he had one secretary, a court reporter, and a law clerk. Jack Peeples was the only deputy marshal. "And that man would have to work day and night. We worked many nights, and then he'd have to go out and serve papers and transport prisoners. And he did this all by himself." There was only one assistant U.S. attorney there (Kendall Wherry), and there were several others who would take turns coming over from Tampa. Many of the cases in the early years were condemnation cases. "There was a great deal of land acquired surrounding the site of the proposed moon shot [space center] so that life and property would not be endangered when the shot went off. We had any number of cases and tried them day in and day out."[23] Francis Rearick was the land attorney. According to Young, "Mr. Rearick had been saddled with all of the condemnation cases all by himself of the entire moon project, over 2,000 cases. He handled every one of them with competence and kept out of trouble."[24] According to court reporter Ted Mack, these trials set many records for time and transcript length because counsel for the landowners often requested that jurors view the premises "so a Jeep Safari of Jurors had to be organized in which all Jurors, the Judge, counsel for all concerned parties, and me went along. I had to be there in case counsel or the Jurors said something in the course of viewing the premises."[25]

The lack of staff in Orlando in the early years necessitated much travel. Before Interstate 4 opened, motorists had to wind their way from Tampa to Orlando on State Road 92. The Tampa to Orlando section of Interstate 4, completed in 1962, facilitated the one-hundred-mile journey. E. J. Salcines remembered, "We had to make that trip between Tampa and Orlando regularly. There was a very popular Broadway production at the time called *Fiddler on the Roof* and one of the popular songs was 'Sunrise, Sunset.' And that was the song of us from the Tampa Division because we had to get up very early. And sunup, as we're traveling east, the sun is in our eyes. And sunset, when George Young would finish up; it was always dark or getting dark, we'd have sunset in our eyes again, coming west." Salcines recalled that when the attorneys and staff drove to Orlando, they carried their typewriters and materials with them.[26]

In 1964, after *Gideon v. Wainwright* (1963), Congress passed the Criminal Justice Act, which required federal districts to formulate plans to provide for persons charged with federal crimes who were unable to afford an attorney. In those early years before the establishment of the Federal Public Defender Act, district judges established ad hoc methods to provide counsel to indigent defendants. Gerald Tjoflat, who practiced law in Jacksonville in the early 1960s, recalled that Judge Simpson "created his own system of public defenders before there was such a system. He would call out a name and tell lawyers to be in court on a Thursday. They would represent 10–15 indigent cases that day out of their own pocket."[27] In Tampa, after he had sworn in young lawyers, Judge Lieb would often approach them and say, "Okay, welcome, you've just been sworn in and if you care to sign up, when there is a case, we will call you."[28] It would only be a short time, however, before the right to counsel would be expanded dramatically, and in this instance judges in the Middle District of Florida would make significant rulings that would have great impact on expanding and extending the public defender system in Florida and elsewhere.

In those years before specialization, many lawyers moved back and forth between federal and state courts relatively easily. Dan Warren of Daytona Beach tried many federal cases in Jacksonville, Orlando, and Miami. When asked about the special challenges of practicing in the federal versus the state courts, Warren recalled that in those early days there

wasn't really that much difference between practicing in the federal courts and the state courts, although you really got a much better trial in the Federal District Court than you did in the state courts. And other than the "Procedural Rules of Evidence," they were virtually the same with differentiations and variations, nuances between the Rules of Criminal and Civil Procedure in the state than those in the federal court. But it wasn't much of a change. One nice thing about our judicial system, it's all based upon the Anglo-Saxon common law, and so most states, if you're familiar with the procedures other than local rules, you're pretty much at home in any court in the United States.[29]

Warren admitted that familiarity with federal statutes would be a whole other dimension of preparation, "but you know, just like researching any other case back then, we didn't have the Internet, so we had to do our research from books. But it took a great deal of research if you were in a complicated case. But other than that," the work was pretty much the same.[30]

Some lawyers remembered a striking contrast of protocol between the state and federal courts. One of the most striking differences was the formality of dress and behavior in the federal court. "You never used anything but dark suits in the federal court. We never used any shirts other than white and maybe a very light baby blue. Never any loud or wild ties, they all were very conservative," one former assistant prosecutor remembered. Also

> you had to stand up whenever you were addressing the court, you had to stand up when you were asking questions of witnesses, if you wanted to make an objection, you could not make an objection from a sitting position. The federal court followed a very strict protocol of the type of demeanor in the courtroom whereas in state court, where you had hundreds of cases, it was a more relaxed environment. You still had to show your respect to the court, your civility to your opponents, etcetera, but you could ask questions from a sitting position, you could object from a sitting position.[31]

FBI agents were also under a very strict dress code that Director Hoover imposed.

> What we now call casual dress never existed and the female employees never had any casual Friday or pants outfits to wear on Fridays. Everything was quite formal. In fact, I remember one of the secretaries of the U.S. Attorney's Office wore gloves and a hat to work, and just as the clock was striking 5:00, she would close her typewriter, fix her

desk, put on her bonnet and put on her gloves and then would walk out as a perfect lady. So the dress in the federal court was a lot more formal than it was in state court.[32]

Because of the rising caseload, the Middle District of Florida frequently used visiting judges in those early years. Clarence Allgood from Alabama and Albert Reeves from the Western District of Missouri were frequently invited to hear cases and were well received. E. J. Salcines remembered Allgood fondly. "He was not a tall man," Salcines remembered. "He was rather short, but he was a perfect gentleman at all times. No matter how boisterous we got in our fights inside that courtroom, he always maintained control and always with a smile, always referred to us as gentlemen."[33] Judge Allgood, Salcines recalled, contributed mightily to reducing the criminal case backlog. Judge Albert Reeves was equally well received. Like Allgood, Reeves made a profound impression on the young lawyer.

> He was one of those mythical federal judges, tall, skinny, lanky with a lot of white hair . . . He would amaze us because he was an elderly judge, but he was so refined. But when it came time for jury instructions, I mean, it looked like he had a teleprompter in front of him because the words just flowed and he gave it to you like, God has spoken. . . . Now, he also had a tendency of closing his eyes and leaning back sideways on the chair. And sometimes the defense attorney would look at me or I would look at the defense attorney or look at the marshal like wondering, hey, is the old man asleep. And then a lawyer would make an objection, and immediately, he would say, overruled, counselor, because of so and so, and cite a rule. So the old man may have appeared that he was half asleep up on the bench, but he was not. He might have been relaxing his eyes, but his ears were all ears in that courtroom.[34]

Reeves came to Tampa with a long, distinguished career behind him. Appointed in 1923, Reeves was born on a farm near Steelville, Missouri, in 1873. He was known for his tough rulings on criminals, he clashed often with Harry Truman, and he was instrumental in breaking Kansas City's Pendergast Machine when he presided over federal vote fraud trials in 1936. Retiring in 1954, Reeves purchased a home in Dunedin in 1961 and often sat in Tampa as a visiting judge. He died in 1971 at the age of ninety-seven.[35]

Salcines remembered that while he reported to U.S. Attorney Boardman, the Justice Department in large part controlled the cases in that they were not allowed to dismiss a case without the approval of the Criminal Division in Washington. As he explained, "we had an FTS system, a telephone system and we knew the chain of command, particularly in the Criminal Division of the Justice Department. We knew who headed up Organized Crime, we knew who headed up General Crimes, and we knew who headed up the Economic Fraud Division, things such as that."[36] Salcines and other prosecutors frequently found themselves on the phone and writing memos as to why this or that case had fallen apart. It was permissible to change the violations as new evidence emerged or substitute this one indictment for another, "but you could not dismiss outright without Washington's approval."[37] The U.S. attorney's office also became involved when civil defendants had agreed to make payments under a settlement and had defaulted. As Salcines explained, "we would get these 'blue bonnets.' We would call them blue bonnets because the Department of Justice, Civil Division, would send you a memo in blue paper and it certainly got our attention when a blue bonnet showed up that said, 'You need to follow up on these cases.'"[38]

Salcines recalled that some of the most numerous criminal cases in those early years were for car theft. "People would steal cars up north and drive to Florida, get busted by the highway patrol or the local sheriff or the local police, and immediately, the FBI was called because the vehicle had come across state lines. And Mr. J. Edgar Hoover had a high priority on those types of cases like he did for armed robberies of banks and kidnapping. We also had some very big counterfeiting cases," Salcines recalled. "The Xerox machines, for lack of a better term, the printing presses of old, had really become refined with new photography . . . [and] as a result, people were experimenting with photography and they were making some good quality twenty-dollar bills and hundred-dollar bills etcetera. And the Secret Service was very active in pursuing those."[39]

Counterfeiting

Boardman's prosecutors pursued two high-profile counterfeiting cases in the 1960s, one in Polk County and another in Brevard County. In 1965 Polk County Sheriff Monroe Brannen raided Willie Plaster's Lakeland residence and found thousands of dollars of counterfeit currency stashed in cardboard boxes and bureau drawers in a bedroom. Brannen led a party of deputies, U.S. marshals, Secret Service agents, and Lakeland police detectives to the house. Plaster, who worked as a postal clerk, was operating a correspondence school in the front of the house. Officers also found engraving tools, a small offset press, and money in a rear room. One of Brannen's deputies had been working on the case for two months, and a search warrant was obtained from the U.S. Marshal's office. Plaster and a female companion were arrested and the U.S. marshal transported the couple to Tampa where U.S. Magistrate Paul Game set their bonds at $20,000 and $10,000, respectively. The couple were eventually tried and convicted in Tampa.[40]

One of the most bizarre counterfeit cases to be prosecuted in the Middle District involved a dentist named Stiles Davis who lived in Cocoa Beach. Dr. Davis was charged with selling $24,000 in $10 bills at 20 cents on the dollar. Davis's Orlando lawyer, J. Russell Hornsby, called his client a "very mentally ill man" who was "attracted to ambitious schemes."[41] Davis had undergone extensive psychiatric treatment including shock therapy for mental illness. A native of Chicago, Davis (forty) had been married four times and had three children. Davis had transferred over $10,000 in cash to a pawnbroker named Harrell, who in turn tried to sell the bogus cash to an undercover Secret Service agent who taped the transaction. The taping occurred at the Cocoa house of the pawnbroker, and once Harrell was discovered, the pawnbroker turned himself in and offered to assist them in setting a trap for Davis, and the dentist was eventually arrested on August 19, 1965. Hornsby's defense was that Davis was temporarily insane and did not know what he was doing. The jury deliberated six hours, went to their hotel, reconvened the next day, and reached their verdict in twenty minutes. Davis was sentenced to eighteen months in prison and three years' probation.[42]

After his conviction, Davis was released on $3,500 bond pending an appeal. Not long after, when it was revealed that Davis owned land in the Bahamas, U.S. Judge George C. Young upped his bond to $50,000. But by that time Davis had absconded. He took his 8-ft skiff on the Banana River and did not return. Davis's wife said she found a suicide note her husband had written, which stated that he would commit suicide by wrapping an anchor and chain around himself. "I am going down to the sea, not to return. This is where I want to remain, eternally," the note stated. Judge Young ordered an international search.[43] Finally, a year later, U.S. Attorney Boardman received notification that Davis had been apprehended in Nicaragua and would soon be returned to Florida.[44]

Davis's case was clouded by contradictory evidence as to his sanity. In 1966 Davis's attorney had solicited a psychiatric evaluation of his client and entered an eleven-page report into the official record. The psychiatrist concluded in the report that Davis "does carry the psychiatric condition of Manic Depressive Reaction, manic type, mild to moderate degree, which he likely has been carrying for many years."[45] In July 1968 Judge Young ordered another psychiatric test of Davis. This time the psychiatrist found that that Davis was found to be competent to stand trial. A new trial was set for July 8, 1968 in Tampa and the jury found him guilty on July 12, 1968. He was sentenced to three years in jail, the sentence to begin after his first eighteen-month conviction.[46]

The Draft

Soon after Lyndon Johnson was elected president in 1964, conditions in Vietnam reached a breaking point, leading to an escalation of American military involvement. Johnson's policy became increasingly unpopular and triggered draft riots and outbreaks on college campuses. When young men resisted their draft notices or refused to take civilian jobs, their cases were turned over to federal authorities and indictments were sought. From 1960 to 1966, one source noted that over fifty Tampa area men had gone to jail rather than face military service or take a civilian job assigned to them under the military draft. Most of those resisting the draft were Jehovah's Witnesses. The Tampa division was viewed nationally as one of the toughest on those who evaded the draft. Judge Joseph Lieb usually sentenced them to the same amount of time in prison as the time that they would have served if drafted. "As long as our young men are fighting and dying in Viet Nam," he said in 1966, "I see no reason why these men should stay home in a safe place and get out of serving time in the military."[47]

Assistant U.S. Attorney Joseph Hatchett joined the U.S. Attorney's office at the height of the Vietnam escalation. Hatchett ended up prosecuting selective service cases. As Hatchett later told an interviewer, "I prosecuted every single case of a draft dodger in the state of Florida. It just turned out that I was the only veteran in the Jacksonville office and the induction ceremony was in Jacksonville so a draftee would be told to step forward to indicate their willingness to enter the service and of course those who did not step forward were arrested right away. So the place of a violation was always Jacksonville for the whole state of Florida. So I tried all the cases." Hatchett became an expert in these prosecutions. "You had to know the classifications," he continued. "You had to know everything anybody who was sitting on the draft board would know. Everybody in the office didn't need to learn all of that so I learned it, the entire draft procedure. So when there was testimony of what had occurred and what was in the file, I would know exactly what it meant and could, before the jury questioned the draft board officer, [explain] the process that took place." Hatchett admitted at the time that he was "gung ho" and saw it as his duty to prosecute these cases to the hilt.[48] Only later, like others, did he question the wisdom of the Vietnam War. "Early on I was ready to take whatever my President said. That was the law and I obeyed it. I had served and my brothers had served when they couldn't even vote. . . . It was just sort of automatic, you protected the country. . . . So it didn't bother me at all to prosecute draft dodgers. I had done my duty and a lot of other people were doing it, why is this guy not doing it?"[49]

Organized Crime

In 1966 the FBI, coordinating with other federal authorities, moved decisively against organized crime activities in Orlando and Tampa. In 1963 a special agent of the IRS, after conducting an investigation and stakeout of a house that suspected gambler Clyde Lee owned in Seminole County, swore out an affidavit and search warrant before a U.S. commissioner. The agent was convinced that the house was the headquarters of an illicit gambling operation, and the raid netted evidence of wagering. A federal grand jury in Orlando indicted Lee on April 26, 1965. Assistant U.S. Attorney Charles Carriere prosecuted Lee on a charge of failure to pay a wagering tax; he was found guilty on January 14, 1966, and was sentenced to six years in prison. Lee's attorney, Edward Kirkland, appealed the case based on the fact that evidence was obtained through illegal means. According to Kirkland's motion, "The defendant alleges upon information and belief that the evidence obtained by the wire-tapping by the Orlando Police Department was communicated to agents, servants or employees of the Internal Revenue Service of the Treasury Department of the United States of America, and that the evidence resulting in the charges brought against the said defendants was obtained by wire-tapping, and therefore, said evidence is inadmissible to federal courts." The bond for Lee pending appeal was set at $20,000. Lee's appeal before the Fifth Circuit Court of Appeals was successful, and Judge George Young vacated the sentence by order of the court in August 1968.[50]

In 1966 a Tampa grand jury issued twenty-four sealed indictments against suspected organized crime suspects. FBI agent J. F. Santoiana arrested Nick Scaglione on federal gambling and liquor law violations. Also arrested at the Tropicana Café was Frank "Cowboy" Ippolito, who was charged with using "interstate facilities for [exchanging] gambling information" between Chicago and Tampa from April to June 1966. A number of others thought to be associated with organized crime were subpoenaed before a grand jury: Henry Trafficante, Frank Diecidue, James "Jimmy" Longo (former body guard of Santo Trafficante Jr.), and Johnny "Scarface" Rivera, former body guard of the slain gambling kingpin Charlie Wall. Prosecuting the case were assistant U.S. attorneys Salcines, Mackenzie, and William Kenney, an attorney from the U.S. Justice Department's Organized Crime Division. Scaglione was already on bond awaiting an appeal from a previous conviction for violating the gambling laws. Scaglione was charged with making five trips from New York City to Tampa transporting 1,000 sheets of flash paper, a chemically treated paper used by bolita peddlers on which bets were written. (The paper dissolved quickly when touched by a match.)[51]

Newspaper reports stated that "Kenney and a special team of organized crime investigators did their work so thoroughly that agents of other federal investigative departments did not even know Kenney's group was in Tampa." Kenney, the report noted, would cooperate "with Salcines to direct the probe of racket money being funneled into local bars, hotels, and other legitimate businesses. The federal prosecutor noted that Tampa's Grand Jury action is only part of the stepped up national campaign against the Mafia."[52] In response to the federal crackdown, Rep. Sam Gibbons praised Atty. Gen. Ramsey Clark and FBI director J. Edgar Hoover in their efforts to apprehend and prosecute those who had been preying on the public for so many years.[53] Scaglione was eventually convicted, and Judge Lieb sentenced him to five years in prison, but his case was overturned on appeal. After all was said and done, Scaglione only served five months in state prison.[54] Prosecution of organized gambling operations was difficult. As will be related in future chapters, Congress would soon provide the Justice Department with new tools to prosecute lawbreakers.

Right to Counsel and Death Penalty

Middle District judges were vigilant when it came to protecting the constitutional rights of defendants or convicted criminals in Florida state courts. In a series of judgments on the right of counsel and the death penalty, judges William A. McRae and Joseph P. Lieb made rulings that were closely watched throughout the nation and would greatly influence criminal prosecution at the state level in Florida. In 1965 Judge Lieb ruled that "indigent persons charged with misdemeanors (and not just felonies) were entitled to attorneys and may appeal the case to get it settled." Dubbed "little Gideon," because of its likelihood of extending the right to counsel as per the Supreme Court's ruling in *Gideon v. Wainwright*, the case in Lieb's court involved a Largo man named James Gaston, who had been sentenced in 1964 to two years in the Pinellas County jail. On a writ of *habeas corpus*, Judge Lieb ordered that a new trial be granted to the Largo man. When apprised of Lieb's ruling and after considering its implications, Florida Atty. Gen. Earl Faircloth mulled the possibility of appealing the decision so that Florida's misdemeanor courts would not have to adjust to the judge's order. State courts consistently argued that the right to an attorney did not apply to indigents in misdemeanor cases. One local justice of the peace (JP) asserted that the ruling would create serious problems. "It's a mighty far-reaching decision," he asserted.[55] The prosecutor for the City of St. Petersburg agreed. "Can you imagine every common drunk and vagrant unable to pay for counsel himself, insisting on an attorney to defend him? We'd never get finished." Another JP added, "We'd never be able to do any business. I can't see how we can practically permit every defendant counsel."[56]

In December 1967 McRae ruled similarly that "Gideon . . . does apply to misdemeanor cases. 'Failure of the Justices to inform petitioner of his right to appointed counsel was a denial of a right guaranteed by the United States Constitution,' he wrote in the case of *Wayne Cloer v. Rodney B. Thursby, Sheriff of Volusia County*." Cloer appeared before a justice of the peace on a misdemeanor charge of carrying a concealed weapon. Although advised of his right to counsel, he had no money and was not assigned one. He was convicted and sentenced to eighteen months and fifteen days in a county work camp. Cloer sought support of the legal services of the OEO. Tom Goldsmith, a young lawyer, took his case. Goldsmith filed affidavits complaining that two justices failed to advise Cloer of his right to counsel, and thus that Cloer's conviction and sentence were illegal. The ramifications of the case would be dramatic for lower courts in Florida. In Volusia County alone, for example, County Clerk James Doyle estimated that it handled 18,000 cases a year.[57]

On April 14, 1967, the *St. Petersburg Times* announced that "a federal judge yesterday blocked the execution of Florida's 50 death row inmates at least through May," and added that the "indefinite stay of execution is believed to be the first of its kind in the United States." The article reported that Judge McRae stayed all executions after hearing pleadings by the American Civil Liberties Union (ACLU) and NAACP in a suit charging that the Florida's capital case trial laws were unconstitutional. Attorneys represented six men, but their petition was filed on behalf of all fifty death row inmates. The attorneys brought the suit on the grounds that under the Florida death penalty law (1) a defendant could only waive a jury trial if he would plead guilty; (2) Florida juries are required to be "death-oriented"— that is, they were not allowed to serve unless they declare they are in favor of the death penalty (3) and under the Florida law, judges are required to sentence defendants to death unless the jury recommended mercy. Lawyers also cited statistics to show that the death penalty was imposed disproportionately against blacks. In early August McRae extended the moratorium on the death penalty and granted ACLU and NAACP lawyers permission to "enter death row and interview all prisoners held with the view of bringing a massive attack against the death chair."[58] McRae's moratorium on Florida executions stood until the Supreme Court, in *Furman v. Georgia* (1972), voided over six hundred death sentences in the United States.[59]

By 1967 Florida's population and the caseload in the Middle District of Florida had grown to the point that Lyndon Johnson was able to appoint two additional judges. Charles R. Scott and Ben Krentzman would be the only two Johnson appointments to the Middle District of Florida. U.S. Atty. Gen. Ramsey Clark was actively involved in Johnson's selection process, as was Asst. Atty. Gen. Nicholas Katzenbach. Johnson was particularly concerned about the civil rights views of his nominees, and he made it a point to order his aides to make a thorough investigation before he officially nominated them. After Clark recommended Charles R. Scott for the opening, he assured Johnson that he had vetted Scott with civil rights leaders in Florida, who "affirm Scott's good reputation."[60]

Born January 13, 1904, in Adel, Iowa, Scott came to Jacksonville in 1923 after graduating from Valparaiso University School of Law. Once in town, Scott took a job selling railroad tickets and worked part time for George C. Bedell, founder of the law firm of Bedell, Dittmar, DeVault, Pillans & Gentry. In 1926 Scott became associated with the Francis P. Fleming law firm, and by 1957 he had formed his own firm. He served for many years as district counsel of Seaboard Air Line Railroad Company and was extremely active in the defense of railroad cases until Gov. LeRoy Collins appointed him circuit judge of the Florida's Fourth Judicial Circuit in 1960. Scott was serving in that capacity when Lyndon Johnson appointed him to the federal bench.[61]

Isaac Benjamin Krentzman was born in Milton, Florida, on March 21, 1914. He attended the University of Florida and excelled in debate; he received his law degree just before the United States entered World War II. Serving in the Pacific theater in the Philippines, Krentzman was awarded a Bronze Star and attained the rank of lieutenant colonel. After the war Krentzman entered private practice in Clearwater and soon began dating a woman from a prominent local family named Wilma McMullen Cransler. Krentzman later joked that his future bride helped his burgeoning law practice. "Well, it helped a great deal . . . that I was going with Wilma because everybody in the courthouse except for one person, and I think that was the tax collector, were McMullens, or related to the McMullens and it made it a lot easier for a young lawyer, they knew that [I] was the one that went out with that McMullens girl." Krentzman flourished in his new environment. He served as city attorney and served in numerous leadership positions in civic clubs and organizations.[62]

Ben Krentzman and Sen. George Smathers had been good friends at the University of Florida. Krentzman remembered years later that Smathers once joked that while the two were in college that, once he became a senator,

> he was going to appoint me a federal judge. Well, it was just a joke because nobody expected him to run and nobody expected me . . . to be a judge . . . and he called me up one day. He said I'm not going to run anymore. I'm tired of this job and if you want to be a judge, this is the last time you're going to get a chance. But I said I never have said I wanted to be a judge. Well, he said, I assumed you did if you had good sense. He said federal judgeship is a great office.[63]

Krentzman discussed the matter with his law partners and they "decided that it was a nice way to cap a career. "My wife and I went up for the Senate Committee hearing and I was nervous as a cat," Krentzman remembered. "I tried to think about how to prepare myself. I had heard that on occasion some senators asked you how you felt about this and how you felt about that, and I was violently opposed to that. I was not going to be committed to anything except just to do justice and follow the constitution." The confirmation was a foregone conclusion. By the time Krentzman's hearing came up, only Smathers and another senator were in the room. Assuming the chair, Smathers asked Krentzman why he wanted to be a district

Middle District Clerk Julian A. Black and Judge Bryan Simpson. William Terrell Hodges Photo Collection, Middle District of Florida Archives, George C. Young Courthouse, Orlando, Florida.

judge—to which Krentzman answered: "'Because a very good senator nominated me.' He said, 'That's good enough for me.' That was it."[64] Judge Lieb swore Krentzman in on June 29, 1967, before well-wishers that included judges Scott, Young, and Whitehurst. Also on hand were Krentzman's law partners, Florida Supreme Court Justice Stephen O'Connell, and former governors LeRoy Collins and Doyle Carlton.[65]

Two years before Judge Krentzman was sworn in, the Middle District of Florida lost perhaps its longest-serving official. Julian A. Blake had worked in Jacksonville in the clerk's office since 1922, becoming the head clerk of the Southern District of Florida in 1952, the same year Harry Truman appointed Judge Bryan Simpson to the court. After Blake announced plans to retire in December 1965, Judge Simpson circulated a letter to his brethren who had worked with Blake all those years, suggesting that they contribute toward the gift of a television.[66] With the money collected and the television purchased, Judge Simpson penned a playful, heartfelt letter to his friend: "Dear Julian: John Holland, Bill Barker, George Whitehurst, Emmett Choate, Joe Lieb, Bill McRae, George Young and I have finally found a matter, after all these years, about which we are all in full accord and agreement. That is your retirement, after many years of loyal and devoted service to your duties and to us individually, should not pass without recognition by this group. You are held in warm and affectionate regard by each one of us. We hope that this portable color T. V. set will provide many hours of pleasure to our old friend and associate in the years ahead."[67]

Simpson's letter to Blake came following one of the most stressful periods in the judge's time on the bench in Jacksonville—the St. Augustine uprising of 1963–64. Conflicts associated with that struggle played themselves out in Simpson's courtroom. It is to this incident and the Middle District's adjudication of issues involving civil rights that we now turn.

3

The Middle District and Civil Rights, 1962–1968

In 1963 legal scholar Leon Friedman wrote,

> There is no more important figure in the Civil Rights Movement than a federal district court judge. As a practical matter, he is the most immediate interpreter and enforcer of federal law. Since most of the claims of Negroes against the authorities of the southern states are based on violations of their constitutional and federal rights—in terms of voting restrictions, segregated schools, discriminatory treatment in public accommodations and other facilities—a federal district court judge has the power to correct a wide range of discriminations and abuses. More important, he can act swiftly and effectively to protect the constitutional rights of those bringing suit, in a matter of days if he chooses.

According to Friedman, there was one judge who exceeded all others in the South "in his speed in enforcing the law and in his willingness to embark on new legal territory to protect Negro rights." And that man was Judge Bryan Simpson, chief judge of the United States Middle District of Florida.[1]

Friedman described Simpson as a "handsome, aristocratic, white-haired southern gentleman, with a personal charm and friendliness that never interfered with his decisiveness and quick intellect in the courtroom. . . . The bar knew him as a competent, hard-working judge, seldom reversed by the court of appeals."[2] Dan Warren, who often practiced before Simpson in the 1960s, described the judge as a "tall, gangly man, with rugged features like those of a working cowboy, one who had been on the open range too long."[3]

Both before and after World War II, Jacksonville, where Judge Simpson held court, had grown to become a shipping, manufacturing, and insurance center. Jobs were plentiful in the dynamic "New South" riverport-seaport. As they had after the Civil War, rural folk from neighboring counties in

Florida and Georgia—white and black—came to Jacksonville during the 1930s and 1940s seeking economic opportunities. By the 1930s the city had become home to the DuPont banking and railroad empire presided over by Ed Ball, the DuPont trustee and brother-in-law of Alfred DuPont. While Jacksonville possessed a relatively large African American middle class, the city still retained elements of the Old South. By 1962 Jacksonville—like its New South sister cities of Atlanta, Savannah, Birmingham, Richmond, Memphis, New Orleans, Nashville, and Charlotte—was still largely segregated. "White" and "Colored" signs over doorways, water fountains, and waiting rooms told the story. Its hotels, restaurants, theaters, and, of course, schools (despite the *Brown* ruling of 1954) still operated on the Jim Crow system sanctioned by the Supreme Court's "separate but equal" doctrine of *Plessy v. Ferguson* (1896). But things were about to change. Carefully interpreting the Constitution, relevant Supreme Court and appeals court decisions as well as federal laws written to address generations of inequality in America, Florida's Middle District judges—bolstered by the Fifth Circuit Court of Appeals—joined other judges across the South in making rulings crucial to the civil rights movement.

While not as well known or sensationally covered as events in Mississippi, Alabama, Georgia, and South Carolina, Florida's experiences in the civil rights movement are still significant. Florida's reputation for moderation is largely due to the behavior and rhetoric of Florida governor LeRoy Collins (1954–1960). Indeed, when compared to Orval Faubus, George Wallace, or Ross Barnett, Collins was the epitome of moderation. Collins' response to the *Brown* decision and the growing demands of African Americans for an end to segregation and for voting rights were measured and thoughtful. In 1957 he also successfully blocked the Florida legislature's "Last Resort Bill," a measure threatening to close the public schools if the courts forced integration.[4] Yet, as one recent study of the civil rights movement in Florida has noted, the "national media and the chroniclers of the times . . . attributed" Collins' "rhetorical restraint to a legacy of moderation and lack of racial turmoil in Florida" when in reality the sentiments of perhaps a majority of white Floridians were just as rigidly determined to maintain traditional customs of racial separation as their "Down South" neighbors.[5] Even if rhetoric was restrained in these early years, Klan violence, bombings, and violent racial incidents in Miami, Orlando, Tampa, and other Florida cities were not uncommon. And the Tallahassee Bus Boycott of 1956, coming soon after the Montgomery one (even though it did not turn violent), served notice that African Americans were no longer willing to accept second-class citizenship. Jacksonville and neighboring St. Augustine were in the center of early rumblings of the civil rights movement in Florida—at least when it came to clashes between the federal courts and state and local authorities. And it was in Judge Simpson's court in Jacksonville that some of these important battles took place.

By 1962 Jacksonville had grown to nearly 400,000 persons, but its urban core was nearly all African American as whites increasingly left downtown residential areas for the suburbs. Jacksonville's network of bridges over the St. Johns River further seemed to divide the city into sections. According to historian Abel Bartley, Jacksonville was a complicated mix of "natives, immigrants, South Georgia transplants, Yankee newcomers, and African American population," and it "reflected well the demographic, social, and racial diversity that was sweeping most of peninsular Florida in the post-*Brown* era."[6] Jacksonville had an active NAACP chapter in 1960 that was determined to challenge the status quo. In December 1960, in one of the first efforts to challenge school segregation in Florida, Jacksonville NAACP attorney Earl Johnson, assisted by Thurgood Marshall and Constance Baker Motley, brought suit against the Duval County School System, claiming it was in violation of the Supreme Court mandate to desegregate.[7] While school officials were largely successful in ignoring these threats, an impassioned leader emerged to challenge the racial status quo. Rutledge Pearson, a thirty-one-year-old Jacksonville native, teacher, and newly elected leader of the Jacksonville chapter of the NAACP, began to organize sit-ins at Jacksonville lunch counters in downtown Jacksonville using nonviolent methods practiced by Martin Luther King Jr. and other civil rights leaders.

Confrontations reached a climax on August 27, 1960, when Ku Klux Klan members from outlying areas arrived in downtown Jacksonville with axe handles, baseball bats, and golf clubs, determined to prevent local merchants and store owners from capitulating to black demands of equal access. Their main target that day was students participating in sit-ins. After about twenty-five students were ejected from the lunch counter at Grant's department store about midday, they were immediately descended upon by whites wielding axe handles, baseball bats, and canes of various kinds. The rampaging whites chased the students through Hemming Park, pummeling as they went, until they reached the black section of town when African Americans counterattacked. Only then did police arrive to restore order. As "Axe Handle Day" seared into the memory of white and black North

Jacksonville Federal Courthouse, ca. 1930s. The U.S. Post Office and Courthouse was completed in 1933. The U.S. District Court for the Southern District of Florida met here until
the creation of the Middle District in 1962; the U.S. District Court for the Middle District
of Florida met here from 1962 until 2003; the U.S. Court of Appeals for the Fifth Circuit
met here from 1948 until 1981. National Archives and Records Administration, Record
Group 121.

Floridians, they pondered the future, even as Pearson and Jacksonville's
strident segregationist mayor, Haydon Burns, eyed one another uneasily.[8]

Over the next four years Jacksonville suffered sporadic violence among
whites and blacks. In early February 1964 Iona Godfrey's house was
bombed. Godfrey was a civil rights worker and the mother of a six-year-old
child who had integrated an all-white elementary school. On March 23 riots broke out in and around Stanton High and nearby Hemming Park. That
evening, in a seemingly random act of violence, Johnnie Mae Chappell, a
thirty-six-year-old African American mother of ten, was gunned down on
U.S. Highway 1 as she walked along the road with a friend. The incidents of
that day touched off several more days of rioting in Jacksonville.[9]

Meanwhile, approximately forty miles south of Jacksonville, racial unrest also buffeted St. Augustine. While local leaders there planned for the
projected 400th-year celebration of America's oldest city, the veil was lifted
over one of the most racially segregated towns in America. A congressional resolution establishing a Quadricentennial Commission and a federal
appropriation of $350,000 in support of the celebration cast a favorable

spotlight on St. Augustine. But local white leaders' determination to exclude African Americans from planning the festivities brought the city unwanted attention of the nation, especially once local NAACP leaders became determined to use the event to demonstrate the town's unfair racial policies. Instead of producing the economic bonanza of tourist dollars its backers had in mind, beginning with Vice President Lyndon Johnson's visit on March 12, 1963, the racial disturbances of the next two years in St. Augustine brought shame to the city's political and law enforcement leaders. It also brought Martin Luther King Jr., Andrew Young, Mary Peabody, Jackie Robinson, J. B. Stoner, Connie Lynch, and a whole host of "outside agitators" that put the national spotlight on the Ancient City.[10]

Years later Dan Warren (who served as state's attorney during the crisis) asserted that "the deliberate exclusion of a major segment of the city's citizens doomed the celebration from the start. The committee's carefully laid plans to encourage a flood of tourists, and their dollars, to attend the event would collapse in chaos. Martin Luther King Jr. and legions of his devoted followers would come as uninvited guests steeled with the determination to end segregation in the business community, the city, and the country. It would also bring the Ku Klux Klan to the nation's oldest city." Warren represents the St. Augustine crisis as the "final battleground in the long struggle for passage of a meaningful civil rights bill." Indeed, most historians now accept the direct link between the St. Augustine crisis and the passage of the Civil Rights Act (1964).[11] And the U.S. Middle District Court of Florida would play a pivotal role in the struggle.

The principal leader of the protests against the St. Augustine authorities' decision to exclude African American participation in the 400th anniversary celebration was Robert W. Hayling, a black dentist. Dr. Hayling was a firebrand who would eventually move far beyond the NAACP's traditional modes of procedure in confronting discrimination. He issued a statement saying that "passive resistance was no good in the face of violence. I and others of the NAACP have armed ourselves and we will shoot first and ask questions later."[12] These statements and the white pushback escalated into violence in the fall of 1963. In November Hayling and others petitioned the federal court in Jacksonville to enjoin the mayor and other city officials from interfering in peaceful demonstrations. Judge William A. McRae denied the petition. The judge stated that the plaintiffs "did not come into court with clean hands. Their leadership and particularly Robert B. Hayling have displayed a lack of restraint, common sense and good judgment, and an irresponsibility which have done disservice to the advancement of the best interests of all the plaintiffs and others in St. Augustine who are similarly situated." McRae continued, "Problems which might well have been solved by intelligent action have been handled with deliberate provocation and apparent intent to incite disorder and confusion."[13] Thus, the petition was dismissed with prejudice because, as McRae declared, the petitioners were not without fault in the controversy.

Rebuffed by the court and with the NAACP's support dwindling, Hayling prevailed on the Southern Christian Leadership Conference (SCLC), at that time meeting in Orlando, to become involved. They agreed, and their leader, Martin Luther King, was soon in St. Augustine. Conservative whites despised King's presence in St. Augustine, especially after he labeled the town "the most segregated city in America."[14] With King and the SCLC working primarily among African American churches, marches and demonstrations escalated. Predictably, St. Augustine authorities responded by arresting a large number of demonstrators, establishing unreasonably high bail and subjecting the prisoners to inhumane confinement conditions.[15] Once again King sought recourse in the federal courts. King's strategy, as Dan Warren explains, was simple: "Throughout the South, from the Montgomery bus boycott in 1955 to Birmingham in 1963, King had relied on local officials to interfere with this basic, constitutionally protected right. Once the right had been denied, he would call upon the federal courts for protection."[16] In other words, King knew that St. Augustine officials would violate the constitutional rights of the marchers.

After the initial mass arrests of the marchers, such as Mary Peabody, wife of an Episcopal bishop and mother of the governor of Massachusetts, civil rights attorneys William Kunstler and Tobias Simon represented the prisoners in the local circuit court. Their goal was to transfer the pending cases to the federal court. Before the removal proceedings, Kunstler paid his respects to Judge Simpson. After an exchange of pleasantries, Kunstler remembered that Simpson had said he was "intrigued" by Kunstler and Simon's petition for removal. "I've had no experience with them at all," he said, "I look forward to hearing your arguments as to why I should retain jurisdiction of all these prosecutions," he told the lawyers.[17] Kunstler and Simon then proceeded to St. Augustine to interview the incarcerated marchers and selected several of them, including Mrs. Peabody, to testify in court as to their treatment. Another of the prisoners was Annie Ruth Evans, a fifteen-year-old African American school girl. In a revealing moment on the first day of the hearings, Judge Simpson ordered the cross-examining defense attorney not to address Evans by her first name, "Annie," but to use the formal "Miss Evans."[18]

The hearings in Judge Simpson's courtroom revealed astonishing facts—not the least of which was the degree to which the St. Johns County Sheriffs' Department was incompetent and had been infiltrated by the Klan. It was clear that the sheriff's department had provided unruly whites an opportunity to attack demonstrators with impunity. Evidence also surfaced that one of Sheriff L. O. Davis' "auxiliary deputies" was convicted moonshiner Holstead "Hoss" Manucy, head of the Ancient City Gun Club, a Klan organization. In pointed questions from the bench, Simpson questioned Davis directly about this situation: "Isn't [Manucy] a convicted felon in this court? . . . Has he had his rights of citizenship restored?" Davis responded, "Not that I know of sir." Simpson followed: "He's good enough to be a deputy sheriff?" Davis responded, "No sir." Simpson: "You have given them cards saying they are Deputy Sheriffs and asked them to help you keep order in your Easter parade; is that correct?" Davis: "Yes Sir." Simpson: "I think, Sheriff, as a law enforcement officer, you can appreciate the danger in a situation like this when you have members of the Klan and allied organizations in your organization as deputies."[19] After lengthy hearings Simpson remanded the prosecution back to the local courts, but he did force the prosecution to agree that no cases would be tried before May 5, so as to give the petitioners "ample opportunity" to appeal his decision to the Fifth Circuit Court of Appeals to have their case moved to the district court. The Fifth Circuit Court eventually did grant the stay—and on May 11 it unanimously reversed Judge Simpson's order of remand.[20]

Meanwhile marches continued, and King and Andrew Young joined the demonstrations. This prompted the City of St. Augustine to ban nighttime marches. Again, attorneys for the marchers were in court asking Judge Simpson's intervention. On June 9, 1964, Simpson's order overturned the city's ban on nighttime marches and the confinement of demonstrators in outdoor holding pens, and also ordered that bonds be reduced from $3,000 to $100. "The basic guarantees of our Constitution are warrants for the here and now and unless there is an overwhelming compelling reason, they are to be promptly fulfilled. . . . The fundamental rights involved here: of speech, of assembly, and of petition are clearly such rights. Prior restraint against their exercise casts a heavy burden upon the Defendants to demonstrate 'clear and present danger.' This burden the Defendants failed to meet." Simpson noted that the sum total of the defendant's claims were that "a small number of youthful agitators or hecklers" had caused "minor disturbances." It was not enough, the judge declared, to simply "assert inconveniences to law enforcement officers in being required to patrol to preserve order, and the loss of sleep to do so." They told the plaintiff and his class that they could no longer protect them, but their proof in court was convincingly to the contrary. "The heavy presumption against the constitutionality of the type of prior restraint indulged in here is simply not met." Finally, Simpson declared that the plaintiffs' "rights of freedom of speech, freedom of assembly, and of petition of redress of grievances, guaranteed by Amendment I and protected against infringement by State action by Amendment XIV to the Constitution of the United States" had been violated. "Preliminary Injunction will issue."[21]

Simpson also declared that the exorbitant amounts for the appearance bonds were arbitrary and capricious, and were clearly meant to harass the plaintiffs. Moreover, in their inhumane incarceration, Davis and his deputies had inflicted "cruel and unusual punishment" on their prisoners. After describing the awful conditions in which Davis's prisoners were held, Judge Simpson, concluded, "More than cruel and unusual punishment is shown here. Here is exposed, in its raw ugliness, studied and cynical brutality, deliberately contrived to break men, physically and mentally. Regardless of their race or color, regardless of divergent political viewpoints, these were Sheriff Davis's fellow Americans, indeed his fellow townsmen."[22]

Simpson reversed the lower court's ruling, ordering that arrested juvenile marchers be turned over to the cognizance of their parents while awaiting trial instead of remanding them to juvenile authorities as wards of the state. Simpson later issued an order commanding the St. Johns County sheriff, the St. Augustine mayor, and chief of police to permit "peaceful and orderly demonstrations by marching in and about the city of St. Augustine and its public streets, sidewalks and parks at any hour in the night time. . . . If law enforcement agencies are willing to let people move in and take over the downtown area it is time for the state to take over. I think the state has the power to police a little place like St. Augustine."[23]

After Simpson's ruling, nighttime marches began taking place immediately, and the situation escalated as King and his associate Ralph Abernathy were jailed. Eventually released, King let it be known that he and the marchers would demonstrate "if it took all summer," unless the city officials were prepared to grant four things: (1) integrate hotels and restaurants; (2) hire black police officers and firemen; (3) drop charges against those arrested for demonstrating; and (4) form a biracial committee. On June

14, 1964, state authorities once again asked Judge Simpson to suspend the demonstrations, and once again Judge Simpson refused, claiming the demonstrators possessed the constitutional right to demonstrate. Simpson put the onus on law enforcement to protect the marchers, with the implication that if local and state authorities were unable or unwilling to protect the constitutional rights of the marchers, then federal authorities would. Ironically, Simpson's order also emboldened the Klan, which began nighttime marches through the black sections of town, and the chances of violent confrontation escalated. Soon Gov. Farris Bryant inserted state authority into the situation. At first Bryant had coordinated all state law enforcement forces under St. Johns County Sheriff L. O. Davis' control, but previous testimony in Judge Simpson's court had proven that Davis' force was unreliable. Bryant then organized all state law enforcement personnel into a special force and named a Florida highway patrol official as its head.[24]

As civil rights demonstrators and Klan marchers marched and countermarched, sporadic violence erupted. On June 21 Governor Bryant issued an executive order banning night marches in St. Augustine. The order was in open defiance of Judge Simpson and thus set up a confrontation between state and federal authority. According to Dan Warren, the issue "was a classic First Amendment confrontation: the state's right to control purely local law enforcement matters versus those rights guaranteed under the U.S. Constitution."[25] Meanwhile both sides ignored Bryant's executive order. Marches continued, as did arrests, as did the scrutiny of the national media. When King's assistant, Andrew Young, filed a petition in the federal court asking Judge Simpson to find the governor, the sheriff, the highway patrol chief, and the St. Augustine police chief in contempt, Simpson issued a summons to all four to come to court to show cause why they should not be held in contempt. Newspaper editorials across that state supported Governor Bryant, urging him to ignore Simpson's "show cause" order. The *St. Augustine Record* reprinted the editorial of the *Tallahassee Democrat* calling for Governor Bryant to defy the order:

The Governor of Florida should ignore the summons of a Federal Judge to defend himself against a possible contempt of court hearing. . . . The federal judge's series of orders and statements from the bench in Jacksonville had done nothing to restore domestic tranquility at St. Augustine. They may have aggravated the situation. . . . Sometime somewhere—and soon—a stand must be made against this recurring attempt of our federal judges to make and direct enforcement of the laws as well as to interpret them and settle disputes which arise under them.[26]

Governor Bryant refused to appear in court. He sent Florida attorney general James Kynes in his place, who argued that the court did not have the right to countermand the governor's order because he was the supreme law enforcement officer in Florida, and this was a local matter. The governor's interest, the attorney general argued, was purely to prevent violence, and in the exercise of his law enforcement authority, the federal court had no jurisdiction.[27] Dan Warren had advised Bryant and his lawyers not to adopt this strategy but instead to stand on a public safety or police power argument (that is, given the circumstances on the grounds that there was no way for law enforcement personnel to protect the demonstrators). Extremely late in the evening, with everyone including Warren believing that Simpson was going to hold Bryant and all of them in contempt, Warren asked for permission to address the court. As Warren recalled, Simpson

Gov. Farris Bryant and Atty. Gen. James Kynes confer over Judge Bryan Simpson's order, June 22, 1964. State Archives of Florida, *Florida Memory*, http://floridamemory.com/items/show/128457.

with a "deep weary sigh, . . . leaned back in his chair, closed his eyes, and said, 'All right Mr. Warren, you go right ahead.'" The lawyer used the opportunity to make an impassioned statement to the court arguing that Bryant's order was necessary because protecting marchers was impossible. "I don't care if you call out every marshal at your disposal . . . Or if you call out the 101st Airborne. You cannot protect the marchers. If they are allowed to march in the old city at night we cannot ensure their safety. There are a hundred places where a sniper can hide and kill a marcher." Warren then added that there were small children marching as well. "I have six children of my own," Warren continued. "I don't want the blood of any of these children on my hands." At this Judge Simpson responded, "Thank you Mr. Warren. That was bothering me too." Warren, it seemed, was on the verge of convincing the judge that it was public safety rather than state's rights that should protect the governor and his agents from contempt. By that time it was past midnight, and Judge Simpson closed the hearing by announcing he would rule on the motion in the next few days. But he never did. The issue was eventually dismissed. Yet violent confrontations between marchers, the SCLC, and the Klan continued, and law enforcement seemed unwilling and unable to stem the tide.[28]

In the following days it became increasingly apparent that the cause of the violence came from the Klan-affiliated groups and their determination to prevent the demonstrators from enjoying their constitutional rights. In fact, state witnesses had to admit that confrontations in the streets, beaches, and elsewhere came from counter-demonstrators from the Klan or other allied groups. Judge Simpson himself stated that peace was not possible until law enforcement authorities forced these groups to comply with the law. He declared,

> There comes a time when, as insulated and as cotton wrapped as the courts are . . . [that even] the Courts almost get to know it. I mean, there comes a point when general knowledge may be equated with judicial knowledge, or the other way around, and I think there's no real secret involved as to the source of what have been called the anti-demonstrators or counter-demonstrators. Whether you call them the Klan, the Ancient City Gun Club, the Citizens Band Radio or Manucy's Raiders, or whatever name you give them. . . . It's pretty clear on this record, made in this and other hearings, that there is this violent resistance to any attempt by this plaintiff and the class that he represents [to assert their constitutional rights]."[29]

Finally, by the end of June, the Senate filibuster of the Civil Rights Act was lifted. President Lyndon Johnson signed the Civil Rights Act into law on July 2. The new federal law outlawing segregation and mandating equal treatment in public and private facilities—all restaurants, motels, hotels, stores, sports facilities, and other places that served the public—provided citizens with access to the federal courts to redress their grievances. Almost immediately the marchers and the SCLC in St. Augustine attempted to integrate twenty-eight businesses but were turned away in twenty-three of them. The Civil Rights Act's passage also steeled the determination of the Klan and others who seemed even more determined to resist integration. The Klan stepped up its actions and openly sought to intimidate all business owners who complied with the law. Violence continued.

In the face of these events Judge Simpson rejected further pleas that the governor and other state officials be held in contempt, but he did issue an injunction against the Klan and the Ancient City Gun Club for actions against the law. Simpson also enjoined the motel and restaurant owners from further violation of the federal law. The ruling opened the way for plaintiffs to bring two suits, filed on July 20, in Judge Simpson's court. The first suit was against the Klan and its affiliated organizations for violation of African Americans' civil rights under the new law. The second asked the federal courts to take jurisdiction over the three hundred or so cases pending in state courts against the demonstrators.

Manucy and the motel and store owners were forced to testify during the trial, and it soon became clear that a conspiracy existed between the Klan and other persons to violate the law. In both cases the plaintiffs were successful. Finally, he issued a protective order that kept hundreds of civil rights protesters from being tried in state courts. Simpson also assumed federal jurisdiction over pending cases, and they were eventually dismissed—but not before Simpson ordered the state to return the excessively high bonds of defendants forfeited by the state judge. Dan Warren noted that Judge Simpson's ruling was the "first ruling by a federal judge under the new Civil Rights Act, it was a dramatic breakthrough that would end segregation in St. Augustine and eventually throughout the South."[30]

Throughout the St. Augustine Crisis of 1964 Judge Simpson held firm on his determination to protect the constitutional rights of the demonstrators, and his rulings are hailed today by Floridians and others as crucial beginning steps of bringing the rights of African Americans in line with all Americans. Yet his rulings were unpopular at the time, and Simpson faced abuse. For example, in response to one of his rulings that forced Sheriff Davis to remove deputies because their of Klan affiliation, South Carolina senator Strom Thurmond labeled Simpson's action "Federal Judicial dictatorship."[31] Simpson received hate mail, death threats, and calls for impeachment. One woman wrote to him saying that if she were a man, she would "beat you to a pulp," and added that she hoped he would be impeached and, better yet, he should just "drop dead and save the expense so the whites can have equal rights again."[32] Another correspondent calling himself "An Irate Taxpayer" excoriated Simpson, claiming that he was apparently a "perverted 'Nigger Lover' and a betrayer of the white peaceful citizens of this small city. It is a wonder that you have not been run out of Jacksonville before this. What an audacity to accept your salary in taxpayer's money and summon the Governor of our state to your court."[33] Also angering many was the degree to which Simpson and the federal court seemed to usurp and cast aside the "sovereign power" of the governor. As one man wrote, "The people of this nation are witnessing the destruction of our judicial system at the Federal level which is without precedent and the substitution of it for a dictatorship of the judiciary based on the cheapest sort of partisan politics. . . . I hope that Governor Bryant has the moral fortitude to make use of the power and authority vested in him as head of this state to resist this completely unwarranted usurpation of his authority and *defy* your unlawful order." While the correspondent had the "greatest respect" for the local and state courts, he thought the "Federal Courts from the highest to the lowest have become so degenerate and utterly remiss in interpreting our laws on the basis of long established principle of legal morality that I can say only one thing. 'Sir, I have nothing but contempt for you and your fellow-travelers of the Federal Oligarchy.'"[34] Simpson later admitted that it was perhaps his "native stubbornness . . . that helped stiffen [his] resolve. . . . I like the idea of being in certain people's SOB book. I never tried to please everybody anyway. There are certain people that I am happy to enjoy their ill will."[35]

Judge Simpson made it a practice not to discuss his decisions outside the courtroom, but the day after his June 9th ruling, he told a reporter. "I'm no innovator. . . . I've never consciously tried to do anything but determine the binding precedent and follow it."[36] Years later Judge Simpson himself recalled the abuse he encountered that summer. He remembered asking the U.S. marshals to watch his car. He got an unlisted telephone number because he did not want his wife or son to answer the phone, "but it wasn't a lot of disadvantages, I guess." His friends accused him of being "overzealous." But he insisted that he was "doing what I thought was right. I got a number of friends who were a little cooler for a while during that time." If anything, Simpson thought that he should have made his decisions in some of his cases a "little tougher. . . . And I think I might stiffen up a few . . . and insist on my view rather than being so accommodating. Whenever I send a proposed opinion to a brother, he would suggest that I take this and that out; a few of them, I wish I had left some of my opinions in the original form instead of softening them up. That's the only regret."[37]

Dan Warren later observed that Simpson, because of his lifetime appointment, was

> free from any political pressure to render justice. And I think that was the hallmark of Judge Simpson. I mean he was interested in one thing and that was preserving the constitutional rights of individuals that appeared before him and especially under the First Amendment. And it really didn't make much difference to Judge Simpson whether he was ostracized by the community in Jacksonville or not but he was going to do justice in the case regardless of the consequences. And to me, his enduring legacy in the federal court was that he rendered justice without fear from any pressure group in St. Augustine or in the judicial system. He was certainly subjected to it, I want to tell you. It was a monumental task.[38]

Following the tense courtroom dramas of the summer of 1964, the governor's lawyer paid Simpson a personal tribute. Florida Atty. Gen. James W. Kynes had appeared in Simpson's court numerous times in defense of Governor Bryant, the final being a complaint filed by Andrew Young against the governor, the head of Florida Department of Public Safety, the St. Augustine chief of police, and the St. Johns County sheriff. By late fall, with the demonstrators out of town, Simpson eventually dismissed the case, and the dismissal prompted a pleasant exchange between the governor's lawyer and Simpson. As Simpson enclosed the dismissal papers, he offered his compliments to Kynes and closed with the statement that "my respect and admiration for you as a man and as a public official have grown through all our contacts." Acknowledging receipt of the documents and Simpson's "kind words," Kynes answered, "I think it has been very obvious that I hold you in great respect. While we had to live through some unpleasant experiences together, I think history will conclude your conduct during some of Florida's most challenging times was in the public's interest. You, perhaps more than any other man in Florida, . . . had to carry a great deal of these burdens. I know it hasn't been pleasant, but your strength and conviction have done so much to resolve these problems."[39] With this distinguished record on the federal bench as district judge behind him, President Lyndon Johnson elevated Simpson to the Fifth Circuit Court of Appeals in 1966.

Simultaneously with Judge Simpson's rulings, other judges in the Middle District began to hear suits brought under the Civil Rights Act when plaintiffs were denied equal access to restaurants, inns, and other public facilities. For example, a federal injunction suit was filed in Judge William A. McRae's court against three clubs in Ocala that refused to serve a "mixed Negro–white group" who were not members. The plaintiffs charged that the Big D Club, the Elliot's Club, and the Four Bs Club were actually restaurants serving the general public. The defendants maintained they were private clubs and not subject to the law because they became private clubs after the passage of the Civil Rights Act.[40]

Discrimination suits in employment were also brought under the Civil Rights Act. In Judge Joseph P. Lieb's court in Tampa civil rights attorney James Sanderlin brought suit in favor of twelve St. Petersburg black police officers who claimed discrimination in work assignments, promotion and pay, and locker room facilities. The plaintiffs sought an injunction against the police department's actions. The city countered that there was no discrimination and argued that the Civil Rights Act was not applicable to the operations of a police department. Lieb called the case "unique" and asked both the City of St. Petersburg and the plaintiffs to file briefs reiterating their arguments, and gave them twenty days to prepare records. One commentator noted, "the non-jury trial is believed to be the first of its kind in the country."[41]

Following a two-day hearing Lieb dismissed the case and opined that "the practice of assigning Negroes to predominantly Negro residential areas for patrol duty was not discriminatory, but for the purpose of police protection and better law enforcement."[42] These decisions, Lieb declared, were up to the chief of police and city manager, and the court "will not substitute its judgment in the matters of operating the police department."[43] Sanderlin appealed Lieb's ruling to the Fifth Circuit Court of Appeals, and the court in New Orleans reversed Lieb's ruling, arguing that the fire department had indeed violated Civil Rights Act in their assignments. They remanded the case back to the Lieb's court, and the judge ordered an "end of racial discrimination in the city police department" and enjoined the St. Petersburg Police department from using "racial discrimination in police assignments and in designating police patrol zones."[44]

The Middle District Court and School Desegregation

While courts in the U.S. Middle District of Florida heard many cases involving the civil rights of citizens, it was school desegregation that would consume the largest measure of their time in years to come. In this work Middle District of Florida judges heard complaints and made rulings in light of the *Brown* decision and subsequent rulings of the appeals courts and the Supreme Court. While blacks protested discrimination in Jacksonville, Tallahassee, St. Augustine, and other towns across Florida and the South, the Supreme Court and the Fifth Circuit Court of Appeals issued numerous decisions that would affect segregation. Yet, as of 1962, school districts in Florida and elsewhere had largely resisted meaningful desegregation. Assessing the situation, one legal scholar observed that "all deliberate speed" had turned into "indefinite delay."[45] Beginning in 1966, however, several cases came down that had profound impact on jump-starting school desegregation.

In *United States v. Jefferson County Board of Education* (1966), the Fifth Circuit Court of Appeals established three principles that guided judges in the Middle District Court of Florida as well as other district judges. In so doing, the court went far beyond what had previously been prescribed. The *Jefferson* ruling ordered that school districts that had practiced de jure racial segregation must do more than adopt nondiscriminatory policies. They must design desegregation plans under Department of Housing, Education, and Welfare (HEW) guidelines. (It would eventually be the case that the failure of schools boards to cooperate with the HEW could result in removal of federal funds.) Detailed instructions regarding methods of correcting current circumstances on nonintegrated districts addressed such matters as pupil assignments, hiring of teachers, and assignment of faculty and staff. The decision also referred to busing as a possible remedy. The goal as set out in Justice John Minor Wisdom's decision was to "eradicate [all] vestiges of the dual system." Finally, the third element in the decision (and this was the most controversial) was compensatory justice—that is, remedies must constitute the "organized undoing of the effects of past segregation."[46]

The *Jefferson* decision was crucial. According to one source, "The Supreme Court accepted *Jefferson* and expanded it. Thus, after more than a decade as a passive agent in school desegregation, the Supreme Court ended 'freedom of choice' as an option in school desegregation plans because it had left segregated schools largely in place."[47] *Jefferson* was also transformative in that it not only initiated the idea of compensatory justice but also envisioned relief to classes as well as individuals. Hugh Davis Graham has argued that "it was radical change. Yet the courts slipped into the compensatory model while inching their way along a frustrating spectrum of implementation, without apparent awareness of the indefinable and perhaps insatiable burdens it would eventually place both on the courts and on society. For requiring present society to 'undo' the effects of the past was to require a remedy for which there was no rational definition, and hence no principled termination point."[48] Few realized at the time (except perhaps district judges) the implications that the ruling would have on the individual district judges who oversaw and ruled on the hard work of desegregating school districts. For, as Graham continued, Judge Wisdom himself "had voiced in *Jefferson* his hope that reliance on HEW guidelines would extricate the courts from the burdensome school controversies. But *Jefferson* had the opposite effect, enmeshing the federal courts ever more deeply in school policies on student transportation, school finance, student remediation, teacher training, and testing."[49]

Two years after *Jefferson*, the Supreme Court fully rejected freedom-of-choice plans as a method of desegregation. The court ruled in *Green v. New Kent County School Board* (1968) that freedom-of-choice plans had resulted in very little desegregation. That system, the court argued, placed the burden entirely on black children and their parents in seeking redress. The *Green* ruling put the onus on the school districts to construct plans to ensure immediate desegregation. Thus, Supreme Court Justice William Brennan declared that any "plan that at this date fails to provide meaningful assurance of prompt and effective disestablishment of a dual system is ... intolerable. ... The burden on a school board today is to come forward with a plan that promises realistically to work, and promises realistically to work *now*."[50]

An even more unequivocal ruling for the immediate desegregation of schools came in 1971 when the Supreme Court issued its decision in *Swann v. Charlotte-Mecklenburg Board of Education*, (1971). The decision openly endorsed busing as a viable remedy for the immediate desegregation of public schools. Added to busing were remedies such as the "use of ratios as beginning guidelines for desegregation; the remedial altering of attendance zones through gerrymandering, [and] clustering, or grouping schools in noncontiguous areas."[51] Also in *Swann* the court held that no more delays were permissible. Immediate action to desegregate must take place. The result of these three decisions had sweeping consequences for district judges everywhere. According to Kermit Hall, "Perhaps the simplest fact about the role of the [Supreme] Court in the implementation of the *Brown* decision was that it lost control over the process. Federal district judges had that task thrust upon them, and many of them acted with courage in the face of substantial personal danger."[52]

Thus it is within the context of these new rulings set down by the Fifth Circuit Court of Appeals and the Supreme Court that district judges in the Middle District of Florida heard and ruled on cases brought by plaintiffs. And so our story up to 1968 follows.

As of 1962 Florida's schools were still largely untouched by the *Brown* ruling. That year a number of plaintiffs in counties throughout the Middle District brought suit against school boards that had made little progress in desegregation up to then. Before the *Green* decision, county school board officials often used the Florida Pupil Assignment Law to slow down the process of integration. The law required individual students to petition school boards to change their school assignments.[53]

It comes as no surprise that Judge Bryan Simpson led the district and the nation in rulings in support of integration of the public schools. In cases involving Duval and Volusia County, Simpson became the first federal district judge to order faculty desegregation, and the Fifth Circuit upheld his order. In *Braxton v. Board of Public Instruction of Duval County*, he was the "first district judge to order a school board to provide a majority-to-minority transfer policy as a part of its freedom-of-choice plan. Such a policy allowed any student in a school where he was a member of the majority race, on request to obtain automatic transfer to a school where he would be a member of the minority race." Simpson approved a plan to provide integration of one grade per year. But as late as 1965 only sixty children were attending integrated schools in Duval County.[54]

Also in 1962, a number of other counties, assisted by the NAACP legal defense fund, brought suit in the federal courts. Suits were brought in favor of plaintiffs in Volusia, Polk, and Pinellas Counties. In March 1962 in Orange County eight black families appealed to the school board to have their children assigned to schools without regard to race, color, or creed; to assign teachers and principals on the same basis; to abolish dual schemes of school attendance; and to abolish practices that based budget policies regarding curriculum, school construction, or any function or administrative duties on race, color, or creed. NAACP attorneys Constance Baker Motley and Francisco Rodriquez brought suit on behalf of the Orange County parents in Judge George Young's court. The plaintiffs claimed that children, teachers, and principals were assigned to schools on the basis of race, and that budgeting, school construction, and administrative functions were similarly determined. The plaintiffs claimed that they were "injured by the operation of a compulsory biracial school system in Orange County and by the refusal of the defendants to reorganize the biracial school system into a unitary non-racial system. The operation of the compulsory biracial school system in Orange County violates rights secured to plaintiffs and members of their class by the due process and equal protection clauses of the Fourteenth Amendment to the Constitution." In response, Judge Young eventually approved a plan for the school board to integrate one grade each year beginning with the first grade.[55]

Litigation regarding school segregation also took place in Judge Joseph P. Lieb's court in Tampa. In 1964 NAACP lawyers filed suit on behalf of Leon Bradley Jr. and his father against the Pinellas County schools, arguing there had been little progress in desegregating schools. The attorney for the school board countered that over one thousand black children were attending school with white children at twenty-eight county schools.[56] By February 1965 Pinellas school superintendent Floyd Christian unveiled its desegregation plan to some two hundred citizens in Clearwater. Christian's plan would begin in the 1965–66 school year and would completely desegregate schools within two years. The plaintiffs' attorney, James Sanderlin, who was present at the meeting, complained that the meeting was "unilateral and not conducive to the exchange of ideas." He and his associates argued that Judge Lieb had ordered both sides to "discuss together the problem and explore solutions to them. We feel very strongly that solutions can be found—but can be found only through negotiation and not through a public hearing." Lieb had ordered both parties to meet together and agree on a plan to submit to him by March 15. After Christian's opening statement, Sanderlin approached the microphone and stated on the behalf of the plaintiffs that they did not consider the public meeting as an appropriate forum for settling the dispute.[57]

In November 1965 both sides were back in court. Sanderlin appeared before Judge Lieb, charging the Pinellas County with not complying with Lieb's desegregation order; he said that "through the issuance of special permits, White children who live in a zone are systematically allowed to go out of their zone to avoid going to schools that are all-Negro schools . . . and Negro children are not afforded an equal opportunity for permits." Sanderlin also charged that discrimination prevented "Negro teachers from being assigned to white schools; Negro children were prevented from getting equal opportunity to use 'special education facilities' and that 'extra-curricular activities are still for the most part maintained on a segregated basis.'" The school board attorney denied knowledge of the charges and said these complaints had never been brought to school authorities. Sanderlin said he had not gone to them because he considered it a "useless gesture." "'But you haven't shown that,'" Lieb snapped. "'Why do you burden me with all this? The federal courts don't run the schools! Why don't you go to the School Board and tell them that little Johnny Jones, colored, can't get a special permit and little Johnny Jones, white, has one?' Lieb asked attorney Sanderlin." "'Am I supposed to run over there every time some kid wants a special permit?'"[58] From that point on, the hearing consisted mostly of Judge Lieb asking questions of the school board attorney, who pled ignorance and invited Sanderlin to present his material to the board, Sanderlin agreeing to do so. In September 1966 Judge Lieb denied a motion by Sanderlin (filed April 15) for further relief under his desegregation order. He said the school board was complying with the plan. Lieb insisted that the plaintiff's evidence failed to show discrimination in hiring and teacher assignment or in admission to special education and extra-curricular activities. Sanderlin eventually appealed Lieb's ruling to the Fifth Circuit Court of Appeals. The Pinellas desegregation case, *Bradley v. Board of Public Instruction of Pinellas County*, would go on for years.[59]

On October 29, 1964, Judge Lieb turned down the Lee County School Board's bid for approval of its school integration plan because it merely provided for integration of one grade per year until all grades are integrated. Judge Lieb said based on other cases in recent decisions that one-year progression plans were inadequate. A suit had been filed the previous August on behalf of twenty-one black children. The school board moved for a summary judgment in its favor on the ground that it had, at its September 16 meeting, adopted a desegregation plan. The attorney for the school board, Julian Clarkson, and Jacksonville attorney Earl M. Johnson for the plaintiffs met in a pretrial conference in Judge Lieb's chambers. Clarkson accepted that schools were segregated in the past and said they were in the process of changing it. Johnson said it seemed that the board had a desire to find a solution. Lieb told Clarkson that he was not able to give him a summary judgment. "It is not a matter that is open and shut," he said. The judge told the attorneys to go back to work to "see if they can work out an integration plan that is mutually acceptable."[60]

In 1963 Judge Lieb heard the complaints of black parents in Polk County asking him to issue a permanent injunction stopping the board from operating a "compulsory biracial school system." Guided in their efforts by Rev. Joel Atkins, the suit filed in November 1963, *Herman H. Mills et al. v. Board of Public Instruction, Polk County, Florida*, occupied sixteen months. On January 15, 1965, after hearing the evidence, Judge Lieb ruled for the plaintiffs and filed a two-page decree giving the Polk County School Board six weeks to produce a plan for removing dual attendance zones and opening the public schools on a "non-racial basis, including the elimination of the assignment of teachers, principals, and other personnel of the defendant on a racial basis." Even so, foot-dragging in Polk continued.[61]

Because of a lack of progress in Polk and other counties, the U.S. Justice Department intervened directly. On March 1967 newly appointed attorney general Ramsey Clark filed suit on behalf of the plaintiffs in Judge Lieb's court. By that time, in addition to Pinellas, Lee, and Polk Counties, Lieb's court had desegregation cases pending in Sarasota, Hillsborough, and Manatee Counties.[62] The next month, in light of the *Jefferson* decision, Lieb summoned all the lawyers and school officials representing plaintiffs and defendants in those counties to appear in conference with him to discuss the new ruling. He ordered the officials to "reduce conflict areas" and "determine the differences and issues presently existing" and report back to him. As the Sarasota County superintendent explained, "The judge called each of the four county cases up and he wanted to see what the attorneys for the plaintiffs wanted and [what] the replies of the school board attorneys [would be.]"[63] The general message relayed in the meeting was that the *Jefferson* case set more stringent guidelines for school desegregation and called for more haste in movement toward desegregating and that school boards could no longer avoid the situation. According to one source, "Federal guidelines for integration stipulate that counties refusing to comply will face loss of federal funds, but even if a county does turn its back on federal funds, the guidelines and subsequent court decisions say that integration must take place anyhow."[64] The source reported that Judge Lieb accepted a general plan outlining desegregation goals for school years beginning in 1967 and continuing through 1969.

In July 1968 lawyers in the Polk County case were back in Judge Lieb's court after the Fifth Circuit Court of Appeals remanded the *Mills* case to the court. As outlined by the court, Lieb ordered that a new elementary school in Lakeland could not be built because it would serve to perpetuate segregation. He ordered that all future school construction in the county be approved by the court. A week later the county decided it would close five black high schools by September 1969 and the remaining black junior high schools by 1971. After commenting on the county's foot-dragging on integration, an editorial in the *St. Petersburg Evening Independent* observed, "A 6-year-old Negro entering the 1st grade in 1954, when the Supreme Court handed down its landmark decision, is now 20 years old. He has passed through elementary school, junior high and high school—all probably segregated. He must wonder how effective the law really is when he saw it flouted for 14 years."[65] In October 1968 Judge Lieb ordered the county to come up with a comprehensive plan for switching to a nondiscriminatory school system.[66]

This brief survey of actions within the Middle District of Florida's courts through 1968 regarding desegregation provides some measure of the hardships and pressures judges were up against in following the mandates of *Brown* and subsequent rulings of the Supreme Court. And these pressures and emotions would grow stronger as years would go by. Not until well into the turn of the century would most county school systems be released from court supervision. In their work, judges and other functionaries of the court faced all manner of hardships in executing the legal mandates. Some attempts at obstruction were serious and might include violence. Others were frivolous. For example, Paul Game, who labored in Tampa as a U.S. commissioner and then as a magistrate, remembered, "People were very inventive trying to jam the court up so the court couldn't move forward in those things." Game received a flood of complaints but "usually they had no standing. There must have been 150 or 200 of those things within several couple of weeks; different people would sign off on them . . . They were frivolous, but that was a genuine attempt to jam the court."[67]

Redistricting—One Man, One Vote

Yet another matter taken up by the federal courts and related in part to civil rights was redistricting. Because the state legislature had failed to take account of the massive population growth in south and central Florida, the state had one of the most unequally represented state legislatures in the United States. Despite the vigorous efforts of Gov. LeRoy Collins to rectify the situation, Florida's "Pork-Chop" legislators (members largely from rural northern counties) blocked all efforts at redistricting. Experience had proven time after time that without action by the federal courts, little change was possible. Even after the Supreme Court's ruling in *Baker v. Carr* (1962), which declared unconstitutional state constitutions that did not provide for "one man, one vote," Florida was slow to act. The current circumstances, the court declared, were in clear violation of equal protection of the laws. After *Reynolds v. Sims* (1964), federal courts mandated that the Florida legislature develop a redistricting plan. But it was in the courts rather than the legislature that made "one man, one vote" become a reality. The federal district courts partially approved a plan drafted by the legislature, but it was only after *Swann v. Adams* (1967)—another Supreme Court case that invalidated Florida's redistricting plan—that substantial progress was made.[68] Judge William A. McRae in Jacksonville headed a three-judge panel and adopted University of Florida political science professor Manning Dauer's plan, and it was ultimately approved by the higher court. In a resourceful play on words one distinguished Florida journalist commenting on Dauer's plan noted that "One Man One Vote Did It All."[69]

As one might expect, Florida legislators took a dim view of the court action that in effect superseded their own work. Florida Speaker of the Florida House of Representatives E. C. Rowell expressed his frustration after the Supreme Court rejected the plan that he and the legislators had worked out in 1966. "The whole thing is a tragedy to the people of the state of Florida when the Supreme Court legislates by judicial fiat to take over state government." The court's action, he complained was a "step toward central government," and he accused the three-judge panel of "merely wanting to please their bosses so they thought they'd better step in and act." The Supreme Court, in Rowell's view, was a "bunch of eggheads."[70]

The effects of the court order were substantial and immediate. Historian Canter Brown has noted that Judge McRae's reapportionment decision carried immense significance for the state and its government. The effect of the decision was to transfer "political power over budget and legislation from north Florida to central and south Florida."[71] The Middle District's involvement in reapportionment battles would continue in years to come. For example, when the validity of a 1972 law passed the Florida legislature, it was immediately challenged, and it came to McRae's court again. This time the judge recommended that the measure go directly to the Fifth Circuit Court of Appeals.[72] But make no mistake about it. Judge McRae's and the three panels' ruling referenced above was the turning point. That decision, along with Florida's shifting demography and national political trends, also cleared the way for a new political landscape in Florida. The days of one party (Democrat) politics in Florida were numbered.

McRae's decision also pushed forward the drive toward constitutional revision. The push to revise Florida's antiquated Constitution of 1885 had stalled, but with the new order of things it gained unstoppable momentum.

Constitutional revision began, and by 1968 voters overwhelmingly ratified the new document. Supporters of constitutional revision had an advocate in Florida's Republican governor, Claude Kirk Jr. Two years earlier Kirk had campaigned on the issue in his run for governor. His election brought change and uncertainty to the Florida political landscape. The first Republican governor since Reconstruction, Kirk was elected because Florida's Democratic Party was in disarray. A maverick with unpredictable tendencies and an eye on national office, Kirk would attempt to "shake things up," and as events would unfold, he would attempt to use defiance of the federal courts as a means to attract attention. Another omen for change of Florida's political landscape was foretold in George Smathers' decision in 1968 not to seek reelection to the United States Senate. That year Democratic stalwart LeRoy Collins emerged battered from a tough Democratic primary to face well-financed Republican Ed Gurney in the general election.

In the shadow of the Johnson's War on Poverty was the inching forward of a military commitment in Vietnam. Growing frustrations with Johnson's liberal agenda, the white backlash against civil rights, violence in the streets, the degenerating situation in Vietnam, and a whole host of other intractable problems convinced President Lyndon Johnson not to seek another term as president. In 1968 the political culture of the United States erupted as Detroit, Los Angeles, Washington, and other major American cities exploded in violence. Martin Luther King Jr. was murdered in Memphis, as was Robert Kennedy in Los Angeles after he had practically wrapped up the Democratic nomination by winning the California primary. A faction-ridden and demoralized Democratic Party unenthusiastically nominated Hubert Humphrey inside the convention center in Chicago while hundreds of protesters were beaten up and teargassed outside.

The resurgence of conservative political forces coincided perfectly with Richard Nixon's candidacy for the Republican nomination in 1968. He called for a restoration of law and order and pledged to address "violence in the streets." The Warren Court's "due process revolution" was denounced as going too far. Nixon pledged to roll back the Great Society. He also hinted at a new and as yet undisclosed strategy for winning the war in Vietnam. The 1968 election also included the vociferous, race-baiting campaign of George C. Wallace of Alabama. Wallace's message resonated with disenchanted white southerners who were life-long Democrats. His "white backlash" message was also popular among working-class districts in the industrial North, who were convinced that the federal government was under the control of "pointy-headed liberals" who were on the side of the criminals, welfare queens, and college professors "who didn't know how to park their bicycles straight." (The Wallace phenomenon continued to surge in the early 1970s. The day after he was gunned down in a Maryland shopping center, he won the 1972 Democratic primaries in Florida, Tennessee, North Carolina, Maryland, and Michigan.)

The primary beneficiary of this unrest was Richard Nixon. One of his main themes was his promise to appoint federal judges who would respect the "original intent" of the Constitution, respect precedents, and not "legislate from the bench." His "southern strategy" directed at disenchanted white Democrats worked, as it did for Ronald Reagan in 1980. Wallace had almost proved the spoiler, but Nixon squeaked by with a victory. Nixon's coattails were long. Gurney also defeated Collins for a seat the U.S. Senate. Americans expected a dramatic shift in the Nixon approach to judicial appointments. His imprint on the Supreme Court and the courts in the Middle District of Florida would soon be felt.

4

Adjudicating Equality Continues

The Middle District and School Desegregation, 1968–1976

Florida experienced tremendous growth after 1968, and this growth brought with it new challenges and opportunities. By 1970 Florida's population had advanced to nearly 7 million, almost 2 million more than in 1960. Probably the most dramatic event that contributed to the population explosion in Central Florida was the opening of Disney World in 1971. Plans for the theme park had been announced jointly by Gov. Haydon Burns and Walt Disney in 1966. Even before the announcement, Orlando was growing by leaps and bounds. The opening of Interstate 4 in 1965, which crosses the Florida Turnpike near the city, spurred growth dramatically. (The confluence of these roads was one of the reasons why Disney had chosen the site in the first place.) The region sported one of the fastest growing populations in the nation. Industrial expansion also occurred, and in 1964 alone eighty new companies moved to Orlando.[1]

Population growth in the Middle District's three largest cities pushed Florida legislators toward creating three new state universities. In 1963 the University of North Florida opened its doors in Jacksonville. Also that year in Orlando—largely inspired by the demand for more scientists and engineers to work at the Kennedy Space Center and by the needs of military contractors such as Martin Marietta—Florida lawmakers founded Florida Technological University (eventually the University of Central Florida). The 1970s witnessed huge expansion to these new universities and to Tampa's University of South Florida as well.

With President Richard Nixon's replacement of Earl Warren with Warren Burger as chief justice in 1969, a new era in the nation's highest tribunal began. While most expected a dramatic shift in the tenor of Supreme Court decisions regarding law enforcement and a tamping down of court-ordered

Orlando Federal Post Office and Courthouse, ca. 1940s. Completed in 1941, the U.S. District Court for the Southern District of Florida met here until the creation of the Middle District in 1962; the U.S. District Court for the Middle District of Florida met here from 1962 until 1974. National Archives and Records Administration, Record Group 121.

desegregation, the Burger Court continued the process unabated. But the Court also upheld stringent congressional measures to deal with crime, initiated in the waning days of the Johnson years. Even tougher federal crime-fighting legislation followed, and the federal courts would apply vigorous federal laws to deal with law-breaking on a mass scale.

Both nationally and in Florida, opposition to the Vietnam War's escalation, the draft, and other war-related policies of the Nixon administration triggered campus protests. The potential for dissention, conflict, and disorder in the area of school desegregation grew even stronger in the Nixon years. Yet the Burger Court's stand on enforcing the mandates established by the Warren Court's rulings did not waver. In fact, some acceleration could be discerned. The Burger Court's commitment to following through with mandated desegregation became clear in October 1969, when the court announced its unanimous decision in *Alexander v. Holmes County*, which stated that every school district had to terminate segregation immediately. Nixon announced that his administration would "carry out what the Supreme Court has laid down. I believe in carrying out the law even though I may have disagreed as I did in this instance. . . . But we will carry out the law."[2] But the Supreme Court went even further in April 1971, when it unanimously affirmed in *Swann v. Charlotte-Mecklenburg Board of Education* that mandatory busing was an acceptable tool for achieving court-ordered desegregation. More importantly, the court ruled that all delays of full integration must end immediately. In response, Nixon reaffirmed his 1968 stand against busing to achieve racial balance in schools. As time went on, both on principle and as a method of courting the votes of conservatives, Nixon would use various means at his disposal to slow down school desegregation, including pursuing antibusing legislation and redirecting the enforcement efforts of the departments of Justice and Housing, Education, and Welfare (HEW). (For the first time in anyone's memory, Justice Department lawyers and civil rights lawyers suing on behalf of private plaintiffs would find themselves on the opposite side of desegregation cases.[3])

Thus, as a Republican courting conservative white voters in the South, Nixon had promised to enforce the law, but not too stringently if it applied to desegregation. The situation put Nixon in a tough position, but he could also blame the situation on the courts. As historian Randy Sanders has asserted, "President Nixon developed a public policy of ambivalence and equivocation while designing an agenda to shift political culpability away from his administration and toward the judiciary."[4] Even so, as president, Nixon had methods at his disposal to slow down the process and demonstrate to conservatives that he was on their side. Nixon announced that he had "ordered HEW and the Justice Department 'to work with individual school districts to hold busing to the minimum required by law,' and he disavowed the plans already put forward by his own administration for busing" in some instances. He still had to contend with George Wallace, who was already planning another presidential run in 1972. Wallace charged that Nixon's HEW and the Justice Department were shot through with liberals who were enthusiastically enforcing busing. Meanwhile, Nixon and his staff worked feverishly to ensure that bureaucrats within these departments were not pushing busing too hard.[5]

And yet, in the last year of his first term, Nixon did push to provide tough federal sanctions to prohibit discrimination against black employment when he favored the amending of the Civil Rights Act to include broader enforcement measures. In March 1972 he signed into law the Equal Employment Opportunity Act, which gave the Equal Opportunity Commission the "authority to seek court enforcement against discrimination and to broaden its scope to ban discriminatory practices of state and local government and educational institutions."[6]

In what may have been one of the first federal cases heard involving this new act, Judge William A. McRae ruled in favor of a pregnant Jacksonville elementary school teacher named Sandra Pocklington, who challenged a Duval School Board rule that required teachers who are more than four months pregnant to take leave of absence. Pocklington claimed that she felt fine and charged that the rule was discriminatory and violated her rights. She asked McRae for an injunction against the board. Her attorney, William Manes, said the "right to become pregnant and to fix the size of the family is a fundamental constitutional right. The school board policy infringes on that right." He added that the rule was "arbitrary and capricious . . . and discriminates solely on the basis of sex." McRae granted the teacher a preliminary injunction, saying that Mrs. Pocklington would be "harmed more if she were deprived of her employment than the school system would be if she keeps on teaching," adding "The law is clear that whereas in the present case, there had been a showing of substantial likelihood that the plaintiff will ultimately prevail, she is entitled to relief." Mrs. Pocklington hailed the judge's decision as a great victory for all female teachers in the future in similar situation.[7]

In yet another case involving constitutional questions, Judges McRae and Bryan Simpson ruled in a three-judge panel (with George C. Young dissenting) that Florida's obscenity law was unconstitutional. (There were twenty cases pending that challenged the law, but the one they heard involved the showing of the film *Vixen* in Jacksonville.) McRae and Simpson found that the basic part of the law designed to regulate obscene written, recorded, and filmed material was unconstitutional and violated the First Amendment, but the court left standing elements of the law that prohibited the sale and distribution of certain material to minors.[8]

McRae, who wrote the opinion, disclaimed any notion that the court condones pornography but added that the "right of free expression is too fundamental to be abridged even by a law of good intent. . . . This court is keenly mindful that pornographic films and publications, often devoid of redeeming social or literary value, are being distributed throughout this state and nation. This problem should perhaps receive study and appropriate constitutional action by Congress and the legislatures." McRae barred the state from seizing "matter it says is obscene without first holding a court hearing on the question of obscenity. It cannot prescribe local rather than national standards of obscenity."[9]

Court-mandated desegregation remained unpopular in Florida. And opponents of desegregation had an advocate in Tallahassee. Since his election in 1966, Gov. Claude Kirk's popularity had waxed and waned. As the decade came to a close, Kirk's bizarre behavior had worn thin among Florida voters. Understanding that public opinion regarding integration was ambivalent at best, he sought to insert himself into local conflicts in the name of protecting Florida's citizens from the "evil mandates" of the federal courts. (The primary example of Kirk's clashes with the federal court was his battle with Judge Ben Krentzman in Manatee County, discussed below.) It is in this context that Middle District judges Krentzman, Joseph P. Lieb, William McRae, Charles R. Scott, and George C. Young continued to hear cases and develop desegregation plans that were in line with higher court rulings. The desegregation cases of each judge from 1969 through 1972 are addressed in turn in the following.

Judge Joseph P. Lieb's cases in Pinellas, Sarasota, Hillsborough, Lee, and Polk Counties continued in his Tampa court during those years. Since 1966, with Bryan Simpson's elevation to the Fifth Circuit Court of Appeals, Judge Lieb also had assumed the duties of chief judge of the Middle District of Florida. In early May 1969 Judge Lieb held hearings for two days on the pros and cons of the Pinellas school desegregation plan. Civil rights attorney James Sanderlin, who filed the original suit in 1964, continued to represent the plaintiffs. Both he and the school board superintendent, Thomas Southard, sparred over maps and district line boundaries. After submitting his plan to Judge Lieb, Southard stated it was the best the county could do without "radically upsetting the education system in Pinellas." The superintendent declared that 49.1 percent of the black students attend integrated schools, and under the desegregation plan the percentage would climb to 53.2 percent. He added that under the plan seventy black and eighty-two white teachers would be transferred the next year to meet the faculty integration requirements.[10] Not satisfied with the board's next submission, Lieb ordered that the school board submit a plan guaranteeing that, by 1970, 12 percent of the faculty of every school in Pinellas County would be black. He also ordered the school board attorney to prepare a plan outlining the intention of the school board to completely desegregate facilities. The court's action triggered opposition by a group of white parents who were determined to protest the action. A group calling itself the United Residents of Pinellas County announced plans to hold a rally at the Seminole High football field on July 29 to protest court-ordered desegregation. William Courtney, a Largo resident and member of the board of directors of the parents group, declared, "The middle classes are getting fed up with the way things are going in this country. We here in the central area of Pinellas County don't have a representative on the School Board and we feel our rights have been infringed upon the way the board is handling this integration thing." The group was raising money to mount a legal challenge if Judge Lieb approved the desegregation plan. "We're fed up with the way the School Board is spending our tax dollars putting in plans nobody really wants," announced Courtney. "We're just little people, but we pay the bills and our rights are being violated."[11] The organization objected to Lieb's decision on the grounds that there was no community involvement in the decision and that moving the children was "unnatural" and a dangerous "inconvenience to parents." Many children who had previously walked to school would now be bused, and this would cost more money than the school could afford. Moreover, Parent-Teacher Association involvement would be "non-existent," and busing would kill after school extracurricular activities.[12]

In a seven-page ruling, Judge Lieb approved the Pinellas School Board's desegregation plan on August 5, 1969. He allowed nine predominantly black schools to remain intact rather than begin widespread busing. He also allowed for the delay of faculty and administrative integration along county racial population ratios until the 1970–71 school year. He said he did not favor "wholesale busing in order to integrate the all-Negro" elementary, junior, and high schools.

> This court finds no feasible alternative to zones for these all-Negro schools in St. Petersburg. . . . Additionally, the court finds the existence of these all-Negro schools is the result of voluntary housing patterns of Negro parents and is no longer a result, in this year of 1969, of state imposed segregation of Negroes in residential areas and schools. . . . The court concludes based on the record and in light of all suggested alternatives, including suggestions from plaintiff's expert, that the defendant board has met its burden of converting the school system to one which is without so-called "white" and "Negro" schools but merely schools, a few of which, statistically, are all-Negro, but none of which are the result of a dual school system.[13]

Lieb believed that the school board had done its best to remedy past discrimination. "The probabilities are that the schools will remain all-Negro until housing patterns change in the area or that new school sites can be selected which will promote desegregation."[14]

In September 1969 Sanderlin and the plaintiffs appealed Lieb's ruling. Sanderlin's appeal argued that "some sort of desegregation" in the all-black schools should be necessary. "About 30 per cent white students in these schools would be a step in the right direction," he insisted. Sanderlin also contended that the "School Board was ordered in 1964 to eliminate all vestiges of a dual school system in Pinellas County."[15] Sanderlin's premise for his appeal insisted that a dual system had not been eliminated because nine all-Negro schools in the inner city virtually still existed. The Fifth Circuit Court of Appeals modified Judge Lieb's decision in the *Bradley* case on July 29, 1970, ordering desegregation of all but three of the county's schools.[16]

The integration of the Pinellas County public schools proceeded with no little disruption over the next several years. By December 1971 the desegregation plan included busing, and three antibusing leaders of the African American community threatened boycotts and other actions for the purpose of disrupting desegregation. Pinellas School Board officials filed contempt of court proceedings in the federal court.[17] In one of his first rulings from the federal bench, U.S. District Judge William Terrell Hodges called the parties into his court and urged the Pinellas officials to drop their accusations. It turned out that most of the evidence against the three came from uncorroborated newspaper accounts. Hodges was careful to remind those in his hearing of the importance of protecting freedom of speech in the matter. "The expression of critical opinion and disfavor is protected free speech under the First Amendment so long as such expression does not create a clear and present danger that the orders of the court will be thwarted." Even assuming that the three had made such the statements alleged by the school board, Hodges announced that "there is no present showing that such statements have causally resulted in any actual, substantial interference with or obstruction of the court's decrees." But Hodges added that his court would take a

> firm stand on interference with court orders and would, if necessary take action without hesitation. The court is well aware of the stress and difficulties experienced by the several members of the School Board in the performance of their duty to obey the orders of this court, particularly on those occasions when the board itself has sought a different result. Suffice it to say that the court has ample power to deal with contemptuous conduct on the part of anyone who seeks to actively interfere with this court or the board in the performance of its duty.[18]

In Sarasota County Judge Lieb announced in April 1969 that he would not extend his court order. Civil rights attorney James Sanderlin had no concerns with the plan as outlined. Yet one month later the decision to close several black schools as part of the implementation of the plan triggered black parent protests. As one newspaper reported, "A threat to fine or arrest about 1,500 black parents who removed their children from public schools was met yesterday by a vow from the parents to jam Sarasota County's jails to get what they want." In response to closing the black schools and busing their children to white schools, black parents formed the Newtown Citizens Committee to boycott the public schools. Their goal was to create "freedom schools" operated by black high school parents and white volunteers from nearby New College.[19] Despite the temporary disruption, by January 1970 most pupils and teachers were integrated under the court approved plan of 1967. A few all-white schools still existed, and there were no black teachers in eight of the nine schools in the southern part of the county. School officials cited inadequate housing in rural areas of the county for teachers and the difficulties of requiring long travel to and from schools. But Sarasota County's work was not complete. On January 21 Judge Lieb ordered school officials to submit a new plan to comply with the Supreme Court's *Green* decision.[20]

In Hillsborough County matters were much the same. Attorney James Sanderlin represented the black plaintiffs in the suit originally filed in 1962. On May 9, 1969, Judge Lieb rejected the Hillsborough desegregation plan, and he ordered officials to present a revised plan in one week. The school board proposed maintaining two all-black high schools and operating on a freedom-of-choice basis. On July 30 Lieb rejected the plan and ordered the officials to submit a completely revised comprehensive school plan based only on geographic attendance zones. The judge ordered that attorneys revise school attendance areas and prepare maps showing how all county schools would have their zones aligned to promote desegregation. Judge Lieb eventually approved a plan that would be put in effect in the fall of 1970. As of January 1970 the plan was still on appeal with the Fifth Circuit.[21]

While he labored on cases in Pinellas, Hillsborough, and Sarasota Counties in 1969–70, Judge Lieb simultaneously heard desegregation cases in Lee, Polk, and Manatee Counties. *Rosalind Blalock et al. v. The Board of Public Instruction of Lee County, Florida* was originally filed in Lee County in 1964. On May 7, 1969, Judge Lieb turned down Lee County's school desegregation plan and ordered total integration for the 1969–70 school year.

He directed Lee officials to close all three black schools and comply with the total desegregation plan. By January 1970, with the case having been transferred to Judge Ben Krentzman's court, the county had submitted a plan that the judge approved.[22] Judge Lieb approved a Polk County plan put into effect in the fall of 1969 and ordered that by September 1970 all remaining black schools in Polk would be phased out and that faculties would be integrated.[23]

All of Judge Lieb's desegregation rulings were difficult, and, despite circumstances peculiar to each county, there were similarities. The challenge was to bring each desegregation plan in line with higher court rulings in *Jefferson, Green,* and *Alexander.* While making these rulings, Judge Lieb continually received extensive abuse and hate mail. According to his son, Lieb received more than one hundred phone calls threatening his life. On one occasion, while shopping at a grocery store, one angry customer hit Lieb in the stomach with a wine bottle.[24]

As of December 1969 one source assessed the scene in Florida. "The effects of the court order for total public school integration by Feb. 1 are spreading in Florida, with Volusia County the latest to feel the impact," the source noted. "U.S. District Judge Charles R. Scott ordered Volusia County Schools to comply with the Feb. 1 total integration deadline. The school board had been prepared to ask delays. Scott said his order will stand unless there is a change in direction from federal courts. None is in sight." When he learned of Scott's order, Governor Kirk lashed out at the judge, calling for his impeachment. The Fifth Circuit Court of Appeals ordered nine school districts in the South (including Orange, Manatee, and Lee Counties in the Middle District) to change immediately to a unitary school system. The report also noted that a court decree similar to the one in Volusia County appeared in store for Alachua, Columbia, and Duval Counties. School boards in those counties had integration cases pending.[25]

On January 17, 1970, in Tallahassee, Governor Kirk and General Counsel Rivers Buford of the State Board of Education presided over a meeting of officials from seventeen counties containing two-thirds of Florida's public school enrollment to discuss ways to delay the U.S. Supreme Court's February 1 total desegregation order. Meanwhile, at Jacksonville, Judge William A. McRae said he would tell Duval and Columbia shortly how to comply with the Supreme Court decision. "I'm prepared to do my utmost to establish guidelines for the school board to aid in compliance with any orders from my court."[26]

By that time McRae had heard cases involving desegregation in Columbia and Duval Counties. The original case in Columbia was filed in 1964 by the Justice Department on behalf of HEW. In August 1969, as the new school year was about to commence, McRae ordered the county to submit a total desegregation plan by December 1. He also ordered the immediate desegregation of buses and the placement of white teachers in black schools where there were vacancies. He also ordered the board to either close down or pair a black school with a white school. Finally McRae set February 1, 1970, as the date for full faculty and pupil integration.[27]

McRae also ordered that teacher reassignment to achieve racial balance begin in Duval County on January 27, before the February 1 deadline. According to one source, schools remained closed while more than six hundred white teachers shifted to new assignments in Duval County. They were to receive orientation from their black predecessors, who went to new jobs in white schools. It was also reported that fifty teachers had resigned.[28]

The previous week Judge Young approved a modified freedom-of-choice plan for Orange County on the grounds that forced transfer solely to achieve racial balance was untenable. Young altered the previous plan to ensure transportation for any black student who desired to transfer to a white school. Schools in Orange were also closed temporarily to allow faculty shifts. Young's ruling also negated the HEW plan, which would have transferred black and white pupils throughout the district by February 1. Young ruled that the HEW plan was not acceptable because it would have been implemented through involuntary busing and disruption of numerous schools in the middle of the school term.[29]

Buoyed in their hopes at delay after studying Young's ruling in Orange County, Volusia County amended its own desegregation plan in light of Young rulings and tried unsuccessfully to set up a hearing before Judge Charles Scott to obtain his approval. School officials, optimistic that a hearing before Scott could be held that week, asked assistance from Governor Kirk and the State Board of Education, but by that time—largely due to Kirk's antics—Scott, while disclaiming any bias in the case, asked to be recused. Without comment, Lieb assigned McRae to the case. Volusia's hopes at delay were dashed when McRae moved decisively. Several days after the February 1 deadline, McRae, less than thirty minutes after hearing the plea, denied the request and ordered that all Volusia schools be immediately desegregated.[30] Volusia officials decided to appeal.

As news on desegregation conflicts circulated the state, front-page newspaper headlines told of Nixon's veto of Congress's education bill, which contained funds for busing. Nixon's televised veto message on the evening on January 26 cited excessive government spending and inflationary scares as the cause for the veto.[31]

The situation in Manatee County was perhaps the most intractable of all. As the year came to a close, the Manatee County superintendent vented his frustration to the press, claiming that he was "sick and tired of being pushed around" by federal courts. He complained that the county had submitted plan after plan, and each time the court made more demands, but each new plan was unsatisfactory. Again the superintendent complained that about 50 white children were sent to all-black schools under the plan. The effect of the court's order was so disruptive that "parents of most of the white children [had] either moved, sent their children to private schools, or are holding them out of school."[32] Despite the superintendent's disgruntlement, Judge Ben Krentzman ordered that the official attend a hearing to review the aspects of the case. But the situation in Manatee would soon reach a breaking point.

In late January 1970 Gov. Claude Kirk decided to insert himself directly into the confrontation between county school boards and the federal courts. It is hard (then and now) not to interpret Kirk's actions as a mere political ploy in an election year to raise his standing among conservative voters. Kirk had gone personally to Washington to file a motion to have the Supreme Court extend the February 1 deadline and replace it with the beginning of the next school year in September. Rejecting Kirk's plea without comment, the Supreme Court merely stated, "The motion of the governor of the state of Florida for leave to intervene and to recall the judgment is denied." When the governor returned to Florida, the state commissioner of education, Floyd Christian, criticized Kirk for this rash move, adding that, "The decision of the court comes as no surprise to me, and certainly should be no surprise to Gov. Kirk. We were all amply advised by the best legal advice in Florida that the governor would not be able to enter this case at the Supreme Court level. The attorneys of the counties involved in federal cases and the general counsel strongly advised against the governor's taking this action. All of them felt it would be lending false hopes to the people." Christian asserted that his department would continue to assist "local school districts in providing that orderly educational programs for our children are maintained at minimum of disruption."[33] These comments came while Judge Krentzman was hearing arguments in the Lee, Manatee, and Sarasota County cases.

Meanwhile Kirk blasted the Supreme Court, promising to persuade Florida's federal district courts to put off Florida school desegregation until September. Earlier Kirk had filed petitions in seven different cases then pending before three different district judges. Kirk even threatened to sign an executive order forbidding school officials from complying with desegregation deadlines after the first of the year. Kirk called the Supreme Court's rejection of his plea a "defeat for all of the children and parents in Florida," charging that there existed a double standard for the North and the South. "Fortunately we still have available to us the system of federal district courts, who have always been closer to the people and therefore more responsive to the real issues which, of course, are the children and the immorality of forced busing," the governor announced. Kirk was "joyous" that some district judges had been setting September deadlines. "They have been, so far, fair."[34] In an executive order pertaining to Volusia and Manatee County, Kirk barred student transfers and busing to accomplish school desegregation and threatened to suspend of any county official who violated his order. This order directly contradicted several court orders currently in force. School officials soon faced a difficult choice: would they face a federal judge's contempt charges, or would they be removed by their governor?

Kirk's hard line and hard talk escalated into a confrontation with Judge Ben Krentzman over the Manatee County situation. Kirk eventually took over the functions of the county school board and physically occupied the school board offices until Judge Krentzman threatened to hold him in contempt of court. The confrontation occurred on April 7, one day after Kirk suspended the Manatee County School Board and superintendent, naming himself to this position. Krentzman issued an order restraining Kirk from any conduct that would impede the desegregation plan. He also ordered Kirk to appear in his court to show cause why he should not be held in contempt. When the governor failed to appear in court on April 11, Krentzman held Kirk in contempt and ordered him to obey the desegregation order or pay a fine of $10,000 a day. Meanwhile, Kirk had ordered the Manatee County sheriff to seize control of the buildings and protect his aides who had occupied facilities. Krentzman responded by ordering U.S. Marshals to reclaim the facilities and arrest the sheriff, his deputies, and the governor's aides. When the marshals arrived on the scene they faced the sheriff and deputies in riot gear forming a barricade outside the superintendent's office. Instead of resorting to violence the marshals merely served arrest warrants on the guards, saying they considered the aides, the sheriff, and his deputes under arrest, even though they were not in custody. Krentzman's tough stand and the Nixon administration's seeming embarrassment over the spectacle put an end to Kirk's defiance. Within a few days, Kirk relented.

As a face-saving measure Kirk announced that he had gotten assurances from Washington that the Justice Department would join Florida in an appeal to the Supreme Court. (Justice Department officials denied this assertion.)[35]

Kirk, Krentzman later recalled, was in campaign mode throughout the confrontation. The judge also remembered that, as far as he was concerned, all he did was consider the Manatee case in light of the "the decisions and opinions, and the judgment" of those other cases. "I don't deserve any great credit for the novelty of it. . . . The same thing had happened [in other places] so I was walking down [a familiar] a pathway," he recalled. "But nobody believed I was going to . . . do it and everybody kept thinking I was going to change my mind. I would back off if it got to be complicated. It was interesting how people began to finally realize that I meant what I said." Krentzman admitted later that "I wasn't going to send him to jail. He didn't know that, but I knew I wasn't going to send him to jail. It was like a briar patch. He was in the briar patch." Krentzman also remembered that the U.S. Attorney, John Briggs, a Nixon appointee, behaved admirably in the crisis. "He was a good man," Krentzman remembered. Briggs understood that it was his duty to support the opinions of the judiciary, and that's what he did. Krentzman asked Briggs to find out how much money Kirk had, and when Krentzman discovered that Kirk could not pay the fine himself, he knew that there was no question that he would comply with the order.[36]

Kirk's antics caused added headaches for the Nixon administration because they came just as Nixon's attempt to install G. Harrold Carswell on the Supreme Court fizzled in the Senate. Nixon had hoped to appoint a conservative southerner both to cancel out a liberal member of the court and to shore up Republican voting strength in the South. As Kirk folded his tent in Bradenton, Nixon announced after it was clear that Carswell would not be confirmed, "I have reluctantly concluded that it is not possible to get confirmation for a judge on the Supreme Court of any man who believes in the strict construction of the Constitution if he happens to come from the South." (Carswell was the second southern nominee in a row to be turned down.) Nixon promised that he would not "nominate another southerner and let him be subjected to the kind of malicious character assassination accorded both Judges [Clement] Haynsworth and Carswell. . . . I understand the bitter feeling of millions of Americans who live in the South about the action of regional discrimination that took place in the Senate yesterday."[37]

Kirk eventually made another attempt to have the Fifth Circuit Court of Appeal delay the Manatee plan. Flying to New Orleans, he personally filed a motion seeking modification of the Manatee County plan, which required some busing across attendance zones. But the court denied Kirk's motion. They upheld Krentzman's desegregation plan.[38] As had Judge Simpson after his rulings in the St. Augustine uprising, Judge Krentzman received continual abuse, even death threats, from angry citizens. Bulging files of angry letters in Justice Department collections in the National Archives attest to the fact. Even so, he refused to buckle. As one lawyer observed, Krentzman remained firm under pressure. "There was no histrionics. Nobody went to jail. The law was administered but it was administered with grace and discretion."[39]

During and immediately following the confrontation between Krentzman and Kirk in Manatee County, Judge McRae also heard desegregation cases in the Volusia and Duval cases. After McRae's ruling in February 1970, Volusia County hired Jacksonville attorneys Chester Bedell and Robert Smith to appeal McRae's ruling. Plaintiff and defense lawyers were back in court to discuss the matter on May 13. The purpose of the hearing was to "gather facts and answer questions raised by the Fifth Circuit Court of Appeals." McRae would also prepare his own evidential brief on the Volusia situation and submit it to the appeals court.[40] After examining the evidence, the court did not foreclose the board from adopting a pairing plan as a viable alternative to busing. Under such a plan one attendance zone around two nearby elementary schools could assign all children of certain grades to one and then children of another grade to the other school.[41]

On August 6, 1970, McRae moved decisively in the Duval case, writing a "sweeping desegregation order . . . eliminating virtually all black schools in the Jacksonville school system." He also made the mayor and councilmen of the City of Jacksonville parties to the suit because they controlled the school district's purse strings. As justification, he cited a rule adopted by the Fifth Circuit Court of Appeals in 1966 saying that "the constitution is color conscious to prevent discrimination being perpetrated and to undo the effects of past discrimination."[42]

McRae refused to postpone his desegregation order while it was being appealed. Jacksonville NAACP president Lloyd Pearson called Duval's decision to appeal a waste of time and taxpayer money. "The records show that every appeal by the school board during the last ten years to maintain segregation in the public schools in Duval County has been lost." McRae's order noted that 79 percent of the "Negro pupils in the county were in all-black schools. School officials estimate that the judge's order would reduce this to 58 per cent."[43] Almost on cue, Governor Kirk soon weighed in. He called on Duval County School Board to appeal and seek a stay of McRae's ruling. Kirk said the "neighborhood school concept has been severely jeopardized and basic educational principles completely cast aside." While he faulted the Supreme Court for not defining what is meant by a "unitary school system," he offered some hope that the higher court might come to its senses. "Hopefully we are now at the threshold of such a decision and while the children remain the unfortunate victims of this litigation we should remain calm and continue to work within our system." Duval School Board attorney Yardley Buckman was not so sure. He said an appeal would be, "an exercise in futility and a waste of taxpayer money."[44]

On September 6, 1970, schools opened across the state generally without incident. In Jacksonville about forty black students who formerly attended the former all-black Eugene Butler High School, which was turned into an integrated junior high school under Judge McRae's desegregation order, picketed the school. Then they went downtown to protest the circumstances to Superintendent Cecil Hardesty. The demonstrators then picketed in front the federal courthouse where McRae's office was located. Many of the students were upset at being transferred to Robert E. Lee High, named after the Civil War general who they called a racist.[45]

Meanwhile, Florida's and the South's political winds were changing toward moderation. In the November elections Floridians selected two Democratic leaders who would have significant impact on Florida. Both Reubin Askew of Pensacola and Lawton Chiles of Lakeland had served in the Florida legislature and had reputations for pragmatism and being able to work with members from both rural and urban districts. Although both were little known and widely considered dark horses, they emerged victorious in hard-fought primaries, and both were elected in 1970 (Askew defeated Kirk's reelection bid, and Chiles filled the U.S. Senate seat vacated by Spessard Holland). Historian Randy Sanders has argued that the 1970 gubernatorial elections marked a turning point in southern politics. In 1970 Askew joined three other southern moderate governors elected that year. Jimmy Carter (Georgia), Dale Bumpers (Arkansas), and John West (South Carolina) downplayed race in their campaigns while pursuing a moderate approach to integration and broad support for education.[46] If anyone doubted that Askew would mark out a far different path to the federal court mandates with regard to desegregation than his predecessors, these questions were put to rest once and for all when the new governor declared in a University of Florida commencement address: "The law demands, and rightly so, that we put an end to segregation in our society."[47]

By the fall of 1970 the Middle District also had a new district judge. Born in Pittsburgh on December 6, 1929, Gerald Bard Tjoflat was the son of a Chilean mother and a second-generation Norwegian immigrant. His parents had met at the University of Wisconsin. The oldest of five siblings, Tjoflat worked many jobs as a youngster growing up during the Great Depression, including at his relatives' dairy farm in Wisconsin. He excelled in baseball, receiving a partial scholarship to the University of Virginia, but family financial problems forced him to withdraw from school. Moving with his family to Cincinnati, Ohio, Tjoflat enrolled at the University of Cincinnati where he earned a bachelor's degree. Not long after entering law school there, he was drafted into the army in 1952 and for two years served in the Counter Intelligence Corps 1953–55. He resumed law school at Cincinnati but later transferred to Duke where he finished in 1957. In Durham he met another student, Sarah Marie Pfhol, and the couple married and moved to Jacksonville, where Tjoflat spent ten years in private practice. A self-described "Taft Republican," Tjoflat was one of only a few Republicans in Duval County when he arrived. In 1968 Republican governor Claude Kirk appointed him circuit judge after the previous judge had been shot. He was unopposed for reelection, and in 1970, when Congress created a federal judgeship, President Nixon nominated him.[48]

Only a few months after his confirmation, he received a call from the chief of the Fifth Circuit Court of Appeals who told him that, with Judge McRae on medical leave, he was being assigned to his school desegregation cases. The most pressing one at the time was Duval County. Since December 1970 Jacksonville school district officials had already been working feverishly to implement Judge McRae's ruling in the *Mims v. Duval County School Board* case, but because Judge McRae's order had left eighteen black schools intact within the core, most understood even then that greater requirements might be required of them. Tjoflat remembered that desegregation "cases had been going up and down on appeal—kind of like a yo-yo. All these cases were sitting there waiting for *Swann*."[49] Then on April 20, like a thunderbolt, the *Swann v. Charlotte-Mecklenburg Board of Education* ruling came down. In a unanimous ruling, with Chief Justice Warren Burger writing the opinion, the court declared that "the objective today remains to eliminate from the public schools all vestiges of state-imposed segregation."[50] The ruling required school districts to use all possible techniques to achieve desegregation, including busing. The forty-one-year old, vigorous, athletic judge acted with dispatch. He was determined to move quickly and decisively. As he recalled later, he understood that "the more you drag a school case out and the more indecisive a judge is, the worse off he is and the worse off the community is."[51]

Soon after being assigned to the case, Tjoflat attended a meeting arranged by Fifth Circuit Court of Appeals Judge Griffin Bell that included the superintendent, school board officials and their lawyers, and NAACP lawyers to discuss a timetable for bringing the county into line with *Swann*. The appeals court set June 23 as the deadline for compliance. The parties were warned that there would no extensions so that appeals could be taken care of before the beginning of the 1971 school year. Tjoflat stressed that it was up to the school board to come up with a plan that would fully dismantle the dual system. "The impression was created that we would solve the problem within twenty days . . . come hell or high water." He also understood that he needed to be prepared to take the heat—that is to have the "monkey on his back. . . . This is because both representatives of the blacks and the whites must satisfy many conflicting interests within their groups. Every move they make must be ordered by the judge so that neither side must accept political blame for the respective shortcomings of the eventual compromise."[52]

Back in Jacksonville, Tjoflat worked closely with school board officials to develop a desegregation plan. Tjoflat likened the inner city of Jacksonville to the "hub of a wheel," with most of the black population in the hub and the white portions outside the wheel. "Over a long period of time, both before *Brown* and after *Brown*, schools kept being built in the outskirts and to a lesser extent in the inner city." Various things were tried previously to deal with white/black concentrations. Freedom-of-choice was tried but did not work. Clustering was also tried. Tjoflat explained,

> If you had a white school near the hub and a black school in the outer part of the hub, [and if] both were grade schools, you can hook them together. You put one through three in one building and fourth through sixth in the next, and that was pairing. Clustering was essentially the same thing: you'd have [grades] one and two [in one school] and then [grades] three and four [in another school] and then five and six [in another school]. Before the case came to me, there had been some pairing and some clustering, but that left in the hub an

awful lot of one race black schools and in the outskirts all the white schools.[53]

Tjoflat remembered that he was blessed with excellent lawyers to work with. Drew Days represented the plaintiffs. An NAACP lawyer, Days was eventually appointed assistant attorney general in the Carter administration and went on to join the Yale Law School faculty. Tjoflat also praised school board attorney Yardley Buckman and school superintendent Cecil Hardesty.[54] Tjoflat remembered that "I got them together, and I told them the school board had the constitutional obligation to have a constitutional system and told them they needed to get with it, drawing a plan." Then, in the company of U.S. Marshals, the chairman of the race relations commission for the city, and other parties, Tjoflat went to every school in the system, even the ones that he closed. "It took me a week," he recalled. "Then by this time people had plans, so I set hearings in the number one courtroom, which if you put them in a jury box, you can get close to 300 people in there inside the rail and standing along the wall." Hearings went from eight to five, and "I listened to everybody that had a plan, pro and con on each plan. I had bus times run from all the parts of Jacksonville in and out of the inner city, over bridges with tolls to find out how long it took to get a bus from the beach to downtown and from downtown to the beach or wherever, eliminating ones that were prohibitive in terms of distance." After deciding the case, Tjoflat discovered that there were not enough buses available to execute the plan, so he amended the decree to allow time for the emergency purchase buses. But the decree "kept the closure of the schools in the inner city that were rotten basically," he remembered. "They were beyond description. As a matter of fact, the expert witnesses for the plaintiffs said at least three of those schools had to go."[55]

Tjoflat remembered that providing the public the opportunity to speak was crucial to the success of the desegregation plan. "There's only one way to handle a case that is so controversial—that is to have hearings so that everyone and every group gets to have their say," he said. "The American people have an enormous sense of justice and fair play." The open hearings, Tjoflat thought, were the "key to the process."[56] After providing ample opportunity for concerned citizens to be heard, Tjoflat issued his desegregation plan. "How you write the opinion is extremely important. You write to your audience. A case like this you are writing to 'Joe Sixpack' without condescending. Everyone knew what the deadline was—June 23. They

were anticipating it." Tjoflat was careful to write a clear understandable ruling. He met with the publisher of the *Jacksonville Journal* and *Jacksonville
Times-Union* to have the ruling published in the paper.[57] "You are in a great
teaching mode when you write opinions," Tjoflat explained.

> You're writing for an audience . . . if you're writing in a voting rights
> case, the audience is huge and the news media is going to communi-
> cate what you've done to the public, so you use language that the me-
> dia understands and the public understands. I wrote the *Mims* case
> because I knew it was going to be printed in whole in the newspaper,
> and they could cut sections out, like the remedy section and print
> it separately, which they did. Also on television that night for about
> three hours or whatever they explained the opinion so a man in the
> street could understand it. . . . There's another thing that gets me go-
> ing, and that is in large measure, opinions are teaching vehicles for
> lawyers and judges . . . and to the extent that the teaching goes on, it's
> a value to society as a whole."[58]

While all sides had some quarrel with parts of Tjoflat's order, most hailed
his decision as fair. Both Jacksonville newspapers applauded Tjoflat's decision. The *Jacksonville Journal* editorialized that the judge

> deserves the praise, we think, of every Jacksonville citizen for the
> manner in which he has sought to erase the remaining vestiges of
> officially imposed racial segregation in Jacksonville's schools. We be-
> lieve that all reasonable citizens, who reflect on the problems that
> confronted Tjoflat as he prepared his ruling in the case will agree
> with us. We recommend that Tjoflat's decision to be read in full. Its
> reasoning seems legally sound to us, and it has the added virtue of
> having been written in language understandable to any reasonably
> well-educated layman. . . . He applied reason and a genuine concern
> for the welfare of all the children of Jacksonville in making judgments
> that weren't strictly dictated by law and precedent.[59]

The judge's decision, the paper continued, was "essentially an endorsement
of the desegregation plan that the School Board has submitted to the court.
This means that the School Board also deserves to be complemented for
having acted in good faith to achieve desegregation."[60]

Likewise, the *Jacksonville Florida Times-Union* editorialized that Tjoflat's
opinion

is in our opinion the most reasonable and realistic one which could be drawn up to comply with the clear and inescapable mandate of the Supreme Court. With impressive logic, Judge Tjoflat proceeded from the premises of past events and the present situation in the local schools, through the pertinent language of High Court rulings which set the prevailing guidelines, to arrive at a strongly supported conclusion of what must be done for the immediate elimination of the vestiges of the *de jure* segregated school system in Duval County.[61]

Readers were reminded that the *Brown* decision in 1954 "at one blow cut away the legal foundation for the tradition of segregated schools, anchored on the long-accepted 'separate but equal' doctrine. What the court has said since has been solely a refinement of that revolutionary decree, pointing to but one possible conclusion. That moment of truth has now arrived, and unless and until modified by due process, Judge Tjoflat's ruling stands as the law with which all parties to the issue must conform."[62]

At a press conference held immediately after Tjoflat's ruling, Superintendent Hardesty announced that unless the decision was overturned on appeal, it was the law for the Duval County school system. "The superintendent of schools and the entire staff," he declared, "now turn to implement the decision both in good faith and in due course. The appropriate time for argument about the merit or details of [the issue] ended late Wednesday afternoon, June 16 when the hearing ended in Judge Tjoflat's court. Now that the court plan has been issued, we will approach our assignment to implement the court plan on a positive, constructive basis. We believe the community will respond in similar fashion."[63]

The NAACP's appeal was unsuccessful. Writing for the appeals court, Judge Griffin Bell affirmed Tjoflat's decision on August 16, noting that there was no "invidious discrimination [in closing the black schools] and that the schools were closed for sound nonracial reasons."[64] As one commentator has noted, "In adjudicating the issues of the case, Judge Tjoflat was careful to take public opinion into account; he knew that persons of good will would enlist in the difficult task of effectively desegregating the school district. And indeed they did. Citizens from all walks of life worked together to make the social upheaval as negligible as possible."[65]

Still, there were bumps in the road. One of the most difficult sticking points in implementing the order was the need to acquire more buses. It soon became clear that the county did not have an adequate number of buses to fully implement the plan by the opening of the school year. Tjoflat called a closed-door meeting between the school superintendent and lawyers for both sides, and they emerged with a signed agreement in which all agreed that the school board would have sufficient buses in place by November 15 for the 1972–73 school year. Controversy also existed as to the cost of busing. Later the city commission—in a thinly veiled attempt to slow down the court order—developed an amendment to the city charter prohibiting the spending of state and local money for busing, and put the measure up for a vote. (Hardesty and school board attorney Buckman protested the move, claiming all along that the measure was in direct conflict with the federal court ruling.) Even so, the amendment was adopted and an election was held that approved the measure by better than a three to one margin. On the evening of the vote school board attorney Buckman moved for a protective order; once the judge was notified of the vote, Tjoflat nullified the election in one minute, ruling that the amendment was invalid because it "violated the equal protection clause of the Fourteenth Amendment and the supremacy clause of Article VI of the Constitution." Tjoflat held firm that the school board must continue to carry out the court orders.[66]

Not surprisingly, as he had all along, Tjoflat took heat for nullifying the election. One antibusing leader remarked, "It's really interesting that the judge didn't even do the people the courtesy of donning a robe and convening court. All he had to do was sit at home and strike down the will of the people."[67] Like judges Simpson and Krentzman, Tjoflat was attacked and threatened. His family also suffered. On one occasion his son was beaten up. On another occasion angered citizens put up a billboard reading "Impeach Tojo!"[68]

Tjoflat also acted firmly when violence broke out in the schools in the spring of 1972. The most serious outbreaks concerned Ribault High, where rioting rocked the school for more than a month. After the disturbances, Judge Tjoflat signed an order that banned the campus to everyone except students, faculty, and persons having specific business there. Judge Tjoflat issued an injunction and had notices personally served on every student who was suspended or expelled. He ordered U.S. Marshals to enforce the peace and ordered that his injunction be read over the school's public address system with the warning that violators of the order would be subject to arrest for contempt of federal court.[69]

In the face of George C. Wallace's growing popularity during the 1972 primary season, Nixon moved to reassure southern conservatives that he opposed the rapid pace of integration as ordered by the courts, especially insofar as busing was involved. On March 16 in a televised address, Nixon called on Congress to "enact a moratorium on busing remedies." He further stated that he was "directing Justice Department attorneys to intervene in pending litigation to oppose further use of such remedies in the interim."[70] Later Nixon spoke favorably of the education bill moving through Congress, which contained antibusing provisions. After Tjoflat's refusal to modify the second phase of integration, Jacksonville mayor Hans Tanzler communicated his displeasure to officials in Nixon's Justice Department. Tepid support was offered, but nothing came of it. Faint hope still existed in an antibusing bill that Nixon had put up. Tanzler added that President Nixon's bill "may be, in the long run, the only vestige of hope we have remaining. And however faint that ray of hope may be, we intend to do whatever we can to try to assist our own state delegation to encourage the passage of that bill and to make sure that Jacksonville is included in any relief that the bill makes possible." Tanzler called busing "tremendously disruptive, tremendously expensive and dangerous—from the traffic standpoint, not to mention the further heightening of racial tensions."[71]

On August 15 Tanzler and school officials with their attorneys flew to Washington to "try to head off court-ordered Phase II busing in Jacksonville with proposed amendments to President Nixon's Equal Education Opportunities Act of 1972. The school board passed a resolution earlier to have Duval included in its antibusing provisions. These include setting guidelines that busing be used only as a last resort and forbidding cross-busing of grade-school pupils." Superintendent Hardesty expressed ambivalence with the move. He had asserted to the school board, "In my opinion Judge Tjoflat has given us a very generous decision on June 23, 1971. . . . The plan Judge Tjoflat gave us was reasonable, fair and good in light of what the Charlotte-Mecklenburg decision said. . . . School opens in three weeks and to start a new plan would be a physical impossibility and would carry the implication that we abandoned this one." Hardesty admitted that there were parts of the plan he did not like but that in "general it was equitable."[72] The Jacksonville delegation was in Washington when the antibusing measure passed the House; the bill eventually died in the Senate.[73]

When the 1972–73 school year opened, there were a few flare-ups of opposition. On September 7, the first day of school, 250 orderly demonstrators marched near the Oceanway School. Later in the afternoon a motorcade of about 175 cars proceeded to the center of town. Some students were clearly staying home. This was the first year that a sizable number of black students were bused to the white school.[74] As the weeks wore on, picketers at Oceanway School became more unruly. After the school administration petitioned Judge Tjoflat to intervene to protect the students, he acted decisively. The petition charged that the picketers had used degrading and insulting language to black seventh grade students and teachers. On one occasion they had blocked movement of school buses and frightened children by pounding on the buses. Tjoflat issued an injunction against such activity:

> While it is clear that the demonstrators have a right protected by the First Amendment to voice their opposition to busing and urge others to join in that opposition, that right stops short of efforts such as those involved here, which are calculated to disrupt the operation of the school system and which jeopardizes the safety of the students and faculty. . . . What was originally a peaceful and orderly demonstration has degenerated into a vigorous and volatile campaign aimed at and intended to prevent the operation of Oceanway School.[75]

"The demonstrators are now relying on the use of insulting and intimating remarks and threatening gestures directed at the students and faculty of Oceanway School. The activities of the members of the campaign constitute a deliberate attempt to prohibit the school from functioning as an educational institution and to frustrate the Duval County School Board in its effort to comply with the final judgment of this case."[76] After Tjoflat's strong stand in the Oceanway crisis, most overt opposition to the desegregation plan melted away. One expert has hailed Tjoflat's ruling and conduct a "masterpiece of judicial diplomacy."[77]

While judges Tjoflat and Krentzman went on to make many more important rulings in subsequent years, it could be argued that, given the circumstances and challenges that presented themselves in the years 1970–72, this was their finest hour. On the occasion of Judge Krentzman's death twenty-seven years later in 1998, Peter Grilli, who clerked for Krentzman, remarked, "There was a small group of courageous federal judges in the 1960s and 1970s who had to endure death threats trying to follow the law and bring about racial justice to the country." Of Krentzman, Grilli noted, "People loved him and people hated him. That kind of courage is a rare thing."[78] The same could have been said of judges Simpson, Lieb, Young, McRae, and Tjoflat.

5

The Middle District and the War on Crime,
1968–1976

In the late 1960s the Middle District Court of Florida was poised for growth. Judges William A. McRae, Joseph P. Lieb, and Charles R. Scott were nearing their seventies, and their ages along with the tremendous population growth and caseload increases presaged new appointments. The district in 1970 reported a backlog of 1,450 cases, up over 300 from the previous year.[1]

Openings would provide President Richard Nixon with the opportunity to fill vacancies with judges who were more in line with his judicial philosophy. During his first two years in office, Nixon appointed four new members of the Supreme Court and selected many district and court of appeals judges. Legal scholar David S. Clarke noted in 1981 that Nixon "expanded the federal bench by a larger percentage than any other Republican President since Warren Harding," with the main "part of the increase [coming] between 1970 and 1972 when the number of district court judges was increased by 18% from 331 to 392 judges."[2] As has already been discussed, one of Nixon's appointments in those years was Gerald Tjoflat. Another was William Terrell Hodges.

But by early September 1971 speculation swirled around one of the Middle District's most respected judges. By that time, with Judge Lieb reaching age seventy and Judge McRae still on medical leave, George C. Young had just become chief judge.[3] It was reported that the Nixon administration was considering the fifty-four-year-old Young for a seat on the nation's highest tribunal. Hugo Black and John Harlan retired within the space of a week, and suddenly Nixon had two seats to fill. Rumors circulated that Judge George C. Young was on Richard Nixon's short list for an appointment to the Supreme Court. Months earlier Sen. Ed Gurney had recommend Young to Nixon for a spot on the appeals bench should G. Harrold Carswell be confirmed for the Supreme Court. When Carswell's nomination went down and he resigned from the appeals court to run for the Senate, Nixon appointed St. Petersburg lawyer Paul H. Roney to the vacancy. Not long thereafter Young's name emerged again—this time as a possible replacement for either Black or Harlan. Although a registered Democrat and Kennedy appointee, Young's reputation as a strict constructionist was certainly to Nixon's liking. Young would also have the support of former senator George Smathers, a close personal friend of President Nixon. True to form, the *Orlando Sentinel* reported, Judge Young was mum on the subject. "He goes out of his way to avoid talking about himself." The report attributed this to Young's "modesty and judicial discretion." Although he had been involved in a number of controversial cases, including segregation cases, the article continued, Young never loses his cool. "He seldom gets angry. When he does, attorneys duck and usually run for cover. But it's not because they're afraid of him, it's more like respect."[4]

Once reports circulated that Young was under consideration, Senators Lawton Chiles and Gurney were asked to make statements regarding their support. When asked, Chiles remarked that Young was an "outstanding jurist with a great deal of experience. He has a fine personality with a fine background and should the president see fit to nominate him I would be happy to support him." While Gurney certainly supported Young, the experience with Carswell compelled him to move with caution. "I think I'll wait for a while," said the senator who had just been appointed to the Senate Judiciary Committee. "I went that route once. I think I'll now let someone else do the nominating."[5] Speculation in Florida ran hot and heavy regarding Young's chances. One source noted that Young was among six others on Nixon's short list. Nixon was known to want an appointee from the South. With Atty. Gen. John Mitchell and his staff, including John Ehrlichman and others, Nixon mulled the situation until finally settling on Lewis Powell of Virginia and William Rehnquist, who at that time was serving as assistant attorney general. Nixon announced the nominations on October 21.[6]

Meanwhile, a vacancy also occurred suddenly in the Middle District when Judge Joseph P. Lieb suffered a fatal heart attack on November 1. On that day Lieb was impaneling a special grand jury to investigate organized crime, and Lieb died in his chambers while taking a nap. Lieb's segregation cases had also unquestionably added to the judge's stress.[7] Immediately after Lieb's death, a young lawyer named William Terrell Hodges in the prestigious Macfarlane, Ferguson firm in Tampa was called into the office of a senior member of the firm. Ed Kohrs had been a strong supporter of Gurney in his senatorial campaign in 1968. Most expected that whenever an opening came along, a position on the federal district bench was Kohrs' to turn down. But as Hodges explained years later, Kohrs was not interested. An expert in real estate, Kohrs did not enjoy the courtroom. When Kohrs asked Hodges if he might be interested in the position, Hodges discussed the matter with his wife and told Kohrs that he would be honored to be considered. Kohrs passed Hodges' name along to Gurney, and eventually the thirty-seven-year-old lawyer traveled to Washington and interviewed with the senator. "I had heard a couple of days before the telephone call came that he had been making inquiries of other lawyers in Tampa on whom I had reason to believe had given him a good report," Hodges remembered. "So when his call came, it was an exciting moment but not wholly unexpected." The call came on November 10, and not long after that, President Nixon nominated him.[8]

Hodges's Senate confirmation hearing was exactly one month later. Both Gurney and Chiles attended his hearing in support. "They were both at my hearing. They both came. It was a very honorable thing," Hodges remembered, "not political at all."[9] Perhaps one of the reasons that Hodges had such an easy time being confirmed was the fact that fellow nominee, Rehnquist, was drawing most of the fire. After his hearing was over, Hodges watched from the Senate gallery that evening as the stormy debates over Rehnquist's confirmation as associate justice of the Supreme Court came to a close. The debates concluded at 6:00 p.m. on Friday, December 10, 1971. A Senate vote to confirm Rehnquist's nomination was held: sixty-eight for, twenty-six against. Both Hodges and Rehnquist's commissions bore the same date, December 15, 1971.[10]

William Terrell Hodges was born in Lake Wales, Florida, in 1934. The son of a barber and citrus grower, Hodges attended Lake Wales High School where he excelled in chemistry, physics, and math. Entering the University of Florida in 1951 with plans to become an engineer, Hodges eventually turned to business as a major. Hodges entered University of Florida Levin School of Law in 1956 and earned Law Review in 1957. A young woman named Peggy Jean Woods was working in the *Law Review* office at that time, and the two eventually married. Hodges graduated in 1958 and took a job with Macfarlane, Ferguson, Allison, and Kelley in Tampa. The young lawyer rose rapidly in the profession.

Attending Hodges' investiture ceremony on December 28, 1971, were Senators Gurney and Chiles and a host of other dignitaries. Perhaps because the ceremony occurred between Christmas and New Year's, the ceremony was even more festive than normal. Peggy and Hodges' law partners,

Ed Kohrs and David C. G. Kerr, presented him his robes. William Reece Smith, president-elect of the Florida Bar, presented the Bible used to swear him in. Senators Gurney and Chiles spoke at length. Hodges acknowledged his "'humble acceptance of the grave responsibility. My singular objective,' he promised, 'will be to hold this position with dedication . . . and objectivity.'"[11]

Hodges's first official act was perhaps more unusual than any other newly appointed Middle District judge ever experienced. His investiture occurred on a Thursday of the holiday week, and the new judge planned a relaxing weekend before officially beginning his duties on Monday or Tuesday. But an alarming call from an assistant U.S. attorney interrupted his repose. On Saturday night, in a driving rainstorm, a shootout in Tampa had ensued between escaped bank robbers and FBI agents. Because all other officials were out of town on vacation, the attorney asked Hodges if he would conduct an initial appearance for those in custody. The attorney offered to bring the suspects to Hodges's house, but the judge told him he would meet him at the courthouse at 8:00 a.m. As Hodges explained, that "gave me about three hours, because, while I had handled some criminal cases by appointment, criminal law was not my specialty or area of much expertise. So I beat it down to the office and got out the rules of criminal procedure and got ready for the hearing. When they came into the room it was some the meanest angriest people I've ever seen, including FBI agents with blood and mud all over them. It was a hectic scene. I thought to myself, if this is what I've gotten myself into, I think I've made a mistake." But in truth Hodges's recalled that in nearly forty years on the bench he never had an experience like that again.[12]

In February 1972 Judge Hodges received a letter from chief judge William McRae asking him to attend a meeting of all the Middle District judges in Homosassa Springs. There was an agenda, and court matters were to be discussed among all the judges. Hodges soon realized that this was the first meeting that had ever been held for all the Middle District judges. Among the matters discussed was the decision to close the courthouse at Fernandina, as nearly all court business there had ceased.[13] Not long thereafter, annual meetings of the judges became a regular occurrence.

One of the issues that some of the judges may have discussed as a group or privately among themselves was the current status of executions in Florida. In 1967 Judge McRae had blocked executions in the state, and the moratorium still held. The issue had come up again in June 1971 when McRae was on medical leave, and McRae's cases were transferred to Judge Charles R. Scott. On June 9, Scott held a hearing to review the death penalty injunction, discover the status of each case, discuss recently decided capital punishment cases, and map out any future proceedings. Present at the hearings was Tobias Simon of Miami, the ACLU attorney representing one of the death row inmates. In May the Supreme Court had upheld death penalty procedures, but McRae's injunction for Florida still prevented any executions in the state. That fall the Supreme Court agreed to take up the death penalty again, and in a five–four decision in *Furman v. Georgia* (1972), the court found the death penalty unconstitutional because it was not administered consistently and fairly and without discriminatory intent or effect. Significantly, only two of the five judges joined the majority on the basis that they found the death penalty to be "cruel and unusual" punishment as set out in the Constitution. Thus on June 30, 1972, over six hundred death sentences in the United States (and roughly fifty in Florida) were voided. Florida, like many other death penalty states, began rewriting its death penalty statutes to meet the standards set down by *Furman*.[14] As of 1975, the status of the death penalty, even in federal courts, was unclear. That year Judge Young ruled out the possibility of that sentence for two suspects should they be found guilty in his court of slaying a postmistress in rural Gotha, Florida. After carefully studying the higher court ruling, Young ruled that "all the provisions of the federal statutory structure to perform the death penalty apparently are voided."[15]

Another question the judges may also have discussed at the conference was the current status of public defenders in the Middle District. The 1964 Criminal Justice Act as amended in 1970 required all federal districts to have a plan in place to provide counsel to indigent defendants in their courts. In January 1971 the district submitted a plan to the judicial council of the Fifth Judicial Circuit that "provides for the continued appointment and compensation of private counsel, who shall defend indigent persons and [provide the] services of an attorney under the Act." The eighteen-page plan, signed by Judges Lieb, McRae, Young, Krentzman, Tjoflat, and Scott, was approved in February by Judge John R. Brown, chief judge of the Fifth Judicial District.[16]

Meanwhile, since Nixon's election in 1968, the decision as to who would succeed Eddie Boardman as U.S. attorney for the Middle District remained unresolved. While a number of Boardman's assistants resigned before and after Nixon's election in the expectation that the new administration would immediately replace the incumbent U.S. attorney, change did not come, and Boardman continued to serve for quite some time after Nixon's election. As someone on the scene at the time explained, that strange situation occurred because of both a misunderstanding among Senators Holland and Gurney and mixed signals from Washington about Boardman's successor. "In those days," the person observed, "the blue-slip system was still being used, and if both senators didn't return a blue slip on someone going through the judiciary committee, they just never came up for a hearing." Thus, the man Gurney urged Nixon to nominate had never gotten a hearing because Gurney had "never run the name through Holland." The issue became a serious problem because U.S. Atty. Gen. John Mitchell would "not allow Boardman to hire any assistants. As assistants left, they weren't replaced, and the office was basically depleted." Eventually "Boardman decided he would resign for the good of the country." Once this occurred, the court appointed Jacksonville lawyer John Briggs to assume the position. Later, at Gurney's behest, Nixon soon nominated Briggs, and he was confirmed easily.[17]

Born in 1919, John L. Briggs grew up in Jacksonville. He attended the University of Florida and served in World War II as a Navy flier. After the war, he continued in the naval reserves, flew jets for Eastern Airlines, and earned a law degree from George Washington University. Briggs had served briefly as an assistant U.S. attorney and at the time of his appointment was in private practice.[18] When Briggs took charge, he found the office depleted. Veteran Kendall Wherry and the youthful Joseph Hatchett remained but many of Boardman's assistants had moved on. Arnold Levine, Don Stricter, Edward Hirsh, Robert Mackenzie, and Charles Carriere had entered private practice. Thomas Wilson had accepted a job in Washington in the Justice Department. E. J. Salcines had been elected Hillsborough County prosecutor.

Briggs was thus tasked with hiring many new lawyers for his office. One of the first was thirty-year-old Brooklyn native and Citadel graduate Harvey E. Schlesinger, who had come to Jacksonville several years earlier after serving three years in the Army Judge Advocate General Corps. Schlesinger remembered that when he joined the office there were only twelve assistant U.S. attorneys in the entire district: five in Jacksonville, five in Tampa, and two in Orlando. There was a huge backlog of cases. On his first day on the job after being sworn in, Schlesinger was ushered in to his office. He saw files piled up on wooden chairs and then was told those are "your cases." In his first year on the job he tried criminal cases as a prosecutor, and "on the civil side—because we did everything in the office, there was no specialization," he tried civil cases as the plaintiff or the defendant. Schlesinger remembered that Briggs's style was to give his lawyers free rein to try their cases. "His basic attitude was you're the lawyer. It's your case. I am not going to interfere with telling you how to handle your case." He recalled very little supervision from Washington except in aviation, admiralty, and civil rights cases.[19]

When Joseph Hatchett was appointed U.S. magistrate, Schlesinger took Hatchett's place as Briggs's chief assistant. Schlesinger remembered that Briggs let the chief assistant "run the office, assign the cases, and I would make sure once a month that the cases were evenly distributed. If one assistant got a little overworked, [I would] take some cases and distribute them to others." Schlesinger recalled that practicing in the Jacksonville federal court was an excellent environment. "The trial atmosphere in Jacksonville is a lot different than in other places around the country. We have what I think is probably one of the best bars in the country. The judges and the lawyers get along very well, and it was very enjoyable practicing before these judges at the time." Judge William McRae was particularly interested in the development of young lawyers. Schlesinger recalled that on occasion McRae "would call you in after a case and say now this is what you did right, this is what you did wrong. It was a nice upbringing."[20]

Schlesinger remembered Briggs as a "very very, distinguished individual. He had a presence and a manner of speaking like Warren Burger. He would walk into a room, he would command attention."[21] Joseph Hatchett also remembered Briggs fondly. Briggs was a "great, great man and a fine United States Attorney. Never let politics interfere with his duty as a chief United States Attorney. He is one of my favorite people." Hatchett also remembered Boardman fondly. "They were both great United States Attorneys."[22]

But both Schlesinger and Hatchett also came to respect Briggs's flying talents as much as his legal talents. An incident that occurred soon after Schlesinger joined the office proved that Briggs could stand up under pressure in the most dangerous of circumstances. Briggs often flew his 1948 Stinson airplane on court business. One afternoon in 1971 found Briggs piloting the aircraft from Tampa to Jacksonville with Schlesinger, Joseph Hatchett, and Judge Gerald Tjoflat on board when the oil line broke. As Schlesinger recalled, "at 10,000 feet over Lake Apopka, we lost our power."[23] Schlesinger muttered to Hatchett that he better start praying. Hatchett responded that he had already been through the whole Bible. Briggs assured his passengers that he had landed a far larger Navy plane under similar circumstances. Negotiating a space between power lines and a barn, Briggs calmly landed the plane in a cow pasture near Eustis.[24]

Another lawyer who joined Briggs and would contribute mightily to the efforts of the U.S. attorney's office in the years to come was Ernst Mueller. Born in Hamburg, Germany, in 1942, Mueller immigrated to the United States as a war refugee at the age of five. Growing up in Philadelphia, Mueller excelled, graduated from Lehigh University, and earned a master's degree in political science from the University of Florida in 1966. After a brief period teaching, Mueller attended Duke University School of Law and after graduation clerked for Judge Warren Jones of the Fifth Circuit Court of Appeals.[25]

The lawyers in John L. Briggs' office faced many challenges in prosecuting violators of federal laws. They also had a new set of tough federal laws at their disposal. Many new developments in crime fighting were ushered in during the Johnson and Nixon years. Increasing concern with crime, particularly the growing problem of narcotic trafficking and the concern that federal policing was needed to help combat this kind of law breaking, pushed Congress to action.

While Nixon strengthened and expanded Lyndon Johnson's federal attack on crime that he had initiated in the waning days of his administration, his predecessor had also moved decisively in this area. President Johnson had formed the President's Commission on Law Enforcement and the Administration of Justice (1965) and the Task Force on Organized Crime, which made its report to the president in 1967. That year the FBI established the National Crime Information Center. Johnson was also the first president to address the problem of illegal drug abuse. He signed into law the first federal legislation in this area. In 1968 Johnson also signed the Federal Gun Control Act, the first comprehensive piece of legislation regulating gun ownership. The crowning achievement of the Johnson administration's anticrime legislation was the Omnibus Crime Control and Safe Streets Act (1968), signed into law the day after Robert Kennedy's assassination.[26]

The mood of the nation clearly favored—indeed, demanded—tougher measures against crime. Historian David J. Bodenhamer notes, "Despite protests that these measures were unconstitutional, popular opinion clearly supported the Congressional action. . . . There had been too much disorder, too many killings and assassinations, too much property destroyed. Order, not rights, was the new public watchword."[27] Another historian commenting on the national trend toward federal law enforcement in the late 1960s noted, "Prodded by public fears, and perhaps emboldened by past successes, federal officials committed the national government to a broader attack on crime. They also launched an assault on illegal entrepreneurs . . . and on white-collar crime. Different strategies were supposed to deal with each aspect of these new responsibilities. The Omnibus Crime Control Act of 1968 created a bureaucratic structure for coordinating a national campaign against crime. Congress allocated enormous sums to improve policing."[28] The new law provided federal assistance to state and local law enforcement agencies in the form of "block grants." The money was used for new equipment and better training for police officers.[29] The act established the Law Enforcement Assistance Administration, a vehicle for channeling huge sums of federal money for training and the purchase of equipment. Because Nixon firmly believed in allowing as much decision making as possible to states and localities, this program was expanded. Such an approach would provide the utmost flexibility to localities. Nixon's revenue-sharing programs, according to one expert, "would send power and resources back to the individual states."[30]

But the problem of effectively prosecuting white collar criminals and drug traffickers was especially difficult because, as one historian explained, these offenders often possessed "social, economic, and political power. Their power rested on the public demand for illegal goods and services. Federal successes, such as the apprehension of an entire drug syndicate, simply created more room for other entrepreneurs to fulfill public demands. On the other hand, the influence which these entrepreneurs have in their local communities complicates efforts to build cases against them. And white collar criminals . . . have considerable power to protect themselves from the consequences of their acts."[31]

As a state attorney in the 1960s, Dan Warren had witnessed this growth of newer, more sophisticated law breaking firsthand. He recalled his frustration with how crime was escalating in Florida and the idea that every single act of a crime spree had to be tried with due process on an individualized basis. "It was becoming more and more apparent to me at that time that something had to give in the criminal justice system."[32] But then Congress passed the Racketeer Influenced and Corrupt Organizations Act (RICO, 1970), also known as the Organized Crime Control Act. The RICO Act authorized the "witness immunity and protection program, extended federal jurisdiction over illegal gambling, and prohibited the investment of income from racketeering in legitimate interstate businesses."[33] The law made it possible for the first time to prosecute an entire gang as engaging in an ongoing criminal enterprise through a pattern of criminal activity. According to Robert J. Kelly, until this statute was enacted, "the investigation and prosecution of organized criminal groups had not been conducted in a coordinated manner. Congress passed RICO with the specific intent of combating the infiltration of organized crime into legitimate businesses. The act provided federal law enforcement personnel with a wide range of tools. Prosecutors employed RICO to imprison heads of crime families, to exact forfeiture based on criminal earnings, and to treble the penalties associated with racketeering."[34]

Attorney Dan Warren thought the RICO statute was the most important innovation in criminal prosecution to appear in his career. "All of a sudden," he remembered,

> it gave federal courts jurisdiction over the bulk of the criminal cases. I don't think you can really underestimate how RICO changed the federal court system and its prosecution of crimes. If you go back prior to RICO, you found only a few federal crimes. . . . All of a sudden, RICO comes in. It just about federalized all of the criminal laws, because RICO went across state lines. . . . See RICO had what we call a relation back theory which states that if you engaged in this pattern; if you committed two or more predicate acts, then you could go back and pick up criminal activity for the past seven years. So I mean it was a statute that really changed the face of how we prosecute crime in this country. It had a great impact on it, no question about it.

It created the concept of "the [ongoing] continuing criminal enterprises. . . . It increased the jurisdiction of the federal courts drastically. . . . And that's the unintended consequences of that act that led to a proliferation of federal cases and changed dramatically the way we prosecute crime in the state," he observed.[35]

Middle District prosecutors and law enforcement personnel had another innovation at their disposal in prosecuting criminals. The "Strike Force" concept emerged in the 1960s. The idea was to have "personnel from several federal agencies who pooled their knowledge and skill to investigate and prosecute underworld figures."[36] The first Strike Force was created in 1966, but the Nixon Justice Department expanded the program dramatically from 1970–71. By the end of 1971 there were nineteen of these operations in the country. Also in the effort to more effectively fight the illegal drug trade, Congress created the Drug Enforcement Administration (DEA) in 1973, which reorganized all of the various agencies involved in investigating drug smuggling and distribution under one umbrella. The agency expanded rapidly. Within two years after its creation, the agency had more than three thousand employees. It also worked closely with the U.S. Customs Service.[37]

Also in 1969, in an effort to standardize and professionalize law enforcement at the federal level, Congress created the U.S. Marshals Service, and by 1976 it achieved bureau status within the Department of Justice. By 1972 the Marshals Service took control of hiring and training all deputies nationwide. Previously, according to one historian, "U.S. marshals enjoyed a surprising degree of independence in performing their duties. No central administration existed to supervise their work until the late 1950s. Even then the Executive Office for U.S. Marshals had no real power over the districts until it was transformed into the U.S. Marshals Service. . . . Before that, each marshal was practically autonomous, receiving only general guidance from the executive branch." They "enjoyed . . . wide latitude in determining how they would enforce the law. For most of them the solution was to go as easy as possible. Few of them wanted to offend their friends and neighbors, particularly because they knew all too well that the job of marshal was temporary. Unless they were prepared to leave their homes after their commissions expired, the marshals struggled to balance the enforcement of federal laws against the feelings of the local populace."[38]

By the late 1960s prosecutors were using the new methods at their disposal to prosecute organized crime. In November 1969 a federal grand jury in the Tampa division indicted thirty-eight persons. Assisting the jury was Miamian James Oliphant, a member of the Department of Justice's newly formed Strike Force to fight organized crime. Judge Lieb set bond before releasing the arrest warrants to federal agents who would apprehend defendants. The probe was aimed at gambling and organized racketeering, and, according to Oliphant, the suspects were accused of using "interstate communications facilities—telephones and telegraphs—to further gambling activities." Santo Trafficante Jr. and members of his family were called to testify, as were FBI agents. One of the main witnesses was Joe Phil Ciccarello. Lieb granted him immunity and warned him to tell the truth on threat of perjury, but not much progress was made in pursuing law breakers.[39]

In late October 1971, in a huge sweep, state and federal agents rounded up fifty suspects in a multimillion-dollar sports bookmaking and gambling ring based in Central Florida. The titular head of the Central Florida operation was Harlan Blackburn, aka "The Colonel" or the "Fat Man." (Blackburn had ties to Santo Trafficante and at that time was serving an eight-year-term in a federal prison in Springfield, Missouri.) Those arrested included Belleview bank president Vincent Razzano and Blackburn's lawyer, Orville Johnson. FBI special agent J. F. Santoiana called the raid the "largest organized roundup in Florida's history." After sealed indictments were issued in Tampa, federal, state, and county officers made arrests in six Central Florida counties and in Miami and New York. Evidence was obtained through wire taps and search warrants turned over to the grand jury by the Florida Department of Law Enforcement. Judge Joseph P. Lieb impaneled a special grand jury at the request of U.S. Atty. Gen. John Mitchell. Gov. Reubin Askew sought federal assistance "because of the interstate scope of the Florida gambling operations and a chain of evidence [that was] said [to go] far beyond" Blackburn's illegal gambling organization. When Lieb died suddenly in November 1971, Judge Gerald Tjoflat inherited the case.[40]

Dan Warren, who by that time had left the state attorney's office, represented two minor players caught in the conspiracy in that first federal RICO prosecution in Florida history. Warren's clients were gamblers making book on football games, and "they were caught up in this massive criminal conspiracy that was being operated out of Tampa and Orlando, that included prostitution and drugs and all different sorts of criminal activity. . . . They were incensed that they were thrown in with this drug crowd and all sordid aspects of criminal activity around the state and they were just out to take bets on football games." But Warren's clients were prosecuted along with the others who were operating within the framework of Harlan Blackburn's mob.[41]

The huge trial in Jacksonville before Judge Tjoflat began on May 15. Some of the evidence was based on wiretaps authorized by Governor Askew, who acted under the authority of the federal RICO statute. The various defendants were charged with using interstate facilities—primarily telephone lines—to violate Florida's antigambling law.[42] The ninety-six page indictment also alleged that Blackburn had twice ordered his twenty-year underworld aide and friend Clyde Lee's assassination. This came after Blackburn discovered that Lee was stealing large sums of money from the lottery operation. Trial testimony also revealed that Blackburn and others had masterminded several post office and bank robberies, netting hundreds of thousands of dollars. It was also disclosed that Martin Segal, a paralyzed Orlando attorney, loaned Blackburn huge sums of money at high interest rates to finance gambling. (At the time, Segal was in Arizona, recuperating from gunshot wounds inflicted by his wife.) Blackburn operated a large check kiting scheme to maintain a delicate balance between gambling income and debts.[43]

The strength of the government case prompted first thirty-eight, then eight more, and then three final defendants to plead guilty. "The avalanche of guilt admissions is considered a triumph for young prosecutor Bernard Dempsey Jr. and for the FBI and FDLE," one source noted. But the same report stated that four Orlandoans still faced indictment, and five others were severed from the case and granted separate trials. Thus, the lengthy trial continued.[44]

On May 22 Beverly Roberts Mathews, Blackburn's former mistress and FBI informant, took the stand and identified persons who she accused of being investors in Blackburn's gambling operations, which spanned three counties and dozens of towns. Among the seven men she identified in her testimony was a Cocoa man named John Newton Fountain, who she claimed had loaned Blackburn more than $80,000. Arnold Levine, Fountain's lawyer, objected frequently to Mathews' testimony. Mathews testified that Fountain frequently bankrolled narcotics operations in the Orlando area. Mathews was unsure about whether "Blackburn himself was involved in dope peddling but he did make loans and covered car payments for 'some of the girls'" involved. "Taking the stand in a powder pink pants suit and an elaborate, piled up coiffure with curls dripping over her shoulders, Blackburn's most trusted confidante began detailing 'the whole thing' about her romance and business participation in the complex gambling enterprise."[45] She said even after Blackburn was hospitalized with a liver complaint, he still managed to run his vast combine with daily messages and reports smuggled back and forth by Altamonte attorney Orville Johnson. In order to shorten her perjury sentence Mathews began giving information to the FBI. She supplied the FBI with a list of Blackburn's creditors and a list of his assets.

She testified that she first met Blackburn at Freddies steakhouse in 1962. She lived with him "in a very close relationship" until 1969.[46] She said she was present at most of the illegal transactions, many of which were conducted at her home in Seminole County or her pawnshop in Longwood. She admitted to prosecutor Dempsey that there was no question that the loans, which carried rates as high as 60 percent, were known to the creditors as going for illegal activity. She often accompanied Blackburn on his rounds to banks in Ocala and was with him the day Fountain handed him $60,000. She said banker "Razzano also obliged by obtaining loans from other banks and passing the funds along to Blackburn at 'shylock' rates."[47]

William Alexander Fox, Blackburn's assistant, also took the stand to provide more details. Levine tried to discredit the veracity of the testimony. He argued that his client loaned Blackburn the money because he thought it was to support his plumbing business. Fox countered that Fountain and the others fully understood what the money was intended for, adding the gambling take was between $50,000 and $200,000 a week. Wagers were taken on football, boxing, horse-racing, baseball, and basketball. Also numbers brought in between $10,000 to $30,000 a week. Fox said he often personally took payoffs of principal and interest, or "juice," to Fountain and the others. Defense attorney Levine charged that assistant U.S. attorney, Dempsey, had "primed" the witness and demanded a new trial and permission to cross examine Fox. Judge Tjoflat denied both requests. "After this trial you can file a grievance against Mr. Dempsey," Judge Tjoflat countered. "A big issue in this case is what the money was used for. You want to say the money was not used for illicit purposes."[48]

Eventually Blackburn himself was temporarily released from prison to testify in the case. Blackburn had already pleaded guilty but had not been sentenced in the current trials. One newspaper account reported that Blackburn was being held in heavily guarded secrecy somewhere in the 33-county federal district. Federal marshals ushered him into the courtroom on May 30. "Still big but shrunken somewhat from the former portliness which won him the underworld code name as 'Fat Man,' the 53 year-old Blackburn walked heavily into the expectant courtroom."[49] When questioned by Levine, Blackburn took the Fifth. Fox later testified that Blackburn's empire was dependent on the constant flow of borrowed money. "If it had not been for Blackburn getting that revenue, the business would have gone broke years ago." Levine continued to hammer away at Fox and Mathews' credibility. Fox had been on the wrong side of the law for thirty years but "had finally seen the light," and Mathews, an admitted perjurer and a "cheap prostitute," had taken the stand for "self-preservation."[50]

John Fountain and four other defendants were found guilty. Tjoflat ordered them free on bond pending an appeal. The sensational trial had had the effect of exposing the dark underworld of organized crime in Central Florida. It also exposed the sordid behavior of some lawyers who had facilitated the illegal operations of organized crime kingpins like Harlan Blackburn. Judge Tjoflat ordered a transcript of the government's sweeping case against Harlan Blackburn's crime syndicate sent to the Florida Bar because of the evidence regarding the conduct of the lawyers in the Orlando area. "Judge Tjoflat declared he would be 'derelict' in his duty if he did not send the record to the legal profession's self-disciplining organization 'forthwith. . . . I hope this jury does not leave this courtroom with the thought that all lawyers in the state are like some of those that have been described in the Orlando area.'"[51]

The federal prosecutions against Blackburn's mob effectively disabled his "Cracker" mafia, but far bigger challenges lay ahead for law enforcement officials in the Middle District of Florida. When compared to the operations of sophisticated drug syndicates of the 1970s and 1980s, Trafficante and Blackburn's mob would seem miniscule indeed. But that is a subject for a future chapter.

One of the most bizarre trials Judge Tjoflat presided over was the mail fraud–conspiracy case of the flamboyant entrepreneur Glenn Turner. Tjoflat recalled that the case was "kind of a zoo. That was a mail fraud case. It was a pyramid. Koscot was a pyramid operation where they sold distributorships; it was cosmetics. Then they shifted to Dare to be Great, which was a cassette arrangement with inspirational speaking."[52] The twenty-eight count federal indictment charging Turner and his associates with fraudulently using the mails to promote his illegal businesses came before Tjoflat on September 17, 1973. Glenn Turner was an eighth-grade-educated son of a South Carolina sharecropper, who rose from being a door-to-door salesman to the owner of his own multimillion-dollar company. Nine lawyers including, F. Lee Bailey (both a lawyer and a defendant in the case), represented the three Orlando-based corporate defendants, Koscot Interplanetary Inc., Dare to Be Great Inc., and Glenn Turner Enterprises Inc. The government called over 150 witnesses, most of whom lost money in various schemes. Trial transcripts ran to more than 16,500 pages.[53] "The problem about this case," Tjoflat later recalled, was that "there were many federal, criminal laws that were violated. There were securities problems. There was securities fraud. There was tax evasion."[54] There were many competing federal agencies: SEC, IRS, Postal Inspectors etc.[55]

As of February 1974 the marathon trial was still under way, and it attracted extensive press coverage. A reporter from the *Miami Herald* noted that, while Judge Tjoflat was once a "hot prospect for the Cincinnati Reds[, his] court room is no ballpark, and if a spectator should as much as remove his coat, a bailiff will descend to enforce the proper attire on threat of expulsion." One person delighted with the length of the trial was court stenographer Sam Rosenfeld, who got "$8 a page with reporters and typists working relays for daily transcripts[;] his bill for 19,000 pages is now $152,000." Bailey and the eight other defendants were staying in an apartment complex with twenty-one apartments at a cost of $4,000 a month. "Outside is the Glenn W. Turner Memorial Basketball Hoop. Inside is a Xerox 7000 with a l-slot collator, two WATS lines, video film equipment, and files galore. (In court the prosecution uses supermarket-styled grocery carts from the Post

Office Department for their files.)" Bailey had taken a $124,000 fee from Turner and was supposed to get a $750,000 Learjet. Bailey's third wife, New Zealand–born Lynda, was also on hand.[56]

The trial eventually ended with a hung jury. At that point Chief Judge George C. Young transferred the proceedings to Judge Hodges. The court had earlier ordered that the case against Bailey be severed from the Turner prosecutions. Proceedings against Bailey would take place in Orlando.[57]

Turner's new trial in Tampa began on August 4, 1975. On that day Turner stunned those present by declaring that he would defend himself. After nearly six weeks of testimony, Turner and three former associates pleaded no contest to federal misdemeanor charges of violating securities and exchange regulations. Each was fined $5,000, the maximum penalty. Judge Hodges accepted the pleas, dropping felony charges on the condition that Turner and the other defendants sign a written statement promising to "refrain from violating any law" and "work regularly at a lawful occupation."[58] Emerging from the courtroom, a tearful Turner announced, "'I've been fighting the government for seven years. . . . My money ran out and I couldn't fight any more. That's what happened.'"[59] Thus, Turner walked free, but he would return to federal court nearly ten years later in a battle with the IRS over tax disputes.

On March 30, 1973, judges, lawyers, and other persons in Tampa associated with the Middle District took time out of a busy day to pay tribute to one of their brethren. Joseph P. Lieb had died about a year and a half before. As he presided over the ceremony, Judge George Young also introduced Bankruptcy Judge Alexander Paskay, Judge Bryan Simpson, and others who offered their memories of Judge Lieb.[60]

Only two months earlier the Middle District had lost another judge when William A. McRae died. With McRae's passing, Judge Young once again became chief judge. With the district's population expected to grow to five million in only a few years, Young made an appeal to Washington for more judges. Testifying before a Senate subcommittee, Young explained that six judges in his district handled an average of 461 cases each in 1972, and this was 98 cases more than the national average. The district's five divisions in Jacksonville, Ocala, Orlando, Tampa, and Fort Myers had almost 1,500 civil and 295 criminal cases pending. One senator responded to Young's request for more judges by suggesting that visiting judges could take of the problem. Senator Gurney immediately countered the assertion. "The clear and compelling need for increased judicial manpower for these districts is apparent and fully justified," he declared.[61] Back in Orlando, when questioned, Young admitted that with the caseload growing by leaps and bounds, there was "no question that the pressure on judges has been greater." There were more cases and more people. "Then, there's more matters that are the subject of litigation than there used to be."[62]

The sudden opening on the court coming on the heels of McRae's death aroused a conflict between Senators Chiles and Gurney. Chiles understood that, as a Republican senator in office at the time of a Republican president, Gurney had the primary responsibility of recommending a name to the president, but Chiles indicated to Gurney that he would like to have some input. Gurney cast aside Chiles' request and even hinted that Chiles had some ulterior motive in the suggestion. Chiles favored the creation of the nine-member panel to select five qualified candidates for the senators to choose from, instead of "the party in power appointing one from its ranks." Without waiting any longer to discuss the matter, Gurney held a press conference announcing the man that he had selected was Orlando lawyer John Alton Reed Jr.[63]

When confronted with a fait accompli, Chiles responded publicly. "Because I do not want to cloud the issue of finding a better way to select our judges and because he seems to be qualified, I am going to support John Reed. . . . . Now all vacancies are filled and for the future, I intend to insist that we find a better way than political patronage. I urge Sen. Gurney to join me in creating the Selection Commission."[64] A number of editorial boards across the state weighed in on Chiles' recommendation that a Florida federal judicial selection commission be established. The *Daytona Beach Morning Journal* rejected Gurney's assertion that to do so would be to disregard the Constitution, arguing that the "proposal does not diminish the President's right to have the final say about who gets the appointment." The journal praised Chiles' plan, which "wants to change the utter political nature of choosing men or women who are going to have life or death power over human beings."[65]

John Alton Reed Jr. was born in 1931 in Washington, D.C. He married Louisa Wardman one year before earning an bachelor's degree from Duke University in 1954. After graduating from the Duke University School of Law in 1956 he relocated to Tampa, where he practiced law for one year and practiced in Orlando from 1957 to 1967. At the time of his appointment Reed was in his sixth year of service of Florida's Fourth District Court of Appeal. After his confirmation, Judge Reed joined Judge Young in Orlando.[66]

One historian has noted that while Nixon's federal campaign on crime produced some "solid achievements, it also caused enormous abuses of police power. The attitudes and methods of the men in charge of specific activities were partly responsible for this mixed record. But Nixon and Attorney General Mitchell bear the greater responsibility because they were not especially concerned about the means their subordinates used to obtain results."[67] These same dubious methods and tools would soon be put to use in the political arena as well. While his position was strong heading into the campaign for reelection in 1972, the Nixon White House was determined to leave no stone unturned to ensure that he won a landslide victory. In January Atty. Gen. John Mitchell resigned his position in the cabinet to head up Nixon's campaign. The Committee to Re-Elect the President (CREEP), headed by Mitchell, soon became the vehicle through which a whole array of "dirty tricks" were orchestrated against Democratic primary candidates.

In the days leading up to the March 14 Florida primary, the Edmund Muskie, Henry "Scoop" Jackson, and Hubert Humphrey campaigns were victimized by a whole host of dirty tricks by CREEP operatives in Florida. The goal was to sabotage the Muskie, Jackson, and Humphrey campaigns with the idea of helping George McGovern, whom they perceived as the weakest challenger. Directing the operations in Florida was thirty-one-year-old Californian Donald Segretti, who, it turned out, was recruited to the task by Dwight Chapin, the president's White House appointment secretary, who in turn worked closely with presidential advisor H. R. Haldeman. Early in 1972 Segretti circuited Florida and hired young people to infiltrate the Muskie and Jackson campaigns and to steal documents, stationery, and other items that could be used for "dirty tricks." As one example, Segretti's operatives mailed hundreds of copies of a letter on stolen Muskie campaign stationery containing false allegations of Jackson and Humphrey's sexual misconduct. (Scoop Jackson had fathered an illegitimate child, and Humphrey had been arrested twice for homosexual acts.) After the primary election Segretti returned to California, but in light of the June 17 Watergate break-in, the FBI questioned Segretti nine days later.[68] After denying any knowledge of the break-in, investigators asked Segretti about his campaign activities in Florida the previous February and March. Segretti explained that in January 1972 he decided to "take a rest" from his law practice and follow "primary elections across the country." As a concerned citizen and a supporter of the president's reelection, he decided "he could best work toward that goal by putting questions to Democratic candidates for the Democratic nomination whenever he had the opportunity, which would require them to discuss their feelings on issues on which their opinion is unpopular, or discuss their voting record on issues of interest to the people where they are speaking." Segretti told the FBI that he considered "his function at these rallies to be that of an organizer who gives direction to people who support the President's policies but who lack direction; however his activities in this regard are a result of his own initiative and are not conducted as a result of any instructions or directions given to him by anyone else." While Segretti did admit to receiving small amounts of "money from persons he does not wish to disclose," he insisted that he "initiated all his travel and activities with respect to the Democratic primaries himself."[69]

Only weeks after Nixon's landslide victory over George McGovern, national and Florida newspapers contained stories of Segretti's and CREEP's "campaign sabotage ring" in Florida.[70] It was soon learned that Segretti's operations were funded by huge sums of money funneled to him by CREEP through Nixon lawyer Herbert W. Kalmbach. With information supplied to him by the FBI, U.S. Attorney John Briggs presented the evidence to a grand jury in Orlando, and the panel indicted Segretti and an accomplice, Tampa man George A. Hearing. On May 4, the same day as the indictment, federal agents arrested Segretti in Los Angeles and returned him to Florida to face the charges of violating federal campaign laws. On the day the indictments came down John Briggs announced, "I think what we have done in Orlando has a national significance. . . . I can't say whether there will be other indictments. There will certainly be additional investigations and I hope they will result in indictments." Briggs added that he was in touch with the grand jury in Washington investigating the Watergate bugging and break-in.[71]

U.S. Attorney John Briggs was also under attack from Senator Jackson, who claimed that he had sat on the case until after the election. Jackson charged that he had turned over the evidence to the official more than a year ago, but "they sat on their hands." He asked Sen. Sam J. Ervin, chair of the select Watergate Committee, to investigate Briggs' handling of the affair. "The conduct of the U.S. attorney is reprehensible. It is important why he did nothing about this until the full bloom of Watergate has reached the point where they are all running for cover these days." Briggs, Jackson charged, did not ask the FBI until late. "I'd like to know whether they were under any orders on this." Briggs responded to Jackson's charges, claiming that the accusations were "unfair" and he resented it because "we've knocked our brains out" and his investigations were not over.[72]

Segretti entered the Tampa court house for his arraignment on May 16.

His attorney asked U.S. Magistrate Judge Paul Game for thirty days to file an appropriate motion, so no trial date was set. Game set Segretti's personal recognizance bond at $10,000. Segretti eventually pled not guilty to the charges and his case was set for trial on October 8, 1973.[73] Meanwhile, one of Segretti's associates pled guilty and supplied another grand jury in Tampa with additional information.

U.S. Special Prosecutor Archibald Cox also began probing the Segretti operation. Cox noted that "we will certainly draw on U.S. attorneys around the country for their assistance. They'll be a break in the normal chain of command at some level in the Justice Department. They will report to me and my assistants exclusively, rather than up the normal channels to the attorney general."[74] Briggs continued to receive criticism about his handling of the case. Responding to a Rowland Evans and Robert Novak column questioning his department, Briggs bristled at the implication that he was slow to investigate. Briggs branded the column as a "direct attack" on the U.S. attorney's office and the people in it. "We didn't drag our feet, we didn't ignore facts, we didn't cover up, and we didn't receive any instructions to do so." Briggs said he wanted to answer the charges because "credibility of this office with the courts, the attorneys, and the general public is essential to its effective performance." He added, "My files are open for scrutiny to the Senate Special Committee, Mr. Archibald Cox or his representatives, or to other authorized personnel. I will gladly go before the Senate Special Committee, should they ask, but before all the facts are made public, we must be given the opportunity to try our pending case."[75]

Not surprisingly, with such allegations and revelations on the Watergate matter breaking every day, Segretti would never make his appearance for trial in Judge Ben Krentzman's courtroom. The Watergate Committee subpoenaed him, and he received limited immunity for his testimony. He eventually pled guilty to some counts and served four months of a six-month sentence.[76]

Back in Florida, Segretti's accomplice, George A. Hearing, was sentenced to one year in prison, but Asst. U.S. Atty. William James recommended to the U.S. Board of Parole that Hearing's sentence be reduced. Hearing had pleaded guilty, claimed James, and had "furnished the FBI and the Federal Grand Jury with information of value concerning political espionage and sabotage." James recommended parole and added that he thought most of "Hearing's problems stem for the fact that he is an alcoholic. I would strongly recommend that he receive some type of psychiatric care for this problem." Judge Krentzman penned a response on the same form: "I agree with the A.U.S.D.A.'s comments, except that I believe service of some time would have a deterrent effect on the others."[77]

If the political strains on Briggs seemed unbearable, they were about to get worse. At some point during the Segretti investigation, Asst. U.S. Atty. Harvey Schlesinger was summoned into his chief's office. As Schlesinger recalled, "I was minding my own business, working one day in the office, when John Briggs came in and told me I needed to be in Washington the very next day to meet with . . . the assistant attorney general who was in charge of the criminal division. He was starting an investigation that in-volved Senator Gurney. Because John was a Gurney nominee, he had to be recused from the case, so the Jacksonville office, other than me, really had nothing to do with the case."[78]

The FBI had been investigating Gurney's office since 1971 after hearing complaints from building contractors who had applied for FHA funding that they were being shaken down for campaign contributions. In Novem-ber 1973 Larry Williams, a campaign fundraiser for Gurney testified, before a federal grand jury in Jacksonville that he had raised over $300,000 from Florida builders who sought FHA loans. He also swore that Gurney was well aware of his activities. "Yes, emphatically," he swore, "I worked for Gurney." As the scheme played itself out, "Gurney's campaign staff would be given advance notice . . . of who was to get FHA and HUD contracts. They would then go to the developer and say. . . . Right, for a $25,000 cam-paign contribution, we can guarantee you're going to get this project. The money was turned over," even though the award had already been made.[79] Williams was seeking immunity for his testimony, and if granted, he would enter a plea of guilty on criminal charges. Also on the hot seat was Tampa federal housing administrator K. Wayne Sweiger. He also cooperated with the grand jury, essentially corroborating evidence gathered by the FBI.[80]

Obvious to everyone was the political ramifications of the case. Gurney was President Nixon's staunchest supporter in the Watergate hearings. Gur-ney nominated Briggs to his current position, which was to expire within a month, and his reappointment to another four years in office was subject to Gurney's approval. Briggs announced, "to avoid even the appearance of conflict," that he had assigned the case to Schlesinger and that he was keeping the case at arm's length. This did not satisfy Sen. Lawton Chiles, who announced that he saw a "clear correlation between this (Gurney) case and the Nixon-Watergate matter." He called for someone from out of state to direct the prosecution of Gurney, "someone with no appointment problems."[81]

Gurney denied any knowledge of the alleged scheme from which his campaign fund benefited. Even so, he was indicted in July 1974 along with six other defendants, several of whom cooperated in the case in exchange for lesser sentences. Sweiger and another federal housing official were also prosecuted. The trial took place in Tampa before Ben Krentzman and lasted from February through August 1975. Schlesinger prosecuted the case vigorously, introducing sixty-nine witnesses. Gurney's attorneys, C. Harris Dittmar and Charles Pillans, defended their client vigorously. At one crucial point in trial, they had the senator himself take the stand. When asked point-blank if he knew anything of the fund-raising efforts of his staff, Gurney deadpanned, "candidates should keep themselves from knowing about what is going on in the fund-raising area."[82] In August 1975 the Tampa jury acquitted Gurney of five felony charges but deadlocked on two others—"that he conspired to extort a $400,000 political fund from contractors, and that he lied to a grand jury when he denied knowledge about illegal fundraising activities."[83] On November 7, 1975, Judge Krentzman refused to dismiss the other two charges. The trial eventually resumed in Orlando because, as a court spokesman in Tampa announced, "We're nearly a year behind in all our civil cases because of the length of the trial here."[84] The trial had also exhausted Judge Krentzman.

The trial on the two unresolved charges (perjury and conspiracy) took place in late October 1976. Previous to the new trial, Judge Young proscribed use of any of the evidence previously used against Gurney in the former trial. In a pretrial ruling, Young asserted, "While the government may charge, try, and convict a defendant with more than one charge growing out of the same transaction, it may not in a second trial relitigate an issue of either ultimate fact or evidentiary fact upon which the defendant was acquitted in an earlier trial."[85] At long last, the federal government's attempt to convict Gurney of perjury failed. Although he walked free, the former senator's career was over. The once proud, powerful senator was now disgraced and bankrupt, and he did not seek reelection. He bitterly recalled that his ordeal in the federal courts was "a never ending nightmare . . . four years of investigation, indictment and trial."[86] But Schlesinger never regretted his prosecution of the case. When an interviewer asked Schlesinger if he thought the prosecution was merited, Schlesinger responded: "Well, from my knowledge of the case I wouldn't have tried it if I didn't think otherwise."[87]

During the four years that Gurney underwent investigation and trial, the political winds in the United States had blown briskly. Richard Nixon resigned from the presidency rather than face impeachment. No one would have imagined that Donald Segretti's arraignment in the Tampa court house as a CREEP operative would have been a harbinger of the Nixon administration's eventual downfall. On August 9, 1974, Gerald Ford assumed the presidency and dutifully sought to carry out the last two years of Nixon's term. Meanwhile, at the time that the charges against Gurney were being dismissed, Ford was locked in a tough presidential race with Democratic nominee Jimmy Carter. Perhaps the Georgia governor's most important step to the nomination was his victory in the Florida primary that March. Carter was different. Not only was he a dark horse, he was also the first presidential candidate in anyone's memory that openly acknowledged his strong religious faith. As a "born-again" Southern Baptist, Carter promised to restore honesty in government.[88] In the election in November 1976 election, Carter prevailed. The post-Watergate era had officially begun.

6

Growing Pains, Constitutional Questions, and Bankruptcy, 1976–1980

In early 1976 Judge George C. Young prepared to vacate his chambers on the second floor of the old Orlando post office building on Jefferson Street. The attractive Mediterranean structure had housed the federal court, post office, and other federal offices since 1941. But now the court and other federal agencies were preparing a move only a few blocks to a shiny new structure on the corner of North Hughey Avenue and Washington Street, adjacent to the I-4 overpass. The new federal building had taken nearly a decade to build. Ten years earlier *Orlando Sentinel* owner and publisher Martin Andersen, just before retiring, extracted a promise from Senators Smathers and Holland to push for an appropriation for a new federal courthouse. In June 1970 Mayor Carl Langford and a team from the General Services Administration (GSA) selected a site for the new structure that was projected to cost ten and half million dollars. In August 1971 architectural contracts were awarded to three Central Florida firms: Schweitzer and Associates of Winter Park, and Smith and Swilley and Wellman-Lord Inc., both of Lakeland. Dignitaries broke ground in February 1974, and within two years federal agencies were ready to move into the new building. On hand for the building's formal dedication on February 1976 were GSA head Jack Eckerd, U.S. Representatives Lou Frey and Richard Kelly, and District Judges Young and John A. Reed.[1]

Court officials were among 500 hundred federal employees to be housed in the new seven-story building. The U.S. Attorney's office and the federal district court staff with its judges and clerks were the last to move in. By that time employees with the Internal Revenue Service; Social Security; Health, Education and Welfare; Housing and Urban Development; Alcohol Tobacco and Firearms; FBI; Secret Service; Selective Service; and U.S. marshal and probation officers occupied the building. So did various agencies within the U.S. Agricultural Department. One description of the new federal courthouse in Orlando noted that the structure had a number of "right angle hallways to be used only by judges and court personnel. There is even a secret elevator to be used only by judges, U.S. marshals and other federal authorities." There were three courtrooms. Judge Young's was the largest, with blue carpeting. Judge Reed's courtroom was smaller, and it had green carpeting, and a third courtroom for visiting judges was the smallest and was decorated, according to the account, in "orangish-tomato soup red." A magistrate courtroom was located on the sixth floor.[2]

While Chief Judge Young was no doubt pleased to move into his new quarters, his primary concern was the need for more judges to handle the rising caseload in the Middle District. In May 1975 he traveled to Washington to attend a convention of the American Law Institute. While there he voiced the need for more judges. The situation in the Middle District was particularly acute because President Gerald Ford had recently promoted Gerald Tjoflat to the Fifth Circuit Court of Appeals. In September 1976 Judge Charles R. Scott was about to undergo heart surgery and was expected to retire soon. While Young was in Washington, Senators Lawton Chiles and Richard Stone were stalemated with the Ford administration over the appointment of judges. Meanwhile the backlog continued to build. Young stated that the district had six judges but needed nine. Young had little concern about the politics of the situation. When asked about recent squabbling, he smiled "benevolently, his twinkling eyes dissolving into slits, and [said]: 'I don't care if they're Republicans or Democrats. I just want more judges.'"[3]

One of the reasons for the backlog of cases was the passage of the Speedy Trial Act in 1974. This new law set specific time limits between various stages of criminal proceedings. The law required that prosecutors file information or indictments within thirty days of a defendant's arrest. If the defendant entered a not-guilty plea, the trial must commence within seventy days. While there were various exclusions from compliance, the new law put greater pressure on prosecutors to move rapidly. The net effect of the law also meant that criminal cases would take priority over civil cases.

In 1977 Congress was considering a bill to add ten new federal judge positions in Florida (three in the Middle District, six in the Southern District and one in the Northern District). But its passage was by no means assured. Rarely one to weigh in publicly, Judge Young did so in this instance, claiming that the situation in the Middle District and in the rest of Florida was in crisis. He claimed that the backlog of cases was so extensive that all of his judges had essentially ceased hearing civil cases because the speedy trial rule gave the government only 120 days to pursue a case after an indictment. Criminal trials had become longer and more complicated. "Many of the cases presently being filed are multi-defendant white collar, or conspiracy cases which are least likely to be terminated by a guilty plea and involve protracted trials." The caseload in the Middle District had more than doubled in the previous five years—despite the fact that the judges of the court had virtually led the nation in bench time. "A judge," Young stated, "needs time off the bench The real work of a judge—so much of it, is off the bench reading briefs, studying files, making decisions, and writing opinions." If no relief was granted in the form of appointing more judges, Young stated, civil cases would be ignored and delayed for years. "If there are not enough judges to handle criminal cases something's going to have to give. Either there will be a reduction of filings, or there will have to be more plea bargaining or cases will have to be dismissed."[4]

Fortunately federal magistrates were available to lessen the burden. In 1968 Congress created the office of magistrate to provide the courts assistance in doing tasks that were increasingly overburdening many judges in various districts of the nation. The new position essentially expanded, extended, and professionalized the office of commissioner. Full-time U.S. magistrates were appointed by district judges for renewable eight-year terms to perform tasks as delegated by district judges. According to one authority, the "magistrate's authority was confined to the limited tasks performed by the old U.S. commissioners, lay judicial officers who handled warrants, arraignments, and petty offenses. . . . Congress subsequently amended the Magistrates Act in 1976 and 1979 to authorize magistrates to assist district judges with a broad spectrum of tasks, including the supervision of complete civil trials with the consent of litigants. After the 1979 Act, magistrates could perform virtually any task undertaken by district judges except for trying and sentencing felony defendants."[5]

Although the law went into effect in 1968, most districts did not begin appointing magistrates until the early 1970s. The Middle District of Florida commissioned its first U.S. magistrates in 1971. Paul Game had been a U.S. commissioner operating in Tampa since 1962. In 1971 he became one of the first eight U.S. magistrates appointed in the Middle District. According to Game, the "scheme was to try it in a few districts around the country as models to see how it worked, to see if we needed to smooth out anything before we went forward, and in 1971, it was generally open to all districts. All of the magistrates in this district were appointed at the same time."

Besides Game, the others appointed were Joseph W. Hatchett, George T. Swartz, Harvey E. Schlesinger, Thomas L. Henderson, John F. Hughes Jr., Young J. Simmons, and Donald Paul Dietrich.[6] Game thought the primary motivation for creating the new positions was economic: "What happened was that Congress wanted a cheaper level, moneywise, level of judges."[7]

Magistrates impaneled juries, handled pretrial motions, issued writs of habeas corpus, and presided over misdemeanors trials of any offense for which punishment was less than a year. Magistrates could also issue injunctions, but Article III judges had to sign off on them. In fact, all magistrates' decisions are appealable to the district judge. In 1971 Joseph W. Hatchett left the U.S. Attorney's office and became one of the Middle Districts first seven magistrates. Remaining in Jacksonville, Hatchett remembered that much of his time consisted of trying misdemeanor cases that occurred on the three navy bases in the area. "Because any misdemeanor that occurred on federal land was a federal offense so I tried those misdemeanor cases: speeding, shoplifting, failing to stop at a stop sign. Not anything very large but all these things occurred on a federal reservation so they had to be tried by a federal judicial official and that was the United States Magistrate." He also recalled that district judges would assign him tasks such as writing reports.[8]

George T. Swartz began his involvement in the federal system as a U.S. commissioner in 1964. Even after his appointment as U.S. magistrate in 1971, Swartz continued with his law firm until 1989 when the position became full time. Based in Fort Myers, Swartz recalled that he was the "only federal presence around, and that wasn't much at the beginning." Swartz's duties grew as time went on. By the late 1980s judicial business had grown in Fort Myers to the extent that the district decided to make the magistrate's duties full time and invited Swartz to apply. He eventually got the position and left his firm.[9]

Congress expanded the powers and the numbers of magistrates as time went on. The Judicial Improvement Act of 1990 made it possible for civil litigants to consent to have their case heard by magistrates. Because of his isolated situation, Swartz had this happen perhaps more often than any other U.S. magistrate in the district. The work was heavy and often tedious. Yet surprises often came Swartz's way. He recalled that one time arrests came, and "we wiped out Everglades City with about eighteen arrests, or I guess it was in the twenties, and took every fisherman that was down there because they were all hauling marijuana off the boats to help their income." On another occasion in 1968, Swartz got a call late one night from

Federal Building, Fort Myers, ca. 1970s. Completed in 1933, the U.S. District Court for the Southern District of Florida met here from 1952 until the creation of the Middle District in 1962. The structure served the Middle District Court until 1999, when the new federal courthouse was opened. National Archives and Records Administration, Record Group 121.

the FBI that they had arrested a man named Krist who was charged with kidnapping Barbara Jane Mackle, the daughter of the wealthy Coral Gables developer. Krist, with $500,000 in ransom money, was chased in a speedboat and crashed on one of the barrier islands off the Lee County Coast. The next morning Swartz held an arraignment in the hospital because Krist had jumped off his boat and was sliced up badly from the barnacles and mangroves. Swartz set Krist's bond at $500,000 to which Krist responded, "'Gee, I just had that amount.' The FBI jumped up and came over and said, what did you say?' He said, 'Gee, I wish I had that amount.'"[10]

While Judge Swartz operated essentially alone in Fort Myers, most magistrates served in Orlando, Tampa, and Jacksonville, where overburdened caseloads strained district judges. Whether Congress intended it or not, magistrates, as one authority has noted, tended to operate as "a kind of 'junior' district judge" because it "was the district court judges themselves who determine the duties and responsibilities of their magistrates."[11] Thus, they can serve as additional judges to hear civil cases. They could serve as specialists—such as Judge Hatchett—who handled certain types of cases exclusively. Or they can operate as a "first line" of entry, handling pretrial matters and preparing cases for trial.[12]

In 1977, events were moving toward a reshaping of the Middle District of Florida bench. That year Judge Charles Scott retired, and, with the court already short, President Jimmy Carter appointed two judges in his first months in office. Carter and his attorney general, Griffin Bell (former judge of the Fifth Circuit Court of Appeals), made careful judicial selection a major priority of the administration. Carter had promised in his campaign to seek judges who were "more representative" of the public at large, meaning that he intended to make it a special priority to identify and appoint women and minorities to the bench. Late in his term Carter proclaimed to an assemblage of woman judges: "Because I knew the power and importance of judges, I was determined to get the very best people possible to serve on the federal bench. I was also determined that women and minorities, whose destinies have so often depended upon the kind of justice our courts provided, should be included in those judgeships." According to one scholar, "The election of Jimmy Carter in 1976 signaled the beginning of some of the most fundamental and historic changes in the selection, screening, and nomination of federal judges in the twentieth century."[13]

The Omnibus Judgeship Act of 1978 created 152 new judgeships and gave President Carter significant opportunities to shape the federal bench during his final year in office. The act also encouraged U.S. senators to establish nominating commissions within their states. This idea had already been put in place two years earlier by Sen. Lawton Chiles and his new Democratic senatorial colleague, Richard Stone. The commission was composed of nine members: three appointed by each senator and three appointed by the Florida Bar. As President Carter said when he signed the act into law on October 20, 1978, "This Act provides a unique opportunity to begin to redress another disturbing feature of the Federal judiciary: the almost complete absence of women, or members of minority groups. Of 525 active judges, only 29 are black or Hispanic, and only nine are women—and almost half of these have been appointed during my Administration." All told, Carter appointed 202 federal district court judges. He appointed more women and minority federal judges than all other presidents combined. But his first two appointees to the Middle District of Florida were not among them.[14]

Jimmy Carter's first appointment to the Middle District—in fact, his first judicial appointment of all—was Howell Melton, who had served sixteen years as circuit judge on Florida's Seventh Judicial Circuit. Born in Atlanta in 1923, Melton moved with his family to Mayo, Florida, a community of about three hundred, when he was one year old. His father's grocery store was right across the street from the Lafayette County Courthouse, and he watched trials when he was a boy. He soon decided he wanted to be a lawyer or a judge. Melton graduated from Lafayette County High School in 1941 and entered the University of Florida. He eventually joined the army in the middle of World War II, serving in the Ninth Infantry Division in Germany. After the war Melton entered the University of Florida Levin School of Law, graduating in 1948. Settling in St. Augustine, Melton married Catherine Wolfe in 1950, the niece of banker and businessman Herbert E. Wolfe, and practiced privately until he became a circuit judge in 1960.

In 1976 Melton applied for an opening of the district court, and the judicial nominating commission recommended him. Senators Richard Stone and Lawton Chiles forwarded his name to the White House as the presidential election came on. As Melton recalled, "I was selected by the senators near the end of the year. I think it was either October or November. I don't recall the exact time. The problem evolved where we didn't know whether it was going to be a Republican or a Democrat [president]. Hopefully, I was going to be the selection of Gerald Ford and hopefully if Gerald Ford was not elected I was going to be the selection of President Jimmy Carter. As things turned out, President Carter was elected as president. I was the first nominee of President Carter." Melton was confirmed and took office on May 12, 1977.[15]

When Melton began presiding in Jacksonville, the Middle District Court was in crisis. He was the only district judge in Jacksonville at that time, and Harvey Schlesinger was the lone magistrate. Judges Reed and Young traveled to Jacksonville to relieve some of the burden but still the caseload stretched far beyond reasonable limits. "I believe there were approximately 2,000 cases on the docket," Melton later recalled.

> Civil cases were not being tried at all except by visiting judges. What they would do if a case was ready to try, if they could get a visiting judge from another district, another state usually, to come in, they would put fifty, sixty, or a hundred cases all on the docket and a lot of those cases would be settled because the attorneys would know they were not likely to get to them anyway. That was the way the cases were handled. Civil cases were not handled at all. They tried to keep up through the magistrate handling the discovery matters and any other matters that the magistrate could take care of. . . . I think there

were approximately 200 cases, maybe, waiting to be filed when I came in. . . . All types of cases. . . . . All of us were working full time. There wasn't any time for vacation or rest. You worked from early morning until late afternoon, sometime into the evening.[16]

The congested situation in the Tampa division was also acute. One assessment in August 1977 found that more than one thousand civil cases in Tampa could not be tried because criminal cases had to take priority. "Civil work here has been suspended for months. . . . Not even pretrial motions are being heard and some have been waiting since December 1976." Judges Krentzman and Hodges each had over five hundred civil cases waiting for them. One official stated, "We've got cases, big cases involving big litigations, which have been pending since 1971. I wouldn't be surprised if they were still pending in 1981. There is simply too much work for two judges to handle."[17]

U.S. Marshal Mitchell Newberger was also understaffed and overburdened. In June 1976 he complained that over 344 arrest warrants were yet to be served because he lacked adequate personnel. Newberger claimed that he did not have "enough deputies to ride herd on all the outstanding warrants in the district's thirty-three counties." Many warrants on fugitives had not been served because Newberger did not have personnel capable of tracking them down. Newberger had twenty-four field officers to cover the thirty-three-county, 26,000-square-mile district. He needed at least eight more. "My manpower ceiling is based on what I consider an obsolete formula based on the number of criminal cases filed in the district," Newberger explained. "The formula is not accurate—it doesn't consider districts like mine," which was so spread out and had district offices in Orlando, Jacksonville, and Tampa.[18]

With such a backload Middle District of Florida, judges had to work long hours, which increasing put strains on their health. For example, Judge Hodges remembers his own time of crisis that occurred in March 1977. "I started off trying criminal cases one after the other. That continued throughout the 1970s. . . . Our criminal docket just monopolized our trial time. I spent almost all my time on the bench, day after day, trying criminal cases of just about every kind. . . . After the jury was excused in the evening, I would be there in the evening for another two or three hours, most of it on the bench." Working long hours, not getting proper exercise, or proper diet brought on a "heart attack for me when I was forty-two years old on March 15, 1977," he recalled. The attack came in his office about 6:00 p.m. after he had sent the jury out to deliberate. Hodges was rushed to Tampa General Hospital and underwent open heart surgery. Hodges was able to return to work several weeks later.[19]

One of the stressful trials that Judge Hodges had dealt with before his heart attack involved the organized crime figure Frank Diecidue, who was accused of participating in a conspiracy to assassinate Tampa policeman Richard L. Cloud. Because of excessive publicity, the trial was moved from Tampa to Jacksonville, where Hodges presided. Diecidue was reputed to be the number two man in the Santo Trafficante operation. The five-week trial netted Diecidue and six other defendants convictions. As well as ordering the contract killing of a rival, the jury found Diecidue guilty of illegal possession of firearms and dynamite and other acts related to assassination attempts. Hodges called the fourteen-count indictment the "most serious indictment that I have seen on this bench."[20] After the conviction Hodges denied the convicted men bail, asserting that they "constitute a danger to the public."[21]

Help was soon on the way for the overburdened district. Jimmy Carter's second appointment in the Middle District was Lakeland attorney George C. Carr, one of Sen. Lawton Chiles' closest friends. They had attended elementary school, high school, college, and law school at the University Florida together. In 1954 Carr, Chiles, and another Lakeland native, William Ellsworth, formed a law partnership. Carr had served as assistant Polk County attorney from 1959 to 1973, and by 1977 he had headed the law practice for four years.[22] Some raised their eyebrows at his appointment, claiming that the forty-eight-year-old lawyer simply owed his appointment to his friendship with Chiles.[23] But all who knew him understood that Carr was a "cut above." Carr, most agreed, was a legal scholar, an intellectual, and he possessed a fine temperament for the bench.

Not surprisingly many Florida Republicans found fault with the commission's choice. Republican leader Bill Taylor blasted Carr's nomination as "just the second part of a deal between Chiles and Stone to appoint their personal friends."[24] And later, when the commission passed over Republican favorite, Circuit Judge Elizabeth Kovachevich, Taylor once again slammed the commission, branding the process a "phony set up to permit senators to continue making their selections on a political basis."[25] But others defended the state-wide commission as submitting names based on quality rather than philosophy. One close observer of the commission's work noted that "not only have the appointments been drawn from both

The Middle District Bench, ca. 1979. *Seated, left to right*: Ben Krentzman, George C. Young, William Terrell Hodges; *standing, left to right*: George Carr, John A. Reed, Susan H. Black, and Howell Melton.

major political parties, a practice unheard of in many states, but the judges have not been readily classifiable in terms of judicial philosophy."[26]

Carr's nomination was confirmed in the Senate with a simple voice vote, and his investiture was set for January 6, 1978, in Tampa. Judge Young, presiding that day, cheerfully received Carr's credentials, responding, "It appears to be properly signed by Jimmy Carter and Attorney General Griffin Bell." One observer commented that Carr looked neat in his "brown hair neatly trimmed save for a short cowlick to complement his smiling boyish, bespectacled face . . . and speaking in his slow, deliberate native drawl." Speaking at his investiture ceremony was Chesterfield Smith, past president of the American Bar Association, who asserted that Carr possessed "those precious qualities that can, in time, make him a great judge."[27]

Dan Warren tried a case before Carr in 1978, one of the first cases the judge ever had on the bench. "I never will forget this one thing as long as I live. I had just made my final closing argument and the jury was out and I got word that my oldest son had been killed in Honduras. And I just went to pieces. And Judge Carr was so nice to me, trying to console me and so forth. But I remember that incident like it was yesterday." In addition to that tragic incident, Warren recalled that Judge Carr was "really, really a fine man. He gave you an excellent trial. You can tell. You know after you have been practicing law as long as I have, you know when a judge is fair and impartial and I mean it's no big secret. But he was a very fair person."[28] After his appointment, Judge Carr first served in the Jacksonville Division and commuted from there to Lakeland on the weekends for a year and a half. Carr was soon assigned to Tampa, where he joined Judges Hodges and Krentzman.

After the Omnibus Judgeship Act's passage in September 1978 Sen. Richard Stone commented that "surely now, with this many judgeship openings, we will be able to consider qualified woman and minority group members for appointment to the federal bench." Members of the nominating commission contended that they sought but were unsuccessful in finding qualified women and minorities. "The problem, according to former nominating commission Chairman Earl Hadlow, a Jacksonville attorney, is that few qualified blacks and women have applied. The reason: Their entry into top-flight law firms and key government legal jobs that provide experience for judges is a new phenomenon. 'I have personally contacted at least eight or 10, urging them to apply,' Hadlow said. 'We feel acutely aware of the problem.'"[29] One African American who drew significant comment was Joseph Hatchett, who had been appointed to the Florida Supreme Court by Gov. Reubin Askew. Chiles and Stone were about to put Hatchett's name forward for a district judge position when President Carter beat them to the punch. The decision to nominate Hatchett to the Fifth Circuit Court of Appeals was an easy one for Carter. Hatchett had just won a hard-fought election to the Florida Supreme Court, his name had been vetted thoroughly, and he had the experience of nearly a decade in the federal system, serving as assistant U.S. attorney and U.S. magistrate. During those years Hatchett had become well known to Atty. Gen. Griffin Bell, and the former appeals judge had a high personal regard for him.[30] Hatchett was easily confirmed. The Floridian became the first African American judge in the Fifth Circuit Court of Appeals.

Because of its size, the Middle District of Florida was entitled to three new judicial positions under the new law. Working with the nominating commission, Senators Chiles and Stone forwarded three names to President Carter in March 1979: Circuit Judge Susan Black, Clearwater lawyer William Castagna, and Hillsborough County state's attorney E. J. Salcines. President Carter nominated Castagna and Black almost immediately, but the White House failed to act on Salcines. Since leaving Eddie Boardman's

U.S. Attorney's office in 1968, Salcines' political career had soared. That year Salcines was elected Hillsborough County solicitor, and then in 1972 he was elected state attorney for the Thirteenth Judicial Circuit. He served as president of the Florida Prosecuting Attorneys Association and vice president of the National District Attorneys Association. By the time Chiles and Stone forwarded his name to President Carter, he had attained national acclaim as a prosecutor, authoring a *Trial Manual on Predicate Questions* (1977), which soon became a standard in the field. The West Tampa native had also built a strong political base in the Latin community, but in a town notorious as an organized crime haven, Salcines made tough decisions that often put him at cross purposes with federal authorities.

The prosecutor had continually clashed with the Tampa offices of the FBI and the Federal Organized Crime Strike Force over the prosecution of criminals. Although the senators said the Justice Department and FBI files had nothing to preclude their consideration of Salcines, his critics soon emerged. One negative newspaper story listed several instances in which federal attorneys successfully prosecuted cases after Salcines declined to do so in the state courts. Chiles answered the criticism against Salcines, arguing that the prosecutor had an outstanding record. "I know there is a blood feud between the U.S. attorney's office and E. J., but he will be screened by the FBI." Stone recognized that the situation was difficult in Tampa. "When names recommended by the commission are made public, they become the target of everyone who has ever been offended. . . . I think tendering Mr. Salcines's name will show that applicants for these jobs will be stood up for. . . . I think what we are saying is that just because a person is controversial is no reason not to consider him." Regarding Salcines' popularity in Tampa's Latin community, an aide to Senator Chiles was quoted as saying, "They like him. They respect him. And how many Hispanic Judges do we have?" For his own part, Salcines was delighted to hear that his old professor at Florida Southern College had forwarded his name to the Justice Department. "I am just elated and very humble and grateful," he said. Salcines admitted that his job as county prosecutor was controversial. Even so, he countered that the *Tribune* article was a rehash of "allegations that were really old news and that were not truthfully reported." Salcines said he expected no problem in being confirmed by the Senate.[31]

Both William Castagna and Susan Black breezed through the confirmation process. Known as one of Florida's top civil lawyers, Castagna was born in Philadelphia in 1924 and attended the University of Pennsylvania. Castagna served in the Air Force during World War II, and after the war he attended law school at the University of Florida. Practicing briefly in Miami, Castagna settled permanently in Clearwater, where he practiced with Judge Ben Krentzman's former firm. In 1954 he married Carolyn Ann Spoto. Castagna had served as president of the Clearwater Bar Association and contributed his time to many community and charitable organizations. He was sworn in on September 14. Castagna was first posted to the Jacksonville Division but eventually moved to Tampa in 1981.[32]

Susan Harrell Black, Florida's first woman federal judge, was born in Valdosta, Georgia, on October 20, 1943, while her father (a native of Mayo, Florida) was in flight training during World War II. She was too young to realize the danger when her father was shot down over Germany and missing in action for many months until her mother finally learned that Lt. William H. Harrell was still alive in a prison camp. Both of her parents, as she says, were "old Florida." She fondly remembered pleasant summers in Mayo and with her mother's family in Lake City.[33]

While her father pursued his career as a U.S. Air Force officer, Susan Harrell attended school in Colorado, Nebraska, Ohio, and Paris, France. In high school she enjoyed history, English, and speech. Harrell attended Ohio Wesleyan University and Spring Hill College before transferring to Florida State University where she excelled in debate, earning her bachelor's degree in 1964. Harrell attended the University of Florida Levin School of Law, and she married Louis Black before graduating in 1967. After taking the bar exam, she taught civics for one semester at Ribault High School in Jacksonville. Her first legal job was as an attorney for the Army Corps of Engineers, who were involved with purchasing land for the cross-Florida barge canal. As she later explained, "Well, I wanted to litigate, and no one in town would hire women to litigate."[34] Her first chance for entering the courtroom came in 1969, when Black joined State Attorney Ed Austin's office, where, as an assistant state attorney in the Fourth Judicial Circuit, she tried cases until 1972, when she became a county judge. In 1975 Black became a circuit judge, serving until 1979, when Carter nominated her.[35]

Unfortunately for E. J. Salcines, support from the Justice Department was not forthcoming. After sixteen months Carter's attorney general, Benjamin Civiletti, wrote Chiles, asking the senator to forward another name. Chiles and Stone were angry and knew that friction between Salcines and Bill James, former assistant U.S. attorney and the head of the Justice Department Strike Force on Organized Crime in Tampa, was at the root of the problem. "I am extremely disappointed," Chiles announced. "When we recommended Mr. Salcines last year I felt he would make a fine and able federal Judge. I still feel that just as strongly today." The FBI and the nominating commission had thoroughly vetted Salcines' background. "All these checks have produced nothing to indicate Mr. Salcines is not qualified to be a federal judge," Chiles said.

> I have been given no information by the Justice Department that questions his credentials for the position. I must assume that the controversy carried forward in the press is the basic reason for the decision. E. J. Salcines has been controversial. We knew that when we recommended him, as did the nominating commission. A good prosecutor on any level has difficult and controversial decisions to make every day within the law to enforce to law, not just to please everyone. It is apparent much of the controversy stems from a situation seen in many jurisdictions where a federal strike force is at odds with state and local authorities regarding investigations and prosecutions.

Chiles said he had urged Attorney General Civiletti to meet with Salcines or to have one of his top assistants do so "in order that any questions or concerns might be aired. That opportunity was never afforded, and I don't understand why it was not." Stone called Civiletti's decision not to pursue a meeting an "outrage." When informed of the Justice Department's inaction, Salcines thanked Chiles and Stone for their support but added, "I can't help but feel there has been a total disregard of fundamental fairness—being held hostage for 16 months," he said. "I am relieved, however, that a decision was finally made. I feel the way I have been treated has been wrong. It has not been fair. I have never been given a forum." He said the senators repeatedly assured him there was no question in their minds as to his qualifications and integrity.[36]

Within a week Chiles and Stone submitted another name to Carter. Jacksonville circuit judge Ralph Nimmons, they asserted, had an "impressive" legal background, which, along with his personal and professional qualifications, would make him a "tremendous asset" to the Middle District.[37] As the next presidential election loomed ahead, the Senate dragged its feet. It adjourned without taking up Nimmons' nomination.

Constitutional Questions

During the 1970s Middle District judges presided over a myriad of cases that involved fundamental constitutional rights. Many of their decisions were controversial. Among the issues confronting the courts were school prayer, nude dancing, job discrimination, standardized testing, and issues involving abortion clinics. When it came to school prayer, tension had been building nationwide since the Supreme Court had ruled the practice unconstitutional in 1962. In 1970 thirty-nine persons from various religious and nonreligious persuasions objected to an Orange County School Board directive requiring compulsory early-morning inspirational readings because they often included Bible readings. Responding to plaintiff's concerns, Judge George C. Young held a hearing on the issue. While he refused to rule in favor of the plaintiffs, he warned the school board that Bible readings and the distribution of Gideon Bibles by the board were unconstitutional. He also ordered that the school board change the name of the five-minute early-morning exercise from "devotionals" to "inspirationals." Even though the board denied that Bible readings were taking place, some parents complained about the practice, and they appealed to the Fifth Circuit Court of Appeals, who returned the case back to Young for a further finding of fact.

Also under scrutiny was a Florida statute that mandated teachers to inculcate to students "by precept and example, the practice of every Christian virtue."[38] Young dismissed the suit, saying that the evidence indicated that the school board had ended the practice of Bible readings. An assistant Florida attorney general defended the Florida statute, claiming that the word "Christian" was "merely a synonym for good practices, which happen to coincide with the Judeo-Christian religion."[39] After hearing the evidence, Young refused to rule the state law unconstitutional, declaring that there was no evidence "of any effort to utilize that section to teach Christian religion or attempt to promulgate in a student the Christian religion or the belief that Jesus Christ is the ruler of the world."[40]

In the 1970s nude dancing clubs began to proliferate in Florida, particularly in Daytona Beach, Orlando, and Tampa. Counties and localities sought to regulate or ban the activity by passing proscriptive ordinances and challenges to the laws. Because such laws were perceived to be violations of the First or Fourteenth Amendment, the questions often found their way into federal court. In 1978, for example, Judge Hodges upheld a Tampa ordinance banning nude dancing in clubs that sold alcohol, citing a Supreme Court case that held it was within the "legitimate powers of the states to regulate the activities of establishments engaged in the sale of alcoholic beverages." The prohibition of nude dancing in such places "was not so irrational as to be an unconstitutional infringement of the minimally protected form of 'speech' under the First or Fourteenth Amendments," he said.[41]

Employment discrimination also became a frequent issue that cropped up in federal courts, especially after the passage of the Employment Opportunity Act in 1972. Despite the city of St. Petersburg's "highly touted affirmative-action program," the city fell short in the hiring of black firemen, and a suit was initiated in 1975. "A stronger remedy is needed," Judge Hodges stated.[42] On September 6, 1979, Hodges ruled that the city must hire one black for every two whites until 9.6 percent of the force is black. As of the end of 1978, 9 of 306 city firefighters, or 2.9 percent, were black. Judge Hodges made his decision on the premise that blacks made up 9.6 percent of the people in the Tampa-St. Petersburg metropolitan area who meet the age and education requirements for becoming firefighters. While he did not accuse the city of discrimination in the hiring of policemen and firemen, Hodges stated that his order was intended to correct previous discrimination by the fire department. "Unfortunately," said Hodges, "the plain answer is that the city's voluntary affirmative action program has not succeeded in eradicating the effect of past discrimination."[43] The city of St. Petersburg eventually began a "federally funded training program to help those persons, particularly minority applicants, who are unable to qualify for the fire department because they cannot pass the required written test."[44] A consent agreement between Pinellas County and the U.S. Justice Department was filed in court on July 25 in which the county pledged to hire more women, blacks and Hispanics for county jobs.[45]

In 1979 Judge George C. Carr heard a case involving the implementation of a standardized test for graduation from Florida public schools. Plaintiffs sued to test the constitutionality of the exam, claiming that it was racially and culturally biased against blacks. As one observer summarized the arguments, "Attorneys for the plaintiffs claim black seniors began their education under a dual system that put them at a disadvantage. Today, schools are still tainted with vestiges of discrimination, the attorneys contend. But the state counters that the test is not discriminatory. It merely measures how well a senior can apply the basic skills of reading, writing and arithmetic to everyday living—such as shopping, writing a check or understanding instructions."[46] Carr ordered that the implementation of the test as a precondition for graduation be postponed for four years to allow for study of the question and to ensure that the state was adequately preparing its students for the exam. Florida's commissioner of education declared Carr's decision to delay the test "a setback in our battle for a better education for Florida's students."[47] "'Everybody's watching this case,' says Stephen F. Hanlon, an attorney for (Tampa) Bay Area Legal Services, the federally funded organization who sued over Florida's controversial literacy test. 'There are 36 other states with some form of competency testing program,' he said, 'but Florida was the first state to try to deny diplomas to students who didn't pass.' Florida's testing program also was the first challenged in court."[48]

Carr eventually ruled that the test was not culturally biased, but in the ruling, he barred the state from withholding diplomas until the 1983 school year so students would have a chance to advance through 12 years of integrated classrooms. In 1983 Carr upheld the test again, claiming in the thirty page ruling that the "test was an integral part of Florida's efforts to boost its public education."[49] Thus in May 1983 the State of Florida refused to award diplomas to 1,300 high school seniors who failed a functional literacy test. Carr refused to interfere with the state's decision. Carr denied a request for an injunction only hours after the state education commissioner in Tallahassee announced results of the test given for that year's graduating class. "The plaintiffs have not shown that the stay will serve the public interest. To the contrary, the public interest would appear to be best served by allowing the state to implement a plan which is the keystone of its new educational policy," Carr's order stated.[50] Attorney Steve Hanlon appealed, seeking a stay until an appeal could be heard. The Eleventh Circuit Court of Appeals refused to overturn Carr's ruling. The test, the higher court asserted, was "instructionally valid and not discriminatory."[51]

Another controversial issue frequently battled over in the federal courts was abortion. Despite the Supreme Court's ruling in *Roe v. Wade* (1973) that affirmed a woman's right to an abortion, numerous cities and county ordinances sought to obstruct the operation of abortion clinics in various ways. In August 1977 Judge George C. Young imposed a temporary restraining order against the enforcement of a City of Cocoa Beach ordinance because it appeared to be aimed specifically at the Aware Woman Clinic. Young asserted that the "likelihood of the ordinance being unconstitutional is great" because it was "ambiguous, vague and overbroad."[52]

In 1980 the Middle District of Florida added a new official position when Congress mandated that each federal district have a public defender. The Middle District judges appointed Robert W. Knight, who had a long career in the FBI and had also been assistant state attorney in Hillsborough County. By 1980 Knight had gone into private practice, but he applied for the new position and the judges selected him. Knight set up his office on the first floor of the Tampa courthouse. The first lawyer he hired was recent Loyola University New Orleans College of Law graduate Mark Pizzo. A second lawyer, James Whittemore, also joined the office, as did an investigator, an administrative assistant, and a secretary.[53]

Bankruptcy

In the 1970s the U.S. economy faltered. Richard Nixon and Gerald Ford battled inflation. In the waning days of Nixon's administration, Arab members of the Organization of Petroleum Exporting Countries, in retaliation for U.S. support of Israel, issued an oil embargo that sent prices soaring. Energy prices, inflation, and unemployment rose as the decade wore on. By the time of the presidential election of 1980, the "misery index" (defined as the sum of inflation and unemployment) hit 22 percent. Interest rates hit unprecedented levels.[54] The result of this economic tumult was a proliferation of bankruptcies.

Under federal law, bankruptcy was under the jurisdiction of the district courts, and in the Middle District of Florida—and perhaps in the nation as a whole in the modern era—any discussion of bankruptcy begins with Alexander Paskay. Coming to Tampa from Miami with Judge Joseph P. Lieb in 1963 and serving until his death in 2012, Paskay was the longest-sitting full-time bankruptcy judge in the nation. During his many years on the bankruptcy court, Paskay witnessed and was part of changes and the evolution of the laws, especially as the litigation became more frequent and complicated. As lawyer Don Stichter recalled some years later, the "atmosphere of the Bankruptcy Court was clearly and dramatically different in 1963" and the "bankruptcy practice was not held in high esteem by practitioners generally. The practice was dominated by attorneys whose primary efforts were in the debt collection business. Many major firms did not have a practice in the Bankruptcy Court and even defined their practices as excluding bankruptcy."[55]

Thus, in the early 1960s the practice of bankruptcy law was not taken that seriously by lawyers or even, at times, judges. To illustrate the point, Leonard Gilbert, who later became one of the leading practitioners in the field, recalled an incident when he was a law student working as a summer intern for one of Tampa's biggest law firms. He remembered that one day his firm was shorthanded and due to represent a client at a hearing, and one of the partners called Judge William Barker asking if Gilbert could fill in.

Even after he was reminded that Gilbert was just an intern and not admitted to the bar, Barker said, "Sure," send him over. Gilbert remembered the incident as "unbelievable. . . . But they did prepare me and I did represent the client as well as I think anybody could under the circumstances." The client, he continued, seemed satisfied because, as Gilbert speculated, the firm "probably charged less to send me." But a dramatic change occurred after Alexander Paskay's appointment as referee, Stichter recalled. Paskay "enforced higher standards of representation from attorneys appearing before him. . . . Attorneys came prepared and quickly acknowledged that they were getting fair, prompt and appropriate results."[56]

When Paskay became a "referee" in 1963, the Bankruptcy Act of 1898 was still in effect. There were two types of proceedings: Chapter 10, which was corporate reorganization, and Chapter 11, for individuals, in which debtors proposed a repayment plan. Over time Congress expanded the judicial responsibilities of the referees, who assumed nearly all the bankruptcy work of the district judges. In 1973, at the Supreme Court's behest, "referees" became "bankruptcy judges."[57]

But the limitations and the obsolete nature of the 1898 law necessitated change. As time went on, referees began handling increasingly complicated cases, yet their jurisdiction under the law "was very limited and restricted." As Paskay explained, "The district judge didn't want anything to do with it, didn't know anything about it, but yet we had no practical jurisdiction and the referee had only jurisdiction over disputes of property, which were in the actual or the constructive possession of the debtor on the date of the filing." Also, under the previous system the referees appointed trustees, which made it awkward in certain instances to rule against a trustee that the referee himself had appointed.[58] In 1973 Congress created a commission to study the problem and propose corrective legislation, and Paskay, as one of the foremost bankruptcy authorities in the United States, was instrumental in formulating the new legislation. The Bankruptcy Reform Act of 1978 established United States Bankruptcy Courts in each federal judicial district and made the new panels courts of record with their own clerks and other staff. The 1978 act determined that the bankruptcy judges would be nominated by the president and confirmed by the Senate, and would serve fourteen-year terms. The act also established the position of U.S. Trustee, who was an employee of the Department of Justice. The U.S. Trustee "establishes a private panel of trustees and they are supposed to be the policemen, supervise the trustees, appoint them, and run the whole system. So we're out of it completely," Paskay explained.[59]

For over a decade after the Middle District's creation, Paskay was its only bankruptcy judge. During those years he traveled to Orlando once a week to hear cases. Years later Jules Cohen, who often practiced before him, recalled, "He'd show up with two bulging briefcases of documents. . . . No secretary, no clerk, no bailiffs, just himself. He was the whole bankruptcy court for Orlando."[60] Paskay remembered that he and Tampa referee Buck Shaw went to Orlando twice a month by bus. Paskay recalled that in his first year there were 123 filings in Orlando and that there were no facilities whatsoever; Paskay held court sometimes in the hallway or in a closet-sized room in clerk's office.[61]

Finally, in 1974 another full-time judge was appointed in Jacksonville. George Proctor, the son of a Jacksonville grocer, was born in 1926. George's father, Jack, was born in Poland and immigrated to New Haven, Connecticut, when he was ten years old. In 1918 Jack married and eventually settled in Jacksonville. George Proctor was one of six boys. He entered the Marine Corps one month after graduating from Robert E. Lee High School in 1943. Proctor fought in the Pacific at Peleliu and Okinawa as a member of the First Marine Division. When Proctor returned to the United States, he entered the University of Florida, earned a law degree, and practiced privately in Jacksonville from 1949 to 1959. In 1959 Gov. LeRoy Collins appointed him deputy commissioner of the Florida Industrial Commission. Proctor acquired a good reputation as a worker's compensation lawyer and was offered an appointment as bankruptcy judge in 1975.[62]

Proctor got his chance to be a bankruptcy judge by happenstance. "I enjoyed my work as a worker's compensation judge, but in regards to the bankruptcy judge where I now sit, I never did bankruptcy practice in my career," he explained. "I had never filed a bankruptcy petition. I had no knowledge in it. I got into the field because my predecessor had a drinking problem, and it became so severe that he fell off the bench. He was really drunk. He literally fell. . . . Now this episode happens in August 1975. They're trying to find someone to take his place. This was not a tremendous job back then. The salary was $33,000 a year." Proctor's wife did not want him to take it, but he eventually accepted after numerous entreaties.

There was nobody, my predecessor was gone, there was nobody here to teach me anything about bankruptcy. I knew nothing about it, so the question becomes, what do you do? Well, I just did my homework every night. I just looked at the cases and decided how they should go. I read up on the law and got familiar with it, and I found this: I became more proficient than ninety percent of the people that came before me because I did my homework and they did not. I knew more about their cases than they did. The ten percent that were left, they were pretty good lawyers involved and that helped me rather than hurt me. So I learned the job. It was as simple as that. I had to learn what to do.[63]

Once Proctor came on the bench, he and Alexander Paskay shared the docket in Orlando. As Proctor explained, there was no Orlando division. All Orlando cases were filed in Jacksonville. At the time of the trial, Proctor brought all the files to Orlando. He had the hearing in Orlando and then took all the files back to Jacksonville. He traveled to Orlando every other week. Proctor eventually took over all the Orlando cases. At that time, Proctor remembered, "we were probably getting 500 cases a year. That included both Orlando and Jacksonville."[64]

His clerk's office in Jacksonville was

no bigger than a library table. The girls who worked that office had their typewriters. There were just two of them, two people. . . . When we would have a hearing here in Jacksonville, the court had to use that hearing table and the chairs for the people who were involved in the hearing, the witnesses, so the secretarial staff actually had to go outside the room. There wasn't room for them to sit in there. They couldn't do any work, they just had to sit and wait. Fortunately for everyone, the business was not heavy.[65]

Proctor's staff used manual typewriters with carbon paper. There were no online databases or computers. "When I had to look up a case . . . I just walked up to the volume and pulled it out, and I had a yellow pad and I'd write down what I wanted to say in there." In the first five years of his tenure, Proctor and Paskay basically ran their offices on their own. As Proctor explained, "Judge Paskay basically ran his show and I ran my show, and we just didn't have any reason to have a common clerk. But when the bankruptcy code became effective in 1979, we decided it would be appropriate to have a clerk. We selected a man named Aaron Nathan. Aaron was a chapter thirteen trustee in Orlando. He was a retired military colonel." He served for five years.[66]

In 1980 the United States was about to take an abrupt shift to the right. Jimmy Carter's popularity had taken a downward turn with the flagging economy, the Iranian hostage crisis, and the growing feeling that the country was in decline. As an antidote to what some called the country's "malaise," Carter offered up little other than shared sacrifice, reduced consumption, and spiritual renewal. Going in to the election of 1980 against confident and vigorous (even though he was nearly seventy) challenger Ronald Reagan, the president seemed tired, petulant, and ineffective. Reagan had many things going for him. The Republicans were well financed. The Democrats were squabbling and demoralized. Carter had failed as a party leader. Traditional Southern Democrats were switching parties in droves. Reagan supporters were even further energized by Christian evangelicals who for the first time organized themselves politically. Ironically, this newly energized force rejected the born-again Baptist Carter (who had inserted religion into the 1976 election) and turned to a divorced former Hollywood actor who had never attended church regularly.

Reagan called for a rollback of the Great Society, the reigning in of government regulations, and massive tax cuts to spur the economy. As Richard Nixon had done in 1968, Reagan targeted the federal courts in the campaign. Like Nixon, Reagan denounced federal court decisions that undermined school prayer and others that supported affirmative action, busing, and abortion rights. Denouncing "law making" from the bench, Reagan promised to reign in the courts and appoint federal and Supreme Court judges who exercised "judicial restraint" and interpreted the Constitution narrowly. Everything seemed to go wrong for Carter, who lost in a landslide to the ever-confident Ronald Reagan. The "Reagan Revolution" in America and in the Middle District Court of Florida was about to begin.

7

A New Era Begins

The Reagan Years, 1980–1988

On January 20, 1981, when Ronald Reagan took the oath of office as president of the United States, the U.S. Middle District of Florida numbered eight judges. George C. Young, Susan Harrell Black, William Terrell Hodges, George C. Carr, William J. Castagna, Ben Krentzman, Howell Melton, and John Alton Reed heard cases in the principal divisions in Jacksonville, Orlando, and Tampa. But judges also occasionally visited Ocala and Fort Myers. A few logistical changes were coming for the district. After 1981 all appeals from the Middle District would go to the newly created Eleventh Circuit Court of Appeals rather than the Fifth. Congress also saw fit to take away and add several counties to the Middle District. In 1978 Madison County was removed from the Middle and added to the Northern District of Florida. Then, ten years later, Congress added Collier, Glades, and Hendry Counties to the Middle District. Thus, in 1988 Middle District inherited jurisdiction of cases in the growing population center of Naples.[1]

During the Reagan years, through retirement and promotions, the composition of the court changed substantially. As would be expected given Reagan's political philosophy, there would be a rightward shift—at least as far as appointees' previous political philosophies were concerned.

Legal scholar Sheldon Goldman has noted that the "Reagan presidency was the mirror image of the Roosevelt presidency. Both Reagan and Roosevelt were enormously popular with the majority of Americans, but their policies and philosophies were opposed and even denigrated by a vocal minority." Both were reelected in landslides. "Reagan, like Roosevelt, spent the first term dealing with economic crises, and both used Keynesian economics (without credit to Keynes in Reagan's case) to nurse the economy back to health." Roosevelt had used social and domestic spending while Reagan used primarily military spending to boost the economy. "Both presidents had a view of the role of government including the courts that was radically different from their immediate predecessors. Both Reagan and Roosevelt sought to change the direction of the government, and both saw the federal courts as frustrating their policy agendas. Both self-consciously attempted to use the power of judicial appointment to place on the bench judges who shared their general philosophy."[2]

When it came to judicial selection, Reagan relied primarily on three men: Atty. Gen. William French Smith, in Reagan's first term; Edwin Meese (who was the president's advisor and attorney general in his second term); and White House counsel Fred F. Fielding.[3] The president created the President's Federal Judicial Selection Committee, which operated within the White House. Fielding chaired the committee, which also included Meese, the White House chief of staff, and others of Reagan's inner circle. "The highest levels of the White House staff thus played an ongoing, active role in judicial selection. Legislative, patronage, political and policy considerations were systematically scrutinized for each judicial nomination to an extent never before seen." The committee acted in proactive fashion as a source of "names of potential candidates and vehicle for the exchange of relevant information. . . . The committee, like the Justice Department, was determined to place on the bench, insofar as it was possible to do so, those compatible with the administration's overall ideological and judicial-philosophical perspective."[4]

For anyone who had any doubt about the Reagan administration's commitment to rolling back judicial activism, Attorney General Smith clarified the situation when—before an assembly of federal government attorneys—he blasted the federal courts for "their liberal activism in creating rights not mentioned in the Constitution and for unwarranted intrusion in the affairs of state and local government." Smith argued that some of these rights were "only implied in the Constitution" and that these expanded interpretations have "become a real base for expanding Federal court authority . . . The right to marry, the right to procreate, the right of interstate travel, and the right of sexual privacy that among other things, may have spawned a right, with certain limitations, to have an abortion. . . . We believe," he continued, "that the application of these principles has led to some constitutionally dubious and unwise intrusions into the legislative domain"[5]

Edwin Meese, who succeeded Smith as attorney general, was even more outspoken against "liberal judges," and promised to make sure that Reagan appointees shared the president's philosophy of judicial restraint. Inevitably, appointments to the courts became ever more politicized, and the

phrase "litmus test" encroached into the vernacular not as a scientific evaluation of a compound but instead as a certification of a judicial candidate's
view on school prayer, busing, abortion, or other politically charged issues.

Reagan's coattails were long in Florida. Newly elected senator Paula
Hawkins, a Republican from Winter Park, defeated Bill Gunter, a strong
Democratic candidate who defeated the incumbent Richard Stone in the
Democratic Primary. She was fully on board with the Reagan judicial
agenda. Hawkins was the first woman elected to the U.S. Senate who did
not immediately succeed a father or a husband. Hawkins opposed abortion rights and the Equal Rights Amendment even while pushing hard for
women's issues. She continually spoke out in favor of harsher measures
against drugs.[6]

By 1980 Florida ranked as the nation's seventh-largest state, with a population of nearly 10 million. While Florida's economy (along with the rest
of the nation in 1980) experienced high inflation and interest rates, Cold
War spending infused the state with federal dollars. Defense spending and
military payrolls in Florida surpassed $15 billion annually. Florida also led
the way in what some scholars have referred to as the "deindustrialization"
of the American economy—that is

> the dismantling and abandoning of much of the nation's increasingly
> obsolete industrial infrastructure. Taking the place of aging Rustbelt
> factory industries [were] the dynamic new industries of the postin-
> dustrial economy—high tech, computerized information businesses
> and the more fully developed (and low paying) service economy. The
> new American economy grew up around services provided by gov-
> ernment, educational agencies, and financial services companies; it
> was spurred also by health care and medical delivery, food service,
> travel and entertainment, and retailing and consumerism. Fast food,
> motel chains, and car rentals, sprawling malls and shopping centers,
> law service and office temps, rent-a-maid and rent-a-nurse—these
> are some of the businesses that have emerged at the low end of Flori-
> da's late-twentieth century economy.

But a new "high end service economy" also emerged. "With computer net-
works and other instantaneous communications, it was possible for major
corporations to relocate" to Tampa, Orlando, Jacksonville, or other Florida
cities. As one commentator observed, "Costs are reduced for company and
employees alike, and all benefit from Florida's low taxes, sunny climate,
and enhanced amenities."[7] One of the most obvious results of the new

deindustrialized economy was to send more and more people to Florida. Thus, as factories folded in the Northern rustbelt, many of the "economic refugees" came to Florida. Their hope (not unlike immigrants coming to America's shores from abroad) was to find some way to make a living in this challenging new time. These new economic realities affected the number and types of cases that appeared in the federal district courts.

In 1981 changes were in store for the Tampa Division of the Middle District of Florida. William Castagna was transferred from Jacksonville, joining Judges Hodges, Carr, and Krentzman. The next year Ben Krentzman took senior status after completing fifteen years on the bench, though he continued to hear cases on a regular basis. When asked what he planned to do with his time, Krentzman responded that he was sixty-five and ready to slow down a bit. "I'll probably work three days a week and go fishing the other two."[8] Upon Krentzman's retirement in 1984 Judge Castagna inherited his courtroom in the old post office building. Castagna remembered Judge Krentzman as extremely conservative on costs in his courtroom. There were old military-issue metal tables and chairs. When women began practicing in his court, he simply had plywood "modesty panels" nailed to the front of the desks. Castagna did some investigating on his own and hired some local carpenters to construct new tables and had the courtroom redesigned in lavish style at an extraordinarily modest cost. Castagna enjoyed a very warm personal relationship with Judges Krentzman, Carr, and Hodges. They had lunch together almost every day.[9]

In 1983 Krentzman, Carr, Castagna, and Hodges welcomed another judge to Tampa. The previous year President Ronald Reagan appointed Elizabeth Kovachevich to the federal bench. Kovachevich was first assigned to Orlando but was transferred to Tampa after one year. Controversial both before and after her confirmation, Kovachevich's name had also been put forward numerous times, even before President Ford nominated her in 1975. Senators Chiles and Stone had refused support, and she was not confirmed.[10] But in 1982, with Senator Hawkins firmly on her side and a new political order in place, her nomination and confirmation went smoothly. The forty-six-year-old Florida circuit judge from St. Petersburg became the second woman to serve in the Middle District.

Moving to St. Petersburg from Illinois at the age of eleven, Kovachevich attended Catholic school and considered being a nun before majoring in finance at the University of Miami. Eschewing the banking world, Kovachevich attended Stetson University College of Law and entered practice. In 1973 she was elected circuit judge, several years after serving a controversial stint as a member of the Florida Board of Regents. In 1971 Kovachevich made state-wide headlines when she referred to coed dorms as "taxpayer whorehouses." At a time of intense student unrest, the phrase resonated with conservative Floridians, and fit perfectly into the backlash politics of the time. But Board of Regents chair Burke Kibler, certainly no liberal, demanded an apology for her remarks, which Kovachevich refused. Kibler later complained that Kovachevich was an overbearing chronic dissenter who turned a majority of the members off. Not surprisingly Kibler, managing partner of the Holland and Knight Law Firm, played no little part in opposing Kovachevich's appointment back in 1975.

Even so, Kibler's law partner, Chesterfield Smith, had formed a different opinion of the judge. The former president of the American Bar Association explained to Sen. Paula Hawkins that, when examining Kovachevich's credentials as a member of Florida's Federal Judicial Nominating Commission back in 1976,

> At most, I had an open mind about her; perhaps it was slightly prejudiced against her. While I had long been acquainted with Judge Kovachevich, I did not know her closely or well, and I had not agreed with all her statements as a Florida Regent. My investigation indicated quite conclusively to me that she had made a splendid trial judge in the Sixth Judicial Circuit of Florida. My peers among the trial lawyers in Pinellas and Pasco counties spoke very well of her and gave her top marks for judicial performance. I came away convinced that she was a very good judge.[11]

The passage of five-and-a-half years had done nothing to change his opinion of Judge Kovachevich. "If she is still under consideration by you for a judicial appointment," Smith wrote to Hawkins, "I would applaud her totally. During all of my adult life, a personal goal has been to secure the highest qualified candidates for judicial appointment. It is my opinion that Judge Kovachevich meets that lifetime personal standard."[12]

With Kovachevich's appointment, the Middle District acquired a nononsense, workhorse of a judge. She soon gained respect as a tireless jurist determined to do justice and wipe out crowded dockets. "We've got all these people waiting to get answers from the court. . . . To me, that's what we're here to perform," she said. Once on the bench, Kovachevich dedicated all her energy to the job of judging. During the year ending in July 1987, Kovachevich disposed of 767 cases, more than any other judge

Judge Elizabeth Kovachevich on the day of her investiture. Looking on are Judges Ben Krentzman and George Young (*back row*) and Gerald Tjoflat and George Carr (*front row*). William Terrell Hodges Photo Collection, Middle District of Florida Archives, George C. Young Courthouse, Orlando, Florida.

in the Middle District.[13] Kovachevich's breakneck pace pleased some and frustrated others.

While not nearly as controversial as Kovachevich, Elizabeth Jenkins also had to overcome barriers in her early years in the legal profession. The Gainesville native had served seven years as assistant U.S. attorney before her appointment as the district's first female U.S. magistrate judge in 1985. After receiving her bachelor's degree from Vanderbilt, Jenkins earned her law degree from the University of Florida in 1976. Joining the U.S. Attorney's Office in Orlando at the age of twenty-seven, she admitted later, "I was shy, but I prepared the hell out of things." She soon matured into one of the district's most talented prosecutors.[14] Jenkins' addition to the Tampa court proved indispensable to easing the crowded docket.

The caseload in Tampa was growing dramatically. According to one account, between 1981 and 1986 the number of civil lawsuits in Tampa and Fort Myers grew by 57 percent and the number of criminal prosecutions went up by 144 percent even as the number of full-time judges (four) remained the same.[15]

With Judge Ben Krentzman's retirement, Hodges inherited chief judge duties. "The chief judge doesn't have any authority to supervise the other judges on the court, thank heaven," explained Hodges. "That's a large misconception among lay people, even some lawyers. But the chief judge is the focal point of communication with the Administrative Office, the support of bureaucracy in Washington. All of the mail comes to the chief judge for dissemination to the other judges in the district office and so forth. The chief judge is generally responsible for the administrative operation of the court from day to day, working with the clerk, the probation office, the marshal."[16] As chief judge, Hodges had no qualms about acting decisively to expedite the operations of the court. In 1985, when he understood that bus shelters in front of the courthouse were hindering the access of jurors and court personnel from coming in and out of the courthouse, he asked the City of Tampa bus officials to take them down. When they failed to act, he ordered a team of seven U.S. marshals and a welder to disassemble them on a Sunday afternoon before court opened the next Monday. Some years later when asked about his decision, Hodges admitted that some in the public and press perceived his move as "an arrogant act, and it may have been," he recalled, "but it was in the best interest of justice, and I'd do it all again if I had to."[17]

But a far more serious matter presented itself to Hodges not long after he became chief judge. From 1981 through 1989 Judge Hodges became embroiled in one of the most controversial episodes in involving the federal judiciary when he and another federal judge filed a formal complaint against Judge Alcee Hastings of the Southern District of Florida. Hodges' decision to act came after an administrative meeting of judges in March 1983. "I felt it was my duty. . . . It was one of the most difficult decisions I have made in my life," he recalled.[18] A Carter appointee, Hastings was the first black federal district judge in Florida history, and one of the first cases over which he presided was a racketeering case involving Thomas and Frank Romano, who were convicted. A year later authorities arrested William Borders, a friend of Hastings, on charges of brokering a bribe between Hastings and the Romanos.[19] According to the allegations, in exchange for the $250,000 payment to Hastings, Borders and other associates had arranged for the Romanos' sentences to be reduced to probation and for their seized assets to be released. In *United States v. Borders*, Borders was convicted of bribery, and his conviction was upheld by the Eleventh Circuit Court of Appeals with Judge Frank Johnson writing the majority decision. Based on evidence developed in the Borders prosecution, Hastings was also indicted for conspiracy, bribery, and obstruction of justice in federal court but was acquitted in 1983. Because they were convinced Hastings was wrongly acquitted, Hodges and Judge Anthony A. Alaimo, chief judge of the Southern District of Georgia, filed a joint complaint of misconduct with the Eleventh Circuit Judicial Council against Hastings on March 17, 1983.[20]

The complaint charged Hastings with lying under oath, obstructing justice, and "odious behavior." It was filed under the authority of the Judicial Conduct and Disability Act of 1980, which was designed to allow the federal judiciary to police itself. Under that law if the chief judge of the circuit found cause to pursue the case, he must appoint a committee composed of himself and an equal number of district and circuit judges.[21] Hastings filed suit in the U.S. District Court for the District of Columbia charging that the accusations against him were racially motivated, and he countered that the Judicial Conduct Disability Act was unconstitutional. Judge Gerhard A. Gesell rejected Hasting's argument and the investigation proceeded.[22] Among those serving on the five-member committee were Appeals Judge Frank Johnson and former Middle District judge Gerald Tjoflat. The committee hired former Watergate prosecutor John Doar, who conducted a three-and-a-half-year investigation and thereupon submitted the committee's report to the Judicial Conference of the United States, which in turn recommended Hastings's impeachment to the House Judiciary Committee. After conducting its own lengthy investigation of the matter, the House of Representatives voted 413 to 3 to send seventeen articles to the Senate. The Senate found Hastings guilty of eight perjury counts. He was removed from office on October 20, 1989. The excruciating ordeal had taken nearly seven years.[23] In 1992, three years after his impeachment, Hastings won a seat in the U.S. House of Representatives, a seat that, as of this writing, he still holds.

By 1980 Judges George C. Young and John Alton Reed had been in the new federal building in Orlando for four years. While the space had grown dramatically, the personnel had not. With Judge Young's retirement in 1981 and Judge Reed's desire to return to private practice, the Orlando division was heading toward a crisis. But help was soon on the way.

On the last day of October 1983 Florida Circuit Judge G. Kendall Sharp had an assistant state attorney and some federal drug enforcement officials in his chambers when his secretary informed him that he had important call. President Ronald Reagan was on the line, and he told Sharp that he had just nominated him for an opening on the court. Reagan congratulated Sharp and told him he was certain that the judge would do a good job. "As soon as he came on the phone," Sharp told a reporter, "it sounded like all the movies, all the TV. There was nobody who could fake it. It was him." Sharp assured Reagan that "he was very honored and challenged" and would "certainly try to do a good job. I know he is a busy man," he said of Reagan, "so I didn't sit around shooting the bull with him." Senator Hawkins, who had recommended Sharp after Ben Krentzman's retirement, was pleased with the nomination. "He is a supremely qualified jurist. He possesses the right combination of experience, judicial temperament, firmness, and compassion when circumstances require."[24] Less than three weeks later Sharp appeared before the Senate Judiciary Committee, and, as he recalled, they "disposed of me rather quickly." Sharp remembered it as a kind of celebratory atmosphere with his family and friends there; "it was like a neat Washington vacation."[25] Sharp made statements that would have been pleasing to the Reagan Justice Department. He promised that would never become a "judicial activist," and he noted that after witnessing the mandated desegregation cases in the 1960s, he had become convinced that the "states should run the states."[26]

G. Kendall Sharp was born on December 30, 1934, in Chicago, Illinois, and attended Phillips Academy in Andover, Massachusetts, where he excelled in football and track. After earning a BA in English from Yale in 1957, Sharp entered Officers Candidate School in the Navy. After receiving his commission he served on the USS *Ranger*, an aircraft carrier, remaining on active duty until 1960. After leaving the Navy, Sharp attended the University of Virginia Law School, graduating in 1963. Relocating to Vero Beach, Sharp practiced privately and also served as Indian River County School Board attorney. One of Sharp's more memorable clients was treasure salvager Mel Fisher. Sharp often accompanied Fisher on his treasure hunts. An avid outdoorsman and athlete, Sharp flew airplanes, hunted, skin dived up to fifty feet, and spearfished. Known as "Hurricane Ken," Sharp was a competitor on the handball and tennis courts. He exuded an infectious energy on and off the bench.[27]

As it would turn out, Sharp would need all the energy he could muster because within a year, with Judge Young's retirement and Judge Reed's resignation, he would find himself the lone sitting judge in Orlando. As the cases mounted, the two openings in Orlando were left unfilled. With Senator Chiles out of the loop and Senator Hawkins sparring with the Reagan White House, things continued to get worse. Hawkins had suggested several likely nominees, but Reagan's men in Washington dragged their feet. By March 1986 more than one thousand civil lawsuits were awaiting trial in Orlando. John Reed, who gave four months' notice before resigning in December 1984, commented on the sad fact, "I feel horrible about the vacancy not being filled." Former Florida Bar president Russell Troutman called the situation "inexplicable," adding, "If diligence had been pursued, we'd have a new federal judge." Senator Hawkins placed the blame squarely on the shoulders of Atty. Gen. Edwin Meese. In a press release, she blasted the Justice Department for ignoring qualified women for judgeships.[28]

Judge Sharp was working overtime to handle the backlog. He was able to handle one hundred civil cases a month, but as one hundred were added every month, little seemed to be accomplished. Sharp complained that one lengthy criminal case could foul up his entire schedule. With civil cases taking three years to be resolved, some lawyers were gaming the system. As an official in the clerk's office explained, "If the little guy files suit in state court against a big corporation, the company's lawyer gets it moved to federal court where he can drag it out forever."[29]

Finally, the likelihood that the one-and-a-half-year vacancy would be filled came when President Reagan nominated Hawkins' first choice, Patricia Fawsett, a forty-two-year-old lawyer from Orlando. On April 8, as he had with Kendall Sharp, President Reagan called her personally to notify her of his nomination. "I am excited beyond words," she said.[30] Although a Republican, Fawcett had the reputation of a nonpolitical, diligent practitioner. At the time of her nomination, Fawcett headed the civil litigation division of the Orlando law firm Akerman, Senterfitt and Eidson. She was the first female president of the Orange County Bar Association, serving from 1981 to 1982. She was born in Canada but grew up in Winter Park and Lake Wales. After graduating from the University of Florida, she taught history and humanities at Valencia Community College and Florida Technological University. She returned to the University of Florida in the early 1970s and was one of eleven women in the law school's 1973 graduating class. One of Fawsett's passions that she continued as a federal judge was riding motorcycles. "I've had a lifelong fascination with motorcycles," she said. "I'm not a person who feels stressed. But I am an outdoors girl and I love to ride on country roads. And through my teens and young adult years I've loved the feel and experience of riding right out into the country."[31]

At the moment Fawsett was chosen, the Senate confirmation process had nearly ground to a halt. The previous month Senate Democrats had blocked Alabama U.S. Attorney Jefferson Sessions' nomination from coming to a vote based on racial remarks he was reputed to have uttered. The Senate Judiciary Committee had confirmed only eleven judges during Reagan's second term, despite sixty vacancies. Comments like those of Democratic senator Paul Simon were frequent. "I am concerned about the quality of recent judicial nominations and I am concerned about their ideological bent," he stated before the National Press Club.[32] Yet most people believed that Fawsett's confirmation would be uneventful. According to David King, a leading member of the Orlando Bar, Fawsett would make a fine judge. "We are fortunate to get Pat over there. . . . She's as good as anybody I'm aware of. . . . She can deal with the little stuff and the big stuff, from the blue collar worker with a wage claim to the most complex litigation."[33]

As predicted, Fawsett's confirmation went smoothly. She was so eager to get to work that she dispensed entirely with the official robing ceremony that was customary for swearing in federal judges. Sworn in on June 30 over the phone by the district clerk in Jacksonville, Fawsett donned a borrowed robe from Judge Sharp and got right to work.[34]

Once she was on the bench, Fawsett and Sharp attacked the backlog with a vengeance. About a week after Fawsett began her duties Chief Judge Hodges decided to send district Judges Howell Melton and Susan Black and U.S. Magistrate Judge Harvey Schlesinger to Orlando to "knock off 160 civil suits in three weeks" beginning on July 7. Hodges had already overseen an "accelerated trial calendar" in Tampa in April to good effect and hoped that it would assist the overcrowded docket in Orlando as well. Since February, when Hodges announced the move in Orlando, over one hundred out-of-court settlements had taken place. Some speculated that the greater likelihood that cases would be heard encouraged some lawyers to "stop negotiating and begin making deals." John Fisher, president of the Orange County Bar Association opined, "Until you get to the courtroom, you can never be sure the other side has gone as far as they could." Walt Postula, assistant U.S. attorney, agreed. "People become more reasonable" once they know a trial is imminent, he said. Not only were the three sixth-floor courtrooms used but makeshift courtrooms were set up in the grand jury room on the fifth floor and in the basement. A witness room and two hearing rooms were converted to temporary offices for Judges Melton, Black, and Schlesinger.[35]

In the Jacksonville division, U.S. District Judges Howell Melton and Susan Black along with U.S. Magistrate Judge Harvey E. Schlesinger also faced a crowded docket in the 1980s. In 1981 Howard T. Snyder, who had a background with the FBI and with the U.S. Attorney's Office in Jacksonville, joined the division as U.S. magistrate judge. Retired judge Charles Scott continued to hear some cases until his death in 1983.[36] The third judgeship position that Congress had created in 1978 had remained unfilled because the Senate had failed to act on Carter nominee Ralph Nimmons. In 1981 Ronald Reagan turned to Florida appeals judge John Henry Moore, who had previously been nominated by Gerald Ford.

Moore grew up in south New Jersey, attended Syracuse University, and majored in business administration. After graduation he joined the Navy and entered Officer's Candidate School. It was there that he first considered the law. "As a junior officer I was assigned to prosecute and defend some cases in Court Martial. I enjoyed the idea of standing on your two feet and having to think and speak extemporaneously. And I enjoyed the argumentative aspect of it, the professionalism of it."[37] Moore served in the Korean War, operating catapult and arresting gear on aircraft carriers. Moore left active duty but remained in the reserves until 1971, retiring as a commander. In the late 1950s Moore moved to Gainesville and enrolled in University of Florida Law School. After graduation he practiced privately in Atlanta and Fort Lauderdale until 1967 when Gov. Claude Kirk appointed him circuit judge of the Seventeenth Judicial District. An appointment to the appeals bench came ten years later.[38]

Moore soon gained a reputation as a demanding judge with a gruff exterior but with a soft, caring side. Moore's clerks and attorneys who practiced before him remembered his three Ps: "Be prepared, be prompt, and be professional."[39] Moore developed a close personal bond with his fellow judges in Jacksonville. Some years later Moore remarked, "We have a most collegial court in Jacksonville. . . . Yes, we go to lunch together every day and we kick things around. If you're going to sentence somebody, do you think this is permissible under sentencing guidelines? Do you think something else should be? And we kick it all around with each other."[40] One of Judge Moore's least important but widely covered decisions in his first few years on the court was his order to have pigeons evicted from his courtroom after they had come in and were trapped behind the walls. Their cooing and droppings were causing distractions. Moore's order prompted a GSA maintenance engineer to go into the crawl space and release them out the window.[41]

Beginning the 1980s significant changes were coming to the federal courts. For example, in 1982 Congress passed the Pretrial Services Act, which greatly enhanced and expanded pretrial service functions as they related to sentencing and probation services. Building on the Speedy Trial Act (1974), the new law ushered in a tremendous expansion of what eventually became known as the "federal probation and pretrial services system." Pretrial service personnel did careful investigations of persons accused of crimes and worked closely with judges before, during, and after trials. Eventually officers were involved in the criminal justice process from the time a person was arrested on a federal charge until he or she completed community supervision.[42]

The advent of the Reagan administration ushered in major changes in the U.S. Attorney's Office. Upon the resignation of John Briggs in 1979, Jimmy Carter had appointed Department of Justice attorney Gary L. Betz, who had an extensive background in civil rights prosecuting voting rights violations. As deputy chief of the Miami Organized Crime Racketeering Section, Betz had brought cases against Meyer Lansky and other reputed organized crime leaders. Raised in Philadelphia, Betz attended Temple University and earned his law degree from American University in Washington. Robert Butterworth, who later hired him in the Florida Attorney General's office, said Betz was "totally incorruptible, and he went after the bad guys as hard as he could."[43] Betz scored several successes. According to one account, "He prosecuted a Russian spy; deported a Lithuanian who took part in Nazi activities during World War II; and brought the government's case against flamboyant restaurateur Gene Holloway, who was accused of faking his own death at sea."[44]

Betz should not have been surprised when the Reagan Justice Department replaced him, but he was. Yet, as they had with judicial nominations, Reagan's operatives moved slowly in vetting candidates; but soon it was reported, first out of Senator Hawkins' office, that Betz and the U.S. Marshal would be replaced. Betz was at first bewildered and then frustrated when he learned that former Pinellas County prosecutor and Justice Department lawyer Robert Merkle would replace him. "I have not spoken to the senator," he said. "She has not officially informed me that she will seek to have me moved or replaced. . . . There are many major investigations and trials that need to be completed." Betz bitterly contested the patronage system under which such appointments are made. "I am the only United States Attorney in Florida selected through a merit process. I have never been a Republican or Democrat."[45] Even so, Betz was out. Hawkins had her man. The White House cleared Merkle's nomination rapidly; he was confirmed by the Senate, and on May 15, 1982, Judge Ben Krentzman soon swore him in. Major changes were in store in the U.S. Attorney's Office.[46]

Robert Merkle was born in Washington, D.C., in 1944, one of nine children of a U.S. Air Force physician. A devout Catholic he was raised primarily in Greenville, South Carolina, and attended Notre Dame University, where he earned a bachelor's degree and, in 1971, a law degree. At 6'2" and

Robert Merkle, ca. 1980s. Appointed U.S. Attorney by Ronald Reagan in 1982, Merkle served until 1988. U.S. Middle District of Florida U.S. Attorney's Office.

240 pounds, Merkle played fullback on the Fighting Irish football team. After working for the U.S. Justice Department, Merkle came to Pinellas-Pasco State's Attorney's Office, working in the Special Prosecution Division. In 1981 Merkle returned to Washington where his strident anticrime and antiabortion views came to the attention of Senator Hawkins.[47] Dogmatic in his beliefs, aggressive and pugnacious in his behavior, the thirty-seven-year-old combative prosecutor would soon earn the nickname "Mad Dog Merkle." Soon after his confirmation, Merkle asserted, "I'm not happy unless I'm in court. I intend to get into court and lead my troops."[48]

Soon after Merkle's swearing in, the new U.S. attorney invited Judge Krentzman and Judge Terrell Hodges to lunch, and "we were happy to go," as Hodges recalled, but the dining became unpleasant when the prosecutor

> announced that his main reason for asking us to lunch was so that he could come to an agreement with us that anybody who got convicted, we would give consideration to imposing maximum punishment in every case. That way justice would be served and there was a likelihood that more crime could be prosecuted. I sat there in some wonderment. . . . In fact, Judge Krentzman just got up and left the table as best I recall. That was the last time we had a conference with Mr. Merkle. I don't say that to denigrate the man, he had his idea

about what his function was and he intended to zealously pursue it, which he did. He rubbed a lot of people I think the wrong way in the process.[49]

Merkle hit the ground running. In his first twelve months on the job, Merkle oversaw 87 jury trials, filed 492 new cases, and closed out 513 investigations.[50] As Merkle hit his stride, one source described him as a "blond, Irish charmer" who danced, sang, and played the piano. "Outside the courtroom, he's a Gregorian choir chanter, a Catholic, a father of seven who wants more, an outspoken critic of abortion, and singer of Irish ballads." But, the source continued, "there are some detractors who will tell you—if you promise not to use their name—that he is an aggressive, intimidating, win-at-all-cost prosecutor who bullies witnesses, defense lawyers and judges." In twelve years, he bragged, he had only lost one case. "I don't like to toot my own horn," he said. "But in candor (I'm) as good as you're going to find."[51]

Since 1969, when John E. Maguire retired, the U.S. Marshal's office had enjoyed stable leadership. Andrew Peeples, Ralph Saucer, Mitchell "Mickey" Newberger, George R. Grosse, and Michael Romanczuk were appointed by presidents Nixon and Carter. Newberger and Grosse served full four-year terms. In 1982 President Reagan appointed retired U.S. Army colonel Richard L. Cox to the post. The forty-six-year-old Cox would serve two four-year terms.[52] During Cox's tenure, the office grew dramatically and faced many challenges.

In the 1980s the U.S. Marshal's Service found themselves in possession of large amounts of property due to seizures. Under the Controlled Substances Act (1984), the federal government was allowed to seize the assets and property of convicted drug dealers and take control of businesses that were thought to be financed with illegal drug money. The revenue from sales went to the National Assets Forfeiture Fund, which provided the Marshals Service with funds to operate and maintain other properties that it confiscated until they could be sold. "Marketing these properties is a real challenge," Cox said. "We're more used to kicking down doors and arresting people. But this gives us a real opportunity to serve in a different manner."[53]

Cox supervised approximately one hundred employees responsible for providing security at federal courthouses, transporting prisoners, and finding federal fugitives. In the 1980s security became more and more difficult as numerous high-level prosecutions of drug smugglers and racketeers went forward. Marshals continually assessed security risks and investigated threats to judges or other court officials. Later in the decade, when Judge Robert Vance of the Eleventh Circuit Court of Appeals was assassinated near Birmingham and other bombs were discovered, security was tightened in federal courthouses around the state.

As time went on, the danger to federal judges grew. Nearly every federal judge experienced serious threats. Judges Simpson, Lieb, Krentzman, and Tjoflat had been threatened because of their civil rights rulings. In the 1980s controversial rulings that judges made in big drug and racketeering cases resulted in threats. Judge Harvey Schlesinger noted that he had constant threats during his thirty or so years on the bench. "I have had disgruntled litigants write nasty letters indicating that you are a marked person. I've had people actually write letters from prison saying that they have got an accomplice on the outside that is going to kill your children or something like that." Judge Susan Black and nearly every other federal judge had the same experience. "I've been threatened," she said, "I've had individuals who've broken out of jail and told their fellow inmates that they were breaking out of jail to come kill me. I've known about that, and things can be done to protect me from that. What can't be done to protect you is someone who decides to kill you over something that you would never think of?"[54]

One of the more onerous duties of U.S. Marshal Richard Cox was providing for the housing of federal prisoners awaiting trial. This problem, combined with jail overcrowding at the county level, grew worse as time went on. In the absence of any federal facility to house prisoners, Cox was forced to work out agreements with county sheriffs to house prisoners. One inducement Cox had for county officials' cooperation was that he could support them in gaining federal dollars for expansion. In November 1985 Cox had 166 prisoners in county and municipal jails scattered through the district. Cox worked continuously with Seminole County Sheriff John Polk, who cooperated with the federal marshal by housing federal prisoners on numerous occasions. Because of its close proximity to the Orlando federal court, Cox relied on the Seminole jail, and Sheriff Polk was cooperative even though he had an excess of county prisoners.[55]

But overcrowding became such a problem that in November 1984 four out of the five circuit judges in Seminole County threatened to block further housing of federal prisoners in the county jail. Cox countered that "we're using every available jail. We have a 200-year history of holding federal prisoners in local facilities. It's not a 'we versus them' situation. Seminole County is as much a part of the country as the rest of the nation. The federal prisoners are not solely the concern of the federal government."

County authorities received $35 a day for housing federal prisoners, and over $300,000 in federal dollars had built additional space. Moreover, Cox insisted that $700,000 of a $6 million appropriation was earmarked for Seminole County in exchange for the county's holding of up to thirty prisoners a day. It was reported that from 1983 to 1986 over $4.24 million federal dollars had been appropriated for jails in the Middle District counties.[56]

By 1988 the situation had worsened to crisis proportions. There were reports that 43 federal prisoners awaiting trial in Hillsborough County were crammed into a prison cell meant for 16 inmates. By that time the average number of federal prisoners exceeded 350 per day. In Sarasota there were inmates reputed to be wielding knives and using jail telephones to transact cocaine deals. According to one account, the "time, money, and logistics involved in delivering the prisoners to court hearings and trials has become an expensive and burdensome waste of time for the U.S. Marshal Service. . . . The average number of federal inmates in custody every day in county jails had more than quadrupled since 1981, from fifty-eight to 265," the account continued. "The average daily number is expected to reach 500 by the end of the year."[57]

There were several reasons for the increase. One was a new federal bail law that made it harder for persons arraigned to get bond. Meanwhile, the prosecutions in Merkle's office had jumped 122 percent (between 1981and 1986, from 388 to 863 annual cases). The U.S. attorney warned that the situation was "rapidly reaching a state of criminal justice gridlock." Judge Elizabeth Kovachevich added that the "whole thing is getting out of control. . . . You are just confronted with a situation where you are expected to do the job, and the taxpayers assume that you have the wherewithal to do the job. And that's an erroneous assumption. We in fact do not have the wherewithal to get the job done and I'm embarrassed and ashamed of the system." Tampa attorney John M. Fitzgibbons penned complaints to Judge Kovachevich, Chief Judge Hodges, and U.S. Marshal Richard Cox. "I think the marshal is frustrated," Fitzgibbons said, "and I think the judges are frustrated. The prosecutors are frustrated and the defense lawyers are frustrated. . . . I hear it from several of my clients, and some of them say that the conditions are just a powder keg and getting ready to blow."[58]

Judge Kovachevich and U.S. Attorney Merkle were trying to convince federal authorities to build a federal detention center, but there was little chance of that happening, and one center serving the nearly four-hundred-mile district would cause even worse logistical problems. As an example of existing logistical problems, some prisoners awaiting prosecution in the

Tampa federal court were being housed in Gilchrist and Hamilton counties. Thus, for federal hearings in Tampa deputies were sometimes forced to drive four hours to pick them up and four more hours to return them to jail.[59]

Fundamental causes for jail overcrowding were increased drug prosecutions, further federalization of crime, and inadequate funding of the system. Citizens wanted "tough on crime" measures but were unwilling to pay taxes for them. State and federal politicians were getting elected on "tough on crime" and "no new taxes" pledges. In the midst of huge tax cuts in the 1980s, deficits rose to proportions never before seen. U.S. Marshal Cox was forced to admit that the U.S. Congress, President Reagan, and taxpayers were unwilling to provide adequate resources. "It's probably the only point I would find serious disagreement between myself and my president," Cox said in 1988. "I wish we had spent two billion on" the needs of the district back in 1980. "It's a question that society will have to face. We may just find more and more crowded prison conditions."[60]

8

Drugs, Drugs, and More Drugs, 1980–1988

The 1980s saw one final push to convict notorious mob boss Santo Traf-ficante in the Middle District of Florida. The aging and ailing mobster was indicted in 1983 for racketeering and conspiracy for giving permission to out-of-state syndicates to run his gambling operations in Florida in return for a share of the profits. The indictment grew out of an FBI sting opera-tion, and the workup for his trial took approximately three years. Because of Trafficante's ill health, the June 1986 trial proceeded only three days a week because of the prisoner's need for dialysis treatments. As they had so many times before, Frank Ragano and Henry Gonzalez defended Traffi-cante. Ultimately the government's case rested on wiretaps from informants and hearsay evidence, much of which was disallowed by Judge William Castagna. Defense moved for a mistrial, and the government did not op-pose. In January 1987 the court found Trafficante too ill to stand trial and rescheduled the trial for February 9, 1987. He died on March 15, 1987.[1]

Perhaps Trafficante's death can be considered the closing chapter of a bygone era in organized criminal activity in Florida. The state's expansion of pari-mutuel betting ended Trafficante's bolita empire, and control of the illicit drug trade had fallen into other hands. If the days of Trafficante and Harlan Blackburn were fast receding, a new and more dangerous threat came from drug trafficking from points outside the United States—from the Medellín and Cali drug cartels of Colombia.

By the early 1980s drug cases began to overwhelm Florida's state and federal courts. Political and judicial authorities were not prepared for the onslaught, remembered Dan Warren, who practiced often in the district. "I don't think they had a handle on it as did most law enforce-ment. . . . They just weren't equipped. In fact . . . there was so much money involved in drugs. . . . It corrupted many state officials with the tremendous amount of money that was flowing through the drug pipeline. Sheriffs, law enforcement agencies, especially in the state systems; you'll find that many of the judges and law enforcement officers were taking kickbacks."[2]

By the 1980s law enforcement personnel and the courts had stronger resources to combat crime, especially drug trafficking, and drug prosecutions increasingly found their way into the federal courts. The Comprehensive Crime Control Act of 1984 provided federal law enforcement and judicial officials with new tools to prosecute drug dealers. The new law included tougher sanctions, tougher reporting of currency and foreign transactions, wiretaps, witness protection and relocation, acquisition of foreign evidence, speedy trials, the forfeiture of assets, and federal grants to states and localities for law enforcement.[3]

The Sentencing Reform Act (1984) also ushered in a massive overhaul of the federal sentencing system. The purpose of the new law was to address problems of disparity, dishonesty, and excessive leniency in sentencing. The new law established the U.S. Sentencing Commission to amend certain sentencing guidelines. In October 1985 President Reagan appointed seven persons as the first members of the commission. Within two years the commissioners had promulgated mandatory sentencing guidelines, and the guidelines were passed into federal law in 1987. The new scheme completely changed the way courts sentenced federal offenders. Not surprisingly, the new guidelines were tested in court and were upheld by the Supreme Court in January 1989. One of the effects of the new law was to require more extensive fact finding and legal conclusions for each case and substantially lengthen the amount of time judges spend on sentencing.[4]

Many judges were critical of the mandated sentencing guidelines. Judge Harvey Schlesinger admitted that while "sentencing guidelines to some extent have led to greater uniformity . . . there is the individual case that has some unusual twist to it which may call for a higher sentence or a lower sentence, and it's not to be found in the guidelines, and you are really in a quandary." Judge George Swartz did not like sentencing guidelines because it took away a judge's discretion for young offenders who become involved in cases for the first time. Judge Howell Melton admitted there was both praise and criticism for the guidelines. "There are many, many cases which a judge, in exercising his or her discretion, would not impose the sentence that the guidelines call for," he said. "The judge's hands are pretty well tied by those guidelines. They're not entirely. There's certainly safeguards that are in place within them, but they're pretty stringent."[5]

The overall effect of the new legislation was to extend federal jurisdiction over more and more crimes traditionally handled by states and localities.

The 1984 laws were only the beginning. The Money Laundering Control Act (1986) gave federal law enforcement authorities new tools to conduct surveillance and prosecute drug dealers. The Violent Crime Control and Law Enforcement Act (1994) further enhanced federal funding for law enforcement and crime prevention and expanded the number of federal crimes. In addition, the Violence Against Women Act (1994) provided funds for research and education to enhance knowledge and awareness for judges and judicial staff in matters involving domestic violence and sexual assault. Plus the measure made "gender-motivated crimes a violation of federal civil rights law." This provision of the law remained valid until the Supreme Court struck down the provision as unconstitutional in 2000.[6]

The overall result of the proliferation of federal involvement in the prosecution of crime was to place added strain on the judiciary to keep pace with the growing flood of criminal cases in their courts. From 1980 through 1992 the number of criminal cases in the federal courts grew by 70 percent and the number of individuals prosecuted grew by 87 percent. Drugs and firearms prosecutions accounted for the lion's share of the increase as both quadrupled in those years. Legal scholar Sara Sun Beale has observed that, as Congress "expanded the reach of federal criminal jurisdiction, it also provided greatly enhanced resources for federal prosecutors," but there was little corresponding rise in judicial resources.[7] The number of prosecutors per federal judicial officer doubled from 1986 to 1996. By 1996 there were nearly four federal prosecutors for every federal judge. As a result of the Omnibus Drug Initiative Act of 1988, the Middle District added eight new prosecutors, bringing the total to fifty-seven. The result was that federal and Middle District judges increasingly spent more and more of their trial time in criminal court. Thus, "criminal cases get priority; civil cases get ADR (alternative dispute resolution). There is a trade-off being made in favor of criminal cases at the expense of civil cases," Beale continued, "which span the gamut from commercial litigation to environmental and civil rights cases."[8]

This tradeoff was particularly apparent in the Middle District of Florida. In a 1989 issue of the *Florida Bar Journal* Chief Judge William Terrell Hodges summarized the challenges facing the district. He reported that 45 percent of the criminal cases filed in the district were drug cases. The percentage had grown every year during the decade. Hodges further added that criminal trials consumed two-thirds of the bench time of the judges as multidefendant trials added complexity to the cases. Yet another added burden occurred when Florida's death row prisoners sought recourse to federal courts when the state judiciary rejected their appeals. Hodges pointed out that the number of capital *habeas* cases filed had perhaps a greater impact on the Middle District than on any other U.S. district court. Hodges observed that in 1989 Florida had more than 300 death row inmates, with roughly 180 falling within the jurisdiction of the Middle District. "The 10–20 petitions filed annually with the court necessarily consume large amounts of judges' time relative to their numbers—time unavailable for other matters before the court." In order to manage the added burden, Judge Hodges noted that arbitration, other alternative dispute mechanisms, optimal use of magistrates, and development of effective local rules would be necessary.[9]

With profits high and risk relatively low, Florida became one of the most popular sites for drug smuggling in the United States. Because of Florida's vast, underpopulated southern regions, it was relatively easy for planes coming from South America by way of the Bahamas or other Caribbean islands to land with large caches of marijuana or cocaine and quickly unload their cargo at predetermined drop points. Glades County Sheriff Roy Lundy recalled that he began seeing lots of drug planes landing in his county by the late 1970s. On one occasion he remembered two huge DC-3 planes loaded with marijuana landing in a cow pasture on two consecutive days. The pilots had run out of gas. From maps on board it was determined that they were scheduled to land in the Big Cypress National Preserve but missed the drop point because of fog. It was clear that the planes had come from South America. Both had bladder tanks for extra fuel. Lundy recalled seizing DC-3s, Queen Airs, Aztecs, Islanders, and other types of airplanes. "I don't remember how many we caught. There were a lot of them," Lundy recalled.[10] Throughout Florida—especially in sparsely settled sections—the experiences of local and federal law enforcement personnel were similar.

On June 13, 1981, U.S. Customs tracked a suspicious plane from the Bahamas and followed it for two hours until it landed in a deserted field near Indian Lakes Estates in west Polk County. The U.S. Customs plane watched from overhead as eleven duffel bags were loaded from the plane to a late-model Cadillac, which immediately sped away. The pilot, a man named Donald Kramer Peterson, from Irvine, California, ran away from the plane after it landed, but Polk County sheriff's deputies captured him in the bushes. The deputies also recovered the Cadillac after it became stuck in an orange grove. The driver of the car got away, as did another man who had bailed out of the plane before it landed. But Peterson was not so fortunate. He was convicted in Judge Hodges's court of smuggling 559 pounds of high-quality cocaine, which one source reported as the second-largest seizure of illicit drugs in U.S. Customs history. Hodges sentenced Peterson to thirty years in jail, declaring, "The evidence presented in this case showed that the defendant is guilty, not beyond a reasonable doubt, but beyond any shadow of doubt."[11]

The I-95 and I-4 corridor served as a major conduit for drug transportation. Judge Elizabeth Kovachevich once nicknamed the route the "cocaine corridor."[12] Florida Highway Patrol and Drug Enforcement Administration (DEA) agents were particularly alert to suspicious automobiles traveling along that route. Agents netted many arrests, but defense attorneys often challenged the constitutional basis of the stops. For example, the well-publicized seizures of popular Volusia County sheriff Robert Vogel brought the officer's tactics under scrutiny. Vogel's deputies seized thousands of dollars' worth of drugs and cash on I-4 and I-95. Sheriff Vogel's methods were soon challenged in court. He was accused of racial profiling, as the vast majority of those stopped by his Selective Enforcement Team were blacks or Hispanics. By the middle 1990s Vogel was investigated by the Justice Department but never officially charged with wrongdoing.[13]

By the latter part of the decade extensive resources and the successful coordination between state and federal agencies provided Middle District prosecutors with the ability to work up cases against some the world's most sought-after drug kingpins. Thus from 1987 to 1989 the Middle District of Florida was the venue for some of the most sensational and successful drug trials in the United States—and none was more significant than the notorious Medellín drug lord Carlos Lehder Rivas. By some estimates Lehder's operatives were responsible for 80 percent of all the cocaine smuggled into the United States.[14]

U.S. Magistrate Judge Elizabeth Jenkins, who began her duties in 1985, likens magistrates to "foot soldiers in the front line" of the federal judiciary. "We take whatever walks through the door," she noted. One afternoon, not long after she first came on the bench, a U.S. Marshal told her as she was leaving work that they were bringing in a Colombian the next day. She really did not pay much attention to the remark until she arrived at the courthouse the next day and saw U.S. Marshals on the roof, inside the courthouse, and patrolling the rear entrance carrying Uzi machine pistols and semiautomatic shotguns. She soon understood something big was up.[15]

Carlos Lehder Rivas was indicted in Jacksonville in 1981, but he was not returned to American soil until February 5, 1987, in Tampa. The day before, Colombian officials had captured Lehder in a gun battle at his ranch in Medellín, and he was immediately turned over to American authorities under a recently approved extradition treaty. Four U.S. marshals brought Lehder in handcuffs and leg shackles before Judge Jenkins for processing. Also in the group were U.S. Attorney Robert Merkle and Mark Pizzo of the federal public defender's office. After preliminary proceedings were concluded, Judge Jenkins in the usual formal manner asked, "Should we consider bail or detention?" At that point Merkle bolted upright, announcing in what Jenkins remembered, was a "snarling" tone. "Your honor, we are going for detention. Mr. Lehder has threatened to kill a judge a week if he was arrested," to which Lehder snapped at Merkle, "That's a lie!"[16]

Born in Colombia, Carlos Lehder Rives was the son of a German father. He immigrated to the United States at the age of fifteen with his Colombian mother. A troubled teen, Lehder stole cars, sold drugs, and eventually landed himself in a federal prison in Danbury, Connecticut, where he plotted a drug-smuggling scheme with fellow inmate George Jung. After their release, the success of their operations reached unbelievable heights. According to Judge Harvey Schlesinger, who handled Lehder's pretrial hearing in Jacksonville, Lehder "invented the transportation system."[17] The Jacksonville and other indictments charged Lehder with smuggling thousands of pounds of cocaine into the United States from Norman's Cay in the Bahamas. The small island served as the drug kingpin's distribution point for the cocaine brought in from Colombia. One of Lehder's drop-off points was an airstrip west of Jacksonville. "That's how we acquired jurisdiction on the case," Schlesinger recalled.[18]

DEA documents alleged that Lehder bribed Bahamian prime minister Lynden Pindling $100,000 a month as a way of continuing his operations. Two other Lehder associates were also brought to Jacksonville to answer the indictment—Jack Carlton Reed, of San Pedro, California, one of Lehder's flyers who was arrested at his Panama jungle hideout; and Edward Hayes Ward, a former Marine and resident of Jacksonville—and a pilot was also in custody. Other indictments charged Lehder with being one of the four leaders of the Medellín Cartel, responsible for numerous murders and assassinations of politicians, judges, and news reporters in Colombia. Lehder was known also for his hatred of the United States. An avowed follower of Adolf Hitler, Che Guevara, and John Lennon, Lehder also aspired to become president of Colombia. He once asserted from his jungle hideout in a television interview that cocaine was the "revolutionary weapon in the trouble against North American imperialism."[19] On another occasion he bragged that cocaine was the "atomic bomb of Latin America," perhaps the most potent weapon of all against the power of the United States.[20]

U.S District Attorney Robert Merkle announced soon after Lehder's appearance in Jacksonville that the drug lord "represents the personal embodiment of the term that's come to be known as the 'narco-terrorist.'"[21] While he admitted that Lehder's arrest would not end cocaine smuggling, it would be symbolic. Addressing the Suncoast Tiger Bay Club, Merkle asserted that the arrest was "an absolutely revolutionary manifestation—in terms of both the will and the courage of the American people and the will and the courage of the Colombian people."[22] Merkle was quick to take credit for the arrest and extradition. He explained how he had personally traveled to Bogota in 1983 to negotiate an extradition treaty with Colombian officials, and that those same officials were targeted for death by the Medellín Cartel. Meanwhile, it was soon learned that Judge Howell W. Melton would hear the case.

The security surrounding Lehder's prosecution was unprecedented. While awaiting his trial he was held in various undisclosed locations some distance away from Jacksonville (which later turned out to be Marion, Illinois, and Talladega, Alabama). While he claimed that all his assets had been seized, Lehder sought to hire his own lawyer, but as his court-appointed attorney explained to Judge Melton, Lehder's undisclosed location not within the "geographic jurisdiction of the court" prevented him from having a "face-to-face conference with persons he wants to interview." Some estimated that private counsel would cost Lehder over $2 million, which of course he had, but some lawyers were reluctant to take the case because they knew that the government might be able to prove that all Lehder's assets were illegally accumulated and thus subject to seizure. With such obstacles in the way, Judge Melton ordered Lehder moved to Atlanta so he could more easily confer with his attorneys. The trial was set for April 20, a date eventually extended to May 18 and then to September 8. Lehder's lawyers, Edward Shohat and Jose Quinon, continued their appeals to have the trial date moved back and also requested a change of venue, arguing that there was no way to be prepared for such a complex case and that their client could not receive a fair trial in Jacksonville. Judge Melton denied the request for a change of venue but postponed the trial one last time to October 5.[23]

Despite heightened security, difficult logistics regarding jury selection, and the ever-present national press scrutiny, the trial began on the appointed date. Robert Merkle assigned himself to the case along with veteran prosecutor Ernst Mueller, who had assisted Merkle in his efforts to convince Colombia authorities to extradite Lehder. Karla Spaulding, one of several assistant U.S. attorneys on hand, recalled that both Merkle and Mueller had around-the-clock protection. Security was unprecedented. Bomb-sniffing dogs roamed the courthouse.[24] Judge John H. Moore recalled that, in the interest of security, marshals even participated in a deception to fool trial watchers. "Every day they would take him upstairs. In the courthouse there's a little holding cell up there and this is in the old courthouse, and they fitted it out with a television set and a more comfortable bed. They housed him there every night and fed him up there, but they'd have somebody with a hood on walk out to the car and drive away like they were taking him back someplace. So the press never knew that he was in the courthouse the whole time."[25] The masquerade went on for seven months.

The jury selection process was excruciatingly drawn out. It took five and a half weeks for a jury of nine women and three men to be selected. "I don't know whether to pass out cigars or ask for a vacation," Merkle muttered as he shook hands with Lehder's lawyer, Edward R. Shohat.[26] Once the jury was set, a list of 213 governmental witnesses was read aloud in court. In his opening arguments before the court, Shohat portrayed his client as the victim of a "'masquerade of horribles' contrived by federal prosecutors and a group of convicted Jacksonville cocaine smugglers to 'secure a conviction at any cost.'" Lehder's conviction had become a "cause celebre like nothing else in law enforcement."[27] Shohat argued that his client's flamboyant behavior and peculiar political beliefs had made him into an easy target for Merkle and federal authorities. His plans to develop Norman Cay into an upscale tourist mecca were legitimate, until Edward Hayes Ward, who occupied the island as a refueling stop for cocaine and marijuana smuggling, wrongly blamed Lehder when he was captured. Shohat argued that Ward and George Jung, Lehder's old associate, who was also brought in to testify against Lehder, were all convicted felons trying to reduce their prison sentences and were willing to say anything to accomplish their goal. Merkle brought in witness after witness to refute Shohat's contentions, but the prosecutor found it difficult to confine himself to arguments inside the courtroom, and began to hold press conferences outside. When the defense complained of these antics, Merkle responded that he discussed no evidence at the conferences. Judge Melton put an immediate end to the practice and warned that he would consider a gag order if the interviews continued. "I just don't see the importance of interviews. I'm just simply not going to make this an interview trial," he said.[28]

The marathon trial placed serious strains on Melton, the attorneys, the jurors, and other functionaries of the court. Melton remembered the trial as the most difficult he ever had. Jurors (identified only by number) were bused to the courthouse every day from a designated spot in Jacksonville and then deposited at the same place at the end of the day. A U.S. marshal was assigned to Melton on his trips to and from court. "They picked me up and brought me to court then took me back home in the evening. It was a difficult time," he recalled. The attorneys, though skilled, were "quite contentious. There were motions throughout the day that you had to rule upon and it was just a very difficult case to try. As a matter of fact, we finally decided that, on motions for mistrial, we reserved up to an hour after the jury was gone each day for the attorneys to make their motions for mistrial. It was such interference for the trial of the case, but we had to come up with something."[29]

Merkle's parade of witnesses included pilots, couriers, and a host of well-known people such as Walter Cronkite, who told of being chased away from Norman Cay when he approached the island with his family in his sailboat. After calling 115 witness during twenty-two weeks of testimony, federal prosecutors rested their case against Lehder and Reed on April 28. In a surprise move the defense rested their case without calling witnesses. Shohat claimed that the charges against Lehder were politically motivated, and that evidence was manufactured by offering convicted drug dealers special deals to testify. "The government has literally given away the courthouse to get our client," he declared."[30]

On May 11 Merkle's final argument lasted five hours, with Shohat objecting thirty-three times, only two of which Judge Melton sustained. Merkle asserted that Lehder's crimes had resulted in untold "human wreckage . . . in Colombia, South Caicos and the Bahamas and the United States." Lehder had left behind a "trail of bribery, corruption, violence and personal debasement."[31] Jury deliberations went on for seven days. Finally, the jury delivered its guilty verdicts on all eleven counts on May 19. In a news conference after the verdicts Merkle addressed a large gallery, "In the immortal words of James Brown," he said, "I feel good. This is a victory for the good guys. I mean the American people." Four hours later attorney Shohat also addressed reporters: "Mr. Lehder and we are obviously disappointed at the verdict. We fully intend to appeal. Mr. Lehder is in very good spirits. He feels very, very strongly about his legal position."[32] With the conviction, federal authorities next moved to seize Lehder's assets, including what remained of his property on Norman's Cay. Revelations at the trial also resulted in the indictment of Panamanian dictator Manuel Noriega and international financier Robert Vesco, who authorities thought was hiding in Cuba. An Orlando grand jury also mulled an indictment of sitting Bahamian prime minister Lynden O. Pindling.[33]

On July 20 Judge Melton sentenced Lehder to 135 years in prison without the possibility of parole. At his sentencing, in a rambling twenty-five-minute statement, Lehder claimed that his arrest and prosecution was illegal and politically motivated. "I have been Mr. Merkle's hostage. I'm a political prisoner." Judge Melton brushed aside Lehder's contention. The judge asserted, "You were not convicted because of your political beliefs, because you are a Colombian." The evidence in the case showed that Lehder's actions were motivated by "money" and "greed," not politics. He added that Lehder's heavy sentence was a "message, a signal to our society that it will do everything it can to rid itself of this cancer." Also present at the sentencing was Merkle's former assistant, Joe Magri, who was pleased at the severity of Lehder's sentence. He called the drug kingpin a "cocaine narcoterrorist" and said that "the judge fairly, justly and appropriately socked it to a hoodlum."[34]

By the fall of 1989, in what prosecutors called the "Son of Lehder Trials," several defendants were prosecuted in Judge John H. Moore's court in Jacksonville for their role in Lehder's drug-smuggling enterprises. One of the nine defendants who pled guilty was Lehder's former wife, Yemel Nacel of New York City. The trial ended with two acquittals and three convictions. Others indicted but not in custody were Colombian drug kingpins Pablo Escobar Gaviria, Jose Rodriguez Gacha, Jorge Ochoa Vasquez, and Fabio Ochoa Vasquez.[35]

The Lehder prosecutions led to still other investigations, indictments, and convictions. For example, Robert Castoro, a man who lived in Orange County, was convicted of drug smuggling and income tax evasion in Judge Patricia Fawsett's court roughly the same time as Lehder's sentencing occurred. Castoro was accused of heading a marijuana and cocaine importation ring from 1977 to 1984 that smuggled 360,000 pounds of marijuana and 440 pounds of cocaine into the United States, mainly from the Bahamas to South Florida but also from Mexico to Texas. Castoro's boyhood friend and partner, Bill Baron, testified against Castoro (as he did in the Lehder trial), and it was revealed in the trial that Castoro's major suppliers were Lehder and Pablo Escobar of the Medellín Cartel. After Castoro's conviction, the IRS and DEA seized millions of dollars' worth of expensive homes, properties, and luxury cars. After the verdict Assistant U.S. Attorney Cynthia Hawkins, who prosecuted the case, announced, "If you want to be a big player in the drug business, you've got to be willing to pay the price—including facing life in prison and losing everything you own."[36] Two months later Judge Patricia Fawsett, in what one source called the harshest penalty ever handed down in a federal court in Orlando, sentenced Castoro to life in prison without parole. "In the court's opinion," Judge Fawsett asserted, "you have introduced more harm and evil to this society than a murderer." Fawsett called Castoro a "cool, detached and very calculating" man who must be permanently "removed from society."[37]

Even if his cooperation and testimony against Castoro and Lehder paid dividends for prosecutors and had the effect of substantially reducing his own eventual sentence on drug convictions, Bill Baron was subsequently convicted in Judge Fawsett's court and was sentenced to fifteen years in prison without parole. "You enjoyed a high standard of living, which included yachts, ranches, paying bribes to a prime minister of a foreign country and law enforcement officers," Fawsett asserted. But at Baron's sentencing hearing, numerous IRS and DEA agents testified that Baron's continued cooperation was indispensable to Lehder's conviction and other ongoing drug investigations, including those under way against Pablo Escobar. Veteran prosecutor Ernst Mueller told Judge Fawsett that protecting Baron's safety in prison was essential. "Unfortunately, all Latin prisoners will view Lehder as a hero," and Baron would require "special handling," he said.[38]

Federal authorities pursued prosecutions against other of Castoro's associates. Two men, one named Andy Yurowitz, a vice president of E. F. Hutton & Co, and another man named Arthur Stein, were indicted for laundering $450,000 of drug proceeds, but Judge Fawsett dropped the charges on Yurowitz and overturned Stein's jury conviction. "I do not set aside jury verdicts lightly," said Fawsett, but "the evidence does not show that Mr. Stein knew that the money which was laundered came from drug smuggling. At most the evidence shows that defendant Stein agreed to launder a sizable amount of cash."[39]

Once in prison, Castoro decided to help investigators in numerous drug-related civil and criminal investigations. His cooperation paid dividends for them and himself. He implicated over three dozen other drug smugglers in the United States, Latin America, and Europe. By 1994 Castoro's revelations had led to the prosecution of 125 drug-smuggling associates and the seizure of over $6 million in assets. Appearing once again in Judge Fawsett's court in January 1994, the prisoner tearfully admitted his wrongdoing, but, most importantly, the judge heard testimonials from investigators of his "invaluable testimony" in the prosecution of other cases. Judge Fawsett carefully considered the testimony in the prisoner's behalf, including that of Cynthia Hawkins Collazo, who originally prosecuted Castoro six years earlier. Fawsett reduced his sentence from sixty-five years to twenty years. Four years later Judge Fawsett reviewed Castoro's case once again, and her decision in effect set Castoro free. "Frankly," she said, "I feel he's been in prison long enough." Due to Castoro's assistance, seventy-six other defendants had been convicted and $8 million in assets seized.[40]

About the same time as the Lehder and Castoro prosecutions, another huge drug trial against three men—Michael J. Tsalickis, a Tarpon Springs importer, and two Colombian accomplices—was taking place in Tampa before Judge George C. Carr. Arrested on May 3, 1988, Tsalickis was accused of smuggling nearly four tons of cocaine into St. Petersburg in hollowed out Brazilian cedar boards. The haul was the second-largest seizure of cocaine in U.S. history. The three men were arrested as they transferred the cocaine-laden lumber from the port to Tsalickis's warehouse in Tarpon Springs. Trial testimony showed that Tsalickis, who had traveled extensively as an importer and adventurer in South America, had contacts with the Cali Cartel. But Tsalickis denied that he knew anything about the drugs. The jury disagreed, and on February 16, 1989, Judge Carr sentenced him to twenty-seven years in jail. "I've thought about this very carefully," Carr told Tsalickis. "When you chose to get involved in such an undertaking to bring in this much contraband, I can only assume your reason must have been one of greed. You let the greed take over."[41]

Closely linked to the Lehder and Castoro prosecutions was the case of Manuel Noriega, captured in Panama in 1989 during Operation Just Cause, the U.S. invasion of that country. In 1988 the dictator and his associate, Enrique "Kiki" Pretelt, were indicted in Tampa, but Noriega was eventually tried in the Miami federal court under other drug indictments. Pretelt was brought directly to Tampa from Panama and faced charges that he had conspired to ship 1.4 million pounds of Colombian marijuana through Panama to the United States. Pretelt eventually pled guilty to planning to smuggle 400,000 pounds of marijuana to the United States, and to helping to launder drug profits in Panama. Pretelt also agreed to testify against Noriega and five international bankers awaiting trial in Miami. On August 16 Judge William J. Castagna sentenced Pretelt to ten years in jail, but the judge granted him immediate eligibility for parole once he testified against Noriega.[42] The deposed dictator was eventually convicted in Miami and sentenced to forty years in prison. Noriega still faced charges in Tampa, and after his conviction in 1992, U.S. Attorney Robert W. Genzman announced,

"It is our present intention to proceed against Manuel Noriega in Tampa." Under the Tampa indictment, Noriega was accused of accepting $4 million in bribes to protect a marijuana smuggling ring, but his case never came to trial because of prosecutions elsewhere.[43]

In the summer of 1987, as Bob Merkle was assembling his Lehder prosecution team, a newly hired prosecutor strolled past Merkle's Tampa office. Douglas Frazier had been working in Orlando and had only been in the Middle District roughly six months, but he had experience as an assistant United States attorney in New Orleans for the U.S. Eastern District of Louisiana. As Frazier happened by that day, Merkle was contemplating expanding the federal law enforcement presence in Fort Myers. The town had grown precipitously and was the center of drug smuggling that had overwhelmed state and county law enforcement. Merkle ordered Frazier to Fort Myers immediately to prosecute a drug-related murder, and, in the process, he eventually established a permanent U.S attorney's office there. As Frazier recalled, "So on July 5, 1987, I drove down to Fort Myers for the first time and went in the courthouse. And there was no security, no marshals." Representative Connie Mack had a small office in the old courthouse. There were two or three FBI agents, a probation officer, an investigator for the Wage and Hour Division of the Department of Labor, and an unmanned National Weather Station. "There was lots of smuggling going on in Everglades City and in Pine Island Sound," Frazier continued. "There were corruption cases. There was a large undercover operation ongoing on a cocaine and crack cocaine distribution network headed by Ronnie Tape. It was just time to put somebody here permanently."[44]

In 1979 Ronnie Lee Tape began selling cocaine in the impoverished Dunbar neighborhood of Fort Myers where he grew up. By 1988 his $100-a-week enterprise had become a multimillion-dollar operation. Tape and his girlfriend, Sandra Hernandez, and several other companions bought, prepared, and packaged cocaine for sale and sold it for Tape as well as for a number of street distributors. By 1985 Tape's distributors brought in up to $20,000 a day for Tape. By that time Tape's operation was the major source of cocaine for South Carolina, Louisiana, Georgia, Dallas, and Los Angeles. By 1988 Tape owned two night clubs in Fort Myers, a recording studio in Los Angeles, and a home in Beverly Hills valued at over $2 million. But that year Tape's drug empire was overthrown as federal agents arrested the "flamboyant businessman" on charges of cocaine distribution, engaging in a continuing criminal enterprise, and attempts to defraud the IRS. Indicted in May 1988, Tape and four codefendants were eventually convicted. After netting the convictions, Douglas Frazier noted, "This was the most signifi-cant conviction of the most significant player in the cocaine, heroin, and crack industry here."[45] Within weeks after Tape's conviction, Larry White, one of Tape's closest accomplices, was captured in Grand Rapids, Michi-gan. White, authorities claimed, was responsible for distribution of crack in Tampa and St. Petersburg. White had been on the run for seven years. U.S. Marshal Richard Cox hailed the arrest. "As far as I'm concerned, Larry White was our most wanted man. . . . He was a national fugitive."[46]

From 1989 to 1993 Judge Elizabeth Kovachevich visited Fort Myers fre-quently to handle the burgeoning criminal caseload brought on by what she remembered as an out-of-control drug trade. She likened law-breaking and the violence associated with it to the "wild west." About the time of the Tape prosecution, recognizing that local authorities were ill equipped to handle the marijuana smuggling operations in Southwest Florida, the Lee and Collier County Sheriff's office and the Florida Department of Law En-forcement, in cooperation with several federal agencies including the DEA, U.S. Customs, and the Coast Guard, formed "Operation Peacemaker"—an effort at coordinating investigations and prosecutions. Also at the time, assistant U.S. attorneys Frazier and Susan Daltuva, in conjunction with other federal agencies, created the Organized Crime Drug Enforcement Task Force. The coordination between state and federal authorities paid off. Between 1987 and 1990 over 180 individuals were charged with smuggling and prosecuted in the federal court in Fort Myers.[47]

Douglas Frazier explained later that federal prosecutions offered many advantages over what had previously been primarily a state function.

> There have been so many instances of which the U.S. Attorney's Office and the federal courts have had to come in and not cover for the state system but be able to do things that the state couldn't do. . . . Well, the tools are different sometimes. And since they're separate sovereigns, sometimes we can come in after they have failed, like O.J. Simpson. And then other times, it's just the tools. When I first came down here, the State wasn't able to make any of these cases. They weren't able because of resources and laws. [The federal government could offer] much better protection of sources and witnesses, and . . . we also had the Sentencing Guidelines, which people knew that this was a pretty severe sentence. . . . And then the Bail Bond Reform Act where they got detained pretrial and didn't get out on bond to go intimidate wit-nesses and commit more mayhem and whatnot. So there have been a

number of times when the federal resources have been able to come in and assist or buttress what the State was not able to do. . . . And that's kind of what happened here.[48]

Everglades City, a village of little over five hundred inhabitants, was perhaps Florida's most strategically located community positioned to serve as a marijuana smuggling point. In the early 1980s fishermen found it easy to sneak out into the Gulf at night and return with bales of marijuana chunked overboard from Colombian boats. With profits so high, many fishermen were tempted by the easy money. In 1983 Operation Everglades swept down and arrested forty-one people. That was only the beginning. More arrests and would follow. In a 1989 case, Assistant U.S. Attorney Daltuva prosecuted a number of smugglers in Fort Myers before Judge Kovachevich. Daltuva complained that the greatest difficulty in successful prosecutions came from the mistaken idea that to inform on lawbreakers was somehow dishonorable. Instead of "outlaw heroes," the men were dangerous criminals who were destroying their communities and harming the country. "It's the attitude of the people of Everglades City that has to change and these men can be part of that change. It shouldn't be a situation where standing up for law and order, standing up for the rights of the American people to have a drug-free society, should be cause for humiliation. It should be a cause for a sense of pride in the community." Judge Kovachevich agreed with the prosecutor's observation, and she sentenced two of the men to forty years in prison. Lecturing the two men who had refused to implicate others who they knew were also involved, Judge Kovachevich stated, "Now, I'm serious gentlemen. You have got your value structure wrong. . . . Your attitude about sticking up for other people is wrong. You're hurting your own country. On Memorial Day this year, when you think about everybody that gave up their life for this country, you think about why they did it. Did they do it so that you could bring drugs into this country? Did they?"[49]

Judge Kovachevich recalled that, in Fort Myers among drug people, the "choice of weapons were explosives." Those especially targeted were cooperating witnesses. The father of one cooperating witness was killed in a car bomb. The sister of a cooperating witness was run off the road and killed. Another went out on an airboat and never came back. On December 16, 1989, the same day a mail bomb exploded in the home of Eleventh Circuit Court of Appeals Judge Robert Smith Vance in Birmingham, Alabama, bombs rocked South Florida as well. One of the bombs blew off the arm of a Miami lawyer whose client had revealed information to Judge

Kovachevich about the death of a man in the witness protection program. Judge Kovachevich and authorities at the time thought there might be some link to the bombings, but it turned out that the Alabama bombings were unrelated to events in South Florida. Even so, the simultaneous bombings put the entire district on edge.[50]

One especially frightful series of incidents in Fort Myers occurred in the spring of 1990 when another drug dealer in Fort Myers Beach, Jeffrey Matthews, threw a pipe bomb though the window of the DEA field office two days after he was indicted by a federal grand jury. The office, along with evidence gathered from numerous drug investigations, went up in blazes. The sensational incident made national headlines, and federal law enforcement personnel descended on Fort Myers. Matthews sold cocaine from his pizzeria on the beach, and was suspected of killing an FBI informant. He immediately dropped out of sight the day of the DEA building bombing but was apprehended two weeks later in Orlando. Judge Swartz remembered the harrowing incident as extremely frightening. On the day of the bombing Swartz and his wife were out of touch on the golf course. The marshal's office frantically tried to find them and called their children, which terrified them. Eventually the marshals guarded the judge at his condo for about a month.[51]

Judge Elizabeth Kovachevich remembered that on the day Matthews was apprehended, she immediately adjourned a trial she was conducting in Tampa and proceeded at once to Fort Myers. The cause for the alarm was that Matthews had threatened to blow up a federal courthouse and authorities had obtained information that indicated he had stashed explosives somewhere for that purpose. The U.S. attorney's office had decided to seek the death penalty because it had evidence that he had killed people that were talking to the police. "He was especially vicious," she recalled. When they hauled Matthews into court, Kovachevich gave him an ultimatum: "I'm leaving and I'm not coming back; make your decision about whether you will tell us where the explosives are." She told him that if he would plead guilty and cooperate, she was prepared to accept a reduction to life in prison, or he could take his chances on the death penalty in a full trial. Matthews cooperated, and explosives were discovered in a storage facility in Gainesville.[52]

A case that involved "homegrown" drugs was the "Myakka Gold" case that U.S. Attorney Robert Genzman called the largest-ever case against domestic marijuana growers. On May 1, 1991, twelve defendants and their twenty-nine lawyers packed into Judge Kovachevich's courtroom to face charges of growing the local weed that had "a national reputation." The indictment charged the defendants with participating in a "nine-year conspiracy to grow, process, and distribute Myakka Gold."[53] Only one of the defendants refused to plead guilty, and that was Donald Clark, who was accused of heading the ring in eastern Manatee County. Clark owned much of the land the pot was found on, had previously been convicted in state courts for growing marijuana, and had served time in prison. He considered his case over and refused to accept any culpability in the present federal case, claiming that he was not involved. Even so, federal authorities came after him again. As one source explained, "Under Operation Trigger-lock federal prosecutors were instructed to comb closed state cases for people who had, in the course of some other crime, violated federal gun or drug laws. Such people would be re-arrested by federal agents, as they walked out of state prison if necessary."[54] The Fifth Amendment protection against double jeopardy did not apply, and Clark was convicted. Judge Kovachevich sentenced him to life in prison.[55]

One of the district's most high-profile drug cases involved baseball star Denny McLain. Few ballplayers had fallen so far or as fast as the former Detroit Tigers pitcher, major league baseball's last thirty-game winner, who led his team to the world championship in 1968. McLain won two consecutive Cy Young awards, but he was rumored to be involved with unsavory elements. (He was briefly suspended from baseball in 1970 for gambling.) Since his retirement in 1972, McLain had worked for Tampa Equities Corp, a subsidiary of First Fidelity Financial Services of Hollywood, Florida. McLain and six other coconspirators were accused of charging customers over 150 percent interest, using the threat of violence to extract payment, taking kickbacks, and taking illegal bets on basketball and football games. The indictment also charged McLain with conspiring to import 400 kilos of cocaine. On March 19, 1984, U.S. Attorney Robert Merkle announced that McLain would soon surrender to authorities in Tampa. Two of those charged were already behind bars, and the others were arrested in Miami, Los Angeles, and Newark, New Jersey.[56]

McLain's trial proceeded in November in Judge Elizabeth Kovachevich's court. After eight days of testimony the judge called a mistrial. The trial resumed once again in March 1985. McLain's lawyer, Arnold Levine, put the defendant on the stand, and the defendant admitted gambling and bookmaking but denied any involvement in extortion or drug dealing. McLain told reporters outside the courtroom, "I'm no altar boy, but I'm not accused of child molestation. Or of assassinating Kennedy. Or kidnapping the

Lindberg baby. I've simply touched a lot of people and unfortunately, got some dirty hands."[57] Levine asserted that his client was the victim of con-men, crooks, thieves, convicts, and deadbeats. Out of court, McLain added also that the case against him was "a conspiracy engineered by Mr. Merkle for headlines." Prosecutor Ernst Mueller countered that McLain was fully responsible for committing the crimes.[58]

After 14 weeks, 350 hours and 26,000 pages of trial testimony, the jury deliberated 30 hours before convicting McLain on March 17 on all counts except the drug smuggling charges. Under the law, McLain could have re-ceived up to 75 years in prison, but Judge Kovachevich sentenced him to 23 years. Levine called the sentence uncalled for and "too harsh." He promised an appeal and predicted McLain would be out of jail in "about 10 months."[59] McLain sat in federal prison for two and a half years until he was granted a new trial by the Eleventh Circuit Court of Appeals. Sharply reprimand-ing prosecutor Ernst Mueller for his personal attacks against McLain's law-yer and citing "plain errors" by Kovachevich, the higher court overturned McLain's conviction. "The facts garnished from the voluminous trial tran-script brand this trial as a classic example of judicial error and prosecu-torial misconduct." Kovachevich's "emphasis on an accelerated trial," the ruling continued, "compounded with the prosecutor's inappropriate and prejudicial comments about the defense counsel's character, denied defen-dants their basic rights to a fair trial. . . . There are numerous examples of how this excruciating trial schedule reduced the effectiveness of the jury." Kovachevich allowed jurors to stand to keep awake during testimony and cross-examination. She brought in coffee and sandwiches during the trial, and the extraordinary pace of the trial exhausted all the participants. In sum, the opinion declared, "It was the cumulative effect of the errors com-mitted by the judge and the prosecutor that denied the defendants a fair trial."[60]

Released on bail, McLain planned for his retrial, but prospects for an impartial trial before Kovachevich were marred by McLain's book manu-script, which branded the judge a "hanging judge" who had it in for him. An anonymous person sent the judge a copy of his autobiography, *Strike-out: The Story of Denny McLain* (1988), and McLain's court-appointed at-torney asked the judge to recuse herself from the case, claiming that the manuscript would prejudice the court. Finally, in October 1988 defense lawyers and prosecutors reached an agreement. In a plea deal agreed to by Kovachevich, McLain pled guilty and would receive a prison term not to exceed twelve years but under the agreement would be eligible for release in nineteen months. In a three-and-a-half hour sentencing hearing, Kovachevich, citing the twenty-nine months he had already served, resentenced McLain to five years of strictly supervised probation.[61]

Both before and after the McLain trial, Kovachevich was both praised and criticized for the swiftness with which she tried cases. The judge admitted that it was her "mission" to attack the backlog of cases that the Middle District was confronted with. Indeed, the challenge was enormous. While on one occasion U.S. Supreme Court Chief Justice Warren Burger had commended Kovachevich for her swiftness in deciding cases, some lawyers criticized the judge, charging that her decisions were unpredictable and that the swiftness of her decisions hampered careful consideration of the cases. "I try to make sure that in the cases that come before me, that justice is dispensed," Kovachevich responded. "I try to always do that. I'm not saying that I don't make mistakes, but I don't deliberately try to make mistakes. I try to be fair and I try to remember that the case belongs to the litigants," she asserted.[62]

The drug cases discussed here constitute only a fraction of the successful prosecutions in the Middle District of Florida in the decade of the 1980s. Intricate banking and money laundering schemes were essential to drug smuggling operations as well as large-scale racketeering enterprises. From 1988 through 1991 Judge Hodges presided over the first major money laundering criminal trial in the United States, and as such it was an important corollary to drug prosecutions. The Bank of Credit & Commerce International (BCCI) was the seventh-largest private bank in the world, investing in seventy-eight countries with assets in excess of $20 billion. In 1988, after a five-year undercover operation, indictments for money laundering, narcotics, and conspiracy charges were filed against fifteen different defendants in Tampa, Florida. Robert Mazur, an undercover agent posing as an underworld high-roller named Robert Musella, infiltrated Colombia's drug cartels and was eventually admitted into the shadowy world of money laundering.[63]

Judge Hodges remembered the *United States v. Awan et al* case as the longest case he ever tried.

> We started in January and finished in the end of July. So it was about seven months from the beginning to the verdict. There were about ten defendants, all of whom had been employed by the Bank of Credit and Commerce International in various offices around the world. The principal defendants were two men who had been employed in

Miami and they were charged with money laundering, that is, taking in cash deposits and then wiring transfers of those funds to offshore branch banks of the BCCI in Panama, Cayman Islands, United Kingdom, France, and all over the world.[64]

Mazur, working undercover,

> posed as a money launderer for a lesser cocaine distributer who worked his way up to laundering money for one of the major cartels. . . . So agent Mazur went undercover and wore a body bug and, of course, spent half of his life on the telephone with these bankers. The government let some $30 million of ill-gotten funds go through to test the extensiveness of the enterprise. He traveled all over the world. . . . with a female agent posing as his girlfriend and she maintained a log of the calls and activities. When they were ready to indict, the question was how do we get all these people who were scattered all over the world in one place, in Switzerland, Pakistan, France, and so forth? The agents then lured them to Tampa by saying they were getting married and that they were inviting them to come to the wedding at Innisbrook Resort in Tampa Bay. They gave them airline tickets for them and their family. . . . They all came to Innisbrook except for one major defendant who was in the United Kingdom who had some conflict and couldn't come. When they arrived, they came at different times. So they were all met by a limousine driven by an FBI agent at that time, driven over to Innisbrook, put up in these luxurious accommodations. Then on Friday night, when they were all there the limousine came to take them, ostensibly, to a bachelor party in Tampa and instead they were taken to the DEA's office and put under arrest.[65]

Two or three years' worth of printed telephone conversations were used in the case. "I have to say," Hodges remembered, "the agent did an amazing job. He could be asked about a given date or a given conversation, and he could reach into this mass of material and pull it right out."[66]

Hodges also remembered that the jury was very attentive. "They knew it was going to be a long case. They were told that of course in the process of their selection. And the evidence was detailed and lengthy in terms of the transcripts of all these conversations. But I think the jury was able to follow what the role was of each of the defendants, at least according to the government's theory of the case. They understood what the alleged offenses were and what the conduct was. The instructions were not that complicated particularly."[67] It took the jury seven days to reach a verdict. The jurors found all the defendants guilty except one. Prosecutors hailed the decision as the first time that international bankers had been convicted under the 1986 Money Laundering Act. Assistant U.S. Attorney Mark Jackowski said, "This case is important to the United States of America because it shows that those who sit in the ivory tower of society, the bankers in the gray suits, they don't touch the dope, but they should know that if they violate the law and they are convicted they're going to jail."[68]

The lead defendant was Amjad Awan, the former head of marketing for the Latin American and Caribbean division of BCCI and the banker of Manuel Noriega. Awan was fined $100,000 and could have been sentenced to up to nineteen and a half years in jail, but Hodges sentenced him to twelve years, citing remorse and lack of a previous record. Awan and the five other defendants were convicted of laundering over $4 million in cocaine profits. The effects of the investigation and the Tampa trial resulted in other nations shutting down BCCI's operations in their countries. The appeals court upheld all of the convictions except one.[69]

One of the eventual outcomes of the many high-stakes drug, racketeering, and complex financial prosecutions was the growing skill and effectiveness of the Middle District's career prosecutors. Veteran trial lawyer Dan Warren witnessed this development firsthand. "Of course, they [assistant U.S. attorneys] had guidelines that they had to follow and their decisions were pretty well made by higher ups. . . . It was very difficult to defend those cases because in the federal courts, conviction ratios in drug cases were ninety-five percent, so you very seldom could win a case in the federal courts except based upon, you know, some motion to suppress or things like that. They were well prepared." The assistant U.S. attorneys "were career prosecutors. So they worked in the highest ethical standards."[70]

Even if career prosecutors in the Middle District were known for their professionalism, U.S. attorneys were highly controversial and often subjected to criticism. While most U.S. attorneys faced criticism during certain periods of their tenure, none were more controversial than Robert Merkle, whose tenure was marked by many successes scored against drug dealers and dangerous criminals but also many ill-conceived, seemingly politically motivated indictments against public officials, which netted few results.

9

Mad Dogs, Spies,
and International Weapons Dealers

Since his appointment in 1982, crusading U.S. Attorney Robert Merkle had set his sights on drugs and organized crime, and in February 1983 he announced that his office would begin a massive investigation of public corruption at all levels of government throughout the Middle District. Judge William Terrell Hodges approved Merkle's request for a special grand jury for the purpose. The announcement came just after the arrest of three Hillsborough County commissioners on charges of soliciting and accepting bribes in return for favorable votes for rezoning.[1]

According to one source, Jerry Bowmer and two other Hillsborough County commissioners "had turned the permitting and regulation process in the county into a grubby little back-street bazaar." Bowmer, Fred Anderson (a former fire chief), and Joe Kotvas (a former policeman) were charged with soliciting bribes from developers who wanted zoning changes. Votes were usually 3–2 with Bowmer, Kotvas, and Anderson outvoting the two other commissioners. The scam worked until January 1983 when Pickens Talley, who represented a developer, was shaken down for a bribe and decided to go to the FBI. Agents wired Talley, who then met with Bowmer and agreed to pay the commissioner $75,000 for the zoning change; the vote went through. When the first installment of cash was delivered, the FBI nabbed Bowmer, and he decided to cooperate. He in turn was wired, and when he delivered the shares to Kotvas and Anderson in the county courthouse, the FBI descended on them. All three were arrested and marched to the adjacent FBI offices and then to the federal courthouse across the street. A federal organized strike force headed by Bill James and Christopher Hoyer had developed the evidence, but soon after the initial arrests the U.S. attorney's office took over the case. Merkle pounced on the defendants, squeezing out more details that led to an indictment against Michael

Sierra, a lawyer who had worked for the three. The three commissioners were convicted on July 19, 1983. Anderson and Kotvas got eight years, but in exchange for further cooperation the corruption investigations, Bowmer received only three years behind bars. Bowmer eventually revealed over one hundred various deals and kickback schemes. He fingered many high-level elected officials and their associates on the Hillsborough County political scene.[2]

The successful prosecution of Bowmer, Kotvas, and Anderson marked the beginning of Robert Merkle's seven-year-long crusade against corruption. His initial success whetted his appetite for uncovering corruption in Hillsborough County and other jurisdictions. He was convinced that the commissioners' cases were only the tip of the iceberg. As will be seen, his use of the ongoing grand jury investigation drew criticism, but the accusations of high-handed behavior only served to convince him that there were even bigger quarry to cage.

Merkle next set his sight on Hillsborough County State Attorney E. J. Salcines. Elected four times to the office since 1968 after leaving Eddie Boardman's U.S. Attorney's office, Salcines had not drawn a challenger since 1972. Salcines had clashed with federal authorities over the years, but Merkle's attacks would escalate matters to a new level. The first hint that Merkle was after the prosecutor came after Salcines met with federal prosecutors regarding a bribery case. A man named Armando Tamargo connected to the Angelo Bedami drug ring had visited Salcines at his house and offered him $75,000 not to prosecute a man named Leon Wood. Salcines promptly threw the man out of his house and told the Hillsborough County sheriff of the incident, but no arrests were made. Salcines prosecuted and convicted Wood along with twenty of twenty-four others of the Bedami organization. "We have acted legally and lawfully and have spearheaded the investigation that got to the core of the [Bedami] organization itself," Salcines said. The remaining four cases were turned over to Merkle's office, which used those cases to probe deeper into the Hillsborough Prosecutor's Office to discover whether members of the Bedami drug ring were trying to fix the outcome of drug cases by bribing or trying to bribe members of the Hillsborough County State Attorney's Office. Under Merkle's direction, the special grand jury took the matter up.[3]

Salcines cooperated with Merkle's investigation until he suddenly realized that he was the target of the probe. In a public letter dated February 17, 1984, Salcines declared, "I am incensed and outraged over the unjust accusations and innuendos that have been irresponsibly hurled at me and my office over the past two weeks. I have done nothing wrong, illegal or un-ethical in carrying out the honored charge of my public responsibilities."[4] Salcines explained that on February 2 he had met with federal prosecutors over the Tamargo case, in which he was a witness, and it became clear to him that he was a "target of an unspecified federal charge."[5] He was im-mediately subpoenaed to appear before the grand jury the next day, but he refused to answer questions. As he stated in a public letter,

> For reasons totally unknown to me, I have been labeled a 'target' of a federal investigation, and in less than one day, I was subpoenaed to appear before the federal grand jury. I have always cooperated fully with federal authorities in their investigations as evidenced by my two voluntary appearances before the grand jury in this matter. However, after learning that Robert Merkle, whom I believe to be an over-zeal-ous and politically motivated U.S. Attorney, was trying to incriminate me, I had no choice but to reluctantly, upon insistence of legal coun-sel, invoke my constitutional rights including the Fifth Amendment and insist upon a fair and impartial forum. This is precisely why I have formally requested that Gov. Bob Graham assign a special state prosecutor to fairly and objectively investigate this matter.[6]

Meanwhile on the same day Salcines took the Fifth, the grand jury in-dicted Salcines' former chief assistant, Norman Cannella, for taking bribes. Stunned and upset at Merkle's vendetta against him, Salcines told a reporter, "I am bewildered and I am incensed."[7]

Merkle's actions also perplexed and gave pause to numerous court ob-servers, especially when they learned that he was planning to use the testi-mony of convicted felons to go after Salcines. One prominent Tampa law-yer noted, "It certainly looks strange to me that Bedami and Wood weren't indicted. It's funny to think that Angelo Bedami is going to testify against anybody." Another lawyer intoned of Merkle, "He's an excellent lawyer in the courtroom—a winner. But I hope he realizes what he's doing when he and his assistants—in open court—name targets of investigations. You're not ever going to bruise the reputation of a drug dealer or a murderer. But we're talking here about people, at least some of them, who are well-respected in the community. Their records are unblemished. Even if they're acquitted, I wonder if they can pick up the pieces." "If Bob Merkle is right and what I hear about all the other indictments that are supposedly coming down are true," another lawyer said, "the man will ride out of here a king. But he better be careful when he drops the net. You don't drop a net that traps innocent people too. I'm not saying that's what happened, but on past occasions, I have sensed a little recklessness on the part of the feds."[8]

While Governor Graham considered the situation, Salcines stood by his decision not to testify, asserting that he would cooperate with any "state prosecutor" Governor Graham may appoint, but in a letter to the grand jury foreman he asserted, "I will not voluntarily assist him [Merkle] in his efforts to destroy me and my office." Graham eventually appointed Richard A. Earle Jr. of St. Petersburg to investigate whether Salcines had lied to a circuit judge in order to secure the early release of a drug smuggler. Earle had served as chair of the Florida Judicial Qualifications Commission that had investigated the Florida Supreme Court scandals in the mid-1970s.[9] Earle's six-month investigation exonerated Salcines, a fact that Graham announced on June 26.[10]

In July Bill James, a man with whom Salcines had clashed on former occasions, resigned from the Organized Crime Strike Force to run against Salcines for Hillsborough state attorney. Commenting on James' candidacy against him, Salcines charged, "We have seen a consistent pattern of trying to get at the local state attorney's office. And now all of a sudden, we have an assistant U.S. Attorney coming from that office to run for this office."[11] That fall as the political contest heated up, Judge Hodges, after hearing nearly two months of testimony against Norman Canella, threw out the case against Salcines's former assistant, declaring that the evidence against him and another defendant was "circumstantial and insufficient."[12] Still the ongoing grand jury investigation of Salcines continued with no end in sight. The embattled prosecutor's attorney wrote directly to U.S. Attorney General William French Smith, charging Merkle with an "insatiable appetite for power" and a "master plan to get Salcines."[13] He also assembled an impressive number of sworn statements of witnesses that accused Merkle and his prosecutors of pressuring them, burglarizing offices for evidence, and even offering drugs to one witness in an attempt to manufacture evidence against Salcines.[14]

By this time Merkle's tactics had aroused numerous complaints from prominent state officials. Among those who complained directly to federal authorities was Jacksonville State Attorney Ed Austin, who called Merkle a "reincarnation of Joe McCarthy." To Austin, Merkle was "an abusive, arrogant, unstable U.S. attorney."[15] The charges against Merkle triggered a Justice Department probe of his conduct in the Salcines investigation.

On the campaign trail Salcines blasted Merkle, accusing him of a political conspiracy to unseat him, and added that James, his Republican

opponent, was a willing tool in the plot. "These political appointees are trying to take over the local law enforcement community. Your constitutional
rights could be at stake. . . . We cannot permit a takeover [by] a federal
agency," Salcines warned.[16] With Election Day on the horizon, Governor
Graham called on the U.S. Justice Department to speed up their investigations of Salcines. "The effect of this unresolved federal investigation and
the recent charges of misconduct against Merkle have been to erode public
confidence in these offices and disrupt the functioning of the criminal justice system within this community of our state," wrote the governor.[17] Years
later Graham recalled that he had a "high regard for E. J. as a human being
and a professional and thought he did a good job. My concern was this was
an investigation without end." The way it was handled was "fundamen-
tally unfair. Salcines was sort of hung out to dry without a way to defend
himself."[18]

In a "preliminary finding" the Justice Department cleared Merkle's office
of wrongdoing. One week later, despite public endorsements of Salcines
from Sen. Lawton Chiles, Gov. Bob Graham, and former governor Reubin
Askew, Bill James defeated the long-time state prosecutor in a close election. As James assumed his new duties, Merkle's office continued its investigation of Salcines and within a year the U.S. Attorney's office indicted
twenty-five current and former Hillsborough County officials. Included
among those charged were sixteen business executives and Tampa defense
lawyer Paul Johnson, chairman-elect of the criminal justice division of the
American Bar Association. And Robert Cannella was indicted once again.
So were formerly charged but previously acquitted Tampa lawyer John
Demmi, businessman-politician Nelson Italiano, and Lawrence Goodrich,
a former circuit judge. Included in the 166-page indictment were charges
of conspiracy, mail fraud, extortion, obstruction of justice, and perjury. "In
short," Merkle proclaimed in a press conference outside the courtroom,
"the entire spectrum of commercial life in this county has been the subject
of bribery. That era has come to an end."[19]

As the indictments in the Hillsborough County case came forward,
Merkle was also shepherding evidence through federal grand jury investigations of Orange-Osceola State Attorney Robert Eagan on charges of
bribery and case fixing. Merkle's investigation of Eagan's office began at the
same time as the Salcines probe. "This thing has gone on long enough, you
just have to wonder how long it can continue, when it will end," complained
Eagan, who was first elected to his post in 1968.[20] The Salcines investigation dragged on. In December 1985 Governor Graham testified before the

Tampa grand jury. Meanwhile, as a sidebar to a subsequent case regarding a drug smuggler, Judge Hodges said there was no proof of corrupt conduct by Salcines. During the trial it was reported that Merkle next had his sights on state representative Elvin Martinez. Merkle urged the grand jury to indict Martinez, alleging that a convicted drug smuggler had supplied Martinez with marijuana and cocaine. Martinez charged that Merkle knew the charge was untrue, "and damn him for trying to destroy me."[21] A perjury indictment against Martinez moved forward. Finally, after three years of investigations, the grand jury probing public corruption in Hillsborough County disbanded without indicting Salcines. Adding insult to injury, Merkle announced, "This office has never made any public charge against Mr. Salcines."[22] Instead, Merkle asserted, it was the former prosecutor and his attorney who assumed that Salcines was a target.[23]

Meanwhile, criticism of Merkle's behavior mounted. Merkle made no attempt to hide his political opinions. One critic charged that his speech to a right-to-life convention criticizing the Supreme Court's *Roe v Wade* decision as "judicial tyranny" put a "chilling effect of the exercise of our reproductive choice. . . . If I were a doctor," Diane Wilkinson state president of the National Organization for Women asserted, "I would be very hesitant in making sure that I didn't cross any line that Bob Merkle has drawn." Abortion, in Merkle's view, differed little from pornography and drug trafficking. He defended himself by asserting that he felt it was the duty of an executive branch appointee to "address wrong Supreme Court rulings" and that he was compelled to speak out against the price society pays because of "crime and violence of which abortion is a part."[24]

Merkle's critics charged that his many prosecutions were politically motivated and misguided. Yet his charges against prominent Tampa leaders continued. In the fall of 1986, while the trial of the indicted officials was taking place, Merkle charged Republican gubernatorial candidate Bob Martinez with taking a bribe while he was Tampa mayor to secure a cable television franchise for a political supporter. Merkle pointed to charges against Martinez as evidence of his nonpartisan behavior, but critics on both sides began to question his tactics. Republican state senator Kurt Kiser noted of Merkle that there "probably is quite a bit of popular support out there for him because there's the perception that he's not playing footsie with anybody. . . . But I'm concerned he's a little fast and loose, using a meat axe when he should be using a surgeon's scalpel." Others were more blunt. Of Merkle, Ed Austin charged, "I think the worst corruption in public office is a prosecutor who abuses the power of his office, and he has abused the power of his office." One Miami defense lawyer observed of Merkle that he suffered from the "Holy War Syndrome. People imbued with the Holy War Syndrome want so badly to go after corruption and illegal activity that they'll do anything, trample anybody's rights, destroy anybody's reputation. Merkle doesn't understand that a prosecutor also has to be concerned for an individual's rights." Merkle's public outbursts and his political statements had, according to many, undermined his effectiveness as a prosecutor and had in effect hurt law enforcement in Central Florida. Again, Duval State Attorney Ed Austin stated that relations between federal and state officials "have declined to a point where cooperation and coordination, even on the biggest cases, such as drug cases, is all but nonexistent. And for that reason I consider him disastrous, even dangerous."[25]

Austin and others renewed their attacks against Merkle after the acquittal of one of Austin's prosecutors on corruption charges. "They've got to get him out of there," Austin stated. "I think he should go. I think he's an embarrassment to his prosecutor's office."[26] A *Tampa Tribune* editorial also called for Merkle's removal.[27]

No one challenged Merkle's talents in the courtroom. One of his assistants who did not particularly like him remembered, "On two occasions, I've see seen him just eat people alive on the witness stand. I mean, they just broke down and cried. Some people think that's bad. But the times I saw it, they deserved it. They were just lying and messing around. And he ate them alive."[28] Judge Hodges remembered that, in the only case the prosecutor tried before him, Merkle "was impeccably prepared" in the courtroom. He was able to make his opening statement, examine and cross-examine witnesses, and make his closing argument "without note one and never missed a beat. So he was capable as a trial lawyer." But as lawyer and as a human being, Hodges noted, "Mr. Merkle appeared to be a person who never saw anything that was gray in color. It was either black or it was white, there was no in between, which was a bit unusual," Hodges thought, especially for a lawyer.[29]

Only four of the sixteen indicted Hillsborough County officials were convicted in July after the five-month trial in Judge George C. Carr's courtroom, and among the four were former commissioners Anderson, Kotvas, and Bowmer. Merkle called Bowmer' testimony against his former associates "heroic," but Carr disputed Merkle's characterization. "I can't characterize you as a hero," he told Bowmer, "because this doesn't quite fit. There might be a word that fits but I don't know what that word is at the moment."[30]

Governor-elect Bob Martinez and Senator-elect Bob Graham discuss issues, November 12, 1986. Photo by Mark T. Foley, State Archives of Florida, *Florida Memory*, http://florida memory.com/items/show/134552.

Less than two weeks after his reelection to the Florida House of Repre-sentatives, Elvin Martinez learned that his trial for perjury in Judge Ben Krentzman's court was set for December 1. The indictment was based on Merkle's charge that Martinez had lied to the grand jury when he denied using or receiving drugs during the past ten years and had lied twice when asked about the drug activities of others. After the week-long trial Martinez was acquitted of three of the four counts, and Krentzman dismissed the remaining charge when the jury deadlocked.[31]

The November elections also brought omens significant to Merkle's ten-ure. Gov. Bob Graham defeated Merkle's champion, Paula Hawkins, for a seat in the U.S. Senate, and former Tampa mayor Bob Martinez was elected governor. Merkle had accused Martinez of accepting a bribe from Tampa businessman Nelson Italiano, and with the political operative on trial, Judge Hodges cleared the way for the governor-elect to testify in his trial. Martinez was slated to testify in the case after he was sworn in, even as out-going governor, Bob Graham, was continually questioned about whether in his new role as senator he would work to have Merkle replaced. Graham refused to comment on whether he thought Merkle's prosecution of Rep. Elvin Martinez was justified. "The questions we must ask," Graham stated, "are not on an individual case basis but on the general operation of the prosecutorial office in the Middle District of Florida. Has it been judicially handled? Is it professionally competent?" Incensed at Graham's remarks, Merkle wrote a letter charging the senator-elect with injecting politics into his investigations.[32]

Gov. Bob Martinez testified in the Italiano case five days after he was sworn in as governor. He denied any wrongdoing in Judge Hodges' courtroom. On the second day of his testimony Martinez grew increasingly testy with Merkle after continual denials and intense questioning. "I don't believe you have dealt with my case properly," he stated.[33] Martinez accused Merkle of leaking information to the media about the governor, which ultimately caused Martinez's subpoena by Italiano's defense counsel. When Martinez emerged from the courtroom, he was obviously agitated. He declared that he was "concerned" about Merkle's conduct and that, with the prosecutor's four-year term having expired, that President Reagan should either resubmit Merkle's name for another four-year appointment and accept the possibility of nonconfirmation by the Senate or appoint someone else. By the time the new governor returned to Tallahassee, Martinez's tone grew harsher. Voicing complaints directly to the White House and working with Senators Chiles and Graham, Republican Rep. C. W. "Bill" Young and others, Martinez called for Merkle's immediate removal. The *St. Petersburg*

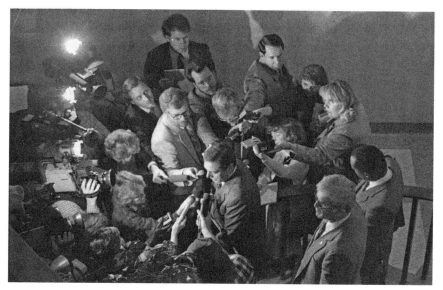

Gov. Bob Martinez fields questions regarding Bob Merkle in the state capitol. January 13, 1987. Photo by Mark T. Foley, State Archives of Florida, *Florida Memory*, http://floridamemory.com/items/show/134490.

Times followed suit on January 13, and three days later the paper editorialized, "The problem with Merkle is not that he is a zealous foe of corruption. On the contrary, the problem with Merkle is that his single-minded vendetta against his political opponents has diverted time and resources from legitimate investigations and prosecutions of official corruption."[34]

Even as Merkle secured the conviction of Nelson Italiano in Judge Hodges' courtroom, Governor Martinez stepped up his attacks against Merkle, arguing that he was unfairly dragged into the case. Martinez's chief advisor, Mac Stipanovich, stated, "There had to come a time when someone with the courage and ability to do something about Bob Merkle does something about Bob Merkle. This is the time and Bob Martinez is the man."[35] Merkle responded to Martinez and other attacks against him in a press conference at his office in Tampa by claiming that they were unjustified and that the newspapers had formed a kind of "lynch mob mentality" against him. "When you go after a public corruption case you're tackling a heck of a lot because . . . whoever the defendant may be he is able to marshal considerable support."[36] Also despite inaccurate reporting, Merkle said he had received great support from the general public in his efforts. One group, calling itself "Concerned Citizens for Merkle," planned to secure at least five thousand signatures and send a petition directly to President Reagan, Edwin Meese, and Senators Chiles and Graham as well as the governor. The group was also mailing out "Support U.S. Attorney Bob Merkle" bumper stickers. Merkle continued to attract wide support in some circles, and his appearance on the CBS program *60 Minutes*, which aired on January 10, 1988, further inflamed the pro and con arguments about the prosecutor.[37]

Despite continual appeals from Governor Martinez and others, the White House refused to act. Speculation as to likely successors for Merkle was printed in the newspapers, but no action was taken. Throughout much of the year Merkle was consumed with the Lehder trial. But more Hillsborough public corruption trials went forward as well. After Italiano's sentencing, Merkle called the former political operative back to testify before the grand jury in what many speculated was one last effort to have him implicate Governor Martinez in the bribery scheme. Italiano not only reasserted his innocence but also denied any criminal conduct by Martinez, even as he prepared himself for his two-year sentence in federal prison.[38]

In June another of Merkle's twenty-five indicted Hillsborough County targets was preparing for trial. As of that time, fourteen of eighteen of those charged that had gone to trial had been acquitted. Prominent Tampa lawyer

Paul B. Johnson faced public corruption charges for inflating his legal fees for a contractor so as to bribe Hillsborough County Commissioner Jerry Bowmer. Johnson's attorney, F. Lee Bailey, contended that his client's prosecution on charges that had previously been dropped was merely Merkle's "personal vendetta" because Johnson had refused to testify in the grand jury's investigation of E. J. Salcines. This was essentially Johnson's defense in his January 1989 trial before Judge George C. Carr.[39]

With the Lehder conviction under his belt by May 1988 and Reagan's second term nearing its end, many speculated that Merkle was poised to resign and seek higher public office. When Sen. Lawton Chiles decided to retire, many speculated that Merkle would enter the Republican primary. Merkle's late June meeting with Edwin Meese, on what the prosecutor called his "future and matters of mutual interest," fueled talk that his resignation was imminent. And indeed it was. Soon thereafter Merkle resigned and announced that he was running for the U.S. Senate.[40]

The front-runner in the Republican primary was the popular U.S. representative Connie Mack from Fort Myers, who refused to debate Merkle. As Merkle circulated the state debating "Cardboard Connie," the Justice Department named Robert W. Genzman U.S. attorney instead of Merkle's trusted assistant, Joseph D. Magri. When he learned of the decision, Merkle expressed betrayal, saying that he had received the "personal assurances" of Attorney General Meese that Magri would get the job. "But for that assurance, I would not have resigned because I was very concerned lest that office be compromised by hidden political agendas."[41] Merkle lashed out at Meese, calling him a liar. He also attacked fellow Republicans Governor Martinez and his opponent, Connie Mack, as "Florida's dynamic duo of sleaze," who had "engineered the witting or unwitting assistance of the Republican delegation [in] a sneak attack on tough, fair, independent law enforcement in the Middle District of Florida."[42] He even suggested that Vice President George H. W. Bush, who was running to succeed Reagan, was a willing participant in the scheme. A Justice Department spokesman answered that Meese had assured Merkle that Magri would be retained as interim head of the office until another replacement could be found, adding, "It is a pity Mr. Merkle should choose to use such virulent language. We can only conclude it's a ploy to attract attention."[43] One of Connie Mack's campaign spokespersons pounced on Merkle's comments. "Merkle's comments are ludicrous and 'Mad-Dog' Merkle obviously is very bitter and a frustrated candidate because he is trailing so badly in the polls and his campaign is going nowhere."[44] The injudicious remarks were the final nail in the coffin in Merkle's unsuccessful bid to win the Republican primary. Merkle was out.[45]

Magri remained interim U.S. attorney until Merkle's successor was sworn in in late September. Robert Genzman had a distinguished background. An Orlando lawyer and graduate of the London School of Economics and Cornell Law School, Genzman had worked for three years in the U.S. Attorney's office before resigning in 1983. In 1987 he had served as minority counsel in the Iran-Contra congressional hearings. After his swearing in on September 26 by Judge Hodges, in what the jurist called a "happy chore," Genzman stated that he was "anxious and enthusiastic about getting started." He promised to be "aggressive, independent, fair and non-partisan in the work that we do."[46] Genzman presented a striking contrast to Merkle. According to St. Petersburg attorney Terry Smiljanich, who worked with Genzman during the Iran-Contra hearings, "Bob is a very low-key individual who does not come on strong with a lot of bombast. Quietly, he is very effective. He gets the job done without making a big show."[47]

As expected, Genzman shuffled his staff, demoting Magri and hiring two other young prosecutors that would eventually make great contributions to the U.S. Attorney's office. Genzman hired Gregory Kehoe away from the Southern District of Florida to replace Magri. Kehoe grew up in Bronx, New York, the son of a policeman, and he earned his law degree from St. John's University. James R. Klindt grew up in Orlando, starred in baseball at Edgewater High School, and attended the University of Central Florida and Florida State University College of Law. Uncertain about his future, Klindt clerked for Judge Howell Melton during the Lehder trial. Witnessing Merkle, Ernst Mueller, and the team of prosecutors in the six-month Lehder trial convinced Klindt that he wanted to be a prosecutor. Also joining the Jacksonville criminal division with Klindt was Stephen M. Kunz.[48] Klindt hit the ground running, scrambling as fast as he could to learn the ins and outs of prosecution. Besides the specific instruction and hands-on training he received, he found former prosecutor and state's attorney E. J. Salcines's predicate evidence handbook extremely helpful. "I wore it out," he said, "used it constantly. It was the most valuable thing in the office."[49]

After George H. W. Bush's and Connie Mack's elections, Florida's entire Republican establishment lined up in support of Genzman for a regular appointment. President Bush acquiesced, and Genzman won Senate approval for a four-year term.[50] As a pathetic finale to Merkle's crusade against Hillsborough County corruption, prosecutions against prominent

Tampa attorneys Paul Johnson, John Demmi, and Lawrence Goodrich went forward. Leading the prosecution against Johnson in January 1989 was the now-demoted Joseph Magri, who sparred with Judge George C. Carr over the testimony of Magri's star witness, Jerry Bowmer. Carr refused to allow Magri to pursue a line of questioning with Bowmer, stating that the former commissioner was "such a liar" that it might put the entire trial in jeopardy. "And he is," Carr insisted. "He's admitted that time and time again." Magri responded by filing a motion complaining that the judge was taking the defense's side in the trial. Carr responded, "I resent some of the things you have said in this motion. It's apparent that you're alleging that I'm being partial as the trial judge in this case, and I resent that."[51] Johnson's attorney, F. Lee Bailey, called numerous witnesses on his client's behalf, including former state attorney Salcines, Sheriff Walter C. Heinrich, state senator Malcolm E. Beard, Tampa lawyer Louis de la Parte, and Hillsborough circuit judge Harry Lee Coe. The construction company executive who retained Johnson's services also testified that, although he was shocked at Johnson's legal fee, he paid it willingly—but was then "browbeaten" by Merkle and Magri to testify against Johnson when they were investigating the defendant. In the end Magri's case hinged on the testimony of Jerry Bowmer, whom Bailey asserted, and few disagreed, was a "pathological liar." The three-week trial ended with the jury acquitting Johnson on charges of conspiracy, extortion, and two of three counts of perjury. The jury deadlocked on the third perjury count, and Judge Carr declared a mistrial on that count. Then, in December, Genzman's prosecutors failed in a third try to convict attorney John Demmi of corruption charges. "Enough is enough," Demmi said after the jury pronounced its not guilty verdict. "I hope this is the last chapter." Demmi's lawyer added, "This prosecution was part of the inheritance left to us by an overreaching and overzealous U.S. Attorney."[52] Finally, Judge William Castagna's dismissal of the corruption case against Lawrence Goodrich in 1990 marked the end of Merkle's public corruption investigations against Hillsborough County officials and lawyers.

Using the grand jury as his personal weapon, the U.S. attorney indicted many public officials and lawyers. While the prosecutions netted no major convictions, they did consume tremendous resources and damaged many reputations. Many years later Hillsborough County circuit judge J. Rogers Padgett, recalling Merkle's seemingly endless probes, said, "He was suspicious of everybody who worked at the courthouse—the judges, the assistant state attorneys, the criminal defense attorneys. . . . He seemed to be convinced there was corruption, and he pursued it, and he found very little."[53]

Even with Merkle gone, the U.S. Attorney's office continued to receive criticism from Washington. On November 21, 1990, U.S. Attorney Robert Genzman called a report by the House Committee on Government Operations "unfair" in its assertion that the Middle District was one of three districts in the country that did not place a high enough priority on bank fraud and embezzlement cases. Genzman countered that such prosecutions were second only to drugs in his office's priority. "Our problems are in, not the lack of quality or allocation of manpower, but the lack of manpower," he explained.[54] Genzman stated that he had the equivalent of fifteen attorneys working full-time on economic fraud, and nine on bank fraud and embezzlement cases, and that this was a proper allocation given the pressing problem of drugs, defense procurement fraud, and Medicare fraud facing the district. Genzman noted that in the last two years ninety-five bank fraud and embezzlement cases had been brought forward and forty-four were still pending.

As further proof of the office's effectiveness, Genzman reported that under his leadership the district took in three times more money in fines and forfeitures than the amount allocated to his office (or $37.3 million versus about $11 million in operating expenses). The next year (1991) Genzman's office also returned to the U.S. Treasury more than $29.3 million in excess of its operating expenses. "We're not in business to turn a profit, but we're happy when our work produces large monetary benefits for the public we service." The money "from our operations gives the taxpayers a break, because this money is used to fund government programs."[55] Genzman noted that the office logged roughly 900 criminal cases the previous year. His offices in Tampa, Orlando, Jacksonville, and Fort Myers employed 187 people, 89 of whom were lawyers. Providing further information regarding the financial operations of his office, Genzman noted that civil collections amounted to $13.2 million, and those included defaulted student loans, federal mortgage foreclosures, and overpayment of agency benefits. Criminal collections amounted to roughly $10 million, and 95 percent of those funds were deposited into the federal Crime Victims Fund, a fund that provided the states money to compensate victims and their families for economic losses. Money from criminal asset forfeitures was also used to finance federal law enforcement programs and prison construction. Local police agencies also were allowed a share in the forfeitures. Justice Department officials ranked the Middle District in the top 20 percent in the nation in terms of money collected.[56]

Nuclear Protests, Spying, and Arms Trafficking

By the middle 1980s both Tampa and Orlando had grown substantially. Large international airports with daily flights to Europe, the Middle East, and Asia linked them to the outside world, and travelers engaged in legal and illegal enterprises found the two cities hospitable venues to conduct business. By the middle 1980s, with the Cold War still running at fever pitch, Orlando's Martin-Marietta Corporation was a manufacturing center for the U.S. Army's Pershing 2 nuclear missiles, Patriot missile launchers, and other sophisticated military hardware.

Before daylight on Easter Sunday 1984 a group of six men and two women calling itself the "Pershing Plowshares Group" cut a hole through a chain link fence, entered the Martin-Marietta production facility, hammered on missile components, smeared blood on them, and tacked up copies of an "'indictment' denouncing Marietta 'for the manufacture for profit of weapons of mass destruction.'"[57] When guards discovered the group inside the facility, they were singing and praying. They asserted that their actions constituted a symbolic act of civil disobedience for their cause. Their purpose was to demonstrate against the factory which they claimed was "engaged in 'immoral activity.'" When brought before Judge George C. Young, the protestors stated that they intended to defend themselves on the basis that production of nuclear weapons was a violation of "God's Law" and that "the break-in was justified on the basis of international law and the necessity of avoiding nuclear confrontations." Young responded sternly, stating that his courtroom was "not a forum for the espousal of political beliefs any more than it would be the forum for persecution of political beliefs."[58] Further, Young forbade any attempt to defend those charged based on the fact they were obeying, as they called it, "God's Law." If convicted of conspiracy and destruction of U.S. Army property, the men and women were facing up to fifteen years in prison. Outside the courthouse and at the entrance to the defense plant, protestors carrying signs picketed daily during the trial while supporters from around the country filled the courtroom.[59]

As expected, the defendants were convicted of breaking and entering, thus joining six other groups of defendants representing the nuclear freeze movement convicted in other federal courts across the country. Even so, one defendant muttered, "It was a moral victory. The truth was told in the courtroom. We expected to be misunderstood and that is what happened."[60] On July 27 Young sentenced the defendants to three years in prison and $2,900 each for damaging the missile-launcher components. "The law is clear," Young declared, "It must be obeyed." After listening to the defendant's statements, Young responded, "This case does not involve a debate between war and peace. No one would dispute the desire for peace or the undesirability of nuclear weapons . . . but in this country the views you have espoused here today can be espoused better to the representatives of the people."[61] As the U.S. marshals led the eight away, they smiled and waved to their supporters who sang "We Shall Overcome."

Far more serious issues for the Middle District courts to consider were several cases involving spying and arms trafficking. In 1981 Judge Susan Black presided over an espionage case involving a man named Joseph George Helmich, who had sold secrets to the Soviet Union for $130,000.00. As Black described the case, during the Vietnam War Helmich had "supplied the enemy with the codes of our black boxes, our cryptographic work, which means that they were able to listen in to our military channels, and rather than stopping after the war . . . he continued to get the money, and he continued to supply information to governments who were not friendly with us." The deception had gone on for seventeen years.[62]

Judge Black remembered that an unusual aspect of the trial was that it was the first time "any judge in the country had used an agreement that was entered into between the Chief Justice of the United States and the White House on how spy cases should be conducted." The problem was that the evidence used in the case was still classified. "I actually had an FBI agent assigned to me who was not permitted to go back and speak to the FBI about anything that was going on, but he took care of the evidence because part of this was still secret. . . . But I didn't understand the technology completely obviously because the military felt that part of it . . . was generational thing, that if you had the whole box you could figure out today's cryptology. The generals in the war testified, and it was an interesting case." Black sentenced Helmich to life in prison for violating the espionage act, and the decision was upheld on appeal.[63]

On June 29, 1984, in Judge Ben Krentzman's Tampa courtroom West German auto mechanic Ernst Ludwig Wolfgang Forbrich was convicted of spying. Forbrich was first apprehended in Clearwater when he put a down payment on the purchase of a classified military document to an undercover federal agent posing as an army captain assigned to the U.S. Central

Command, headquartered at MacDill Air Force Base. It was revealed at the trial that Forbrich intended to sell the documents to East Germany, as he had done in similar fashion for the previous fifteen years. Forbrich lived near the U.S. military base at his home in Goeppingen, West Germany. His success in obtaining documents in Germany ultimately encouraged Forbrich to use his contacts to put him in touch with officials at MacDill. The taped conversation about the down payment was used against the defendant, but jurors also listened to other secretly taped conversations between Forbrich and the former wife of an army major who had access to classified documents at the military base. The tapes revealed that Forbrich had urged her to steal the documents and sell them to him. Forbrich was eventually sentenced to a total of fifteen years in prison.[64]

The Tampa courthouse was also the scene of another dramatic spy trial in 1991 when ex-sergeant Roderick Ramsey pled guilty to stealing sensitive Western military secrets and selling them to Eastern Bloc nations. According to the FBI, which had been cooperating with Ramsey in the hope of arresting others involved in the scheme, the sale of sensitive documents in the early 1980s to Hungarian and Czechoslovakian agents represented an "unprecedented" breach of Western security. Ramsey had been stationed with the 8th Infantry Division headquarters in Bad Kreuznach, West Germany, and was assigned to guard sensitive military plans. He was recruited into the spying activity by his supervisor, Clyde Lee Conrad, who was already serving a life sentence. After Ramsey's guilty plea, U.S. Attorney Robert Genzman argued that Ramsey deserved a stiff sentence because the sergeant had sold "plans for the defense of Central Europe; documents outlining the location and use of NATO's tactical nuclear weapons; and technical manuals and information about the ability of the alliance's military communications." Calling Ramsey's crimes the "most serious criminal offense one can commit," Judge Hodges sentenced Ramsey to thirty-six years in prison. Genzman praised Hodges' tough sentence. "We can't afford to have people giving out military secrets to the enemy. We feel the sentence is appropriate."[65]

Soon two other Ramsey associates, Sgt. Jeffrey Rondeau, stationed in Bangor, Maine, and Jeffrey Gregory, stationed in Alaska, were both arrested and brought back to Tampa in 1994. Both pled guilty to selling U.S. Army and NATO secrets to Hungary and Czechoslovakia in 1985. Both were sentenced to eighteen years in federal prison. Finally, in 1997 yet another suspect in the Conrad spy ring was taken into custody. Kelly Therese Warren was arrested in Warner Robins, Georgia. Warren was charged with preparing classified documents for distribution during the ten-year period she was stationed in West Germany. In February 1999, in Judge Elizabeth Kovachevich's court, she was found guilty of spying and sentenced to twenty-five years in prison.[66]

Also in Tampa retired Army Reserve colonel George Trofimoff was prosecuted for espionage. Charged with a twenty-five-year conspiracy of selling secrets to the Soviet Union, Trofimoff, seventy-three years old, was arrested in a sting operation in Tampa on June 14, 2000. The colonel formerly headed the Nuremberg Joint Interrogation Center in Germany, which interviewed refugees and other émigrés from Russia and other Eastern Bloc countries. He had a top-secret security clearance and worked in military intelligence from 1959 through 1994. Prosecutors alleged that Trofimoff received between $250,000 and $300,000 in payoffs for passing sensitive information to the Russians. After thirty-five years in the military, Trofimoff retired to Brevard County. After a lengthy investigation, the FBI lured Trofimoff to Tampa, posing as Soviet agents offering to pay him for what he thought he was still owed, and he was immediately arrested. The indictment charged Trofimoff with thirty-two overt acts of conspiracy from 1969 through 1995. Trofimoff had given the Soviets "documents, photographs, photographic negatives and information relating to national defense of the United States, with intent and reason to believe that the same would be used to the injury of the United States and to the advantage of a foreign nation."[67]

At Trofimoff's bail hearing Assistant U.S. Attorney Terry Furr alleged that the defendant was "responsible for a huge hemorrhage of information that had come out. . . . There's no telling how many documents went over." Included in the twenty-five years worth of secrets was information about chemical weapons, battle strategies, and NATO intelligence needs. Worse still, Furr had audio- and videotape of Trofimoff, the son of Russian immigrants to the United States, telling undercover agents, "Russia is my homeland," and pounding his chest while saying, "I'm not American in here."[68]

Trofimoff's trial began approximately ten months later. One of the leading witnesses for the government was "John Doe," an agent for the British Secret Service, MI6. Also used in the trial were secret KGB records recovered from a former agent who defected to England in 1992. Given a chance to testify on his own behalf, Trofimoff accused the witnesses of lying, claiming that his entire family was killed by the Bolsheviks. "I hated them and so did my whole family."[69] He told of growing up in Berlin and being raised with another boy who eventually became an official in the

Russian Orthodox Church. (Trofimoff was accused later of conspiring with the official to sell secrets to the Soviets.) Trofimoff eventually immigrated to New York in 1947 and enlisted in the U.S. Army the next year. Of the tapes, Trofimoff said he concocted the whole story. "The whole story was based on the need of money and the offer of money. That's why I did it. I'm not proud of it."[70] The jury convicted Trofimoff on all counts. Three months later a stern Judge Susan Bucklew addressed the convicted spy: "I think you concocted a story, you committed perjury in your testimony . . . and I think life is an appropriate sentence for the crime you committed."[71] Trofimoff appealed his conviction on three separate occasions to the Eleventh Circuit Court of Appeals, failing each time. His life sentence behind bars became a certainty in 2004 when the Supreme Court refused to consider his case.[72]

Central Florida was also the venue for illegal arms trafficking activity, and the Orlando and the Tampa courthouses were sites of several high-profile arms trafficking cases. Since the passage of the Arms Export Act (1979) in response to the Iranian revolution and hostage crisis, the United States had banned arms sales and other commerce with Iran. Yet with that embattled nation's war with Iraq and lots of oil cash available, the inducements to sell Iran weapons tempted many. In August 1985 federal agents arrested Paul Sjeklocha (aka Paul Cutter) of San Jose, California, a Lebanese importer-exporter, and four others at a hotel near Orlando International airport. A seventh suspect was arrested at the Orlando airport after flying in from London. The seven men were charged with arms trafficking. Also arrested in California and Virginia were two Iranian nationals, a U.S. Army lieutenant colonel, and an artillery expert assigned to the Pentagon. FBI officials claimed that Cutter and his Lebanese accomplice were in Orlando to finish the deal to buy antitank weapons for over $9 million to be sold to Iran. At Cutter's bail hearing U.S. Magistrate Judge Donald Dietrich heard testimony describing the suspect as a naturalized American citizen born in Yugoslavia. He had worked for the U.S. Information Agency in Moscow in the 1960s, had been detained four and a half years in Yugoslavia on suspicion of spying for the United States, and since that time had returned to California and worked as a writer and publisher of several military-science magazines. An FBI agent testified that many incriminating documents were seized from Cutter's briefcase including a communiqué sent from Cutter to the Defense Ministry of the Iranian Islamic Republic on the proposed sale of five thousand tube-launched, optically tracked, wire-guided (TOW) missiles sent from Cutter to them for $50 million.[73]

Within two weeks Paul Cutter and six others were indicted by a federal grand jury in Orlando for conspiring to defraud the U.S. government, wire fraud, and bribery in trying to illegally ship arms and other military goods to Iran. The Middle District of Florida's trial version of "Iranscam" went forward in Orlando on December 1985 before Judge Kendall Sharp. Most of the evidence in the case was developed through informants and the undercover taping of customs officials, FBI agents, and other unidentified sources who posed as thieves who had access to the missiles.[74] Assistant U.S. Attorney Stephen Calvacca portrayed Cutter as an "international con man extraordinaire" who masterminded the arms deal.[75] The defense attorneys for the other defendants charged that Cutter convinced them that he was assisting the U.S. government in a secret weapons deal to Iran to prevent Iraq and the Soviet Union from taking over the vast oil-rich Persian Gulf. The defense also accused the government's chief witness, Anthony Romano, a man with a Mafia past, as well as another man in California with making death threats against the defendants if they refused to go through with the deal. Romano and an undercover FBI agent posed as Mafia figures with access to stolen TOW missiles. The jury convicted Cutter and arms dealer Charles St. Claire. The five others accused were acquitted.[76]

Cutter and St. Claire bitterly contested the verdict, claiming that the U.S. government had recently done several "under-the-table" deals with Iran. Cutter called his arrest "lousy and strictly illegal." He charged that Mafia figures working for the government intimidated and in effect forced him and Cutter to make the deals.[77] The fact that only two of seven defendants in the high-profile case were convicted brought the FBI and the undercover informant's behavior under close scrutiny after the trial. Several of the jurors expressed discomfort over the FBI and the prosecutor's office use of Romano. Romano's shady past in the Mafia, his continued assertions that the arms deal were sanctioned by the government, and his threats to kill the defendants if they refused to cooperate was troubling to many of the jurors. One defense attorney also criticized Robert Merkle for approving the use of Mafia figures to pose as weapon's suppliers. "He is the Darth Vader of the criminal justice system for approving the use of the Mafia in an undercover operation," the attorney asserted. Even so, Cutter was sentenced to five years in prison, and his corporation was fined $100,000.[78]

St. Claire was sentenced to eighteen months in jail, but St. Claire and Cutter had served only two months when they were freed on the grounds that they were prosecuted at the same time that the White House was conducting secret arms sales to Iran. On November 13 in a televised address, President Ronald Reagan admitted clandestine arms deals to Iran in order to fund Nicaraguan Contra rebels. As more information began to surface after the conviction, jurors began to express misgivings about their decision to convict Cutter and St. Claire. Responding to legal papers filed the previous month and to a statement by the jury foreman that he felt "duped" by the president, Judge Sharp dismissed the former convictions and granted the men a new trial. (The juror publicly stated that he would have acquitted the defendants if he had known of the government's secret decision to sell arms to Iran.) "The court is convinced that this new evidence warrants a new trial," asserted Sharp.[79] Prosecutors appealed Sharp's decision. Because of President Reagan's disclosures, it was also reported that six pending arms smuggling cases with Iran were under review. Then, more than a year later in April 1988, the Eleventh Circuit Court of Appeals overturned Sharp's decision and ordered the men back to jail, ruling that the judge should not have considered the juror's statement as evidence in overturning the verdict in granting the men a new trial.[80]

Years later Cutter appealed his conviction once again, claiming that the Reagan administration's illegal clandestine operation of selling arms to Iran should absolve his guilt. But the Eleventh Circuit Court of Appeals cast aside this logic. "Although many Americans may possibly have felt betrayed and disappointed by the revelations concerning the Government's involvement in the sale of arms to Iran and the funneling of the proceeds to Contra rebels in Nicaragua, such anguish, however great, is an insufficient basis on which to ignore constitutional laws enacted by Congress," the court declared.

> The defendant's participation in a conspiracy to sell to Iran and his other related illegal activities do not become less illegal simply because the Government for reasons of its own security engaged in the transfer of arms and munitions to Iran. The Government's diplomatic conduct of international negotiations or its policies in affairs of state do not excuse a person's violation of federal criminal laws. As the Government aptly noted in its brief, "[h]ad Oliver North sold crack to the Contras, other drug dealers would not get a break in their sentences." The defendant's conduct was illegal—a crime; the Government's covert activities involving Iran in no way justify or excuse defendant's wrongful acts.[81]

The Iranscam case points out how difficult it was to gain convictions in arms trafficking cases. Yet another complex case was tried in Judge Patricia Fawsett's court in 1990 against the backdrop of an impending war with

Iraq when a German optometrist and a Spanish businessman were tried
on charges that they conspired to sell arms to Iraq and several other Middle Eastern countries. Claus Fuhler and Juan Martin Peche-Koesters were
charged with violating the Arms Export Control Act for conspiring to sell
antitank missiles to Iraq and Libya, who were identified by the U.S. State
Department for promoting Middle Eastern terrorism. The two men were
arrested in Orlando by customs agents posing as arms dealers eleven days
after Saddam Hussein invaded Kuwait, and the trial was scheduled a month
before the deadline set by the UN Security Council authorizing the use of
force to expel Iraq from Kuwait. Their purpose in coming to Orlando, the
indictment stated, was to finalize a deal to sell four hundred TOW missiles to Libya. A year earlier a manufacturer had tipped off authorities that
the defendants were seeking to buy ten thousand TOW missiles for $160
million.[82]

The trial began in Judge Patricia Fawsett's courtroom on December 4,
and after two weeks of complicated testimony, including sixty cassette-tape
conversations in German and Spanish between the defendants and government agents, Judge Fawsett threw out three of the five charges against
Fuhler and Peche-Koesters. Similar to the Iranscam case, the issues in the
trial came down to the behavior of the undercover agents. Defense lawyers
claimed that the government led the defendants to believe that the sale was
legal. In the process of the sting, the government set up a fake company and
the agents assured the defendant that "this exportation was going to be an
official government to government deal following all the legal channels."[83]
Even though the two men may have suspected they were negotiating illegal
sales, that did not satisfy the law. "Just because the air reeks of something
foul is not proof of specific intent," the judge asserted.[84] Defense counsel
praised Fawsett's strict interpretation of the law adding that the men were
foreigners and "naïve amateurs." They were unacquainted with the law and
did not know what they were discussing was illegal. Assistant U.S. Attorney
Ricardo Pesquera deplored Fawsett's dismissal, saying, "There's no doubt
that they knew what they were doing was illegal. But she ruled we didn't
prove it. It was a technicality."[85] With the crux of the government's case collapsed, all that was left was to decide on the final count against the men, and
Judge Fawsett did so on December 21. That day she directed the acquittal of
the two men, ruling that there was not enough evidence to prove intent or
a conspiracy to smuggle the weapons.

Judge Fawsett's decision was a serious setback to customs officials, who
stated the arrests were the result of a year-long sting operation code-named

Operation Dragon. U.S. Attorney Robert Genzman publicly announced that the acquittals would not deter his office from prosecuting illegal arms dealers. "We accept the court's decision but we also want to stress the importance of pursing arms traffickers who jeopardize our national security interests."[86] Defense attorneys charged that the government's trumpeting of the arrest of the men in the wake of the U.S. invasion of Iraq had backfired. The Customs Service had called news conferences in Orlando and Washington to proudly announce the arrest of the men in August, noting that the case was "'clearly' linked to the invasion of Kuwait." U.S. Atty. Gen. Dick Thornburgh had called the men the "merchants of death," and a customs official referred to them as the "brokers of destruction."[87] Defense counsel charged the prosecutors and others connected with the case were "grandstanding from the very beginning. . . . The problem was there was never any case. The government imagined the whole thing," one lawyer charged.[88]

Three years later Genzman and his prosecutors experienced a similar setback when Judge Kendall Sharp threw out conspiracy charges against four persons accused of selling antitank missiles to Uganda. The four, who also were suspected of conspiring to send helicopter parts to Libya, were arrested as part of a sting operation conducted by U.S. Customs agents posing as unscrupulous arms dealers. Sharp threw out the case as it was about to go to the jury. "In this case we had a lot of talk . . . but there was never any agreement, any contracts." There was no "substantial act" to conclude the deal, he stated. Genzman expressed frustration over Sharp's directed acquittal. "We vigorously disagree with the court's ruling on factual and legal grounds. Unfortunately, because the court did not allow the case to go to the jury, the government cannot appeal."[89]

The international nature of these prosecutions points to the fact that population within the Middle District of Florida had grown substantially. By the 1980s the urban centers within the district, particularly metro Orlando and Tampa, had become tourist meccas and travel destinations for domestic and international visitors. The region's growth and development also lured transient residents seeking fun, relaxation, and, increasingly, business opportunities. These new dynamics posed numerous challenges to the judges and other functionaries of the U.S. Middle District of Florida because the new circumstances offered many new varied opportunities for adjudicating commercial disputes and prosecuting federal law breaking.

10

Income Tax Evasion, the Death Penalty, the
Environment, the AIDS Epidemic, Desegregation,
and Voting and Employment Discrimination,
1980–1988

During the 1980s Florida's Middle District judges, prosecutors, and law enforcement officials were involved in numerous important criminal and civil cases. This chapter provides a broad overview of some of those cases while highlighting certain features of the cases that are emblematic of the district's growth dynamics and increasing commercial complexity.

Income Tax Evasion

One important case that symbolizes Orlando's transformation from a sleepy town into a thriving metropolis was the income tax evasion case of one of the city's most well-known entrepreneurs. When Champ Williams came to Orlando as a boy with his family from Black Rock, Arkansas, in the 1930s, the town had only about twenty-eight thousand inhabitants, but by the time of Williams' prosecution for income tax evasion in the 1980s the city had grown to over one million. His rise to riches in post–World War II Orlando mirrored the transformation of City Beautiful from a sleepy backwater to a growing dynamic community suited to Williams' entrepreneurial skills. With a keen knack for business, Williams flourished. First he opened a string of tobacco stores. Then came success in the restaurant business. In 1948 he opened the White Turkey on Mills Avenue. Four years later he contracted with the city to open the Skyline Restaurant at the Orlando Municipal Airport. In 1963 another restaurant followed at McCoy Airport. Eventually the emerging restaurant empire encompassed twenty-three food outlets that brought in huge amounts of cash. Williams, meanwhile, kept loose books. In 1986 a federal grand jury indicted him, his wife, and a daughter for "skimming" over a ten-year period.[1]

Williams' principle antagonist proved to be his estranged son, Bruce, who had revealed the father's crimes to the IRS in 1984. Bruce and his wife were already under investigation for irregularities in their returns; this, combined with disputes with his father, contributed to the son's cooperation with prosecutors. That cooperation was needed. Over the years Champ Williams had aided many philanthropic causes, enjoyed local celebrity, and possessed so many local business and political contacts that trying him proved difficult. Judges Kendall Sharp and Patricia Fawsett, for instance, recused themselves because of their own relationships with family members or their attorneys. In the end, visiting Judge James Watson heard Bruce recount that he, his father, his mother, and his siblings had buried cash at their home. When cash got wet and moldy, he related, they baked it in the oven until it was "nice and crisp." Assistant U.S. Attorney Stephen Calvacca asserted that the skimming not only had cost the federal government hundreds of thousands of dollars but also that the City of Orlando in effect was robbed because the rental leases were based on the revenue of the enterprises. Williams' attorneys charged that the son was mentally unstable. When denied exclusive control of the company, the argued, Bruce "committed the 'ultimate self-destructive act' by going to the government."[2]

The trial resulted in the conviction of the seventy-three-year-old businessman for not reporting an estimated $3 million in revenue. Williams' other son and daughter were also convicted, but his wife was spared. The IRS then decided to pursue a civil case. At the sentencing hearing, Judge Watson, according to a published account, "read a lengthy dramatic statement reciting his philosophy on sentencing." He called the Williams case the "most difficult trial I've heard in twenty-five years I've been on the bench" but intoned, "One of the big rules is not to cheat the silent partner in all businesses: the government of the United States."[3] Williams and his son received two and one-half years in prison. Daughter Susan Williams Wood received one year and a day. Each was fined $10,000.[4]

Another high-flying entrepreneur who waged a decade-long battle with the IRS was Glenn Turner. Though he had escaped jail in a plea bargaining deal in Judge William Terrell Hodges' court in 1975, he had lost his three companies, and the IRS came after him for back taxes. At issue was his seventy-nine-acre property in south Seminole County known as "Turner's Castle." To avoid its seizure, Turner had transferred the multimillion-dollar property to another company he owned. In 1983 Judge George C. Young sided with the IRS and voided the transfer. Even so, Young stayed a request to immediately foreclose on the property because only a fraction of its worth could be obtained at that moment. One month later, after ruling favorably in a Federal Trade Commission suit against Turner, Judge John Reed ordered Turner to buy national advertising in newspapers to alert more than thirty thousand former distributors of his cosmetics company that he was liable for over $40 million of their losses.[5]

As of April 1988 Turner's Castle had still not sold, and he was serving a seven-year sentence in an Arizona federal prison for fraud and once again operating an illegal pyramid scheme. That month Judge Young considered several offers on the property. He finally approved a sale for $1.8 million, a sum insufficient to satisfy the judgments against Turner. The IRS had levied nearly $10 million in tax liens, and Seminole County demanded back tax payments because Turner had not paid since 1979.[6]

Death Penalty Habeas Corpus Litigation

One of the added burdens that Middle District of Florida judges faced in the 1980s involved the growing number of capital habeas cases filed after the U.S. Supreme Court, in *Proffitt v. Wainwright* (1982), upheld the constitutionality of Florida's death penalty statute. Originally a case presided over by Judge Hodges, *Proffitt v. Wainwright* had reached the supreme tribunal after the Eleventh Circuit Court of Appeals affirmed Hodges' decision.[7] Because Raiford—Florida's state prison—sat in Bradford County within the Jacksonville division, judges there heard all the capital habeas cases. Judge Howell Melton remembered: "You used to get a case on Friday before the execution was scheduled for the following Wednesday. Sometimes you were lucky to get it on a Wednesday. But usually it would be on a Friday. So you worked night and day to get that case out. You tried to get it out by Monday, if you could. Tuesday, of course, was the last day before the execution, so that it could be appealed to the court of appeals." Eventually Melton and the other judges decided that the "cases should be turned over to their original venue for disposition." He added, "That was a tremendous reduction in the difficulties for the judges in the Jacksonville division."[8]

One very controversial capital habeas appeal involved the Miller and Jent case. Earnest Lee Miller and William Riley Jent (half brothers) were convicted in 1980 of rape and first degree murder of a Pasco County woman and sentenced to death largely on the testimony of three eyewitnesses. The

Florida Supreme Court upheld their conviction, but—only sixteen hours before their execution—on July 18, 1983, Judge George C. Carr issued a stay.[9] When the case came before him, Judge Carr was filling in for Judge William Castagna. "I want to go to the merits as soon as possible," Carr declared. "I will handle it personally. I won't assign it to a magistrate." The decision elated Jent's attorney, Eleanor Jackson Piel of New York. "You don't have to conclude they are innocent today," she reacted. "Just give us time." Piel and Howardene Garrett, who represented Miller, challenged witness credibility, alleging they were heavy drug users that state prosecutors had pressured into making the allegations.[10]

Gruesome details emerged. Witnesses swore that the men had brutally beaten an unidentified woman called "Tammy" on the banks of the Withlacoochee River during a motorcycle club party. They raped her repeatedly, put her in Miller's car, and then—the next day while she remained alive—took her to the Richloam Game Preserve in Pasco County, doused her with gasoline, and set her on fire. Miller and Jent were heavy drug users and had been associated with motorcycle gangs, but Piel and Garrett found another witness who swore that the two were not present when he saw another man named Dodd choke his girlfriend and set her on fire. Meanwhile, two witnesses recanted, claiming that a detective had forced them to testify.[11]

Eventually more revelations about the mismanagement of the original investigation along with possible wrongdoing by prosecutors came to light. First, the identity of the dead woman was revealed as Linda Gale Bradshaw, the girlfriend of the man named Dodd, who, it turned out, had recently been charged with the Georgia killing of a girlfriend in a similar manner. In February 1987 Miller's and Jent's attorneys demanded a new trial and demanded that original lawyer's notes, state attorney's files, and grand jury testimony be made available. When objections resulted, Judge Carr snapped, "Given what has gone on in this case, given the recantations of testimony, I think we ought to hang it all out. . . . There needs to be a search for the truth, whatever that may be."[12] Carr subsequently concluded that the prosecutors broke federal law when they withheld evidence that might have shown the defendant to be innocent. Also, another government witness not revealed at the original trial put Miller and Jent at the Tampa airport the night of the killing. Judge Carr threw out the previous convictions and ordered another trial.[13]

Repercussions followed. One week later Carr issued a scathing order denouncing the manner with which Pinellas-Pasco State Attorney James T. Russell had handled the case. "The Court finds the failure of the state to produce material that is the subject of this order deeply troubling," he exclaimed, "by withholding such favorable evidence, the state has demonstrated a callous and deliberate disregard for the fundamental principles of truth and fairness that underlie our criminal justice system." The state had failed to observe its duties and obligations under federal law. He continued, "The Court would remind the state . . . that society wins not only when the guilty are convicted but when criminal trials are fair; our system of the administration of justice suffers when any accused is treated unfairly."[14]

A new trial was scheduled to take place in the state circuit court within ninety days. The short timeframe made preparation difficult for both sides. Miller's attorneys insisted that they needed to take depositions from forty-five to seventy-five witnesses. Since 1979, many of the witnesses had moved away or were in poor health. One key witness, the original detective in the case, had relocated to Saudi Arabia.[15] Ultimately, following an eleven-minute hearing on January 15, 1988, Carr set Miller and Jent free after they pled guilty to the second-degree murder of Linda Gale Bradshaw. The deal, reached between the prosecution and defense, meant freedom for Miller and Jent given the eight years they had served on death row. As the pleas were voiced, lawyer Piel handed out a statement proclaiming their innocence. Miller and Jent then appeared at a televised press conference. "Well, the only thing I could think of was just getting it over with and finally being glad to be out again," said Jent. "No, I can't say I'm bitter . . . I'm disappointed because I had to stand up there and swear to a lie. They framed us once. What was keeping them from doing it again?" Miller added, "We was going up against the same system that did it last time." One of Miller's attorneys summarized the man's dilemma. "What would you do," he asked, "if you were offered a chance to walk out of death row after eight years if you were facing another possible death sentence and your lawyers couldn't guarantee 100 percent that you could win your case?"[16] Miller and Jent received small settlements from the Pasco County Sheriff's Office for their wrongful arrest; most of the money went to attorney's fees.[17]

While the Miller and Jent cases wound their way through Judge Carr's courtroom in Tampa, a no-less-sensational capital habeas case hearing unfolded in Orlando during December 1987 before Judge Kendall Sharp. Since his conviction for the murder of twelve-year-old Kimberly Leach and two Florida State University coeds in 1979, Ted Bundy and his attorneys had been appealing his death penalty convictions. His appeal in Judge Sharp's courtroom involved claims that Bundy had been mentally unstable at the time he committed the murders. Judge Sharp had rejected the appeal a year earlier, but the Eleventh Circuit Court of Appeals had remanded the case, concluding that the judge had improperly denied Bundy an evidentiary hearing. Sharp now lashed out at manipulation of the appeals process. When asked if he had received some of the documents supporting the appeal, Sharp snapped, "There are boxes and boxes of this stuff. We send them off and then they send them back. Who knows whether we have them at the moment?"[18]

Sharp sent Bundy back to death row and to the appeals court, calling him a "diabolical genius. Certainly he was able to understand the proceedings and was able to assist in the preparation of his trial," the judge declared. "I don't believe there is anybody in this courtroom that seriously questions Mr. Bundy's competence," Sharp commented after five days of testimony. "It's not really competence on trial here. It's the death penalty—everybody knows that." The jurist voiced the impatience felt by many when they argued that the death penalty system was broken. "The deterrent effect is diminished so much when these killers persist ten or twelve years in this process," he asserted. "The legislature or appellate courts, both of which have the power to change the system, need to speed up the process. They either should abolish the death penalty itself or change the procedure." In an interview later that afternoon the exasperated judge again blasted the process. The court system would be shut down, he exclaimed, if every death row inmate "milked the system" as Bundy had; "it would shut down the courthouse." The paperwork in Bundy's appeal weighed eighty pounds, he estimated, and "we had to read every damn page." One source observed, "Sharp used one word to sum up the whole process, 'Bullshit!'"[19] Bundy, one of Florida's and America's most notorious serial killers, eventually was executed on January 24, 1989.

Another case, that of Judi Buenoano, also took many years to go through appeals in the Orlando division. Dubbed the "Black Widow," Buenoano was sentenced in 1985 to die in the electric chair in an Orange County Circuit Court for the 1971 poisoning murder of her husband, a retired naval officer. One year earlier an Escambia County Circuit Court had sentenced her to life in prison for drowning her paralyzed son and attempting to poison her boyfriend with arsenic. Authorities discovered that Buenoano was the beneficiary of two hefty life insurance policies on the two. When her husband's body was exhumed, traces of arsenic were found in the corpse. Her case came up to Judge Patricia Fawsett on appeal in 1990 and 1992. In the first instance, Fawsett temporarily halted the woman's execution because, during a previous execution, the head electrodes on the electric chair had malfunctioned causing the condemned man's head to burst into flames. In 1992 the Eleventh Circuit Court of Appeals ordered that Fawsett grant Buenoano another hearing to determine whether her defense attorneys had provided an adequate defense because they had failed to reveal in her original trial that she had spent most of her childhood in foster homes and had been sexually abused. The appeals ultimately proved unsuccessful.[20] In 1998 Buenoano became the first woman executed in Florida since 1848.[21]

Environmental and Wrongful Death Litigation

During the 1980s one growing area of federal jurisdiction and litigation federal courts assumed concerned environmental issues. Passage of the Endangered Species Act (1973) had provided for the conservation of sensitive ecosystems upon which threatened and endangered species of fish, wildlife, and plants depended. It also authorized the determination and listing of species as endangered and threatened while providing authority to acquire land for conservation of listed species and prohibiting the possession, sale, and transport of endangered species.[22]

When egregious instances of pollution or dumping occurred, cities, counties, and municipalities sought recourse in the federal courts—sometimes even against federal agencies themselves. For example, in 1982, when two federal agencies—the Corps of Engineers and the Environmental Protection Agency—began dumping millions of cubic yards of dredged material thirteen miles off Tampa Bay on sensitive coral reefs, the Manatee County Commission, the City of Anna Maria, and the City of Holmes Beach first opposed and then sued the agencies in federal court. The dumping, they claimed, irreparably harmed the reef, which nurtured a vital snapper and grouper fishery. Judge George C. Carr ordered that the dumping be stopped immediately and chided the Environmental Protection Agency for not making proper studies before the dumping began. "If it were not for its tragic environmental implications," he declared, "the designation and use of the site for ocean dumping could best be described as a comedy of errors." While Carr's ruling did not halt Tampa Bay dredging work, he did place a temporary moratorium on the dumping until the "federal defendants . . . properly considered the effects of disposal at the site." The order failed to bring permanent resolution, and over the next several years the parties continued to spar over the location and circumstances of the dumping.[23]

Passage of the Endangered Species Act produced numerous prosecutions for taking endangered species that found their way into the federal courts. Most cases resulted in light sentences, suspension of commercial licenses, or probation for those convicted. In 1986, however, Judge John H. Moore sentenced a sixty-one-year-old Homosassa fisherman to jail for possession of six green sea turtles with the intention of selling one. Prosecutors charged that the man had been catching and butchering sea turtles and selling the meat for five dollars a pound for many years. The fisherman's public defender admitted that his client did intend to sell the one turtle but argued that the defendant merely was intending to relocate the others so they would not foul his nets. The fisherman appealed to the court for community service instead of jail time. Judge Moore was not impressed and sentenced the fisherman to six months.[24]

Jacksonville, too, saw environmental cases at issue. In 1988, in U.S. Magistrate Harvey Schlesinger's courtroom, two local men faced possible three-year jail sentences and $300,000 in fines for violating the Endangered Species Act. Charges included possessing three alligator hides and conspiracy to transport the mounts of a grizzly bear, a mountain sheep, a mountain goat, and an Alaskan brown bear. The men also had traded alligator hides, the use of a Florida condominium, and tickets to car races in exchange for costly hunts in Alaska for the purpose of circumventing laws protecting grizzly bears, mountain sheep, and mountain goats. Even though alligators were taken off the endangered list in 1986, Schlesinger found the men guilty of illegal hunting and shipments of big-game trophies, fined them $10,000 each, and placed the men on three years' probation. He banned them, as well, from hunting for one year and ordered them to complete one hundred hours of community service to a wildlife conservation organization. When one of the men complained that he had already purchased a one-year hunting license in Montana, Schlesinger responded, "If you don't get your $200 back, chalk it up to sorrow."[25]

During the 1980s the Middle District Court of Florida was the scene of two extensive civil cases following man-made disasters that resulted in complicated lawsuits. In both instances numerous plaintiffs sought recourse for family members who lost their lives. The first case involved the collapse of Tampa's Sunshine Skyway Bridge on May 9, 1980, claiming the lives of over thirty victims who plunged to their deaths after a 608-foot phosphate freighter *Summit Venture* plowed into a span in a blinding rainstorm. The criminal prosecutions against pilot John Lerro for negligence involved perhaps the Tampa Bay area's greatest man-made disaster. Lawsuits over the next several years filled state courts. By 1982 the federal court hosted additional litigation. "Everyone is suing everyone," one account noted. "The state of Florida is suing the ship owners for damage to the bridge. The ship owners are suing the state for allegedly building a defective bridge. Greyhound is suing both the state and the ship owners. And the families of the dead are suing the state, the ship owners and Greyhound. Forty-three law firms have a piece of the action."[26]

Judge George C. Carr prepared to hear the civil litigation pertaining to the accident. According to one account, "In U.S. District court claims and counter-claims fill nearly a 2-foot stack of fat file folders. They include documents filed on behalf of owners of the *Summit Venture*, the Florida Department of Transportation, which built the bridge, Greyhound, persons who were killed or injured in the collapse and even ships that couldn't use the channel under the bridge until the mangled bridge structure was pulled from the water." It added, "The claims in federal court are so complicated that Judge George C. Carr appointed a committee of five lawyers to work out details of gathering evidence. Nearly three dozen attorneys showed up for the initial court hearing last November."[27]

The State Board of Pilot Commissioners cleared Lerro of wrongdoing, but despite this and the pilot's claim that the weather blew the ship into the bridge, Carr eventually found John Lerro negligent because he failed to anchor "when a squall suddenly whipped up in Tampa Bay, dropping visibility below the minimum needed to proceed safely." The ruling came during the pretrial phase of suits filed for wrongful death, survivor injuries, and bridge damages. "A mariner is supposed to be going slow enough in poor visibility to be able to stop his ship in half the distance he can see ahead," the judge observed. "Lerro has said at one point he couldn't see beyond the bow of his ship." Carr continued, "Mr. Lerro at least [two miles from the bridge] failed to comply with the rules of the road. No matter how bad it got further on, he should have anchored and stopped it. . . . It is obvious to the court that there was some negligence by Mr. Lerro." The wrongful death claims eventually settled at about $12 million.[28]

When the space shuttle *Challenger* exploded soon after taking off on January 28, 1986, families of seven of the victims sued the United States and Morton-Thiokol, the builder of the solid-fuel booster rocket, for damages under the Federal Tort Claims Act. Originally passed in 1946, the law gave citizens the right to sue the federal government in cases of personal injury and wrongful death. On February 26, 1988, Judge Patricia Fawsett denied astronaut Michael Smith's widow the right to sue the U.S. for her husband's wrongful death because he was considered a member of the military. The ruling fell in line with a 1950 a Supreme Court decision that effectively barred military personnel who were injured or killed while in service from suing the government. Smith, a Navy captain, had been selected and trained by military agencies for service as an astronaut. Judge Fawsett set aside contentions that this bar should not apply because Smith was not on regular military duty but was working for NASA, a civil agency, when he died. Judge Fawsett, to the contrary, accepted government lawyers' contentions that the families of military personnel losing their lives in the line of duty already received generous death benefits. Smith and the families of six others received settlements from Morton-Thiokol and death benefits from the government.[29]

Prison Overcrowding

Mark Lender, writing about New Jersey federal courts, noted a trend also applicable to the Middle District of Florida. In the era after the 1964 Civil Rights Act, he noted, "the public has looked, in agreement or disagreement, to the federal courts as arbiters of questions of individual rights and equality. Significantly, it was also the period in which the court finally and confidently embraced its role in this regard."[30] Throughout the 1980s the Middle District served as a place of recourse for plaintiffs who charged that their civil rights were being violated. All manner of cases were litigated, including ones involving school desegregation, minority set-asides, voting discrimination, employment disputes encompassing discrimination in the work place and sexual harassment, and prisoner rights as defined in habeas corpus provisions of the Civil Rights Act as amended.

In 1993 Judge Susan Black closed a case that had been litigated in the Middle District Court since 1972, when Judge Charles R. Scott had first presided over it. The landmark case *Costello v. Wainwright* began that year when inmates Michael V. Costello and Robert K. Celestino filed separate pro se complaints alleging prison overcrowding and inadequate physical and mental health care in the Florida prison system. The plaintiffs petitioned the court to examine the state's criminal justice system and determine whether their federal constitutional rights had been violated. They asserted they were entitled to sue under the Civil Rights Act of 1971 that created "federal statutory right to bring a civil suit for damages and appropriate equitable relief against state actors who violate federal constitutional rights." The federal law granted the federal courts the right to supervise state criminal justice administration.[31] Judge Scott agreed with the plaintiffs. He observed that the prisons in question exceeded their "emergency" capacity by nearly three thousand inmates each. According to attorney William Sheppard, Judge Scott "enforced settlement agreements between the parties regarding the prison population, medical care, sanitation and food service. The overcrowding settlement agreement, which finally codified the prison system's maximum capacity, mandated the population of the prison system could never exceed its maximum capacity."[32]

Litigation linked to the case, including a suit that Sheppard pursued on behalf of an inmate against Duval County Sheriff Dale Carson, ran for nearly two decades. Complaints asserted Eighth Amendment violations, and a class of all present and future Florida prison inmates achieved certification. When Judge Black inherited the matter a number of years later—by that time it was styled *Celestino v. Singletary*—it was, as the judge recalled, a "class action, and it covered all prisons in the state of Florida." She commented, "That was happening quite a bit in the late 1970s. . . . There were class actions where you would have all the school systems, all the prisons. This was one, all the prisons in the state, and . . . it covered everything having to do with the prison." After studying the situation, Black determined that the remaining problems were local ones. "The system was functioning," she recalled. "With some changes and with some oversight from within the system, the federal courts could get out of it and come back in if a particular prison had a problem." The judge then appointed as special master University of Florida law professor Joseph R. Julin to work with her and another expert on prisons on the terms of a settlement.[33] To Black, Julin proved more than a mediator. He had "access to funds, and I could charge the parties to pay for it if you needed an analysis of a particular institution by a third party who was not involved in the litigation, he could pay for that," she explained. "He stayed with it, he persevered, and was able to put together a settlement agreement that we were able to work with and to close the case."[34] Part of the settlement required the creation of a correctional medical authority under Florida law to assist in the delivery of health care services for inmates and to serve as an advisory board to the governor and legislature. The authority possessed broad powers and was envisioned as a replacement for the court as the guarantor of continued compliance with the standards of physical and mental health. In 1990 Black relinquished the physical health care survey function to the authority. Finally, she closed the lawsuit on March 5, 1993, returning the control of Florida's prison health care to the state.[35]

In a similar case Judge Howell W. Melton lifted federal oversight of the Duval County jail after nearly twenty years. In 1974 an inmate had sued in federal court, charging that he was among four hundred prisoners being held in a facility designed for one hundred prisoners. The next year Judge Charles R. Scott, likening the inmates' condition to being "trapped in a dungeon," ordered city officials to reduce overcrowding. Fourteen years later Judge Melton inherited the case, and after attorney William Sheppard filed a complaint, he called the officials into his courtroom. "I don't want a report that says, 'We're doing the best we can.' I want something concrete, not platitudes," Melton announced as he demanded that the officials address the situation immediately. "The handwriting is on the wall," Sheppard observed. "The judge recognizes the problem, and if he is forced to do something, he will."[36] Melton eventually held city officials in contempt and appointed a monitor to oversee jail operations. Finally, on May 18, 1994, Melton announced that the oversight was ended. "The initial constitutional concerns that were raised nearly 20 years ago have been resolved," he said. Sheppard expressed delight at Judge Melton's order. "I know somewhere Judge Scott's looking down here with a smile on his face," he said.[37]

Desegregation

From 1968 to 1980 Florida had made dramatic progress in desegregating its schools. One 1980 national study rated Florida among the top three states that had made the largest percentage increase in integration. The study found that by 1980 roughly 60 percent of blacks in Florida attended predominantly white schools, whereas the percentage in 1968 was slightly over 23 percent.[38] Even so, by that time the push to integrate schools had reached its high-water mark. In ruling after ruling, the U.S. Supreme Court began to revise its original determination that the federal courts have an important role in ensuring that race was a factor in pupil placement. Fewer suits were initiated. and the pace of activity in the federal courts regarding desegregation slowed unless it applied to enforcing court orders that had been issued subsequent to *Swann*. In such circumstances some districts began to resegregate.

Throughout the 1980s and early 1990s many county school boards within the Middle District Court of Florida were under some phase of continued supervision of court-ordered desegregation, and from time to time parties sought redress in the courts. Under the arrangements reached in the first suits, county school boards were required to submit timely updates on the progress of desegregation. Time after time school officials were sent back to the drawing board to construct plans that addressed concerns of different parties, and federal judges were forced to rule on plans and establish guidelines and time lines.

In many counties both white and black parents began to resist busing, especially if they perceived, as many blacks did, that black children were experiencing the brunt of it. This was the case in Manatee and Orange Counties. Moreover, in cases such as *Milliken v. Bradley* (1974), the Supreme Court seemed to back away from mandated busing as a required method for desegregation. Changing neighborhood patterns during the decade exacerbated the problem of resegregation, especially as whites and blacks increasingly favored neighborhood schools over busing to achieve racial balances. Some counties began to develop "magnet school" schemes, special enrichment programs in inner-city schools to attract white pupils who opted to attend.[39]

Following a decade of friction between various federal agencies, the Department of Justice brought suit against the Marion County School Board in 1978. Five years earlier the Department of Housing, Education, and Welfare had threatened to cut off federal funds because of the failure to desegregate. Judge Susan Black subsequently ordered the Marion School Board to submit to her names of three experts on desegregation to assist the district in the development of a desegregation plan. The county and the Department of Justice worked out a plan that provided, among other things, that two inner-city black schools be converted to magnet schools. Judge Black eventually approved the plan in December 1983 but also stipulated that the plan would be examined again in 1988 to make sure that it had been properly implemented.[40]

The situation in Polk County is instructive of the often tortured path some counties took toward desegregation from the 1970s to the 1990s. Judge Joseph P. Lieb had issued the initial order in 1971 just before he passed away. Not much happened until 1975 when Judge Hodges "ordered information and recommendations for the school board to desegregate nine schools in 1975."[41] Hodges found the county's response unsatisfactory and ordered the board to develop a clustering plan. When none was forthcoming, he summoned school board attorney C. A. Boswell and Justice Department attorneys to his chambers to work on a plan. Finally, on August 8, 1977, Hodges ordered that 2,100 Polk County students in nine elementary schools must be bused by the opening of the school year to ensure racial integration in three all-black schools. Hodges asserted that "the right of black students in the county outweighed any disadvantages the school board may face setting up the clustering proposal."[42]

As the 1980s progressed, the percentage of black enrollments in some schools in Polk inched above the 50 percent limit established by Judge Hodges in his 1978 order. In 1989 Hodges ordered Polk County to develop a new plan to address the rising percentages. The district answered that they expected that the problem would be resolved once more schools were constructed.[43] Polk school board officials appointed a twenty-member panel composed of parents, educators, business people, clergy, NAACP members, and representatives of the Department of Justice. The panel eventually submitted a plan to the school board, which in turn submitted the plan to Hodges. The plan involved some busing, but it also included a new magnet school plan that was expected to also aid in the rebalancing. In February 1992 Hodges hosted attorneys for the Polk County School Board, the NAACP, and the U.S. Justice Department, and negotiations on the plan took place. The NAACP opposed converting two predominantly black schools into magnet schools, but the plan was eventually approved, only to be revisited again a decade later.[44]

The AIDS Epidemic

Also during the era, the Middle District of Florida was forced to balance an individual student's rights to attend school against the health concerns of other pupils. No public health issue was more volatile than the AIDS epidemic. In 1986, when three brothers with hemophilia who lived in Arcadia, Florida, were diagnosed with AIDS, the DeSoto County public schools barred them from attending school. Lawyers for the brothers—Ricky (10), Robert (9), and Randy (8) Ray—appealed to the federal court in Tampa, claiming that their civil rights were being violated. In one of the first such cases in the country, Judge Elizabeth Kovachevich agreed, stating that the boys had suffered "irreparable injury" and ordered that the school board allow them to attend school.[45] The Ray family was ostracized from their community and within a month after Kovachevich's ruling and only days after the new school year opened, arsonists burned down the Ray house, forcing the family to relocate, first in Sarasota and later Orlando.[46]

Within one year, Kovachevich heard a similar case when Eliana Martinez, a six-year-old developmentally handicapped child with AIDS, sued the Hillsborough County Public Schools to be admitted to school. Born prematurely in Puerto Rico in 1981, Eliana contracted AIDs after an intensive battery of blood transfusions in the hospital. Adopted by Rosa Martinez, a Tampa nurse practitioner, Eliana was ready to begin school, but school officials blocked her attendance based on the fact that Eliana was not toilet-trained and sucked her fingers, and thus might spread her virus. Eliana's mother and her lawyers disputed the scientific veracity of the claim and insisted that Eliana have the right to mingle freely with other children and enjoy all aspects of the education process. Rejecting the county's offer of a private tutor for Eliana at home, Martinez sued the county in the federal court to have her daughter attend the Hillsborough County public school facility for handicapped students.[47] After evaluating the evidence, Kovachevich ordered that Eliana be admitted to school but ordered that she remain isolated from other children in a specially built glass enclosure until she was potty-trained and stopped sucking her fingers. The eight-by-ten-foot glass-enclosed isolation booth would contain a toilet, desk, and sound system. An aide would be assigned to Eliana full time. Martinez and her attorney, Steve Hanlon, objected to the restrictions, arguing that Eliana's introduction to the classroom provided no threat to the other children and that such isolation would have the effect of preventing needed interaction, stimulation, and socialization with other children. "I said to myself, 'There's no way I'm going to do that, see her behind a cage watching other children and wanting to get out and play with them," claimed Eliana's mother. The decision pleased no one. One school board member called the judge's remedy "cruel," adding, "If we did this in any other school setting . . . , the courts would have us there for child abuse."[48]

Mrs. Martinez appealed Kovachevich's decision to the Eleventh Circuit Court of Appeals, which sent the case back to Kovachevich for review. At issue was the medical risk that the girl posed to the other children. The higher court declared that "remote" or "theoretical" risk was not sufficient to bar Eliana from the classroom. Further hearings revealed that the girl's "risk that the mentally handicapped child could transmit AIDs to other students is too remote to justify excluding her from school or separating her from other children." Delighted at the outcome in this nationally significant case, Hanlon remarked, "I think the case establishes, once and for all, that children with AIDS cannot be excluded from school rooms unless they pose a significant risk to other children. The risk they pose is nothing more than a remote or theoretical risk." Eliana attended her first day of school on April 27, 1988, but unfortunately she died only seven months later.[49]

Years later Kovachevich remembered the case as one of the most difficult of her career. The problem, she recalled, was balancing the rights of the children with the rights of society at large. Plus there was little scientific knowledge of the disease at the time. "The climate of people at the time was very different. AIDS was treated as if it were the plague, and you have to get the mindset of people at the time. . . . We didn't know what we were dealing with. . . . In retrospect, people may look at that and say well, 'why were you so careful?' Well we didn't know what we were dealing with, and there were a lot of concerns."[50]

Voting and Employment Discrimination

The 1980s saw a number of voting discrimination cases reach the federal courts. In February 1983 Judge Hodges ruled that, beginning in 1957, the City of Fort Myers' at-large voting process had unfairly discriminated against blacks. Hodges' ruling came after a four-year-long NAACP suit against the city. Finding that it took a city-wide majority to elect a candidate, and that voters usually vote along racial lines, Hodges reasoned that since blacks made up less than 40 percent of the electorate, they were thus disadvantaged in the polling process for city commissioners. Hodges ordered city officials to come up with a new plan within sixty days.[51] Hodges' decision that the at-large decision disadvantaged blacks had important repercussions. Fort Myers was the third city in the nation, after Pensacola, Florida, and Mobile, Alabama, to lose an election suit. There were six more suits pending in Florida cities and counties. Civil rights attorney David Lipman hailed the decision. "Throughout the South, at-large elections have barred blacks from running for office. Now that we have won this case, I predict suits against at-large elections will sweep the South like a prairie fire."[52]

In the late 1970s black residents brought suit in federal court if the black districts of the city were not receiving the same municipal services as white sections. In 1981 Judge Charles R. Scott ruled that the City of Apopka had intentionally denied blacks equal services. He impounded the city's revenue-sharing funds and ordered that no money be spent on white sections until black sections reached parity. The City of Apopka appealed Scott's order, but the case was finally settled in May 1983. The terms of the settlement were that the city would spend nearly $89,000 in upgrades to the black sections, and it would also be monitored by the court for five years to ensure that it provided municipal services in a nonracially discriminatory manner. From a cynical standpoint, it could be argued that the City of Apopka won the five-year battle: the original suit brought by the NAACP was for $1.5 million, and city's total cost of the extended litigation and the final amount agreed to in the settlement was slightly below $350,000.[53]

In June 1985 Lake County settled a twelve-year-old discrimination case— one of the longest civil rights suits in the nation. In 1970, when the county ended its segregated schools system under court order, some schools were closed, some black principals and administrators lost their jobs, and significant reassignment of teachers took place. In 1973 a number of black teachers and administrators charged the county with discriminating against them in their applications for administrative jobs. *Walter Berry et al. v. the Lake County School Board* crawled its way through the system until Judge Charles Scott ruled in 1981 that two of the plaintiffs had been discriminated against and ordered that they be placed in administrative jobs, adding that the "school's personnel decisions were 'tainted by a racially discriminatory intent to, as least temporarily, shut out black school principals and assistant principals.'" Two years later the county school board and the plaintiffs reached an out-of-court settlement.[54]

A 1983 federal law provided that in order to address past discrimination, a city or county could "set aside" a certain percentage of contracts to let to minority companies, defined as blacks, Hispanics, Indians, Eskimos, Aleuts, and the disabled. During the decade many such programs were put in place in Florida and elsewhere. Charges of reverse discrimination were common, and ultimately these challenges found their way into federal court. In 1989 a Jacksonville contractors association, after the Supreme Court had ruled that some minority set-aside programs were an unconstitutional form of discrimination, sued in federal court to have the Jacksonville set-aside program ended. On April 7 Judge John H. Moore issued a temporary restraining order shutting down the program and scheduled a hearing to consider the case. He eventually issued an injunction while the hearings went on, and in May 1990 he ruled that the program did not meet the constitutional standards as set out in the 1989 Supreme Court rulings. In February 1992, on appeal, the Eleventh Circuit Court of Appeals reversed Moore's decision and ordered the city to decide whether to revive or revamp the program.[55]

By the 1980s federal courts began to rule that the sexual harassment in the workplace is a form of illegal discrimination, forbidden by Title VII of the Civil Rights Act. In *Robinson v. Jacksonville Shipyards* (1991), a case initiated in 1986, Judge Howell Melton ruled that nude photos and sexually suggestive pinup calendars represented sexual harassment of welder Lois Robinson and other female employees. Management continually ignored her complaints and as such created a "hostile environment."[56] The company, claimed Melton, created a "visual assault on the sensibilities of female workers including pinup calendars and close-ups of women's genitals posted on the walls. . . . A pre-existing atmosphere that deters women from entering or continuing in a profession or job is no less destructive to and offensive to work place equality than a sign, declaring men only."[57] Such practices had the effect of keeping women out of the shipyards. Melton recalled years later that the case had profound ramifications in future cases involving sexual harassment in the workplace. "It was picked up all over the country," he remembered. It had "a lot of newspaper and magazine type publicity, colleges, and so forth with regard to that sex discrimination case. . . . It was a case that was of interest to other organizations and other people who had what they believed to be similar situations."[58] Indeed, as one recent commentator has observed, Melton's ruling was the first in the "country to hold that the presence of pornography in the workplace—by itself—could constitute a hostile working environment for women, actionable under Title VII of the Civil Rights Act of 1964."[59]

Another nationally significant employment case adjudicated in the Middle District of Florida involved a Nassau County schoolteacher named Jean Arline who sued under the federal Rehabilitation Act (1973) after the school district fired her in 1981 when she contracted tuberculosis. The act prohibited discrimination against the handicapped in schools that were the recipients of federal funds. Judge John H. Moore dismissed Arline's case, claiming that he did not believe contagious diseases came within the purview of the law.[60] On appeal, the Eleventh Circuit Court of Appeals reversed Judge Moore's ruling, arguing that Arline's illness did indeed constitute a handicap, which the school board was forced by law to accommodate. Finally, in 1988, writing for the majority of the Supreme Court, Justice William Brennan upheld the appeals court ruling: "We hold that a person suffering from the contagious disease of tuberculosis can be a handicapped person within the meaning of the Rehabilitation Act of 1973, and that the respondent Arline is such a person. We remand the cause to the District Court to determine whether Arline is otherwise qualified for her position. The judgment of the Court of Appeals is affirmed." Judge Moore found Arline otherwise qualified and gave the school board the choice of rehiring

Arline with back pay of $125,470 or sever all relations with her and pay her $768,724, the equivalent of what she would earn as a teacher for the rest of her career.[61]

The Middle District of Florida heard one of its first right-to-privacy cases when a 1986 lawsuit challenged the State of Florida's law requiring motorcyclists to wear helmets. In *Picou v. Gillum* (1986), David L. Picou sued the Pasco County sheriff, Jim Gillum, claiming that he had the right to privacy and the right "to be let alone" and freedom of choice—arguments similar to those that led to the landmark case *Roe v. Wade* (1973). Judge William Castagna dismissed the suit and found that the constitutional right of freedom of choice does not extend to motorcyclists who want to ride without helmets in Florida. Judge Castagna wrote, "The area of the right to privacy has been limited to areas of child-rearing, education, procreation, marriage, contraception and abortion. . . . Not by any stretch of the imagination does the claim raised (by Picou) fall in one of these categories." The Eleventh Circuit Court of Appeals affirmed the decision in 1989.[62] Even so, motorcycle helmet laws in Florida were on their way out. Numerous challenges continued during the 1990s and "freedom to ride motorcycles bareheaded" groups rallied and convinced state legislators that forcing them to wear helmets violated their individual rights. In 2000 Florida governor Jeb Bush signed a measure into law that allowed motorcyclists the right to ride bare-headed if they carried at least $10,000 worth of personal injury insurance. If such matters seemed trivial, they do point up the fact that the federal courts remained a forum for contesting the perceived constitutional rights of individuals and groups.

11

New Judges, New Challenges, 1988–1992

In January 1989, when George Herbert Walker Bush was inaugurated president of the United States, the Middle District of Florida was suffering under the strains of an expanding caseload, and the primary cause was the dramatic increase in criminal cases. The docket had grown exponentially because Congress had expanded federal criminal jurisdiction. The federal law enforcement establishment expanded, and so did the number of prosecutors. Even though U.S. magistrates took on more duties and trial work, the number of judges remained constant. As had been the case in the early 1980s, civil cases dragged on and on because "speedy trials" for criminal defendants took precedence. And the number of criminal cases grew and grew. A General Accounting Office study in 1989 found that nearly 1,200 criminal defendants were awaiting trial in the federal system. By the next year the backlog had increased to 7,400.[1]

The situation was particularly acute in the Middle District of Florida. For example, in 1985 in the Orlando Division, Judges Kendall Sharp and Patricia Fawcett had 117 criminal cases pending in the Orlando Division. By 1989 they had 213. From 1985 to 1989, narcotics cases had jumped from 11 to 47, fraud from 8 to 47, and firearms from 5 to 16. The effect was that civil cases often took years to try.[2] Judge Sharp likened the explosion of drug cases to a kind of "funnel." (In Sharp's tenure as judge beginning in 1983, the Orlando Division grew from three to seventeen prosecutors. But no more judges were added.) And because federal penalties for the crimes were more severe, more cases were filed there than in state courts. "We're not making any inroads," Sharp lamented. "It's so insidious."[3]

The political reality was that it was a lot easier to pass tougher federal criminal statutes and appropriate dollars for more law enforcement officers and prosecutors than it was to appoint more judges. Even members of Bush's own party expressed frustration at the slowness with which the president moved to appoint judges. Senator Alan Simpson (R-Wy.) complained,

"We fought like dogs to get a drug bill. You can talk about gun control and . . . capital punishment, but all that pales before the action of having a defendant appear in court for a trial—and they can't appear in court for a trial if there is not a judge on the bench. It's absolutely absurd."[4]

The rising caseload also placed added strains on budgets to hire court-appointed attorneys. Appropriated dollars were insufficient to cover the costs. "Our fear is that this may be a pattern which could cause the quality of defense to go down," noted a spokesman for the Administrative Office of the U.S. Courts in Washington.[5] The Middle District Public Defenders Office had a $300,000 budget deficit. In contrast to the U.S. Attorney's Office, which had expanded from fifty to ninety-five prosecutors in the previous four years, there were only fifteen public defenders for the whole district.[6]

Judges were under extreme pressure to move cases forward. But as Karla Spaulding, an assistant U.S. attorney at that time, remembered, "The court was frustrated . . . that we were pushing so much work their way. Of course they had a civil docket that they couldn't move because the Speedy Trial Act was just backing everything up."[7] According to Mike McMahon, president of the Orange County Bar Association, they were handling twice as many cases as they should, and this was resulting in "outrageous delays." Judges were forced to take "shortcuts that are time-savers for them but basically result in them being unable to handle the cases the way they, the public, and lawyers would prefer." McMahon observed that judges often rejected a motion in a case but, because of a lack of time, were unable to explain the decision, and lawyers were left in doubt as to what approach was acceptable. By any measure, Middle District judges were handling far more than their share of cases. In 1989, for example, Judges Sharp and Fawsett each had roughly six hundred civil cases, but the national average was about four hundred.[8]

With such a backlog of cases in Florida and in the nation, President Bush was soon in a position to appoint many new judges. Most expected the president to appoint conservative judges to the bench. Indeed, during the campaign, he had stated that he was "firmly committed to appointing judges who are dedicated to interpreting the law as it exists, rather than legislating from the bench." Although not as ideological as his predecessor, Bush was the third nonlawyer in a row to be elected to the presidency, and thus, even more than his predecessors, he relied on his advisors and members of the Justice Department to help him in the selection process. Generally, he moved cautiously and slowly.[9]

Another factor in the uncertainty surrounding judicial selection was newly elected Republican senator Connie Mack of Fort Myers who, along with Democratic senator Bob Graham, would oversee the process by which names were forwarded to the Bush Justice Department. No one knew for sure what role Mack would play. Would he agree to continue the nominating commission that Senators Lawton M. Chiles and Graham had established even though he was in a favored position because he was a Republican senator and his party controlled the White House? Senator Graham would soon get his answer when openings on the Middle District were contemplated. From the very beginning, Graham later recalled, "Connie and I had an excellent personal and professional relationship. My experience is that staff was frequently the source of friction. Connie and I took a firm position that that kind of conduct would be unacceptable. . . . It was more difficult for Connie to continue this system since he was a Republican and had a built-in advantage in regard to judicial preferences, but despite this," Graham said, "he stayed true to the system." Each time "we agreed on three names to send to the president."[10] Thus, even as the appointment process grew more and more partisan at the national level and in the incoming years would almost shut down entirely, Mack and Graham worked together in nonpartisan fashion.

When Bush became president, the Supreme Court was in its second year of William Rehnquist's tenure as chief justice. Rehnquist was known for his conservative opinions and likable, collegial personality. Even among the more liberal judges remaining on the Court, such as William Brennan and Thurgood Marshall, Rehnquist was well-liked and praised for his fair dealings and efficient administrative abilities. In general, during his eighteen years as chief justice, the Court moved to the right. Rehnquist opposed the Court's continued supervision of school desegregation; opposed expanding abortion rights, workers' rights against employers, and prisoners' rights against the government; and, in conflicts between states and the federal government, he usually came down on the side of the states. He also believed that the courts had expanded the application of the Fourteenth Amendment far beyond its original meaning to protect minorities.

While the broad outlines and general approach of the Rehnquist Court are interesting and instructive, it was left to the individual judges in the Middle District to rule in specific cases to the best of their ability and then, if their decisions were appealed, have their decisions evaluated by the Eleventh Circuit Court of Appeals or U.S. Supreme Court. Nine full-time judges were hearing cases at the time: Judges Howell Melton, Susan Black, and John Moore in Jacksonville; Judges William Terrell Hodges, George C.

Carr, Elizabeth Kovachevich, and William Castagna in Tampa; and Judges Kendall Sharp and Patricia Fawcett in Orlando. Everyone understood that more judges were necessary to handle the overwhelming burden, especially once it became clear that one of their number was seriously ill.

Over the 1988–89 holiday season, Judge George C. Carr began suffering from debilitating headaches, and a February 17 brain scan revealed a mass. A three-hour surgery five days later resulted in the removal of a malignant brain tumor. After the surgery, Judge Hodges announced that Carr would undergo chemotherapy and added, "We are hoping for happy results," but most understood that Carr's situation was grave.[11] Even so, Carr returned to work intermittently, as best he could, and in October he became chief judge after Hodges left the post. Unfortunately, Carr's condition worsened and he was readmitted to the hospital after the first of the year. When Carr died on January 26, 1990, Judge Hodges noted, "He tried to function as long as his condition allowed. He showed incredible courage." Hodges then assessed Judge Carr's humanity as both a person and a judge. "First of all, he was as honest—purely honest—as anyone I've ever known . . . And he brought to the work of the judiciary, I would say, a sensitivity for others and for the importance of his work in terms of its impact on the lives of people."[12]

On April 27, 1990, Judge Hodges, his fellow judges, court officials, and distinguished members of the bar took time out from a busy schedule to attend a portrait ceremony memorializing Judge Carr. Presiding over the ceremony was new chief judge Susan Black. Also on hand was Carr's childhood friend, former law partner, and the man who had made his elevation to the court possible, former senator Lawton M. Chiles. His comforting remarks soothed all those present, including Carr's children and his widow, Susie.[13]

Even as Carr's friends and associates in the Middle District grieved over their loss, the caseload of the Middle District of Florida continued to grow. Meanwhile, Howell Melton announced his retirement, and so did U.S. Magistrate Paul Game.[14] Replacing a magistrate was far easier than filling an Article III judicial post. Once Game announced his retirement, the process for his replacement moved swiftly. A selection committee reviewed thirty-six applications, chose nine finalists, interviewed them, and forwarded five names to the judges of the Middle District of Florida. The applicant that the judges eventually selected was Charles R. Wilson, an African American Hillsborough County judge. Wilson's selection leaked out prematurely. When asked, Chief Judge Susan Black acknowledged the fact. "There's no secret about it. Pretty soon the FBI and the IRS will be talking to his neighbors, and other judges and everyone he knows," she said.[15] Wilson brought significant qualifications to the position. Born in Pensacola, the son of a civil rights lawyer, Wilson grew up in Tampa, attended Tampa Jesuit High School, excelled, and was elected student body president. After receiving undergraduate and law degrees from Notre Dame University, Wilson clerked for Judge Joseph Hatchett at the Eleventh Circuit Court of Appeals. Later Wilson entered private practice in Tampa and was employed as an attorney for Hillsborough County. In 1986 then-governor Bob Graham appointed him Hillsborough County judge. Just before his appointment as magistrate, Wilson was named co-winner of the Outstanding Young Lawyer award by a local bar association.[16]

Wilson would soon be on duty in Tampa, but his presence did little to address the overwhelming caseload that had piled up. As of October 1990 Congress had passed the Judicial Improvement Act, which authorized two new judgeships for the district, but President Bush would not sign the bill until December 2, and no nominations had been made.[17] Even though visiting judges shared some of the burden, and in Orlando, retired Judge George C. Young heard cases on a part-time basis, the situation had reached crisis proportions. The Orlando Division had slightly over 1,000 civil and criminal cases pending, Jacksonville had over 1,100, and Tampa had nearly 3,000.[18]

The selection process for a new judge was excruciatingly slow. One study noted that it took an average of 504 days from the time a seat is open to the time a new judge was confirmed by the Senate. In May 1990 Senator Mack had forwarded four names to the Justice Department to replace Judge Carr, but as of the first of the year, no action had been taken. The new law authorized eleven judgeships for the Middle District. (The Judicial Conference of the United States recommended an additional judgeship, but Congress ignored the recommendation.) Even so, with Judge Carr's death and Judge Melton's promotion to senior status, the district only had seven full-time judges to handle the entire load.[19]

By the first of the year, the Middle District was eventually authorized a full complement of twelve district judge positions, but with nomination and confirmation of judges far in the distance, Chief Judge Black and the other judges voted in January to stop hearing civil trials to clear up the criminal division in Tampa. Federal law required that criminal defendants be tried within seventy days of arrest and indictment. The judges were concerned that unless something was done, the charges against some criminal defendants would have to be dismissed. District judges from Orlando and

Jacksonville traveled to Tampa and some cases in Tampa were transferred to other locations.[20] In January it was reported that the Tampa Division had 68 percent of the felony criminal defendants awaiting trial, or 962 of 1,408. Its criminal caseload had increased by 240 percent over the previous five years.[21] Addressing a Hillsborough County Bar Association gathering several month later, Judge Elizabeth Kovachevich admonished her audience of lawyers for not speaking out against the crisis. "I see a lot of people in this audience who have a lot of clout. Why are you not rapping on the doors of Senators Graham and Mack? We needed more judges yesterday. I have 332 defendants awaiting trial before me alone. We cannot even begin to function reasonably. No folks, I expect you to do something about this."[22]

The crisis placed added strain on Chief Judge Susan Black. "We are running from one place to the other to put out fires," noted Judge Black. "Once you start pulling judges out of the other two cities, you are creating a potential crisis in those areas. With only seven active judges, it's difficult." The rush to get these cases through the system, Black complained, prevented judges from adequately preparing their cases for trial. Ideally, she said, judges should spend half their time out of the courtroom in preparation, but in such circumstances, this was impossible.[23] In a move to alleviate the Tampa court's crowded docket, even if it would take time to accomplish, Judge Hodges announced that he would be relocating to Jacksonville after twenty years in Tampa. As the veteran judge explained, he was making the move to gain an additional judgeship for Tampa. Under the plan, a permanent replacement would fill Hodges' position, and Tampa could receive a second judge when Hodges opted for retirement in eight years. But Hodges would stay put until a replacement was found.[24]

The answer to who would fill the Middle District openings was beginning to take shape. In April 1991 Senator Mack and the Justice Department agreed on three names to submit to President Bush: Tampa lawyer Steven Douglas Merryday, Florida appeals judge Ralph "Buddy" Nimmons, and U.S. Magistrate Judge Harvey E. Schlesinger.[25] President Bush nominated all three in late May. Soon thereafter Bush selected Orlando lawyer Anne Conway to fill a fourth vacancy.

Sitting U.S. Magistrate Judge Harvey Schlesinger had been a mainstay in the Jacksonville division since joining the U.S. Attorney's Office there in 1970. By the time of his appointment, Schlesinger had served as magistrate for over fifteen years, gaining an enviable reputation as a skilled mediator. Years later Schlesinger recalled the long, drawn-out appointment process.

Senators Mack and Graham, he remembered, formed a merit selection panel of twenty-two lawyers from around the state. They advertised and received ninety applicants for the job. "They did their due diligence and then interviewed somewhere in the neighborhood of about twenty. Then they whittled down to about seven. Senator Mack interviewed all seven." Senators Mack and Graham reached a consensus on Schlesinger. "I got a call from Attorney General Richard Thornburgh . . . who explained the process to me." Schlesinger was then interviewed by a number of lawyers from the Deputy Attorney General's Office and the Office of Legal Policy. The FBI and IRS then did their investigations. By May it "got into the White House." Finally, he recalled, I "got a phone call from President Bush asking me if it was okay to nominate me. I was nominated the next day. . . . The last thing that he said, and it was about a twenty minute conversation, and he said, well, once you get nominated I've done all that I can do and the rest, you are on your own."[26]

Schlesinger was assigned a "mentor in the Justice Department whose job [was] to get you through . . . They send you materials, transcripts of recent hearings, what the current vogue is, what questions senators are asking, and then you get invited to come to Washington for a hearing." Schlesinger was encouraged to bring his family to the hearings—especially children. "Well I had a granddaughter who was born in March and this was June, so we took Hannah and put her in the front row. Of course, they just drift in and out of the hearing, other than the person who is presiding over the hearing, and then there is a member of the minority party, but everybody else just kind of drifts in and out because they probably have a lot of committee hearings at the same time, so they all stopped to play with Hannah." Schlesinger's hearing only lasted about an hour.[27]

Ralph Nimmons had been among one hundred of Jimmy Carter's 1980 nominees who were stranded when the Senate adjourned without taking action. His dreams of becoming a federal judge were dashed when Ronald Reagan chose not to renominate any of Carter's choices. But his chance finally came again in 1991 when Bush nominated him. By that time Nimmons was serving on the First District Court of Appeal in Tallahassee. Nimmons was born in Dallas, Texas, in 1938, attended the University of Florida where he earned bachelor's and law degrees. Nimmons went into private practice in Jacksonville and in 1965 became one of Jacksonville's first assistant public defenders. Nimmons then joined the Jacksonville state attorney's office where he specialized in public corruption cases. Nimmons was eventually elected circuit judge in the Fourth Judicial Circuit, where he served until 1983 when Gov. Bob Martinez appointed him to the appellate bench in Tallahassee.[28]

Steven Douglas Merryday was born in 1951 in Palatka, Florida. According to those who knew him, he had "just the right balance of smarts, experience, conservatism, and personality to get the job."[29] After attending junior college, Merryday received a scholarship to the University of Florida, where he majored in political science, graduated Phi Beta Kappa, a was Rhodes Scholar finalist, a member of Blue Key society, and student body president. Merryday attended the University of Florida Levin School of Law and during the summers worked construction. Merryday's first job after graduation was with Holland & Knight in Tampa; later, with four other colleagues, he formed another firm where he specialized in commercial litigation, personal injury, and malpractice. Merryday's hard work ethic and intelligence, many agreed, made him an excellent candidate for the federal bench. "He's not flamboyant, just a very cerebral lawyer," stated one of his former associates. "And he's got a constrained, conservative judicial philosophy." Ron Russo thought his law partner was an "anomaly. On one hand, he's a country boy from Palatka. On the other hand, he's this brilliant mind. A real scholar. He's the most literate guy I know. He reads constantly."[30]

A native of Cleveland, Ohio, Winter Park lawyer Anne Conway was the granddaughter of a part-owner of the Cleveland Indians and the daughter of a lawyer. Conway became a lifetime enthusiast of baseball, other sports, and the law. After earning her bachelor's degree from John Carroll University, Conway enrolled in law school at the University of Florida. After graduation she clerked for Judge John Reed in the Orlando Division. After two years she entered the entered private practice in Orlando, eventually joining Carlton, Fields, Ward, Emmanuel, Smith, and Cutler, for whom she worked for nearly ten years. Conway was confirmed by the Senate on November 21, 1991. At her swearing-in ceremony, before three hundred guests at Orlando's Expo Centre on January 10, 1992, numerous old friends and dignitaries were present, such as Senator Mack, Representative Bill McCollum, and Judge Reed.[31]

Schlesinger, Nimmons, Merryday, and Conway moved immediately to their prospective posts. Because of the excessive criminal caseload in Tampa, all four judges were initially assigned to Tampa. Schlesinger eventually transferred to Jacksonville. Merryday inherited Judge Hodges' cases in Tampa. Conway commuted from Orlando to Tampa for nine months before being permanently located in Orlando. As he was preparing for his

The Middle District Bench, ca. 1991. *Left to right*: Judges Howell W. Melton, Anne Conway, Ralph W. Nimmons, G. Kendall Sharp, John H. Moore, William Terrell Hodges, Susan H. Black (chief judge), William J. Castagna, Elizabeth A. Kovachevich, Patricia C. Fawsett, Harvey E. Schlesinger, and George C. Young. William Terrell Hodges Photo Collection, Middle District of Florida Archives, George C. Young Courthouse, Orlando, Florida.

swearing in, Steven Merryday worked closely with Judge Hodges, observing the veteran jurist's demeanor and skills. In a rare interview, Merryday revealed that he was grateful for the opportunity. "He's a nationally known and respected trial judge with an admirable demeanor in the courtroom," Merryday said of Hodges. Certain things Merryday had to learn, such as accepting a guilty plea, "have become second nature to [Hodges]. . . . The substantive law is relatively simple, but the actual dialogue with the defendant and method of inquiry" was all new to Merryday. "They don't teach that in law school." Merryday was sworn in on May 27. At forty-one, he was the youngest judge in the district.[32]

By the time Merryday donned his robes, Judge Hodges was settling into to his new surroundings in Jacksonville. The jurist's transfer from Tampa after twenty eventful years on the bench constituted a kind of watershed event in the history of the Middle District of Florida. At an emotional going-away party courthouse employees honored Judge Hodges with a cake decorated with the American flag. Many lawyers and court officials were also on hand for the event.[33] With Hodges' departure and new judges Merryday, Nimmons, and Conway's arrival, the old Tampa federal building was the scene of a "game of musical benches." Judge Kovachevich inherited Judge Hodges' chambers and his prominent courtroom on the first floor. Judge Conway occupied Judge Kovachevich's old chambers. Judge

Merryday occupied space on the second floor, and Judge Nimmons was on the first floor. Although the old federal building's refurbishment was moving along rapidly, it was not intended to permanently meet the needs of the expanding court needs of the Tampa Division. Work on two large courtrooms in a nearby building was under way, and according to court clerk David Edwards, "They represent a temporary fix to the space problem in Tampa."[34]

Beginning in the summer of 1991, lawyers, city officials, and others began touting St. Petersburg as the site of a new federal courthouse complex. Citing congressional authorization for a federal courthouse in the city in 1963 and massive filings in Pinellas County, Rep. Bill Young insisted that St. Petersburg be considered as the new site. Other supporters argued that Pinellas was the only county of the seven most populous in the state without a federal courthouse. In June 1991 the St. Petersburg City Council offered to donate a prime 4.6-acre tract downtown, and the following February Pinellas County offered a huge county court annex as a rent-free temporary facility. While politics, long-standing rivalries between Tampa and St. Petersburg, and disputes about operating costs were bandied about, Chief Judge Susan Black appointed a three-judge panel to examine the issue in March 1992. Largely on the strength of a report by Judges Patricia Fawsett, William Castagna, and John H. Moore, a majority of the thirteen judges voted down St. Petersburg's request, stating that the cost was not justified.[35]

But the issue was not dead. Undaunted, Representative Young argued that the ultimate decision was up to Congress, and he began lining up support. He organized a public hearing in St. Petersburg on April 27 with prominent members of Congress moderating the hearing. Judge John H. Moore attended the meeting, as did a host of lawyers, the Stetson law school dean, the St. Petersburg mayor, and other city and county officials.[36] When it was his turn to speak, Judge Moore explained that even with all the inexpensive land and property offered by the city and the county, guaranteed congressional appropriations would be necessary to make the move feasible. "Don't leave us like the state of Florida, building new prisons and not having money to fund them. Without more judges and personnel, we can't manage it."[37] Even so, by the end of the day, Judge Moore seemed to come around to the idea. Moore admitted that the final decision was up to lawmakers. "We do not oppose you," he said.[38]

Despite the momentum building in St. Petersburg, the new federal courthouse would remain on the other side of the bay two blocks north of the existing courthouse between Polk and Cass Streets. Scheduled for completion in 1996, the 240,000-square-foot, $84 million complex would rise to the height of a thirty-story building, with sixteen floors and nineteen courtrooms. The structure would house one thousand federal employees. Tampa planning director Robert Wehling predicted that the structure would revitalize the area by stimulating retail development. "There should be a lot of spinoff from it," he said. The new courthouse would have almost four times the space of the existing one, but the older facility would continue to operate as a site for senior judges' chambers and trials and as space for the U.S. attorney and Marshals Service.[39]

The sixteen-year-old federal courthouse on Hughey Avenue in Orlando was also overcrowded. Judge Patricia Fawsett stated that the new facility would save the taxpayers money in the long run because the design of the current structure made remodeling and expansion almost impossible. Still, the judges and their staff coped as best they could with the shortcomings. In addition to the five regular courtrooms, trials were held in a basement conference room, a grand jury room, and other rooms throughout the building. A makeshift courtroom called the "bowling alley" was currently under construction and engineers had reconfigured a series of bathrooms, storage rooms, and vacant offices. Fawsett complained that her current courtroom was so small and poorly designed that it was denying defendants their basic constitutional guarantee—the right to confront their accusers.[40]

While the Tampa and Orlando divisions pondered overcrowded courtrooms, the Middle District was about to lose its chief judge. On March 10, 1992, President George H. W. Bush nominated Judge Susan Black to the U.S. Court of Appeals for the Eleventh Circuit, and on August 11, the U.S. Senate unanimously confirmed the nomination. In a statement from his office in Washington, Sen. Connie Mack announced that "Judge Black is a person of exceptional capability and integrity. . . . I believe her 20 years of service to the state and federal judiciary as well as her commitment to the law have qualified her to be elevated to the Court of Appeals."[41] Thus, along with Judges Bryan Simpson, Joseph Hatchett, and Gerald Tjoflat (who swore her in on September 3), Black became the fourth Middle District judge to be elevated to the appeals bench. Judge Black admitted before being sworn in that her elevation to the Court of Appeals was a kind of bittersweet experience. "I spent most of my career saying I never wanted to do it because I absolutely love being a trial judge. . . . I like the courtroom. I like the attorneys. I like the give and take." Even so, she admitted that at this point in her career, she was "ready for it."[42]

With Judge Black's elevation, Judge John Moore took on chief judge duties. Not that long thereafter President Bush bestowed an honor on Senior District Judge George C. Young when he signed into law a congressional bill naming the Orlando federal building after Young. Young had been the first permanent judge stationed in Orlando when he began hearing cases there in 1962. Senator Mack and Representative McCollum sponsored the bill at the request of the Orlando Chapter of the Federal Bar Association. For the seventy-six-year-old veteran jurist, who still heard civil and criminal cases part time, the honor was a surprise. On June 2, in an elaborate ceremony in the six-story structure on Hughey Avenue, over two hundred friends, dignitaries, and associates assembled to honor Judge Young in his old courtroom.[43]

By that time two more U.S. magistrate judges had joined the Middle District. John Edwin Steele was assigned to the Jacksonville division and David A. Baker was assigned to the Orlando Division. Steele had attended the University of Detroit, graduating with a BA in urban affairs (1971) and a law degree (1973). He worked as a county prosecutor before joining the U.S. Attorney's Office for the Western District of Michigan. In 1981 he became assistant U.S. attorney for the Middle District in Jacksonville. After a brief stint in private practice with Mahoney, Adams, and Criser in Jacksonville, Steele was appointed magistrate.[44]

David A. Baker was born in Arlington, Virginia, and attended the University of North Carolina and later the University of Virginia School of Law where he earned law review. After graduation he clerked for U.S. District Judge Joseph Clavitt Clark Jr., in the U.S. District Court for the Eastern District of Virginia. From 1977 to 1991, before his appointment, Baker was in private practice with Foley and Lardner in Milwaukee and Orlando. Baker received high marks from a survey of defense lawyers and prosecutors in Orlando.[45]

Even with the additional personnel to hear cases, the Middle District of Florida was still understaffed, with the Tampa Division most of all needing more judges. The division had an average of 495 cases per judge, more than 70 above the national average. Under federal guidelines Tampa was entitled to seven district judges while Congress only approved five for the division and eleven for the whole district. The division muddled along as best it could. Even though William Castagna had taken senior status, he still took on a full load of cases. "We're doing the best we can with what we've got," Judge Kovachevich stated.[46] In December 1992, as court officials and Congress pondered the advent of the Clinton administration, the length of the nomination and confirmation process for new judges gave court-watchers pause. The tempestuous Clarence Thomas confirmation hearings had further poisoned the political environment between the president and the Senate. After the hearings President Bush severely restricted congressional access to FBI files, and the Senate retaliated by not acting on pending district judge nominations. The grueling ordeal only added to the partisanship, and most expected that even greater obstacles would be put in the path of nominees from the Democratic president.[47]

More congressional legislation that would broaden federal criminal jurisdiction was on the way. In October 1992 Congress passed a federal carjacking law, making it a federal crime to steal a car with a weapon. Only one month after the law was in effect two Polk County men and one minor were indicted in Orlando for the grisly murder of two people committed during the theft of a pickup truck. The men were successfully prosecuted in Judge Patricia Fawcett's court, resulting in the first conviction in the United States under the new law.[48]

Before he left office President Bush also signed into law the Child Support Recovery Act of 1992. The new legislation made it a federal crime to willfully fail to pay support for a child living in another state, and required federal prosecutors to work with state and local agencies to prosecute wrongdoers.

By far the most wide-ranging legislation that expanded criminal jurisdiction in the federal courts was the Violent Crime Control and Law Enforcement Act (1994), which authorized a total of $30 billion in funding for one hundred thousand police officers and provided block grants to the states for law enforcement. The act added fifty new federal crimes, increased the number of federal crimes punishable by death, and established a "three strikes" provision requiring a sentence of life imprisonment for violent three-time federal offenders. As the act's nickname, the "Brady Bill," connoted, it prohibited the manufacture of semiautomatic assault weapons for a period of ten years. It also outlawed the possession or transfer of assault weapons if they were not lawfully possessed as of the date of the act, and the law permitted the prosecution of juvenile offenders as young as thirteen who committed federal crimes of violence or federal crimes involving a firearm. Title IV of the act broadly expanded federal authority to combat violence against women.

The Violence Against Women Act (1994) provided nearly $2 billion for the investigation and prosecution of violent crimes against women. With this new federal legislation, the caseload and duties of the federal courts grew even larger.[49] The act, according to one critic, substantially increased "federal jurisdiction in ways that duplicated state authority and posed the additional threat of compromising the traditional mission of the federal courts by crowding the dockets of the federal courts with new categories of criminal prosecutions." The act drew criticism from many judges, including Chief Justice William Rehnquist, who opposed expansion of federal jurisdiction into areas that had previously been the province of state courts.[50]

In December 1990 there was much speculation over whether U.S. Marshal Richard L. Cox would seek another term. The cocksure marshal who wore a Stetson hat and cowboy boots was dogged by a number of embarrassing accusations: he had attended law school full time at Stetson University in his first term as marshal. He also used official stationery to help a friend in a legal dispute. He also used a seized airplane without proper authorization. Cox eventually decided not to seek another term, resigning his position. At the time Cox resigned, the Middle District U.S. marshal earned $57,000 a year and oversaw forty-five employees, including thirty-five deputies and twenty-two courthouse bailiffs. While his primary duties were to protect the federal court system, arrest fugitives, and manage seized assets, he also bore a new enhanced responsibility—protecting persons in the growing witness protection program. The marshal's office had a $440,000 discretionary budget, and the money was used to pay for equipment, part-time guards, and overtime.[51]

The appointment of Cox's successor was largely in the hands of Senator Mack. Once Mack learned of Cox's resignation, he appointed a ten-person advisory commission to provide him with candidates. President Bush eventually settled on Pinellas County jail director Charles Felton, whom he nominated in August 1992. Unfortunately for Felton, his candidacy for the position went down when Bush lost his bid for reelection against Democrat Bill Clinton. The Senate failed to take up Felton's nomination in its last session before the inauguration of the new administration. Once the new administration came into office, Senator Graham was in the driver's seat regarding nominations, and his selection committee once again recommended Felton, who, although a registered Republican, considered "himself a Democrat in spirit" and was "a longtime Graham supporter."[52]

But the man the Clinton administration eventually turned to was former Marion County Sheriff Don Moreland, a Democrat. Moreland had been elected five consecutive times before losing his post to a Republican a year earlier. He began his thirty-plus years in law enforcement with the Ocala police department in 1956. Sporting his trademark flat-top haircut, Moreland stated soon after his nomination that his long career in law enforcement had prepared him for the marshal's job.[53] Confirmed and sworn in by February 1994, Moreland announced after a few months in office, "The heritage of this organization is so strong you can feel it. . . . I'm just honored to be trusted with the star." The fifty-eight-year-old former sheriff would serve two full terms with distinction.[54]

In March 1993, roughly two months after Bill Clinton was inaugurated as president, Middle District U.S. Attorney Robert Genzman announced that he would resign. He had almost a year to go on his four-year term, but he said he would comply with new Atty. Gen. Janet Reno's request that he and other Republican U.S. attorneys resign, as was customary in each new presidential administration when the opposite party won the White House. The forty-one-year-old Genzman had been appointed in 1988 to replace the embattled Robert Merkle. Looking back over a productive tenure in the office, Genzman noted, "It's been a period of tremendous growth. I'm proud because of the professional atmosphere in the office."[55] During Genzman's tenure the office grew from 50 to 95 prosecutors with a total staff of 200 and an operating budget of $13 million. Genzman recalled a number of successes. His office had been among the top in the nation in drug convictions and asset forfeitures. He had organized task forces on environmental crime, telemarketing fraud, and firearms violations. His staff had also successfully prosecuted the BCCI case and had secured convictions in the nation's first carjacking case under the new federal law. After leaving the post, Gentzman joined the Akerman, Senterfitt & Eidson law firm in Orlando. Genzman's assistant, Douglas N. Frazier, was sworn in on June 19 and would serve as interim until President Bill Clinton's nominee could be confirmed.[56]

Meanwhile, as Genzman was pondering his life in the private sector, a blue-ribbon panel calling itself the Civil Justice Reform Act Advisory Group and consisting of leading lawyers practicing in the Middle District asserted that the shortage of judges and growing numbers of cases had the federal court system in central Florida headed toward "meltdown." Their report cited a number of causes for the crisis: fast-growing metropolitan areas, a long coastline ideal for drug smuggling, an overflowing state prison system, and a total of thirty-two recently failed financial institutions. The district's authorized number of judges was eleven, but only nine seats were filled. Cases had increased so rapidly that the panel insisted that the district should be entitled to two more judges for a total of thirteen. The panel submitted a number of recommendations to Chief Judge John Moore: (1) one judge in each division should hear civil cases full time; (2) there should be a more stringent route to the federal court for inmates complaining of civil rights; (3) a deadline was needed for judges in acting on pretrial motions; (4) attorneys should be allowed to fax pleadings to the courthouse; (5) the federal court system should be computerizing; and (6) attorneys should be persuaded to let federal magistrates rather than district judges hear their cases. Judge Moore said he and the other eight judges would consider the recommendations. "We don't have to adopt all the recommendations, but I think if we don't adopt them, we have to explain why," he said.[57] While the many solutions to the overcrowding problem lay in the hands of the judges themselves, the Middle District, like all others in the United States, relied on help and guidance from the administration in power, Congress, and the Judicial Conference of the United States. It is there that we shall turn in the next chapter.

12

The Court Expands and Confronts
Antigovernment Activity, 1992–2000

In his 1992 campaign for the White House Bill Clinton promised that, if elected, he would appoint men and women to the federal courts who possessed "unquestioned intellect, judicial temperament, broad experience and a demonstrated concern for, and commitment to, the individual rights protected by our Constitution, including the right to privacy."[1] As usual, the character of judicial nominees was an important issue in the presidential campaign. Clinton charged that the Reagan-Bush administrations had skewed the federal courts to the far right. While candidate Clinton's prescription for the courts was necessarily vague, his supporters hoped that the Arkansan would restore balance to the court. Both before and after Clinton's election, his opponents charged that his administration's agenda was to pack the federal courts with liberals and activist judges. Organizations like the Judicial Selection Monitoring Project pledged vigilance against the likely onslaught of liberal judicial nominees. They sounded the alarm, began raising money, and lined up supporters in Congress to oppose Clinton's nominees.[2]

While their parties and priorities differed Clinton and George H. W. Bush were similar in some ways. Both eschewed "litmus tests" for their judicial nominees and both moved exceedingly slow in nominating judges. In Clinton's case this slowness aggravated members of his own party. Clinton had promised to nominate more women and minorities to the bench. He had a pro-choice agenda, and during his term there were several abortion flashpoints between him and his opponents in Congress. One of his first acts as president was to issue an executive order lifting the ban on abortion counseling in federally funded family planning clinics and restoring the use of fetal tissue for medical research. As Clinton explained, "Our goal is to protect individual freedom, while fostering responsible decision making, an approach that seeks to protect the right to choose, while reducing the number of abortions." In short, abortions should be legal, safe, and rare. Yet congressional conservatives struck back. In what some branded a blatant election-year political ploy, conservative legislators put forward the partial-birth abortion bill in 1996, which Clinton vetoed, claiming that the ban failed to take into account the life of the mother.[3]

Clinton also took nuanced approaches to two other issues that had polarized the American voting public: religious liberty and affirmative action. Clinton favored what he called "religious expression" and was determined to set out a workable balance to the school prayer controversies that continued to find their way into the federal courts. Clinton also came out strongly in favor of affirmative action programs while denying that quotas were necessary in carrying them out. "I'm against quotas," he said, "I'm against giving anybody any kind of preference for something they're not qualified for. But because I still believe that there is some discrimination and that not everybody has an opportunity to prove they are qualified, I favor the right kind of affirmative action." While recognizing that some affirmative action programs had been less than perfect, he was not in favor of abandoning the project. "Mend it but don't end it," became the mantra.[4]

As the foregoing implies, Clinton sought the middle ground on some of the most perplexing issues facing Americans in the 1990s. In the end many liberals became disenchanted with his moderate stances, and this was also the case with many of his judicial selections. Clinton's White House Counsel, John Quinn, admitted that some groups might have been disappointed by the president's refusal to "do the mirror-image of what the Republicans had done, that is, fill the courts with liberal and progressive candidates in order to bring the courts back from their lunge to the right. . . . Our mission," Quinn continued, "is not to counteract the conservative appointment of the Reagan and Bush years. . . . This president is a moderate, who brings mainstream, Main Street values to the job of selecting judges."[5] Clinton would get his chance to appoint judges soon enough.

When Clinton took office in January 1993, there were 123 vacancies on the federal bench. Yet he moved slowly. As of June he had still not sent any nominees to the Senate Judiciary committee.[6] Meanwhile, the caseload of the Middle District of Florida continued to grow even as the court's allotted number of eleven judges remained two short. Competition for the two slots was keen. Almost sixty applicants filled out the long application form. Lawyer Robin Gibson chaired a thirty-nine-member state-wide nominating group created by Sen. Bob Graham. Among the applicants were Tampa lawyer Marvin Barkin, ever-popular former state prosecutor E. J. Salcines, assistant U.S. attorney Gregory Kehoe, Stetson University College of Law dean Bruce Jacob, federal magistrates Charles R. Wilson and Thomas G. Wilson, and state circuit judges Susan Bucklew and Richard Lazzara. On April 17, for the first time ever, twenty-nine of the applicants were interviewed in public, and five days later the nominating commission referred six names to Graham who would recommend two names to President Clinton. In July Graham forwarded the names of circuit judges Susan Bucklew of Tampa and Henry Lee Adams of Jacksonville from among the group that included Salcines, Lazzara, Barkin, and Duval State Attorney Harry Shorstein. Background checks on the two began immediately.[7]

Both Susan Bucklew and Henry Adams were barrier breakers, and both had been appointed by then-governor Bob Graham to their circuit court positions: Bucklew was the first woman circuit judge in Hillsborough County, and Henry Adams became the first African American circuit judge in Duval County in 1979. Susan Bucklew came to the law gradually. An English major at Florida State University, the Tampa native taught the subject at Plant, Hillsborough, and Chamberlain high schools over a ten-year period while attending law school at Stetson University. After graduation she worked in the legal department at Jim Walter Homes before becoming Hillsborough County's first female county judge. Her appointment as circuit judge came in 1986. In her years on the bench Bucklew gained the reputation as a hardworking judge and someone who set high standards for herself and those around her. Bucklew was confirmed by the Senate in November 1993, and she took the oath of office in a private ceremony before Judge Elizabeth Kovachevich on December 8.[8]

At the time of his appointment to the U.S. Middle District Court of Florida, Henry Lee Adams had been serving for fourteen years as circuit judge of the Fourth Judicial District of Florida, covering Clay, Duval, and Nassau Counties. Born in 1945, the Jacksonville native was one of three children in a household that stressed hard work and education. At a young age he was inspired by Jacksonville civil rights lawyers Ernest Jackson and Earl Johnson, who were successful in using the federal courts to attack segregation and discrimination. "They were getting good results," he remembered." By the tenth grade, he said, "I want to be like them," and he set himself to work to get there. Adams attended Florida A&M University, earning his bachelor's degree in political science in 1966. As a student he had been involved in civil rights demonstrations in Tallahassee. Later he attended Howard University School of Law where he excelled. After graduation in

Middle District and 11th Circuit Bench, ca. 1994. *Front row, left to right*: Bankruptcy Judge George L. Proctor, Magistrate Judges John E. Steele, Howard T. Snyder, Donald Paul Dietrich, Charles R. Wilson, and David A. Baker, and Bankruptcy Judge Jerry A. Funk; *second row, left to right*: District Judges Henry L. Adams and Howell W. Melton; Circuit Judge Joseph W. Hatchett; District Judge Harvey E. Schlesinger; Circuit Judge Susan H. Black; District Judges Susan C. Bucklew and William J. Castagna; *third row, left to right*: District Judges Patricia C. Fawsett, Elizabeth A. Kovachevich, John H. Moore, II; Chief Circuit Judge Gerald Bard Tjoflat, District Judges William Terrell Hodges, G. Kendall Sharp, and Ralph W. Nimmons. William Terrell Hodges Photo Collection, Middle District of Florida Archives, George C. Young Courthouse, Orlando, Florida.

1969 Adams returned to Jacksonville and worked in legal services and then in the public defender's office. He learned how to try cases and how to use a court, and, as he recalled later, "It was a great way to meet people." In 1972 he and Jacksonville attorney Bill Sheppard formed the first integrated law firm in the State of Florida, and from 1972 through 1976 they did mostly civil rights work and criminal defense.[9]

Adams' excellent service on the circuit bench, plus Graham's knowledge of him, along with the Clinton administration's high priority for identifying highly qualified minority candidates made Adams an obvious choice for one of the two openings on the Middle District bench.[10] The Senate confirmed Adams just shy of three weeks after Clinton's nomination. In a ceremony symbolic of the historic occasion, Judge Joseph Hatchett swore in Adams as the Middle District of Florida's first black district judge. After being sworn in, Adams was first assigned to the Tampa division where he worked closely with Judge William Castagna, whom he later called a mentor.[11]

In 1994 and 1995 two additional U.S. magistrate judge positions were added. To fill the vacancies in Tampa, the Middle District judges selected Thomas McCoun and Mark Pizzo. McCoun, a Miami native, graduated from Georgia Tech in 1973, earning a degree in industrial management. After graduating from Stetson University College of Law McCoun became assistant state's attorney in the Sixth Judicial District of Florida. Then, from 1980 until the time of his appointment, McCoun practiced privately in St. Petersburg. Mark Pizzo had been a mainstay in the federal courthouse in Tampa since 1980, when he became one of the first assistant public defenders in the Middle District of Florida. The Tampa native had only recently joined the U.S. attorney's office when his appointment came down on May 22, 1995.[12]

President Clinton and Atty. Gen. Janet Reno moved to fill the U.S. Attorney's office. In an interim appointment, President Clinton had named Larry Colleton the new U.S. attorney. Colleton took the oath of office in December 1993 in Jacksonville, and his official Senate confirmation was expected in February of the next year.[13] The thirty-five year old Colleton was among an impressive list of U.S. attorney candidates that Sen. Bob Graham's screening committee vetted in the summer of 1993. An assistant federal prosecutor in Orlando, Colleton grew up in rural South Carolina, earned undergraduate and law degrees from the University of South Carolina, worked in Georgia legal aid services, and joined the Navy, serving as a lawyer for six years before moving to Central Florida. Colleton's three years in the Orlando office earned him an impressive reputation as a prosecutor. He handled drug, bank robbery, fraud, weapons, and many other kinds of cases. When it was rumored that Colleton had gotten the nod, his former boss was delighted at the choice. "I hired Larry as a federal prosecutor, and I think he'd make an outstanding U.S. Attorney," Robert Genzman noted. "He's a gentleman with wisdom beyond his years. He's aggressive but fair, and very versatile. I know the troops would welcome him."[14] When news of Colleton's nomination became official Sen. Bob Graham added that Colleton was "an experienced professional with high integrity. I am confident" that he "will serve with distinction."[15] Clinton's choice was historic. Colleton became the first African American U.S. attorney in Florida history.

In the brief period before taking office, Colleton made positive overtures to the Tampa legal community, who hoped that one of their own would receive the appointment, and who felt that the Merkle-Genzman prosecutors had unfairly targeted Tampa officials over the years with politically motivated ethics prosecutions. At a meeting of the Tampa Bar, Colleton announced that he was calling a "truce" between the U.S. Attorney's office and the local criminal bar. The "olive branch" was well received. It was reported that the "group broke out in spontaneous applause."[16] After attending a meeting of new U.S. attorneys in Washington presided over by Attorney General Reno, Colleton explained that he agreed with Reno's message that each U.S. attorney needed to "build partnerships" in their communities. "We're not just about prosecution. We've got to get involved in prevention. We're going to be more visible as volunteers."[17] He later added that his top priority would be violent crime. But also he pledged to address bank, health care and telemarketing fraud, and the war "that seems never ending against drugs; environmental crimes and civil rights."[18]

Unfortunately, for a lawyer with so much to bring to the position, Larry Colleton's tenure as U.S. attorney for the U.S. Middle District of Florida was highly controversial and brief. As was often the case and expected in this instance, many high-level members left the office once the new U.S. attorney took office. Chief assistant Gregory Kehoe resigned in Tampa. Shake-ups were in store for the Orlando office. There were also significant rumblings in the Jacksonville office. On February 8 long-time Jacksonville head Curtis Fallgatter resigned and was escorted out of the office the same day. (Fallgatter had already been demoted by interim Douglas Frazier, but Colleton refused to reinstate him, and relations between the two degenerated.)[19] Most Florida newspapers carried stories of the historic event of Colleton's official swearing in on March 21 in Orlando. Just one month later they also contained information about an angry confrontation that saw Colleton grabbing and striking a Jacksonville television reporter at a judicial conference at Ponte Vedra Beach. The scuffle had been captured on video.[20] Colleton and his office were under considerable pressure at the time because of the prosecution of a Jacksonville judge for receiving illegal pornographic material in the mail. Later it was learned that similar films had also been mailed to the household of one of Colleton's recently promoted assistant prosecutors, Michelle Heldmyer. When her husband was not charged and it was learned that the company's mailing address was sealed as part of a plea bargain, many in Jacksonville cried foul. The outcry became louder after the judge committed suicide. A group of lawyers in Jacksonville filed a grievance petition against Colleton's office in early April, asking for a full investigation of the matter.[21]

But the reporter who triggered Colleton's angry reaction was asking the U.S. attorney about other things. At that time Colleton was having difficulty in the Jacksonville office. Many of the prosecutors in the Jacksonville office (especially those loyal to Fallgatter) opposed Colleton's changes. There were numerous disputes over personnel changes, office space, and other matters, and the tension between Colleton and some of the senior prosecutors spilled over into the courtroom.

On May 2, four days before the confrontation with the reporter, assistant U.S. attorneys James Klindt and Kimberly Selmore told Judge Harvey Schlesinger in open court that Colleton had pulled Klindt off an important drug case that he had been working on for over two years. When Schlesinger recessed the court and called Colleton to inquire why he had taken Klindt off the case, Colleton responded bitterly, "Are you trying to tell me how to run my office?"[22] Schlesinger blasted Colleton's decision during the hearing:

> It's just beyond my wildest imagination that something like this could happen. To come into court and be told, well, you can't set foot in here because you've been switched to another division . . . whatever you call it . . . is just unbelievable to me. . . . It's an abomination for anybody in management to take a prosecutor off a case that he's worked on for two years on the day of the sentencing," the judge continued.[23]

"I think the people of the United States ought to start worrying about what's going on now, and that's enough at this juncture."[24] Colleton was later quoted as saying that Schlesinger was "ranting and raving." Conditions between Colleton and his staff were so poisonous that some suspected that Klindt and Selmore had staged the incident to provoke a confrontation between the judge and Colleton in open court and before reporters. These suspicions proved untrue.[25]

The reporter filed a complaint with the St. John's County Sheriff's Office, and as the state attorney mulled whether to file misdemeanor battery charges against Colleton, the prosecutor was granted a thirty-day leave of absence to fulfill his naval reserve obligation. Meanwhile, a Justice Department investigation of Colleton's behavior took place. Justice Department officials named Donna Bucella, a thirty-seven-year-old Washington official who had previously worked in the U.S. Attorney's office in the Southern District of Florida, as interim U.S. attorney.[26]

After Bucella's swearing in on May 12, she met briefly with Chief Judge John H. Moore. When Judge Moore emerged from the room, he told reporters, "I briefed her on what was going on and answered some questions she had. I was very impressed with her. I think she's a dedicated prosecutor and a no-nonsense leader. Plus, she's really interested in getting the ship back on an even keel."[27] Even as the prosecutor apologized to the reporter and the complaint was dropped, Colleton's friends and foes alike debated his future: friends claimed he was the victim of a dysfunctional office in Jacksonville, hostile federal judges, Jacksonville defense lawyers, and the media. Critics charged that he was an ill-tempered amateur, in over his head. Moore announced that court rules required him to appoint a seven-member grievance committee to examine Fallgatter's charges against the Jacksonville office. Moore admitted the current situation was a "mess" but denied that he was attempting to intrude upon the management of the U.S. Attorney's Office. "The problems of that office in Jacksonville started long before Larry Colleton took office," he said.[28]

Acting U.S. Attorney Bucella reassigned some of Colleton's top aides. She asked Greg Kehoe to return as her executive assistant in Tampa, and she relieved Colleton's head in the Orlando office of some of his duties.[29] As Attorney General Reno's review of Colleton dragged on throughout the summer, his detractors spoke out but numerous supporters also came to his defense. T. H. Poole, head of the Florida NAACP, said the situation resembled a "witch hunt." The charges of Colleton's mismanagement were ludicrous, he said, considering that Colleton was only in office five months. "It's a sad day for the Justice Department," he said, "when they let a small group of people in Jacksonville control the department and that appointment." In a telegram to Janet Reno, Poole wrote, "Larry deserves the same support you got in the Waco incident," referring to Reno's controversial order to storm the Branch Davidian compound, resulting in the death of seventy-five people.[30] Judge Moore expressed regret at Colleton's dilemma: "I think it's a sad situation. Larry had a lot of promise as U.S. Attorney. He may have made a mistake or two, but I'm not sure it's reason enough to remove somebody. It's tragic."[31] In the end, faced with what Colleton's attorney called "an offer he couldn't refuse," Colleton resigned his office and accepted a position in a juvenile justice program in Washington. In a letter to President Clinton, Colleton stated, "My decision to resign is based upon the opportunity to be of even greater service to the public. . . . I see this as an opportunity to be an active participant in carrying out this administration's goals and objectives with respect to criminal prosecution, crime prevention, and education."[32]

With Colleton's resignation, speculation as to who would take his place began immediately. The name that eventually percolated to the top was Charles Wilson, who had been serving as a U.S. magistrate judge since 1990. Senators Graham and Mack quickly coalesced around the choice, and

President Clinton appointed the second African American U.S. Attorney for the Middle District in a row. Senator Mack was particularly impressed with Wilson: "I'm extremely pleased with the President's nomination. . . . He has the demeanor, judgment, and intellect to be an outstanding public servant." Attorney General Reno noted that "Judge Wilson has an excellent reputation as to character and integrity." But one candidate during the first search and also critical of the second wrote a public letter to Reno charging, "Your selection of Magistrate Wilson has nothing to do with qualifications and everything in the world to do with skin color."[33] The *St. Petersburg Times* editorialized that the charge was ill-founded and predicted that Wilson's "quiet, steady demeanor" would "help calm the storm Colleton had created in his well-intentioned but ham-handed effort to take control of an entrenched and Republican-dominated office. Wilson has neither the baggage nor the political inclination to start another bloody battle. He can unite rather than divide."[34] In his acceptance of the position, Wilson took a pay cut and lost the job security that came with serving as a magistrate, but the new position elevated his stature and responsibilities. When asked why he took the job, Wilson responded, "I can't imagine turning down an opportunity like that. . . . I kind of felt I was called into service. If the Department of Justice and the President thought I was the man for the job, I was willing to do it."[35]

Wilson moved deliberately to shore up the Tampa, Orlando, and Jacksonville offices. He replenished the ranks with many new hires. He hired as his chief assistant University of Florida law professor Michael Seigal, who had extensive experience as a tax and fraud prosecutor and had led a strike force prosecution of Francesco Gambino's drug trafficking conspiracy trial in Philadelphia. Seigal replaced Gregory Kehoe, who had taken a new special assignment: to prosecute Bosnian War criminals in the UN tribunal at The Hague.[36] Wilson's new hires were praised. One Tampa attorney who was formerly in the office noted, "I see a real positive force over there. A year ago it was total chaos." Another similarly situated lawyer agreed: "What people were looking for was stability, and Chuck Wilson has given it to them."[37]

Other changes were on the horizon for the Middle District of Florida and their judges. Judge Moore's tenure as chief judge was nearing its end, as was his eligibility for senior status. The new chief judge would be Elizabeth Kovachevich and thus Tampa would soon become the location of the new clerk's office. David Edwards, who had been with the clerk's office since 1983 and had headed the office since 1989, had decided to resign. The district replaced him with Richard D. Sletten, at that time clerk of the Ninth Judicial District in Orlando. Sletten had come to Orlando from Fargo, North Dakota, six years earlier. Judge Ralph Nimmons transferred to Jacksonville once Moore took senior status.[38]

Elsewhere, Judge Hodges' growing national stature among active federal judges was reflected in his appointment to the Judicial Conference of the United States, a prestigious appointment that Hodges continued until 1999. The Conference in effect served as the governing board of directors of the federal judiciary. Hodges also lectured frequently to new district judges at their orientation classes at the Federal Judicial Center, the educational arm of the federal judiciary. Matters covered were managing a civil docket, scheduling cases for trial, conducting pretrial conferences, and instructing a jury.[39]

The caseload of the U.S. Middle District of Florida remained high. A report of the 1995 management statistics produced by the Administrative Office of the U.S. Courts noted that the judges of the Middle District ranked sixth of ninety-four when it came to caseload. The average Middle District judge juggled 623 cases, a number down from 729 in 1993. The national average was 448 cases per judge. "Nobody can accuse us of being lazy," Judge Elizabeth Kovachevich said. "There ought to be a few accolades."[40]

The workload was also impressive in the U.S. Attorney's office, which filed more criminal cases and collected more money in civil cases than it did in the previous year. "Despite necessary cutbacks, our employees responded to the challenge with enthusiasm, professionalism and traditional hard work," noted Charles Wilson in a prepared statement. "I am extremely proud of our efforts as evidenced by our accomplishments in fiscal year 1996." Wilson's prosecutors filed 887 criminal cases. Among these were 76 fraud cases, 270 drug cases, 73 illegal immigrant cases, 34 counterfeiting cases, and 11 child pornography cases. His prosecutors also conducted 113 criminal trials. Criminals forfeited over $20 million, and the office collected almost $32 million from civil judgments and settlements.[41]

January 1996 saw the official passing of chief judge's gavel from Judge Moore to Judge Kovachevich. As was customary, after the current chief judge turned sixty-five, the position was passed to the most senior district judge who had not yet turned sixty-five. Chief Bankruptcy Judge Alexander Paskay predicted that Kovachevich would be an effective advocate for the district in the area of increased funding. "She's got energy, spunk, caring and know-how. . . . I think she'd be an effective administrator in any field." Judge Kovachevich was determined to increase the courts' efficiency. Increased security was a concern. "I've got everyone off on a project," she said. Kovachevich would control operations at all the courthouses in Tampa, Orlando, Jacksonville, Ocala, and Fort Myers. One of her major priorities was to monitor the progress of the new Tampa courthouse under construction.[42]

Aside from her new responsibilities as chief, Judge Kovachevich inherited a crisis. When Judge Kovachevich became chief judge on January 1, the second installment of the government shutdown was into its fifth day. The Middle District, and all other federal agencies and branches were in the middle of a government shutdown over a budget impasse between President Clinton and House Republicans led by Speaker Newt Gingrich. In the 1994 congressional elections Republicans swept into control of the House of Representatives for only the third time since 1931. Gingrich and others had run on the "Contract with America," a sweeping agenda that, among other things, pledged to cut government spending. The first shutdown occurred on November 14, 1995, after President Clinton vetoed a government spending bill, claiming it would have cut spending on Medicare, education, and the environment. The effect of the shutdown was to furlough many federal employees including court personnel. It was estimated that approximately half of the 2.1 million federal civilian employees were furloughed. As an example, Middle District U.S. Attorney Charles Wilson furloughed about a quarter of his 220 employees, including 12 of his 100 prosecutors.[43]

Within a week a temporary restoration of funding allowed federal agencies and facilities to reopen, but the frustrating game of chicken between the president and the House Republicans resumed again on December 19, when President Clinton once again vetoed a budget bill. Contained in the failed proposal was court funding, and by the end of the year the situation was critical. According to one source in Tampa, "court officials braced for layoffs and the prospects of working without pay to keep the courtrooms running." Charles Wilson said his employees were being paid for only one of the past two weeks and expected to get nothing on the next pay day. "It's had a catastrophic effect on employee morale," Wilson noted. Chief Justice William Rehnquist appealed to both the House and Senate leadership to maintain funding for the courts, arguing that not to do so could "damage our judicial system." But Rehnquist's appeal, an official from the Administrative Office of the U.S. Courts had to admit, had "gotten nowhere." At that moment, the official explained, "the courts had been operating on fees and fines that are normally turned over to the U.S. Treasury. That money will run out on Jan. 7." After that, the official explained, "it will be up to each court to decide what level of service to provide." On his second to the last day as chief judge, Judge John Moore announced, "We'll be open, but with reduced staff. . . . The damn thing is ridiculous. . . . . This is typical of the way Congress and the executive branch looks at the third branch of government. . . . They treat us as an agency, not an equal branch."[44]

Finally, by the middle of January, Congress and the president resolved their differences to the extent that federal workers and court officials could go back to work. But the ordeal was but one more reminder of the polarized nature of the American political process. As it did in all facets of American life, this polarization reflected itself in ambivalent attitudes about government in general, and specifically the U.S. courts. Judge Kovachevich sensed this. "There's a sense of great dislike about courts, particularly in Congress, where judges are sometimes accused of making law. We're interpreting the Constitution. Maybe the detractors don't have a full appreciation of what's in that document."[45] Some also pointed to a growing lack of faith in traditional American institutions. Particularly alarming was the degree to which some individuals and groups were willing to lash out against symbols of federal authority—especially judges and the courts. Going back to the 1960s, judges had always been targeted for their decisions—especially in the area of civil rights, but the nature and dimensions of the these threats in the 1990s were different.

On April 19, 1995, a devastating explosion rocked the federal building in Oklahoma City, killing 168 persons and injuring nearly 700 more. This homegrown terrorist attack along with the rising tide of militia-type organizations brought many to the realization that these groups had the firepower to do significant harm to those engaged in the civil administration of the law. By the early 1990s militia groups arose on the scene in various parts of the nation as well as Florida. In early 1991, for example, federal authorities in Jacksonville filed a sixteen-count indictment against U.S. Army sergeant Michael Tubbs, a member of the Knights of the New Order, which professed to be "lifeguards of the gene pool." The previous November law enforcement personnel discovered five caches of weapons including TNT, land mines, grenades, and antiaircraft weaponry stolen from Fort Campbell, Kentucky, and Fort Bragg, North Carolina. Investigators also recovered notes in Tubbs' father-in-law's car near Fort Campbell, where the sergeant was stationed, indicating that newspapers, television stations, and minority-owned business would be targeted for attack—and were "within our operational range." Tubbs eventually pleaded guilty to theft of the weapons and ultimately served four years in federal prison.[46]

Labeling themselves "patriot" organizations, groups rallied around government conspiracy theories, opposition to gun control, antiabortion causes, and ways to resist the Internal Revenue Service. One of the increasingly popular methods of protest against the government was the use of bogus liens—a method to slow down, clog up, or obstruct the state or federal law enforcement system. For a minimal filing fee persons could file documents in state or federal court against officials, and it often took the official time and money to answer the lien in court. The method was intended as a weapon of protest and revenge against a system that they opposed.

In November 1994 in Central Florida, five days after he had led a rally promoting the formation of a militia, Grant McEwan, a former Marine and the owner of a lucrative Castleberry collection agency, was arrested by federal agents on charges of filing bogus liens against the IRS and threatening to take over one of its offices and auctioning off the contents.[47] McEwan was released on $100,000 bail and scheduled to stand trial in late January 1996 on twenty-two counts of fraud, tax, and weapons charges. But he failed to appear on the date of the trial. While on a cruise, McEwan vanished, but he left behind a note to his wife denouncing Judge Patricia Fawsett, who had denied motions to throw out the government's case against him on the grounds that the IRS was an illegal organization. McEwan contended that the case was manufactured because he had tried to expose government fraud. "The fraud and conspiracy as relates to the lien is pure and simple a blatant injustice and a lie as far as the charges are concerned," he wrote. "Any judge who is not a puppet of this conspiratorial fraud by the International Racketeering Service (IRS) would have thrown this whole case out. . . . Those of us who are fighting for justice are not the criminals, and those who deny us justice are the real criminals."[48]

McEwan was eventually arrested in Pennsylvania after being at large for eighteen months. Brought back to Orlando, McEwan pled guilty to six of the twenty charges, including filing bogus liens against the IRS, failure to file tax returns from 1991 to 1993, threatening IRS employees, and bond jumping. The government dropped the other charges because of his decision to cooperate and because he showed remorse. When questioned by U.S. Magistrate Judge David Baker about why he did what he did, McEwan called it a mixture of protesting the tax system and stupidity. "It was stupid," he admitted. McEwan's lawyer told the court that his client had "made the realization that he made some serious mistakes in judgment. . . . And he would like to get this behind him as soon as possible."[49] Moreover, McEwan's attorney noted as his client was taken to jail, McEwan was eager to cooperate with the government by telling what he had learned of patriot organizations throughout the country. Three months later Judge Patricia Fawsett sentenced McEwan to two years in prison and two years' probation.[50]

Another man successfully prosecuted for plotting to commit an act of domestic terrorism was Donald Beauregard, a general in a group calling itself the Southeastern States Alliance. Beauregard led a group that hatched a plot called "Worst Nightmare," a plan to steal explosives from a National Guard armory in Haines City and blow up power lines, paralyzing Central Florida and Atlanta with blackouts. Beauregard's militia activity dated back to 1995. On December 27, 1997, federal agents who had the leader under surveillance said that he called for "simultaneous attacks on power lines and utility towers feeding Atlanta and St. Petersburg, including a bombing at the Crystal River nuclear plant."[51] Beauregard had been under surveillance for five years before he was arrested in December 1999. Once in custody Beauregard told the FBI that he had given up on legal forms of protest. "They don't listen to our people. . . . They don't listen to our yells, our cries," he said. "We tried the ballot box. I've tried everything, even tried the cash box. We got to figure out a way to force our enemies' hand so they could show their true colors. And I think if we can do that, maybe—and it's always a maybe—some of the sheep in this country will wake up and see what's really going on."[52] Beauregard was indicted on six counts and eventually pled guilty in Tampa to "conspiracy to degrade government property, destroy energy plants and provide material support to terrorists." He was sentenced to five years in federal prison.[53]

In the 1990s antigovernment sentiment was voiced in outbursts and threats against judges and the institutions they represented. In 1993 and 1994 three individuals were charged with plotting to kill Judge Steven Merryday. One was a disgruntled man that Merryday had sent to jail. The next year a man named Jason Weeks and his mother were charged with a plot to kill Merryday while they were undergoing a securities fraud trial.[54] Threats against judges continued. In 1996 there were eleven documented threats to judges, magistrates, or courthouses in the Middle District. While he refused to comment on specific instances, U.S. Marshal Don Moreland noted, "We're consistently vigilant on a daily basis."[55]

On August 3, 1994, in Orlando, Judge Anne Conway sentenced Ronald Barbour to five years in prison for threatening to kill President Clinton.

Barbour had continually told neighbors of his plan to shoot the president while he was jogging and even took a gun and ammunition with him to Washington for that purpose. After listening to testimony over the course of several days, the jury took just over an hour to convict Barbour on May 27. One juror remarked after the verdict that she found no evidence that he was joking, and she was convinced that Barbour would have carried out his plan if given the chance. At his sentencing hearing Barbour asserted that his arrest itself violated his right of freedom of speech, and he criticized government's condoning of abortion, slavery, the internment of Japanese during World War II, the firebombing of Dresden, and intervention in Korea and Vietnam.[56]

When it came to antigovernment activity, perhaps the most bizarre defendant ever to set foot in a Middle District of Florida courtroom was Emilio Ippolito. Born in Tampa in 1925, Ippolito was a graduate of the University of Tampa and World War II veteran as well as one of Hillsborough County's largest property owners. In the late 1980s he ran into a series of disputes with county and city regulating agencies over code violations at many of his rental properties. Ippolito's continued refusal to comply with orders and pay fines resulted in continued court appearances and Ippolito's defiant behavior. As time went on the disputes escalated beyond what most would consider any rational basis.

Ippolito's first appearance in federal court was before Judge Harvey Schlesinger. After the Florida Bar and the Hillsborough County Circuit Court had sanctioned Ippolito and his daughter, Susan Mokdad, for practicing law without a license, Ippolito brought suit in federal court claiming that they had been deprived of their constitutional rights to represent themselves. Judge Schlesinger threw out Ippolito's complaint. While he had some sympathy with Ippolito's argument that he should be able to represent himself, Schlesinger reasoned that the continual changes in property law and its complexity necessitated trained legal professionals to represent clients. "Seemingly essential tasks—research and evidence—overwhelm many experienced attorneys. . . . Laymen undertaking representation of another would be handicapped beyond imagination." A trained professional, licensed with the bar, Schlesinger asserted, was essential to the protection of the rights of all Americans. "Too often," the judge asserted, "the rights of minorities—the first Amendment right to advocacy and petition for redress of grievances, and the 14th Amendment's requirement of equal justice—are rendered meaningless because they are helpless to assert their rights without assistance."[57] Subsequently, the Florida Supreme Court found Ippolito and Mokdad in contempt for practicing law without a license, and they served four months in jail.[58]

Ippolito's crusade against state and federal government authorities escalated to the extent that he and others formed a Central Florida branch of the American National Freemen organization, which held meetings in Orlando, Tampa, and Kissimmee. In order to fight what they thought was the unjust treatment by the government, Ippolito and his associates formed the Constitutional Common Law Court. Operating from Ippolito's home in Tampa and at storefronts in Orlando, the "court" printed up legal forms and conducted legal proceedings. One of the documents promulgated from the court called for the arrest of Judge Elizabeth Kovachevich. Ippolito's Common Law Court of the People summoned her to answer "Criminal Complaints of Treason." The federal grand jury indictment in Tampa charged Ippolito and others with conspiracy, jury tampering, and obstruction of justice.[59]

Because of Ippolito and his companions' history of threatening jurors, Judge Merryday moved cautiously. He ruled that the jurors' names would be kept secret, the first such instance in the history of the federal court in Tampa. They were bused in during the two-and-a-half month trial from an undisclosed parking site.[60]

Ippolito's trial was the scene of frequent outbursts and other bizarre behavior by the defendant. On June 5 as the prosecutor was outlining the charges against Ippolito, he jumped up and charged treason against the court. Judge Merryday immediately sent the jurors out of the courtroom, ejected Ippolito, and forced him to watch the trial on closed circuit television.[61] The marathon trial ended with Ippolito and his daughter being convicted on fourteen of eighteen counts and eleven of fifteen counts, respectively. Only one of the seven defendants was acquitted. The jury deliberated three and a half days over the ten weeks of testimony. A number of the jurors were visibly shaken by the ordeal. Judge Merryday congratulated them on their service, calling it "heroic" and "inspiring." "If it were not unseemly," he added, "I would run over and hug each of you for sticking with the case."[62] U.S. Attorney Charles Wilson praised his prosecutors, Tony Peluso and Robert Monk, who not only showed "impressive legal ability, but patience, professionalism and composure—which especially in a case like this are difficult to maintain."[63] Fran Carlton, Orange County Clerk and one of the many officials that Ippolito and the others had threatened, was also pleased at the verdict. "I think it's important to send a message to anti-government types that they are simply not at liberty to threaten government officials."[64] Ippolito was sentenced to eleven years in federal prison. His daughter was sentenced to ten.

One of the most dangerous defendants to be prosecuted in the Middle District court in Orlando was white supremacist Todd Vanbiber, whose plot to plant bombs at the Lake Eola Fourth of July celebration in Orlando and at other Independence Day parties involving blacks and federal employees was aborted when one of the bombs he was working on exploded in his face at a Winter Park storage facility. When federal agents searched the contents of his storage unit they discovered weapons, ammunition, munitions manufacturing guides, Nazi memorabilia, and membership materials from the National Alliance, a right-wing, white supremacist group.[65] While awaiting trial in jail, Vanbiber told an undercover agent that his ultimate goal was to "start a race war." Six months later on October 20, Judge Patricia Fawsett sentenced Vanbiber to six and a half years in federal prison for possessing fourteen unregistered explosives and illegally constructing explosives. In a subsequent trial three persons linked to Vanbiber swore that the bombings on the Fourth of July were to serve as diversions for bank robberies in Orlando. The accomplices said they had participated in a 1996 bank robbery with Vanbiber in Danbury, Connecticut, and were with Vanbiber when they visited the National Alliance Headquarters in Hillsboro, West Virginia, to donate some of the stolen money to its leader, William Luther Pierce, to "support the cause." Pierce was the author of *The Turner Diaries*, which is often cited as the blueprint for the Oklahoma City federal building bombing.[66] Two of Vanbiber's accomplices were eventually convicted in Judge Fawsett's court. She sentenced them variously to forty-eight and seventy-eight months in prison.[67]

13

Bankruptcy in the Middle District, 1984–2000

In the 1970s bankruptcy practice and the laws were poised to undergo massive revision and expansion. Commercial litigation became increasingly complicated, and bankruptcy became an integral part of it as never before. Tampa lawyer Leonard Gilbert, who was involved in some of the largest bankruptcy litigation cases in the 1980s such as the Eli Witt, Uiterwyk Shipping, and Gardinier Phosphate companies, remembered that as specialization and attorneys' fees began to mount, law firms in Florida and around the country began to hire people or train people to handle bankruptcies. "That became the way of dealing with large financial problems beginning in the 1960s and continuing on. . . . We were just small-time at that time. But when the big banks started having these problems, they looked around for people and they found that their own law firms didn't have anybody so they had to hire somebody" and people began creating whole law firms specializing in the practice.[1]

Bankruptcy cases grew in number and complexity, and with the 1978 Bankruptcy Act in place, everything seemed in order. And then suddenly in September 1982 the whole system was thrown into chaos when a Minnesota district judge in *Northern Pipeline v. Marathon Pipeline* ruled the jurisdictional grant of the 1978 act unconstitutional. As U.S. Bankruptcy Judge Alexander Paskay explained, "It was out the window." Having followed the crafting of the law carefully, Paskay actually anticipated the ruling. He and others understood that the law was unconstitutional as written because it gave the bankruptcy courts "unlimited jurisdiction" when in actuality only district courts were granted that power.

> Everyone knew that was unconstitutional because the judicial power in the United States is reserved to adjudicate cases and controversies by judges who are appointed by the president with the advice and consent of the Senate. . . . . Everyone wondered what on earth was

going to happen here. . . . At that point there was no court in the United States, neither bankruptcy court nor the district court, who had any jurisdiction over any matter dealing with bankruptcy. At that time, there were half a million cases pending, some of them very big ones.[2]

The Supreme Court granted a stay to October. Then they extended it to December 26. Congress did nothing.

Then on December 26, Paskay remembered, he interrupted his case: *Jesus Loves Incorporated* vs *Christ Is the Answer*. Everyone walked out of the courtroom. Finally, the Ninth Circuit resolved the issue by the "emergency model rule," in which they "suggested each district court adopt it as a local rule, doing what Congress couldn't do by a local rule promulgated by district judges." Paskay called the situation,

> Unconstitutional as hell again, no question about it. So we all got the command, adopt a local rule, we just kept going and operating. . . . That was giving lip service to the Constitution, in the sense that we can do everything as before, but always under the supervision of the district court, and the ultimate supervision and *imprimatur* will be by district court, and so forth. And they have the right to *de novo* review anything we are doing. . . . Anyway we labored under the emergency model rule until BAFJA (Bankruptcy Amendments and Federal Judgeship Act) was adopted in 1984.[3]

With BAFJA the current bankruptcy system within the jurisdiction of the federal district courts took shape. The new law provided that bankruptcy courts were units within the district courts, and that bankruptcy judges be appointed by the courts of appeal to fourteen-year terms. The new law provided that bankruptcy judges were judicial officers of the district court, and that district judges had review authority of their decisions.[4]

Chapter 11 allowed businesses to reorganize themselves and pay back creditors over a period of time, while Chapter 7 liquidated a failed company's assets, distributing the proceeds to creditors all at one time. According to Robert Young, an Orlando bankruptcy attorney, Chapter 11 is more than just a place where companies increasingly go when they are in trouble. Increasingly, he stated in 1985, it had become a "business planning tool. It's an accepted method of handling business. It's a viable alternative to help solve business problems," a method of managing debt load, borrowing money, and issuing stock. In such instances companies often used the court as a protection to make decisions regarding pending contracts and personnel that they could not easily do outside Chapter 11 bankruptcy court protection. Individuals could file for bankruptcy under Chapter 7, which allowed for immediate liquidation of assets to creditors, or Chapter 13, which allowed individuals to pay creditors from future income.[5]

The vast majority of the bankruptcy cases were simple individual Chapter 7 cases, and these cases mounted in the 1980s and 1990s. The number of bankruptcies doubled from the 1970s to the 1980s and doubled again from the 1980s to the 1990s. By the 1990s, one source commented, bankruptcy filings had become a "torrent," with as many as two hundred or three hundred in a day. Under Florida law, debtors could keep their car and personal items, and hearings typically last about five minutes, some as few as sixty seconds. Many speculated on the cause of the growing bankruptcies. The stigma of personal bankruptcy was certainly diminished from older times. Attorney advertising was posited as a cause. Most attributed the skyrocketing rate to easy access to credit cards.[6]

In 1985 the Middle District of Florida had two full-time bankruptcy judges. Alexander Paskay sat in Tampa, and George Proctor sat in Jacksonville. On alternate weeks Proctor was sitting four days in Orlando while Paskay heard cases there one day every two weeks. Judge Paskay also traveled to Fort Myers to hear cases. Because Orange, Lake, Brevard, Seminole, Osceola, Volusia, and Brevard Counties were some of the fastest-growing counties in Florida, bankruptcy filings in the Orlando division had nearly doubled over the two previous years. Linda Middleton, the division manager of the Orlando bankruptcy court, predicted in May 1985 that 1,800 bankruptcy petitions would be filed there by year's end. Middleton's four-person staff was stretched to the limit. The law required that the first hearing in bankruptcy cases be held within forty days of the filing of the petition, and that notices of the filing be sent to every creditor involved within twenty days.[7]

Judges Paskay and Proctor were on the bench at a time of increasing professionalization, sophistication, and respectability of bankruptcy practice in the United States. This new attitude was reflected in the differing terminology associated with the judicial officials. L. Ralph Mecham, who became director of the Administrative Office of the United States Courts in 1985, observed some years later that he was determined to reverse a bias against bankruptcy judges that had crept into the administrative office procedure. "We had a policy manual here in this agency that said we couldn't refer to bankruptcy court as a court, or a bankruptcy judge as a judge." Instead, he said, "we started treating all judges like judges regardless of whether they were bankruptcy judges or Article IIIs."[8] Due to Mecham's reforms, bankruptcy courts retained much more autonomy, especially in budgetary matters, as they functioned within their district courts.[9]

Judge George Proctor spoke of the increasing professionalization and rising status of bankruptcy judges after the 1984 act. He noted a marked respect for the court. "When I first came aboard, first of all, around the country, many judges were not wearing robes. I've always thought robes make a real contribution to the dignity of the court." He was determined to ensure that persons who practiced before him appreciated the dignity of his court. "Right from the beginning, I wouldn't let them in the courtroom if I didn't have a robe on and the people didn't have ties and coats." He also maintained that when he first began practicing law and even after he became judge, few people were in the field because of the lack of money in it. Large firms ignored it. But by the 1980s that changed. "Once the money began to become attractive, they got into it," he said.[10]

Judge Alexander Paskay's ultimate goal, as he saw it, in his bankruptcy cases was to salvage what he could of the failed enterprise. "If there's a meaningful, salvageable economic value, hard core, which merits salvaging, to keep it alive, [and] keep the jobs. [It's] much better for society if you have a vital—ultimately emerging, a vital economic entity which is good for society than something put on the block and chopped up and just liquidated."[11] Paskay was respected and feared by lawyers in his courtroom. He often came down hard on lawyers who came to his courtroom unprepared. He admitted, on one occasion, that many lawyers "hate my guts. . . . But I'm not running for Miss America. I don't have to kiss babies, run for election. I don't worry about that stuff."[12] Paskay often rebuked law firms who charged outrageous fees. It was part of his discretion as judge to approve fees. In 1990, for example, Paskay slashed $2 million off a $5 million legal fee, scolding the seven law firms and three accounting firms in a written decision that they were not entitled to such huge fees. "Congress didn't design Chapter 11 as a relief chapter for attorneys," he said. Of the accounting firms' fees, he charged that they "approach the annual budget of a small country and indicate to this court nothing else but efforts by the applicants to get while the getting is good and while the creditors of these debtors are held at bay and wait with no relief in sight."[13]

By the middle 1980s Judge Paskay was handling something like seven thousand cases a year.[14] The Tampa court was one of the busiest in the nation. But help was on the way. In 1987 the Eleventh Circuit Court of

Appeals appointed Thomas E. Baynes to the Tampa Division. At the time the forty-year-old lawyer was practicing with the Peterson Myers law firm in Lake Wales. Baynes was born in New York City but moved to Augusta, Georgia, at a young age. He earned a bachelor's degree from the University of Georgia and law degrees from Emory University and Yale University. He served seven years in the U.S. Navy and thereafter served in the Naval Reserves as a commander in the Judge Advocate General's Office. In 1976 Baynes spent a year in Washington, D.C., as a judicial fellow for Chief Justice Warren Burger. He also taught at the Shepard Broad Law Center at Nova Southeastern University. Known as a man with varied interests, including music, baseball, and literature, he also wrote legal history.[15]

Also appointed at that time was Lionel H. Silberman. Orlando's first full-time bankruptcy judge was born in Baltimore and grew up in Flushing, New York. Silberman attended Emory University, earning a bachelor's degree in 1949. Settling in Orlando, he managed a chain of retail clothing stores for twenty years before entering Emory University School of Law in 1968. After graduation in 1970 Silberman returned to Orlando and specialized in bankruptcy law, often serving as a trustee in Chapter 7 liquidation cases. Tragically, after only five months on the bench, Silberman died suddenly while jogging.[16] To replace Silberman in Orlando, the Eleventh Circuit Court of Appeals judges turned to Tampa lawyer C. Timothy Corcoran. A specialist in business litigation, the forty-three-year-old Corcoran was born in Kansas City, Missouri, and attended the University of North Carolina. After graduation, he served in Vietnam as a naval electronics specialist and intelligence officer. He soon thereafter entered the University of Virginia School of Law, earning his degree in 1973. Corcoran first came to Tampa as a law clerk for Judge William Terrell Hodges and then subsequently joined Carlton, Fields, Ward, Emmanuel, Smith, and Cutler.[17]

When Corcoran joined Judges Paskay, Proctor, and Baynes on the Middle Florida bankruptcy bench, filings began to skyrocket. As of June 1990 the Tampa Division had almost fourteen thousand bankruptcy cases pending—both Orlando and Jacksonville had nearly six thousand each. Statistics showed that Paskay and Baynes were handling twice the national average of cases. In October the Tampa Division recorded its ten-thousandth filing, up 38 percent over the previous year. Paskay attributed the rise in filings to lawyer advertising. "There's an awareness by the consumer that they can save their home through Chapter 13 (voluntary personal reorganization). And that awareness is there because of lawyer advertising."[18] To address the crisis U.S. Rep. Sam Gibbons filed a bill in the House of Representatives

U.S. Bankruptcy Judge Alexander L. Paskay, ca, 1988. Catherine Peek McEwen Collection.

for two more bankruptcy judge positions in the Middle District. Senators Bob Graham and Connie Mack filed companion bills in the Senate.[19] Unfortunately, the bill never passed. When he learned the bad news, Paskay remarked that his "workload is tremendous. We have to work every night, and I don't believe it's in the contract I have with the government that I have to take home two suitcases of paper every night."[20]

Shortly thereafter, in an opinion piece in the *Tampa Tribune*, Paskay addressed the crisis, pointing out that the national average for bankruptcy judges was two thousand cases (with one hundred Chapter 11 cases). He and Baynes each had more than eight thousand cases (and close to four hundred Chapter 11 cases each). Judges Proctor in Jacksonville and Corcoran in Orlando each had approximately five thousand cases pending, including nearly two hundred Chapter 11 cases each. "My colleagues and I are now forced to work overtime, including Saturdays and Sundays and holidays. Frankly, we are rapidly reaching the point, just like the district judges did, that we are no longer willing to continue this routine in order to accommodate parties of interest and the attorneys. Maybe if the system reached the point of complete paralysis," he said, "some action will be taken without any further delay."[21]

Yet filings soared with no relief in sight. In 1991, after another bill to authorize more bankruptcy judges failed, filings in Tampa surpassed the previous year's record by a 30 percent increase. Baynes had over 9,600 active cases and Paskay had over 10,000. "He's No. 1 in the country, and I am No. 2," Baynes quipped.[22] In August 1992 Congress finally approved four new bankruptcy judges for the Middle District, two for Tampa and one each for Jacksonville and Orlando. Even with the congressional bill ready for the president's signature, it would take more than a year before new judges were in place.[23]

Paskay remembered that during that time the stress of his job was nearly unbearable—"it was just murder, really bad, bad, bad. . . . You know the responsibility was tremendous. I got hit with [four] mega-cases. . . . The four of them going, I mean, would drive anybody crazy. It was just pretty bad stuff. I was in hearings after hearings every Saturday and every Sunday. . . . But it had to be because there were always emergencies, you know."[24] At one point in the fall of 1992 Paskay and his clerks even worked before and after he went into surgery. A makeshift courtroom was set up in his hospital room, where the judge signed orders and consulted with clerks only moments before entering the operating room. For three weeks after the procedure, Paskay worked on piles of legal papers at his home, brought in by his secretary and clerks.[25]

Like their counterparts in the district courts, bankruptcy judges depended on the assistance of hardworking clerks and professional staff to assist them, especially as caseloads mounted. One indispensable functionary in the Tampa Division was federal bankruptcy trustee Christopher C. Larimore, who was appointed Chapter 13 trustee in 1979. As a trustee, Larimore supervised hearings for creditors, worked out payment plans for debtors, and made frequent recommendations to the judges relevant to approval of plans. He also supervised the office that handled millions of dollars in payments. On January 4, 1993, Larimore collapsed in court and died. Judge Paskay said of Larimore, "Everybody liked him very well. . . . He was a decent and very honest person. We're going to miss him very sorely." When he died Larimore, had 3,500 cases under his supervision.[26]

Bankruptcy judges sometimes appointed examiners in some of the very big cases. Examiners conducted investigations and reported to judges the history, alleged improprieties, possible fraud, or any pending possible suits in cases. "It's a very big job," Paskay explained. Examiners often worked on cases for years. "He'd report to the court, and then he reports back [his] recommendation: should be liquidated, should be permitted to attempt to reorganize, should the management be kicked out, should the management be retained in part, whatever the case may be," Paskay noted.[27]

By the 1980s and 1990s Florida had acquired the unsavory reputation as a place to escape creditors. Florida earned this dubious distinction as a "paradise for bankruptcy" largely because the Florida Constitution excluded homesteads, whether modest or mega-mansions, from seizure in bankruptcy proceedings. Well-publicized stories of debtors moving to Florida and buying huge homes and then declaring bankruptcy to dodge creditors pushed Florida lawmakers to pass legislation addressing the abuse. In 1991 substantial efforts were made to insert monetary exemption caps and waiting periods for new Florida residents, but no success was achieved. Judge Paskay explained that in Florida the homestead exemption is "untouchable." The homestead exemption was a constitutional question, and voters would never approve a change. "It's like apple pie and motherhood," he said.[28]

Even so, one way that the most egregious abusers of the system could be reached was through the bankruptcy courts. In 1993 the Florida legislature passed a law that said that if a person sells an asset and uses the proceeds to buy another asset protected under Florida law with the intent to defraud creditors, creditors were entitled to seek to nullify the sale or seek other relief. Even before the passage of this law, in several well-publicized opinions Judges Paskay and Corcoran voided exemptions for those seeking bankruptcy protection on account of fraud. In June 1993, for example, Paskay denied a Winter Haven couple bankruptcy protection, ruling that they made an improper transaction seeking to shield their creditors from collecting on a debt. The deal, Paskay asserted, was made with specific intent to defraud a creditor. The attorney for the creditor hailed Paskay's ruling. "It should be a precedent nationally," he said.[29]

Only months later, in another important ruling in Orlando, Judge Timothy Corcoran denied a Winter Park couple the benefit of the Florida exemption after moving to the state, buying a huge home, and declaring bankruptcy. Corcoran concluded that the couple moved from Wisconsin to Florida as part of a "well-considered and carefully orchestrated series of maneuvers for the purpose of shielding their assets from the reach of their creditors." Corcoran's ruling forced the sale of the home and allowed the couple to keep $40,000 of the proceeds, the amount allowable under

Wisconsin law. Commenting on the importance of Paskay and Corcoran's decisions, Daniel C. Johnson, an Orlando lawyer noted, "These decisions are very noteworthy. . . . Before a lot of people assumed that their Florida homestead would be automatically protected. People can no longer make that assumption—especially people who convert their nonexempt assets to exempt assets."[30]

Meanwhile, by fall 1993, at long last, the Middle District of Florida had four new bankruptcy judges: Jerry A. Funk, Paul Glenn, Karen S. Jennemann, and Arthur B. Briskman. Funk, Glenn, and Jennemann were all Jacksonville lawyers, and most understood that veteran jurist George Proctor was instrumental in their appointment. Indeed, one source noted that area bankruptcy lawyers "deem the selections an honor and a credit to" Proctor.[31] All three attended the same investiture ceremony in Jacksonville on January 13, 1994. On the occasion Karen Jennemann said, "I'm ecstatic. I've wanted to do this for a long time." Funk likewise intoned enthusiastically, "You want to do something to leave your mark in the community. Hopefully, I'll be able to do that."[32] All four were appointed to fourteen-year terms with salaries of $123,000 per year. Not long thereafter it was also announced that Judge C. Timothy Corcoran would move from Orlando to Tampa.[33]

A native of Dalton, Georgia, Jerry A. Funk earned his bachelor's degree from the University of Georgia and his law degree from the Cumberland School of Law in Birmingham. Relocating to Jacksonville, Funk had practiced law there since 1970. Not long after he arrived in Jacksonville, Funk met George Proctor while Proctor was still a workman's compensation judge. Proctor encouraged Funk to get into bankruptcy and then put him on the list of trustees once he became judge. Funk became proficient in the practice and, at Proctor's urging, applied for the opening.[34]

Paul Glenn was born in Thomasville, Georgia, and attended Florida State University, where he starred in basketball. After graduation he entered Duke University School of Law, earning his law degree in 1970. From 1970 to 1981 Glenn was an associate and partner with Mahoney, Hadlow and Adams. In 1985 he became president and CEO of Mobile American Corporation and was an executive in other various insurance companies until joining the Dale and Bald law firm in 1989 as a partner.[35]

At the time of her appointment, Karen Jennemann was a bankruptcy specialist practicing with Mahoney, Hadlow & Criser in Jacksonville. She organized and served as the first president of the Jacksonville Bankruptcy Bar Association. A native of Louisville, Kentucky, she attended Northern

Arizona University and taught special education for three years before entering law school at the College of William & Mary. She lived with her son, Thomas, in Atlantic Beach. She was a skier, scuba diver, and billiard player. Jennemann was assigned to Orlando.[36]

Also assigned to Orlando was Arthur B. Briskman. At the time of his appointment, Briskman was already serving as U.S. Bankruptcy Judge for the Southern District of Alabama. Briskman attended the University of Alabama and Cumberland School of Law, graduating with his law degree in 1972. After serving in various city and municipal judgeships in Mobile and Chickasaw, Alabama, from 1977 to 1985, Briskman moved to Washington, D.C., where he served as counsel for six years to the U.S. Senate Judiciary Committee.[37]

Before Funk, Glenn, Jennemann, and Briskman heard their first cases, and in the midst of the worst period of bankruptcy court overcrowding in the Middle District's history, Judge Paskay presided over one of his most complicated and contentious cases. Walter Industries, a Tampa-based housing and building supplies conglomerate with annual sales of nearly $1.5 billion annually, sought bankruptcy protection in 1989. At that point Kohlberg, Kravis, Roberts, & Co, a leveraged buyout firm, bought the company and over the next two years tried to reorganize its $2 billion debt. Celotex Corp., a former subsidiary of Walter Corp., was also under bankruptcy protection and was facing thousands of lawsuits by people claiming asbestos-related injuries. The plaintiffs sought to recover losses from Walter Industries, even though Walter Industries had sold Celotex in the interim—thus, the plaintiffs sought to "pierce the corporate veil," or establish the liability of the parent corporation for their subsidiary's actions. Paskay would have to decide if the legal shield between the two companies could be pierced. It would be Paskay's duty to sort out the complicated transactions creating subsidiaries and determine the degree to which the Jim Walter Company was liable for the asbestos claims. Bankruptcy lawyer Leonard Gilbert, who represented Kohlberg, Kravis, and Roberts, recalled that the case went on for years and "involved a lot of lawyers. All the bond holders had their lawyers. A lot of the creditors had their lawyers. . . . There was over a billion dollars in claims."[38]

On August 25, 1992, Paskay denied Walter Industries' request for a summary judgment to dismiss the case, setting the stage for a trial. Paskay refused to rule on the issue without hearing testimony. A company spokesman seemed relieved at Paskay's decision to proceed with the trial. "We can't emerge from Chapter 11 (bankruptcy) until this issue reaches finality," he stated. "We've got to have a ruling as to the liability question before we can emerge."[39] Finally, the trial began on December 13.[40] The five-day trial included testimony from 9:00 a.m. to 5:00 p.m. on most days. There were dozens of documents and charts and numerous debates about accounting methods, corporate control, and asset sales. Mountains of papers were submitted. At one pointed Paskay observed, "You've heard that Napoleon said, 'Paperwork will be the downfall of Western Civilization?' Folks we're getting close." Finally, at the end of the proceeding, Judge Paskay noted, "I've been sitting on the bench for 31 years. This is the most complex, interesting, difficult and best-tried case I've ever had. I have never had the pleasure of such professionalism, both from attorneys and from their helpers and assistants."[41]

On April 18, 1994, Judge Paskay issued his ruling in thirty-eight pages: the plaintiffs had failed to prove that Walter was responsible for the Celotex products. Thus, the thousands of asbestos victims were not entitled to seek damages from Walter. "Having considered the entire record," Paskay wrote, "there is no doubt that in the matter under consideration there is a lot of smoke, but not sufficient fire and the proof presented in support of the veil-piercing claim is a slender reed, indeed, upon which to hang a sword with sufficient strength required under law to pierce the corporate veil." Paskay's ruling provided a clear path for Walter to reorganize itself and get out of bankruptcy court.[42] Even so, after the plaintiffs filed an appeal of Paskay's decision, a substantial number of Walter's creditors sought immediate resolution of the asbestos claims, asking Paskay to approve a reorganization plan that included a $525 million settlement to asbestos victims to end future litigation over the issue. Representatives of Walter opposed the creditors' plan on the grounds that Paskay's decision had released them from paying those same claimants.[43]

In October, after months of failed negotiations between Walter and the creditors, the exasperated judge urged the combatants to come to terms. He stated that if he rejected the asbestos settlement, the heart of the creditor's plan, then his remaining choices would result in disaster. "That would mean either dismissal, which would be utter chaos, or Chapter 7 liquidation would be the same." Or he could reject the plan and "start a whole new ballgame. That would also be just as disastrous in my mind," he said.[44]

About that time Paskay called company founder, Jim Walter, and Henry R. Kravis, whose firm controlled the company, into his chambers. As Paskay told an interviewer later, "I told them, I don't want any lawyers here. Now, Mr. Walter, you people have to make some peace with these people because I cannot give you any more leeway. Unless you're able to get a confirmation, I will have to just throw it in litigation and forget about it." Kravis responded to Paskay, "Judge, you ruled in our favor they are not entitled to a dime," to which Paskay responded,

> Listen, Mr. Kravis, that lawyer's fee in that litigation was $10 million bucks, okay? You can spend $100 more million bucks, and ultimately you might win. But ultimately though you win, you are going to be down under, you are finished, just litigating. . . . Dead, dead. So, why don't you talk to these guys. . . . Jim Walter said "Judge these people, the lawyers are killing me to death, please, do something." I said: there is nothing I can do. I tell you, I will give you a few hours, go out and talk to them. It's three o'clock in the afternoon, come back at five o'clock.[45]

Finally at seven o'clock they reached a settlement.[46]

"The deal," as Paskay described it some years later,

> is Henry Kravis and Kohlberg give their shares, eighty percent interest in the corporation. Give these personal injury victims stock in the newly organized corporation. A piece of paper, right? Kravis retained twelve percent. Confirmed. Kravis went back to the guy—like you are a victim and said: "I'll give you three hundred dollars right now, give me your stock." "Oh sure." In six months, they regained control the same that they had before. A very successful . . . stock exchange, you know, did pretty good.[47]

Paskay approved the formal agreement on March 17, 1995. The plan resolved all asbestos-related litigation and settled more than $2.6 billion in creditor claims. Soon, Paskay recalled, the company "came back in the stock market smelling like roses."[48] Paskay considered the successful resolution of the *Walter* case one of his proudest moments as a judge. "Jim Walter, after the case came to me and said: 'Judge, let me shake your hand. . . . You are patient and you did a fantastic job and I appreciate it. It saved a lot of people a lot of grief and a lot of jobs, and I'm sure they appreciate it.' It just makes you feel good, you know."[49]

Problems continued for Celotex Corporation which, like Walter, had also filed for Chapter 11 protection. The corporation faced more than 380,000 asbestos-related claims, with plaintiffs demanding as much $200 million. Judge Thomas Baynes approved a settlement in which an asbestos settlement trust fund was established by the company with funds approaching

$1.5 billion. A board of five independent trustees would be in charge of satisfying all asbestos claims that might be brought in the coming decades. It was also agreed that the board would control current and future settlements with insurers. Judge Ralph Nimmons eventually approved the plan, ending the six-and-half-year case involving hundreds of billions of dollars.[50] The Fifth Circuit Court of Appeals and the U.S. Supreme Court upheld Baynes' Celotex ruling.[51]

Another case that came just after the *Walter* case was the Lykes Brothers Steamboat Shipping Company case. Founded in 1900, the company had deep roots in Tampa and was a division of the famed Lykes family empire. In October 1995 the company filed for Chapter 11 reorganization. At the time Lykes had hundreds of ships en route to various destinations all over the world. It had $201.7 million in debts and $229.7 million in assets and employed nearly three hundred people in Tampa. The case was particularly complex because Lykes had creditors all over the world. Days after filing for Chapter 11 the company's attorneys came to Paskay asking him to issue a global injunction enjoining Lykes' foreign creditors from attempting to seize any of ships that were en route with cargo. Paskay had never done anything of the sort before. "I thought about it, I can't" he remembered, "I can't enforce that, I don't have an army. What are you going to do? No, just give it, that's all right. So they posted my injunction on every ship, with my signature in every language, whether Chinese or what have you. And it worked for a while." The first challenge to Paskay's order came after a "German creditor sold his claim to a Norwegian guy. The Norwegian guy got a writ of attachment and grabbed one of the ships in Antwerp. They came to me and said: 'Help us.' I said, 'I can't, I don't have an army, what am I going to do? I can't help.'"[52] Even so, armed with Paskay's injunction, the company lawyers went to the Belgian court and the judge released the ship.

On May 8, 1996, Paskay turned down a request from a consortium of Lykes creditors, who were owed over $13 million, to convert the case to a Chapter 7 liquidation. The plaintiffs, he stated, "were woefully lacking in any evidence" that the company was incapable of reorganizing itself. The conversion would have instantly collapsed the company that employed nearly 450 people. Paskay's refusal saved the company from disaster. A Lykes official predicted what the result would have been: "Vessels headed to port or staying in port would be seized, cargo will be stranded, truckers will hold on to cargo and containers. Customers will not pay, employees will start quitting."[53] While the immediate disaster was averted, what was necessary was a viable business plan to either get the company out from under bankruptcy or sell assets to a company that could.

After months of negotiations the massive case was resolved with Judge Paskay confirming a reorganization plan in which most of the assets were sold to a Canadian firm. Montreal-based Canadian Pacific Ltd., paid $34 million for Lykes cargo operations, and the company received all Lykes assets except eleven of its ships. With the settlement, the nearly one-hundred-year family interest in the company was over. The money from the sale was distributed among seventeen different classes of creditors. Bankruptcy attorney Harley Riedel expressed satisfaction at the resolution of the case. "It's a good result. Creditors didn't get paid as much as one would have hoped, but it was better than liquidation, by far, for everybody."[54]

Throughout the 1990s Paskay handled a number of other high-profile and extremely complex cases, including Bicoastal Corp-Singer (1995), Eli Witt Co. (1997), and Optical Technologies (1998). In 1999 the nation's foremost bankruptcy expert had decided to retire from full-time status when his current term expired in September. On March 19 at a brief ceremony in his courtroom where he announced his decision, the seventy-six-year-old jurist assured his hearers that he would continue to serve as judge as needed. "If they ask me to sit in Hawaii, I'm sure I would accept that." Harley Riedel of Tampa, who tried many cases before Paskay, spoke for many when he observed, "He's the dean. . . . He's very outspoken in his opinions, and he has ruled against each and every one of us on numerous occasions. And sometimes, in no uncertain terms, he has told us what he's thought of our arguments." Despite his decision not to seek another term, most observers predicted that Paskay would book a full-time case load, and they were correct. (Paskay would actually be appointed to three successive three-year terms.)[55]

Even during what he called, his "hot and heavy days," the period in the late 1980s when he handled up to fourteen thousand cases a year, Paskay managed to score a number of remarkable achievements. He published several books on bankruptcy law that became standards in field.[56] He had advised Congress and the Supreme Court, and had lectured widely across the nation and the world on bankruptcy matters. Paskay intended to continue teaching at Stetson University College of Law, mentoring generations of students as he had since 1974. As of this writing, the school's distinguished "Judge Alexander L. Paskay Seminar on Bankruptcy Law and Practice," in its thirty-eighth year, still flourishes.

Over Paskay's career on the bench, beginning in 1963, the Middle District's bankruptcy calendar grew to become one of the nation's busiest. Paskay began in the paper, typewriter, and law book age. Computers, the Internet, and law databases came next. Finally in 1997 the district was the second in the nation to install video conferencing equipment, enabling lawyers and judges to conduct motion hearings on television screens instead of traveling miles to meet in one room. After the turn of the century, numbers of cases and the stature of its judges continued to rise. In the upcoming years the district's Bankruptcy Court would continue to be on the cutting edge of innovation. That story will be taken up later.[57]

Since its inception in 1962, the Middle District had served as the first point of entry for litigating issues involving the First Amendment (church and state controversies), abortion rights, class action suits for various kinds of discrimination including employment bias, and. finally, the desegregation of the public schools. During the 1990s various Middle District Court courtrooms continued as forums for various constitutional questions that arose throughout the decade. At this point the narrative will turn to the lawyers, judges, plaintiffs, and defendants grappling with these questions.

14

First Amendment, Abortion Rights, Employment
Discrimination, and School Desegregation
Litigation Runs Its Course, 1992–2000

First Amendment Rights

Conflicts over the constitutionality of praying and Bible readings and the
degree to which students, teachers, and administrators could represent
Christianity at graduation ceremonies, athletic contests, and convocations
in public schools continued to reach the courts of the Middle District. The
Supreme Court in *Engel v. Vitale* (1962) banned prayer in public school ex-
ercises. The High Court held that such activities violated the Establishment
Clause of the First Amendment. Yet Florida school districts, especially in
rural areas, chose to ignore the Court's mandates.[1]

Middle District judges, like their counterparts elsewhere, evaluated the
facts of each plaintiff's case and ruled on its constitutionality. Such cases
were always contentious and often drew significant comment in the press.
In September 1990, for example, when a Nassau County elementary school
teacher opened her class each day with Bible readings and said prayers
every day before lunch, one of her student's parents complained to the
principal and then to the school board that the practice violated the First
Amendment to the Constitution. When the board took the matter up, they
voted 5–0 to allow the teacher to continue. The American Civil Liberties
Union brought suit, seeking an injunction to halt the practice. The issue
appeared before Judge John H. Moore in Jacksonville, who ruled in favor
of the ACLU. Moore brushed aside the school board attorney's contention
that the Bible was a book of literature. "Do these stories deal with Jesus?
Is Jesus not a religious figure? Suppose she was reading from the Moonies

book, Hare Krishna book or the Buddha Book?" The judge continued, "Albeit that the defendants may have good motives, the practices violate the Constitution of the United States as interpreted by the Supreme Court."[2]

Many Nassau County residents reacted angrily to Judge Moore's order banning a practice that had been going on for many years in at least six other Nassau County classrooms. Some principals at the schools admitted they knew the daily practice was illegal, but school officials, they explained, had never compelled them to abide by the law. After issuing the new policy banning the practice, the Nassau County School Board heard complaints from many parents urging the county to appeal the decision, but upon discussing the merits of the case with attorneys, the board declined to pursue an appeal.[3]

Yet carefully crafted school board policies did not rule out the discussion of religion as long as the school board, teachers, or its officials were not seen as endorsing or supporting religion. And this was especially the case if public statements or expressions of this nature came from students rather than administrations or faculty. In 1993, for example, Judge William Terrell Hodges ruled in *Adler v. Duval County School Board* that the school board's policy of allowing students to decide the type of graduation speech they would like to hear, and to allow a student-led graduation prayer without faculty review of the speech or prayer, did not violate the First Amendment's Establishment Clause. The week before June 1993 graduation ceremonies Adler and other plaintiffs asked Hodges to issue an injunction barring the student presentations. Hodges denied the request, saying that he did not have enough evidence to determine whether or not the activity was a violation of the First Amendment.[4] When the matter arose again the next year, Hodges again denied the injunction, noting that "the United States Supreme Court has only held state action unconstitutional where it has found excessive entanglement of government and religious institutions. By requiring that graduation messages be voted on by the students and written and presented by a student volunteer, the guidelines effectively exclude institutional entanglement." An ACLU attorney, disappointed at the decision, stated that he "respectfully disagreed" with Hodges' "interpretation of the law" and planned to file an appeal, which he did, but the cause died because the plaintiffs graduated before a decision could be reached.[5]

The issue resurfaced again four years later in Hodges' court under nearly the same circumstances. In that lawsuit, filed only two weeks before the 1998 school year graduation, civil rights attorney William Sheppard represented plaintiffs who would not graduate for several years. Representing the Duval County School Board was former assistant U.S. attorney Ernst Mueller, currently senior deputy general counsel for the City of Jacksonville. Both Sheppard and Mueller favored streamlining the case to move it more speedily toward appeal, as both predicted that because of its national implications, the case could end up in the Supreme Court. Mueller defended school board policy based on the fact that the students were the ones deciding whether there would be a message and who would give it, adding that the free speech rights of the students would be violated if Hodges granted the injunction. Sheppard countered that the plaintiffs were not trying to censure speech, arguing instead, "I'm not comfortable with the district censoring anything. This is about prohibiting prayer." Under the current guidelines, Sheppard added, at graduation the will of the majority would subject the minority to prayer of their choosing. Sheppard sought not only an injunction but monetary damages from his clients, claiming that they had been "ostracized by their peers for taking a stand."[6]

Hodges denied the motion for the injunction and the plaintiffs appealed his decision, but the Eleventh Circuit Court of Appeals did not issue its decision until a few weeks before the next year's graduation. At that point a three-judge panel ruled that Judge Hodges had erred in denying the injunction. The school policy, the panel asserted, was an unconstitutional attempt to circumvent federal law. School board counsel filed a petition requesting that the issue be heard before all twelve members of the appeals court. The petition asserted that the panel contradicted previous decisions of the Supreme Court. The case was important, the petition argued, because "'it presents fundamental constitutional issues of nationwide significance as to whether, and, if so, how public school officials may accommodate the free speech and free exercise of religion rights of graduating seniors without violating' the First Amendment."[7] The Eleventh Circuit Court of Appeals, in an en banc decision, upheld Hodges' 1999 ruling and remanded the case to the district court. The case ultimately went to the Supreme Court, which vacated the appellate decision and sent the case back to the Eleventh Circuit to decide the case again in light of the Supreme Court's ruling in *Santa Fe Independent School District v. Doe* (2000), which banned school prayer at football games. By an 8–4 vote, the appeals court once again upheld Hodges' original decision that the school board did not violate the Establishment Clause of the First Amendment because it retained no control over the content of the student speech. Hodges' ruling stood when the Supreme Court refused to hear an ACLU appeal.[8]

Abortion Rights

Few issues in society and law are more contentious than abortion rights. This is so because the intermixing of religious faith and notions of morality often conflict with what the law defined as the constitutional rights of privacy. Ever since *Roe v. Wade* (1973), abortion rights and right to life advocates have battled one another in the streets, churches, and airwaves. The right to life and the right to choose have no middle ground. Because the issue involves fundamental rights as protected by the Constitution, matters relating to abortion are often adjudicated in the federal courts. Yet under the *Roe v. Wade* ruling, states retain the power to regulate the procedure. Whenever there are disputes, conflicts are litigated in the federal courts. One of the most contentious questions regarding the regulation of abortion has involved parental consent laws.

In 1975 the Fifth Circuit Court of Appeals struck down a parental consent law passed by the Florida legislature in 1973. Another passed in 1979 and was struck down in 1981 by the same court.[9] In 1988 Gov. Bob Martinez signed another consent law requiring judges to decide whether or not the girl was mature enough to make her own decision. Seven days after the law went into effect, Judge John H. Moore stayed the law, saying that his "order would stay in effect . . . until the state Supreme Court issues rules 'it considers necessary relating to the confidentiality of proceedings, anonymity of petitioners and expeditiousness of judicial proceedings.' The order stands, until 'further order of the court.'"[10] Predictably, foes of abortion deplored Moore's ruling, and advocates of abortion rights praised it. William Sheppard, counsel for the plaintiffs, praised the decision, saying, "It means young women of Florida can do what they want with their bodies and exercise their constitutional right to have an abortion."[11] A lawyer for the Florida Catholic Conference countered that he was "very disappointed, because [he] really felt strongly that the law was well-drawn."[12] Politics almost always intruded into abortion questions. Governor Martinez denounced the "liberal" ruling and used the occasion to remind Floridians that this was just one more "reason that we must make certain we elect a conservative president, to make certain that judges we have in the future had a more conservative viewpoint."[13] The governor seemed to be unaware that Moore was a Reagan appointee.

Once the Florida Supreme Court promulgated rules guaranteeing confidentiality, Judge Moore lifted his stay, allowing the law to go into effect. On March 2, 1989, a Jacksonville abortion clinic filed an appeal of Moore's decision, claiming that the new rules did not adequately address petitioners' confidentiality, failed to provide for filing initial petitions, and failed to provide for expeditious resolution of petitions. In *Jacksonville Clergy Consultation Service v. Martinez* (1989) the Eleventh Circuit Court of Appeals upheld Moore's decision.[14]

In 1994 Congress passed the Freedom of Access to Clinic Entrances Act in response to numerous instances in which angry demonstrators had blocked access to citizens seeking abortion services. Section 2 of the act asserted that Congress had the "affirmative power" to "enact this legislation under Section 8 of Article I of the Constitution, as well as under section 5 of the Fourteenth Amendment to the Constitution. It is the purpose of this Act to protect and promote the public safety and health and activities affecting interstate commerce by establishing federal criminal penalties and civil remedies for certain violent, threatening, obstructive and destructive conduct that is intended to injure, intimidate or interfere with persons seeking to obtain or provide reproductive health services."[15] The law included tough federal penalties of fines and jail time for violators. In a recent decision the Supreme Court also ruled that, in conspiracy cases, prosecutors could use federal antiracketeering laws to sue militant protesters and collect damages for clinics. Only two months after President Clinton signed the act into law, a minister in Pensacola shot to death an abortion doctor and his escort. An abortion clinic in Falls Church, Virginia, was firebombed, and similar violent episodes occurred at abortion clinics across the county. In response, Atty. Gen. Janet Reno deployed federal marshals to guard clinics in Texas, Kansas, Mississippi, and Florida. Without specifying details, U.S. Marshal Don Moreland admitted that he had dispatched marshals at various locations to protect clinics.[16]

One of the most controversial figures to appear as a defendant in the Middle District courts during the 1990s was Maryland-born doctor James Scott Pendergraft, who operated many women's clinics in Florida. His first appearance in federal court involved a five-year dispute beginning in 1996 with the City of Orlando over the right to perform second-trimester abortions at his clinic. The City of Orlando had declared that second-trimester abortions violated zoning laws because the recovery time of patients exceeded the time allowed for medical offices and homes as provided by the zoning laws. Pendergraft's lawyer sought an injunction against the enforcement of the zoning law. Judge Patricia Fawsett granted the request, calling the city's behavior "arbitrary and capricious," adding, the Orlando City Council "had reached the decision that it did not want Dr. Pendergraft to open his facility . . . and then searched for a method to deny his applications."[17] Because Pendergraft had been battling the city for seven months, he sought $1 million in damages for lost wages and attorney fees. The city eventually agreed to pay Pendergraft $325,000 in exchange for dropping the suit.[18]

Meanwhile, Pendergraft began opening clinics in other cities, and two years later he filed suit again in federal court against the City of Ocala, the Ocala Police Department, and the Marion County Sheriff's Office, claiming that his rights for equal protection of the law under the Fourteenth Amendment were being violated when they refused to guard his Ocala abortion clinic. Pendergraft's lawyers also sued a minister and several other protesters he said were harassing clinic personnel and patients. But Pendergraft's suit soon began to fall apart when his lawyer failed to respond to motions filed by his adversaries.[19]

Soon the government turned the tables on Pendergraft. Within a year he and his lawyer, Michael Spielvogel, were indicted for conspiring to extort millions of dollars from Marion County government by making false and fraudulent statements in the previously mentioned civil lawsuit. They had attempted, the charges asserted, to shake down the county, and force the county to pay them not to open an abortion clinic. The indictment also alleged that the FBI had secretly filmed a meeting between Pendergraft's lawyer, a city commissioner, and the county attorney in which the lawyer threatened to bankrupt the county by suing it for $100 million. As well as extortion, the indictment also charged the doctor and his lawyer with lying under oath, mail fraud, and making false statements to the FBI.

Judge Hodges presided over the trial in Ocala, which began on January 1, 2001. Pro–abortion rights picketers paraded in front of the courthouse and pro-life picketers paraded in front of Pendergraft's clinic two blocks away.[20] As the trial proceeded, attorneys sparred over the admissibility of the tapes and letters that passed between Pendergraft's lawyer and county officials. Pendergraft's attorney charged that his client was being persecuted because he was offering abortion services to the poor. Assistant U.S. Attorney Mark Devereaux charged that the case was not about abortion but about two men trying to extort money from the City of Ocala and Marion County. Throughout the trial Hodges continued to assert that the trial did not involve the question of abortion. In his instructions to the jury, Hodges declared that while the jurors could consider how the issue influenced the witnesses' behavior, abortion itself was not at issue in the case. "There is no issue in this case [about] whether abortions are right or wrong and you should not be influenced by your own feelings about abortion, whatever your view might be."[21]

On February 1, 2001, the jury returned a verdict of guilty on all five counts. Both men were released without bail. Dr. Pendergraft announced that he was "disappointed in the justice system as far as saying I'm guilty. But I will continue to fight that, and in the interim I will take care of women in their most difficult time."[22] He vowed to keep his two clinics in Orlando and three others in the state open despite the verdict. Pendergraft was sentenced to forty-two months in prison but remained free on bail pending appeal, although he did go to prison for several months before the Eleventh Circuit Court of Appeals overturned all but one of his convictions. The court remanded the single conviction back to the court. In subsequent litigation Pendergraft pled guilty to one count of accessory after the fact and another count of making a false statement.[23]

Employment Discrimination

In the 1990s numerous employees filed employment discrimination lawsuits, and federal judges in the Middle District considered motions to certify them as class actions. After Judge Henry Lee Adams certified a class action sexual bias lawsuit against Publix Super Markets in March 1996, an attorney for employees of Albertsons grocery stores requested that Judge Ralph Nimmons likewise certify their suit as a class action. Both suits alleged that the grocery stores had systematically bypassed female employees for promotions because of their sex.[24] Meanwhile, the Winn-Dixie grocery chain also was being sued by female and African American employees for discrimination. Court documents contained allegations that the company had denied minorities promotions and that "racial and sexual jokes were tolerated. Some who repeatedly complained about rude and insensitive behavior were reprimanded. A few were fired. Some who sued were then assigned the least favorite shifts and fewer hours. One plaintiff said her boss tried to 'sabotage' her job by shorting the cash in her register."[25] In July 1999 Winn-Dixie's lawyers and the plaintiff's lawyers reached a settlement of $33.5 million for up to fifty thousand employees who could join the class action as claimants. Winn-Dixie, though agreeing to the settlement, steadfastly denied the allegations.[26]

In 1995 St. Petersburg bakery worker Deborah Crutcher was one of twelve women who filed suit in the Middle District against Publix Super Markets for sexual discrimination, claiming that women had been denied promotion on account of their sex. Publix, they claimed, had denied women the opportunity for advancement and steered them into low-paying, dead-end jobs. The Equal Employment Opportunity Commission (EEOC) also filed a motion to join the suit on the plaintiffs' behalf. The EEOC had interviewed hundreds of employees and obtained other documents showing that 98 percent of Publix store managers were men. One EEOC official called the Publix suit the "biggest sexual discrimination case that the EEOC has ever been involved in in the state of Florida . . . and it has the potential for being the biggest . . . nationwide."[27] This was especially so once Adams certified the case as a class action because it could affect between 45,000 and 150,000 women employees. Adams eventually allowed the EEOC to enter the suit, but only on behalf of the twelve plaintiffs, not as a class action.[28]

Publix countered that the suit was brought on by the United Food and Commercial Workers Union in an attempt to retaliate against and discredit the company when non-union Publix challenged grocery stores in Atlanta who were unionized. According to a company spokesperson, the Publix defense team intended to "show how strong the relations are between the plaintiffs' lawyers and the union." Defense counsel asserted that the union had "influenced and controlled the selection of the women's legal team," and "therefore, cannot fairly represent thousands of woman as a class." The plaintiffs' lawyers denied the charges, asserting that the union had nothing to do with the lawsuit.[29] Adams seemed to agree, finding that "the court has not been presented with evidence demonstrating that the UFCW has any agreement with plaintiffs or their counsel concerning the funding, or conduct of this litigation. At this preliminary stage," Adams continued, "Publix's own practices cause the court to discount the 'self-selection' argument. Publix does not post job openings. Instead it relies on the 'tap on the shoulder' system in which managers subjectively determine which of their employees should be chosen for the position."[30] In his ruling Adams also stipulated that any woman employed by Publix had the right not to participate in the class or testify in favor of Publix. Finally, the judge hastened to add that if the case made it to trial, it would be a jury and not a judge that would decide the case. Thus, his decision to certify the case as a class "should not be viewed as a prediction that [the] plaintiffs will ultimately prevail on the merits of the action."[31] Even so, Judge Adams' ruling meant that more than one hundred thousand women in Florida, Georgia, and South Carolina could be included in the suit. Adams ordered both sides to mediate the question but, if they could not settle, the trial would begin in the summer of 1997.

As the suit dragged on, many Publix employees rallied behind their company, and the company launched a publicity campaign to counter the charges. On January 26 many demonstrators congregated outside the courthouse in support of Publix. "I'm here because I'm part owner in this company," one woman employee announced. "And I think this case has no foundation at all."[32] But the woman's claims were countered by one Orlando woman employee who joined the others in the law suit, claiming she was "pushed to the limit and I knew that, if I didn't do something, I would probably lose my job." Her former boss had charged she was a trouble-maker for complaining about discrimination. "Not wanting to lose everything and start over again, I fought back," she said.[33]

Throughout the summer little progress was made in mediation. In November 1996 Adams denied the defense's motion to reconsider his class action certification, and the trial date was moved back to November of the next year.[34] Finally, in January 1997, a settlement was reached. Though it denied that it "engaged in any policy, pattern or practice of unlawful gender discrimination," the company agreed to pay $81.5 million to settle the case.[35] Under the agreement worked out between the company, the EEOC, and the attorneys for the plaintiffs, the plaintiffs would share $63.5 million and the plaintiff's attorneys would receive $18 million in fees. Contained in the 120-page settlement agreement was a new system that guaranteed women the opportunity to move into positions they were qualified for. The settlement agreement was also written in the form of a court order that Judge Adams and a magistrate would monitor and enforce for the next five to seven years. Even though Publix CEO Howard Jenkins had consistently asserted that he favored taking the case to trial, he and the board relented. "Through the process of mediation," he explained, "we realized we could agree on quite a few things."[36] On May 23, when Adams agreed to the settlement, which involved periodic hearings to ensure compliance, he declared, "I will not hesitate to bring this case to trial in two, three or four years" if the company did not comply with the settlement.[37] Years later, Adams expressed satisfaction at his role in the settlement. "I think within ten months I was at a new Publix in Georgia and this picture of this woman manager was up there and it makes you feel good and you find them all over the place."[38]

No sooner had Publix agreed to a settlement in its sex discrimination lawsuit than another lawsuit was filed in federal court against the company charging it with racial bias in hiring and promoting African Americans. In support of the suit was the National Baptist Convention, an African

American church organization with over 8 million members. Publix denied the allegations and asserted that it had worked with the Southern Christian Leadership Conference and other organizations in advancing African Americans into management positions.[39] As the case was filed once again in Tampa, there was a one-in-five chance that Adams would hear the case. Judge Adams again won the lottery. When Publix spokeswoman Jennifer Bush learned that Adams, who had made some unfavorable rulings against Publix in the previous case, would again hear the case, she stated, "We respect Judge Adams and we will respect his decisions."[40] On June 16, 1998, U.S. Magistrate Thomas McCoun, in a forty-two page ruling, recommended that Adams certify the case as a class action, and the judge eventually approved the recommendation on March 23, 1999.[41] Talks dragged on for almost a year and a half until finally the parties reached a negotiated settlement on December 29, 2000. Publix agreed to settle the class action racial discrimination case for $10 million. Publix admitted no wrongdoing in the case. Instead a Publix spokesperson announced that the "settlement really builds on what we already put in place to settle the earlier discrimination case."[42]

In 1995 another large corporation defended itself in the Middle District Court of Florida on charges that it had discriminated against its employees on account of age. More than 117 former employees sued Florida Progress Corporation after they were laid off under a redeployment program. The plaintiffs alleged that they and other employees over forty years of age had been systematically laid off to reduce the company's retirement and health benefit payments. The question of class action status turned largely on whether or not the principle of "disparate impact" could be used in the case—that is, whether a disproportionally large number of older employees were laid off during the 1992–96 reorganizations. Judge Hodges certified the suit as a class action but changed his mind after subsequent objections by lawyers for Florida Progress. The plaintiffs appealed the ruling to the Eleventh Circuit Court of Appeals, which upheld Hodges's ruling. The plaintiffs received the rare opportunity to have their case heard before the Supreme Court only to have the case dismissed after oral arguments. Back in Ocala, after the first successful suit, Hodges suggested that the parties settle the pending suits. Settlements were eventually reached.[43]

Desegregation (1990s to the Present)

Most academic studies note that school integration peaked in 1988 when about 43 percent of black students attended white majority schools. A series of Supreme Court cases from 1991 to 1995 had the effect of reversing this trend to the extent that Gary Orfield, cofounder of the Civil Rights Project at UCLA, noted in 2008, "Every year since 1990 schools have become more segregated. We are back to where we were in the late 1960s."[44] The following three Supreme Court decisions seemed to represent a retreat on segregation.

Dowell v. Oklahoma City Board of Education (1991) allowed school districts to end court-ordered integration efforts if they had done everything to end past discrimination over a reasonable period of time and if they had been "ruled unitary by a federal court." In this instance, the court affirmed the right of the Oklahoma City Board of Education to subsequently vote to "return to segregated neighborhood schools. The Court held that 'unitary status' released the district from its obligation to maintain desegregation." The ruling, in effect, "makes it easier for school systems to be released from court supervision."[45] In *Freeman v. Pitts* (1992), the court held that "school districts can be released from certain aspects of court supervision, even if other racial disparities continued to exist" and "even if integration had not been achieved in all the specific areas outlined in the *Green* decision." Then, in *Missouri v. Jenkins* (1995), the Supreme Court ruled that "some racial disparities are beyond the authority of federal courts to address, reaffirming the court's desire to return control of schools to local authorities." The ruling also stated the "Millikan II equalization remedies should be limited in time and extent and that school districts need not show any actual correction of the education harms of segregation. The Court defined rapid restoration of local control as the primary goal in desegregation cases."[46] Finally, in *Parents Involved in Community Schools v. Seattle School District No. 1* (2007), the Court ruled that "districts can take voluntary steps to promote diversity and avoid racial isolation in schools, but places limits on the use of race to achieve those goals."[47]

Citing the results of these four cases as evidence of retreat of the goals of *Brown*, a 2003 report on the status of school desegregation noted that "many of the nation's decisions in the courts have changed from being on the leading edge of desegregation activity to being its greatest obstacle. Since the Supreme Court changed desegregation law in three major decisions between 1991 and 1995, the momentum of desegregation for black students has clearly reversed in the South, where the movement had by far its greatest success."[48]

Middle District judges continued to hear petitions, motions, and pleadings relevant to various county schools that remained under their supervision. Their decisions, as they always had been before, were guided in large part from their interpretation of various appeals court and Supreme Court decisions. As of 1990 Duval, Hillsborough, Marion, Lee, Polk, Pinellas, and Orange counties were still under court supervision. Various rulings by Middle District judges pushed these counties closer and closer toward unitary status.

In 1992, when a Hillsborough County parent group filed a petition in state court challenging busing for desegregation purposes, Judge Elizabeth Kovachevich "'permanently enjoined' the lawyers and the circuit judge involved in the case from proceeding or 'interfering with the jurisdiction of this (federal court).'"[49] When given the opportunity, the parents voiced their frustrations with busing to Judge Kovachevich in August 1993. "Why can't everyone, white or black, go to their neighborhood schools in their younger years?" one woman asked. "Why are they sending my kids way down there? There are several schools nearby." Judge Kovachevich admitted that the woman's points had been raised by a succession of parents. "The reason that all of you are here today occurred about 40 years ago," the judge explained.[50] But she also admitted that until the goals of the *Brown* decision were achieved, the battles over desegregation would continue, and she ultimately refused to alter the busing plan the petitioners complained of.

One year later Warren Dawson of the NAACP Legal Defense Fund and an attorney for plaintiffs complained that the school district had failed to comply with the twenty-three-year-old court order by allowing several schools to become "racially identifiable" and "re-segregated." During the hearing a school board official admitted that some schools had drifted back toward majority black schools, but that was because of shifting neighborhood and housing patterns, and it was not the responsibility of the school to address these changes. In fact, the official even cited a conversation that he had had with Judge Krentzman several years earlier that the judge had assured school officials that they need not address the problem. As the official explained to U.S. Magistrate Judge Elizabeth Jenkins, one day during a hearing Judge Ben Krentzman asked the official why a couple of schools that had once been desegregated had growing percentages of black students. The now retired school official said they had not done anything but that the neighborhood had changed, to which the judge said, "If you haven't changed anything . . . then just let it alone."[51]

In November 1994 U.S. Magistrate Judge Elizabeth Jenkins ordered the plaintiffs and the school board into mediation. But the mediation went nowhere. At a hearing seven months later, the school board official once again invoked Judge Krentzman's statement to the school board official as the reason why they had not moved children around. And the policy had been continued. As the current official noted, "I was indoctrinated with that: the judge said leave it alone," he said. Warren Dawson hotly contested those facts. He told Judge Jenkins that he was "shocked, surprised and frankly, I don't believe that happened." Such a conversation would have been improper and Judge Jenkins interrupted him saying, "Judge Krentzman has served in this court with honor and distinction and he gave a substantial part of his life as a judge to this case, to monitoring this case." Krentzman oversaw the monitoring himself. "Whatever was done was done with the sincere objective of achieving compliance with his court order."[52] In line with recent Supreme Court decisions, Judge Jenkins in a report and recommendation to Judge Kovachevich, decided that Hillsborough County was not in violation of the 1971 court order (even though some of its schools had populations of up to 90 percent black), as long as the racial imbalances were caused by demographics and not by action of the school district.[53]

In November Kovachevich stated, "Today the Court notes that the case is approaching four decades on the active docket, and . . . supervision . . . may well extend into the next millennium. It is this Court's express intention to avoid such a result."[54] Thus, Kovachevich issued an order calling both sides to come together within thirty days to schedule hearings to determine whether the Hillsborough County schools have achieved "unitary status." Kovachevich sent the case back to Jenkins who issued a ninety-page report in August 1997 recommending to the judge that the court order be lifted and that government supervision be ended. Jenkins stated that while there were some resegregating circumstances in some schools, the cause was the "result of demographic changes in the community." Jenkins asserted that the "district had eliminated segregation to the extent practicable in the areas of student assignment, faculty, transportation, extra-curricular activities and quality of education."[55]

Then, on October 26, 1998, Kovachevich dropped a bombshell. In a 110-page order, the judge rejected Jenkins's recommendation, saying that the county had not been aggressive enough to address segregation. Though she said the county had a "short road to travel," they were not there yet. "While the Court finds that the racial imbalances in the schools are not the result of a deliberate attempt by the school officials to fix or alter demographic patterns to affect the racial composition of the schools, officials' apathy over the years demonstrates a lack of good faith compliance. . . . Officials failed to fully discharge their affirmative duty to desegregate the school system." Because the "School Board unilaterally determined that they were not responsible for the racial balances," they decided "there was no need to take affirmative steps." Judge Kovachevich also recognized that the "unfortunate" and "inappropriate" off-the-record comments that Judge Krenzman had given the school officials might have contributed to the school board's apathetic attitude. Finally, she admonished the school board to work more closely and share information with the NAACP Legal Defense Fund and other interested parties so that they could make their own independent analysis and make their own recommendations.[56] Kovachevich's ruling raised many eyebrows, including Harvard professor Gary Orfield. "Most Judges do a very superficial job looking at the statements because they want to get rid of the cases," he said. "This was obviously not the case here."[57]

Many of the Hillsborough County School Board members were stunned over many of the elements in Judge Kovachevich's order. They asked for clarification and guidance from the court. In a thirteen-page order, the judge "lashed out at the board for focusing too much on hurt feelings and not enough on its failings over the year to ensure a unified school system."[58] Kovachevich asserted that it was not the court's purpose to prescribe to the board specific solutions but warned the board that if it was unable to achieve results that the court would hire its own experts at the school system's expense. The school superintendent assured the judge that would not be necessary. Desegregation "has always been our goal and will continue to be our goal," the official assured the judge.[59] Over the next couple of years the school board actively pursued input from parents groups, the NAACP, and other interested parties. They also sent delegations to neighboring counties struggling with the same challenges.[60]

Throughout the summer and fall of 1999, school and community leaders aired and received input on a desegregation plan they intended to submit to Kovachevich. Simultaneously, they pursued an appeal of Kovachevich's order before the Eleventh Circuit Court of Appeals. They submitted the plan in December 2000, and then suddenly, on March 19, 2001, as Kovachevich was considering the new plan, the appeals court reversed Kovachevich's 1998 ruling, saying that it was "tainted and infected by reliance on an incorrect legal standard."[61] The district, the appeals court ruled, "no longer needs busing, race ratios, or federal supervision for desegregation. . . . We hold that the Appellants have achieved unitary status. We reverse and remand for the district court to enter judgment in accordance with this opinion, declaring the Hillsborough County school system to be unitary."[62] Even though they were no longer bound to do so, the Hillsborough County School Board officials declared they would abide by the plan they submitted to Kovachevich. The NAACP Legal Defense Fund appealed the ruling to the Supreme Court, but it refused to hear the case, once and for all ending the litigation.[63]

Judge Steven D. Merryday inherited Judge Joseph Lieb's 1965 court-ordered Pinellas County desegregation plan from Judge Hodges. In 1998, in a hearing to approve a magnet school proposal, Merryday admonished school board officials to begin working decisively toward a plan to end court oversight. "My polite but firm and respectful message to the school board is it will be done . . . this year," he bluntly told the superintendent. After the hearing Merryday told the superintendent and others, "I was trying to help" the superintendent "with his school board and kick the old mule down the road a bit."[64] The effect of Merryday's message was to order the school board to work with the NAACP Legal Defense Fund to work out an agreement, which they did by December. Finding the agreement too vague, Merryday appointed a mediator to push the parties to a more concrete agreement. Both parties agreed to the settlement, and Merryday declared that the county had achieved unitary status on August 10, 2000.[65] Elsewhere, Merryday granted Polk County unitary status in 2000. He essentially did the same for Lee County in August 1996.[66]

In Duval County, officials also struggled to have the court supervision lifted. Though they finally succeeded in 2001, the path was not easy. In January 1996 conflicts between the warring parties seemed so intractable that a new lengthy trial seemed a certainty until Judge Hodges ordered twenty school board members and NAACP officials into mediation before Judge Harvey Schlesinger. Hodges had inherited the decades-old case from Judge John H. Moore, whose order to cease busing had been overturned in 1988. The Duval County public schools were operating under a desegregation agreement between the school board and the NAACP signed in 1990 in which the school was forced to create magnet educational programs designed to draw whites into inner-city schools, but since that time numerous disputes had occurred. In 1994 negotiations had broken down.[67]

When the mediation sessions began on January 29, 1996, one of the most contested issues involved school overcrowding in the suburbs. The school board wanted to build more schools, even though schools in the inner city were not fully occupied. Building those schools, the NAACP argued, would violate a 1990 agreement that pledged to keep elementary schools at least 20 percent black.[68] Judge Schlesinger asked the school board to postpone the vote on the building measure. Talks continued throughout February and into March when finally an agreement was reached. Under the pact the basic elements of the 1990 agreement remained intact but both sides got something: The school board was able to build eight new schools to relieve suburban overcrowding, and the NAACP received assurances that no predominantly black schools would close and that millions of dollars would be poured into inner-city schools to attract white pupils.[69] But when the school board met and voted to alter the plan, NAACP lawyers blasted the move and said revisions would undermine the agreement. "The changes are totally unacceptable," stated NAACP attorney Michael Sussman, who had been a primary negotiator in the agreement.[70] At that point Judge Schlesinger called Sussman and the school board attorney back together, and they were able to agree on new language in the agreement that would satisfy both sides.[71] Still, the plan appeared in jeopardy because, while the national NAACP offices accepted the plan, the local NAACP branch opposed it. Then, in August, negotiations resumed in Washington between Sussman, school board attorney Ernst Mueller, NAACP general counsel Dennis Hayes, and Maree Sneed, a Washington attorney and consultant for the board, but the efforts to revive the plan were unsuccessful.[72]

The month before, also in Washington, Chief Justice William Rehnquist conferred a distinct honor on the presiding judge of the Duval segregation case when he named Hodges chair of the executive committee of the Judicial Conference of the United States. Along with his usual judicial duties, the twenty-year veteran would now assume leadership of the chief policymaking body of the federal courts. The appointment made him the second-ranking federal court official behind Rehnquist. The Conference met twice a year. It approved the judiciary's annual financial plans and advised Congress on new laws and how they affected the courts. It also set federal court policy on such matters as sentencing guidelines and cameras in the courtroom.

Back in Jacksonville, with the negotiations stalled, the school board returned to court and asked that the district be granted unitary status. In October school board lawyers filed a motion in Judge Hodges' court to that effect, but the NAACP hotly contested the school board's contention that it had fully desegregated and should be relieved of oversight. In April 1997 Michael Sussman and Ernst Mueller were back in court in front of Judge Hodges. Sussman wanted Hodges to block school construction, asserting that once the schools were built in predominantly white neighborhoods, there would be no incentive for white students to leave their neighborhoods. Mueller countered that the new schools would open racially balanced. "The notion that these schools are intended just for white people is just dead wrong," he said.[73] Hodges refused to block the construction plan because the NAACP failed to prove it would cause irreparable harm to the students.[74]

The nonjury trial before Hodges began on August 18. On that day, in opening arguments, Duval County School Board attorney Ernst Mueller announced, "The evidence will show the district, in good faith, has done what was required and more."[75] Sussman countered that time and again school officials, when given the chance to adopt policies to assure compliance, did not do so because they were "perceived as politically unpopular and unsafe for elected officials. Increased, not diminished, court supervision is required if . . . desegregation is ever to be achieved in Duval County."[76] Much of the trial testimony centered on the efficacy of the use of magnet schools and their ability to attract white students to inner-city schools to enhance integration, but the reality of the situation was that most parents, white or black, chose neighborhood schools, and the result was tilted toward resegregation because of housing patterns. But the school board introduced a demographic study to show that more and more blacks were moving to the suburbs, and thus the new schools would include African American pupils as well as whites.[77]

Finally, on May 27, 1999, Hodges dismissed the thirty-nine-year-old case, ruling in a 140-page opinion that the Duval County public schools were being run without racial discrimination "to the maximum extent possible." While the school board had not reached many of the goals it had set, Hodges asserted that students are treated equally "in all respects" regardless of race.[78] Hodges cited the magnet school program and the presence of African Americans in the district's power structure as "an important factor to a finding of good faith on the part of the board" and a "factor that can be expected to help prevent regression to a dual system. . . . The board has simply not contributed to or perpetuated the current imbalance [in certain schools] in any way. . . . To the contrary, the board has made enormous efforts to counter the effects of past discrimination."[79] Hodges added, "The NAACP has failed to present any persuasive evidence demonstrating that such racial imbalance existing at any elementary, middle and senior high schools is the result of anything other than racial isolation in housing patterns and the continued existence of 'white flight' in Duval County."[80] The NAACP appealed the case, arguing that the school board had yet to meet the goals of the 1990 desegregation agreement reached by both parties and endorsed by the court, but the Eleventh Circuit Court of Appeals affirmed Hodges' ruling on November 19, 2001.[81]

In 2004 Judge Schlesinger began hearing appeals from the Marion County superintendent and school board to release it from court supervision. That year, after a week-long trial, Schlesinger issued a modified decree instead of dismissing the suit.[82] Schlesinger heard testimony regarding the 1978 court order for three more years from school officials, U.S. Justice officials, and various national experts. Each time Schlesinger admonished the school board to address certain issues, until finally on January 15, 2007, the judge granted Marion County unitary status, thus ending the twenty-eight-year-old segregation lawsuit.[83]

Orange County had the longest-standing desegregation court order in the Middle District of Florida. In 2008 school board attorneys and the NAACP Legal Defense Fund renewed negotiations to end the case. Both parties worked out a plan, but while Judge Anne Conway rejected their plan, she eventually decided that the district had met the requirements to have the case dismissed. Finally, on August 2, 2010, by declaring the Orange County System unitary, Conway put an end to the case that had begun in 1962. "The School Board is now entitled to reclaim full control over its affairs. The duty now falls upon the political system to ensure that the discrimination which triggered this action does not once again percolate."[84]

The shifting social conditions and attitudes among Floridians and other Americans regarding the wisdom of court-ordered desegregation seemed light years away in 2012 from what they had been fifty years earlier when the Middle District of Florida was created. Some African Americans saw integration as a dismantling of black communities because with it came the closing of many inner-city schools. In 2008 one African American woman from Orlando asked the question: "Was it worth it? Not for me. We lost community. Segregation had to end. But the decline of the community didn't have to come with it."[85] There was a growing sense among some elements in the African American community that integration at any price was no longer worth the cost. In 2008 Evelyn Ellis Snipes, in whose name the original desegregation case in Orange County was filed in 1962, questioned the wisdom of school desegregation at all costs. "I'm not sure what we did was the right thing. My father is probably rolling over in his grave to hear that. I am a proponent of neighborhood schools. I'm as opposed to school busing as my father was in favor of it."[86]

15

Drugs, Outlaws, Fraud, Pollution, Endangered
Species, and a Baby Named Sabrina

Drugs

On September 1, 1992, U.S. District Judge G. Kendall Sharp flew into a rage
when he learned that the Eleventh Circuit Court of Appeals reversed his
decision to dismiss a drug case from his court. The appellate court had ruled
that Sharp had erred when he dismissed the case on the grounds that the
defendant should have been prosecuted in state rather than federal court.
"I think it sucks—and you can quote me on that," Sharp told a reporter.
"They might as well shut down the state courts. Just like big brother, the
government wants us to do everything. The only reason they do is because
of the breakdown of the state prison system. Everyone knows that." Sharp
had dismissed the case because it did not involve large-scale distribution or
smuggling and thus was not of the magnitude to take up time in the federal
courts. Yet, because the new federal statutes allowed drug prosecutions in
federal courts, state authorities were increasingly turning to federal courts
because state prisons were overcrowded and because of harsher penalties
and greater conviction rates in the federal courts.[1]

If Sharp was one of the most outspoken judges who voiced frustration
at the growing number of "piddly" state criminal cases transferred to an
already clogged federal court system, he was not the only one.[2] Throughout
the 1990s federal judges chaffed at the added burden placed on the federal
courts because Congress saw fit to pass tougher and tougher federal sanctions against drug dealers. In addition, the DEA, FBI, U.S. Customs, and
other federal agencies had more effective tools to go after criminals—all of
which led to more and more prosecutions of crimes that traditionally had
been reserved for the state courts. If violent criminals and drug dealers

were targeted by federal laws, so were deadbeat dads. Despite the opposition of the Judicial Conference of the United States, in 1992 Congress passed the Child Support Recovery Act, which gave federal prosecutors the ability to prosecute deadbeat parents who crossed state lines. Even as court challenges of the law's constitutionality went forward, Atty. Gen. Janet Reno in 1996 declared the law's enforcement a top priority.[3]

One of the most vocal critics of the trend toward federalizing crimes was Chief Justice William Rehnquist. In his 1998 report on the state of the federal courts, Rehnquist noted that the

> trend to federalize crimes that traditionally have been handled in state courts not only is taxing the Judiciary's resources and affecting its budget needs, but it also threatens to change entirely the nature of our federal system. The pressure in Congress to appear responsive to every highly publicized societal ill or sensational crime needs to be balanced with an inquiry into whether states are doing an adequate job in these particular areas, and ultimately whether we want most of our legal relationships decided at the national rather than local level. Federal courts were not created to adjudicate local crimes no matter how sensational or heinous the crimes may be. State courts do, can, and should handle such problems. While there certainly are areas in criminal law in which the federal government must act, the vast majority of localized criminal cases should be decided in the state courts which are equipped for such matters.[4]

Rehnquist cited a 15 percent increase in the number of criminal filings in the federal courts. Resources in the federal courts had not kept pace; neither had the number of judges.[5] The needs were particularly acute in the Middle District, which had one of the highest ratios of cases per judge in the nation.

Increasing overcrowding and retirements on the Middle District bench gave President Clinton the opportunity to appoint more judges in his second term. The six district judges that Clinton appointed would have a profound impact on the makeup of the court. Indeed, when added to the three judges that Clinton appointed in his first term, the total of nine gave Clinton the distinction of appointing more Middle District judges than any other president. Before the circumstances of these new appointments are discussed, however, it is now necessary to discuss several important cases during these years in the Middle District that involved drugs, the Outlaw motor cycle gang, fraudulent business practices, environmental pollution, endangered species, and one of the most sensational kidnapping cases in American history.

As they had in the 1980s, Middle District of Florida prosecutors initiated many major drug prosecutions. For more than fourteen years, three drug kingpins known as the "Miami Boys" had distributed drugs from Miami to Jacksonville, the Atlanta area, and other southeastern cities. The first two conspirators, Causey Bryant and Ike Florence, were convicted in 1989 and 1993, respectively. Leading the prosecution of Michael K. Delancy, a third conspirator convicted on November 5, 1999, was Assistant U.S. Attorney James Klindt. On January 31, 2000, Judge Ralph W. Nimmons in Jacksonville sentenced Delancy to life in prison without parole for conspiracy to distribute cocaine, crack cocaine, and heroin.[6]

On November 20, 1996, the *Orlando Sentinel* reported that "drug agents hit the mother lode Tuesday in their efforts to dig out heroin and cocaine dealers involved in the smugglers' pipeline between Puerto Rico and Orlando."[7] Twenty-one search warrants were issued for homes, businesses, and storage warehouses in Orlando, Kissimmee, Fort Myers, and Puerto Rico. After more than 120 police officers made dozens of arrests, U.S. Attorney Charles Wilson announced, "We think this will cripple the ring . . . and make a dent in the heroin-trafficking problem in Central Florida."[8] A grand jury indictment listed Jorge Alicea as a ring leader. Millions of dollars of cash was seized from his home and that of his relatives. Alicea eventually pled guilty to nine federal violations ranging from conspiracy to import cocaine, distribution, and money laundering.[9]

On October 8, 1998, after a ten-month investigation, federal agents arrested "untouchable" west central Florida crack dealer Stephen Bush. For four years authorities were certain that Bush was providing cocaine to dealers in Volusia and Putnam Counties. Drug enforcement personnel arrested him at his Deltona home and confiscated cash, cocaine, guns, and financial records. Bush was eventually convicted in Judge Patricia Fawsett's Orlando courtroom on December 17 for operating a narcotics network for eleven years. When the conviction was announced, Managing Assistant U.S. Attorney Rick Jancha said Bush had five prior felony drug convictions in Florida and expressed delight in the fact the "this will be his last. Mr. Bush said he was untouchable." Jancha continued, "I guess that he's been reached out and touched." Judge Fawsett eventually sentenced Bush to three life sentences to run concurrently.[10]

Numerous drug and other criminal prosecutions launched in the middle 1990s led to the seizure of millions of dollars worth of cash, gems, automobiles, real estate, and other property from criminals. In fact, in 1997 the Middle District of Florida led the nation in dollars and assets forfeited. Overseeing the federal forfeiture program in the district was Assistant U.S. Attorney Virginia Covington, whose office seized over $39 million worth of property in the first nine months of 1997. This total already exceeded the $21 million of the year before. According to Covington, "We take away the reasons they committed that crime in the first place. I think it's very difficult for defendants to part with the assets from their criminal activity. Money motivates most of the crime." Covington worked hand-in-hand with the prosecutors and case agents. She recalled the biggest ever seizure in the district involved over $70 million netted from a deceased Colombian cocaine trafficker. "It was pretty staggering," she said.[11]

Outlaws

Closely connected to the scourge of drugs was the proliferation of gang activity in Florida. In the 1990s Tampa became the scene of numerous prosecutions of Outlaw Motorcycle Club members. Federal prosecutors could reach the Outlaws because their law-breaking often crossed state lines and thus was subject to federal RICO laws.

The Outlaws Club began in Illinois in 1935 as a fraternal brotherhood of motorcycle enthusiasts who shared a love of the open road and the free lifestyle associated with it. By 2000, the Outlaw Club had grown to include chapters in seventeen states, Europe, Canada, and Australia. Not all members broke the law, but as time went on the club became identified with various law-breaking activities that its "counterculture" lifestyle became synonymous with, such as the drug culture and the attendant modes of violence associated with it.

In 1981 Florida prosecutors netted their first conviction of an Outlaw gang that operated an interstate prostitution ring between Tampa and Meridian, Mississippi. The leading defendant in the case was Wilson Tony "Roadblock" Harrell, of Jacksonville, the former Florida chapter president.[12] Harrell was sentenced to five years in prison but was also a defendant in a subsequent trial seven months later involving twelve other conspirators with nicknames like "Harpo," "Quick Carl," "Ahab," and "Louis the Lip." Their lawyers defended the bikers by arguing that their clients were being persecuted for their counterculture way of life. "The government has portrayed nothing but a lifestyle to prejudice you. . . . They don't conform to traditional lifestyles, but they're not on trial for that." Lead prosecutor

Lee Atkinson disagreed. In his closing argument against the defendants, he reminded jurors, "The guilt of these defendants was exemplified and emblazoned on their creed: 'God Forgives; Outlaws Don't.' These are words of terror, words of revenge."[13] All told, Harrell and his codefendants received sentences ranging from twenty to forty years behind bars for various crimes including murder, drug trafficking, extortion, and prostitution.[14]

Even as some Outlaw gang leaders were successfully prosecuted, others arose to take their place. The gang was particularly strong in Florida, and by the middle 1990s it had become an even more sophisticated and threatening menace. According to one commentator, the Outlaws gangs "resembled multinational corporations, albeit one where the income comes from drug dealing and loan sharking. As prosecutors have sent top gang leaders to prison, they are quickly replaced by an established line of successors."[15] One law enforcement officer likened the Outlaws to cancer. "If there are any cells left, it will come back and regenerate." Thus, after a two-and-a-half year investigation by a host of state and federal officials called Operation Shovelhead, a new crop of Outlaw gang members were tried in Judge Susan Bucklew's courtroom from April through August 1995.[16] Twenty members from clubs in Daytona Beach, Tampa, and St. Petersburg were accused of more than fifty individual crimes, including fire bombings, murder, kidnapping, drug running, and weapons violations—all as part of an ongoing criminal enterprise. It was the longest and most extensive Outlaw trial in the United States. It involved unprecedented security problems for the Tampa court. Marshals stood watch on rooftops. Sixteen others were in the courtroom at all times.

As in previous trials, defense counsel defended their clients based on the fact that prosecutors were attacking their lifestyle. They represented their clients as "aging hippies." "They look like a bunch of Willie Nelsons. . . . If anything they should plead guilty to political incorrectness," one of the lawyers stated.[17] According to the defense, the Outlaws' supposed "sex slaves" were willing girlfriends, and the drugs they were accused of trafficking were actually supplied by undercover government agents. Yet the grand jury indictment alleged that the "Outlaw Motorcycle Club is a violent, racist, misogynistic gang that relied on beatings, kidnapping, bombings, and even murder to perpetuate 25 years of criminal enterprise."[18] As if to emphasize the point, in his opening statements in the trial, Stephen Kunz, one of the lead prosecutors asserted, "This is not a bunch of good old boys riding motorcycles with their hair blowing in the wind trying to be different."[19] In the five-month trial, federal prosecutors Kunz and Walter

Furr presented hundreds of tapes containing secretly recorded evidence and over two hundred witnesses. On August 14, with final arguments completed, the jury began its deliberations. Finally, after more than two weeks, the jury reached its verdict: fourteen men were convicted of various crimes while two of the men were cleared of all charges.[20] All received long prison terms. Yet a number of jurors found fault with the government's tactics in the case. One juror stated, "I think the government overstepped its bounds. It really didn't wash with a bunch of us."[21] On the eve of the sentencing, seven jurors even wrote a letter to Judge Bucklew saying they regretted their decision to convict, asking that the defendants get another trial, and asserting that they disagreed with the tactics of law enforcement in entrapping several of the defendants. Another juror disagreed. "I think they had complete knowledge of what they were doing."[22]

No sooner were the fourteen convictions handed down than a grand jury handed down an eighteen-count racketeering indictment on ten other Outlaw members for seven murders, two attempted murders, and six separate conspiracies to murder rival gang members and others. In all, forty-three violent crimes and sixteen drug offenses were included in the fifty-seven-page indictment. U.S. Attorney Charles Wilson announced that the indictments came as a result of cooperation of Outlaw members convicted in the previous year. "We've worked our way up the ladder to the regional bosses and presidents of clubs around Florida. We think this eliminates the Outlaw Club as a significant threat to Florida," he said.[23] Heading the list of those indicted were ex-regional heads Clarence "Smitty" Smith and Wayne Hicks, who eventually pled guilty and promised to testify against the others.[24] Smith's and the others' convictions in the six-week trial gave U.S. Attorney Charles Wilson cause to proclaim that the convictions "shattered . . . this violent gang" in Florida.[25]

Hicks' testimony also led to indictments of other members in numerous states across the country, including one-time Outlaw president Harry "Taco" Bowman of Michigan. Subsequent to his indictment, Bowman had made a dramatic escape even as federal agents broke through his well-defended Outlaw headquarters near Detroit with a tank. Eventually captured in 1999 after two years on the FBI's 10 Most Wanted List, Bowman was brought to Tampa to face the September 1997 indictment for murder, bombing, and drug dealing. Bowman was eventually convicted on eight counts, including conspiracy to commit two murders, racketeering, and various drug charges. Judge James S. Moody Jr. sentenced Bowman to life in prison. Because of Hicks' cooperation with prosecutors, Judge Bucklew reduced his sentence to slightly over twelve years. But Hicks and the other informants understood that, with their cooperation, they were marked men and would need to remain in the government's witness protection program for the rest of their lives. Hicks told Judge Bucklew, "My greatest fear has been the Outlaws' ability to harm my family. . . . Because of my cooperation the threat of danger will never end for me."[26]

Soon, according to one commentator, Tampa became the "epicenter of [national] Outlaw prosecutions because of sweeping cases brought against the gang in the mid-1990s."[27] One more important trial commenced in Tampa in 2003. Once again due to the cooperation of informants, authorities were able to capture and prosecute Bowman's successor, James Lee Wheeler, of Indianapolis. The sixty-one-year-old biker was convicted in 2004, seemingly ending the more than fifteen-year battle between the federal authorities and the Outlaws in the Middle District of Florida.[28]

Fraud Prosecutions

In July 1997 Jay Jarrell, Michael Neeb, Robert Whiteside, and Carl Lynn Dick—mid-level executives with Columbia/HCA—were indicted on charges of Medicare fraud. The defendants were charged with cheating government health care programs of $2.8 million by overbilling for services and then trying to cover up the inflated costs. The work-up for the trial took two years, and the prosecution assembled a sixty-person witness list as well as expert witnesses on handwriting, accounting, and Medicare cost reimbursement. Overruling defense counsel's request for more time to study the documents, Judge Susan Bucklew ordered the parties to be ready for trial on May 3, 1999.[29]

The Tampa case against the four mid-level executives was only part of the biggest health care investigation in U.S. history in terms of scope and money at stake. While billing records at Port Charlotte's Fawcett Memorial Hospital were being scrutinized in the Tampa case, the FBI and the Justice Department had already cited many other hospitals owned and operated by HCA in six states. The corporation was in settlement talks with federal officials. Some speculated that the wrongdoing could result in a fine to the corporation of over $1 billion.[30] The complexity of the Florida case raised many challenges for the twelve jurors. Assistant U.S. Attorney Bob Mosakowski warned jurors about the task ahead. "You are going to learn more about Medicare reimbursements, cost reports, and accounting practices than you ever wanted." Still, he maintained to jurors, the case boiled down to the simple question: Did the defendants file accurate reimbursement reports to the federal government? And when an auditor mistakenly gave a hospital more money than it deserved, did the defendants conspire to keep the government from finding out?[31]

One of the government's chief witnesses in the case was John Schilling, a whistleblower who made hours of recordings of conversations between himself and several of the defendants. The prosecutors and defense attorneys sparred over whether all the tapes could be shared with defendants. Prosecutors maintained that to do so would jeopardize ongoing investigations of other HCA wrongdoing. Judge Susan Bucklew reviewed the tapes and denied the defense's request to review the tapes on the grounds that they were not relevant to the trial. She also cast aside the defense's motion that not sharing the tapes would constitute a mistrial. Defense attorneys attempted to discredit Schilling's testimony on the grounds that he stood to gain financially from the whistleblower lawsuit he filed if the defendants were convicted.[32]

Finally, after nearly two months of testimony and mountains of trial documents, the jury convicted two of the executives, acquitted one, and could not reach a verdict on the fourth. Jay Jarrell and Robert Whiteside were convicted on six counts of conspiracy and fraud. Michael Neeb was acquitted of all charges, and the jury could not reach a verdict on Carl Lynn Dick. "We're pleased. The agencies involved in this put in a tremendous effort and did a tremendous job," noted Assistant U.S. Attorney Bob Mosakowski. The lone acquitted defendant, Mike Neeb, after embracing his wife stated, "I think a great injustice was done today. Two innocent people were found guilty. I pray for them and hope things can be resolved properly."[33] Judge Bucklew sentenced Whiteside to two years in jail and Jarrell to thirty-three months in prison, but she allowed the defendants to remain free while their case was on appeal.

In March 2002 the Eleventh Circuit Court of Appeals reversed the convictions of the two executives, finding that the case against them had not been proven. Tampa Attorney Peter George, who represented Jay Jarrell, asserted that the appellate court recognized that the regulations were too vague to prosecute his client on. "Basically, what the court of appeals is saying is that if prosecutors are going to bring a criminal case based on regulations, the regulations can't be ambiguous, and they must be crystal clear. That's just common sense."[34] Whiteside's attorney, Charles Lembcke, was equally gleeful at his client's acquittal, noting that he "feels vindicated because throughout this entire case he really had a hard time understanding why they went after him. He was always troubled by the fact that he never had any inkling the government was even looking into him."[35] While Whiteside and Jarrell escaped jail, Columbia/HCA eventually paid $1.7 billion in criminal and civil fines to the federal government, the largest health care fraud settlement in U.S. history.[36]

Another fraud case involves William and Chantal McCorkle, who lived the life of the rich and famous, driving luxury cars, cruising around in yachts, flying in private jets, taking vacations at exotic destinations, and living in mansions in Orlando and other locations throughout the world. They had Cayman Island bank accounts stashed with millions gained through a nationwide telemarketing scheme designed to lure customers on the promise of quick riches through buying and selling real estate. The McCorkles' ten companies promised instant wealth to customers who purchased information packages for between $69 and $2,400, which accounted for roughly $5 million to $6 million a month in revenue to the pair. In hundreds of television infomercials that ran from 1994 to 1997, William McCorkle, a rags-to-riches real estate investor from Orlando, and his British-born wife, Chantal, told thousands of viewers that they too could get rich quick if they purchased the packages. But the empire came crashing down on March 6, 1998, when a federal grand jury indicted the McCorkles and two associates in a ninety-count fraud and money-laundering indictment while the couple was in Mexico on vacation. Nearly a year earlier, after the Florida attorney general and U.S. postal inspectors received hundreds of complaints, federal agents raided the McCorkles' offices on Edgewater Drive in Orlando. Meanwhile, federal agents also seized twenty-three bank accounts, nine parcels of real estate, four luxury cars, and roughly $5.3 million in Florida and Cayman bank accounts. On the day of the indictment, Rick Jancha, head of the U.S. Attorney's Office in Orlando, announced, "It was a nationwide telemarketing scheme designed to defraud those who wanted to gain financial independence. And the only ones who got rich were the McCorkles."[37]

The McCorkles were arrested and arraigned immediately after they returned from vacation. The McCorkles' two high-profile defense attorneys were F. Lee Bailey and Mark Horwitz. (Bailey had flown his own plane to Mexico to pick up the couple to face the indictments in Orlando.) The trial began before Judge Patricia Fawsett on September 3.[38] Bailey and Horwitz charged state and federal agents with wrongdoing. It was the seizures and raids, they argued, that damaged the company to the point that it was not able to make refunds or operate in a successful fashion.[39]

Assistant U.S. Attorney Jancha charged that William McCorkle's systematic lying and his deceitful assertions on television had netted him and his wife millions at the expense of defrauded customers who fell for his get-rich-quick schemes. He had concealed a bankruptcy by using an alias and a bogus social security number. Trial testimony also revealed that Bailey had assisted the McCorkles in concealing millions in off-shore bank accounts, and that he controlled a trust fund that once contained $2.1 million set up to pay their attorneys. Finally, after eight weeks and nearly two hundred witnesses, the defense rested on October 28, and the prosecution summed up its case against the McCorkles on November 2.

Two days later a jury found both McCorkles guilty of eighty-two counts of fraud and money laundering. William McCorkle collapsed when he heard the verdict. F. Lee Bailey bolted upright announcing, "My client needs attention." As the defendant was wheeled out of the courtroom, his wife's reaction to her guilty verdicts on all sixty-nine charges was no less dramatic. Chantal McCorkle wept loudly and fell into attorney Mark Horwitz's arms. The next day the jury stripped the McCorkles of nearly all their worldly possessions amounting to approximately $10.6 million. The seizure also included the special fund set aside to pay Bailey and Horwitz.[40] Judge Fawsett sentenced the husband and wife to twenty-five years in prison each. Under sentencing guidelines the McCorkles could have received up to thirty years. Judge Fawsett remarked, "This case is troubling. The Defendants are young. They have no prior records. . . . This is a very stiff sentence and it gives me great pause." Judge Fawsett also added that she would not oppose Chantal McCorkle serving her time in a British prison after her appeals had run out.[41]

Before long McCorkle attorney F. Lee Bailey found himself in legal trouble because he could not account for the money he had deposited on behalf of the McCorkles in the Cayman bank account. Though the account was intended as a legal trust fund, the judgment against the McCorkles ordered the account forfeited to the government. Thus the court determined that the contents of the accounts represented Bailey's clients' ill-gotten gains. "If the court does not enter an order requiring Bailey to remit the sum to the United States," Assistant U.S. Attorney Marie DeMarco argued, "the property may be lost forever." A magistrate ordered Bailey to turn over the money by May 3 or face contempt charges, but the lawyer responded that he had already spent most of the money defending the McCorkles.[42]

May 3 came and went with Bailey still insisting that he would not comply with the order. In a sixty-eight-page report the magistrate blasted Bailey, stating that he had "no right to accept fraudulently obtained and laundered money in payment of a fee. The government has a right to recover all forfeited attorney's fees from Bailey, even the fees that Bailey has spent." The magistrate added that, "having observed Bailey's testimony for many months, this Court had no confidence in its truth. Bailey's testimony about assets and income was evasive, inconsistent, strident, argumentative and lacking in credibility."[43] In her ruling, Fawsett was forced to recognize that while Bailey had wrongly spent much of the money in the fund, the prosecutors could not seize unrelated assets to make up for what was missing. But Bailey was still facing a contempt charge, and she ordered him to post bond to appear in court on August 17, and on that date to provide a full accounting of the money disbursed from the legal fund. Fawsett eventually found Bailey in contempt but did not send him to jail or force him to pay a fine, preferring instead to refer his case to the Florida Bar for discipline. Fawsett recommended that prosecutors sue Bailey civilly for the money. But Assistant U.S. Attorney Virginia Covington told the judge that the "lawyer was so debt-ridden that it was impossible to find any assets traceable to the McCorkle money that weren't tied up in loans." His home, airplane, even his computer were mortgaged. "If we seized these assets," she explained, "it would, in essence, hurt the people of the United States. . . . Our goal is to realize a profit so we have sufficient money available to pay victims."[44] Things went from bad to worse for Bailey. In 2001 the State of Florida disbarred him, and federal prosecutors won a $2 million judgment against him in Judge Anne Conway's courtroom in Orlando. The bill for Bailey, including the judgment and fines, totaled $5 million.[45]

On August 21, 1997, U.S. Attorney Charles Wilson announced that his office had launched an investigation of Rev. Henry J. Lyons, president of the National Baptist Convention U.S.A. (NBC), an African American religious organization with over 8.5 million members. Also being scrutinized was his relationship to convicted embezzler Bernice Edwards, an associate in the organization. Lyons and Edwards had purchased a house in Tierra Verde and other property together using church funds. It was also revealed that a $500,000 mortgage was obtained through the promise of a $4,000 per month rental fee from the convention.[46] The investigation of Lyons gained momentum after Lyons's wife, in a rage over her husband's suspected infidelity, set fire to the Tierra Verde home and was charged with arson. The incident led to the discovery of the Baptist Builders Fund, an off-the-books account from which Lyons and Edwards purchased other property, bought jewelry and cars, and paid utility bills. Even though there seemed to be plenty of evidence of financial wrongdoing, federal prosecutors moved gingerly in their investigation because of the need to protect First Amendment rights. As a former assistant U.S. attorney explained, "The government has to be particularly sensitive with a religious group, because of the constitutional problems."[47]

For twelve months a Tampa federal grand jury scrutinized Lyons' spending patterns and tax returns. Admitting that he had "erred" and "sinned" and had "displayed human weaknesses and human frailties," the embattled Lyons pledged to fight the criminal charges and announced that he would not step down from his leadership post in the church organization.[48] Finally, on July 2, the Tampa grand jury indicted Lyons on fifty-six counts. As the handcuffed Lyons was led into the courtroom to hear the charges against him, U.S. Attorney Charles Wilson addressed the assembled news media gathering outside: "The message . . . we're sending . . . to leaders who hold positions of trust [in] charitable or religious or civil organizations who have access to large sums of money . . . is that [we are going] to hold them accountable for their actions." Edwards, Brenda Harris, and two other associates said to be romantically involved with Lyons were also indicted. Among the charges listed in the indictment against Lyons included wire fraud, bank fraud, mail fraud, tax evasion, extortion, money laundering, and conspiracy. Lyons, the indictment continued, had in effect stolen from banks, corporations, government agencies, and groups dedicated to registering black voters and repairing burned African American churches. As they had throughout the investigation, Lyons and his attorneys insisted that the charges were merely an example of government's assault on prominent black leaders, an accusation that Wilson addressed head on: "I am convinced that the vast majority of black Baptists in this country are sickened and disgusted by the conduct that is alleged in this indictment and they are, in fact, today cheering the return of this indictment."[49]

After Lyons's conviction in state court on February 27 on charges of state racketeering and grand theft charges, Lyons and his attorneys entered into plea negotiations with federal prosecutors. On the day after resigning his presidency of the NBC, and in exchange for a guilty plea on five of the fifty-four counts, the other charges were dropped. The result was that Lyons acknowledged "committing bank fraud, submitting forged documents to the federal government and failing to report $1.3 million in income from his deals with corporations eager to obtain church business."[50] He also forfeited his ill-gotten cash, cars, jewelry, and property. U.S. Attorney Charles Wilson asserted that Lyons "did the right thing." He also challenged the notion that his office had been too lenient on Lyons. "I don't characterize it as too generous. I characterize it as fair. . . . He's pleading to two 30-year felonies, and three five-year felonies," Wilson continued. The agreement was "fair, reasonable, in the best interests of the United States and in the best interests of Rev. Lyons."[51] As Lyons began serving his five-and-a-half-year state sentence, federal officials began pouring over stacks of trial testimony and other data in preparation of their recommendation for Judge Henry Adams's sentencing of Lyons. On June 18 Judge Adams sentenced Lyons to four and a half years in prison, the lightest sentence permissible, to run concurrently with his state conviction.[52]

Prosecuting Polluters and Protecting Endangered Species

On April 22, 1997, at a news conference on the twenty-seventh anniversary of the first Earth Day, U.S. Attorney Charles Wilson announced a number of environmental crime indictments and plea agreements. "We've made environmental crime one of the top priorities of white-collar crime," he said. Wilson promised that he and his prosecutors were pledged to "make sure polluters obey the law and clean up their act."[53] Among the list of six huge environmental cases Wilson referred to was the case against Ocean Chemical Carriers and one of its captains, who admitted under oath that he had given the order to dump over 60,000 gallons of oily waste from his Tampa-bound tanker into the middle of the Atlantic on April 7, 1993. The prosecution came under the Act to Prevent Pollution from Ships (1990). It was the first reported prosecution under the law in history. The company agreed to pay a $50,000 fine, $200,000 in restitution, and publish a public apology in the *Tampa Tribune*.[54]

In another case a Miami company agreed to pay a $50,000 fine for discharging fuel and garbage into the St. Johns River from one of its cargo vessels.[55] With fines and settlement payments totaling nearly $300,000 from these and other prosecutions, Wilson set up an environmental trust fund to restore polluted areas, with the proceeds to be administered by a nonprofit foundation headed by the Jacksonville Community Foundation, the University of Florida College of Law, and the environmental studies program at the New College of the University of South Florida. The program was the first of its kind in the nation established by a U.S. Attorney's Office.[56]

Prosecution of polluters continued. In November 1998 a Mulberry, Florida, company and its general manager were convicted of improperly treating contaminated soil, making false statements to customers, and other crimes. The company was the first in the nation to be prosecuted under enhanced criminal provisions of the Clean Air Act. Judge Susan Bucklew fined Specialty Environmental Corporation $500,000 for numerous violations of the Clean Air Act and mail fraud. Seven months later, after no installments had been paid on the fine, the company president was brought to court to answer why his firm had not begun payment of the fine. Despite periodic fact-finding hearings, it became clear that the fine could never be paid as the company ceased operation and had no assets. Three years after her original ruling, Judge Bucklew was forced to terminate the case.[57]

On August 16, 1999, Gary Benkovitz, who prosecutors described as an "incorrigible and unrepentant polluter for more than an decade, was sentenced to thirteen years in prison" for "releasing more than four million gallons of contaminated water and more than 636,350 pounds of sludge as a result of an industrial drum-washing operation" and letting them into bodies of water leading into Tampa Bay.[58] Benkovitz's company, Bay Drum and Steel Inc., cleaned, reconditioned, and resold fifty-five gallon drums for commercial use. According to Teri Donaldson, assistant U.S. attorney in charge of environmental prosecutions, Benkovitz had "shown a total lack of remorse, and worse than that, he had continued to damage the community."[59] In addition to his jail sentence, Benkovitz was fined $300,000, but an exhaustive FBI search for assets yielded nothing. Thus taxpayers were forced to pay for the cleanup.[60]

While polluters were prosecuted in the Middle District courts, those seeking to protect endangered species from harm also sought recourse in federal court. In July 1995 New Smyrna Beach residents Shirley Reynolds, Rita Alexander, and their attorney, Lesley Blackner, asked Judge Anne Conway to force Volusia County authorities to ban beach driving during the summer nesting season of loggerhead and green turtles. The plaintiffs also asked the judge to order county authorities to impose stringent lighting restrictions along the beach because turtles, both egg-laying females and hatchlings, were often disoriented by the lights. Blackner and her clients had filed suit several weeks earlier, but on July 21 the plaintiffs argued before Conway that an immediate injunction banning cars from Volusia Beaches was justified under the Endangered Species Act. "The hatchlings are starting to emerge right now," Blackner asserted to Conway on July 21. "The turtles are being harmed as we speak."[61] Volusia County attorney countered that the ban was unnecessary, asserting that the county had already been working with the U.S. Fish and Wildlife Service to make the beaches safer for the turtles. Moreover, the move would unjustly curtail a right that had been enjoyed by citizens for over ninety years. Conway took the matter under advisement and promised to rule within a few days.[62]

The day after the hearing, an incident occurred that underscored the dangers of both lights and cars to the tiny creatures. One hundred hatchlings, mistaking streetlights for moonlights and star lights, crawled up a beach ramp onto State Road A1A and were crushed by cars passing by. Only twenty of the one hundred survived. "There were tons of turtles in the road," claimed one restaurant worker who dashed out late that night to save the turtles. "I was frantic."[63] On August 1 Conway banned night driving on the beach during nesting season (May–October) and ordered Volusia County officials to forbid cars in dune areas where turtles typically build nests. The Volusia County manager, Larry Arrington, hailed Conway's ruling as "balanced" and "prudent." "I think it's a great victory for common sense."[64] Predictably, Conway's ruling did not sit well with many property owners, restaurant owners, and merchants along the beach. After County Manager Arrington explained the new rules to the county commissioners, he warned them that "compliance with this order is going to be disruptive. You are going to get phone calls. You are going to get complaints. But we have no choice. . . . There are three things you don't mess with: grizzly bears, lightning, and federal judges." For the time being, the new restrictions would be put in place.[65]

The trial that would determine the future of beach driving was postponed until Volusia County could develop a sea turtle nesting conservation plan. The county had also applied for an "incidental take" permit from the U.S. Fish and Wildlife Service to allow the county a certain number of human-caused turtle deaths on Volusia's beaches. Conway granted a delay so that the plan could be put in place and so that the Wildlife Service would have the time to evaluate the permit. Meanwhile Conway reimposed the regulations for the upcoming nesting season.[66] Throughout the summer the plaintiffs complained that the county was not adequately enforcing the restrictions and asked the judge to issue a total ban on beach driving as a way of protecting turtles before the October trial. In response Conway contradicted the plaintiffs' assertions, adding that Volusia County had "fully complied with the court's Aug. 1 [1995] order," and that the county's efforts in "enforcing its 'zero tolerance' policy (toward violators) were to be commended." Conway also chided the plaintiffs, whose "time," she asserted, "would be better spent in working with the county to educate the public about the damage that violations of the conservation zone cause to the sea turtles and in helping the county to identify the beaches where the most frequent violations occur, in a spirit akin to a neighborhood-watch program."[67]

Finally, after several postponements, Judge Conway dismissed the case in December 1996, ruling that the plaintiff's suit was moot after the U.S. Fish and Wildlife Service approved the requested "incidental take" permit and the county closed off nine miles of its shoreline to beach driving. The plaintiffs appealed because beach lighting was not taken into consideration in the judge's ruling. In a 2–1 ruling, an Eleventh Circuit Court of Appeals panel agreed. It sent the case back to the district court to address the beachfront lighting.[68] As the parties were preparing for a new trial, in December 1998, the Volusia County attorneys filed a petition to the U.S. Supreme Court asking it to invalidate the appeals court ruling, claiming that the ruling encroaches on the authority reserved to local government by the Tenth Amendment, but the High Court refused to hear the case.[69]

With neither side budging, the case dragged on. On numerous occasions Judge Conway granted delays. Finally, the second trial began on May 1, 2000. After days of testimony, Conway on May 18 once again dismissed the plaintiffs' suit, ruling that Volusia County was doing all it could to protect the turtles under the federal Endangered Species Act. This time the plaintiffs decided not to appeal because they concluded that they had succeeded in getting the county to implement new restrictions on lighting and enforce its own regulations. They declared they had accomplished their mission of forcing the county to protect the turtles. "The county had a lighting ordinance as far back as 1989 but there was virtually no enforcement," one of the plaintiffs explained. "They didn't really get serious until last year because they thought the lawsuit would go away." The five-year case came to an end.[70]

Baby Sabrina

On November 21, 1997, Steve and Marlene Aisenberg tucked William (eight), Monica (four), and tiny Sabrina Paige (five months) into bed in their house in Brandon, Florida. When they awoke the next morning, they found the baby's crib empty. Frantic, Marlene Aisenberg called 911 and then ran next door to their neighbors yelling, "My baby's gone, my baby's gone." That afternoon the parents made an emotional plea that aired on the evening news: "This morning someone came into our home and took our baby Sabrina Paige out of her crib and took her out of our home. I'm begging that person to please bring our baby back to us."[71] The Aisenbergs, as was their habit, had left their garage door open that night but no one, not even their German shepherd mix who slept in the house, was awakened. There were no clues at all. As one source noted, there was "no ransom note, no witnesses, no signs of forced entry, no obvious family custody issues."[72] First on the scene that morning was the Hillsborough Sheriff's department. The FBI and Florida Department of Law Enforcement soon followed. Deputies conducted a door-to-door search of the neighborhood and brought in a canine tracking team. They dusted the automobiles in the garage and questioned the neighbors. Suspicion soon fell on the parents themselves.[73] After one particularly lengthy and unpleasant interrogation, the Aisenbergs hired high-profile defense attorney Barry Cohen, who directed them to end their talks with the Hillsborough County Sheriff's Office.[74]

The search for Baby Sabrina continued from Thanksgiving, through Christmas, and into the New Year with no results. On February 4, after the Aisenbergs were subpoenaed before a federal grand jury, Cohen said of the sheriff's department, "They're doing a half-ass job trying to find Sabrina, and spending more time trying to build a case against Marlene and Steve."[75] For the moment, at least, because the kidnapping was not certain to involve the crossing of state lines, the Aisenbergs avoided testifying before the federal grand jury. But this changed a week later after Judge Henry Adams summoned Cohen, the Aisenbergs, and Assistant U.S. Attorney Stephen Kunz into his chambers for a hearing. Forty minutes later Marlene went into the grand jury chamber alone for fifteen minutes. Her husband followed in like fashion. Amid CNN and other national news media broadcasting from the other side of the closed doors, Cohen and the Aisenbergs filed out of the courthouse. Legal experts outside speculated that fifteen minutes was only time enough for both Aisenbergs to plead the Fifth. For now the Aisenbergs were "subjects" and not "targets" of the grand jury.[76] But this would soon change. The previous month, after steadfastly refusing to speak to the press, the Aisenbergs began what could only be called a media tour, appearing on CNN, *Larry King Live*, the *Today Show*, *Dateline NBC*, *Oprah*, the *Geraldo Rivera Show*, and *Good Morning America*. On April 2, 1999, the Baby Sabrina story appeared on the CBS program *Unsolved Mysteries*. The Aisenbergs and the search for "Baby Sabrina" had captured the attention of the entire country.[77]

The search for Baby Sabrina went on throughout the year, and so did the investigation. Amid the sheriff's department's attempt to question the Aisenbergs further regarding the disappearance of their daughter, the couple decided to move to Maryland to get away from the leering gaze of the media. Sheriff Lt. Greg Brown told reporters on May 3, 1999, that he had six full-time detectives on the case and that the Hillsborough County Grand Jury looking into Sabrina's disappearance was still "very active. We have followed up to 1,900 leads and conducted over 6,000 interviews," the lawman said. They had followed leads to every state except Nebraska, as well those in Canada, Costa Rica, Germany, Mexico, the Bahamas, and England. The Aisenbergs, he said, had still "not been ruled out as suspects." Speaking for his clients, Cohen stated that it's "very, very difficult to live in this environment, a constant reminder of the loss of your child," and also "having to deal with some people who stare and some people who make comments that are insensitive. But by and large the people have been very supportive. Steve's got to go where he can make a living too." Cohen and Lt. Brown disagreed about the degree of cooperation the Aisenbergs had provided to the police department. Cohen stated that they had met with detectives for three hours the previous month. Brown countered that "they still have not provided a formal interview, and they have refused spontaneous interviews throughout the investigation."[78]

Little information on the investigation's progress leaked out. Then on September 10, 1999, screeching headlines told the story: "Aisenbergs Arrested," "Baby Sabrina's Parents Indicted." A federal grand jury indicted the Aisenbergs not for murder but for conspiracy and making false statements regarding the disappearance of their daughter. The crux of the indictment rested on secret recordings made at their home that were alleged to evidence a cover-up after Steve Aisenberg had killed the baby while high on cocaine. In the indictment Marlene Aisenberg is quoted as telling her husband on December 23, one month after Sabrina's disappearance: "The baby's dead and buried. . . . It was found dead because you did it," to which Steve Aisenberg responds, "There is nothing I could do about it. We need to discuss the way we can beat the charge."[79] Assistant U.S. Attorney Rachelle DesVaux Bedke told a U.S. magistrate in Greenbelt, Maryland, where the Aisenbergs were living, that the husband had admitted to the crime in the taped recordings: "I wish I hadn't harmed her, it was the cocaine," Bedke quoted Aisenberg as saying. "The evidence has shown, after a long and torturous investigation, that the baby was not kidnapped. . . . The baby is, in fact, dead, and they had some hand in it," Bedke contended.[80] The indictment contained incriminating dialogue between the husband and wife from December 16, 1997, to February 17, 1998 (during which time they discussed the cover-up. Aisenberg attorney Barry Cohen steadfastly defended his clients. "I think the indictment is made up, frankly of a bunch of innocent acts and innocent statements that are taken out of context. There are a lot of half-truths in there. . . . I have every confidence that these people are not responsible for what they've been charged with."[81] When the FBI came to arrest the Aisenbergs at their Bethesda home, Marlene refused them entry, but the agents forced the door open. They were brought before the magistrate to hear the charges against them and released on $25,000 bond to answer the charges in Tampa.[82]

As both sides prepared for trial, Cohen's and Assistant U.S. Attorney Bedke's bickering became so annoying that on May 23 Judge Steven Merryday warned both sides to tone down their rhetoric. "Provocations stand out on both sides," the judge told them both, adding that they could not count on the "leniency you have received so far."[83] During the run-up to the trial it seemed increasingly apparent that the prosecution's case depended almost entirely on the testimony on the tapes. Yet experts who had reviewed the tapes had testified that they could not make out significant portions of the tape. Once the trial began, defense counsel contended that the tapes were entirely inaudible. "You can listen to this time and time again," Todd Foster told Merryday, "You're never going to hear any conversation." Judge Merryday decided to hear for himself, and he did so behind closed doors.[84]

Then, in a heavy blow to the prosecution's case, on November 13 Judge Merryday announced in court that after listening several times to the recordings he found them "largely inaudible," and added that random noise and distortions of various kinds "materially obscure large portions of most or all of these recordings." He also suggested that he doubted whether some of the other evidence provided to the grand jury existed. Local experts agreed that Merryday's statement was a major setback to the government's case. "I think Judge Merryday is letting the government know he has some significant problems with those tapes and he just may be inclined to rule that they are inadmissible," former federal prosecutor Stephen Crawford added. "The judge is giving prosecutors a little time to rally the troops and get their supervisors together and see what they want to do with this case."[85]

Prosecutors turned over enhanced versions of the tapes that they contended were more audible. They also provided revised transcripts of the tapes. Arguing that the tapes should be admissible, the prosecution declared: "None of the recorded conversations is unfairly prejudicial or deceptive, and in no instance is there unfair prejudice that substantially outweighs a recorded conversation's probative value. The defendants are free to attempt to rebut the incriminating nature of the conversations with innocent explanations for those conversations."[86] Yet problems continued with the tapes. In a hearing conducted on December 19, U.S. Magistrate Mark Pizzo found the new versions no more audible than the other ones. Also brought into question was the truthfulness of the evidence presented to the judge who authorized the taping in the first place. Then, on February 15, 2001, Judge Pizzo, after carefully considering the evidence in the case, found that the Hillsborough detectives "deliberately misled" the circuit judge who authorized the wiretap. "They omitted information and distorted conversation. . . . They included statements [in their applications for extensions] which the defendants did not say or cannot be heard. . . . The detectives report conversations no reasonably prudent listener can hear, quote conversations that do not appear in the supporting transcript . . . and deliberately or with reckless disregard summarize conversations out of context." Pizzo recommended that Merryday throw out the tapes.[87] Within forty-eight hours Merryday authorized Pizzo to hold hearings on whether or not the indictment against the Aisenbergs should be thrown out completely. Instead of pursuing the case further, the U.S. Attorney's Office, on February 21, decided to file papers seeking permission to drop the seven-count indictment.[88]

With Pizzo's ruling and the subsequent collapse of the case, attention turned to the behavior of the Hillsborough County detectives and the U.S. Attorney's Office. The case's collapse inspired even more calls for an official investigation of misconduct. Did detectives intentionally fabricate the evidence in order to secure the wiretaps? Or were they just inept? Did they intentionally falsify the transcripts in order to build a case? How was it possible that such mistakes in building the case against the Aisenbergs could go so far? When they learned of the case's dismissal, the Aisenbergs immediately began contemplating a lawsuit against the government. Federal law allowed persons prosecuted by the government to sue for attorney's fees and damages if the prosecution was "frivolous, vexatious, or in bad faith."[89]

The Aisenbergs, through their attorneys, sued the federal government in Merryday's court for $7 million—three times the cost of their defense, arguing on October 22, 2002, that "it is important to keep the system honest." The four-day hearing examined the facts of the federal government's botched investigation. There was considerable argument over whether the Aisenbergs were entitled to more than their legal fees. Merryday admitted that "there was a number of ways to look at this statute."[90] On January 31, 2003, Merryday awarded the Aisenbergs $2.9 million. In a ninety-four-page order, the judge charged that parts of the indictment were "trivial," "gratuitous," and "misleading." He stated that, despite prosecutors' insistence for months that they had incriminating statements on tapes, "no such taped statements exist."[91] Merryday also ordered release of all grand jury transcripts so the public could learn how the case was improperly handled. "The public has an interest in inspecting these troubled investigations to determine the source of the United States' misdirection."[92]

The government eventually appealed Merryday's decision, claiming that his insistence on making grand jury transcripts public would be to surrender the principal weapon in the government's ability to fight and investigate crime. Over the course of several weeks, after allowing the government many opportunities to show why release of the transcripts would be damaging to ongoing investigations, and after "reading every syllable of the grand jury proceedings" himself, Merryday ordered the release of the transcripts, claiming, "The United States has defaulted its obligation and defied the request of the district court to establish the existence of some ongoing criminal investigation of the disappearance of Sabrina."[93] The Eleventh Circuit Court of Appeals reduced the Aisenbergs' award to $1.5 million and reversed Merryday's order that the grand jury transcripts be released.[94] Efforts of the Aisenbergs to prosecute Kunz and Bedke for wrongdoing failed. Judge Merryday ruled on July 20, 2004, that "federal prosecutors' official actions are protected by 'absolute immunity, even if tainted by ill-will or ineptitude.'"[95] Over the years periodic claims of Sabrina sightings or other evidence in the case would be investigated. As of this writing the search for Baby Sabrina, who if alive would be sixteen years old, continues.

16

"It's a Tidal Wave . . . and I'm Not Kidding about It!"

Only months after Bill Clinton's reelection in 1996, the Middle District Court of Florida faced a familiar problem—excessive caseloads due to an inadequate number of judges. While the district's population had grown to nearly 8 million residents, and while the Judicial Conference had recommended four additional judges in 1994, Congress had not provided them. In 1996 the district's judges handled more cases than judges in any other district in the United States except one. The national average of weighted cases per judge was 448; the Middle District average was 623. The district's plight was made even more acute because its eleventh judicial position was yet unfilled. Election-year politics in the Senate had stalled Clinton nominee Florida Second District Court of Appeal judge Richard Lazzara.[1]

With one year as chief judge under her belt, Judge Elizabeth Kovachevich was determined to make the crisis known to members of Congress. "The volume of cases here in Tampa is tremendous," she said. "It's a tidal wave. It's overwhelming, and I'm not kidding about it." Judge Kovachevich was so determined to make Congress understand the necessity of funding more judges that she decided to break tradition and go directly to Washington and lobby Congress. She did so in July, and she planned another trip in the upcoming year. Senator Bob Graham needed no convincing on the need for more judges. He was confident that the recommendation would be approved. "Normally, these recommendations are not highly controversial. Creating a new judgeship certainly has an expense to it," he continued. "But in the scale of a federal budget, which is about $1.3 trillion, we can afford to maintain one of the attributes of a civilized society."[2]

As of May 1997, when Judge Kovachevich returned to Washington, the situation had changed little, and the Senate had yet to act on Lazzara's second nomination. Though he waited again for nearly a year, a hearing had still not been scheduled. Statistics showed that by nearly every measure the district ranked as one of the busiest in the nation: 5,975 lawsuits were filed in the district in fiscal year 1,996—543 per judge, the sixth-heaviest in the nation. Records also revealed that in the previous year 844 criminal cases were filed, 79 per judge, the eighteenth-heaviest criminal caseload in the nation. Also 2,008 prisoners filed lawsuits, and there were 1,249 civil rights lawsuits. As if to put an exclamation point on the statistics, Judge Kovachevich told the House Judiciary Subcommittee on Courts, that growth rates in the Middle District were "unparalleled in the country."[3]

If more Article III judges were not immediately forthcoming, help was soon on the way. In 1996 and 1997 Congress approved a total of four more U.S. magistrate positions, and the Middle Districts judges moved quickly to select them. For the eight-year positions in Jacksonville and Orlando, the judges selected Timothy Corrigan and James G. Glazebrook. Corrigan, a Jacksonville native, attended Notre Dame University and Duke University School of Law. After graduation in 1981 Corrigan clerked for Judge Gerald Tjoflat, from whom he learned, as he once stated, a "fierce independence of thought and decision-making." Corrigan's time with Tjoflat was life-changing and convinced him that he wanted to be a judge someday. Even so, he entered private practice in Jacksonville.[4] Glazebrook earned a bachelor's and a law degree from Middlebury College and a law degree from Case Western Reserve University. Glazebrook clerked for Judge John A. Reed from 1980 to 1983 before entering private practice in New York. He returned to the district as a federal prosecutor in 1990, serving in that capacity until his appointment.[5]

For magistrate openings in Orlando and Tampa, the judges turned to two women: Karla Spaulding, a successful prosecutor, and Mary Scriven, a law professor who had taken a two-year leave of absence from one of Florida's power law firms. As an undergraduate at Western Michigan University, Spaulding's ambition was to become a history professor, but circumstances pointed her toward entering law school at Northwestern University. After graduation Spaulding took a job with Baker and Hostetler in Cleveland until realizing that the high-powered corporate legal practice was not for her. Desiring courtroom experience, in 1983 Spaulding cast a wide net to secure a job in a U.S. attorney's office. After a number of interviews she joined the office in Tampa and was fortunate to work on some high-profile cases, including the Lehder and Noriega trials. Spaulding advanced rapidly. From 1989 to 1992 she served as chief of the Tampa U.S. Attorney's Office of drug and appellate divisions.[6] After joining U.S. attorney's offices in Michigan and Texas, Spaulding returned to Tampa and entered private practice. After a few years in Tampa, Spaulding noticed an announcement in the *Florida Bar Journal* listing two magistrate openings. She decided to apply.[7]

Mary Scriven was the first African American woman to sit on the federal bench in Florida. Two days after her appointment, Scriven told a reporter that she was "honored" and acknowledged feeling "anxiety, happiness, and excitement."[8] Born and raised in Macon, Georgia, the daughter of a minister and a nurse, Scriven attended Duke University and then Florida State University College of Law. While at the Carlton Fields law firm Scriven specialized in what she called "money law"—corporate litigation, banking, franchising, and civil forfeiture.[9]

Even with the addition of Glazebrook, Corrigan, Spaulding, and Scriven, the caseload in the Middle District seemed out of control. At a bar luncheon on August 28, 1997, Judge Kovachevich announced that the next summer she would call all ten judges to Tampa to tackle a huge backlog in excess of 4,500 pending civil cases. There were simply not enough judges to hear cases.[10] Judge Kovachevich similarly addressed a gathering of federal lawyers in Orlando, admonishing them to lobby Congress for more judges. Again sharing her plan to reduce the civil case load in Tampa, Kovachevich added that under current formulas the district was entitled to almost eleven more judges.[11] If her purpose was to encourage many of the trial lawyers to settle their civil cases, the strategy worked. By April of the next year hundreds of the cases had either been settled or dismissed. Even so, Kovachevich still planned to pursue her "rocket docket" plan. The remaining cases still needed prompt resolution, and filings had not abated either. They were "not going away," she said. "The simple math is that we need more judges. And we aren't getting them now." Kovachevich understood that this scheme was not to the liking of the bar, but she asserted that her plan was the only way to get the docket under control.[12]

Judge Kovachevich's accelerated trial calendar (ATC) began on June 1, 1998. The nine-month period before the ATC began was, as one source noted, one of "intense preparation." Approximately 850 cases were designated to the ATC. "The district's 12 magistrate judges handled dispositive motions and related pretrial matters. . . . The district's four senior judges, with the voluntary services of senior and active judges from the Northern and Southern Districts of Florida were enlisted to handle the criminal dockets during the planned trial months of June, July, and August. This cleared the way for the six district judges in Orlando and Jacksonville to relocate temporarily to Tampa to handle the master trial docket." In the end only 75 of the original 850 cases went to full trial. Most of the others were settled or mediated. While she hailed the ATC a success, Kovachevich asserted that it "highlighted our inability to maintain the pace necessary to handle the high caseload" because, as she added, "weighted case filings continue to remain at levels that are more than 55 percent higher than the national average."[13]

By the time the "Rocket Docket" began, there was a new judge on the bench. The Senate had finally confirmed presidential nominee Richard Lazzara on Friday, October 26, 1997, and then he was hastily sworn in early the following week. On the day the Senate voted on Judge Lazzara's confirmation, Sen. Patrick Leahy (D-Vt.), ranking member of the Judiciary Committee, addressed the Senate: "Mr. President, I am delighted to see two more hostages released by the Republican majority to serve the American people as Federal judges." Leahy used Lazzara's case as yet another example of Republican foot-dragging. He had waited for over a year for the Senate to grant him a hearing. Lazzara was an experienced judge who had served at nearly every level of the state judiciary with distinction. He had received the highest possible rating from the American Bar Association. Both Senators Graham and Mack had wholeheartedly endorsed his nomination. There simply was no excuse for the holdup. Leahy said,

> I know that the chief judge in that district, Elizabeth Kovachevich, has been speaking out about the workload, backlogs and vacancies in her court. Judge Kovachevich has noted that serious crimes are up 28 percent in her district and civil filings are up 25 percent for the second straight year leading to a growing backlog of over 3,200 cases. Both Senator Graham and Senator Mack were strong supporters of this nominee at his hearing in early September. I was struck that Senator Mack called the situation one of "crisis proportions" and pointed out that the district is having to take unprecedented steps to deal with a backlog growing "at an alarming proportion."[14]

Leahy deplored the Republican majority's unwillingness to move forward on Clinton's nominees, arguing that the confirmation rate in President Bush's last year in office when the Democrats controlled the Senate resulted in the confirmation of fifty-nine of seventy-two nominees. Thus far in the session, Leahy continued, forty-seven of sixty nominees had not even been given a hearing. "Those who delay or prevent the filling of these vacancies," he declared, "must understand that they are delaying or preventing the administration of justice. We can pass all the crime bills we want, but you cannot try the cases and incarcerate the guilty if you do not have judges. Mounting backlogs of civil and criminal cases in dozens of districts . . . are growing taller by the day."[15]

While Congress continued its sparring over the confirmation process, the Middle District Court in Tampa celebrated two important milestones on December 12, 1997. On that day onlookers gathered for Judge Lazzara's investiture and for the official dedication of the new Tampa courthouse. The Sam Gibbons Federal Courthouse was named in the honor of the congressman who worked tirelessly to secure that appropriation. The shiny new seventeen-story structure incorporated the latest technology, including computers, television monitors to display documents, and sound and teleconferencing equipment.[16] In a guest opinion column appearing in the *Tampa Tribune* on the day of the courthouse's opening, Senators Graham and Mack celebrated the opening but also recognized the "growing judicial crisis in Central Florida." Graham and Mack asserted that for ten years they had worked in bipartisan fashion to confirm judges, but political gridlock had hindered their work. "Unfortunately," the senators argued, "the number of federal judges responsible for this area has not grown adequately to keep up with the population—and this stagnation has had a devastating effect on Middle District caseloads. For example, Central Florida judges are forced to handle 49 percent more criminal defendants than colleagues in other parts of the nation." Graham and Mack pledged to continue their bipartisanship to ensure that the district's needs were met.[17]

Born in Tampa in 1945, Richard Lazzara was one of four high-achieving sons of Anthony Lazzara. Brother Robert was a heart surgeon. Brother Tony left a thriving medical practice in Atlanta to run a medical clinic for the poor in Peru. And brother Michael ran the family oil business. Richard Lazzara majored in history at Loyola University New Orleans and attended the University of Florida Levin School of Law graduating in 1970. After working in the Hillsborough County solicitor's office, he entered private practice in 1975. After serving briefly as a county judge, Lazzara became a circuit judge in 1988. Finally in 1993 Gov. Lawton Chiles named him to the Second District Court of Appeal.[18]

In March 1999 Senators Mack and Graham introduced the Florida Federal Judgeship Act, a bill providing for four new Middle District judgeships. The bill's introduction came on the heels of a Judicial Conference of the United States recommendation that the new judgeships be added. Among twenty-six members of the conference was Judge William Terrell Hodges, who had served as chair of the executive committee since 1996. In

1998, flanked by U.S. Courts Administrative Office director L. Ralph Mecham and Federal Judicial Center director Judge Rya Zobel, Hodges testified before the House Judiciary Subcommittee on Courts and Intellectual Property that "one of the greatest challenges confronting the federal judiciary is to continue providing just and timely adjudication of a burgeoning federal docket." Caseloads had expanded because of new legislation federalizing additional crimes. "The workload of the federal courts keeps growing . . . despite productivity gains by judges," he explained. There had been no increases in Article III judgeships since 1990 and there were "a large number of unfilled judicial vacancies. Many courts are simply congested with too much work and growing backlogs."[19]

U.S. Attorney Charles Wilson agreed with the judge—especially as these circumstances pertained to the Middle District. "I believe we have some of the hardest working judges in the country here in the Middle District of Florida and I think they would agree judicial resources have not kept pace with growth." Statistics compiled by the Administrative Office of the U.S. Courts proved Wilson's point: their studies showed that the district ranked second nationally in the number of cases filed per judge each year, at 805.[20]

In March 1999 Judge Kovachevich and a delegation of legal officials traveled to Washington to lobby for the passage of Graham and Mack's bill. With state representatives Charles T. Canady, R-Lakeland; Porter Goss, R-Sanibel; Bill McCollum, R-Longwood; and Bill Young, R-St. Petersburg, chair of the House Appropriations Committee, in her corner, Judge Kovachevich made her case. Representative Goss later commented that "Judge Kovachevich eloquently drove home what we all know to be true. Southwest Florida needs a federal judge and the sooner the better. It's unacceptable that Southwest Floridians have to drive hundreds of miles for a trial, especially as a new $25 million federal courthouse sits unused in our back yard." The House overwhelmingly passed the judicial bill. Senate action was not expected until the summer. Some speculated that the trouble was that the GOP-led Senate, which had just narrowly acquitted Clinton in his impeachment on February 12, did not want to provide the wounded president with an opportunity to appoint more judges.[21]

The new courthouse that Representative Goss had referred to was the new six-story, 167,000-square-foot federal courthouse that had opened a week earlier. The new structure was only a few blocks away from the old one. It housed offices for the U.S. attorney, the public defender, the federal bankruptcy court, the U.S. Marshal's Office, and other federal court and law enforcement agencies. With Senator Mack and about two hundred onlookers in attendance, Chief Judge Kovachevich presided over the official dedication ceremony on August 14.[22] Although U.S. Magistrate Judge George Swartz continued to hear cases in Fort Myers as he had since 1964, the location still lacked a permanent sitting district judge. Since 1989 semi-retired Southern District of New York Judge Lee Gagliardi had been hearing cases during the winter in Fort Myers. But in November of 1999 the eighty-year-old jurist passed away.

That same month Judge Kovachevich visited Fort Myers to rally the local bar there to lobby for a full-time judge. "We need muscle and I hope I'm looking at muscle out here. I'm here today to see an attack squad put together." Judge George Swartz, who was nearing retirement, stated that the lack of a permanent district judge had caused the civil and criminal bar to suffer. "It's extremely expensive litigation, and it's going to get worse because the caseload increases on a daily basis." Fort Myers lawyer Joseph Coleman voiced the frustrations of many when he said, "Bricks and mortar don't dispense justice." Referring to the new courthouse as a "hollow chamber until we get it filled," he said that "justice delayed is justice denied, and justice is being denied now in Southwest Florida."[23]

Even as the crowded court docket absorbed everyone's rapt attention, the Middle District Court establishment took time out to recognize several important milestones. First, on March 29 court personnel learned of the death of former Judge Ben Krentzman, who died at his home at the age of eighty-four from complications of a stroke. News of Krentzman's passing brought out numerous public statements of condolence and recollections. Peter Grilli, one of his former clerks, said the judge was among "a small group of very courageous federal judges in the '60s and '70s who had to endure death threats trying to follow the law and bring about racial justice to the country. . . . People loved him and hated him for it. That kind of courage is a rare thing."[24] Terry Smiljanich, another of Krentzman's former clerks, remembered that the judge always "followed the law but approached everything from a compassionate point of view" and was always concerned that justice was done. But above all, Smiljanich remembered, Krentzman was most concerned about the First Amendment; he always carried a copy of the document in his pocket. Smiljanich said that the only time he ever saw the judge lose his temper in court came one day when a prosecutor referred to a "mere violation" of the First Amendment of the Constitution. Krentzman snapped. "'Counsel! Don't you ever come into my courtroom and say a mere violation of the Constitution' and picked up a copy of the Constitution and then threw it at him and hit him right the chest."[25]

In the spring of 1999 the Middle District marked another milestone when one of its most distinguished jurists decided to take senior status. On April 5, 1999, Judge Hodges wrote President Clinton, "My years on the bench have confirmed my conviction that no greater honor can be bestowed upon any American than the privilege of serving on good behavior as a United States judge, and I will now look forward to the opportunity of continuing in the capacity—and enjoying that honor—as a working senior judge."[26] Hodges was also nearing the end of his six years of service on the Judicial Conference, and the accolades for the judge began rolling in. That spring his alma mater, the University of Florida, honored him with an honorary doctorate. Among the letters of support the university received in Hodges' favor was one from the Supreme Court Chief Justice. "I have the highest respect for Judge Hodges' abilities, judgment, and commitment to public service," Rehnquist wrote. "He is prompt, thorough and performs countless tasks for the judiciary without fanfare. . . . Judge Hodges has brought honor and recognition to the University of Florida. It certainly would be most fitting, in my view, for the university to honor him."[27] Perhaps Hodges' greatest honor came on September 15 when the Judicial Conference honored him with a special resolution in his behalf.[28]

Hodges looked back at his service on the Judicial Conference as some of the most gratifying and enriching experiences of his career. Not only had he made important contributions to the administration of courts, he had also made lasting friendships that he treasured all his life. As he told an interviewer, Hodges saw his service on the conference as both a "diversion and a challenge. It's a diversion in the sense that it affords a perspective from which all judges can profit. And it's a challenge in the sense that the work being considered by the Conference is very important work." Service on the Judicial Council had afforded Hodges the opportunity to "participate in the decision making process relating to the governance of the courts. . . . The judges I have met on Judicial Conference committees have been inspiring to me, and many have become close personal friends. . . . For me, the experiences had been the highlight of my work as a judge."[29]

Also about that time Orlando's Kendall Sharp announced that he would take senior status. Since his appointment in the early 1980s by Ronald Reagan, the blunt, outspoken, and often controversial Sharp had been a stalwart workhorse in Orlando, hearing an average of 600–700 criminal and civil cases a year.[30] With Hodges' and Sharp's decisions, the pressure for more judges grew even more intense. And rumors circulated that U.S. Attorney Charles Wilson was being considered for an opening on the

Eleventh Circuit Court of Appeals. Wilson's mentor, Joseph Hatchett, had announced that he would retire on May 14. Since taking over the U.S. Attorney's Office from the embattled Larry Colleton on October 1, 1994, the forty-four-year-old prosecutor had served with distinction.[31] On April 15 the *Tampa Tribune* referred to Wilson as the "presumptive nominee," adding that while he "has been criticized by letters on these pages for the questionable actions of some of his prosecutors"—an oblique reference to the Aisenberg case—Wilson "has overseen mostly successful prosecutions. He has brought health care fraud to the forefront in Tampa and undertaken difficult prosecutions for environmental crimes. He has investigated allegations of local government corruption and continued prosecutions of drug dealers." The paper praised Wilson as a "man of convictions whom we can trust to act fairly and wisely. . . . If there was ever a person both sides of the political [spectrum] could support, we think he is Charles Wilson. We urge a quick recommendation, nomination and Senate approval."[32]

President Clinton nominated Wilson in May, but that only meant that the prosecutor could take his place in line with other nominees in the Senate logjam. Since the session had begun in January no hearing had been held for the forty-one other pending nominees and none had been scheduled. Even so, Wilson was upbeat. "That's beyond my control. I'm optimistic. I've always had strong bipartisan support. . . . I expect that, consistent with the past, I will continue to have bipartisan support in the Senate." Senators Graham and Mack both whole-heartedly supported Wilson. "He had maturity," said Graham, "but also the enthusiasm of a relatively young man. . . . He will be an important part of the federal judiciary for many years to come." Mack agreed, adding, "I will do everything I can to move this nomination. . . . He's a good candidate we'd like to get through."[33]

With Graham and Mack leading the charge, the Senate took up Wilson's case surprisingly rapidly. In the middle of July Wilson found himself with both senators at his side being grilled by Senate Judiciary Chairman Orrin Hatch regarding his views on judicial activism, the death penalty, and affirmative action. When asked how he would apply civil rights laws with regard to employment, college admissions, and scholarships, Wilson responded that the Supreme Court had subjected "affirmative action plans" to "strict scrutiny analysis . . . They must be narrowly tailored to further a compelling government interest." Wilson pledged that he would be faithful to the laws Congress enacts and follow precedents set by the U.S. Supreme Court. Wilson's answers and his demeanor impressed the senators. Within two weeks the full Senate confirmed Wilson on July 30.[34]

Moving with dispatch to fill the U.S. Attorney's Office, Senator Graham recommended Department of Justice official Donna A. Bucella to the White House. The forty-two-year-old former prosecutor had worked in the Southern District of Florida before becoming acting U.S. attorney in the interim between the time of Colleton's leave of absence and Wilson's official appointment. Bucella served admirably in that brief period. "It was a most unfortunate thing all the way around so it was good she was here. She did a very fine job," said Judge Elizabeth Kovachevich. Since returning to Washington Bucella had worked closely with Atty. Gen. Janet Reno. In 1997 Reno had honored her with the Attorney General's Exceptional Service Award, given annually to one employee. Charles Wilson also praised his likely successor. "She will be a great asset." Clinton nominated Bucella, and she was scheduled to be sworn in as interim U.S. attorney in September.[35]

At long last, on October 20, 1999, the House and Senate approved the bill authorizing four more judges for the Middle District. That same day President Clinton nominated Hillsborough Circuit Judge James Whittemore to fill the vacancy created by Hodges taking senior status. He was assigned to Tampa because Judge Henry Adams had moved to Jacksonville.[36] The forty-seven-year-old Whittemore announced, "My family and I are very appreciative of the confidence President Clinton has in my judicial qualifications and my ability to contribute to the federal judiciary."[37] Whittemore was born in Walterboro, South Carolina, but moved to Florida at a young age and was living in Temple Terrace at the time of his nomination. Whittemore attended the University of Florida and Stetson University College of Law. After law school he worked in the federal public defender's office in Tampa and then was in private practice until becoming a circuit judge in 1990.[38]

On February 19, 2000, two months after he had officially taken senior status, over four hundred well-wishers assembled at the Orlando federal courthouse on the occasion of Kendall Sharp's portrait unveiling. On hand were the judge's wife, Mary, two daughters, and a granddaughter. Also in attendance was H. Manuel Hernandez, president of the Federal Bar Association in Orlando, many lawyers, court officials, and several of Sharp's Navy buddies who came from as far away as Hawaii and Boston. Depicted in the portrait of Sharp were a law book and the Bible as well as a 1715 Spanish gold coin fashioned into a tie clasp—all of which have great significance in the judge's life. The coin symbolized Sharp's love of the sea and his former legal client, treasure salver Mel Fisher. When the emotional Sharp addressed the gathering, he said of the Bible and the law book, "If the people

Senators Connie Mack and Bob Graham, ca. 2000. During the 1990s Mack (Rep.) and Graham (Dem.) worked together in bipartisan fashion to secure Senate confirmation of Florida district judges. P. K. Yonge Library of Florida History, University of Florida.

who have been here had read it and the Ten Commandments . . . they probably wouldn't have been here. . . . The law is black and white to me. I don't see the shades of gray all the litigants are bringing up today."[39]

The same day Sharp's friends were honoring him, Judge Whittemore was preparing for his Senate Judiciary Committee hearing scheduled for Feb. 22. Once again in a demonstration of bipartisanship, Graham and Mack accompanied their man, assuring their colleagues of Whittemore's qualifications. Committee chairman Orrin Hatch was impressed with all the nominees. He assured them that he would make every effort to confirm them. Even so, the mood in the Senate was extremely poisonous. Several Republicans had pledged to hold up all Clinton nominees. Yet Mack was confident that he and Graham would be able to move the nominations forward. "There are two aspects of politics—there's rhetoric and there's action. Senator Graham and I have shown through our action that we can fill those positions."[40]

Meanwhile, on February 9 Clinton had already nominated another well-qualified applicant, John Antoon II, a former Brevard County circuit judge who was serving as a judge on Florida's Fifth District Court of Appeal. Both Whittemore and Antoon were slated to fill the vacancies left by Hodges and Sharp.

Chairing Antoon's hearing before the Senate Judiciary Committee was Sen. Strom Thurmond. Sen. Bob Graham introduced Antoon to Thurmond and his Senate colleagues. Graham asked that Senator Mack's statement endorsing Antoon's confirmation be inserted into the record.[41] Despite the ongoing tension in the Senate, Antoon, like Whittemore, had little trouble in his confirmation hearing. The full Senate voted to confirm both judges on May 24. Antoon was able to watch his confirmation on C-SPAN on the television in his office.[42] Some speculated that the vote on Whittemore, Antoon, and fourteen other nominees was part of a deal with the administration to confirm an ultraconservative member of the Federal Elections Commission. Regardless of that possibility, Clinton White House spokesman Joe Lockhart said, "We hope today's votes represent a new beginning on the road toward full and fair consideration of all nominations currently pending before the Senate."[43]

Antoon, the judge that would fill Sharp's vacancy in Orlando, was born in 1946 in Bakersfield, California but came to Florida at an early with his family. He excelled in academics and basketball at Satellite Beach High School, and he pursued both with energy at Florida Southern College in Lakeland. Before graduating in 1968 Antoon was president of his senior class and was a member of the college's student supreme court, student government, Omicron Delta Kappa, ROTC, and other organizations. After attending law school at Florida State University, Antoon privately practiced in Cocoa until 1984, when he was elected circuit judge in Florida's Eighteenth Circuit. In 1995 Gov. Lawton Chiles appointed him to the appeals bench. Known as an athletic, cerebral, deep thinker, Antoon continued his quest for learning well beyond his law degree, continuing his studies at the Florida Institute of Technology and the University of Virginia, even while on the bench. Through his time as a private lawyer and judge, Antoon had earned many accolades and awards. In 1988 lawyers gave him the highest rating of all other lawyers in his circuit.[44]

Meanwhile, Graham and Mack's special vetting panel forwarded nine names to the senators to consider for the four new judicial positions authorized by Congress. Four candidates that eventually emerged as recommendations to the White House were Gregory Presnell, James Moody Jr.,

John Steele, and Richard Gilbert. Presnell (Orlando) and Gilbert (Tampa) were both lawyers in private practice. Moody was a circuit judge from Plant City, and Steele was a U.S. magistrate judge in Jacksonville.[45] All but Gilbert were eventually nominated by Clinton.

Graham and Mack's bipartisan work continued to pay dividends. Hearings for nominees Presnell, Moody, and Steele were scheduled July 12. Lake Wales attorney and past chairman of the Federal District Court Nominating Commission for Florida Robin Gibson stated, in the current climate of gridlock in Congress, Graham and Mack's success in moving the nominations forward was remarkable. "This is being done during a time when the process is shut down," he said. "In a presidential year with presidential politics, attempts to get new judges appointed is almost unheard of."[46] Yet on the appointed day, all three appeared before the Senate Judiciary Committee with their families. Once again Senators Graham and Mack read statements in support of the nominees, and their hearings went smoothly. The full Senate confirmed all three just over two weeks later on July 21.[47]

When the newly confirmed James Moody learned that he would serve in Tampa, he stated, "I'm very excited about that. None of us knew where we would be. This is my home." The fifty-three-year-old Plant City native was from one of the town's oldest families. The son of a Florida legislator and a well-respected circuit judge, Moody possessed an understated, plain-spoken personality and a droll sense of humor. Graduating from the University Florida School of Law with honors in 1972, Moody practiced with the Plant City firm of Trinkle, Redman, Moody, Swanson, & Byrd until his election to the circuit bench in 1995.[48] Moody was the only lawyer who practiced east of Highway 301 ever to be elected president of the Hillsborough Bar Association.

A fourth-generation Floridian, Gregory Presnell was born in St. Petersburg in 1942 while his father was fighting in World War II. After graduating from the College of William and Mary in 1964 with a degree in economics, Presnell attended the University of Florida Levin College of Law. He excelled, earned law review, and after graduation in 1966, he joined the Akerman, Senterfitt law firm when it had only ten lawyers. Presnell helped build the law firm into one of Florida's largest and most prestigious. At first Presnell specialized in transportation-related practice, and he also did commercial litigation. For seven years during the 1980s Presnell served as managing partner of the firm, specializing at that time in power and energy litigation. Presnell had served as the youngest president of the Orange County Bar Association and in that capacity strived to provide legal access to the poor and pushed for pro bono requirements for bar members. Described as a "meticulous," "skillful," "well-prepared" lawyer "with a social conscience," years earlier Presnell had said, "The thing I like about being a lawyer is that you are able to intervene to protect the individual from government power that is being abused. This is what makes our country different. It's what makes it all worthwhile."[49]

Since his appointment as U.S. magistrate in 1991, John E. Steele had served in Jacksonville with distinction. Within days after his confirmation Judge Elizabeth Kovachevich announced that Steele would become Fort Myers' first full-time district judge. Kovachevich explained that Steele would hear cases but also manage them as well. "The management is the really significant thing for Fort Myers," the judge explained. "Until now, the logistics have discouraged the filing of federal actions. Lawyers didn't want the travel that came with these cases. The court was in a horrible position." Steele was sworn into office in Tampa on July 28 and was expected to begin his duties in Fort Myers in September.[50]

Welcoming Judge Steele in Fort Myers was U.S. Magistrate Judge Douglas Frazier. Frazier was sworn in as U.S. magistrate judge on January 7, 2000, the day George Swartz stepped down. The forty-nine-year-old Frazier attended the Naval Academy and then earned a law degree from the University of Mississippi. When he left the service he became a prosecutor in New Orleans briefly before joining the U.S. attorney's office in Orlando and later Fort Myers in the 1980s and early 1990s. Atty. Gen. Janet Reno had appointed Frazier interim U.S. Attorney in 1993, and he later continued his career as a prosecutor in Nevada before assuming a post in the Justice Department in Washington. Frazier enjoyed arguing cases in the courtroom immensely but admitted that "any attorney who has an affinity for the courtroom would always want to become a judge. It's sort of a logical extension of a whole life of public service."[51]

Another federal judge named about that time, Gary R. Jones, became the first full-time judicial official in Ocala when he was appointed U.S. magistrate. A graduate of the University of Miami School of Law, Jones also earned a master of laws degree in international law from the New York University School of Law. In 1999 Jones left the firm of Hickey and Jones, which he helped found in 1988, to become a U.S. magistrate in Gainesville. The next year he was transferred to Ocala.[52]

With five district judges confirmed, robed, and ready to take on the overwhelming case load of the Middle District of Florida, Senators Graham and Mack could take satisfaction in the fact that their bipartisan work had contributed mightily to the administration of justice in the Middle District of Florida. Somehow they had both convinced their colleagues to set aside their differences to help resolve the backlog crisis. They had rallied Florida's house delegation to their cause. As Graham recalled, "Connie and I sat down and agreed that we would fill those on a bipartisan basis to ensure that the nominations had the best chance of getting confirmed. We worked to impress upon Sen. Hatch, Sen. Grassley and other key people on the Senate Judiciary Committee that the situation in the Middle District was desperate." Their collaboration was unusual. As one Judiciary Committee staffer noted, "Florida is a unique situation, because Senators Graham and Mack work so well together" even though they were not from the same party.[53] Florida Bar president Herman J. Russomanno summarized the results of Senators Mack and Graham's accomplishment: "Because of their extraordinary determination and hard work they have achieved what no other state has even come close to accomplishing in recent years concerning the appointment of U.S. district court judges. Because of their dedicated service," he continued, "Florida has been blessed with competent, experienced, compassionate, and highly professional judges. These individuals bring to the court the highest standards and strong commitments to the administration of justice."[54]

Looking back on these difficult times, Judge Kovachevich also praised Graham and Mack's cooperation, but she also recognized the assistance of many others. "I can't say enough for all the personnel," she recalled, "the federal bar associations, what they did, their efforts individual at their own cost and expense, flying to Washington and staying in Washington, giving up their time, giving up time from the practices. I mean, everybody just put their shoulder to the wheel because it was the right thing to do. And it serves and still serves the people of the Middle District of Florida by all of their efforts."[55] Unfortunately, this strong bipartisan relationship that had produced so much for Florida, including not only judgeships but also many other important dividends, would be tested in January 2001, when Connie Mack retired from the U.S. Senate.

17

Into the New Century, 2000–2004

No sooner had Sen. Bob Graham and outgoing Sen. Connie Mack succeeded in their work of shepherding through the Middle District judicial nominations than the United States was faced with one of the greatest political and judicial crises in its history. Everyone expected the presidential election of 2000 that pitted incumbent Vice President Al Gore against Texas governor George W. Bush to be close. But few would have predicted how close. With the deficit transformed into a surplus and the economy booming, Al Gore was certainly in a strong position. Yet the wonky Gore's association with the unsavory aspects of Clinton's misdeeds in the previous eight years dragged down the Gore-Lieberman ticket. In contrast, Bush seemed likeable, down to earth, and the GOP poured huge resources into his campaign.

On Election Day Al Gore polled five hundred thousand more votes than Bush, but the fate of Florida's twenty-five electoral votes—and thus the election—hung in the balance. The uncertainty went on for weeks. Bush's less-than-one-thousand-vote majority in Florida triggered a recount under state law. The Florida Supreme Court ordered recounts in some south Florida counties where election officials painstakingly scrutinized "hanging chads" and "butterfly ballots" with lawyers and party functionaries looking over their shoulders. Finally, after two weeks the U.S. Supreme Court ordered the counting stopped. In a 5–4 decision, the court ruled in *Bush v. Gore* (2001) that the Florida Supreme Court's method of recounting ballots violated the Equal Protection Clause of the 14th Amendment because there was no state-wide standard for counting votes. The higher court accepted the state canvassing board's previous decision to certify Florida's electoral vote total for Bush. Thus, George W. Bush became the forty-third president of the United States.[1]

At one point during the electoral crisis a Middle District judge heard pleas from plaintiffs and defendants on behalf of Bush and Gore. On

November 14 newly appointed Judge John Antoon rejected a request by Bush attorneys to stop the recount. Antoon noted that "federal courts had been reluctant to interfere with state election procedures, and he was not convinced that state court remedies had been exhausted."[2] The plaintiffs appealed Antoon's ruling to the Eleventh Circuit Court of Appeals. On December 6 the higher court, in a split decision, affirmed Antoon's ruling, but on December 12 the Supreme Court issued its *Bush v. Gore* ruling, halting the recount—thus awarding the Presidency to George W. Bush.[3]

Once the election controversy was resolved, the new Bush-Cheney administration moved rapidly to fill important cabinet positions. As attorney general they chose former Missouri governor and U.S. senator John Ashcroft, who had just been defeated in his Senate reelection campaign. One of the Senate's most conservative members, Ashcroft was a strident opponent of abortion and a vocal advocate of gun owners' rights. Ashcroft's justice department would take a decisive rightward shift, but nothing would alter the disposition of federal law enforcement—and indeed American society—more than a catastrophic event that occurred only nine months into George Bush's presidency.

On the morning of September 11, 2001, U.S. District Judge Richard Lazzara was hearing testimony in a sexual discrimination suit in Tampa when suddenly the judge ordered that the court adjourn for the day. News had reached the bench that two airplanes had hit the Twin Towers of the World Trade Center in New York. Another plane had hit the Pentagon. It was clear that the United States was under attack by terrorists. Within minutes the news spread though the courthouse. Some employees left the building. Others gathered in a conference room to watch live coverage of the event on television. Frightened federal employees in the Tampa courthouse—like other employees in courthouses in the Middle District and throughout the nation—had no way of knowing whether other attacks against federal facilities or courthouses might occur. Some speculated that the attack might have been the work of a homegrown domestic terrorist organization. After all, had not this been the case in the attack on the Alfred P. Murrah Federal Building in Oklahoma City six years earlier? That afternoon U.S. Middle District Marshal Don Moreland announced in a brief statement without elaborating that his officers were taking necessary steps to protect federal property.[4]

The attacks were soon determined to be the work of the radical Islamic organization al-Qaeda, led by Osama bin Laden. That evening President Bush announced to the American people: "Today our fellow citizens, our way of life, our very freedom came under attack in a series of deliberate and deadly terrorist acts."[5] The Bush administration's reaction to the attacks, its subsequent "War on Terror," the passage of the Patriot Act, and the war in Iraq had a transformative effect on American society. The need to protect America from another attack consumed the Bush administration and influenced its every policy decision, both domestic and foreign. Most Americans would come to understand that the periods before and after 9/11 represented two different worlds.

Even so, judges, their staffs, and other members of the Middle District workforce, like other Americans, struggled to do their duty in the days following the 9/11 national calamity. Several judges who had been only recently confirmed moved into their new chambers. Judges John Antoon and Gregory Presnell joined Judges Anne Conway, Patricia Fawsett and senior Judges George C. Young and Kendall Sharp in Orlando. In Tampa Judges James D. Whittemore and James S. Moody Jr. joined Judges Richard A. Lazzara, Steven D. Merryday, William J. Castagna, and Chief Judge Elizabeth Kovachevich. Judge Henry Adams transferred to his hometown, Jacksonville. In Fort Myers newly appointed Judge John E. Steele, the lone district judge there, presided over an ever-expanding caseload.

As of the election of 2000, the Middle District still had one judicial vacancy to fill. The situation proved to be sticky as Bob Graham and newly elected Bill Nelson, both Democrats, represented Florida in the U.S. Senate. In April 2001 Gov. Jeb Bush, the new president's brother, alongside GOP representatives C. W. "Bill" Young and Clay Shaw announced the formation of a new Florida federal judicial nominating commission. Governor Bush's selections to the commission resulted in a decisive Republican tilt. Many wondered if the decade-long bipartisan cooperation on judicial nominations had come to an abrupt end.[6]

The dawn of the new century found many Middle District Court personnel either occupying new spaces or ready to vacate old ones. The new Sam Gibbons Courthouse in Tampa had opened in 1997. Judge William Castagna remained behind in the old 1905 federal building, occupying his cherished courtroom until 2001, when he reluctantly moved to the new facility. By that date the grand old building was almost entirely abandoned. On September 25, 2003, the General Services Administration (GSA) deeded the building to the City of Tampa. Mayor Pam Iorio proudly received the keys, declaring, "This courthouse is really a symbol of Tampa." She and others looked forward to the day when the ninety-nine-year-old structure would be refurbished. Also on hand that day was Judge Castagna, who said of his old courtroom, "I have always felt it was the nicest courtroom in the Southeast. . . . The walls and the building are steeped in atmosphere."[7]

But there were glitches in the new Tampa courthouse. Only months before Judge Kovachevich's "Rocket Docket" had blasted off in June 1998, pipes burst in the new building, sending gallons of water down a wall and onto the floor. Then a leak in the glass roof resulted in water pooling in the building's lobby. In December 1998 Judge Kovachevich found that the ledges outside her seventeenth-floor window made an excellent roost for buzzards. Judge Kovachevich noted that their crashing, scrapes, thumps, and scratching at the windows were particularly annoying at night. "It's a little eerie, but I'm starting to get used to it," she said.[8] Turkey vultures migrated to Tampa in the winter months from the North, and since their departure, $25,000 had been spent to clean up the mess. The next year they were back in force, eighty strong. Electric wires were installed to ward away the unwanted scavengers. The $80,000 remedy was soon in place, but not before the problem made national headlines. The GSA was deluged with suggestions: smear the ledges with grease, blast a shotgun in the air, tether bird dogs on the roof.[9] Yet far more serious problems, such as leaks, mold, mildew, and bad air, plagued the courthouse in years to come. Many workers complained of respiratory problems and headaches.[10]

Indeed, as early as 2001, a study commissioned by the Administrative Office of the U.S. Courts found all five courthouses in the Middle District to be suffering from some form of "sick building syndrome." In September the Middle District planned town hall meetings in Fort Myers, Jacksonville, Ocala, Orlando, and Tampa where experts would discuss the findings. All courthouses had problems with air circulation, ventilation, and a lack of dehumidified air. Leaks plagued all the buildings, and experts found that moldy files transferred from the old structures in Fort Myers and Tampa were also a culprit.[11] In December 2001 in Jacksonville Judge Harvey E. Schlesinger and the other district judges there demanded that the GSA take action immediately to address the air quality in the sixty-seven-year-old courthouse. Many of the courthouse staff, he asserted, were suffering from "diseases or allergies, we know what it's caused by. There's a 75-foot patch they just put over my chambers, and it's still leaking in there," he said.[12] The health risks associated with the courthouse, Schlesinger and others maintained, was threatening current and future trials.

The complaints continued as new courthouses went up in Jacksonville and Orlando. In 1999 officials broke ground on a new Jacksonville courthouse. By the fall of 2002 the new structure was ready for occupation. In

Orlando the federal building built in 1975 was showing its age. Not only was the old structure inadequate for the expanded Orlando division but the rundown structure had suffered from overuse and neglect in many areas. In 1996 Congress appropriated $9.5 million to acquire land adjacent to the current structure and to draw up plans to build a new structure that was projected to cost more than $50 million. When negotiations over the 3.9-acre tract broke down, the U.S. attorney filed condemnation proceedings in the Orlando court to seize the property in March 1998. Judge Kovachevich asked Eleventh Circuit Court of Appeals Chief Judge Joseph Hatchett to appoint an outside judge to hear the case.[13]

Meanwhile, sparring between the GSA and the judges over the selection of architects and the design of the structure threatened the project. Judges, legislators, and Orlando mayor Glenda Hood opposed the design, which featured large glass windows facing I-4. Disputes over the design continued and threatened to destroy the whole project. Rep. John Mica (R-Winter Park) warned on February 1, 2001, "Unless the GSA meets the design and security requirements and concerns that have been expressed by the judiciary and the law-enforcement community, it will not be funded."[14] Finally, by August 2001, after prodding by the GSA, Boston architect Andrea Leers presented a new design that drew support from all sides. "I think it's going to be one of the most beautiful buildings in downtown Orlando," Judge Patricia Fawsett stated. "It's a gorgeous complex that has a modern building with classical elements. It's identifiable as a courthouse, and it's secure." The new plan also called for a new entrance for the current courthouse and an enclosed walkway that would connect to the old structure.[15]

Many in Orlando anticipated that the new structure—as well as the new Florida A&M University College of Law to be built adjacent to the federal court complex—would help in the revitalization of the lower-income Parramore neighborhood.[16] Approval of the plan proved none too soon. The current courthouse's dilapidated nature came to light once again on February 13, 2002, as Judge John Antoon was forced to order everyone out of his courtroom (often referred to as the "bowling alley") when he learned that a six-by-five-foot concrete slab had shifted out of place. "This building is structurally unsound," he declared. "I want you all to evacuate the building."[17]

With the design agreed upon, Congress approved a nearly $80 million appropriation for the new courthouse in February 2003. Finally, on April 5, 2004, Judge Patricia Fawsett, other judges, and employees participated in a ground-breaking ceremony. Judge Fawsett eagerly followed the project's construction as the year progressed. In celebration of the first phase of construction, she exchanged her judicial robes for blue jeans and sneakers as she grilled hot dogs and hamburgers for the 180 construction workers on the site. After completing her work Judge Fawsett announced, "These are hard-working Americans who are here. I watch them from my office. They are here, sometimes in the rain, and they worked around hurricanes last year. They are so dedicated."[18]

By the fall of 2007 the sparkling new six-story structure with a cost that had ballooned to $101 million was completed and ready for occupation. "We've been released from a dungeon," Judge Fawsett noted of the other building. One source called the building on the corner of West Central Boulevard and Division Street that faced south toward the city's warehouse district and the Parramore neighborhood as "part government building, part art museum, and part cathedral." The most identifiable feature of the building was a fifty-by-twenty-foot stained glass window based on the watercolor paintings of internationally known artist Al Held. The glass was handblown in Germany and cut and assembled in China.[19] On hand for the official ribbon-cutting and opening on September 21 were Supreme Court Justice Clarence Thomas, Judges Fawsett, Kovachevich, a host of politicians, and current and senior district judges.[20]

With the new administration, most understood that a new U.S. attorney would be selected. Donna Bucella had led the U.S. Attorney's Office since 1999, when she took over the office after Charles Wilson's elevation to the appeals bench. Since coming to the U.S. Attorney's Office, the forty-four-year-old Bucella worked to develop a better dialogue among local, state, and federal law enforcement and prosecutors. Most were impressed with her work.[21] But a few missteps by her prosecutors dogged her. One of her prosecutors had allowed a witness to testify under a false name. Another prosecutor had knowingly allowed untruthful affidavits to be used in drug prosecutions. The actions drew stern rebukes from Judge Steven Merryday, U.S. Magistrate Elizabeth Jenkins, and the Eleventh Circuit Court of Appeals.[22]

In anticipation of President Bush's decision to name a new U.S. attorney, Bucella resigned her post effective on May 1, 2001. Florida's Federal Judicial Nominating Commission selected three finalists for the post, and the person who eventually got the recommendation from Gov. Jeb Bush and Representatives Clay Shaw and Bill Young was Jacksonville attorney Paul I. Perez.[23] The forty-six-year-old Perez had a strong background and qualifications. A Cuban American, Perez came to the United States at the age of five in 1960 with his family. Settling in Jacksonville, Perez attended Bishop Kenney High School and then Jacksonville University, where he majored in history. After earning a master's degree in Latin American studies from the University of Florida, Perez served as a park ranger at the Castillo de San Marcos in St. Augustine. Perez eventually attended the George Washington University Law School, graduating in 1984. Returning to Jacksonville, Perez clerked for Judge John H. Moore before taking a job as assistant U.S. attorney in Jacksonville. Perez entered private practice in Jacksonville and specialized in federal criminal defense. Fellow Jacksonville lawyer Mark Rosenblum hailed Perez's selection not only because of his integrity but because he understood both sides of the process. "Because Paul was a criminal defense lawyer following his tenure with the U.S. Attorney's Office, I expect him to bring to the table two crucial qualities—the ability to represent the government zealously while at the same time appreciating the devastating effect being charged with a crime has on a human being and his family."[24]

Even before his confirmation, Perez announced that he would carefully access the needs of the office and make changes where necessary. He also noted that his priorities would be in line with Atty. Gen. John Ashcroft's priorities: terrorism in the wake of 9/11, illegal immigration, drugs, and convicted felons who buy guns. Confirmed by the U.S. Senate on March 8 and sworn ten days later in Tampa by Chief Judge Elizabeth Kovachevich, Perez oversaw a U.S. attorney's office that stretched four hundred miles from the Georgia line to Naples. As law professor Michael L. Seigal explained, the Middle District was "so big that it ends up almost being a microcosm of the United States. It's got urban regions. It's got rural regions. It's got drug crimes. It's got everything. . . . We used to say when I was there, if there's a crime, a type of crime committed anywhere, it's also committed in the Middle District of Florida."[25] Perez would supervise 110 attorneys and 90 support staffers and oversee a $17 million budget—all in the immediate post 9/11 environment.

Perez chose Jim Klindt in the Jacksonville office as his chief assistant. Klindt had been honored in 1998 for his stellar performance in successfully prosecuting drug dealers and corrupt public officials.[26] Klindt had only recently successfully secured drug-related convictions of former sheriffs Laurie Ellis of Nassau County and Joe Newmans of Baker County as well as several Jacksonville police officers accused of corruption. Perez soon announced other important personnel changes in the office. Terry Zitek, who had been chief of the criminal division for more than seventeen years, was named executive assistant U.S. attorney and would oversee prosecution

guidelines, victim-witness programs, training, and policies and procedures. Robert O'Neill was appointed chief of the criminal division and
would oversee criminal prosecutions in Tampa, Orlando, Fort Myers, and
Jacksonville. One of Perez's newest initiatives in line with the directives of
the Attorney General's Office was to create a special prosecution unit to
handle terrorism-related crimes. "Our first priority will be terrorism and
preventing terrorist attacks," he said. The importance of the new unit was
emphasized in a November visit to Tampa by Attorney General Ashcroft.[27]

Also with George Bush's election as president, longtime U.S. marshal
Don Moreland announced in May 2001 that he would step down. Moreland had served since his appointment by President Clinton in 1993. There
were many applicants for the position. The person President Bush selected
from among the nomination commission's recommendations was Orange
County public safety director Thomas Hurlburt, who had also served as
Orlando police chief. Hurlburt had many powerful supporters, including Orange County state attorney Lawson Lamar, Orlando mayor Glenda
Hood, and President Bush's cabinet secretary of Housing and Urban Development and Orlando native Mel Martinez. Hurlburt was eventually nominated, confirmed by the Senate, and sworn in late the spring of 2003.[28]

One of the most sensational police corruption cases in Florida history
was tried soon after Perez became U.S. attorney. The case involved several
Jacksonville police officers charged in a number of crimes, including the
slaying of convenience store owner Sami Safar. Jacksonville police officer
Karl Waldon was accused of the 1998 kidnapping and slaying of Safir in a
staged traffic stop. (Safir's abandoned car was found near a bank the day
after he withdrew $50,000. His corpse was also found nearby.) After an
extensive grand jury investigation of the Jacksonville police department,
Waldon and several accomplices were arrested in December 2000. Prosecutors charged that Waldon strangled Safir in the back of his squad car
after robbing him of $50,000. They also alleged that Waldon and his ring of
police officers invaded homes, kidnapped victims, robbed, stole drugs, and
obstructed justice—all while wearing their uniforms. Three other police
officers had pled guilty and swore that they acted in concert with Waldon
in the Safir case and other crimes. Jim Klindt tried the case before Judge
Henry Adams in Jacksonville. Authorities in Washington directed prosecutors to seek the death penalty against Waldon.[29]

The trial began on October 15, 2002. In his opening arguments, Klindt
portrayed Waldon as a greedy killer using his authority as a police officer to coordinate a three-and-a-half-year crime spree, including drug

thefts, heists, and other crimes. "He used his badge and authority as weapons. . . . He used them to injure innocent citizens, kidnap innocent citizens and eventually kill an innocent citizen, all for the almighty dollar. . . . The good guys became the bad guys," Klindt continued, "police officers stealing, robbing, invading homes, kidnapping and eventually committing murder. It was all too easy. They did think they were invincible. Once they crossed the line, their lawlessness knew no bounds." Waldon's attorney questioned the veracity of the government's witnesses, charging that they had lied about Waldon's leadership role in the conspiracy to save their own skins.[30]

The most dramatic moment in the trial came on October 17 when two accomplices that participated with Waldon in Safir's slaying described how their plan to rob Safir during a traffic stop went awry when Safir refused to leave his car without the money. Waldon handcuffed Safir, took him to a deserted school parking lot and strangled him with a rope in the back of the squad car. Splitting the money among themselves, the accomplices helped Waldon dispose of Safir's body.[31] After several more days of testimony the prosecution rested its case on October 24, and closing arguments by both sides took place five days later. After deliberating for nearly a week the jury found Waldon guilty on fourteen counts.[32] In January Judge Henry Adams sentenced Waldon to life in prison, and the other five accomplices who testified against Waldon were sentenced variously to time served, four years and three months, nineteen years, five years, and seventeen years. Later that year, in a special ceremony with other honorees in Washington, James Klindt received the Attorney General's Director's Award from John Ashcroft.[33]

Middle District prosecutors succeeded in convicting another corrupt law enforcement officer, this trial taking place three hundred miles away at the other end of the district in Judge John E. Steele's Fort Myers courtroom. Assistant U.S. Attorney Doug Malloy used the testimony of a sheriff captain who pled guilty, drug dealers, numbers runners, and numerous others in Immokalee to convict Sgt. Glendell "Pee Wee" Edison of the Collier County Sheriffs Department of conspiracy, extortion, and cocaine trafficking. Over his eighteen years in the sheriff's department, according to testimony, Edison had extorted money from drug dealers, tipped them off when busts were imminent, and threatened Haitian immigrants with deportation if they refused to pay protection money. In his closing statement Malloy called Edison "not crafty or wise. . . . He was greedy. He was drunk with power." He was no different than the other criminals. He used his badge to extract money from criminals. "He'd become one of them." The seven-day trial resulted in Edison's conviction on five counts of "conspiracy to commit extortion under color of official right, possession with intent to distribute powder and crack cocaine, and three counts of extortion under color of official right." Four months later Judge Steele sentenced Edison to fourteen years in prison.[34]

Two other high-profile federal corruption cases involving administrators of federal housing funds also took place in 2004–5. In one of the cases in Orlando, Judge John Antoon sentenced Orlando Housing Authority accountant Courtney Escoffery to two and a half years in prison for helping to bilk more than $424,000 in agency funds. Escoffery was also ordered to repay $205,185 and serve three years' probation after his release and perform 150 hours of community service. "This was motivated by greed. . . . You were entrusted with responsibility by the government," Judge John Antoon told the defendant as he sentenced him. A contrite Escoffery responded: "I deeply regret my actions. . . . I've let down my family, this country and my co-workers."[35]

Convicted in similar fashion a year before for using their positions to enrich her and her husband, Lynne LaBrake, instead of accepting her guilt, blamed the media for their prosecution. Government prosecutors charged that the LaBrakes used their positions in the Tampa housing authority to extract personal favors from contractors, including one who performed substantial improvements to their house. In exchange, Steven LaBrake helped a contractor win bids from his agency for inflated contracts for city housing. As the contractor on the witness stand told Assistant U.S. Attorney Robert O'Neill in Judge Richard Lazzara's Tampa courtroom, "I got paid back on some of the new houses. . . . They would pay me back by giving me more money on the houses than what the normal contract rate would be." The contractor performed any number of personal tasks for LaBrake. "He was the boss of everything in the city"—implying that to refuse LaBrake meant that he would get no more city construction work.[36]

The sixty-count indictment against the LaBrakes and another housing and banking official alleged a conspiracy to commit bribery and wire fraud. After nearly four weeks of testimony the jury found Steven guilty on thirty counts and Lynne guilty on twenty-eight counts. At her sentencing hearing Lynne LaBrake appeared defiant, proclaiming to the judge that she was devastated "to see my dream house on TV as the media made a name for themselves at my expense. I've never set out to defraud anybody or have anything handed to me. I feel I've been punished enough through the loss of everything I achieved, including my reputation."[37] Judge Lazzara stopped

LaBrake's tirade, warning her attorney that she was harming her plea for leniency. The judge was also frustrated by the couple's lack of remorse for damaging the cause of low-income housing in Tampa. "What strikes me about both LaBrakes," he said, "is it seems that the culture that permeated their work environment appears to be, 'You do me a favor, I'll do you a favor,' even though it violated the public trust."[38] Judge Lazzara sentenced Steven and Lynne LaBrake to five and three and a half years in prison, respectively.

As 2002 drew to a close Chief Judge Elizabeth Kovachevich prepared to pass the leadership of the Middle District Court to her successor, Judge Patricia Fawsett. Under Kovachevich's leadership the district experienced one of the most difficult overcrowding crises in its history. Not content to just sit back and let matters grow worse, Kovachevich effectively sounded the alarm to the district's lawyers, congressional representatives, and other stakeholders. While it could be argued that she may have gone beyond traditional means to admonish lawmakers and others responsible for providing help to the overburdened district, her efforts paid off in the appointment of five new judges in some of the most difficult political times anyone could remember. Moreover, Kovachevich's leadership was also visible in that five new courthouses were either designed, under construction, or opened during her tenure as chief judge. Kovachevich continually strived to maximize the district's output and continually sought ways to improve the court's efficiency. She was also open to nontraditional innovations. For example, less than a month after the 9/11 attack, Judge Kovachevich, allowed CNN legal commentator Greta Van Susteren to moderate a panel discussion between herself, lawyers, journalists, and judges Susan Bucklew, Patricia Fawsett, and Harvey Schlesinger about allowing cameras into federal courtrooms. Such open discussion about decisions that only the chief justice of the United States and the U.S. Judicial Conference could make was bound to ruffle feathers. "I hope we will do it in the future," she said.[39]

Only a week before Judge Kovachevich made these remarks the U.S. Senate acted to confirm the nomination of Timothy Corrigan as U.S. district judge. Nominated in May, Corrigan filled the seat that had remained unoccupied since its creation in 1999. Corrigan had served in Jacksonville as a U.S. magistrate judge since 1996 and would remain there in his new position. Only days after his confirmation, U.S. Circuit Judge Gerald Tjoflat, for whom Corrigan clerked after graduating from law school in 1981, swore the new judge in.[40]

Only months after Judge Patricia Fawsett's official tenure as chief judge began, word reached the district that one of its most distinguished judges had received yet another award. According *Tampa Tribune*, "no judge in Florida . . . commands more respect from his peers than William Terrell Hodges." That was why, the paper reported, Hodges received the twenty-first annual Devitt Distinguished Service to Justice Award from the American Judicature Society—an award that recognized Hodges' lifetime of achievements and work on the bench, his administrative contributions and public service, and his "fairness, decency, and knowledge of the law."[41]

While the Middle District Court community celebrated Judge Hodges' national recognition, several months later they expressed collective sorrow at the passing of one of their favorite judges. U.S. District Judge Ralph Nimmons was diagnosed with terminal liver cancer in March 2003 but worked almost until the very day he died, on November 24. Nimmons' old boss, former Jacksonville prosecutor and mayor Ed Austin, was particularly saddened by Nimmons' passing. "I didn't have a better friend in the world and I don't know of anyone who had it together as well as Buddy did. . . . He was an outstanding lawyer and judge and the young lawyers scrambled to get in his courtroom because they knew they could learn so much from him. He loved the law and he was the greatest credit to the profession." Circuit Court of Appeals Judge Susan H. Black had known Nimmons going all the way back to their days as state prosecutors in the early 1970s. "He helped me prepare my first case for trial. . . . He remained a part of my personal and professional life ever since. When you mention his name I think of the gentleman, a scholar and a man devoted to his family and his faith."[42]

Meanwhile, one matter that the district faced that was particularly acute was the overcrowding situation in Fort Myers. Even after the Fort Myers Division added a second U.S. magistrate to join U.S. Magistrate Judge Douglas Frazier and District Judge John E. Steele, the cases began to mount far beyond acceptable levels. Judges Gregory Presnell and Anne Conway came from Orlando to assist Steele and others, but still the cascade of cases from Collier and Lee Counties grew. At a weighted caseload of 958 (more than double the 430 average for district judges), Steele was believed to have the heaviest case load in the Eleventh Circuit. Chief Judge Fawsett said that 864 weighted cases were filed in 2001, and 760 were filed in 2002. Steele expected to put a dent in the backlog, but even so, it grew and grew. "I figured, 'Give me a year and I'll get this number down. I'm a hard worker.'" Yet in March 2004, four years after his appointment, he was forced to admit the reality. "We haven't hit the downside yet. I don't see the number going down," he said. The need for a second district judge in Fort Myers seemed obvious, but that did not automatically translate into action. Even so, that year Sen. Orrin Hatch had sponsored a bill to add three more district judges for the Middle District, but it would take three years before a similar measure passed.[43]

Stepping into this Fort Myers maelstrom of cases a year earlier was Sheri Polster Chappell. In the fall of 2002 the Judicial Conference authorized another magistrate position for Fort Myers. Chappell was one of the names that emerged from the merit selection committee, and after extensive interviews the Middle District judges selected her to fill the post in April 2003.[44] Chappell had a degree from the University of Wisconsin and earned her law degree from Nova Southeastern University of Fort Lauderdale. She served as assistant state attorney for the Twentieth Judicial Circuit of Florida until being appointed Lee County judge in 2000 by Gov. Jeb Bush.

While Fort Myers lacked adequate judgeships, three additional magistrate judges were added in Jacksonville. In 2001 the district judges appointed Thomas E. Morris, a graduate of the University of Missouri and the University of Florida Levin College of Law. Two years later they appointed Marcia Morales Howard and Monte C. Richardson to the bench. Howard was the daughter of Cuban immigrants, had degrees from Vanderbilt and University of Florida Levin College of Law, and had practiced privately for thirteen years. Monte C. Richardson, a native of Valdosta, Georgia, became the fourth African American U.S. magistrate appointed in the Middle District of Florida. Richardson had compiled an admirable record as assistant U.S. attorney in the Middle District of Florida since joining the office in 1988. Both Howard and Richardson were sworn in together in a lavish ceremony, surrounded by their families and friends in Jacksonville's historic Florida Theater.[45]

By the spring of 2004, the judicial nominating committee had forwarded several names to President Bush to replace Judge Ralph Nimmons. In April President Bush nominated Florida's Second District Court of Appeal judge Virginia Hernandez Covington. Covington's father was a well-known history professor at the University of Tampa, and her mother had emigrated from Cuba in 1953. Covington attended the University of Tampa, earning bachelor's and master's degrees in the 1970s. In 1980 she earned her law degree from Georgetown University and worked briefly for the Federal Trade Commission before joining the U.S. attorney's office in her hometown. In the 1980s Covington headed the asset forfeiture section in the office. In

2001 Governor Bush appointed her to the appeals bench, making her the first Cuban American woman ever appointed to a Florida appeals bench.[46]

During Covington's confirmation hearing on September 7, Judiciary Committee Chair Orrin Hatch and ranking member Patrick Leahy warmly recommended her swift confirmation. As Senator Hatch related to his Senate colleagues, Covington lectured widely and participated in seminars on asset forfeiture and money laundering with "prosecutors, law enforcement personnel, and judges in Chile, Argentina, Mexico, Venezuela, Colombia, Costa Rica, and Honduras. As a U.S. Department of Justice liaison, she also helped the Bolivian government establish its narcotics-related asset forfeiture program."[47] With such glowing words by both sides of the aisle, Covington's confirmation was secure. With longtime friend and judicial colleague Second District Court of Appeal Judge E. J. Salcines by her side, she watched on C-Span as she received a unanimous ninety-one to zero vote. "I'm very humbled and very, very grateful," she said a day later. "I've always wanted to be a lawyer—well before high school, maybe sixth or seventh grade. . . . It seemed like an interesting and fulfilling career. I haven't been disappointed."[48]

When she learned of Covington's confirmation, Chief Judge Patricia Fawsett praised the bipartisan cooperation of the Senate, especially coming as it did during a time when a Republican was in the White House and Florida had two Democratic senators. Senators Graham and Nelson, she stated, had been instrumental in ensuring Covington's confirmation. "It shows a great deal of statesmanship by all those involved," she said. While Covington's slot was originally intended to replace Judge Nimmons in Jacksonville, Judge Fawsett announced that Covington would be assigned to Fort Myers, where the need for another judge was most acute.[49]

Meanwhile, the Middle District Court of Florida achieved an important milestone for which it had been preparing for more than a decade. Several years earlier Judge Kovachevich appointed Judge Susan Bucklew to create an automation committee to explore the feasibility of moving away from paper filings for the court. In 2004 the court went paperless when it launched the Case Management/Electronic Case Files System (CM/ECF). Developed by the Administrative Office of the U.S. Courts, the system allowed courts to maintain case documents in electronic form and gave lawyers and judges the ability to file pleadings, motions, and petitions with the court over the Internet. The first implementation of the system in some federal courts began in 2001 in bankruptcy courts and then in some district courts by 2002. CM/ECF revolutionized the daily operation of court functions, especially as it related to managing cases and dockets. As Judge Richard Lazzara explained, the new system allowed judges access to important files at the click of a mouse. "It's just wonders. . . . when I go home in the evening, I'll go online at home—because I'm hooked up at home—and I'll see whether anything's been filed. That kind of prepares me for the next day. It's just super, super efficient. . . . I remember the old days where you had the paper files. You had to go through the file and look for the motion, etcetera. Now, you just go down, you click on it, there it is, you can print it out."[50]

No sooner had the new paperless system been put in place than three major hurricanes slammed through the Middle District of Florida that fall. Hurricanes Charley (August), Frances (September), and Jeanne (September) all carried the potential of disrupting the courts' operations, especially in Orlando and Tampa, where all three storms caused substantial damage. Clerk Sheryl L. Loesch rapidly organized her staffs in Orlando, Tampa, Jacksonville, and Fort Myers to maintain the newly installed CM/ECF system that had been put in place only months earlier. They installed emergency power generators, and the main server remained operational throughout the crisis. In recognition of her staff's hard work, Loesch nominated a number of them for awards. Despite the danger to their own families, many of her employees left their own families during this time of great fear and anxiety, "left their homes that were likely to sustain damage, to go into the courthouse to make sure that generators functioned properly. . . . Some employee lost the roofs to their homes, some employees lived without electricity and water for weeks. It was a horrific time, yet everyone continued to maintain the mission of the court, despite any personal hardships they were experiencing." Eight of Loesch's staff received the Administrative Office Director's Award for Extraordinary Action.[51]

In her new role as chief judge, Patricia Fawsett, as had her predecessor, did her best to alert all interested parties of the need for more judges to the overburdened district. But, as usual, politics, budget shortfalls, and the reluctance of Congress to create more Article III judgeships would get in the way. In the upcoming years the Middle Florida district courts faced challenges other than a lack of man- and womanpower—not the least of which was the difficulty of adjudicating complex, politically charged constitutional cases that involved some of the most controversial issues facing contemporary American life. It is to these matters we now turn.

18

Contesting Sentencing Guidelines,
the Patriot Act, Terrorism, and Cases Involving
International Questions

Since coming on the bench in 2000 Judge Gregory Presnell adjusted well to his new role as a district judge. One of the state's most outstanding commercial litigators when he was appointed by President Bill Clinton, Presnell had never been a judge before, but he worked hard to master the intricacies of the job. "In some ways," he reflected some years later, "it's good to have experienced lawyers as judges—good to bring people in fresh." Presnell admitted that he "had to work at the criminal side. I knew the civil side." By all accounts Presnell's hard work was well received. A 2002 survey of federal lawyers practicing in Orlando rated Presnell extremely high.[1] Yet the lack of civility among lawyers was something that Presnell complained about both before and after he came on the bench. In one of his cases, after bickering attorneys could not agree on a minor issue in a pretrial hearing, Presnell issued an order that the matter be decided by a game of Rock, Paper, Scissors. The silly dispute was covered extensively in the newspapers, and the chastened lawyers eventually resolved the question.[2]

But a far more serious matter stuck in the judge's craw almost immediately upon becoming a judge. What was particularly troubling to the new judge were sentencing guideline disparities, namely the disparity of sentences for those convicted of using crack versus powder cocaine. Powder cocaine was the drug of choice for the well-to-do addict while crack was the drug of the streets. After studying the issue, Presnell became convinced that the Sentencing Reform Act of 1984 that took judicial discretion out of the process was a setback for justice. Sentencing guidelines, he complained in one of his opinions, were "at best schizophrenic and at worst contrary to the basic principles of justice."[3] They had "rendered judges meaningless participants in the sentencing process."[4] "I went out on some limbs. . . . I wasn't hamstrung by the procedures. . . . I did a lot of writing on sentencing issues, and I think it made an impact positively," he recalled.[5] Presnell was right. The U.S. Supreme Court accepted Presnell's rationale in *United States v. Booker* (2005) when it ruled mandatory sentencing guidelines unconstitutional. The guidelines, the court ruled, should be advisory and not mandatory. The ruling provided district judges the flexibility to argue why guidelines did not apply to the case at hand and then impose sentences above or below the guidelines.

Judge Presnell exercised this new flexibility in *United States v. Hamilton* (2006) when he refused to follow guidelines in sentencing a defendant convicted in his court because of what he called the "arbitrary and discriminatory disparity between powder and crack cocaine. . . . Unless one assumes the penalties for powder cocaine are vastly too low," the judge asserted, "then the far-higher penalties for crack are at odds with the seriousness of the offense. The absence of a logical rationale for such a disparity and its disproportionate impact on one historically disfavored race promotes disrespect for the law and suggests that the resulting sentences are unjust. Accordingly, these statutory factors weigh heavily against the imposition of a Guidelines sentence."[6] Also in *U.S. v. Williams* (2005), *U.S. v. Delgado* (2005), and *U.S. v. Pancheco* (2006), exercising the discretion established in *Booker*, Presnell ordered sentences below the range established by the sentencing guidelines.

On December 11, 2007, in an effort to fix the sentencing disparities between crack and cocaine sentences, the U.S. Sentencing Commission voted to reduce the prison terms of hundreds of inmates convicted of a crack cocaine offense. Of the nearly twenty thousand inmates eligible for early release nationally, roughly four hundred of those had been sentenced in Middle Florida courts, the second-highest number of any district in the nation. The amendment to the guidelines excluded career offenders and those serving mandatory-minimum prison terms.[7] Taking into consideration the growing body of evidence of the unfairness in sentencing, Congress passed the Fair Sentencing Act (2010). The law reduced the disparity between the amounts of crack cocaine needed to trigger federal penalties.

While prosecutors may not have liked this new order of things, the Patriot Act, passed in 2001 as a counterterrorism measure after 9/11, gave them new resources to fight terrorism. The act gave federal agencies far greater latitude in gathering intelligence, particularly as it applied to surveillance and monitoring electronic financial transactions. The law expanded the government's power to investigate individuals and groups, and facilitated more efficient sharing of information among federal agencies. As one commentator noted, the Patriot Act gave "the Justice Department and law enforcement new powers to combat domestic activities of terrorists, including broad wiretapping powers, indefinite detention of noncitizens suspected of terrorist activities or links to terrorists, enhanced abilities to trace Internet activity and library borrowing, and other provisions."[8] From the beginning the law was controversial, and opposition to the law grew as time went on. Critics claimed the law gave too much power to the federal government to search personal information without a court order. In an op-ed piece contributed to numerous Florida newspapers, U.S. Attorney Paul Perez defended the Patriot Act, calling it a "reasonable" and "appropriate measure" to "increase security after the deadly attacks on our citizens on September 11, 2001." In another piece, Perez referred to the Patriot Act as a "common sense tool that has helped law enforcement and intelligence communities coordinate, communicate and uncover terrorist operations." Perez's piece inspired numerous rebuttals on letters-to-the-editors pages throughout the district.[9]

Middle District judges were soon interpreting the law in their courtroom. On two separate occasions U.S. Magistrate James Glazebrook rejected Patriot Act search warrants in child-pornography cases, ruling that the act was specifically designed only for cases that involve terrorism or domestic security. Judges Kendall Sharp and Gregory Presnell reversed Glazebrook, with the latter judge ruling that while the "statutory language is ambiguous . . . , the court ultimately comes to a determination regarding the meaning of this language, but by no means is it clearly, unambiguously, or precisely written."[10]

Given the law's ambiguity and their concern for the new powers it gave prosecutors, Presnell and other Middle Florida judges were particularly vigilant of prosecutorial misconduct in their courtrooms. In 2001, for example, Judge Patricia Fawsett sided with the defendant in a counterfeiting case when she learned that four Secret Service agents repeatedly threatened him and violated his rights to remain silent and to see a lawyer. "His version of the events . . . is by far more plausible than the tightly constructed, seemingly rehearsed, almost verbatim testimony of the four agents who testified," she wrote as she threw out the case. Also in 2001 Judge Anne Conway threw out a case against a laborer when the U.S. Border Patrol picked him up simply because he "looked Mexican."[11]

One of the most high-profile cases of prosecutorial misconduct involved

Antonio "Nino" Lyons, a popular clothing store and nightclub owner, convicted in Judge Gregory Presnell's court in Orlando in the fall of 2001 of selling cocaine. The evidence in the trial consisted entirely of testimony from twenty-six convicted felons but did not include any seized drugs, videotaped drug deals, wiretaps, or other physical evidence. During the trial Judge Presnell accused the lead prosecutor of withholding evidence that might have served the defense. After, he discovered that some of the evidence in the case had been destroyed, Judge Presnell overturned the conviction based on prosecutorial misconduct. The Eleventh Circuit Court of Appeals reversed Presnell's ruling, but the judge persisted in an effort to discover the full facts of the case.[12] He ordered U.S. Magistrate David A. Baker to investigate the prosecutors, and the judge found numerous instances of wrongdoing.

Baker discovered that in numerous instances prosecutors encouraged witnesses to lie under oath. Thus, it was "virtually impossible," Baker wrote, "to reassure all concerned that the defendant received a fair trial." Not unexpectedly, Lyons' lawyer welcomed Baker's report. "This is a case that was concocted completely on the testimony of convicted felons, telling the government what it wanted to hear. It becomes extremely upsetting and shocking that the government knew these people were not telling the truth." Even so, Chief Assistant U.S. Attorney James Klindt denied intentional wrongdoing on the part of the government. "We have conceded from the outset that mistakes were made in this case. We did not turn over some things we should have. . . . We're disappointed that the court views our mistakes as prosecutorial misconduct because prosecutorial misconduct suggests intentional or purposeful wrongdoing."[13]

Five months later Klindt was back in court. "We strive to do the right thing in every case and the right thing to do in this case is to ask the court to dismiss the drug-conspiracy case because of the mistakes that were made," he told Judge Presnell. "The mistakes go to the credibility of the witnesses and the defense's ability to cross-examine them effectively."[14] The government, he said, would not ask to retry the drug charge but continued to assert Lyons's guilt in two other charges: selling counterfeit clothing and carjacking. In a ruling four months later, Judge Presnell dismissed all the charges against Lyons. "The court refuses to be the government's rubber stamp of single-minded injustice. . . . The government would be well-served to guard the esteem of its offices with greater vigilance. . . . The government cannot now change the fact that, through aggravated violations of its prosecutorial duties, it destroyed Lyons's character and credibility, and, with that, confidence in the jury's verdict on the carjacking count."[15] Although he was acquitted, Lyons' reputation had been destroyed, and he had lost thousands of dollars in the process of defending himself against the wrongful prosecution. In 2010 he appeared in federal court again seeking damages against the wrongful conduct of the government under the Unjust Conviction Act; he was eventually granted a Certificate of Actual Innocence and awarded $140,000.[16]

Despite the controversial nature and the ambiguity of the Patriot Act, it did assist prosecutors in going after terrorists, drugs dealers, and spies. Most importantly, however, it was essential in building the case against one of the Middle District's most controversial defendants: University of South Florida (USF) engineering professor Sami Al-Arian, who was accused of being a leader of the Palestinian Islamic Jihad (PIJ).

Al-Arian, a Kuwait-born Palestinian, first came to the United States in 1975 to study engineering, eventually earning a doctorate from North Carolina State University. Since coming to USF in 1986, he had not been shy about expressing his sympathy for various Palestinian causes. In 1988, while employed by USF he created the Islamic Concern Project, an umbrella organization that included the Islamic Committee on Palestine, a charity devoted to Palestinian causes. Another of its purposes was to inform Americans about the intifada, the insurrection against Israeli occupation in the Gaza Strip and the West Bank. Three years later, Al-Arian founded World Islam and Studies Enterprise (WISE), a think tank at the university to study Islamic thought and political theory. Throughout his tenure at USF, Al-Arian's outspoken criticism of Israel and his defense of organizations that the United States had labeled "terrorist" often tested the bounds of academic freedom. By 1996 numerous critics had charged that Al-Arian's two organizations were fronts for Palestinian terrorist groups. In fact Ramadan Abdullah Shallah, a WISE director, resigned to become head of the PIJ in Damascus. USF placed Al-Arian on paid leave while a federal investigation probed Al-Arian's association with known terrorist organizations. (Al-Arian was reinstated two years later.) Also in 1996, after the Immigration and Naturalization Service denied Al-Arian U.S. citizenship on account of evidence that he had fraudulently voted, the professor sued the INS in federal court. Judge Henry Lee Adams threw out the suit.[17]

Not surprisingly, after 9/11 Al-Arian's activities came under even closer scrutiny. His appearance on Fox News channel's *The O'Reilly Factor* on September 26 brought more unwanted attention to USF. Responding to criticism from students, alumni, and others, university president Judy Genshaft suspended Al-Arian on the grounds that his outside activities disrupted the life of the university. Al-Arian sued the university in federal court, alleging that he was being persecuted because of his religion, ethnicity, and political beliefs. As his dispute with USF over his suspension played itself out in federal court, the U.S. Attorney's Office confirmed that federal law enforcement was conducting an investigation of Al-Arian, and on February 20, 2003, an indictment was filed. (Within a week Genshaft fired Al-Arian.) The indictment charged that Al-Arian was a leader of the PIJ and that he and nine others were involved in a criminal enterprise that had conspired to kill and maim others abroad. The fifty-count indictment also charged Al-Arian and the other defendants with conspiracy to commit racketeering and murder and with having plotted to maim or injure persons at places outside the United States. Al-Arian and his associates had also conspired to provide material support to terrorists by raising funds for their use and benefit. They had also unlawfully used the mails and had illegally attempted to procure citizenship for themselves and others.[18]

Prosecutors planned to try Al-Arian using the Racketeer Influenced and Corrupt Organizations Act. Atty. Gen. John Ashcroft credited the Patriot Act as essential to Al-Arian's prosecution because it removed barriers to sharing intelligence with law enforcement and provided law enforcement with new tools to investigate terrorist activity. Indeed, much of the evidence for the indictment was developed through declassified national security wiretaps that detailed dozens of intercepted telephone calls and faxes between the defendants. The indictment, claimed Ashcroft, sends a message. "We will hunt down the suppliers of terrorist money, we will shut down their sources and we will ensure that both terrorists and their financiers meet the same swift, certain justice of the United States of America." For his part, Al-Arian denied his guilt, claiming the charges were political, that he did not condone violence against civilians; his attorney referred to his client as a political prisoner.[19]

U.S. Magistrate Judge Mark Pizzo refused Al-Arian bail at his arraignment. As he was taken back to jail, Al-Arian proclaimed once again that he was a "prisoner of conscience." Jesus, he said, like himself, had "always questioned power and spoke out." As he was being led away, he handed a prepared statement to his seventeen-year-old daughter, who read the statement to the reporters outside the federal courthouse: "I'm prisoner because of the hysteria engulfing the country in the aftermath of the 9/11 tragedy. . . . And because there are very powerful political groups which are thirsty for my blood. I'm not an enemy, but the forces of intolerance and exclusion are."[20]

Al-Arian's prosecution attracted national media coverage. It shared headline space with President Bush's attack on Iraq, launched on March 19, 2003. The next day Al-Arian was brought into Judge Pizzo's courtroom to participate in his bail hearing. Prosecutor Walter Furr called Al-Arian the "lifeblood" of the PIJ. For a time, Furr asserted, "Al-Arian . . . was as powerful as any member of the Islamic Jihad on the planet." After considering much testimony, Pizzo eventually denied Al-Arian bail, noting that the evidence against him was "substantial and convincing." Al-Arian and his codefendants were substantial flight risks, plus, as he explained in his twenty-nine-page ruling, "based on the government's strong presentation," the defendants "repeatedly assisted, promoted, or managed the Palestine Islamic Jihad (PIJ), an organization which indiscriminately murders to achieve its goals . . . and both did this for years, regardless of the risks, risks apparent to all." Pizzo went on to admit that while the defendants were "prominent leaders and models of civic involvement in their respective communities," they "hid and obfuscated their PIJ association. This dichotomy, a private life versus a public one," the judge continued, "reveals much about their character and the tenacity of their commitment to a pattern of deception toward achieving the PIJ's goals. . . . This assumption of the risks, this willingness to push all the PIJ's goals, is telling. . . . It means each valued the PIJ more than family or lifestyle."[21]

While prosecutors prepared their case against Al-Arian and the other defendants, the lottery system in place at the time determined that Judge James Moody would hear the case. Mounds of evidence in the form of nearly one thousand reels of taped conversations, faxes, bank transfers, seized computers, and compact discs containing counterintelligence surveillance recordings—all gathered as a result of 152 separate warrant applications to a secret court—had yet to be analyzed. Thirty computers were seized. Prosecutor Furr estimated that 99 percent of the conversations and the data were in Arabic.[22] While Al-Arian remained in jail, the case continued to receive attention in the national media and even during a nasty senatorial race between former USF president Betty Castor and Mel Martinez. The former Bush cabinet member accused Castor of being soft on terrorism because she didn't fire Al-Arian when she led the university. Castor countered that she left USF in 1999 and that Al-Arian was involved in President Bush's successful 2000 campaign and was even invited to the

White House at one point. Given the publicity and other concerns, Judge Moody postponed the trial until April 2005. He eventually rejected a defense motion to move the trial, and jury selection began on May 16, 2005. Judge Moody ordered his courtroom closed to the public, but a video feed with the camera turned away from the jury candidates was shown next door.[23]

The trial finally got under way on June 6. Security was tight. Large plastic barriers surrounded the courthouse as did armed federal law enforcement officers. In his opening statement, Al-Arian's attorney, William Moffitt, proclaimed that his client was a nonviolent advocate for the rights of Palestinians, and that his prosecution was an assault on the fundamental rights of free expression. Moffitt claimed that Al-Arian's involvement in the PIJ diminished markedly after 1994, after he had failed to convince the Islamic movement to move away from politics toward religion and nonviolence. Moreover, the group was not declared a terrorist organization until 1995. The attorney found nothing wrong with Al-Arian's efforts to raise money for the orphans of suicide bombers or those in prison. "Labeling people PIJ orphans means they should be denied charity for the political beliefs of their relatives. . . . I suggest that's not the American way, and it's not something that should be embraced in this courtroom." Finally, Moffitt asserted, "The evidence will show that Dr. Al-Arian is an unrepentant supporter of the liberation of Palestine. . . . The evidence will show that Dr. Al-Arian's choices were always nonviolent ones." Prosecutor Furr strongly contested Moffitt's assertions, countering that PIJ was one of the "most violent terrorist organizations on earth." And for a time, he told jurors, "Al-Arian was the most powerful man in this organization. . . . The stock and trade of the PIJ . . . is murder and maiming. . . . These people were above the level of any fool who's going to get on a bus and blow himself up, killing other people. . . . Other people did that. They funded the organization. They gave it life, saved it when it was in trouble."[24]

The trial included over eighty witnesses and went on for more than five months. Federal prosecutors portrayed Al-Arian as a sort of crime boss assisting the terrorist organization with financial support, but defense countered in closing arguments that the government did not prove that Al-Arian did anything but speak. The defense argued that the First Amendment protected Al-Arian's actions and that the government had no evidence that he planned a single attack. Judge Moody instructed the jurors that mere association or sympathy for a criminal organization is not illegal.[25] Jury deliberation lasted nearly two weeks. Finally, on December 6, the jury acquitted Al-Arian on eight counts and deadlocked on nine others, prompting Judge Moody to declare a mistrial on the other counts. The not-guilty verdicts included conspiracy to murder or maim citizens outside the United States and providing material support to the PIJ.

Visibly shaken, U.S. Attorney Paul Perez left the courtroom with several of his staff. He told reporters that his office would consider whether to refile charges on the counts the jury could not reach a unanimous decision. In the end one juror remarked that the government did not prove the case. Another added, "A lot of it, I felt it was hearsay." Outside the courtroom, Al-Arian's wife, Nahla, beamed. "This is America and everybody has the right to speak out. . . . Above all, I'm so grateful to God, the God of justice; he was with us."[26] Moffitt's co-counsel, Linda Moreno, added, "We worked very hard—two lawyers against the federal government in what many people described as the biggest terrorist case in the country. . . . Dr. Al-Arian's positions on the struggle of his people in Palestine, while unpopular, are protected in this country."[27]

Al-Arian remained in federal custody while the government decided whether to pursue removal proceedings against him or perhaps try him again. In April 2006 Moody approved the broad outlines of a plea deal between Al-Arian and prosecutors in which he pled guilty to conspiring to help a terrorist organization in exchange for Al-Arian agreeing to be deported after serving a sentence that was little more than time served. (The agreement seemed to confirm several of the charges against Al-Arian and contradict the findings of the jury.)[28] Even so, approximately twelve days later at Al-Arian's formal sentencing, Judge Moody sentenced the defendant to fifty-seven months in federal prison—the maximum allowable under the plea agreement.

When provided the opportunity to speak, Al-Arian praised the PIJ, held forth on the true meaning of democracy, and launched into the integrity of the jury system when Moody snapped. "Dr. Al-Arian, as usual, you speak eloquently. . . . I find it interesting that here in public in front of everyone you praise this country, but yet in private you refer to this country as the Great Satan . . . but it's just evidence of how you operate. . . . You are a master manipulator."[29] Moody accused Al-Arian of lying about the extent of his leadership in PIJ and blasted him for calling his work "charity for widows and orphans. . . . When it came to blowing up children and women on buses, did you leap into action? No. You lifted not one finger. On the contrary, you laughed when you heard about the attacks."[30] Finally, referring to a 1995 double-suicide bombing that Al-Arian had praised at the time, Judge

Moody declared, "Anyone with even the slightest bit of human compassion would be sickened. Not you. You saw it as an opportunity to solicit more money to carry out more bombings."[31] Obviously, Moody's views on Al-Arian differed markedly with the jury that had acquitted him. U.S. Attorney Paul Perez contended that Moody's statements and the sentence vindicated the criminal prosecution.

Al-Arian's problems continued. In 2006, when he refused to testify before a grand jury in the U.S. Eastern District of Virginia regarding an Islamic think tank with which he was associated, he was convicted of contempt, and more jail time was added to his sentence. Though eventually released under house arrest, as of this writing he is still facing contempt charges for his connection with alleged involvement in terrorist activity.

While the Al-Arian trial was probably the most sensational trial to address international issues during this time period, there were other cases that involved such matters as immigration, the abuse of immigrants, illegal trafficking of animals, émigrés charged with war crimes, and espionage. Florida continued to be a destination where immigrants came legally and illegally to engage in business activity or even just to better their living conditions, and this created circumstances that often led to federal prosecutions. Most vulnerable were illegal immigrants coming from Haiti, Mexico, or other impoverished nations who were taken advantage of. For example in 2002, Eric Bruno was indicted and convicted in Fort Myers for posing as a FBI agent and soliciting bribes of over $25,000 from fellow Haitian immigrants to help them handle their immigration problems. Assistant Prosecutor Doug Malloy said that Bruno "chose his victims because of their lack of familiarity with the system here." The victims, he continued, were particularly vulnerable because they were used to paying bribes to government officials in their former country. After Bruno's conviction for impersonating a federal agent, Judge John E. Steele sentenced him to three years in federal prison, one year for each count of false impersonation.[32]

In 2004 the federal government prosecuted Palestinian millionaire Jesse Maali and two codefendants, M. Saleem Khanani and David Portlock, for money laundering, tax evasion, hiring illegal immigrants, and creating shell companies to pay employees off the books. After Maali's arrest Assistant U.S. Attorney Cynthia Hawkins, citing Maali's ties to groups in the Middle East who supported violence, asked that the defendant be denied bail. Even so, a U.S. magistrate set his bail at $10 million.

Born in Palestine, Maali immigrated to Venezuela, New York, and then to Orlando in 1986. Investing in stores and shops primarily on International

Drive, Maali was reputed to be worth over $70 million. Federal prosecutors contended that much of Maali's wealth came through income tax evasion and employing illegal immigrants off the books. Maali's lawyers contended that their client was wrongfully targeted because of his political beliefs and the post-9/11 hysteria that was sweeping the country. They also argued that the two hundred federal agents who had seized hundreds of boxes of documents and 3 million computer files in November 2001 had exceeded constitutional bounds against unreasonable search and seizure. When asked to rule on the defense's motion, Judge John Antoon noted, "To be sure, the warrants are broadly worded to encompass many documents. However, warrants of such breadth have been upheld, especially in white-collar crime cases involving fraud where a 'paper puzzle' must be assembled."[33] Judge Antoon ordered Maali's personal papers returned, however. Months later Antoon cast aside charges that Maali was the victim of selective prosecution because of his Arab heritage, or that he was targeted because of his charitable giving and advocacy of Palestinian causes. Even so, Antoon granted a severance of Maali's prosecution from the two other defendants because Maali was undergoing chemotherapy and radiation treatments for cancer.[34]

One month after a jury convicted Maali's codefendants, Khanani and Portlock, of breaking immigration laws, tax evasion, and fraud, Jesse Maali died while undergoing cancer treatments. After he learned of Maali's death, U.S. Attorney Paul Perez sent out his condolences to Maali's family but defended his office's prosecution, adding that it had nothing to do with ethnicity or religion. "In this case, we firmly believe we had a righteous prosecution."[35] Perez also pointed out that Maali's coconspirators had been recently convicted on the same evidence: Khanani got five years in prison and $275,000 in fines; Portlock got four years and a $15,000 fine.[36]

Illegal immigrants were often susceptible to abuse by those eager to exploit their labor in agricultural enterprises. Often paid in cash and cheated out of their wages in various ways, those without proper identification were vulnerable because they had entered the country wrongfully and thus lacked proper documentation to seek employment. Other laborers in Florida were victimized in similar ways. Some contractors charged exorbitant costs for housing, food, cigarettes, drugs, and alcohol—entrapping laborers into enormous debt. Because it was a major producer of citrus and vegetables, Florida continually faced the challenge of protecting low-paid laborers from predatory contractors who exploited them. Such practices not only resulted in a modern-day debt peonage but in some cases these conditions led to human trafficking. In 2004 U.S. Attorney Paul Perez, responding to directives from the Justice Department, announced a major federal crack-down on human trafficking and further spoke out frequently about federal efforts to enforce the Trafficking in Victims Protection Act of 2000.[37]

On June 3, 2005, federal agents raided an East Palatka labor camp, seiz-ing drugs and financial records documenting an illegal operation in which homeless people, drug addicts, and illegal immigrants were lured into a form of peonage by forcing them to work off debts from credit purchases of cocaine, cigarettes, and beer. Robert Evans, his son, his wife, and several others were eventually captured and charged with human trafficking, drug dealing, and making false statements to Labor Department investigators. Evans' laborers stayed in Northeast Florida from December to June, cut-ting cabbage and grading potatoes, and then were transported and housed under similar operations in North Carolina. Evans' son pled guilty to sup-plying the workers with cocaine. Eventually prosecuted in one of the largest human trafficking cases in American history, Evans, his wife, and son were convicted in Jacksonville of various federal crimes. Evans received thirty years in prison.[38]

While the Evans family's operation was local and unsophisticated, large companies and corporations were also prosecuted for similar wrongdoing. In 2007 Judge Henry Lee Adams, after determining that Florida tomato producer Ag-Mart had intentionally violated federal rules, ordered Ag-Mart to pay $500,000 in damages to agricultural workers who were forced to live in substandard housing while harvesting crops. The successful pros-ecution came under the Migrant and Seasonal Agricultural Worker Pro-tection Act. Extensive trial testimony revealed how the company housed workers in broken-down motels that lacked facilities for cooking, refrig-eration, or laundry in violation of federal law. At the same time Ag-Mart also forced workers to buy prepared food. The successful class-action suit was brought by the Migrant Farmworker Justice Project of Lake Worth and Tallahassee.[39]

As it had since the 1980s, Orlando and Tampa attracted numerous im-migrants and other persons who conducted all manner of legal and illegal business enterprises. By the 1990s, with daily international flights to Eu-rope, Latin America, the Middle East, and Asia, entrepreneurs (legal and illegal) could come and go, meet clients with ease, or even set up temporary headquarters. Drug dealers had been doing this since the 1980s. Increas-ingly one of the scourges that had arisen in the 2000s was the black market smuggling of exotic animals into the United States. In January 2002 one of the international kingpins of the illegal traffic, Lawrence Wee Soon Chye, a native of Singapore, was apprehended as he was attempting to establish temporary headquarters for his operation in Orlando. Nearly a year later Chye pled guilty in Judge John Antoon's court to smuggling hundreds of endangered and protected creatures into the United States. In a blistering statement to Chye, Antoon stated, "Your crimes are reprehensible. They not only are a form of animal cruelty, they also endanger public health." The crime not only threatened many endangered birds, reptiles, and mammals with extinction but it also presented numerous health risks to Americans because the animals brought in many dangerous germs and diseases. Although Antoon considered Chye deserving of a long jail sentence, he sentenced Chye to the maximum allowable under sentencing guidelines, thirty-seven months.[40]

In the 1990s Alejandro Ballen, a Colombian engineer who lived in the drug-infested Cali area, fled to the United States after guerillas had murdered his father. Abandoning his property, Ballen settled in Kissimmee with his wife—also an engineer. By 2002 their family included three children. In 2002 Ballen made a serious mistake. In January 2003 Ballen was arrested on Orange Blossom Trial with over $1 million in counterfeit currency, one of the largest seizures in Florida history. A prospective buyer of Ballen's farm, who also headed one of the largest counterfeiting operations in the Americas, offered Ballen $15,000 to help move the counterfeit money to New York City. Once he was apprehended, Ballen cooperated with Secret Service. With his assistance, authorities seized over $20 million in bogus currency. After pleading guilty to his crime, a remorseful Ballen appeared before Judge John Antoon. "I want to be a good man again," he said. Secret Service Agent Kevin Billings spoke in Ballen's favor. Ballen had put his life at risk in assisting the federal government, the agent explained. "The United States has been trying to close down this counterfeiting ring for a quarter of a century." Judge Antoon sentenced Ballen to twenty-three months, roughly half of what sentencing guidelines provided for.[41]

The federal courts also served as forums for which persons accused of war crimes could be prosecuted. Adolph Milius, a seventy-nine-year-old gynecologist from Lithuania, came to the United States in 1947, became a naturalized American citizen in 1955, and served two years as a doctor in the U.S. Army. After spending most of his career in Chicago, Milius relocated to St. Petersburg Beach in 1979. In 1998, armed with documents from Lithuania's archives, the Justice Department's Office of Special Investigations accused Milius of being a member of the dreaded Saugumas, a unit of the Lithuanian Security Police charged with rounding up Jews during the Nazi occupation in 1941. The accusation charged that for five months Milius, a medical student, worked for the organization that was responsible for sending over thirty-three thousand Jews to their deaths. Although Milius' lawyer, Paul Johnson, argued that his client was only a clerk for a brief time, and that it could be proven that Milius was personally responsible for apprehending only about a dozen individuals, Judge Henry Adams decided that such activities were sufficient to revoke Milius' citizenship. "Although Milius may have performed his duties as gently as possible, and may not have personally injured anybody, his participation in the above events nonetheless constituted persecution." Milius returned to Lithuania and he died there in 1999.[42]

In 2006 Branko Popic, a recent immigrant to the United States who had found his way to St. Petersburg, was indicted for lying about his service in the Serbian Army on his application for U.S. citizenship. Popic's arrest was part of a nationwide sweep of Serbian immigrants who participated in the massacre of Srebrenica during the Balkan conflict. Popic was charged with fraud and making false statements, but attempts to convict him resulted in a mistrial when the jurors could not agree on his guilt. A second attempt to prosecute Popic was also unsuccessful. Even so, Popic remained in federal custody until 2011, when he was eventually deported to Bosnia.[43]

Foreign governments also sought recourse to the U.S. Court for Middle District of Florida in disputes involving American companies. Such was the case in 2007 when Spain sued in Tampa to have nearly $500 million in gold returned to its nation after it claimed a Tampa-based salvage company had wrongfully recovered more than fifty thousand coins and other artifacts. The cache amounted to nearly seventeen tons of silver and gold from the nearly 1,700-foot-deep site off the coast of Gibraltar. The Odyssey Marine Exploration Company had salvaged the treasure from the *Nuestra Señora de las Mercedes*, which had been sunk off Gibraltar by a British warship during the Napoleonic Wars. Spain sued Odyssey, claiming that the gold came from the *Mercedes*, which was within Spanish territorial waters and thus was protected under the Foreign Sovereign Immunities Act. When Odyssey disputed the claim, U.S. Magistrate Judge Mark Pizzo ordered the company to reveal the contents of the find in a confidential manner so experts could identify the wreck and the treasure. Subsequent investigation determined that the wreck was indeed the *Mercedes* that lay off the coast of Portugal within the territorial limit and was subject to Spanish sovereign immunity. In a thirty-four page ruling, Judge Pizzo ordered the treasure returned to Spain. "More than 200 years have passed since the *Mercedes* exploded. Her place of rest and all those who perished with her on that fateful day remained undisturbed for two centuries—until recently. International law recognizes the solemnity of their memorial, and Spain's sovereign interests in preserving it."[44] Pizzo also cast aside Peru's claims of being entitled to the treasure. (Peru had argued that it was entitled to the treasure because the gold was wrongfully extracted from its mines by a colonial power.)[45]

Not surprisingly, Spanish officials were delighted with Pizzo's ruling, even though it still had to be confirmed by a district judge. "We are very happy," said Spanish Culture Minister Angeles González-Sinde. "This decision is very important. I am glad the judge has really seen that the ship and the treasure belong to Spain."[46] Odyssey argued that the ship's identity was not confirmed by the evidence and even if it was, the commercial nature of the *Mercedes* would nullify its claims because most of the bullion on board was owned by private merchants, not the government. In Judge Steven D. Merryday's ruling affirming Judge Pizzo, the judge dismissed the argument that the *Mercedes* was merely a cargo ship transporting specie for private merchants. "The ineffable truth of this case," Merryday stated, "is that the *Mercedes* is a naval vessel of Spain and that the wreck of this naval vessel, the vessel's cargo, and any human remains are the natural and legal patrimony of Spain." When Odyssey transported the treasure to Florida, he continued, it did so "without the consent of Spain and athwart venerable principles of law."[47] In September 2011 the Eleventh Circuit Court of Appeals issued an opinion affirming Judge Merryday's ruling. The U.S. Supreme Court refused to hear the case, and thus the treasure was returned to Spain.

By their very nature, drug prosecutions often involved foreign nationals, like one prosecuted in Tampa that began as an attempt to sell Strontium-90, a nuclear material used for making dirty bombs. The Eleventh Circuit Court of Appeals noted that the facts underlying the prosecution of English subject Christopher J. Benbow and others "began like something out of a James Bond novel but soon morphed into an international drug conspiracy ring." The plot began in 2003 when Benbow, who owned houses in Miami and Estonia, offered to broker the sale of some $220 million worth of the radioactive material from former Russian KGB agents. Benbow and others began negotiating with undercover federal agents in Miami, Tampa, Belgium, London, and other locations, and it was eventually decided to sell cocaine to raise cash to buy the Strontium-90. Thus, Benbow and three other conspirators, including one man affiliated with one of England's most prominent organized crime families, were charged with possession with intent to distribute $8 million worth of cocaine as part of the conspiracy. All four were extradited to Tampa to face the grand jury indictment.[48]

Benbow and one of his accomplices, Peter S. Davidson, pled guilty to the charges, and Benbow told the court that he thought he was dealing with Israeli agents who would steer the materials away from terrorists. Assistant U.S. Attorney Anthony Porcelli also told the court that he could neither corroborate Benbow's claims nor locate the nuclear materials. In fact, he was not even sure if the nuclear materials even existed. Benbow was sentenced to life in prison by Judge Elizabeth Kovachevich. His life sentence was overturned on appeal, and his case was sent back to Judge Kovachevich, who reduced the sentence to eleven years and three months.[49]

America's war on drugs continued in the new century, and the Middle District continued prosecuting smugglers engaged in bringing drugs from offshore to Florida. In 2000 federal authorities in Tampa launched Operation Panama Express, which targeted the head of the Cali cocaine cartel, and prosecutors netted numerous seizures and convictions. The new craft of choice for Colombian drug smugglers was the "go-fast" boat—a boat that could outrun most regular drug interdiction vessels. Decoy boats were also often used to attract the attention of law enforcement vessels away from those carrying drugs. In April 2002 a jury in Judge Susan Bucklew's court in Tampa convicted the captain of a decoy boat involved in helping another boat smuggle cocaine into the United States. Prosecutors proved that Luis Albeiro Lopez-Ramirez, the captain of the *Barlovento II*, was acting as a lookout and decoy for the *Recuerdo*, a boat loaded with cocaine thirty miles away. The coast guard captured both boats about eight hundred miles off Colombia. On board the *Recuerdo* was over nine tons of cocaine, worth over $162 million.[50]

Because of population growth and its easy access to world travelers, the U.S. Court for the Middle District of Florida would continue to hear cases involving foreign plaintiffs and defendants, and its courtrooms served as forums where constitutional questions were adjudicated. It is to these subjects we now turn.

19

Constitutional Questions
of the Twenty-First-Century Court

The new millennium saw many constitutional disputes reach the Middle District Court—some serious and some seemingly not so serious. For example, an attorney representing Cyberzone, an Orlando dance club featuring "rave" dancing, asked Judge Patricia Fawsett to issue an injunction against a city ordinance forbidding rave clubs to stay open past 2:00 a.m., bringing it in line with clubs that sell liquor (even though the club did not sell liquor). "This is a regulation that prevents adults from dancing," the attorney for Cyberzone argued, and "music is protected under the First Amendment." The assistant Orange County attorney countered that the ordinances were put in place not against dancing but to curtail drug activity at the club. Moreover, he claimed, "recreational dancing is not protected by the First Amendment. . . . It's still conduct that can be regulated." After hearing the evidence in the case Judge Fawsett agreed. She refused to issue the injunction.[1]

The federal court also heard many cases that involved nude dancing. Clubs that offered such entertainment in Daytona Beach, Orlando, and Tampa fought an ongoing battle with religious groups and municipal politicians who sought to ban the practice by local ordinance. Some municipalities banned the sale of alcohol and otherwise tightly regulated adult-entertainment establishments, claiming that they were responsible for an increase in crime, violence, and blight and the loss of property values. In January 2006 Judge John Antoon found two Daytona Beach antinudity ordinances in violation of the First and Fourteenth Amendments, claiming that city officials did not prove that the Lollipops Gentleman's Club was responsible for an increase in crime and violence. The city's claims, Antoon noted, were based on "anecdotal evidence or opinions based on highly unreliable data. . . . Gone are the days," he continued, "when a municipality may enact an ordinance ostensibly regulating the secondary effects on the basis of evidence consisting of little more than the self-serving assertions of municipal officials."[2]

The next year, in a similar case involving an Orange County adult-entertainment code, Judge Antoon invalidated the enforcement of some elements of a code that restricted dancers' movements on stage. In a forty-four-page ruling, Antoon asserted that "the criminal provisions challenged here regulate the very movements an erotic dancer can make during a performance. . . . Because the ordinances criminalize the protected expression conveyed through erotic dances, the ordinances chill the dancers' exercise of free expression."[3] Antoon added that the "First Amendment cannot both protect the expressive element of erotic dancing and also restrict and contort it by prohibiting the very movements that contribute to its erotic message. . . . While the public en masse many not approve of such explicit performances, the First Amendment does not turn on generally accepted views of propriety."[4]

As it had since the 1960s, the Middle District Court continued to hear disputes regarding local governments or schools endorsing religion. In March 2007 Senior District Judge John H. Moore ordered a lighted cross removed from atop a municipal water tower in Starke, Florida, because it violated the federal and state constitutions prohibitions against endorsing religion. The cross had been on the water tower since the 1970s but was unchallenged until 2005 when a Bradford County citizen, along with American Atheists Inc., filed suit in the federal court. Citing local petition drives, bumper stickers, and letters to the editor, the plaintiffs proved that the symbol had a municipally financed religious purpose. It was also revealed that city funds had been used to repair, maintain, and light the cross.[5] In his ruling Judge Moore asserted, "We cannot close our eyes to the light of the cross on the ground that it represents only a minor encroachment of this constitutional command, for the breach of neutrality that is today a trickling stream may all too soon become a raging torrent. . . . If ever there was a clear case of excessive governmental entanglement with religion, this is it." The American Atheists leader hailed the decision, calling it "a great victory for the First Amendment separation of church and state. . . . No government, whether federal, local or state, should be promoting sectarian religion and using public money to build and maintain religious displays."[6]

In a similar First Amendment case involving religious expression, Judge Harvey Schlesinger ruled that two teachers and a principal violated the constitutional rights of two third graders when they made them choose between practicing what he called a "proselytizing" and "sectarian" country music song for a year-end assembly or sitting out the entire performance. Judge Schlesinger's ruling came after the children's parents filed a suit against the St. Johns County School District. William Sheppard, an attorney for the plaintiffs, maintained that compelling the students to rehearse the lyrics of the song *In God We Still Trust* was in violation of the doctrine of the separation of church and state. After studying the lyrics, Schlesinger noted that the song violated that constitutional principle. "'In God We Still Trust,'" the judge noted, is a "song overtly espousing a specific religious viewpoint and attacking those who do not share in the same belief." Plus, the judge added, the third graders "were easily influenced by their teachers" and "extremely sensitive to signs of disapproval and disappointment from the same teachers and their classmates." The teachers, the judge asserted, had in effect "ostracized the objecting students from their classmates and effectively penalized them for exercising their constitutional right to object."[7]

In May 1999, in an effort to improve discipline and learning it its public schools, the Polk County School Board joined a growing number of other school districts across the nation in deciding to implement a school dress code for elementary and middle school students. The policy required students to wear navy blue or white shirts and khaki, blue, or black bottoms. The policy did not include an opt-out option. After the policy's implementation, a group of parents formed a parental action committee, hired attorney Robert Norgard, and sued the county in September, claiming that the policy violated the students' right to freedom of speech and expression, and that the mandatory school uniform policy hinders parental rights. In January 2001 Judge James Whittemore dismissed some of the plaintiff's claims but allowed them to pursue the lawsuit.[8]

The trial proceeded in July. Attorney Norgard asserted before U.S. Magistrate Judge Thomas Wilson that the mandatory dress code "is an issue of free speech."[9] But after considering the evidence Judge Wilson upheld the policy. While admitting that the dress code fell under the First Amendment, it "survives appropriate constitutional scrutiny" because the policy served a higher purpose. Citing precedents in other rulings, Judge Wilson ruled that the "defendants have demonstrated that the dress code furthers an important or substantial government interest. The dress codes themselves contain detailed findings showing that they were designed, among other things, to improve discipline and academic performance, reducing violent, disruptive and distracting behavior and to improve school spirit. . . . These are clearly important interests."[10] Of course, Judge Wilson's ruling had to be confirmed by Judge Whittemore, and the spokesman for the plaintiff parents noted, "I don't see this as a setback. . . . It's just a recommendation. And even if it's struck down, we still have the individual claims. If just one of those is ruled in our favor, it's no more uniform policy."[11] Less than ten days later Judge Whittemore adopted Wilson's recommendation, but the plaintiffs decided to pursue the case based on inconsistent enforcement of the dress code. Once Judge Whittemore threw out those claims before another hearing could proceed in November, the litigation ceased.[12]

Gordon Johnston, a sixty-year-old high school civics teacher and Tampa Bay Buccaneers season-ticket holder, had a problem. Tired of being patted down by rent-a-cops when he entered football games, Johnston, with counsel supplied by the American Civil Liberties Union, sued the Tampa Sports Authority in October 2005, claiming that the patdowns violated his constitutional right of unwarranted search and seizure. Florida circuit and an appeals court blocked the patdowns for the remaining games of the season. Before the next football season started, the case was heard on July 13 in federal court, and Judge James Whittemore upheld the state courts' rulings. "A generalized fear of terrorism should not diminish the fundamental Fourth Amendment protection envisioned by our Founding Fathers," Judge Whittemore ruled on July 28. "The Constitution requires more." Whittemore further stressed that the constitutional threshold of the policy was not met. "It is not about the wisdom of the patdown policy, whether the average fan supports or objects to the patdown searches, or whether the judge believes the patdowns are wise." People may have become more tolerant of searches in the wake of 9/11. But that did not allow the Transportation Security Agency (TSA) the permission to ignore constitutional protections of privacy. "Utilizing mass suspicionless patdowns simply goes too far," Judge Whittemore ruled. Johnston was ecstatic at Whittemore's ruling. "I felt like the Constitution was on my side, and the law was on my side. . . . It's great to know that in our society today, when something is wrong, you can still try to make it right."[13]

After mulling Whittemore's decision, the TSA appealed the case to the Eleventh Circuit of Appeals, and in July 2007 a three-judge panel set aside the ruling and sent it back to Whittemore, claiming that because Johnston had submitted to the patdowns before, he could not object to it later. "It's sort of like telling Rosa Parks, 'You've been riding on the back of the bus for so many years, you can't do anything about it now,'" one of Johnston's lawyers remarked.[14] The plaintiffs appealed to the Supreme Court in 2009, but it refused to hear the case. The patdowns resumed and continued until 2012 when the TSA replaced the mandatory patdowns of fans with sweeps from magnetic wands.[15]

Florida's continued population growth, immigration patterns, and demographic shifts spurred challenges to existing voting methods at the local level. By 2005 Hispanics made up 35 percent of Osceola County's population. That year the United States Justice Department sued the county and its supervisor of elections, claiming that the at-large election system for county commissioners diluted Hispanics' voting power and violated the 1965 Voting Rights Act. The Justice Department suit asserted that a single-member district system would be fairer to Hispanics because they would make up a majority in at least one district and thus would have a voice on the county commission. (The Justice Department began studying Osceola County in 2000 after a number of Hispanic leaders filed complaints with them.) The Justice Department asked for an injunction from the federal court to stay the commissioners' election until the case was resolved. On June 26, 2006, Judge Gregory Presnell granted the request to postpone the elections until a system was in place to guarantee Hispanics' voting rights. In addition, he gave the county and the Justice Department until July 18, when a trial would begin, to work out a compromise that included electing commissioners from individual districts, and he called for a status report on July 12. In his order Presnell asserted that "the Board of County Commissioners has steadfastly maintained its opposition to single-member districts because they point to parochialism," but the current system of at-large voting also ensured parochialism, he maintained. "It's a rationalization or a pretext for diluting the Hispanic vote in Osceola County." "I'm very disappointed by the approach used by the federal government," one former commissioner responded when he learned of Presnell's ruling. "It's very disheartening but not a surprise. . . . There's a level of arrogance in Washington and in the legal system that goes beyond normal. What is more bothersome to me than anything else is the federal government telling local people in the community that their vote is meaningless."[16]

Osceola County officials remained defiant. On June 27, citing a 1996 election in which Osceola voters adopted the at-large voting system (the same year that Osceola elected its only Hispanic commissioner under the single-member district system), they rejected Judge Presnell's suggestion that they establish a single-member district system. An attorney for the county declared they intended "to proceed with the defense of this case." When he learned of the commissioner's decision to defy Judge Presnell, Armando

Ramirez, a county commission candidate and the person who had filed the original complaint with the Justice Department in 2000, blasted the commissioners. "They're making a big mistake. . . . When they became aware of the rapid and extraordinary growth of the Hispanic community, they began a crafty plot to bring back the at-large system. They knew the at-large system would put obstacles in front of Latino candidates. . . . The reason why they did that is they wanted to prolong the dynasty."[17]

Ten days before the scheduled trial date, Judge Presnell granted the county's motion for a two-month extension.[18] The three-day hearing took place in September. One month later, on October 18, citing a "history of discrimination against Hispanic voters," Judge Presnell ordered the county to submit a plan within five weeks that would overhaul the way it elects county commissioners.[19] The current voting structure, Presnell insisted, penalizes Hispanics in violation of the Voting Rights Act of 1965. Both the county and the Justice Department filed proposals for a new voting structure, and Judge Presnell ordered a hearing to consider them. After spending more than $2 million in defending against the Justice Department suit, Osceola County finally accepted the inevitable. They adopted a single-member district voting plan.[20]

Among all the cases that came before the Middle District of Florida, none was more controversial or politically charged and none made more national headlines than the Terri Schiavo "right to die" case. In 1990, at the age of twenty-six, Mrs. Schiavo suffered a heart attack that cut off the blood supply to her brain, leaving her in a comatose vegetative state. Since the attack Mrs. Schiavo was connected to a feeding tube, was unresponsive to stimulation, and required around-the-clock care. In 1999, nine years after her heart attack, her husband, Michael Schiavo, and her doctors determined that Terri's condition was irreversible; believing that she would not have wanted to continue living that way, they made the decision to remove her feeding tube. Terri's parents, Bob and Mary Schindler, sued in state court to block the move. Pasco-Pinellas State Circuit Judge George Greer ruled in the husband's favor, and Florida's Second District Court of Appeal upheld the lower court ruling. When the Florida State Supreme Court refused to hear the case, the Schindlers turned to the federal court in April 2001, but when the Schindlers appeared in Judge Richard Lazzara's Tampa courtroom, he told them that he had no jurisdiction in the case, and that the U.S. Supreme Court was the proper forum to contest the Florida Supreme Court's ruling. He also took issue with their comparison of their daughter's case to that of a death row inmate facing execution without a lawyer to defend her. Even so, Judge Lazzara gave the plaintiffs three days to make an appeal.[21]

After an appeal failed, the Schindlers once again filed suit in state circuit court on April 26, and Terri's feeding tube was reinserted so that a new trial could determine whether new therapies might help her. Over the next year conflicting physician opinions led to Judge Greer once again ordering removal of the feeding tube. While an appeal was going forward, the Schindlers again sought recourse in federal court, asking Judge Lazzara to issue a temporary restraining order blocking the removal of the feeding tube. Rebuffed again by Judge Lazzara on the same grounds as before, the judge allowed them ten days to refile a more carefully worded plea. The Schindlers eventually filed suit against their son-in-law in federal court, asking that he be removed as the guardian of their daughter.[22]

By this time, after six years of litigation, Terri Schiavo's case was making national headlines, and right-to-life and right-to-die advocates had made the issue a cause célèbre for their movements. As of this point the Florida appeals court had issued four rulings that consistently found that Michael Schiavo had established convincing evidence that his wife did not wish to be kept alive by artificial means. Even so, Florida governor Jeb Bush, responding to entreaties from tens of thousands of constituents, inserted himself into the situation and filed a brief in the federal court in the Schindlers' favor. "In light of the seriousness of this matter," Bush's brief stated, "and the inability to remedy an improper outcome, the governor has a strong interest in ensuring that Terri Schiavo's fundamental right to life is not deprived without due process of law."[23] Judge Lazzara refused to rule on the case, stating once again that the Schindlers must look to the state court of appeals. Lazzara also noted that despite Governor Bush's petition, he had no authority to intervene in the state case, stating the Tenth Amendment to the U.S. Constitution forbade him from doing so and that recent federal appeals court rulings had verified that fact. "Frankly, even if I were to find jurisdiction . . . I would be abusing my discretion if I issued an injunction. . . . To say I have not been tempted . . . would be an understatement. I must resist temptation."[24]

At this point the six-year battle to keep Terri Schiavo alive reached a new level as the Florida legislature, at Governor Bush's urging, passed "Terri's Law," a law that allowed the governor to override a state judge's order to remove her feeding tube, and enjoined the state circuit court to appoint a guardian ad litem to make recommendations to the governor and the court about her care. Thus, on October 22, Bush countermanded the judge's order, and Terri Schiavo remained on life support. Michael Schiavo's lawyer, George Felos, and many legal experts considered "Terri's Law" unconstitutional. Felos asked a state circuit judge to declare the law unconstitutional, arguing it violated the right to privacy and that it violated the constitutional separation of powers between the executive and judicial branches. When asked to weigh in on the constitutionality of the law, legal experts were queried. Joe Little of the University of Florida Levin School of Law stated, "The Law allowed the governor and the legislature to take over the courts, and that is profound. . . . When has that ever been done in the state of Florida? Never. Think of the possibilities: All of a sudden we have a tyrant who can do whatever he wants, and the courts cannot protect you." Bruce Rogow of Nova Southeastern University demurred. "Is it a bizarre act of the Legislature? Absolutely. . . . Is it a violation of the separation of powers? Arguably. But does the Legislature have the right to pass a statute to remedy an ongoing situation? I think the answer to that is probably. So I dissent on the constitutional argument but concur on the profound absurdity."[25] On May 6, 2004, State Circuit Judge Douglas Baird declared Terri's Law unconstitutional. Four months later, on September 23, the Florida Supreme Court concurred with the lower court and struck down the law. Then, once the U.S. Supreme Court refused to review the ruling, the case seemed over. The Schindlers then resumed their battle in the state courts, contesting the removal of their daughter's feeding tube on a number of grounds.[26]

Then on March 8, 2005, newly elected U.S. senator Mel Martinez and Rep. Dave Weldon introduced federal bills in Congress extending due process rights to incapacitated persons and giving the Schindlers new federal powers to sustain nourishment to their daughter. Similar bills made their way through the Florida legislature. On March 21, with the entire nation watching, President George W. Bush signed a congressional law, "For the Relief of the Parents of Theresa Marie Schiavo Act," that was intended to get Terri Schiavo reconnected to the feeding tube while a federal court reviewed the case. If the law did not confer any "new substantive rights," it did put the matter back in the federal court because it empowered a federal judge to determine whether any of Terri Schiavo's rights were violated by a state court. The next day, with the national media descended on Tampa's Sam Gibbons Courthouse and the four days after Terri Schiavo's life support had been removed, Judge James Whittemore heard the impassioned testimony of both sides. "The mother and father are pleading with this court, as they pleaded with Congress and the nation," the Schindlers' lawyer told

Whittemore.[27] The judge should rule in their favor on three grounds: (1) The state judge had denied Terri Schiavo a fair trial because he had become an advocate for Terri's death; (2) Terri Schiavo had been denied due process because the state judge had not appointed an independent attorney for her; and (3) Terri had been denied her right to religious freedom because voluntary death was contrary to her Catholic religion. Whittemore was not impressed with these contentions. He was not convinced there was a "substantial likelihood" of eventually winning the case and thus the threshold for issuing a preliminary injunction could not be obtained.[28]

Michael Schiavo's lawyer, George Felos, called the federal law passed only days later a "horrific intrusion" generated by "popular political clamor. . . . What you are asked to do," he told Judge Whittemore, "is to overturn seven years of judicial work of the State of Florida, countenance a severe invasion of her body and force a procedure against her will, trampling on her right of choice." On March 22 Judge Whittemore refused the Schindlers' request to reinsert the tube. Whittemore ruled on narrow grounds. While admitting that the federal law empowered him to issue an injunction in the matter, he declined to do so on the basis that the Schindlers' cause had little chance of success if he conducted a full hearing.[29]

As expected, Whittemore's decision drew passionate criticism. The Vatican weighed in to keep Terri Schiavo alive. Some Catholic leaders likened Whittemore's ruling to capital punishment. The ruling had condemned Terri Schiavo to "an atrocious death: death from hunger and thirst." An editorial in the Vatican newspaper pronounced: "After all, Terri's destiny appears not unlike that of many men and women who in the United States get capital punishment for their crimes. . . . But Terri has committed no crimes" other than being considered "'useless' to the eyes of a society incapable of appreciating and defending the gift of life."[30] As before, the federal law and Judge Whittemore's ruling inspired political debate at the state and national level. While generally it could be said that the Republican Party's right-to-life faction was the driving force behind the bill, not all Republicans agreed with this course. Intervening in state court matters ran against the grain for many Republicans. Summarizing this position, Virginia Republican senator John Warner said he voted against the legislation because it violated his conservative principles of federalism. "The misfortunes of life visited upon Theresa Schiavo are a human tragedy," he stated, "no one can deny. I said my prayers, as did many Americans, when we attended religious services this Palm Sunday. . . . I believe it unwise for the Congress to take from the state of Florida its constitutional responsibility to resolve issues in this case."[31]

The Schindlers appealed Whittemore's decision to the Eleventh Circuit Court of Appeals in Atlanta even as Florida State senator Daniel Webster lobbied state legislators to pass another state law in favor of keeping Terri Schiavo alive.[32] Both attempts failed. On two more separate occasions within the next nine days the federal appeals court and the U.S. Supreme Court refused to hear the case, and Terri Schiavo died on March 31.[33] Not unexpectedly, the aftermath of the Schiavo case roiled state and federal politics as interest groups and the politicians that they opposed and supported were caught in the crossfire of arguments over the right to die, state's rights versus federal power to intervene, and the independence of the judiciary.

At an event honoring Judge Whittemore and Florida circuit judge George Greer, Florida attorney general Charlie Crist made state headlines when he praised both judges. "You are heroes to all of us," he said, "and your defense of the judiciary and what is right is beyond admirable." Some days later, after being given a chance to retract his statement, Crist responded, "It's important that those checks and balances exist. Our system of government needs to have that." Crist's statements were forthright for a person seeking the Republican gubernatorial nomination in 2006. Yet many who equated Whittemore and the circuit judge's decisions as murder were not silent when they heard the remarks. The executive director of the Center for Reclaiming America, a grassroots Christian political group, denounced Crist's statements. Others questioned Crist's commitment to the sanctity of life.[34] The issues involved in Terri Schiavo case was yet one more contributor to polarization of American society—a polarization that continued to play itself out in the federal courts as it did in other areas of civil society.

The political controversy regarding U.S. attorney general Alberto Gonzales and his firing of numerous U.S. attorneys nationwide in the winter of 2007 is yet another example of this political polarization. Political pressure in the Attorney General's Office had been building since the passage of the Patriot Act. Gonzales' predecessor, John Ashcroft, had called upon his prosecutors to monitor closely which judges imposed more lenient sentences than federal guidelines recommended.[35] But political controversy and the degree to which it affected the U.S. Attorney's Offices' ability to do their jobs perhaps reached a crescendo with the appointment of Gonzales. A Bush loyalist, Gonzales succeeded John Ashcraft as attorney general, taking office in February 2005. Prior to serving in this office, Gonzales had served Bush when he was governor of Texas and joined him as White House counsel after the 2000 election. Involved in numerous controversial policies regarding the interrogation of prisoners in the administration's War on Terror, Gonzales had also fought successfully to keep Vice President Dick Cheney's energy task force documents secret. A vocal advocate for the Patriot Act, Gonzales was attorney general when Congress passed a new version of the law in March 2006. The Justice Department's use of the Patriot Act to uncover personal information on U.S. citizens continued to be controversial, but Gonzales' most controversial act involved the firing of a number of U.S. attorneys throughout the country for no apparent reason. Critics charged that the firings were merely attempts to create a cadre of compliant U.S. attorneys throughout the country. While U.S. attorneys serve at the discretion of the president, many were fired unexpectedly and seemingly for no reason before they had served their four-year terms.

As the controversy reached its peak, Middle District U.S. Attorney Paul Perez announced that he would resign effective March 30, 2007, to take a position as chief compliance officer for Fidelity National Financial Inc., a Jacksonville-based financial services firm. Perez admitted that the timing of his leaving looked bad, but the opportunity to accept this position with a Fortune 500 company was too good to pass up. He adamantly denied that his decision had anything to do with Gonzales' ongoing controversies in the Justice Department, but with Bush's second term nearing its end, most understood he needed to seek new opportunities. Perez's five years in office were certainly eventful. He took over the U.S. Attorney's Office in the aftermath of the 9/11 attacks and after the failed Aisenberg prosecution. Morale was low, but Perez hired new people and infused the office with new blood. Supporters pointed out that Perez's office had initiated Operation Panama Express, which hobbled drug cartels. The office had gone after human trafficking rings, and the Al-Arian prosecution (while largely unsuccessful) had exposed the USF professor as what Perez called a "white collar terrorist." St. Petersburg attorney Pat Doherty praised Perez for running his office free of any political partisanship. "He ran his office as ethically as it can be run." Tampa attorney Bill Jung agreed: "He's one of those people you scratch your head: Is he a Republican? He's non-political. I've never seen politics enter the decisions he's made."[36]

Not surprisingly, many of Perez's critics and those critical of the Bush administration were suspicious and saw things differently. While Tampa attorney Rochelle Reback praised Perez for his fair and ethical conduct, she observed that some had criticized Perez for his lack of vigor in prosecuting white collar crimes. Was Perez under pressure from Washington not to pursue such cases? "I would hate to think that what we thought was laziness was really fear," Reback said.[37] Not surprisingly, Democratic leaders were suspicious of the circumstances of Perez's departure. U.S. senator Bill Nelson, who had already called for Gonzales to step down, wanted Congress, which was already investigating Gonzales' office, to look into the causes of Perez's resignation. Nelson pointed to a letter that Perez and sixteen other U.S. attorneys had signed complaining to the Justice Department of its slowness in implementing a data-sharing system for law enforcement agencies. Several of those who had signed the letter had been fired. Still, Perez was adamant in insisting that his departure was in no way related to the firing scandal.[38]

Meanwhile, it was announced, as Perez had hoped, that James Klindt would take over the office on an interim basis. A mainstay in the U.S. Attorney's Office since 1988, Klindt was the natural choice to head the office. "Jim has been by my side since I took office five years ago this month, and he has been a tremendous asset and good friend," Perez stated.[39] Klindt would serve seven months while a permanent successor to Perez could be found. Klindt insisted that morale in the department was good despite the controversy in Washington. "I think everyone in the office is keeping our eye on the ball," he noted.[40]

When the call went out for applicants for the U.S. attorney post, the response was less than overwhelming. Very few applicants lined up for the job. Seigel attributed the lack of interest to the "attorney general's awful performance in defending the actions the department took in firing eight U.S. attorneys. I think the politicization of the department—a lot of people are not interested in getting in the middle of that."[41] But from his new corporate office Perez challenged this contention. "I think that's an inside the beltway issue. . . . That doesn't affect what's going on in the field. That shouldn't keep qualified people from applying for U.S. attorney."[42] Most understood that a successful applicant could only expect to serve two years. And after leaving office, they would not be able to try cases in the district for two years and could not take part in any trials involving investigations launched during their term. "For a person in private practice," said former assistant U.S. attorney Greg Kehoe, "that's a significant sacrifice."[43]

As the days of Klindt's temporary tenure as acting U.S. attorney wound down, politics in Washington again reared its head. Senate Judiciary Committee Chair Patrick Leahy charged that the Bush administration was stalling in its refusal to nominate a permanent replacement for Perez. Senators

Martinez and Nelson had forwarded the administration three names, but the White House had refused to nominate anyone. Leahy charged the administration with attempting "to circumvent Congress and the law" because it was replacing its fired U.S. attorneys with long-term replacements in a way that evaded congressional approval through a provision in the Patriot Act allowing the president to name interim U.S. attorneys without Senate confirmation. Congress had overturned that language in the bill, but still the Bush administration continued the course. "I had hoped when the Senate voted overwhelmingly to close this loophole," asserted Leahy, "it would send a clear message to the administration to nominate Senate confirmable U.S. attorneys and begin to restore an important check on the partisan influence in law enforcement. . . . But regrettably, it did otherwise." With Klindt's tenure about to run out, it seemed that they would try to reappoint him again temporarily, as with the others, to avoid a Senate confirmation process.[44] But only days before his brief tenure was to expire, the district judges named Klindt U.S. magistrate judge and assigned him to Jacksonville.[45]

Instead of nominating a replacement for Perez, Bush named another interim U.S. attorney, Robert O'Neill, on October 26. The son of Irish and German immigrant parents, O'Neill had served in many capacities in his nineteen years in the U.S. Justice Department. Raised in Bronx, New York, O'Neill attended Fordham University and New York University School of Law and began his career as a prosecutor in Manhattan. He worked in Miami in the Southern District of Florida before eventually joining the Middle District U.S. Attorney's Office in Tampa in 1993. When notified of his appointment, O'Neill was elated. "I really do love . . . representing the United States. . . . It's something that never grows old."[46]

Finally, on July 15, 2008, only four months before the next presidential election, President George Bush nominated Holland & Knight lawyer Brian Albritton to become the next U.S. attorney for the Middle District of Florida. "He probably has the best judgment of any lawyer I know," said fellow lawyer Jack Fernandez of Albritton. "He's smart, he's tenacious. He's been aggressive without being overly aggressive in defending cases. He's an extraordinary guy."[47] Another lawyer predicted that Albritton was so respected that he could even serve beyond the current president's term. A native of Tampa, Albritton attended New College in Sarasota, Harvard Divinity School, and Boston College Law School. Returning to Tampa, he clerked for Judge William Terrell Hodges and then joined the Holland & Knight Law firm in 1990.[48]

Despite the political gridlock during his last two years in office, President Bush was able to nominate and confirm two new judges to the Middle Florida bench. The first opening was to fill a slot created by the retiring judge Harvey E. Schlesinger in Jacksonville. Marcia Morales Howard had been serving as U.S. magistrate judge in Jacksonville since 2003 when Bush nominated her. Both Senators Nelson and Martinez warmly endorsed Howard's appointment, and Howard was easily confirmed on February 20, 2007.[49]

Because Judges Susan Bucklew and Patricia Fawsett had decided to take senior status, the Middle District had two more openings to fill. By November thirty-six applicants had applied for the two openings.[50] Of the list that Martinez and Nelson recommended, Bush nominated sitting Tampa U.S. magistrate judge Mary Scriven for one of the openings. If confirmed, Scriven would be the first African American woman district judge ever for the Middle District. Scriven, forty-five, had been serving as U.S. magistrate judge in Tampa since 1997.[51] With both Senators Nelson and Martinez, the Senate confirmed her nomination on September 26, 2008.[52]

Also about that time another U.S. magistrate judge was added in Orlando after James Glazebrook died unexpectedly on a trip to New England on May 3, 2007. On July 11, 2008, the district judges selected Gregory J. Kelly. A native of Buffalo, New York, the forty-seven-year-old Kelly was a longtime civil lawyer with Akerman Senterfitt in Orlando.[53]

The fall of 2008 marked two particularly important milestones for the Middle District of Florida. First, in an official ceremony, the Jacksonville courthouse was named for one of the district's most distinguished jurists, and the district also welcomed a new chief judge. On August 11 with Rep. Corrine Brown, Rep. Ander Crenshaw, U.S. Circuit Judge Gerald Tjoflat, and a host of other dignitaries on hand, the six-year-old federal courthouse on Hogan Street was named for Judge Bryan Simpson. "He integrated not only Duval County's school system but also Daytona's," Brown said. Sam Jacobson, who had practiced before Simpson in the 1960s, said, "Bryan Simpson was the giant of the federal legal system in Jacksonville in the 20th Century. He personified the federal courts in this area from the period of the '50s into the '80s. . . . He was a person of huge courage as far as racial matters were concerned and had just an exquisite sense of fairness." Wayne Hogan, another lawyer, noted that Simpson's "decisions both in public accommodations and education were the models for decisions after that."[54] Finally, Judge Gerald Tjoflat perhaps summed up Simpson's legacy best when he called the judge an "icon. . . . He was, by far, the best trial judge in the state if not the southeast."[55]

Judge Harvey E. Schlesinger Portrait Hanging. *Front row, left to right*: Karen S. Jennemann, Paul M. Glenn, Jerry A. Funk; *second row, left to right*: Harvey E. Schlesinger; John H. Moore, Howell E. Melton, William Terrell Hodges, William J. Castagna, G. Kendall Sharp; *third row, left to right*: Timothy J. Corrigan, John Antoon II, Henry Lee Adams, Steven Douglas Merryday, Patricia C. Fawsett, Anne C. Conway, Richard A. Lazzara, James D. Moody, Virginia M. Hernandez-Covington; *fourth row, left to right*: Monte C. Richardson, Howard T. Snyder, Elizabeth A. Jenkins, Mary Stenson Scriven, Thomas B. McCoun, Thomas E. Morris, Gary R. Jones, Mark Pizzo, Marcia Morales Howard. Middle District of Florida Archives, George C. Young Courthouse, Orlando, Florida.

Also in August 2008 Judge Patricia Fawsett handed over chief judge duties to Judge Anne Conway.[56] Since coming on the bench in 1991, Conway had made a number of important rulings. In 2002 Conway had ruled that unauthorized depiction of relatives of real people in the movie *The Perfect Storm* did not violate the "right to privacy," and that plaintiffs had no grounds to sue Warner Bros. because the film was protected under the First Amendment.[57] Her rulings regarding the protection of sea turtles on Volusia County beaches were landmarks in the environmental field. Conway's current docket included the largest multidistrict litigation matter in the history of the Middle District of Florida that contained roughly 6,200 personal injury and product liability filings involving claims against the makers of the antipsychotic drug Seroquel.[58]

Anne Conway and her fellow judges in the Middle District would hear many cases in the first decade of the twenty-first century that involved complicated business controversies, taxes, tax evasion, white collar crime, and medical fraud. They would also adjudicate matters regarding the environment, wetland protection, and endangered species. It is to these matters we now turn.

20

Income Tax Evasion, Medicare Fraud, Organized Crime, Environmental Disputes, and Bankruptcy

Income Tax Evasion

On October 17, 2006, the U.S. Attorney's Office for Middle District of Florida announced that African American actor Wesley Snipes was wanted for conspiracy to defraud the Internal Revenue Service of more than $12 million. An indictment charged Snipes and two others who had assisted the actor with an unlawful scheme to avoid paying income taxes. Eddie Ray Kahn and Douglas P. Rosile were the founders of American Rights Litigator and Guiding Light of God Ministries, two groups that sold fraudulent tax schemes that helped persons evade income taxes. Snipes, an Orlando native and Hollywood star of more than twenty-five movies, had been affiliated with the organizations since 2000.[1]

Snipes' case eventually ended up in Ocala before Senior Judge William Terrell Hodges. But before that could happen, there was legal sparing over a number of subjects. Snipes' attorneys charged that he was a victim of selective prosecution. And because Ocala had a heritage of racial discrimination, an impartial jury could not be obtained. In a formal answer to the first allegation, Judge Hodges responded, "From a prosecutor's point of view, especially in tax cases, the primary objective in deciding who to prosecute is to achieve general deterrence. Here, Defendant Snipes is admittedly a well-known movie star, a person of apparent wealth, whose prosecution has already attracted considerable publicity. . . . Since the government lacks the means to investigate every suspected violation of the tax laws, it makes good sense to prosecute those who will receive, or are likely to receive, the attention of the media." In the same ruling Hodges also denied Snipes' counsel's request to move the trial from Ocala to New York City. Snipes had a home in Windermere, the judge reasoned, and the two organizations under investigations were located in Florida.[2]

Despite a long, drawn-out process, a jury was impaneled and the trial began on January 17, 2008. On that day Assistant U.S. Attorney Robert O'Neill presented the government's opening arguments. "Snipes, Kahn, and Rosile agreed to defraud the United States by not paying taxes due," O'Neill charged.[3] Defense counsel countered that Snipes was a victim of unscrupulous advisors as well as of the IRS. Snipes, his counsel asserted, was only one of thousands of clients Rosile and Kahn served and was not correctly advised. "Wesley Snipes has never had any intention to defraud the government. He has never been a conspirator. He has never been a tax protestor, and he has never been a cheat. He has never, ever defrauded anyone."[4] Snipes remained silent during the trial, but after each day he was mobbed by autograph seekers as he made his way slowly from the courthouse to his Cadillac Escalade. On one of those days Snipes addressed the crowd outside the courthouse: "No money, no problems. The problems always follow the money. That's the way it goes," he said.[5]

After nearly fifteen days of complicated, grueling trial testimony, the jury convicted Snipes on February 1, 2008. On April 24, at his sentencing hearing, Snipes apologized to the court for "mistakes and errors" and called himself a victim of "jackals and wolves" that were attracted to fame and money. "I am an idealistic, naïve, passionate, truth-seeking, spiritually motivated artist, unschooled in the science of law and finance. . . . Newly acquired wealth does not endow one with immediate wisdom, nor does it make one immune to a good hustle."[6] Prosecutors challenged Snipes' rendition of events, arguing that he deserved harsh prison time and that he owed over $20 million in back taxes. The jury pronounced Snipes guilty, and Hodges sentenced him to three years in jail. Kahn and Rosile drew harsher sentences: ten and four and a half years, respectively. Snipes remained free on bail as he appealed his case. Finally, after the Eleventh Circuit Court of Appeals upheld Hodges' decision, the judge ordered Snipes to jail on November 18, 2010.[7]

Medicare Fraud

Florida's popularity as an appealing home to retirees has also made it an attractive place for unsavory medical professionals who trick or scam seniors by falsely diagnosing illnesses for the purpose of filing Medicare claims. Usually such practitioners are new arrivals to the state and have shady backgrounds. This was not the case with Dr. Michael Rosin, a dermatologist who had been practicing in Sarasota for many years and had graduated from the University of Florida medical school in the early 1970s and trained at the George Washington University Medical School in Washington, D.C. Rosin descended from one of the region's most distinguished families (his grandfather came to Arcadia in 1905). Even so, in 2004 the physician came under scrutiny. Numerous elderly patients had accused the dermatologist of falsely diagnosing skin cancers and performing unnecessary surgeries. Responding to the allegations, federal law enforcement agents raided Dr. Rosin's office and seized patient files. Soon the Florida Department of Health, the FBI, and the U.S. Department of Health & Human Services launched a full-scale investigation of the doctor. Eventually a federal grand jury indicted Rosin on counts of health care fraud and making false statements. The indictment was based on information presented by patients and office personnel who alleged that Rosin continually made false diagnoses in order to collect over $3 million of Medicare claims. Indicted in April 2005 and released on bail, Rosin continued his practice while awaiting trial.[8]

Dr. Rosin's seventeen-day trial on the twenty-seven count indictment began in February 2006 before Judge William Castagna in Tampa. One of the chief witnesses against Rosin was his office manager, Carolyn Ferrera, who, after addressing her concerns to Rosin, had been told to mind her own business. She sued Rosin in 2004 under the False Claims Act (Whistleblower Act) and began talking to investigators.[9] While the defense called many character witnesses for Rosin who cited his strong religious faith and numerous charitable activities, other testimony revealed that Rosin had led a double life. Several of his office staff testified that Rosin often complained that he had seven children to support and that he needed to clear $10,000 a day. Employees told investigators that Rosin made diagnoses of cancer in 100 percent of cases, even diagnosing as positive chewing gum and plastic foam specimens.[10]

Rosin steadfastly denied the allegations, but in the end it was the biopsy slides seized from Rosin's office that resulted in the conviction. More than 865 of the slides examined of biopsies of elderly patients showed no cancer even though Rosin eventually performed surgeries on them. After two days of deliberation, on March 3, 2006, the jury found Rosin guilty on all counts. On October 4 Judge Castagna sentenced Rosin to twenty-two years in prison. While apologizing to his patients for things that went on in his office, Rosin never admitted his guilt. Instead he blamed his office staff, even claiming that they had orchestrated a conspiracy against him. Judge Castagna countered that Rosin's testimony was "clearly and deliberately false." The doctor had lied on the stand and caused serious bodily injuries to his victims. Rosin was also ordered to pay $46,866 to his patients, $3.6 million to the Medicare trust fund, and a $3.7 million fine.[11] On January 16, 2008, the Eleventh Circuit Court of Appeals affirmed Castagna's decision and found Rosin's appeal "to be largely without foundation. The trial itself was fundamentally fair, and Rosin's sentence was reasonable in all respects."[12]

One year after Dr. Rosin began his jail sentence, another dermatologist was accused of falsely diagnosing skin cancers and overbilling Medicare for services she provided. Dr. Marsha Lynn Hoffman-Vaile of Lakeland was eventually convicted in Judge Susan Bucklew's Tampa courtroom on forty-four counts of health care fraud, forty-four counts of submitting false claims, and one count of obstruction of justice. At her trial, prosecutors provided the court with a list of 250 of Hoffman-Vaile's patients upon whom she had performed unnecessary operations. At her sentencing hearing, Hoffman-Vaile showed remorse and asked for mercy. "This is the most difficult and traumatic day of my life. I'm embarrassed and humiliated and humbled to stand here in front of you today. I have worked my entire life to make a better life for my children."[13] Even so, Judge Bucklew sentenced the doctor to seventy-eight months in jail, reasoning that she knew what she was doing was wrong and she kept doing it. Judge Bucklew also ordered the doctor to pay over $1 million in restitution to patients, Medicare, and insurance companies.[14]

Organized Crime

As detailed in previous chapters, Florida, especially Tampa, had long been home to organized crime. With the death of Santo Trafficante in 1987 and the incarceration of Harlan Blackburn, this sordid legacy seemed over. But as Ken Sanz, a special agent for the Florida Department of Law Enforcement explained in 2006, organized crime was still a problem in Tampa even if it had morphed into different forms. According to Sanz, "mobile groups called 'crews' migrate to Florida and work independently, making payments to heads of families in New York or New Jersey." Sanz asserted that organized crime is "alive and well. . . . It's probably not comparable to what it was in the '80s, the '70s or the '60s, but it's here." Central and South Florida, Sanz continued, had become "open territory. . . . Any crime family can come down here now and do business." And that "business" included murder, racketeering, robbery, and extortion. Thus, in 1993 Ronald "Ronnie One Arm" Trucchio, who had been a member of the Gambino mob in

New York, came to Tampa as part of a scheme to establish a base of operations in Tampa. With New York money, Trucchio invested in valet parking companies and in the process linked his operation with Terry Scaglione, the grandson of former Trafficante operative Nick Scaglione. In a relatively short time the Tampa "crew" was sending a steady stream of cash back to New York.[15]

By 2006 Trucchio was already serving a twenty-year sentence for running a crew in South Florida. In May of that year a Tampa federal grand jury indicted Trucchio and five other codefendants for operating a Central Florida crew for eighteen years that committed "multiple acts and threats" involving murder, robbery, armed home invasions, extortion, and drug dealing. The other defendants were John Alite, Steven Catalano, Kevin McMahon, Terry Scaglione, and Michael Malone. Malone accepted a plea deal and decided to cooperate with prosecutors.[16]

After several delays the trial finally went forward in Judge Susan Bucklew's Tampa courtroom on October 15, 2006. Security was especially tight in the one-month trial. In the trial's first week Trucchio's lawyer, Joseph Corozzo, denied that his client was involved in the Tampa operation, claiming that defendant John Alite led the scheme. (Alite had escaped to Brazil but was in custody there fighting extradition.) Corozzo also charged that the government's key witnesses were facing huge prison sentences themselves and had every reason to lie.[17] After five days of deliberation the jurors convicted Trucchio and three of his codefendants, McMahon, Catalano, and Scaglione. Carl Whitehead, special agent in charge of the Tampa FBI, hailed the verdict as a "big blow to organized crime in the Tampa area" and to the Gambino family's New York operation in general.[18] Bucklew sentenced Trucchio to life in prison. Codefendants Catalano and Scaglione received sixteen and five years, respectively.[19]

In an interesting aftermath to the Trucchio prosecutions, a federal grand jury indicted John Gotti Jr., the alleged leader of the Gambino family's attempts to expand their influence into Tampa. The charges stemmed from his attempts once again to muscle his way into the Tampa crime scene by entering the valet parking business. Prosecutions in Tampa went forward after Manhattan juries had deadlocked in three trials in a row. Gotti was arrested, arraigned, and lodged in the Pinellas County jail on August 28. Gotti cooled his heals until his case came before Judge Steven Merryday. At his hearing on December 2, Gotti's lawyers charged that the case against Gotti belonged in New York rather than Tampa, alleging that federal prosecutors were merely jury-shopping to find a venue more likely to convict the suspects. Judge Merryday agreed. Gotti, he said, should be tried in New York. Thomas Ostrander, a lawyer familiar with the circumstances of Gotti's prosecution, predicted that Gotti's failed prosecution in Tampa would raise his chances of getting an acquittal in New York "100 percent, because now he's going back to an area where the jurors have been desensitized to these types of cases." True to form, after his indictment and three-month trial in New York, the government failed to convict Gotti—even with the key government witness—the recently extradited John Alite.[20]

Environmental Litigation

As they had in previous decades, Middle District judges ruled on environmental questions in the first decade of the twenty-first century. In 2005 one newspaper likened federal judges to football players "anchoring a goal-line defense of the environment" against a development-minded governor, state legislature, accommodating local government officials, and the Army Corps of Engineers. Issues such as manatee protection, wetlands protection, and massive developments that violated existing rules and generally threatened the environment were often before federal judges.[21] Middle District judges were also often asked to adjudicate endangered species questions as well.

In 2010 Judge Henry Adams issued a temporary restraining order against Mosaic Fertilizer Corporation's attempt to expand its South Fort Meade phosphate mine, ruling that the federal permit to destroy wetlands was probably issued illegally. Judge Adams' ruling came as a result of the suit brought by the Sierra Club, ManaSota-88, and People Protecting the Peace River, which claimed that the Army Corps of Engineers had wrongfully issued the permit without conducting an Environmental Impact Statement. The permit allowed the company to excavate 543 acres of wetlands and nearly 10 miles of streams adjacent to the Peace River. Adams' ruling stated that the environmental groups would likely be able to prove that the Corp's issuance of the permit was "in violation of the Clean Water Act and the National Environmental Policy Act." Mosaic spokesman Russell Schweiss told reporters that he was confident the lawsuit was without merit. The project, he asserted, had undergone "intense local, state, and federal regulatory scrutiny" and was "based on science and meets or exceeds all legal and environmental requirements."[22]

Adams' ruling was unpopular among many. For some workers the choice was clear: jobs should prevail over the environment.[23] On July 22, less than a week before Adams' temporary restraining order was to expire, Mosaic attorneys argued in his Jacksonville courtroom that halting the expansion of its Fort Meade mine would result in the layoff of 220 workers and cost Hardee County $5 million in tax revenue. Halting the mine would also result in a global shortfall of fertilizer. Plaintiffs once again countered that the Corps of Engineers improperly granted the permit without proper study of environment impacts. At Adams' suggestion, both parties consented to mediation, and on February 2012 a settlement was reached. The deal allowed Mosaic to mine 7,000 acres of land near Bowling Green in return for roughly 4,200 acres of parkland and other environmental protections along Peace River.[24]

In 2007 the Florida Builders Association sued the U.S. Fish and Wildlife Service, claiming that its backlog of endangered and threatened species status reviews had caused unfair construction delays and inflated housing prices. With over one hundred such listed species, Florida had the third-highest of any state in the nation. Attorneys for the agency defended the agency before Judge John Antoon by claiming that budget cuts had made it impossible for them to carry out congressional mandates to review the status of each endangered and threatened species every five years. Antoon cast aside the excuse, ruling that the agency should take up the problem with Congress rather than let "mandatory deadlines expire with inaction." Antoon ordered that the agency complete reviews of eighty-nine plant and animal species on the list by three years.

While the attorney for the plaintiffs had called for a one-year deadline instead of three, Steven Gieseler hailed Judge Antoon's decision as a "landmark" and a "great win for property owners in Florida." He said the ruling once and for all compelled regulators to follow the letter of the law in assessing the health of listed species every five years.[25]

The federal courts also adjudicated disputes over the management of large Florida companies that had stockholders from out of state. In 2004, for example, Cox Enterprises, an Atlanta-based corporation that owned a 47.2 percent interest in the *Daytona Beach News-Journal*, Florida's last family-owned newspaper, sued the company in federal court for violating its fiduciary interest toward its investors. In 1969 Cox had purchased about $5 million dollars worth of shares in the *News-Journal*. Since 1928, when Julius Davidson and his son, Herbert, purchased a majority share in the newspaper, the journal had been one of the state's most respected newspapers. When Herbert Davidson died in 1985, control of the newspaper fell to his son, Herbert "Tippen" Davidson Jr.[26]

A classically trained violinist with a degree from Julliard School of

Music, Davidson never lost his passion for the arts, even after joining his father's newspaper in the 1960s. Throughout the 1970s, 1980s, and 1990s, Davidson threw his and the newspaper's influence behind support of Daytona's music scene. In 1977 he founded the Seaside Music Center, and since 1982 he has funded an annual visit of the London Symphony to Daytona. Eventually, Davidson put together a board of directors to build a new performing arts center, and from his News-Journal office personally lobbied county commission members to vote for a $2.4 million grant to build the center. As fund-raising for the new center fell short in 2003, Davidson and News-Journal attorney Jon Kaney developed a plan that they were certain would benefit both the newspaper and the arts community in Daytona. They would pay $13 million toward the enterprise in exchange for having the newspaper's name on the building for twenty-six years.[27]

The Cox Corporation had been monitoring Davidson's spending habits on the arts for quite some time, and the News-Journal's expenditure on the naming opportunity triggered a lawsuit. They claimed spending newspaper money to support Davidson's hobby violated its fiduciary responsibility to its stockholders. Davidson and Kaney responded to the suit by exercising an option to buy out Cox's shares. Thus began the six-year dispute in Judge John Antoon's Orlando courtroom over the ownership of the News-Journal Corporation.[28]

By the time of the grand opening of the $29 million Daytona Beach News-Journal Center on January 26, 2006, lawyers for Cox and the News-Journal Corporation had submitted hugely divergent estimates for Cox's shares to Judge Antoon: News-Journal lawyers said the shares were worth $29 million, and Cox's lawyers put the value at $145 million. Cox also demanded $15 million in damages. In hearings held to determine the value of Cox's holdings, one of the corporation's attorneys, John DeVault III, noted that since 1992 the News-Journal had spent over $31 million in cultural arts initiatives that were largely founded and run by the Davidson family, an amount that exceeded Cox's dividends from the News-Journal. Whatever the eventual valuation of the Cox shares, Tippen Davidson refused to sell the newspaper. He pledged to borrow whatever money was necessary to pay off Cox. "Paying off a sum like that, over and above your operating need," he said, "is going to be a strain. But that was anticipated when we took that option."[29]

After studying the issue carefully, Judge Antoon made his ruling: Cox's shares were valued at $129.2 million, and the News-Journal could satisfy its obligation to Cox in installments over a five-year period. Meanwhile, any expenditures of the newspaper of over $500,000 would have to be approved by Cox or the court. Newspaper attorney Jon Kaney was gratified that Judge Antoon was allowing the company to make installment payments instead of the lump sum settlement. Even so, he said, with Antoon's evaluation, the company was in "dire straits." While an appeal of the judge's evaluation of Cox's shares moved forward, Tippen Davidson died in January 2007.[30] Finally in December, the Eleventh Circuit Court of Appeals upheld Antoon's evaluation. The appeals decision was a potentially fatal blow to the News-Journal Company. With very little hope of meeting the installments to Cox, they eventually decided to work with Cox to find a third-party buyer for the paper, and Antoon adjusted the payment schedules to Cox. Then, after overruling excessive "golden parachute" severance packages for News-Journal executives, Antoon named a receiver to run the newspaper and oversee its sale.[31]

Meanwhile, the newspaper's value plummeted. The recession, advertising revenue shortfalls caused by the drop in real estate, and the faltering economy generally all played a role. When receiver Jim Hopson told Antoon that Halifax Media Acquisition LLC's offer of $20 million was the best that could be had, Antoon ordered an appraisal before he authorized the sale. After studying the appraisal, Antoon reluctantly acceded to the sale. "I'd like to wait and hope that things will change, but I'm in no position to speculate," he noted.[32] Thus, the paper that was valued at over $300 million in 2006 was sold for a fraction of that amount four years later. Most of the assets from the sale went to Cox. Not long after the sale the Pension Benefit Guaranty Corp. filed a claim of almost $15 million on behalf of the defunct News-Journal Company's employees.[33]

Bankruptcy

If the fate of the Daytona Beach News-Journal Company was unfortunate, given the condition of the economy in the decade of the 2010s, it was not unusual. The final recourse of individuals and corporations, if they found themselves in hopeless financial straits, was bankruptcy. The Middle District's bankruptcy caseload and personnel expanded in this period.

As the new century dawned, the Middle District boasted some of the most widely respected bankruptcy judges in the United States. Alexander Paskay, though slowing down at age seventy-eight, still maintained an impressive caseload, as did George Proctor, who relinquished the chief judge duties to Thomas Baynes in the Tampa Division in 2000. Also that year

Michael G. Williamson, appointed on March 1, joined the Tampa Division. A Duke University (1973) and Georgetown University Law Center (1976) graduate, Williamson had earned an enviable reputation as a commercial litigator in Orlando. He was president of Maguire, Voorhis & Wells when it merged with Holland & Knight in 1998. In 2003 the Orlando Division added another judge when the Eleventh Circuit Court of Appeals appointed Duke University School of Law graduate K. Rodney May to the bankruptcy bench.

Also by 2003 the Middle District of Florida Bankruptcy Bench had a new chief judge. Paul Glenn had served on the Middle Florida Bankruptcy bench since 1994 and had earned an excellent reputation during that time.[34] In 2005 bankruptcy judge Thomas E. Baynes decided to retire. By that time Baynes was stricken with the onset of Lou Gehrig's disease. Judge Glenn presided over Baynes' retirement gathering on June 8. He echoed his fellow judges' sentiments when he referred to Baynes as a "man for all seasons" and "Renaissance man," whose "interests are limitless. Glenn also reminded his hearers that Bayne was a prolific author. One of his most well-known books was *Baynes on Florida Mortgages* (1999), which was perhaps the most referenced work among practitioners in the field. Finally, Glenn recalled Baynes' important Celotex ruling that was upheld by the Fifth Circuit Court of Appeals and the U.S. Supreme Court. The ruling, he observed, had a great impact on broadening the jurisdictional reach of the Bankruptcy Courts.[35] Despite his illness, Baynes remained as active as his disease would allow. Only two days before he died on December 18, 2009, Baynes was able to attend a ceremony honoring him at the Sam Gibbons courthouse in Tampa. Although burdened by his wheelchair Baynes, thanked the assembled gathering as they named his old courtroom in his honor.[36]

Replacing Baynes in 2005 on the Middle Florida Bankruptcy bench in Tampa was Catherine Peek McEwen. Born in Washington, D.C., in 1956, McEwen had been interested in politics and law from a very young age. When she was born her father was an aide to Sen. George Smathers. McEwen earned a bachelor's degree from the University of South Florida and then attended Stetson University College of Law where she took classes from Alexander Paskay. She graduated and was admitted to the bar in 1982. Judge Michael Williamson welcomed his new colleague, calling her "one of Central Florida's hardest-working and finest commercial litigators." A sole practitioner, she frequently served as a bankruptcy court mediator and served as president of the Tampa Bay Bankruptcy Bar Association.[37]

When McEwen joined the district's seven other bankruptcy judges in 2005, the Middle District, with over 55,000 filings that year, was third largest in the nation. It also accounted for one quarter of all the filings in the Eleventh Circuit. The Jacksonville and Orlando courts handled roughly 13,500 cases each while the Tampa Division handled almost 25,000 cases. The district's nine bankruptcy judges each heard between 5,000 and 7,000 cases per year. Also the district had one of the most innovative bankruptcy courts in the nation. In October 2004 the district went "paperless," converting to electronic filings.[38]

In 2005 the national bankruptcy laws were about to undergo sweeping changes. A provision of the Bankruptcy Reform Act (1994) provided for the establishment of an independent Bankruptcy Reform Commission to investigate and study issues relating to the Bankruptcy Code and submit a report to the president, Congress, and chief justice of the U.S. Supreme Court. The commission, composed of legislators, judges, practitioners, and representatives from the academic community, was authorized to hold public hearings and take testimony from experts. As one of the nation's foremost bankruptcy judges, Alexander Paskay served as a senior advisor to the commission. Although he provided his input, Paskay was disappointed with the final result. "The credit card industry was screaming bloody murder that the '78 act was tilted toward debtors," he recalled.[39] Within two years the commission had issued their report but, as Paskay explained, Congress disregarded the recommendations "completely." In the end the Bankruptcy Abuse Prevention Consumer Protection Reform Act of 2005 (BAPCPA) was largely influenced by the credit card industry.[40]

The new law made it more difficult for individual filers to declare bankruptcy. The BAPCPA represented a transformation. The new law gave the U.S. Trustee Program new responsibilities in overseeing means testing for debtors and conducting audits. One of the law's most enthusiastic supporters was President George Bush. As he signed the bill into law on April 19, 2005, he announced that the new legislation would prevent frivolous filings of persons abusing the system. Paskay disagreed with this characterization because in his view the law unwisely disregarded the basic foundation upon which the American bankruptcy system was founded. "Well, for 100 years, actually from day one," Paskay explained, "contrary to the English system, the basic principle was that every person who's eligible for relief has an absolute right to file bankruptcy and doesn't need the permission of the creditors, his spouse, his church, or anybody else. The basic idea was that he is entitled to seek relief to be relieved of his oppressing debts, in exchange

U.S. Sen. Bill Nelson and Judge Alexander L. Paskay, ca. 2010. Catherine Peek McEwen Collection.

for giving up his assets to be liquidated for the benefit of creditors." The 2005 law overturned this right because, unlike before, the debtor "must establish to the satisfaction of the court that he, in fact, needs the relief and he has no wherewithal of money to repay any of his creditors. . . . It's a crazy mathematical formula. It turned the whole thing upside down. It's just unbelievable. . . . If he flunks the means test, the filing is presumed to be abusive and should be thrown out unless he converts to a Chapter 13 repayment plan."[41]

Since the turn of the twenty-first century the Middle District bankruptcy courts heard many important cases that not only had profound impact on the economic history of the state but also influenced the development of bankruptcy litigation in the United States. Among several important cases that had huge significance for the commercial life of Florida was the Winn-Dixie bankruptcy case. Founded in 1925 by the Davis family in Jacksonville, the grocery chain was one of the most important employers and grocery chains in Florida. By 2003 the company found itself in financial difficulty, largely due to competition from Publix and Wal-Mart. In February 2005 Winn-Dixie filed for bankruptcy protection under Chapter 11 and announced the sale or closure of 326 of its nearly 1,000 stores and a loss of over

22,000 jobs. At the time of its filing, the company employed nearly 80,000 employees. The Winn-Dixie bankruptcy case actually consisted of twenty-four individual cases, consolidated into one main case. The case was originally filed in the Southern District of New York, but a judge there ordered the case transferred to Jacksonville in the Middle District, and Judge Jerry A. Funk assumed control of the case. In June 2006 Winn-Dixie attorneys submitted a page reorganization plan to Funk. On November 9, 2006, Funk approved Winn-Dixie's reorganization plan, which allowed the company to obtain financing to support the changes it needed to compete effectively.[42]

On November 18, 2007, Jacksonville and the Middle District of Florida lost one its most beloved judges when Judge George Proctor passed away at the age of eighty-one. The next year the Eleventh Circuit Court of Appeals appointed Caryl E. Delano to the Tampa Division. A Tampa native, Delano graduated from the University of South Florida (1976) and Indiana University Maurer School of Law (1979). After practicing privately in California for fourteen years, Delano returned to her hometown pursued a practice in commercial litigation and bankruptcy.[43]

Bankruptcy continued to grow as recession conditions continued in Florida. In fact, 2010 Middle District filings grew 8 percent from the previous year, nearly reaching a total of 67,000.[44] But two years later, due in part to the improving economic situation, bankruptcy filings in the Middle District of Florida were at their lowest level in four years. Even with the downturn in filings, the district still had roughly 68,000 cases that were unresolved. And many were concerned that the downturn in filing was only temporary. St. Petersburg bankruptcy attorney Charles Moore observed, "I think we're going to be in for a huge storm. . . . I think we're in a weird, artificially created low. . . . All of us are asking why (bankruptcy filings) are so low right now. The economy didn't magically get better over the last two years." One reason for the lull in filings may have been the "robo-signing" scandal over foreclosures, and the fact that many foreclosures had to be refiled, and this gave delinquent homeowners a reprieve by extending the process. According to bankruptcy lawyer Ed Whitson, ever-complex real estate financing arrangements had further complicated bankruptcy proceedings and had begun to transform older procedures. "You're seeing bankruptcy courts morph into more of a hybrid. You have loan modifications taking over bankruptcies. The mediation program is being built into bankruptcy," Whitson said. To expedite cases, judges were increasingly ruling from the bench, finding ways to eliminate lengthy hearings,

Middle District of Florida Bankruptcy Bench, ca. 2013. *Left to right*: Paul M. Glenn, Arthur B. Briskman, Jerry A. Funk, Catherine Peek McEwen, Karen S. Jennemann (Chief Judge), K. Rodney May, Caryl E. Delano, Cynthia C. Jackson, and Michael G. Williamson. Catherine Peek McEwen Collection.

and working with case managers to keep the cases moving—all the while dealing with budget cuts and declining staffs. "We've had a cutback in staff. We've had a freeze of new hiring. . . . We're down a judge; we're down case managers," observed Judge Catherine McEwen in November 2012.[45]

As the Middle District bankruptcy judiciary, bar, and other practitioners pondered the future of their profession, they said good-bye to a man who, through his rulings, academic writings, and pronouncements, had shaped bankruptcy laws and its practice for nearly half a century. On May 5, 2012, at the Sacred Heart Catholic Church in Tampa, the bench, bar, and assembled friends and family said paid their respects to Alexander L. Paskay, who died on April 27, 2012. On that day, as she announced the sad news to her fellow bankruptcy judges, Chief Bankruptcy Judge Karen Jennemann noted that Paskay had served as a Middle District bankruptcy judge with "distinction, intellectual vigor, and honor" since 1964, nearly half a century.[46]

Accolades and remembrances of the distinguished jurist began to flow almost at once. According to one account, Paskay had handled more than 154,000 cases since 1986. Commercial lawyer Leonard H. Gilbert had known Paskay even before he became a judge. "Even when he was a young clerk," Gilbert recalled, "you could tell he was extremely smart. . . . He'd be listening to both sides of a case and reach up for a book on the shelf, show the judge a page, and you'd be wondering, 'Oh boy, is that in my favor or the other guy?' . . . It's hard to say someone is one-of-a-kind, but he was." Jules Cohen of Akerman Senterfitt in Orlando recalled the days when Paskay would drive to Orlando each week. "He'd show up with two bulging brief-cases of documents. . . . No secretary, no clerk, no bailiffs, just himself," Cohen said. "He was the whole bankruptcy court of Orlando."[47]

Judge Paul M. Glenn gave the eulogy at Judge Paskay's funeral service. Glenn spoke of Paskay's many accomplishments as a judge, scholar, teacher, and mentor. After recounting Paskay's early life in Hungary, his immigration to the United States, and his early years as Judge Joseph P. Lieb's clerk, Glenn noted that when Paskay joined the Middle District of Florida in 1963 as its sole bankruptcy referee, fewer than 450 cases were filed in the district. By 2012 that number had grown to over 60,000 filings annually heard by eight judges. Paskay, Glenn told his listeners, was one of the most prolific writers among bankruptcy judges in the country. Westlaw had over 1,800 of his decisions on its website. Paskay authored standard handbooks and treatises in the field. "His many opinions and treatises," Glenn noted, "provide significant guidance for the interpretation and application of the Bankruptcy and commercial laws." Glenn also summarized Paskay's service on commissions and committees that had helped fashion current bankruptcy laws and rules in the United States and internationally.[48]

Glenn presented a picture of man who was demanding of himself but also of those who practiced before him. "When you were in his courtroom," he said, "you saw a man who loved challenges and debate—who raised questions to test the breadth and depth of your knowledge, and of his own knowledge." Paskay was a "man who cherished fairness and equity," Glenn continued. "He was fair to the law, and fair to the parties. And on both legal and non-legal matters, he was a person with a strong sense of right and wrong—a strong sense of fairness and equity." Finally, Judge Glenn concluded his remarks by stating the obvious: Judge Paskay's "passing is truly the end of an era."[49]

21

Closing Arguments and Taking Stock

Fifty Years of Justice

As the 2008 presidential election neared, Americans faced a bleak set of realities. After a series of breathtaking successes in its initial phases in the spring of 2003, by 2006 the war in Iraq had ground down to a quagmire. A Democratic sweep in the midterm elections spoke to the voter rebellion and to the disapproval of George Bush's war policies. Worse still, one of the most critical economic crises in American history loomed on the horizon. The 2000 budget surplus had become a huge deficit, and in the fall of 2007 the housing bubble that was based on subprime mortgages burst. The collapse sent home equity values plummeting. Mortgage borrowers defaulted. Foreclosures soared and banks lost billions on these and other loans. Credit froze, banks stopped lending, people stopped buying, and businesses stopped selling. Then in the fall of 2008, as the presidential campaign was in full swing, the bottom fell out of the stock market, the Dow Jones Industrial Average lost a third of its value. Despite emergency measures enacted in the final days of the Bush administration, the situation grew worse.[1]

Like other Americans, the judges, attorneys, and others in the Middle District of Florida looked upon these dire omens and braced themselves for what would come next. With the economy in such disarray, the possibilities for the Democrats looked promising in the upcoming presidential election. Hillary Clinton was the front-runner for the nomination, but the person who caught fire in the primaries was the one-term African American senator from Illinois, Barack Obama. The son of a white Kansan mother and a Kenyan father, Obama was born in Hawaii and raised by his mother and white grandparents. A Harvard Law graduate, Obama was poised, confident, young, energetic, and presented himself as a "conciliator who could inspire and unite a diverse people and foster bipartisan collaborations."[2]

He eventually bested Clinton for the nomination. Obama's Republican opponent, John McCain, by contrast was seventy-two years old and had been a mainstay in Congress for twenty-five years. Obama's message of "change" and "hope" proved a compelling one. On election night Obama became the first African American president in American history. Four years later voters elected him to a second term.[3]

The new president selected Eric Holder as attorney general, the first African American in U.S. history to hold this post. As other attorney generals before him, Holder would oversee the U.S. attorneys and set a crime-fighting agenda for the department. He would also work closely with the White House on the selection of judges, U.S. attorneys, and other important officials. Despite the optimism that greets most new administrations, bipartisan cooperation in the judicial selection process was generally not achieved. Even so, Florida Senators Bill Nelson (Dem.) and Mel Martinez (Rep.) worked together well when it came to supporting nominees for Florida.

In 2009 the Middle District continued as one of the busiest in the nation. But with so many judges in the district taking senior status and still maintaining heavy dockets, the district benefited from the fact that, once a judge reached senior status, the district was allowed another judge. Thus, the net effect was to provide the district with additional judges. Judge Patricia Fawsett (2008) and Susan Bucklew (2009) added to a growing number of senior judges. Like many of her other senior status brethren, Judge Bucklew expected to carry a heavy case load.[4]

Still, President Obama moved slowly in the nomination of judges. In June 2009 President Obama finally selected his first nominee to the Middle District bench from a list of five provided by the Florida Federal Judicial Nominating Commission. Charlene E. Honeywell would become the second African American woman to serve as district judge in the Middle District of Florida. President Obama called Honeywell "hardworking, fair-minded, tenacious and dedicated." She represented the "very best that our country has to offer in the way of excellence and public service," he continued.[5]

The fifty-one-year-old Honeywell was a native of Fort Lauderdale and graduated from Howard University and the University of Florida Levin School of Law in 1981 with honors in legal research, writing, and appellate advocacy. After graduation Honeywell worked in the Leon and Hillsborough County public defender's office. She then joined the city of Tampa's legal staff, serving from 1987 until 1994, when Gov. Lawton Chiles appointed her to fill a sudden judicial vacancy in Hillsborough County. After serving briefly as county judge, Honeywell ran for the position as an incumbent but lost a close election for the post. She then became the first African American partner of the Hill, Ward, and Henderson firm in Tampa, where she gained valuable experience in numerous forms of litigation. Then in October 2000, Gov. Jeb Bush appointed her Hillsborough County circuit judge, and she served ably in that post until her nomination to the federal bench in 2009.[6] Hundreds of friends, family, and well-wishers—including her former elementary school principal—attended Honeywell's investiture ceremony at the Tampa Theater on January 30, 2010.[7]

Three months later, the day after his sixty-fifth birthday in April 2010, Judge Henry Lee Adams took senior status. In a ceremony at the Simpson Courthouse in Jacksonville, Adams was honored in a ceremonial portrait unveiling sponsored by the Jacksonville Chapter of the Federal Bar Association. While Adams still intended to hear cases, he admitted that "it is time to back away a bit."[8] Upon Judge Adams assuming senior status, President Obama nominated commercial litigator Roy Bale "Skip" Dalton Jr. for the opening on November 17, 2010. Along with his wife, Linda, their four children, and his eighty-six-year-old mother, Senators Bill Nelson and Marco Rubio introduced Dalton to the Senate Judiciary Committee on March 2, 2011. The full Senate eventually confirmed him by unanimous consent on May 2, 2011.

Born in 1952 in Jacksonville, Dalton earned a bachelor's degree and a law degree from the University of Florida. Practicing primarily in Orlando, Dalton earned the reputation as one of the state's most respected lawyers and, although a Democrat, he practiced with Mel Martinez from 1989 to 1998. When Martinez was elected to the U.S. Senate in 2004, Dalton served him in Washington in 2005.[9] Jacksonville attorney Buddy Schulz introduced Dalton to a welcoming gathering of the Jacksonville Chapter of the Federal Bar Association. Referencing Dalton's extensive experience in the courtroom, Schulz noted, "In the 1970s and 1980s, there were a handful of trial lawyers in our state getting a significant number of verdicts on a regular basis, who a bunch of people like me kept their eyes on. . . . Skip Dalton was among that handful of lawyers who set the standard for the rest of us." Over more than thirty-five years Dalton had tried products liability, medical malpractice, criminal, environmental, securities, business, probate, and other cases. He had argued appeals, operated his own real estate development firm, and been a founder and director of a bank.

After thanking Schulz for his introduction, Dalton noted that he was

Middle District Judges on the occasion of Roy Dalton's investiture, ca. 2010. *Front row, left to right*: Judges Harvey E. Schlesinger, William J. Castagna, Susan C. Bucklew; *second row, left to right*: Roy B. Dalton Jr., Marcia Morales Howard, Timothy J. Corrigan, James D. Whittemore, Elizabeth A. Kovachevich, Anne C. Conway, Richard A. Lazzara, Gregory A. Presnell, Virginia M. Hernandez-Covington, Mary Stenson Scriven; *third row, left to right*: Donald Paul Dietrich, Gregory J. Kelly, Monte C. Richardson, James R. Klindt, Karla R. Spalding, Joel B. Toomey, Catherine Peek McEwen, Michael G. Williamson, Karen S. Jennemann, Arthur B. Briskman, David A. Baker, Thomas E. Morris, Elizabeth A. Jenkins. Middle District of Florida Archives, George C. Young Courthouse, Orlando, Florida.

delighted to be in Jacksonville and ready to get to work. The Jacksonville division, he observed, had roughly 11,200 filings in 2010. "We are No. 1 in the district and fifth among districts throughout the country. So you can see that the work before the Middle District is not only incredibly important and significant, but there is quite a bit of it."[10]

The Middle District judges also added four additional U.S. magistrates. Joining the Tampa division was Stetson University College of Law graduate Anthony Porcelli, a veteran in the U.S. Attorney's Office. Porcelli had been involved in some of the district's recent high-profile criminal cases.[11] Joining the Jacksonville Division in July 2010 was Joel B. Toomey, who earned his law degree from Duke University School of Law in 1982 and immediately thereafter clerked for Judge Gerald B. Tjoflat of the Eleventh Circuit Court of Appeals. Toomey then entered private practice before serving in the State Attorney's Office.[12] On July 25, 2011, Thomas B. Smith joined the

Orlando Division as U.S. magistrate. Smith had worked for three years as an assistant state attorney in the Ninth Judicial Circuit of Florida before joining the Maguire, Voorhis & Wells law firm in Orlando. In 2001 Gov. Jeb Bush appointed Smith a circuit judge in Orange County. Joining the Ocala Division on July 2, 2012, was Philip R. Lammens, who earned a bachelor's degree and law degree from the University of Florida. Lammens clerked for Judge Joel F. Dubina in the Eleventh Circuit Court of Appeals in Montgomery, Alabama, and then later clerked for Judge William Terrell Hodges in Ocala. Lammens then became a trial attorney for the U.S. Department of Justice.

By the summer of 2009 the Middle District of Florida was receiving applications for U.S. attorney. The person who President Obama eventually nominated was well known to those familiar with the U.S. Attorney's Office for the Middle District of Florida. Robert O'Neill first joined the U.S. Attorney's Office in Tampa in 1993. During his sixteen years in the office, O'Neill had participated in many important trials and had headed the office's criminal division and public corruption sections. In March 2007 he had served as acting U.S. attorney after Paul Perez's resignation. A permanent replacement for Brian Albritton, who resigned in October 2008, had been long in coming, and just before he swore O'Neill in on October 5, Judge Steven Merryday quipped, "Like the Treaty of Paris, this ends a sort of protracted time of turbulence. . . . And it's good to have it over." O'Neill was sworn in during his lunch break, and about thirty of his colleagues were on hand to congratulate him. When the official swearing was concluded, Judge Merryday asked O'Neill if he was "going to give a speech to your assembled fans." O'Neill demurred. He had no time. He was scheduled to give closing arguments in an important case that afternoon.[13]

International Initiatives

Middle Florida judges often joined other American jurists who participated in international symposiums and conferences, sharing elements of American jurisprudence with those attempting to establish the rule of law in former totalitarian countries. One of the pioneers in these efforts, as has already been recounted, was U.S. Bankruptcy Judge Alexander Paskay. Exchanges and visits accelerated after the creation of the Open World Russian Leadership Program in 1999. The purpose of the program, funded by Congress and sponsored by the Library of Congress, was to bring emerging leaders from Russia, Ukraine, and other former members of the Eastern

Bloc to the United States for intensive exchanges with their professional counterparts. The rule of law component of the program brought "Eurasian judges to the U.S. to learn about the American judicial system" and "examine major aspects of the U.S. judicial system including court proceedings, case management, law enforcement, legal education, judicial ethics, and the relationship between federal and state courts with their American counterparts." The program aimed to offer insight to the visitors into how the U.S. political system promotes and protects judicial independence and the rule of law. The Middle District's involvement in the program was spurred in large part by U.S. Magistrate Judge Elizabeth Jenkins' membership in the Judicial Conference Committee on International Judicial Relations. Chief Justice William Rehnquist appointed Jenkins to the post in October 2001.[14]

In November 2002 a delegation of judges from St. Petersburg, Russia, visited Tampa and St. Petersburg, Florida, to examine the U.S. judicial system with their federal and state counterparts. Judge Elizabeth Kovachevich and Judge Jenkins hosted the Russian delegation, who met with congressional members and observed proceedings of U.S. district court and bankruptcy proceedings. The visiting judges participated in a mock trial performed by Stetson University law students. They also received briefings from the U.S. attorney, the U.S. public defender, the U.S. chief probation officer, and members of the Stetson law faculty. Before traveling to Florida, the Russian jurists participated in an intensive two-day orientation session in Washington with Kovachevich, other U.S. judges, and officials of the Administrative Office of the U.S. Courts.[15]

Other exchanges followed. In 2004 Judge Patricia Fawsett and U.S. Magistrate Judges James G. Glazebrook and David A. Baker hosted five Russian judges. The delegation visited a naturalization ceremony, examined U.S. anti–money laundering laws, met with officials at the Orange County jail and with Chief U.S. Probation Officer Elaine Terenzi.[16] In 2008, 2011, and 2012 Judge Harvey Schlesinger joined others in hosting delegations of judges from Russia and other Eurasian countries in Jacksonville. On the 2011 visit Judge Schlesinger served as a tour guide for visiting judges from Tatarstan as the group visited the Florida Coastal School of Law, the Duval County Courthouse, the Holland & Knight law firm, the Bryan Simpson U.S. Courthouse, and the D. Ray James Correctional Facility in Folkston, Georgia.[17]

In 2010 the Middle District of Florida joined district courts in Kentucky, Tennessee, Washington, Minnesota, and several other states when they embarked on an interesting sister-court relationship with the Ljubljana

District Court in Slovenia. The goal was for the two courts to learn from each other and share innovative ideas. In November 2010 Chief Judge Anne C. Conway and District Court Clerk Sheryl Loesch, paying their own airfare, traveled to Ljubljana to sign a formal agreement establishing the relationship on their first visit. Conway and Loesch kept in touch with their workloads back home by using remote access to the district's Case Management/Electronic Case Files System (CM/ECF). "During the trip, I came to appreciate even more the benefits of the exchange," said Conway. "Our experiences will make our judiciaries more effective and productive for our respective citizens." Judge Conway saw the innovative relationship as a great "opportunity for an exchange of ideas. . . . Through sister-court relationships, lessons and experiences of international visits are extended and solidified, resulting in greater cross-border understanding. Overall the establishment of sister-court relationships assists judges in our quest to enhance the rule of law." Loesch was able to explain to her counterparts how her staff assisted judges in managing settlement conferences, handling backlogs, and keeping the cases moving. Judge Conway thought that "we can learn a lot from each other in case management, court governance, and dispute resolution." Loesch observed, "We have the best justice system in the world. . . . I think it is incumbent upon us to share what we know and to learn from exchanges with the judicial systems of other countries."[18]

One of the most significant contributions of Middle District judges from an international standpoint came through the work of U.S Bankruptcy Judge Michael G. Williamson, who served on the international relations committee of the Judicial Conference of the United States. Williamson took a special interest in the commercial development of foreign countries wracked by war and social and economic instability. Williamson's travel overseas began in 2002. Working under the auspices of the U.S. Department of Commerce Commercial Development Program and the U.S. Agency for International Development (USAID)'s Commercial Legal and Institutional Reform Assessment (BizCLIR), Williamson traveled often to developing countries as a BizCLIR team member assessing the legal and institutional business climate in Zimbabwe, Uganda, and Rwanda. Williamson also went on missions to Macedonia, Azerbaijan, and, most importantly, Afghanistan, where he visited on seven separate occasions from 2007 to 2012 and made trips to study and assess the nation's attempt to build legal and commercial institutions. As of this writing, Williamson and his colleague Charles G. Case II, U.S. bankruptcy judge for the District of Arizona, are assisting in writing Afghanistan's bankruptcy law.[19]

Historical Initiatives

In the early 2000s an important initiative that the Middle District developed to forward and implement important joint goals and initiatives of the district as well as its bar was the creation of the Bench and Bar Fund. In the process of implementing the CM/ECF; Judges Gregory Presnell, Patricia Fawsett, and Susan Bucklew along with staff from the clerk's office visited other districts to study the implementation of the system. On one such occasion on a visit to a courthouse in a different district, they saw a historical display that was very professionally done. They soon learned that the exhibit was funded from the district's Bench and Bar Fund, a special fund derived through applications and renewals from attorneys who paid a fee to practice in the district. At the time the Middle District had a one-time fee to practice in the district, and many of the attorneys had either moved or ceased to practice in the court. Judge Presnell developed the idea of creating an annual renewal fee. This not only brought in more money, it also provided accurate addresses and contact information for the attorneys practicing in the district.[20]

Thus, on October 31, 2003, the Middle District of Florida's Bench and Bar Fund was established, and Presnell became chair of the Bench and Bar Committee, which, among other duties oversees the expenditure of the funds. Judge Presnell continued to serve as chair or vice-chair until 2011. Under the charter, the chief judge appointed one district judge from each division, two magistrate judges, two bankruptcy judges, and six members of the Middle District bar to the Bench and Bar Committee. With an excess of fifteen thousand dues paying members paying $15 for admission and a $20 biannual renewal fee, the Middle District soon had funds to pay for historical exhibits in courthouses and educational programs for teachers and students. Plans also moved forward to fund a historical book on the district. Proceeds from the Bench and Bar Fund also provided for special events of the court, such as investitures, portrait hangings, and retirement ceremonies. Monies also paid for cost reimbursement for pro bono expenses for lawyers who undertook work for the court.[21]

The Middle District Historical Committee recommended to the Bench and Bar Committee historical and other appropriate uses of the Bench and Bar Fund. From 2009 through 2011, the Historical Committee created historical exhibits in the Jacksonville, Tampa, and Orlando courthouses. The exhibit in the Bryan Simpson Courthouse in Jacksonville presented photos, documents, and explanations showing the establishment of the court in 1962 along with key issues and cases facing the court in its early years, including the court's involvement in the civil rights movement in the 1960s and 1970s. On the eleventh floor other exhibits explained the workings of the federal court system. The committee hoped the exhibits would serve as an effective teaching tool for elementary and high school teachers. Chief Judge Anne Conway opened the ceremony and Judge Harvey Schlesinger opened the exhibit. Also giving presentations were Phillip Buhler, president of the U.S. District Court Historical Society, Judge Timothy Corrigan, and Judge Karen Jennemann, who acknowledged the many people who helped bring the project to fruition.[22]

One year later, on June 4, 2010, exhibits in Tampa's Sam Gibbons Courthouse were unveiled. Once again Chief Judge Anne Conway opened the ceremony by providing an overview of the committee's origination and goals. "The purpose is to inform and also to educate," U.S. Magistrate Judge Elizabeth Jenkins announced to the full gathering. "Our hope is that these exhibits will be used by the community at large, but in particular, students who are today more than ever in need of civics education." Judge Susan Bucklew then gave credit to the judges and lawyers who selected the important cases that were featured on the exhibits. "Selecting a few cases to be highlighted was a challenge," she said, "because the court has seen everything from espionage and public corruption to social issues such as the right to die and allowing children with AIDS to attend school." Retired U.S. representative Sam Gibbons participated in the ceremony via video conferencing telecast. "I'm so proud of this courthouse and the people who work in it and what they do for law and justice," noted the World War II veteran and D-day paratrooper. "We have reached a point in civilization where we can begin to think about the rule of law replacing the rule of force. I will rest in peace knowing that there is a group of people in our country who want to not impose world government on anybody, not do something by fiat, not do some magic snap of the fingers," he said.[23] The Historical Committee marked another major accomplishment with the unveiling of the exhibits in the George C. Young Courthouse in Orlando in November 2011.[24]

Through its fifty years of existence the U.S. Middle District Court of Florida, although experiencing both continuity and change, has remained an important part of its region's social, economic, political, and—of course— legal life. When the district was created in 1962 Florida was on the threshold of its most rapid growth phase, the Warren Court was at its zenith, and the civil rights movement was about to take off. The time of the Warren,

Burger, Rehnquist, and Roberts courts saw Florida's population nearly quadruple from roughly 5 million in 1960 to over 20 million in the first decade of the twenty-first century. Indeed, in 1962 the state's social, political, and economic characteristics resembled its Deep South neighbors more than the multicultural melting pot that it is today. Thus was formed a complex society composed of people with different values, economic pursuits, religions, and cultures. With this unbelievable growth came a caseload reflecting numbers, degree of complexity, and diversity that few could have predicted. Indeed, as this book shows, the Middle District of Florida was the scene of some of the most significant criminal and civil trials in the United States—many with national and international implications.

Even for those Florida citizens who have never been a plaintiff, a defendant, a juror, or even a spectator in its courtrooms, the U.S. Middle District of Florida has touched the lives of its citizens through its decisions. It has adjudicated economic disputes. It has protected the environment. It has overseen schools and prisons. It has protected civil rights. It has adjudicated the limits of religious expression as well as the limits of freedom of speech. It has prosecuted dangerous drug dealers. As of this writing, twenty-five district judges (twelve active and thirteen senior status judges), sixteen U.S. magistrate judges, and eight bankruptcy judges strive to do their duty much in the same fashion that the district's first three judges— Bryan Simpson, George C. Young, and Joseph P. Lieb—did over fifty years ago. While the diversity of their caseload and precedents are different, their goal is the same: resolve conflicts, interpret the laws and the Constitution to the best of their ability, and always do justice.

Appendix

Judicial Officers, Middle District of Florida

U.S. District Judges

Name	Birthplace	Education
John Milton Bryan Simpson (1903–1987)	Kissimmee, Fla.	University of Florida School of Law
Joseph Patrick Lieb (1901–1971)	Faribault, Minn.	St. Thomas College; Georgetown University Law Center
William A. McRae (1909–1973)	Marianna, Fla.	University of Florida; Christ College, Oxford
George C. Young (1916–)	Cincinnati, Ohio	University of Florida; University of Florida School of Law
Charles R. Scott (1904–1983)	Adel, Iowa	Valparaiso University School of Law
Isaac (Ben) Krentzman (1914–1998)	Milton, Fla.	University of Florida; University of Florida School of Law
Gerald Bard Tjoflat (1929–)	Pittsburgh, Pa.	University of Cincinnati; Duke University School of Law
William Terrell Hodges (1934–)	Lake Wales, Fla.	University of Florida; University of Florida School of Law
John A. Reed (1931–)	Washington, D.C.	Duke University; Duke University School of Law
Howell W. Melton (1923–)	Mayo, Fla.	University of Florida; University of Florida School of Law
George C. Carr (1929–1990)	Lakeland, Fla.	University of Florida; University of Florida School of Law
Susan Harrell Black (1943–)	Valdosta, Ga.	Florida State University; University of Florida School of Law
William J. Castagna (1924–)	Philadelphia, Pa.	University of Pennsylvania; University of Florida School of Law
John H. Moore (1929–)	Atlantic City, N.J.	Syracuse University; University of Florida School of Law

Preappointment career	Years of Service	Appointing President
Private practice; assistant state attorney (AUSA); state circuit judge	1963–66, chief judge; appointed to Fifth Circuit Court of Appeal (1967)	Harry Truman
FBI investigator; assistant US attorney; private practice	1963–71; chief judge 1966–71	Dwight D. Eisenhower
Private practice	1963–73; chief judge 1971–73	John F. Kennedy
Private practice	1962– ; chief judge 1973–81; senior status 1981	John F. Kennedy
Private practice; state court of appeals judge	1966–83; senior status 1976	Lyndon Johnson
Private practice	1967–98; senior status 1982	Lyndon Johnson
Private practice	1970–75; appointment to the Fifth Circuit of Appeals, 1975	Richard Nixon
Private practice	1971– ; senior status 1999	Richard Nixon
Private practice; state district court of appeals judge	1973–84; resigned 1984	Richard Nixon
Private practice; state circuit judge	1977– ; senior status 1991	Jimmy Carter
Private practice; city attorney	1977–90; chief judge 1989–90	Jimmy Carter
assistant state attorney; state circuit judge	1979–92; chief judge 1990–92; appointed to Eleventh Circuit Court of Appeal, 1992	Jimmy Carter
Private practice	1979– ; senior status 1992	Jimmy Carter
Private practice; state circuit judge	1981– ; chief judge 1992–95; senior status 1995	Ronald Reagan

(continued)

U.S. District Judges—*Continued*

Name	Birthplace	Education
Elizabeth A. Kovachevich (1936–)	Canton, Ill.	University of Miami; Stetson University College of Law
G. Kendall Sharp (1934–)	Chicago, Ill.	Yale University; University of Virginia School of Law
Patricia C. Fawsett (1943–)	Montreal, Canada	University of Florida; University of Florida School of Law
Ralph W. Nimmons (1938–2003)	Dallas, Tex.	University of Florida; University of Florida School of Law
Harvey E. Schlesinger (1940–)	Brooklyn, N.Y.	The Citadel; University of Richmond School of Law
Anne Conway (1950–)	Cleveland, Ohio	John Carroll University; University of Florida School of Law
Steven Douglas Merryday (1950–)	Palatka, Fla.	University of Florida; University of Florida School of Law
Henry Lee Adams (1945–)	Jacksonville, Fla.	Florida A&M University; Howard University School of Law
Susan Bucklew (1942–)	Tampa, Fla.	Florida State University; University of South Florida; Stetson University College of Law
Richard A. Lazzara (1945–)	Tampa, Fla.	Loyola University; University of Florida School of Law
James D. Whittemore (1952–)	Walterboro, S.C.	University of Florida; Stetson University College of Law
John Antoon II (1946–)	Bakersfield, Calif.	Florida Southern College; Florida State University College of Law

Preappointment career	Years of Service	Appointing President
Private practice; state circuit judge	1982– ; chief judge 1996–2002	Ronald Reagan
Private practice; state circuit judge	1983– ; senior status 2000–	Ronald Reagan
Private practice	1985– ; chief judge 2003–8; senior status 2008–	Ronald Reagan
Private practice; state circuit judge; state appeals judge	1991–2003	George H. W. Bush
JAG Corp; AUSA, U.S. magistrate judge	1991– ; senior states, 2006–	George H. W. Bush
Private practice	1991– ; chief judge 2008–	George H. W. Bush
Private practice	1991–	George H. W. Bush
Private practice; state circuit judge	1993– ; senior status, 2010–	Bill Clinton
Private practice; county judge; state circuit judge	1993– ; senior status, 2008	Bill Clinton
Assistant county solicitor; private practice; county judge, state circuit judge; state appeals judge	1997– ; senior status 2011	Bill Clinton
Federal public defender; private practice; state circuit judge	1999–	Bill Clinton
State circuit judge; state appeals judge	2000–	Bill Clinton

U.S. District Judges—*Continued*

Name	Birthplace	Education
John E. Steele (1949–)	Detroit, Mich.	University of Detroit; University of Detroit Mercy School of Law
James S. Moody Jr. (1947–)	Plant City, Fla.	University of Florida; University of Florida School of Law
Gregory A. Presnell (1942–)	St. Petersburg, Fla.	College of William & Mary; University of Florida School of Law
Timothy J. Corrigan (1956–)	Jacksonville, Fla.	Notre Dame; Duke University School of Law
Virginia M. Hernandez-Covington (1955–)	Tampa, Fla.	University of Tampa; Georgetown University Law Center
Marcia Morales Howard (1965–)	Jacksonville, Fla.	Vanderbilt University; University of Florida School of Law
Mary Stenson Scriven (1962–)	Atlanta, Ga.	Duke University; Florida State University College of Law
Charlene Edwards Honeywell (1957–)	Deerfield Beach, Fla.	Howard University; University of Florida School of Law
Roy B. Dalton Jr. (1952–)	Jacksonville, Fla.	University of Florida; University of Florida School of Law
Sheri Polster Chappell (1962–)	Kiel, Wisc.	University of Wisconsin; Nova Southeastern Shepard Broad Law Center
Brian Davis (1953–)	Jacksonville, Fla.	Princeton University; University of Florida School of Law

Preappointment career	Years of Service	Appointing President
AUSA; U.S. magistrate judge	2000–	Bill Clinton
Private practice; state circuit judge	2000–	Bill Clinton
Private practice	2000–	Bill Clinton
Private practice; U.S. magistrate judge	2002–	George W. Bush
AUSA; state court of appeals judge	2004–	George W. Bush
Private practice; U.S. magistrate judge	2007–	George W. Bush
Private practice; U.S. magistrate judge	2008–	George W. Bush
Assistant public defender; private practice; state circuit judge	2009–	Barack Obama
Private practice	2011–	Barack Obama
AUSA; U.S. magistrate judge	2013–	Barack Obama
State circuit judge	2013–	Barack Obama

(continued)

U.S. Magistrate Judges

Name	Birthplace	Education
Joseph W. Hatchett	Clearwater, Fla.	Florida A&M; Howard University School of Law
Thomas L. Henderson	Trenton, N.J.	University of Florida School of Law
John F. Hughes Jr.	—	—
Young J. Simmons	Daytona Beach, Fla.	University of Florida School of Law
Paul Game Jr.	Tampa, Fla.	Duke University; Duke University School of Law
Donald Paul Dietrich	Buffalo, N.Y.	State University of New York at Buffalo; Duke University School of Law
George T. Swartz	Dallas, Pa.	Michigan State University; Washington University School of Law
Harvey E. Schlesinger	Brooklyn, N.Y.	The Citadel; University of Richmond School of Law
Thomas G. Wilson	Detroit, Mich.	Michigan State University; Duke University School of Law
Howard T. Snyder	Miami, Fla.	Stetson University; Stetson University College of Law
Elizabeth A. Jenkins	Gainesville, Fla.	Vanderbilt University; University of Florida School of Law
Charles R. Wilson	Pensacola, Fla.	University of Notre Dame; Notre Dame Law School
David A. Baker	Arlington, Va.	University of North Carolina; University of Virginia School of Law
John Edwin Steele	Detroit, Mich.	University of Detroit; University of Detroit Mercy School of Law
Thomas B. McCoun	Miami, Fla.	Georgia Tech; Stetson University College of Law
Mark A. Pizzo	Tampa, Fla.	Loyola University; Loyola University New Orleans College of Law
James G. Glazebrook	New York, N.Y.	Middlebury College; Case Western Reserve University School of Law

Preappointment career	Years of Service
AUSA	1971–75
Private practice	1971–74
—	1971–74
Private practice	1971–74
Private practice	1971–90
Private practice	1971–96
Private practice	1971–2000
AUSA	1971–91
Civil Division, U.S. Dept. of Justice; AUSA	1979–
FBI	1980–
AUSA	1986–
Hillsborough County Judge	1990–1994
Private practice	1991–
AUSA	1991–2000
Private practice	1994–
Assistant federal public defender; AUSA	1995–
AUSA	1996–2007

(continued)

U.S. Magistrate Judges—*Continued*

Name	Birthplace	Education
Karla R. Spaulding	Breckenridge, Mich.	Western Michigan University; Northwestern University School of Law
Timothy J. Corrigan	Jacksonville, Fla.	Notre Dame University; Duke University School of Law
Mary Stenson Scriven	Macon, Ga.	Duke University; Florida State University College of Law
Gary R. Jones	Philadelphia, Pa.	Boston University; University of Miami School of Law; New York University School of Law
Douglas N. Frazier	Los Angeles, Calif.	U.S. Naval Academy; University of Mississippi School of Law
Thomas E. Morris	St. Joseph, Mo.	University of Florida; University of Missouri School of Law
Marcia Morales Howard	Jacksonville, Fla.	Vanderbilt University; University of Florida School of Law
Monte C. Richardson	Valdosta, Ga.	American University Washington College of Law
Sheri Polster Chappell	Kiel, Wisc.	University of Wisconsin; Nova Southeastern Shepard Broad Law Center
James R. Klindt	Orlando, Fla.	University of Central Florida; Florida State University College of Law
Gregory J. Kelly	Buffalo, N.Y.	SUNY-Buffalo; University of Toledo College of Law
Anthony E. Porcelli	Rhineback, N.Y.	Stetson University; Stetson University College of Law
Joel B. Toomey	New York, N.Y.	SUNY-Buffalo; Duke University School of Law
Thomas B. Smith	Muskegon, Mich.	University of Florida
Philip R. Lammens	Queens, N.Y.	University of Florida; University of Florida School of Law
Patricia D. Barksdale	Washington, D.C.	University of Florida; University of Florida School of Law

Preappointment career	Years of Service
AUSA	1997–
Private practice	1997–2002
Private practice	1997–2008
Private Practice	2000–2010
AUSA	2000–
AUSA	2001–13
Private practice	2003–7
AUSA	2003–
Assistant state attorney; county court judge	2003–13
AUSA	2008–
Private Practice	2008–
AUSA	2009–
State attorney; private practice	2010–
Assistant state attorney; private practice; state circuit judge	2011–
U.S. Justice Dept.	2012–
AUSA	2013–

U.S. Bankruptcy Judges

Name	Birthplace	Education
Alexander Paskay	Mohacs, Hungary	University of Budapest; University of Miami School of Law
George L. Proctor	Jacksonville, Fla.	University of Florida; University of Florida School of Law
Thomas E. Baynes Jr.	New York, N.Y.	University of Georgia; Emory University School of Law; Yale Law School
Lionel H. Silberman	Baltimore, Md.	Emory University; Emory University School of Law
C. Timothy Corcoran III	Kansas City, Mo.	University of North Carolina; University of Virginia School of Law
Arthur B. Briskman	Philadelphia, Pa.	University of Alabama; Cumberland School of Law
Karen S. Jennemann	Louisville, Ky.	Northern Arizona University; William & Mary Law School
Jerry A. Funk	Chattanooga, Tenn.	University of Georgia; Cumberland School of Law
Paul M. Glenn	Thomasville, Ga.	Florida State University; Duke University School of Law
Michael G. Williamson	West Point, N.Y.	Duke University; Georgetown University Law Center
K. Rodney May	Huntington, W.Va.	University of Florida: Duke University School of Law
Catherine Peek McEwen	Washington, D.C.	University of South Florida; Stetson University College of Law
Caryl E. Delano	Tampa, Fla.	University of South Florida; Indiana University Maurer School of Law
Cynthia C. Jackson	Jacksonville, Fla.	Florida State University; University of Florida School of Law

Preappointment career	Years of Service
Law clerk	1963–2012
Private practice; workman's compensation judge	1975–2007
U.S. Navy JAG Corps; private practice	1987–2005
Private practice	1988
Private Practice	1989–2003
Reassignment from Southern District of Alabama	1985–
Private practice	1993–
Private practice	1993–
Private Practice	1993–
Private practice	2000–
Private practice	2003–
Private practice	2005–
Private practice	2008–
Private practice	2013–

U.S. Attorneys

Name	Birthplace	Education
Edward F. Boardman	New York, N.Y.	University of Florida; University of Florida School of Law
John L. Briggs	Jacksonville, Fla.	University of Florida; George Washington University Law School
John J. Daley Jr.	Jacksonville, Fla.	Florida State College of Law
Gary L. Betz	Philadelphia, Pa.	Temple University; American University Washington College of Law
Robert W. Merkle	Washington, D.C.	University of Notre Dame; Notre Dame Law School
Robert W. Genzman	Orlando, Fla.	University of Pennsylvania; London School of Economics; Cornell Law School
Douglas N. Frazier	Los Angeles, Calif.	U.S. Naval Academy; University of Mississippi School of Law
Larry H. Colleton	Round O, S.C.	University of South Carolina; University of South Carolina School of Law
Donna A. Bucella	New York, N.Y.	University of Virginia; University of Miami School of Law
Charles R. Wilson	Pensacola, Fla.	University of Notre Dame; Notre Dame Law School
Donna A. Bucella	New York, N.Y.	University of Virginia; University of Miami School of Law
Michael A. "Mac" Cauley	Pittsburgh, Pa.	Bethany College; University of Pittsburgh School of Law
Paul I. Perez	Cuba	Jacksonville University; George Washington University Law School
James R. Klindt	Orlando, Fla.	University of Central Florida; Florida State University College of Law
Robert E. O'Neill	Bronx, N.Y.	Fordham University; New York University School of Law
Brian Albritton	Tampa, Fla.	New College; Boston College Law School
Robert E. O'Neill	Bronx, N.Y.	Fordham University; New York University School of Law

Years of Service	Appointing President
1962–69	John Kennedy
1969–78	Richard Nixon
1978–79	Jimmy Carter
1979–82	Jimmy Carter
1982–88	Ronald Reagan
1988–93	Ronald Reagan
1993	Bill Clinton
1993–94	Bill Clinton
1994	Bill Clinton
1994–1999	Bill Clinton
1999–2001	Bill Clinton
2001–2	George W. Bush
2002–7	George Bush
2007	George W. Bush
2007–8	George W. Bush
2008–10	George W. Bush
2010–	Barack Obama

U.S. Marshals

Name	Years of Service	Appointing President
John E. Maguire	1961–65	John Kennedy
Andrew J. F. Peeples	1969–72	Richard Nixon
Ralph B. Saucer	1972–73	Richard Nixon
Mitchell A. Newburger	1973–77	Richard Nixon
George R. Grosse	1977–81	Jimmy Carter
Michael Romanczuk	1981–82	Ronald Reagan
Richard C. Cox	1982–86	Ronald Reagan
James Tassone	1990–91	George H. W. Bush
Lonnie R. Hickey	1991–94	George H. W. Bush
Don Moreland	1994–2003	Bill Clinton
Thomas Hurlburt	2003–11	George W. Bush
William Berger	2011–	Barack Obama

Abbreviations

FJC	Federal Justice Center, Washington, D.C.
LCCFH	Lawton M. Chiles Jr. Center for Florida History, Florida Southern College, Lakeland, Florida
MDFA	Middle District of Florida Archives, George C. Young Courthouse, Orlando, Florida
NARA	National Archives and Records Administration
NARA-CP	National Archives and Records Administration, College Park, Maryland
NARA-MG	National Archives and Records Administration, Morrow, Georgia
PKYL	P. K. Yonge Library, University of Florida, Gainesville, Florida
RG	Record Group
SPOHP	Samuel Proctor Oral History Program, University of Florida

Notes

Introduction

1. Elizabeth Kovachevich Oral History, 8–9, 28.
2. Lyles, *Gatekeepers*, 3.
3. Jackson, *Judges*, 249–50.
4. Ibid., 248; John R. Barry, "Judge's Star Still Rising," *Florida Times-Union*, October 15, 1961.
5. Howell W. Melton Oral History, 24.
6. Richard Lazzara Oral History, 34.

Chapter 1. From the Southern to the U.S. Middle District of Florida, 1950s–1962

1. Hall and Rise, *From Local Courts to National Tribunals*, 111–12.
2. Denham, *"Rogue's Paradise,"* 24–25; and Hall and Rise, *From Local Courts to National Tribunals*, 21–29.
3. Denham, *"Rogue's Paradise,"* 42, 149; and Bogart, "History of Federal Courts in Florida."
4. Hall and Rise, *From Local Courts to National Tribunals*, 64, 79, 91, 101–2, 149–50; and Bogart, "History of Federal Courts in Florida."
5. Denham, *"Rogue's Paradise,"* 34.
6. Johnson, *American Law Enforcement*, 168–77.
7. Hall and Rise, *From Local Courts to National Tribunals*, 111–12.
8. John Crews, "The Hands Are Busy but So Is the Mind," *Daytona Beach Morning Journal*, December 27, 1960.
9. Paul Game Oral History, 13.
10. Elizabeth Jenkins to Patricia Fawcett and Karen Jennemann, e-mail, September 8, 2005, folder "Interviews with Senior Judges," Historical Committee Files, MDFA, Orlando.
11. George T. Swartz Oral History, 15.
12. Mack, "Some Recollections," 7–8.
13. Ibid.
14. Ibid.
15. George T. Swartz Oral History, 16. Hall and Rise, *From Local Courts to National Tribunals*, 173–74;; John T. Carlton, "Pepper Stalling Judicial Appointment," *Miami News*, August 5, 1950; Buck, "George W. Whitehurst"; and

16. E. J. Salcines Oral History, July 26, 2010, p. 8, LCCFH.

17. Ibid., 9.

18. William Terrell Hodges Oral History, May 29, 2012, LCCFH.

19. John R. Barry, "Judge's Star Still Rising," *Florida Times-Union*, October 15, 1961. See also Ander Crenshaw, "New Jacksonville Courthouse Named for Judge Bryan Simpson," *11th Circuit Historical News*, 5 (Fall 2008); Corrine Brown, "'A Man of Great Courage and Exquisite Fairness,'" *11th Circuit Historical News*, 5 (Fall 2008): 12–14; and Hall and Rise, *From Local Courts to National Tribunals*, 170–71.

20. *Florida Times-Union*, August 30, 1950.

21. "Proceedings Attendant upon Induction of Hon. Bryan Simpson as United States District Judge, for the Southern District of Florida at Jacksonville, Florida," October 6, 1950, at 11:00 A.M., MDFA.

22. George Proctor Oral History, 17.

23. Crews, "The Hands Are Busy"; and F. T. MacFeeley, "I'm No Innovator," *Jacksonville Journal*, June 11, 1961.

24. United States District Court, Middle District of Florida, "Memorial Proceedings for the Honorable Chief Judge Joseph P. Lieb," Tampa, March 30, 1973, 358 F. Supp.; Hall and Rise, *From Local Courts to National Tribunals*, 164; and Buck, "Joseph P. Lieb."

25. E. J. Salcines Oral History, 7.

26. Thomas Wilson interview with author, October 14, 2010.

27. Hodges Oral History, May 29, 2012.

28. Alexander Paskay Oral History, 1–18.

29. Leonard Gilbert Oral History, 4.

30. Dan Warren Oral History, 7.

31. Finkelman, "Earl Warren," 827–28.

32. Ibid. See also Patterson, "Rise of Rights," 213–14; and Wilson, *Rise of Judicial Management*, 7.

33. Manley, Brown, and Rise, *Supreme Court of Florida*, 256–58.

34. Roy Mills, "Private Schools Seen Key Source of Future Leaders," *Florida Times-Union*, November 16, 1958.

35. Quoted in Crews, "Hands Are Busy."

36. Quoted in Johnson and Wolfe, *History of Criminal Justice*, 243.

37. Graham, quoted in Johnson and Wolfe, *History of Criminal Justice*, 244–45.

38. Finkelman, "Earl Warren," 827.

39. Cooper and Terrell, *American South*, 748.

40. Quoted in Bill Rufty, "Local Leaders Recall Meeting John Kennedy," *Lakeland Ledger*, November 22, 2003.

41. Clark, *Red Pepper and Gorgeous George*, 96–98.

42. Goulden, *Bench Warmers*, 298.

43. Hall and Rise, *From Local Courts to National Tribunals*, 165–66; and "William McRae Is Nominated as U.S. Judge," *St. Petersburg Times*, February 21, 1961.

44. Leonard Gilbert Oral History, 8.

45. George C. Young Oral History, June 2003, SPOHP, 1–10, 14, 16; Jim Leusner, "George Young: A Life of Sound Judgment," *Orlando Sentinel*, July 28, 2008; and Hall and Rise, *From Local Courts to National Tribunals*, 174.

46. George C. Young Oral History, June 2003, SPOHP, 10–11; and George C. Young Oral History, August 4, 2010, LCCFH.

47. George C. Young Oral History, June 2003, SPOHP; and George C. Young Oral History, August 4, 2010, LCCFH.

48. George C. Young Oral History, June 2003, SPOHP; and George C. Young Oral History, August 4, 2010, LCCFH.

49. Salcines Oral History, July 26, 2010; and Orlando *Sentinel*, December 20, 1990.

50. George Young Oral History, June 2003, SPOHP, 12.

Chapter 2. The U.S. Middle District of Florida, First Years, 1962–1968

1. Hall, *From Local Courts to National Tribunals*, 104, 112–13.

2. Johnson, *American Law Enforcement*, 174; and Jim Leusner, "George C. Young: A Life of Sound Judgment," *Orlando Sentinel*, July 28, 2008.

3. Wilson, *Rise of Judicial Management*, 6. See also Clark, "Adjudication to Administration."

4. Reeves, *President Kennedy*, 658–59.

5. E. J. Salcines Oral History, July 26, 2010, 1.

6. Brinkley, "Great Society," 470–72.

7. Todd Perkins, "Bar Hassle Triggers 'Walkout,'" *Orlando Sentinel*, August 1966.

8. Simpson, quoted in F. T. McFeely, "I'm No Innovator—Simpson," *Jacksonville Journal*, June 11, 1964.

9. Leusner, "George Young."

10. Dan Warren Oral History, 13.

11. E. J. Salcines Oral History, July 26, 2010, 9–10.

12. Horwitz, quote in Leusner, "George Young."

13. Author conversation and Tampa Court House visit with E. J. Salcines, July 29, 2010.

14. E. J. Salcines Oral History, July 26, 2010, 2.

15. Virginia Ellis, "Boardman Running Uncle Sam's Law Office Here at a Profit," *Tampa Times*, July 23, 1966.

16. Ron Hutchinson, "U.S. Court Activity Zooms," *Tampa Times*, August 8, 1967.

17. Boardman, quote in Ellis, "Boardman Running Uncle Sam's Law Office."

18. Marlene Davis, "Pam Linquist—Tampa's Civil Service Celebrity," *Tampa Tribune*, January 8, 1968.

19. Joseph Hatchett Oral History, 4, 14, 30, 31; Criminal Dockets, 1967, Middle District of Florida, Jacksonville Division, Criminal Dockets, 1907–1968, RG 21, Box 10, NARA-MG.

20. Ron Hutchinson, "Federal Attorney Adds Two to Staff," *Tampa Times*, August 3, 1967.

21. Joseph Hatchett Oral History, 36.

22. Mack, "Some Recollections," 5–6.

23. George C. Young Oral History, 13.

24. Presentation of Portrait of the Chief Judge Emeritus, The Honorable George C. Young, Orlando, October 23, 1981, 530 F. Supp., LXXXI.

25. Mack, "Some Recollections," 6–7.

26. E. J. Salcines Oral History, July 26, 2010, 9–10.

27. Tjoflat, quoted in Joe Wilhelm, "Courthouse Named after Civil Rights 'Pioneer,'" Jacksonville *Daily Record*, August 12, 2008.

28. E. J. Salcines Oral History, July 26, 2010, 13.

29. Dan Warren Oral History, 2.

30. Ibid.

31. E. J. Salcines Oral History, July 26, 2010, 6.

32. Ibid.

33. Ibid.

34. Ibid., 11–12.

35. Larson, *Federal Justice in Western Missouri*, 126–30, 165–86, 223–24.

36. E. J. Salcines Oral History, July 26, 2010, 14.

37. Ibid., 15.

38. Ibid.

39. Ibid., 4, 16.

40. Don McKay, "$750,000 in Bogus Cash Seized; Pair Jailed," *Tampa Tribune*, December 3, 1965.

41. Thom Wilkerson, "Agents Tell of Buying Bills from Cocoa Beach Dentist," *Cocoa Florida Today*, November 23, 1966

42. Georgia Harbison, "Jury Finds Davis Guilty on Two Charges," *Orlando Sentinel*, December 3, 1966.

43. Todd Persons, "Missing Dentist Vowed Suicide, Letter Reveals," *Orlando Sentinel*, January 18, 1967. See also George Tomlinson, "Convicted Dentist Missing," *Orlando Sentinel*, January 16, 1967.

44. J. F. Santoiana to Edward F. Boardman, March 1, 1968, in *U.S. v. Stiles Richard Davis*, 1965 #66-35-Orl-CR., Orlando Division, U.S. Court for the Middle District of Florida, RG 21, NARA-MG.

45. Arthur M. Blood MD to J. Russell Hornsby, August 19, 1966, in *U.S. v. Stiles Davis* #67-91-Orl-CR, Orlando Division, U.S. Court for the Middle District of Florida, RG 21, NARA-MG.

46. "Dentist Given 3 Years in Jail," *St. Petersburg Times*, July 20, 1968. The case was later reversed on appeal based on Davis's mental illness. Davis v. United States 413 F. 2d 1226 5th Cir. 1969. *Stiles R. Davis Appellant v. US Appellee* No. 25037, RG 21, NARA-MG.

47. Virginia Ellis, "Men Choosing Jail over War Sincere," *Tampa Times*, October 4, 1966.

48. Joseph Hatchett Oral History, 32–33.

49. Ibid., 35.

50. *United States v. Clyde Lee*, Case # 65-26-ORL CR, Middle District Court of Florida (1965–1969), Box 44, RG 21, NARA-MG.

51. Mike Willard, "U.S. Nabs 'Cowboy' Ippolito," *Tampa Times*, October 26, 1967; "5 of Tampa Underworld Post Bond after Arrest," *St. Petersburg Times*, October 27, 1967; Charles Hendrick and Dennis McClendon, "Federal Agents Seek Mafia Inroads with Tampa Arrests," *Tampa Tribune*, October 27, 1967; and Henry Gonzalez to Judge Joseph P. Lieb, July 25, 1968, *United States of America v. Scaglione et. Al.* Case No. 65-87, Tampa Division, U.S. Middle District Court of Florida, RG 21, NARA-MG.

52. Ronald Hutchinson, "Jury's Crime Probe Prelude to Further Action," *St. Petersburg Times*, October 29, 1967.

53. "Gibbons Urges U.S. to Keep Up Crime Attack," *Tampa Tribune*, October 31, 1967.

54. "4 Tampans Face Trial on April 21," *St. Petersburg Times*, March 13, 1969; and Deitche, *Cigar City Mafia*, 126–28.

55. David Schultz, "Faircloth to Study Judge Lieb Ruling," *St. Petersburg Times*, November 26, 1965.

56. Paul Schnitt, "Gideon Rule Praised, But Problem," *St. Petersburg Evening Independent*, December 3, 1965.

57. Mabel Norris Chesley, "Volusia Case May Set Legal Precedent," *Daytona Beach Morning Journal*, December 9, 1967.

58. "Judge Blocks Execution of 50 Florida Convicts," *St. Petersburg Times*, April 14,1967; and "Judge Opens Door on Execution Ban," *Salt Lake City Deseret News*, August 10, 1967.

59. Radelet, Bedau, and Putnam, *In Spite of Innocence*, 210.

60. Clark quoted in Goldman, *Picking Federal Judges*, 170. On Johnson and the selection of judges, see McFeeley, *Appointment of Judges*; and Lyles, *Gate Keepers*, 90–94.

61. DeVault, "'Counsel, You are Dangerously Close to Violating Rule 13!'"

62. Ben Krentzman Oral History, 1–8.

63. Ibid., 6–8.

64. Ibid.

65. "Krentzman Dons Robes as New Federal Judge," *St. Petersburg Times*, June 30, 1967.

66. Bryan Simpson to John Holland, Bill Barker, George Whitehurst, Emett Choate, Joe Lieb, Bill McRae, George Young, December 9, 1965, Correspondence, 1965–1969, box 6, Simpson Papers, PKYL.

67. Bryan Simpson to Julian A. Blake, December 20, 1965, Correspondence, 1965–1969, box 6, Simpson Papers, PKYL.

Chapter 3. The Middle District and Civil Rights, 1962–1968

1. Friedman, "The Federal Courts of the South," 187, 193.

2. Ibid., 193.

3. Warren, *If It Takes All Summer*, 138.

4. Dyckman, *Floridian of His Century*, 161–71; and Karl, *The 57 Club*, 123–30.

5. Winsboro, "Brotherhood of Defiance," 9.

6. Bartley, "From Old South to New South," 48.

7. Ibid., 50.

8. Ibid., 53–63.

9. Ibid.

10. Warren, *If It Takes All Summer*, 5–7. On the St. Augustine crisis, see Hall and Rise, *From Local Courts to National Tribunals*, 130–34; Read and McGough, *Let Them Be Judged*, 418–24; Belknap, *Federal Law and Southern Order*, 130–34; Kunstler, *Deep in My Heart*, 271–304; Colburn, *Racial Change and Community Crisis;* and Garrow, *Bearing the Cross*, 316–44; Garrow, *St. Augustine, Florida, 1963–1964*; and Branch, *Pillar of Fire*, 283, 326–27, 333, 338, 382, 396. For personal insights on participants in the St. Augustine crisis, see Saunders, *Bridging the Gap*, 227–42; and Slate, "Battle for St. Augustine."

11. Warren, *If It Takes All Summer*, 1–2.

12. Hayling, quoted in ibid., 8. Hayling denied ever saying these words, arguing that he was misquoted by hostile newspapers. See Due and Due, *Freedom in the Family*, 205.

13. McRae, quoted in Warren, *If It Takes All Summer*, 28; see also Friedman, "Federal Courts of the South," 194; and Read and McGough, *Let Them Be Judged*, 419.

14. King, quoted in Warren, *If It Takes All Summer*, 86.

15. Friedman, "Federal Courts of the South," 196–97.

16. Warren, *If It Takes All Summer*, 93.

17. Kunstler, *Deep in My Heart*, 273.

18. Ibid., 279; and Branch, *Pillar of Fire*, 283.

19. Friedman, "Federal Courts of the South," 198; and Read and McGough, *Let Them Be Judged*, 420–21.

20. Kunstler, *Deep in My Heart*, 282.

21. Ibid., 296. See also *Andrew Young v. L. O. Davis et al.* No. 64-133-Civ-J., US MD of FL, Findings of Fact and Conclusions of Law and Preliminary Injunction, June 9, 1964, folder entitled "Andrew Young," Box 1, Judge Bryan Simpson Papers, PKYL.

22. Friedman, "The Federal Courts of the South," 200–201.

23. Warren, *If It Takes All Summer*, 93, 88.

24. Ibid., 96, 111, 113; Belknap, *Federal Law and Southern Disorder*, 132–33; Friedman, "Federal Courts of the South," 202–3; and Farris Bryant, Executive Order No. 1, June 15, 1964, Box 1, folder entitled "Andrew Young," Judge Bryan Simpson Papers, PKYL.

25. Warren, *If It Takes All Summer*, 126.

26. Ibid., 128–29.

27. Belknap, *Federal Law and Southern Order*, 133; and James W. Kynes, Return to Order to Show Cause and Response to Order to Show Cause, June 22, 1964, in *Andrew Young v. L. O. Davis, et al.* No. 64-133-Civ-J, Box 1, folder entitled "Andrew Young," Judge Bryan Simpson Papers, PKYL.

28. Warren, *If It Takes All Summer*, 137–38, 145.

29. Simpson, quoted in Garrow, *St. Augustine, 1963–1964*, 27; and Friedman, "Federal Courts of the South," 205.

30. Warren, *If It Takes All Summer*, 158, 165, 167–69; see also Branch, *Pillar of Fire*, 382–83, 396.

31. Thurmond, quoted in Friedman, "Federal Courts of the South," 210.

32. Quoted in Branch, *Pillar of Fire*, 338.

33. "An Irate Taxpayer" to Bryan Simpson, June 24, 1964, box 2, folder entitled "Correspondence & Clippings Unfavorable to Judge Simpson," Bryan Simpson Papers, PKYL.

34. William W. Woodward to Bryan Simpson, June 22, 1964, in ibid.

35. Simpson, quoted in Read and McGough, *Let Them Be Judged*, 423.

36. Simpson, quoted in F. T. MacFeeley, "I'm No Innovator—Simpson," *Jacksonville Journal*, June 11, 1964.

37. Bryan Simpson Oral History. See also Read and McGough, *Let Them Be Judged*, 423–24.

38. Dan Warren Oral History, 4.

39. James W. Kynes to Bryan Simpson, December 18, 1964; and Bryan Simpson to James W. Kynes, December 28, 1964, Bryan Simpson Papers, PKYL.

40. "Decision Due on Motions in Club Suits," *Ocala Star-Banner*, March 8, 1965.

41. Paul Schnitt, "'Cops' Suit Goes to Judge," *St. Petersburg Evening Independent*, January 18, 1966.

42. Dan Millott, "Suit Filed by 12 Negro Policemen Is Dismissed, *St. Petersburg Times*, April 1, 1966.

43. Ibid.

44. "Police Zoning Ordered by Judge, *St. Petersburg Times*, October 4, 1968. See also Ronald Hutchinson, "Sanderlin Asks $8,000 City Fee in Police Case," *St. Petersburg Times*, October 25, 1968.

45. Hall, *Magic Mirror*, 327.

46. Cooper and Terrell, *American South*, 765. On *Jefferson*, see Read and McGough, *Let Them Be Judged*, 436–45; Wilkinson, *From* Brown *to* Bakke, 111–14; and Couch, *History of the Fifth Circuit*, 136–39.

47. Cooper and Terrell, *American South*, 765.

48. Graham, *Civil Rights Era*, 373.

49. Ibid., 374.

50. Brennan, quoted in Green, "The School Busing Case," 404. On *Green*, see Wilkinson, *From* Brown *to* Bakke, 108–18.

51. Green, "The School Busing Case," 405.

52. Hall, *Magic Mirror*, 327.

53. Hall and Rise, *From Local Courts to National Tribunals*, 135; and Couch, *History of the Fifth Circuit*, 108.

54. Read and McGough, *Let Them Be Judged*, 424, 510; Hall and Rise, *From Local Courts to National Tribunals*, 135; and Jung, "The Last Unlikely Hero," 30.

55. *Ellis et al v. R. Earl Kipp, Superintendent of the Board of Public Instruction of Orange County Florida*, Case No. 62-CV-1215, Orl.(1962); "Orange County Desegregation Timeline," *Orlando Sentinel*, February 27, 2008; and Jeff Kunerth, "They Taught Schools a Lesson in Equality," *Orlando Sentinel*, February 24, 2008.

56. "U.S. Judge Studying Pinellas School Suit," *St. Petersburg Times*, October 1, 1964.

57. "Integration Plan Explained; Presentation Criticized," *St. Petersburg Times*, February 24, 1965.

58. "Desegregation Hearing Brings No Firm Action," *St. Petersburg Times*, November 16, 1965.

59. "Court Upholds School Zones in Pinellas," *St. Petersburg Times*, September 21, 1966. See also Schnur, "Desegregation of Public Schools in Pinellas County, Florida," 5–7.

60. "Lee Integration Plan Rejected by Court," *St. Petersburg Times*, October 30, 1964.

61. Robin Williams, "Courts Push Polk through Slow Process," *Lakeland Ledger*, August 31, 1982; and Brown, *None Can Have Richer Memories*, 133–34.

62. "U.S. Sues to Speed School Integration in Polk County," *Sarasota Herald-Tribune*, March 2, 1967.

63. Fred McCormack, "Desegregation Talks Rescheduled April 7," *Sarasota Herald Tribune*, March 4, 1967.

64. Ibid.

65. "A Legal Message for Polk County, *St. Petersburg Evening Independent*, July 23, 1968.

66. Couch, *History of the Fifth Circuit*, 141; and Robin Williams, "Courts Push Polk through Slow Process," *Lakeland Ledger*, August 31, 1982.

67. Paul Game Oral History, 20.

68. For an overview of the redistricting question in the federal courts, see Wainscott, "From the 'Political Thicket,'" 124–32; and Couch, *History of the Fifth Circuit*, 105–7. On Florida, see Colburn and deHaven-Smith, *Government in the Sunshine*, 41–45; Skene,

"Reapportionment in Florida," 178–82; and Colburn and Scher, *Florida's Gubernatorial Politics*, 178.

69. See Johnson, *I Declare*, 73–74.

70. Powers, *E. C.*, 62.

71. Brown, *None Can Have Richer Memories*, 147.

72. "Reapportionment May Go Before 3-Judge Panel," *Ocala Star-Banner*, June 21, 1972.

Chapter 4. Adjudicating Equality Continues

1. Thompson, "Orlando's Martin Anderson," 505.

2. Ambrose, *Nixon*, 316–17.

3. Ibid., 460; and Lyles, *Gatekeepers*, 94.

4. Sanders, "Rassling a Governor," 332.

5. Ambrose, *Nixon*, 460–61.

6. Lyles, *Gatekeepers*, 93.

7. "Maternity Leave Rule Contested," *Daytona Beach Sunday News-Journal*, April 20, 1972; "Pregnant Teacher Wins Right to Keep Working," *Sarasota Herald-Tribune*, April 22, 1972; and "Pregnant Teacher Wins Suit," *Palm Beach Post*, June 15, 1972.

8. "Court Rules Florida's Obscenity Law Unconstitutional," *Daytona Beach Morning Journal*, July 23, 1970.

9. Ibid.

10. "Desegregation Plan Ruling Is Delayed," *St. Petersburg Independent*, May 12, 1969; and "'Best Possible,' Southard Says," *St. Petersburg Times*, May 9, 1969.

11. Courtney, quote in John Lankford, "Mass Rally Called to Protest Integration Plan," *St. Petersburg Evening Independent*, July 29, 1969. See also John Lankford, "12 Per Cent Faculty Desegregation Ordered," *St. Petersburg Evening Independent*, July 28, 1969; John Lankford, "Pinellas School Desegregation 'Mistake' Fixed," *St. Petersburg Evening Independent*, July 24, 1969; and John Lankford, "Integration Plan to Be Altered," *St. Petersburg Evening Independent*, July 24, 1969.

12. Brad Sabel, "Desegregation Fight Planned," *St. Petersburg Times*, July 29, 1969.

13. "Desegregation Plan Approved for Pinellas," *St. Petersburg Times*, August 6, 1969.

14. Ibid.

15. "Desegregation Plan Appeal Filed," *St. Petersburg Evening Independent*, September 16, 1969.

16. James A. Schnur, "Desegregation of Public Schools in Pinellas County, Florida."

17. *Palm Beach Post*, November 5, 1971; and "Student Transfer Is Planned," *St. Petersburg Times*, December 30, 1971.

18. Kathy Scott, "Contempt-of-Court Action in School Battle Is Cancelled," *St. Petersburg Times*, January 26, 1972. See also Schnur, "Desegregation of Public Schools," 7.

19. "Arrests Threatened in School Boycott," *St. Petersburg Times*, May 8, 1969. See also Dora Walters, "Judge Won't Consider Extending School Order," *St. Petersburg Times*, April 5, 1969.

20. "Florida County-by-County: Desegregation Situation," *Sarasota Herald Tribune*, January 26, 1970.

21. "Hillsborough Plan Is Rejected," *St. Petersburg Times*, May 10, 1969; "Hillsborough School Plan Turned Down, *St. Petersburg Times*, July 31, 1969; and "Florida County-By-County: Desegregation Situation," *Sarasota Herald Tribune*, January 26, 1970.

22. "Lee Integration Plan Rejected," *St. Petersburg Times*, May 8, 1969; "Florida County-By-County: Desegregation Situation"; and Winsboro, "Brotherhood of Defiance," 78–81.

23. "Florida County-By-County: Desegregation Situation," *Sarasota Herald Tribune*, January 26, 1970; and "New Judge Named for Volusia Case," *St. Petersburg Times*, February 7, 1970.

24. Buck, "Joseph P. Lieb."

25. "Manatee, Volusia Feel Impact of Integration Order," *Sarasota Journal*, December 19, 1969; and "U.S. Judge Charles R. Scott Ruling on Busing and Prisons," *New York Times*, May 14, 1983.

26. "School Boards' Lawyers to Discuss Schools," *Sarasota Journal*, January 16, 1970.

27. "Columbia Mix Plan Ordered," *Ocala Star-Banner*, August 27, 1969; and "Florida County-By-County: Desegregation Situation," *Sarasota Herald Tribune*, January 26, 1970.

28. "Teacher Shuffle On," *Ocala Star-Banner*, January 27, 1970.

29. "Florida County-By-County: Desegregation Situation," *Sarasota Herald Tribune*, January 26, 1970; and "Orange County Desegregation Timeline," *Orlando Sentinel*, February 27, 2008.

30. "Teacher Shuffle On," *Ocala Star-Banner*, January 27, 1970; and "Judge McRae also Says Desegregate," *Daytona Beach Sunday News Journal*, February 7, 1970.

31. "Nation Watches Veto," *Ocala Star-Banner*, January 27, 1970.

32. "Manatee, Volusia Feel Impact of Integration Order," *Sarasota Journal*, December 19, 1969.

33. "High Court Rejects Desegregation Delay: Kirk Motion Denied," *St. Petersburg Times*, January 27, 1970.

34. Kirk, quoted in Martin Dyckman, "Kirk Strikes Out with School Suit at Supreme Court," *St. Petersburg Times*, January 29, 1970.

35. For Kirk's battle with Krentzman in the Manatee County conflict, see Sanders, "Rassling a Governor," 345–59; Houston, "Voice of the Exploited Majority," 258–86; and Kallina, *Claude Kirk and the Politics of Confrontation*, 168–83.

36. Ben Krentzman Oral History, 8–11.

37. Nixon, quoted in Ambrose, *Nixon*, 337–38. See also Haldeman, *Haldeman Diaries*, 146–47. On Kirk and communications with the Nixon administration during the crisis, see Houston, "Voice of the Exploited Majority," 272–75.

38. "Manatee School Desegregation Upheld," *St. Petersburg Evening Independent*, June 27, 1970.

39. Craig Basse, "U.S. District Judge Ben Krentzman Dies," *St. Petersburg Times*, March 3, 1998.

40. Ray Ruester, "Volusia Pupil Plans Aired for Judge," *Daytona Beach Morning-Journal*, May 14, 1970.

41. "'Pairing' Might Prove the Solution," *Daytona Beach Morning Journal*, July 25, 1970.

42. "Duval Desegregates—McRae Writes Order," *Daytona Beach Morning Journal*, August 7, 1970.

43. "Judge Refuses Delay in Duval Mix Case," *Sarasota Herald-Tribune*, August 12, 1970.

44. "Appeal Integration Ruling, Duval School Board Told," *St. Petersburg Times*, August 8, 1970.

45. Schools Open Peacefully in Fifteen Florida Counties," *St. Petersburg Times*, September 9, 1970.

46. Sanders, *Mighty Peculiar Elections*.

47. Askew, quoted in Dyckman, *Reubin Askew and the Golden Age*, 89–93; Askew's speech is printed in full in Askew, "The Law Demands, and Rightly So."

48. Mauldin, "Hon. Gerald Bard Tjoflat," 24–28; Gerald B. Tjoflat Oral History.

49. Judge Gerald B. Tjoflat interview with the author, May 27, 2011.

50. Quoted in Read and McGough, *Let Them Be Judged*, 525.

51. Ibid., 515.

52. Ibid.

53. Gerald B. Tjoflat Oral History, 45–48.

54. Judge Gerald B. Tjoflat interview with the author, May 27, 2011.

55. Gerald B. Tjoflat Oral History, 45–48.

56. Judge Gerald B. Tjoflat interview with the author, May 27, 2011.

57. Ibid.

58. Gerald B. Tjoflat Oral History, 60–61.

59. "A Reasonable Decision," *Jacksonville Journal*, June 25, 1971.

60. Ibid.

61. *Florida Times-Union*, June 25, 1971.

62. Ibid.

63. Quoted in Jim Davis, "NAACP to Appeal Integration," *Jacksonville Journal*, June 24, 1971.

64. Read and McGough, *Let Them Be Judged,* 517. See also Davis, "NAACP to Appeal Integration"; and *Mims v. Duval County School Board*, 329 F. Supp. 123 (1971).

65. Jung, "Last Unlikely Hero," 30–34.

66. Martin Crutsinger, "Judge's Quick Order Hit by Busing Foes," *Jacksonville Journal*, December 1, 1971. See also Otis Perkins, "Duval Is Given Year's Delay for Most Busing," *Florida Times-Union*, September 3, 1971; and Bill Foley, "Court Acts after Vote Backs Ban," *Florida Times-Union*, December 1, 1971.

67. Crutsinger, "Judge's Quick Order Hit by Busing Foes."

68. Jung, "Last Unlikely Hero," 30–34.

69. "Court Order Here May Be a First," *Jacksonville Journal*, March 6, 1972; Otis Perkins, "Outsiders, Dissidents Cited in School Woes, *Florida Times-Union*, March 6, 1972; Otis Perkins, "End to Disruptions at Schools Ordered by U.S. Court Here: Judge Tjoflat Acts on Petition From Hardesty," *Florida Times-Union*, March 6, 1972. See also Read and McGough, *Let Them Be Judged*, 518–20.

70. Nixon, quoted in Lyles, *Gatekeepers*, 95–96. On Nixon and Wallace's candidacy, see Carter, *Politics of Rage*, 422–26.

71. Tanzler, quoted in Otis Perkins, "Judge Tjoflat Refuses to Delay Busing Order," *Florida Times-Union*, August 11, 1972; and Rachel Bail, "Tanzler May Seek Busing Aid in D.C.," *Florida Times-Union*, August 10, 1972.

72. Rachel Bail, "Busing Fight Taken to D.C.," *Florida Times-Union*, August 15, 1972.

73. Rachel Bail, "Nixon Antibusing Bill Raises Hope of Local School Groups," *Florida Times-Union*, August 19, 1972. According to Kevin Lyles, the primary purpose of Nixon's Equal Education Opportunities Bill was to "limit the court's jurisdiction and 'autonomy' in formulating desegregation plans. This bill, in addition to delaying existing court orders for desegregation, prohibited courts from further ordering or transferring pupils further than

the 'next closest school' to his or her own neighborhood or from increasing the busing in the school district." Under the bill the school boards would be permitted to "reopen existing court orders, subsequently permitting the resegregation of many schools. See Lyles, Gatekeepers, 96; and Ambrose, *Nixon*, 523–24.

74. "Protests, Boycotts Continue at Oceanway," *Florida Times-Union*, September 8, 1972.

75. Bill Humphrey, "Parents Continue Oceanway Picket," Jacksonville *Journal*, November 14, 1972.

76. Otis Perkins, "Protest Halt Is Ordered," *Florida Times-Union*, November 14, 1972.

77. Read and McGough, *Let Them Be Judged*, 516.

78. Grilli, quoted in "Ben Krentzman, Judge, Dies at 84," *Tampa Tribune*, March 31, 1998.

Chapter 5. The Middle District and the War on Crime, 1968–1976

1. Tom Twitty, "Federal Court Here Meeting Challenge of Heavy Docket," *Orlando Sentinel*, November 21, 1970.

2. Clark, "Adjudication to Administration," 137.

3. "Young Acting Chief," *Orlando Sentinel*, September 9, 1971; and "Judge Young Becomes Chief Judge," *St. Petersburg Times*, September 10, 1971.

4. Andy Williams, "Judge Young Respected by Attorneys," *Orlando Sentinel*, July 26, 1971.

5. Dennis Beal, "Gurney Lauds, Won't Push, Young," *Orlando Sentinel*, September 21, 1971.

6. Ambrose, *Nixon*, 468–71; and Haldeman, *Haldeman Diaries*, 367, 357.

7. "Suspects Nabbed in State Roundup," *Sarasota Herald-Tribune*, November 3, 1971.

8. William Terrell Hodges Oral History, July 10, 2006, SPOHP, 25–26.

9. Ibid.

10. Ibid., 72–73.

11. "Judge Vows Dedication, Objectivity," *St. Petersburg Times*, December 29, 1971.

12. William Terrell Hodges Oral History, July 10, 2006, SPOHP, 27–28.

13. Ibid., 34.

14. Crew, "Death and Resurrection of Capital Punishment"; Radelet, Bedau, Putnam, *In Spite of Innocence*, 210; Bodenhamer, *Fair Trial*, 133–34; and Friedman, *American Law in the Twentieth Century*, 219–20.

15. Dianne Selditch, "Judge Rules U.S. Can't Ask Death in Gotha Slaying," *Orlando Sentinel*, September 27, 1975.

16. Plan of the United States District Court for the Middle District of Florida Pursuant to the Criminal Justice Act of 1964, as Amended, January 27, 1971, MDFA.

17. Harvey E. Schlesinger Oral History, 10.

18. "Ex-U.S. Attorney Briggs Dies 'Great Lawyer,' Former Airline Pilot," *Florida Times-Union*, April 9, 1999; and Harvey E. Schlesinger Oral History, 10.

19. Harvey E. Schlesinger Oral History, 12.

20. Ibid., 6.

21. Schlesinger quoted in "Ex-U.S. Attorney Briggs Dies 'Great Lawyer,' Former Airline Pilot," *Florida Times-Union*, April 9, 1999.

22. Joseph Hatchett Oral History, 30–31.

23. Harvey E. Schlesinger interview with author, May 24, 2011.

24. Ibid.; and "Ex-U.S. Attorney Briggs Dies 'Great Lawyer,' Former Airline Pilot," *Florida Times-Union*, April 9, 1999.

25. Joe Wilhelm, "Mueller Receives Ehrlich Award," *Jacksonville Daily Record*, June 7, 2010; David Hunt, "Ernst Mueller, 1942–2011: Jacksonville Lawyer's Fairness Inspired Others," *Jacksonville Times-Union*, July 23, 2011; and "Ernst Mueller, 1942–2011," *Jacksonville Times-Union*, July 24, 2011.

26. Johnson, *American Law Enforcement*, 178; Bodenhamer, *Fair Trial*, 127; and Marion, *A History of Federal Crime Control Initiatives,* 46–50, 56–57.

27. Bodenhamer, *Fair Trial*, 127.

28. Johnson, *American Law Enforcement*, 182.

29. Johnson and Wolfe, *History of Criminal Justice*, 237. On Lyndon Johnson's and Richard Nixon's crime control policies, see Marion, *A History of Federal Crime Control Initiatives*, 37–102.

30. Marion, *History of Federal Crime Control Initiatives*, 80.

31. Johnson, *American Law Enforcement*, 182.

32. Dan Warren Oral History, 17–18.

33. Johnson, *American Law Enforcement*, 178.

34. Kelly, "Organized Crime," 593–94.

35. Dan Warren Oral History, 17–18, 22.

36. Johnson, *American Law Enforcement*, 178.

37. Ibid., 178–79.

38. Calhoun, *Lawmen*, 6–7. See also Sabbag, *Too Tough to Die*, 53.

39. Ron Hutchinson, "Grand Jury Probes Rackets, Gambling," *St. Petersburg Times*, November 7, 1969.

40. "Suspects Nabbed in State Roundup," *Sarasota Herald-Tribune*, November 3, 1971.

41. Dan Warren Oral History, 15.

42. "2 Plead Guilty to U.S. Gaming Count," *Florida Times-Union*, May 4, 1972.

43. Charlie Jean, "Blackburn Ordered Lee Murdered, U.S. Charges," *Orlando Sentinel*, May 5, 1972.

44. Peggy Poor, "4 Accused 'May Gamble' on Trial or Guilty Plea," *Orlando Sentinel*, May 19, 1972.

45. Peggy Poor, "Backburn's Ex-Girl Friend 'Tells All,'" *Orlando Sentinel*, May 23, 1972.

46. Ibid.

47. Ibid. See also Otis Perkins, "Woman Testifies to Blackburn's Insolvency," *Florida Times-Union,* May 23, 1972.

48. Peggy Poor, "Aide to Blackburn Tells of Dope Trade Financing," *Orlando Sentinel*, May 30, 1972.

49. Peggy Poor, "Blackburn Pleads '5th' After Call to Testify," *Orlando Sentinel*, May 31, 1972.

50. Otis Perkins, "Jury Scheduled to Get Gambling Trial Today," *Florida Times-Union*, June 1, 1972.

51. Otis Perkins, "4 Convicted for Gambling: They Remain Free on Bond," *Florida Times-Union*, June 2, 1972.

52. Gerald Tjoflat Oral History, 58–59.

53. Otis Perkins, "Turner Trial: 5 Months Old, Growing," *Florida Times-Union*, January 20, 1974.

54. Gerald Tjoflat Oral History, 58–59.

55. Perkins, "Turner Trial."

56. Gene Miller, "As Trials Go, This One's a Lallapalooza," *Miami Herald*, February 10, 1974.

57. "Turner Trial Is Transferred," *Sarasota Herald-Tribune*, November 7, 1974. Bailey's trial began on July 30, 1975, before Judge John A. Reed. The judge eventually dismissed the case. "Judge Dismisses Some Charges against Turner," *Sumter (S.C.) Daily Item*, July 16, 1975; and "Federal Judge dismisses Charges against Bailey," *St. Petersburg Times*, August 9, 1975.

58. Angel Castillo, "Turner Pleads No Contest to Misdemeanor, Is Fined $5,000," *St. Petersburg Times*, September 17, 1975.

59. "$5,000 Fine Set as Turner Weeps," *Milwaukee Sentinel*, September 17, 1975; and

60. Memorial Proceedings for the Honorable Chief Judge Joseph P. Lieb, March 30, 1973, 358 F. Supp.

61. Ormund Powers, "Young Appeals for 2 More Judges," *Orlando Sentinel*, February 8, 1973.

62. David Wilkening, "Judge Young 'Portrait of Constructionist,'" *Orlando Sentinel*, February 11, 1973.

63. "Friends and Judges, *Lakeland Ledger*, March 32, 1973.

64. "Chiles Seeks Better Way," *Lakeland Ledger*, March 24, 1973.

65. "It's up to Gurney to Aid Judicial Selection Reform," *Daytona Beach Morning Journal*, March 17, 1973.

66. Hall and Rise, *From Local Courts to National Tribunals*, 168.

67. Johnson, *American Law Enforcement*, 178.

68. On June 17, 1972, a team of five burglars composed of G. Gordon Liddy, E. Howard Hunt, and James McCord Jr., chief of security for CREEP, were arrested while breaking in Democratic National Headquarters at Watergate. Ambrose, *Nixon*, 558.

69. FBI Report on Donald Henry Segretti, June 29, 1972, No. 73-66, Cr. T-K, No. 73-153 Cr. T-K, RG 118, Records of the U.S. Attorneys, NARA-MG.

70. John Perry, "Second Brock Aid Linked to Campaign Sabotage Ring," *Tampa Times*, November 24, 1972.

71. Robert Fraser and Margaret Leonard, "Segretti Indicted for 'Muskie Letter,'" *St. Petersburg Times*, May 5, 1973. See also "Big Break Expected Today in 'Muskie Letter' Case," *St. Petersburg Times*, May 4, 1973.

72. Jackson and Briggs, quoted in Robert Fraser and Margaret Leonard, "Segretti Indicted for 'Muskie Letter,'" *St. Petersburg Times*, May 5, 1973.

73. Joann Schulte, "Segretti Pleads Not Guilty," *St. Petersburg Evening Independent*, May 17, 1973. See also Robert Johnson and Joe Registrato, "Tampan Says Hearing Paid Anti-Demo Activity Expenses," *Tampa Tribune*, June 1, 1973; and Robert Fraser, "Hearing Details Wide Sabotage for GOP," *St. Petersburg Times*, June 3, 1973.

74. Cox, quoted in John Barbour, "Cox Promises Full Probe of Segretti Case," *Tampa Tribune*, June 8, 1973.

75. Rowland Evans and Robert Novak, "Florida Segretti Case Bypassed or Bungled?" *Tampa Tribune*, June 29, 1973; and Joe Registrato and Robert Johnson, "Briggs Offers to Open 'Letter' Files," *Tampa Tribune,* July 1, 1973.

76. "Segretti Pleads Guilty," *St. Petersburg Times*, October 2, 1973; and *Clearwater Sun*, November 6, 1973.

77. William James, "Report of Convicted Prisoner by United States Attorney to U.S. Board of Parole," September 11, 1973 in No. 73-66, Cr. T-K, No. 73-153 Cr. T-K, RG 118, Records of the U.S. Attorneys, NARA-MG.

78. Harvey E. Schlesinger Oral History, 13.

79. Robert Johnson and Charles Hendrick, "Williams Says Gurney Got Election Funds," *Tampa Tribune*, November 28, 1973; and Harvey E. Schlesinger Oral History, 13.

80. Johnson and Hendrick, "Williams Says Gurney Got Election Funds."

81. Ibid.

82. Gurney, quoted in Hall and Rise, *From Local Courts to National Tribunals*, 120.

83. "Gurney Hearing Called; Case Shifts to Orlando," *Orlando Sentinel*, November 19, 1975.

84. Ibid.

85. Randy Harrison, "Gurney Judge's Ruling Could Scuttle Retrial," *Orlando Sentinel*, July 24, 1976. See also Randy Harrison, "Gurney's Motions Denied, Trial On," *Orlando Sentinel*, September 18, 1976.

86. Harrison, "Gurney Judge's Ruling Could Scuttle Retrial"

87. Ibid. See also Harvey E. Schlesinger Oral History, 12–13.

88. Bourne, *Jimmy Carter*, 294–300.

Chapter 6. Growing Pains, Constitutional Questions, and Bankruptcy, 1976–1980

1. Powers, *Martin Andersen*, 396; Dick Marlow, "Downtown Sites Viewed for Federal Building," *Orlando Sentinel*, June 9, 1970; "Federal Building Possible in 3 Years," *Orlando Sentinel*, April 21, 1972; Bruce Dudley, "Sen. Gurney Breaks Ground for Orlando Federal Building, *Orlando Sentinel*, February 15, 1974; Tom Twitty, "Agencies Set to Move into Federal Building," *Orlando Sentinel*, January 14, 1976; and "Eckerd, Others to Attend Federal Building Dedication," *Orlando Sentinel*, February 26, 1976.

2. Twitty, "Agencies Set to Move," undated, unidentified, newspaper clipping.

3. "Young Cuts Party Line on Judges," *Orlando Sentinel*, May 25, 1975. See also "Scott's Surgery Puts U.S. Courts in Crisis," *Orlando Sentinel*, September 15, 1976.

4. Judy Doyle, "Federal Judgeships a Florida Must, Young Says," *Orlando Sentinel*, June 26, 1977.

5. Smith, "From U.S. Magistrates to U.S. Magistrate Judges," 210. See also Carp, "United States Courts," 176; Carp and Stidham, *Federal Courts*, 74–78; and Smith, *United States Magistrates in the Federal Courts*, 15–28.

6. Hall and Rise, *From Local Courts to National Tribunals*, 181–82.

7. Paul Game Oral History, 13–19.

8. Joseph Hatchett Oral History, 36–37.

9. George T. Swartz Oral History, 16–17.

10. Ibid., 27, 46–47.

11. Lyles, *Gatekeepers*, 18–19.

12. Elizabeth Jenkins interview with the author, October 13, 2010.

13. Carter, quoted in Lyles, *Gatekeepers*, 117; and Goldman, *Picking Judges*, 240–84.

14. Lyles, *Gatekeepers*, 123; Statement by the President, October 20, 1978, Box 121, folder entitled Judges Seeking Appointments, Chesterfield Smith Papers, PKYL; and Goldman, *Picking Judges*, 242.

15. Howell Melton Oral History, 1–8, 12–14; and Hall and Rise, *From Local Courts to National Tribunals*, 166.

16. Howell Melton Oral History, 14–15.

17. Patricia Templeton, "More than 1,000 Civil Cases Wait," *St. Petersburg Evening Independent*, August 20, 1977.

18. David Smith, "344 Warrants in Jeopardy," *St. Petersburg Evening Independent*, June 29, 1976.

19. William Terrell Hodges Oral History, 28–29; and Lucy Morgan, "Fatolitis Jury Still Undecided," *St. Petersburg Times*, March 18, 1977.

20. William Nottingham, "7 Found Guilty, One Acquitted in Rackets Trial," *St. Petersburg Times*, November 13, 1976.

21. Ibid. See also William Nottingham, "Climax Near in Trial of 8 Accused in Probe of Murder, Rackets," *St. Petersburg Times*, November 9, 1976.

22. Hall and Rise, *From Local Courts to National Tribunals*, 157.

23. "Chiles, Stone Blasted for Choice," *Ocala Star-Banner*, September 22, 1977; and "Lakeland Lawyer Picked for Federal Judgeship," *Lakeland Ledger*, September 9, 1977.

24. "Chiles, Stone Blasted for Choice," *Ocala Star-Banner*, September 22, 1977.

25. Charles Stafford, "Controversial State Attorney Recommended as Federal Judge," *St. Petersburg Times*, March 10, 1979.

26. Robert Ryan, "Process May Reshape Judicial System," *Boca Raton News*, September 24, 1978.

27. Keith Moyer, "Carr Beaming at Federal Judgeship Rite," *Lakeland Ledger*, January 7, 1978. See also Keith Moyer, "County Attorney Carr Becomes Federal Judge," *Lakeland Ledger*, December 16, 1977.

28. Dan Warren Oral History, 9.

29. Robert Ryan, "Process May Reshape Judicial System," *Boca Raton News*, September 24, 1978.

30. Joseph Hatchett Oral History, 57–59.

31. Charles Stafford, "Controversial State Attorney Recommended," *St. Petersburg Times*, March 10, 1979.

32. Elligett, "Judge William Castagna"; *St. Petersburg Times*, September 15, 1979; and Hall and Rise, *From Local Courts to National Tribunals*, 157–58.

33. Susan Black interview with the author, May 23, 2011.

34. Susan Black Oral History, 10.

35. Ibid.; Joe Wilhelm, "U.S. Judge Celebrated for 30 Years of Service and Advancement of Woman in Law," *Jacksonville Financial News & Daily Record*, July 12, 2010; Hall and Rise, *From Local Courts to National Tribunals*, 155; and Susan Black interview with the author, May 23, 2011.

36. Charles Stafford, "Rejection of Salcines for Judgeship Angers Senators," *St. Petersburg Times*, June 27, 1980.

37. Rochelle Jones, "Jacksonville Judge Picked for U.S. Court Vacancy," *St. Petersburg Times*, July 3, 1980.

38. Charles Ryan, "Court to Decide on 'Inspirationals,'" *Orlando Sentinel*, September 9, 1973

39. "Judge: Finds 'No Evidence' of Misuse of Devotionals," *Orlando Sentinel*, January 9, 1975.

40. Ibid.; see also "Judge Young to Preside at Hearing," *Orlando Sentinel*, December 4, 1973; "Orange Schools' Religious Policy under Fire," *Orlando Sentinel*, December 4, 1974.

41. Patrick McMahon, "Enforcement Ban on Nude Dancing Okayed by Judge," *St. Petersburg Times*, April 4, 1978.

42. Patrick McMahon, "Fire Department Ordered to Hire More Blacks," *St. Petersburg Times*, September 8, 1979

43. Ibid.

44. Kay Masters, "Program Boosts Recruitment of Firemen," *St. Petersburg Evening Independent*, April 4, 1980

45. "Minority Quotas," *St. Petersburg Times*, July 26, 1980.

46. "Literacy Test Questions Defended," *Palm Beach Post*, May 30, 1979.

47. Deborah Blum, "U.S. Wants Indefinite Delay in Florida's Literacy Test," *St. Petersburg Times*, December 2, 1980; see also "Appeals Arguments Begin in Literacy Test Delay Case," *Lakeland Ledger*, December 16, 1980.

48. Ken Klein, "Hearing on Florida Literacy Test Monday," *St. Petersburg Evening Independent*, December 13, 1980.

49. "U.S. Appeals Court Upholds Florida Literacy Test," *Palm Beach Post*, May 19, 1983.

50. "Florida to Deny Diplomas to 1,300," *Bangor, Maine, Daily News*, May 18, 1983.

51. "State Literacy Test Upheld by Federal Appeals Court," *Miami Herald*, April 28, 1984; see also "Around the Nation: 1,300 Florida Seniors Are Denied Diplomas," *New York Times*, May 18, 1983.

52. Judy Doyle, "Abortion Clinic Given New Life," *Orlando Sentinel*, August 25, 1977.

53. Mark Pizzo interview with the author, October 13, 2010.

54. Brands, *America since 1945*, 167–72, 175–76, 188.

55. Don Stichter to William L. Norton Award Nominating Committee, 2007, Alexander Paskay Papers, box 1, fo. 10, MDFA.

56. Ibid.; and Leonard Gilbert Oral History, 3.

57. Alexander Paskay Oral History, 21–22.

58. Ibid.

59. Ibid.; "History of the Federal Judiciary, Landmark Legislation, Establishment of Bankruptcy Courts," FJC. On the Bankruptcy Act of 1978, see Carp and Stidham, *Federal Courts*, 29–30; Blum, "Bankruptcy," 54–55; Nimmer, "Bankruptcy: Personal," 55–56; and Nimmer, "Bankruptcy: Business," 57–59.

60. Richard Mullins, "Federal Bankruptcy Judge Alexander L. Paskay Dies," *Tampa Tribune*, April 28, 2012

61. Ibid.; and Alexander Paskay, "Life and Times in the Wild and Wooley World of Bankruptcy," 2005, 4–5, box 2, fo. 7, Paskay Papers, MDFA.

62. George Proctor Oral History, 1–11; Sandra Fish, "Bankruptcy Judge George Proctor Respected for No-nonsense Style," *Jacksonville Times-Union*, November 1, 1987; and Paul

Ivice, "Judge Revisits Site of World War II Battle," *Jacksonville Financial News and Daily Record*, July 4, 1995.

63. George Proctor Oral History, 10–11.

64. Ibid., 11.

65. Ibid., 11–12, 18.

66. Ibid., 13–14, 16.

Chapter 7. A New Era Begins

1. Lori Rozsa, "Officials to Realign Judicial Districts, *Miami Herald*, March 26, 1988; and 28 USC §89, http://www.gpo.gov/fdsys/pkg/USCODE-2008-title28/html/USCODE-2008-title28-partI-chap5-sec89.htm.

2. Goldman, *Picking Federal Judges*, 285–86. On Reagan and judicial appointments theory and practice, see Lyles, *Gatekeepers*, 129–46.

3. Goldman, *Picking Federal Judges*, 291.

4. Ibid., 292. See also Lyles, *Gatekeepers*, 138–39.

5. Smith, quoted in Goldman, *Picking Federal Judges*, 297.

6. David Stout, "Paula Hawkins, 82, Florida Ex-Senator Dies," *New York Times*, December 4, 2009.

7. Mohl and Mormino, "The Big Change in the Sunshine State," 339–41.

8. "Judge Ready to Go Fishing," *Lakeland Ledger*, May 28, 1982.

9. Judge William Castagna interview with the author, October 14, 2010.

10. Hall and Rise, *From Local Courts to National Tribunals*, 114; and Goldman, *Picking Federal Judges*, 210–11, 220–21.

11. Chesterfield Smith to Paula Hawkins, January 11, 1982, box 123, folder entitled "Elizabeth Kovachevich," Chesterfield Smith Papers, PKYL.

12. Ibid.

13. Milo Geyelin, "Judge Pushes for Swift Justice," *St. Petersburg Times*, August 30, 1987.

14. Elizabeth Jenkins interview with the author, October 13, 2010.

15. Geyelin, "Judge Pushes for Swift Justice."

16. William Terrell Hodges Oral History, 36.

17. "Tampa Judge Axes Shelters at Stop," *Orlando Sentinel*, May 7, 1985; and William Terrell Hodges Oral History, 70.

18. R. A. Zaldivar and Stephen Hedges, "Panel Criticizes FBI Tactics in Hastings Bribery," *Miami Herald*, May 26, 1988.

19. Hall and Rise, *From Local Courts to National Tribunals*, 140–41; and Bass, *Taming the Storm*, 429–47.

20. Bass, *Taming the Storm*, 438; and Peter Slevin and Eric Rieder, "Judges Want Hastings Impeached," *Miami Herald*, July 18, 1983.

21. Carp and Stidham, *Federal Courts*, 126–27.

22. Paul Anderson, "Hastings' Challenge of Misconduct Probe Rejected," *Miami Herald*, July 26, 1984.

23. Hall and Rise, *From Local Courts to National Tribunals*, 140–41; Bass, *Taming the Storm*, 438–47; Stephen J. Hedges, "Hastings Prepares to Clear his Name," *Miami Herald*, March 16, 1987; "A Hastings Chronology: 1979–1988," *Miami Herald*, July 8, 1988; Larry Lipman, "Hastings Stripped of Judgeship—Senate Votes 69–26 to Impeach on Eight

Counts," *Palm Beach Post*, October 21, 1989; and Tony Pugh, "The Honorable Alcee Hastings," *Miami Herald*, December 13, 1992.

24. "Vero Judge Chosen for U.S. Bench," *Miami Herald*, November 1, 1983.

25. Judge Kendall Sharp interview with the author, July 28, 2010.

26. "Senate Confirms Judge from Vero," *Miami Herald*, November 17, 1983.

27. G. Kendall Sharp Oral History; and Presentation of Portrait, Honorable G. Kendall Sharp, George C. Young Courthouse, February 18, 2000, MDFA.

28. Craig Crawford, "Long Wait for Judge Leaves Court Short," *Orlando Sentinel*, March 30, 1986.

29. Ibid.

30. Craig Crawford, "Fawsett Named to U.S. Judge's Post in Orlando," *Orlando Sentinel*, April 10, 1986.

31. *Orlando Magazine*, January 2006, 88; see also Jim Leusner and Robert A. Liff, "Orlando Lawyer out of Contention for 1 Judgeship," *Orlando Sentinel*, August 16, 1985; and Stuart, "Grit and Grace," 15–19.

32. Crawford, "Fawsett Named to U.S. Judge's Post in Orlando."

33. Craig Crawford, "Fawsett Eager to Begin Work as New Federal Judge," *Orlando Sentinel*, April 20, 1986.

34. Craig Crawford, "Orlando Lawyer to Ring in 1st Day as a Federal Judge," *Orlando Sentinel*, June 30, 1986; and "New Federal Judge Faces 1,000-Case Backlog," *Miami Herald*, July 2, 1986.

35. Dan Tracy, "Orlando Court Speeds Up, 160 Cases Judges Goal Is to Finish Processing Trials in 3 Weeks," *Orlando Sentinel*, July 8, 1986.

36. "Senior U.S. Judge Suffers Stroke," *Miami Herald*, May 12, 1983; and "U.S. Judge Charles Scott, 79," *Miami Herald*, May 13, 1983.

37. Stuart, "He Ain't No Heavy," 19.

38. Ibid.; John H. Moore II Oral History, 33; and Hall and Rise, *From Local Courts to National Tribunals*, 114, 167.

39. Stuart, "He Ain't No Heavy," 22.

40. John H. Moore Oral History, 39.

41. "Judge Orders Pigeons Evicted," *Miami Herald*, October 28, 1984.

42. "Beginnings for Probation and Pretrial Services," United States Court website, http://www.uscourts.gov/FederalCourts/ProbationPretrialServices/History.aspx.

43. Larry Dougherty, "Gary Betz, Longtime Prosecutor, Dies at 63," *St. Petersburg Times*, February 9, 2000.

44. "Deaths Elsewhere," *Lakeland Ledger*, February 10, 2000.

45. "U.S. Attorney Angered as Replacement Hinted," *Palm Beach Post*, January 8, 1982.

46. "White House Clears Merkle Nomination," *St. Petersburg Evening Independent*, March 12, 1982; and "New U.S. Attorney Sworn In," *Lakeland Ledger*, March 16, 1982.

47. Patti Bridges, "Top Assistants to State Attorney Are Moving to Other Positions," *St. Petersburg Evening Independent*, March 17, 1981.

48. Cassio Furtado, "'Mad Dog' Attorney Attacked Corruption," *Tampa Tribune*, May 7, 2003.

49. William Terrell Hodges Oral History, May 29, 2012.

50. Michael Richardson, "Overburdened Prosecutor Merkle Needs Help," *St. Petersburg Evening Independent*, October 15, 1983.

51. "Merkle Knows How to Win, But He Could Use a Little Tact," *Lakeland Ledger*, November 6, 1983.

52. "Area's Top Marshal Is Calling It Quits," *Orlando Sentinel*, September 8, 1990.

53. "Drug Runner's Mansion a Bust on Auction Block," *Boca Raton News*, March 9, 1987.

54. Harvey E. Schlesinger Oral History, 33–34; and Susan Harrell Black Oral History, 47.

55. Jim Robison, "Federal Prisoners Push Jail to Its Limit," *Orlando Sentinel*, November 10, 1985.

56. "Jail May Get $1 Million, Sheriff Will Ask County to Sign Federal Contract," *Orlando Sentinel*, February 9, 1986.

57. Milo Geyelin, "Federal Prisoners in County Jails/Lack of Detention Center Escalates Overcrowding," *St. Petersburg Times*, February 28, 1988.

58. Ibid.

59. Ibid.

60. Geyelin, "Federal Prisoners in County Jails."

Chapter 8. Drugs, Drugs, and More Drugs, 1980–1988

1. "Mobster Is Healthy Enough for Trial Starting June 16," *Miami Herald*, April 24, 1986; "Trafficante Case Ends in Mistrial," Miami Herald, July 10, 1986; and Jim Leusner and Tom Scherberger, "Florida's Reputed Don, Santo Trafficante, Dies," *Orlando Sentinel*, March 19, 1987.

2. Dan Warren Oral History, 18.

3. Beale, "Federalizing Crime, 49.

4. Nagle, "Federal Sentencing Guidelines, 884–85; Reitz, "The Federal Role in Sentencing Law and Policy," 116–17; Alexander, *Place of Recourse*, 336–37n44; and Geib and Kite, *Federal Justice in Indiana*, 197.

5. Harvey Schlesinger Oral History, 34; George Swartz Oral History, 39–40; and Howell Melton Oral History, 20.

6. "Crime Control Acts," *Free Dictionary* by Farlex, http://legal-Dictionary.thefreedictionary.com/Crime+Control+Acts; and *United States v. Morrison*, 529 U.S. 598, 120 S. Ct. 1740, 146 L. Ed. 2d 658 (2000).

7. Beale, "Federalizing Crime," 45.

8. Ibid., 50–51. See also "Middle Judicial District to Get More Assistant Prosecutors," *St. Petersburg Times*, December 2, 1988.

9. Hodges, Edwards, and Walsh, "Middle District of Florida," 19–21.

10. Sheriff Roy Lundy Oral History.

11. "Smuggler Gets 30 Years for Cocaine Run," *Lakeland Ledger*, September 12, 1981.

12. Elizabeth Kovachevich Oral History, 37.

13. Jim Leusner, "Judge Slaps Tough Terms on Coke Toters," *Orlando Sentinel*, October 22, 1985; Charles Fishman, "A Few Moments with Sheriff Bob Vogel, He's the Mayor of I-95, and a Terror to Drug Smugglers," *Orlando Sentinel*, August 11, 1991; Joseph Ditzler, "'We Won Every Battle' over I-95 Stops, Vogel Says," *Daytona Beach News-Journal*, June 6, 1997; and Bo Poertner, "Vogel Book Brings Back Sad Chapter," *Orlando Sentinel*, May 3, 2001.

14. "Cocaine Smuggler Sentenced to Life," *New York Times*, July 21, 1988.

15. Judge Elizabeth Jenkins interview with the author, February 3, 2012.

16. Ibid.; and Milo Geyelin, "'Drug King' Ordered Held—Agents Alerted for Reprisals After Extradition Action," *St. Petersburg Times*, February 6, 1987.

17. Harvey E. Schlesinger Oral History, 42.

18. Ibid. See also Sydney P. Freedberg, "Drug King Goes to Court Millionaire Gets Public Defender," *Miami Herald*, February 6, 1987.

19. Marcus, "Lehder Trial Testimony Sheds Light on Vast Cocaine Empire," *St. Petersburg Times*, February 21, 1988.

20. Ibid.; Gugliotta and Leen, *Kings of Cocaine*, 28–29; and Ruth and Milo Geyelin, "'Drug King' Ordered Held—Agents Alerted for Reprisals after Extradition Action," *St. Petersburg Times*, February 6, 1987.

21. Milo Geyelin, "Lehder Says He Was 'Hunted' Man," *St. Petersburg Times*, February 10, 1987.

22. Milo Geyelin, "Merkle: "Lehder Arrest 'Symbolic,'" *St. Petersburg Times*, February 12, 1987.

23. "Security Hampers Lehder in Hiring Lawyer, Court Told," *Fort Lauderdale Sun-Sentinel*, February 14, 1987; "Accused Drug Kingpin Moved," *Miami Herald*, March 11, 1987; "Judge Orders May Opening of Lehder Trial," *Miami Herald*, March 26, 1987; and "Trial Won't Be Moved for Lehder Judge: Fair Jury Can Be Found," *Miami Herald*, September 11, 1987.

24. Karla Spaulding Oral History, 12–13.

25. John H. Moore Oral History, 51. See also Milo Geyelin, "Lehder Trial Begins," *St. Petersburg Times*, October 5, 1987.

26. "After 5½ Weeks, Jury Is Seated in Smuggling Trial," *St. Petersburg Times*, November 11, 1987.

27. Milo Geyelin, "Defense Says Victim in Drug Trial Is Lehder," *St. Petersburg Times*, November 18, 1987.

28. Ibid.

29. Howell Melton Oral History, 18.

30. "Defense Rests; No Witnesses in Lehder Trial," *Fort Lauderdale Sun-Sentinel*, May 3, 1988. See also Jeff Leen, "Cronkite Describes Chase from Island at Lehder's Trial," *Miami Herald*, January 29, 1988; "Prosecution Rests Case in Lehder Drug Trial," *St. Petersburg Times*, April 29, 1988.

31. Jeff Leen, "Lehder's Legacy Called 'Human Wreckage,'" *Miami Herald*, May 11, 1988.

32. Jeff Leen, "Cocaine Czar Lehder Guilty Colombian Trafficker Could Face Life Term for Drugs," *Miami Herald*, May 20, 1988.

33. Jeff Leen, "Prosecutor Calls Conviction 'Shot in the Arm to Everybody,'" *Miami Herald*, May 20, 1988; and Jeff Leen, "U.S. Faces Dilemma in Pindling Case," *Miami Herald*, May 30, 1988.

34. "Cocaine Smuggler Sentenced to Life," *New York Times*, July 21, 1988.

35. "'Son of Lehder' Indictment Adds Fugitive Vesco to List," *Orlando Sentinel*, April 18, 1989; "Drug Lord's Former Wife Pleads Guilty," *Fort Lauderdale Sun-Sentinel*, September 2, 1989; "Jury Selection Proceeding Slowly in 'Son of Lehder' Smuggling Trial, *Miami Herald*, September 13, 1989; and "'Son of Lehder' Drug Trial Ends with 2 Acquittals, 3 Convictions," *Fort Lauderdale Sun-Sentinel*, October 27, 1989.

36. Jim Leusner, "Castoro Convicted on All Counts," *Orlando Sentinel*, July 6, 1988; see also Jim Leusner, "Drug Tale: Smuggling and Bribes Surprise Witness Tells His Story to Lehder Jury," *Orlando Sentinel*, February 12, 1988.

37. Jim Leusner, "Life without Parole for Pot Kingpin," *Orlando Sentinel*, August 30, 1988.

38. Jim Leusner, "Partner of Castoro Gets 15 Years," *Orlando Sentinel*, September 1, 1988.

39. Kirsten Gallagher, "Judge Kills Jury's Money-Laundering Conviction," *Orlando Sentinel*, November 4, 1988. See also Jim Leusner, "Case Dismissed against Man Linked to Castoro," *Orlando Sentinel*, October 21, 1988; Kirsten Gallagher, "New Yorker Guilty of Helping Castoro Launder Drug Profits," *Orlando Sentinel*, October 28, 1988.

40. Jim Leusner, "Helpful Convict's Reward: Freedom," *Orlando Sentinel*, May 27, 1998. See also Mike Oliver, "Drug Smuggler Castoro Decides to Help, Not Fight the U.S.," *Orlando Sentinel*, February 1, 1990; "Follow-Up: Robert Castoro," *Orlando Sentinel*, June 28, 1992; Jim Leusner, "Helpful Drug Smuggler Gets Shorter Sentence—Robert Castoro's Term Was Cut to 20 Years from Life Plus 65 Years," *Orlando Sentinel*, January 21, 1994.

41. Jennifer Stevenson, "Tsalickis Gets 27 Years for Smuggling Cocaine," *St. Petersburg Times*, February 17, 1989. See also "Judge Won't Ban Opening Arguments in Trial after All," *Miami Herald*, October 6, 1988; "Importer May Draw Life Sentence on Cocaine-Smuggling Conviction," *Miami Herald*, November 4, 1988; Milo Geyelin, "2 Colombians Convicted of Drug Smuggling," *St. Petersburg Times*, December 3, 1988.

42. "Ex-Partner May Tell on Noriega," *Miami Herald*, January 19, 1990; Bruce Vielmetti, "Panamanian Pleads Guilty in Drug-Smuggling Case, *St. Petersburg Times*, June 9, 1990; and Tom Brennan, "Noriega Drug Partner Receives 10-Year Term in Prison," *Tampa Tribune*, August 17, 1990.

43. Tom Brennan, "Next Stop Is Trial in Tampa," *Tampa Tribune*, April 10, 1992; see also Tim Collie, "Noriega Gets 40 Years, *Tampa Tribune*, July 11, 1992.

44. Douglas Frazier Oral History, 4, 5.

45. "Businessman Convicted on Drugs, Tax Evasion Charges," *Sarasota Herald-Tribune*, January 20, 1989; see also 921 F.2d 1569, *United States of America, Plaintiff-Appellee, v. Sandra Hernandez, a/k/a "Cha Cha," Ronnie Lee Tape, Karen McCalvin, Rodney Gilmore, Rickey Rogers, Defendants-Appellants*, No. 89–3395, United States Court of Appeals, Eleventh Circuit, January 30, 1991; and George T. Swartz Oral History, 41.

46. Milo Geyelin, "Alleged Leader of Drug Ring Arrested—Man Accused of Heading Group that Distributes Crack in Tampa," *St. Petersburg Times*, February 2, 1989; see also "Fugitive Nabbed, Returned to State," *Miami Herald*, February 8, 1989.

47. Elizabeth Kovachevich interview with author, July 5, 2012; Elizabeth Kovachevich Oral History, 23; David Waller Oral History, 2–3; and Douglas Frazier Oral History, 7.

48. Douglas Frazier Oral History, 25–26.

49. Jeffrey Good and Bruce Vielmetti, "Smuggling 'Has Destroyed our Hometown': Once a Fishing Haven, Everglades City Saw Profit in Drugs—and Now Pays a Price," *St. Petersburg Times*, May 14, 1989.

50. Elizabeth Kovachevich interview with author, July 5, 2012; Elizabeth Kovachevich Oral History, 23–25; David Waller Oral History, 2–11; Barry Millman and Dave Nicholson, "Drug Case Witness Is Killed," *Tampa Tribune*, April 5, 1989; Jose Bermudez, "Drug

Witness Dies in Bomb Blast," *Sebring News-Sun*, April 5, 1989; Jose Bermudez, "Neighbors Knew Little of Collins, Brumett Families," *Sebring News-Sun*, April 9, 1989; "Truck Bomb Explosion Kills U.S. Drug Witness," *Miami Herald*, April 6, 1989; and "Attorney Well-Known for Drug-Case Work Hurt in Miami Blast," *Fort Myers News Press*, December 16, 1989.

51. Tom Lassiter and Jeffrey Rubin, "Federal Agents: Drug Suspect Threatened DEA Office Bombing," *Fort Lauderdale Sun-Sentinel*, March 19, 1990; George T. Swartz Oral History, 42.

52. Elizabeth Kovachevich interview with author, July 5, 2012.

53. Bruce Vielmetti, "Pot Trial May Be too Big for Court," *St. Petersburg Times*, May 2, 1991.

54. "Donald Clark Faces Life in Prison without Parole if Convicted of Conspiracy to Cultivate Marijuana," *Sarasota Herald-Tribune*, December 14, 1991.

55. Elizabeth Kovachevich Oral History, 45–46.

56. "McLain Draws Conspiracy, Drug Charges," *Miami Herald*, March 20, 1984.

57. L. Robertson, "Ex-Pitcher Hopes to Avoid a Strikeout," *Miami Herald*, March 10, 1985.

58. Ibid.; "Mistrial Declared by McLain Judge," *Miami Herald*, November 9, 1984; and "McLain Defense Rests," *Miami Herald*, March 7, 1985.

59. "Repentant McLain Gets 23-Year Term, Ex Pitcher Says He Has Learned His Lesson," *Orlando Sentinel*, April 26, 1985. See also Billy Bowles, "Ex-Pitcher Found Guilty on 4 Charges," *Miami Herald*, March 17, 1985.

60. Milo Geyelin, "Ex-Pitcher McLain Wins New Trial on Drug Charges," *St. Petersburg Times*, August 8, 1987.

61. "Attorney Seeks New Judge in Denny McLain Retrial," *Fort Lauderdale Sun-Sentinel*, July 28, 1988; "McLain Makes His Pitch at Judge," *St. Petersburg Times*, September 28, 1988; "McLain, Prosecutors Hit Deal That Includes a Guilty Plea," *Orlando Sentinel*, October 19, 1988; Milo Geyelin, "McLain Gets Probation in Racketeering Case," *St. Petersburg Times*, December 16, 1988; and McLain and Nahrstedt, *Strikeout,* 84–85, 107–32, 130–32, 159–90, 277–80. Judge Kovachevich addresses the case in her oral history. See Elizabeth Kovachevich Oral History, 18–22.

62. Milo Geyelin, "Judge Pushes for Swift Justice," *St. Petersburg Times*, August 30, 1987.

63. The BCCI case and its connection to international criminal banking conspiracies has been the subject of a number of larger studies. See Beaty and Gwyne, *Outlaw Bank*; Adams and Franz, *A Full Service Bank*; and Block, *Organized Criminal Activities*.

64. William Terrell Hodges Oral History, 52–53.

65. Ibid., 54.

66. Ibid. On the wedding ruse and the arrests, see Adams and Franz, *Full Service Bank*, 233–37.

67. Ibid., 56.

68. "Drug Lords' Bankers Convicted, One Had Ties to Noriega; U.S. Claims Big Victory," *Orlando Sentinel*, July 30, 1990.

69. "Noriega Aide Gets Softened Penalty," *New York Times*, December 2, 1990; "Eight Nations Hit BCCI for Fraud, *Tampa Tribune*, July 6, 1991; Tom Brennan, "Court Upholds

4 of 5 BCCI Convictions," *Tampa Tribune*, July 30, 1992; and *United States v. Awan et al.* Case No. 88-330-CR-T-13B, 966 F. 2d 1415 (11th Cir. 1992).

70. Dan Warren Oral History, 9, 10.

Chapter 9. Mad Dogs, Spies, and International Weapons Dealers

1. "Jurors to Probe Public Officials in Central, FLA," *Miami Herald*, February 9, 1983.

2. Orrick and Crumpacker, *Tampa Tribune*, 423–24; "Ex-Official Works Out a Deal, Pleads Guilty," *Miami Herald*, May 4, 1983; Anders Gyllenhaal, "Trial to Show Just the Tip Tampa Bribery Probes," *Miami Herald*, June 12, 1983; "Witness Outlines 'Deal' for Votes in Tampa Trial," *Miami Herald*, June 15, 1983; "Jury Hears FBI Tapes in Corruption Case," *Miami Herald*, June 17, 1983; and "2 Ex-Officials Get 8 Years for Selling Their Votes," *Miami Herald*, September 16, 1983.

3. Mary Jo Melone, "Jury Indicts Tampa Father, Son in Bid to Bribe U.S. Prosecutor," *St. Petersburg Times*, November 8, 1983.

4. "Salcines Puts His Case to People in Ad," *Sarasota Herald-Tribune*, February 20, 1984.

5. Ibid.

6. Ibid.

7. Anders Gyllenhaal, "Corruption Runneth over Tough Prosecutors, Drug Trade and Informants Mean Record Number of Cases," *Miami Herald*, April 29, 1984. See also "Graham Seeks Advice on Salcines Options," *Miami Herald*, March 6, 1984.

8. Bentley Orrick, Andy Taylor, and Kevin Kalwary, "Federal Probe Digs Deeper into County Courthouse," *Tampa Tribune*, February 5, 1984.

9. "Graham Names Prosecutor to Investigate State Attorney," *Miami Herald*, April 13, 1984; "Prosecutor Rejects 2nd Grand Jury Invitation," *Miami Herald*, March 10, 1984; and Dyckman, *Most Disorderly Court*, 52.

10. "Prosecutor Cleared in State Case," *Miami Herald*, June 27, 1984; and "Special Investigator Clears Salcines of Lying Charges," *Sarasota Herald-Tribune*, June 27, 1984.

11. "Salcines Charges Interference," *St. Petersburg Evening Independent*, July 16, 1984.

12. "Ex-Hillsborough Prosecutor Wins as Judge Orders Charges Dropped," *St. Petersburg Evening Independent*, October 2, 1984.

13. "Prosecutor Seeking Probe of Own Office," *Palm Beach Post*, October 19, 1984.

14. See also "Prosecutors Attacked by Salcines," *Miami Herald*, October 12, 1984.

15. Anders Gyllenhaal, "Tampa Race a Thicket of Accusations, Prosecutor Center of Bitter Dispute," *Miami Herald*, October 23, 1984.

16. "Prosecutors Attacked by Salcines," *Miami Herald*, October 12, 1984.

17. "Speed up Investigations, Justice Department Urged," *Miami Herald*, October 19, 1984.

18. Bob Graham interview with the author, March 30, 2010.

19. "Grand Jury Indicts 25 Civic Leaders," *Orlando Sentinel*, May 24, 1985. See also "Agency: U.S. Attorney Didn't Abuse Power," *Miami Herald*, November 2, 1984; "Prosecutor Salcines Ousted after 16 Years," *Palm Beach Post*, November 8, 1984; "Newcomer Defeats Salcines," *Miami Herald*, November 8, 1984; "Federal Grand Jury Indicts Hillsborough Civic Leaders," *Orlando Sentinel*, May 23, 1985.

20. Roger Roy, "Eagan Argues Case for End to Corruption Investigation," *Orlando Sentinel*, January 12, 1986.

21. "Lawmaker Upset by Drug Allegations, He Says Prosecutor 'Trying to Destroy Me,'" *Orlando Sentinel*, February 21, 1985.

22. "Grand Jury Calls It Quits after 3 Years," *Orlando Sentinel*, March 1, 1986.

23. Jim Leusner, "Anti-Drug Leader Wants a Little Help from His Foes," *Orlando Sentinel*, September 18, 1985; "Graham Speaks to Grand Jury Probe Focuses on Hillsborough Corruption," *Miami Herald*, December 21, 1985; Pat Leisner, "Graham Questioned on Meeting with Salcines, *Lakeland Ledger*, December 21, 1985; and "Lawmaker, Former Client Indicted by Federal Jury," *Miami Herald*, February 28, 1986.

24. "U.S. Prosecutor Criticizes Abortion Ruling as Tyranny," *Orlando Sentinel*, November 18, 1985.

25. Paul Anderson, "'Mad Dog' Prosecutor 'Cleaning House' in Tampa," *Miami Herald*, March 3, 1986.

26. "State Attorney Says Prosecutor Should Resign," *Miami Herald*, March 27, 1986.

27. Ibid.; see also Roger Roy, "Merkle—Reviled by Establishment, Revered by Public," *Orlando Sentinel*, April 20, 1986; and "U.S. Attorney Merkle Must Go," *Tampa Tribune*, March 23, 1986.

28. Roy, "Merkle—Reviled by Establishment."

29. William Terrell Hodges Oral History, May 29, 2012.

30. "Ex-Commissioner Gets 3 Years for Bribes," *Miami Herald*, November 18, 1986. See also "Three Guilty of Racketeering Jury Convicts 2 Former Hillsborough Commissioners," *Orlando Sentinel*, July 20, 1986.

31. "Lawmaker's Federal Trial Set December 1," *Miami Herald*, November 19, 1986; and "Martinez Cleared of Perjury Acquits Lawmaker of Lying About Drugs," *Orlando Sentinel*, December 9, 1986.

32. "As Senator, Graham Will Scrutinize Work of Merkle," *Orlando Sentinel*, December 23, 1986; see also "Martinez to Heed Ruling, Testify," *Miami Herald*, December 17, 1986; "Graham: I'm Not Out to Get Merkle," *St. Petersburg Times*, January 3, 1987; and Paul Anderson, "Graham's Tallahassee Farewell Marked by Questions on U.S. Attorney's Letter," *Miami Herald*, January 3, 1987.

33. Milo Geyelin, "Martinez Spars with Merkle During Cross-Examination," *St. Petersburg Times*, January 10, 1987.

34. "Fire the U.S. Attorney," *St. Petersburg Times*, January 13, 1987; see also "Mighty Merkle at the Bat," *St. Petersburg Times*, January 16, 1987; see also Milo Geyelin, "Gov. Martinez Denies Bribe in Cable Deal—Aide Takes Jab at Prosecutor," *St. Petersburg Times*, January 9, 1987; Tom Scherberger and Maya Bell, "Martinez Warns Merkle: Abuse Will Cost You Job," *Orlando Sentinel*, January 10, 1987; and Paul Anderson, "Martinez to Reagan: Oust Prosecutor, Graft Charge Infuriates Governor," *Miami Herald*, January 14, 1987.

35. Tom Scherberger, "Merkle Hits Press, Martinez Attack Comes as Jury Finds Italiano Guilty," *Orlando Sentinel*, January 15, 1987.

36. Tom Scherberger, "Merkle: I'm Not Going to Give Up," *Orlando Sentinel*, January 16, 1987.

37. See also Milo Geyelin, "Merkle Criticizes Media Coverage," *St. Petersburg Times*, January 16, 1987; Kimberly D. Kleman, "Merkle Backers Launch Drive to Stave off His Detractors," *St. Petersburg Times*, January 18, 1987; Joshua L. Weinstein, "'60 Minutes' Cameras Catch Merkle at Work," *St. Petersburg Times*, March 24, 1987; and Mary Jo Melone,

"CBS Spotlights 'Mad Dog Merkle': U.S. Attorney on '60 Minutes,'" *St. Petersburg Times*, January 11, 1988.

38. Milo Geyelin, "Italiano again Questioned on Corruption," *St. Petersburg Times*, April 16, 1987.

39. Milo Geyelin, "Defendant Says Merkle Has Grudge against Him," *St. Petersburg Times*, June 19, 1987.

40. Chris Reidy, "Merkle Meets Meese, Fueling Senate Talk," *Orlando Sentinel*, June 26, 1988.

41. "Merkle's Top Aide Left off List of Nominees for Post," *Miami Herald*, July 23, 1988.

42. "Merkle: Meese Lied about My Successor," *Miami Herald*, August 6, 1988.

43. Ibid.

44. Ibid.

45. See also "A Cardboard Candidate," *Orlando Sentinel*, August 7, 1988; Milo Geyelin, "Orlando Lawyer Picked to Replace Merkle," *St. Petersburg Times*, August 5, 1988; and Kenneth S. Allen, "Merkle Assails Politicians over His Replacement," *St. Petersburg Times*, August 6, 1988.

46. "Genzman Says He'll Be Tough U.S. Attorney," *St. Petersburg Times*, September 27, 1988.

47. Milo Geyelin, "Prosecution in a Lower Key: Interim U.S. Attorney No 'Mad Dog,'" *St. Petersburg Times*, January 2, 1989. See also Milo Geyelin, "Orlando Lawyer Picked to Replace Merkle," *St. Petersburg Times*, August 5, 1988.

48. Milo Geyelin, "U.S. Attorney Demotes Top Aide," *St. Petersburg Times*, December 13, 1988; "Genzman Supported for U.S. Attorney," *Miami Herald*, January 25, 1989; Alessandra Da Pra, "From Bronx Boy to World Class Litigator," *St. Petersburg Times*, July 25, 2008; and James Klindt interview with the author, May 23, 2011.

49. James Klindt interview with the author, May 23, 2011.

50. "Genzman Wins Senate Approval for 4-Year Term," *Orlando Sentinel*, November 2, 1989.

51. Milo Geyelin, "Prosecutor, Judge Swap Barbs at Lawyer's Trial," *St. Petersburg Times*, January 18, 1989.

52. Bruce Vielmetti, "Two Lawyers Acquitted," *St. Petersburg Times*, December 6, 1989. See also Geyelin, "Prosecutor, Judge Swap Barbs"; "Milo Geyelin, "Officials Testify in Lawyer's Perjury Trial," *St. Petersburg Times*, January 25, 1989; and Milo Geyelin, "Tampa Lawyer Found Innocent, Jury Clears Johnson of Extortion, Perjury," *St. Petersburg Times*, January 28, 1989.

53. William R. Levesque, "Bulldog Attorney Dies," *St. Petersburg Times*, May 7, 2003.

54. Tom Brennan, "U.S. Attorney Calls Critical Report 'Unfair,'" *Tampa Tribune*, November 22, 1990.

55. Tom Brennan, "U.S. Attorney Boasts Collections Are Triple Costs of Running Office," *Tampa Tribune*, November 24, 1990.

56. Ibid.; Tom Brennan, "Agency Returns $29 Million," *Tampa Tribune*, December 24, 1991; and "Crime Pays U.S. Prosecutors Bills Federal Attorney's Office Seizes $42.5 Million, Posts 'Profit,'" *Orlando Sentinel*, December 31, 1991.

57. "Trial Begins for Pershing Missile Plant Protesters," *Miami Herald*, July 10, 1984.

58. Ibid.

59. Ibid.; "Plowshares Cite 'God's Law,'" *Miami Herald*, July 11, 1984; and Anders Gyllenhaal, "Protesters, Weapons on Trial," *Miami Herald*, July 12, 1984.

60. Anders Gyllenhaal, "Protesters Guilty of Break-in at Missile Plant," *Miami Herald*, July 15, 1984.

61. "8 Protesters Dealt 3 Years in Prison," *Miami Herald*, July 27, 1984.

62. Judge Susan Black Oral History, 46. See also Jim Leusner, "Spying Suspect Held in Florida," *Orlando Sentinel*, July 16, 1981; "Helmich 'Guilty' in Plot," *Orlando Sentinel*, September 29, 1981; and *Boca Raton News*, September 29, 1981.

63. Judge Susan Black Oral History, 46; Jim Leusner, "Spying Suspect Held in Florida," *Orlando Sentinel*, July 16, 1981; "Helmich 'Guilty' in Plot," *Orlando Sentinel*, September 29, 1981; and *Boca Raton News*, September 29, 1981.

64. "German Pleads Innocent in Spy Case," *Miami Herald*, March 30, 1984; Jury Seated in Trial of Mechanic Charged with Selling U.S. Secrets," *Miami Herald*, June 26, 1984; "German Said to Tout Spying for Profit," *Miami Herald*, June 27, 1984; "W. German Guilty of Spying, Jury Says," *Miami Herald*, June 30, 1984; and "E. German Spy Sentenced to 15 Years Imprisonment," *Miami Herald*, August 4, 1984.

65. "Ex-Sergeant Gets 36 Years for Selling Secrets," *Fort Lauderdale Sun-Sentinel*, August 29, 1992; see also Bruce Vielmetti, "Ex-Sergeant Pleads Guilty to Espionage," *St. Petersburg Times*, September 18, 1991; and Tom Brennan, "Army Recruiter Accused of Espionage," *Tampa Tribune*, October 23, 1992.

66. Vielmetti, "2 Plead Guilty to Selling Secrets"; David Sommer, "Soldiers Get 18 Years for Passing Military Secrets to Communists," *Tampa Tribune*, June 25, 1994; Gragido and Pirc, *Cybercrime and Espionage*, 104–5; and "25 Years Ordered in Spy Conspiracy Ex-soldier Plotted with Warsaw Pact," *Florida Times-Union*, February 14, 1999.

67. Tamara Lytle, "Brevard Retiree Is Accused of Espionage, *Orlando Sentinel*, June 15, 2000.

68. Jim Leusner, "Spy Secrets Unravel for Military Retiree," *Orlando Sentinel*, June 21, 2000.

69. Dong-Phuong Nguyen, "Trofimoff: I Grew up Hating Communists," *St. Petersburg Times*, June 22, 2001.

70. Dong-Phuong Nguyen, "Trofimoff Repudiates Taped Spy Statements," *St. Petersburg Times*, June 23, 2001.

71. Paula Christian, "Spy Sentenced to Life in Prison," *Tampa Tribune*, September 28, 2001.

72. Paula Christian, "British Secret Agent Testifies," *Tampa Tribune*, June 19, 2001; Gwyneth K. Shaw, "Retiree Found Guilty of Spying for KGB," *Orlando Sentinel*, June 27, 2001; and Gwyneth K. Shaw, "Justices Will Leave Spy in Prison," *Orlando Sentinel*, May 25, 2004. On the case, see Susan Bucklew Oral History, 34–38; and Byers, *Imperfect Spy*.

73. Jim Leusner, "Suspect: Agents Threatened Death, 7th Person Sought in Arms Plot Surrenders at Orlando Airport," *Orlando Sentinel*, August 6, 1985.

74. Jim Leusner, "7 Charged with Trying to Sell Arms to Iran," *Orlando Sentinel*, August 21, 1985.

75. Jim Leusner, "Attorney: Plot Ran on Greed," *Orlando Sentinel*, December 10, 1985.

76. Jim Leusner, "Jurors in *Iranscam* Let 4 Go but Convict 2 Arms Dealers," *Orlando Sentinel*, December 17, 1985.

77. Leusner, "Jurors in *Iranscam* Let 4 Go but Convict 2 Arms Dealers."

78. Jim Leusner, "Defense Attorneys, Jurors Say Iranscam Was Handled Poorly," *Orlando Sentinel*, December 18, 1985; see also Jim Leusner, "*Iranscam* Figure Gets 5-year Term Convicted Weapons Dealer Calls FBI Sting Operation a 'Cockeyed Affair,'" *Orlando Sentinel*, January 22, 1986.

79. Craig Crawford, "Judge Frees Dealers in Arms-to-Iran Case," *Orlando Sentinel*, February 20, 1987.

80. Ibid.; and Kirsten Gallagher, "Missile Dealers Lose Retrial Iran Arms Sellers to Return to Prison, *Orlando Sentinel*, April 28, 1988.

81. *United States of America, Petitioner-Appellant, v. Paul Sjeklocha, a.k.a. Paul Cutter, Respondent-Appellee*, No. 96-2642, 11th Circuit, Appeal from MD of FL, (No. 85-65-Cr-ORL-18), May 30, 1997.

82. Bob Levenson, "Arms Trial of 2 to Include Talk about Deal with Iraq," *Orlando Sentinel*, December 3, 1990; and "Weapons Case Ends in Directed Acquittal for 2," *Miami Herald*, December 22, 1990.

83. Levenson, "Arms Trial."

84. Bob Levenson, "Judge Rejects 3 Arms Deal Counts Europeans Still Face 1 Charge Each," *Orlando Sentinel*, December 21, 1990.

85. Ibid.

86. "Weapons Case Ends in Directed Acquittal for 2."

87. Bob Levenson, "Judge Dismisses Case over Weapons Dealing," *Orlando Sentinel*, December 22, 1990.

88. "Weapons Case Ends in Directed Acquittal for 2."

89. Jim Leusner, "Judge Throws out Missile Charges," *Orlando Sentinel*, February 3, 1993.

Chapter 10. Income Tax Evasion, the Death Penalty, the Environment, the AIDS Epidemic, Desegregation, and Voting and Employment Discrimination, 1980–1988

1. Pamela Mercer, "Champ Williams Dies at Age 88," *Orlando Sentinel*, August 13, 2000; and Jim Leusner, "Family Trial Called Greed vs. Hatred," *Orlando Sentinel*, May 29, 1987.

2. Leusner, "Family Trial." See also Roger Roy, "Judge Steps Down from Champ Case, *Orlando Sentinel*, August 8, 1986; Jim Leusner, "Bruce Says He Helped Bury Cash," *Orlando Sentinel*, June 2, 187.

3. Jim Leusner, "Champ, Son Get 2½ Years, Daughter Gets Year and a Day—All 3 Are Fined $10,000," *Orlando Sentinel*, November 14, 1987.

4. Jim Leusner, "Champ Guilty of Tax Evasion, Jury also Convicts Restaurateur's Son, Daughter," *Orlando Sentinel*, July 25, 1987.

5. "IRS Wins Victory in Tax Battle with Turner, *Miami Herald*, January 17, 1983; and Jim Leusner, "Judge Orders Glenn Turner to Buy Ads," *Orlando Sentinel*, February 25, 1983.

6. Jim Leusner, "Turner Castle Falls after Long IRS Siege," *Orlando Sentinel*, April 6, 1988; Elizabeth Wasserman, "Orlando Company Paying $2.1 Million for Turner Castle," *Orlando Sentinel*, July 8, 1988; and "Castle Brings $1.8 Million," *Miami Herald*, December 2, 1988.

7. *Proffitt v. Wainwright*, 756 F. 2d 1500 (11th Cir. 1985); see also 685 F.2d 1227 (11th Cir. 1982). These decisions, along with *Proffitt v. Florida*, 438 U.S. 242 (1976), determined the

validity of Florida's death penalty system, the same system that is still used today. See "685 F.2d 1227: Charles William Proffitt, Petitioner-appellant, v. Louie L. Wainwright, Secretary, Florida Department of Offender Rehabilitation, Respondent-appellee, United States Court of Appeals, Eleventh Circuit.—685 F.2d 1227, Sept. 10, 1982.Concurring in Part and Dissenting in Part Opinion Sept. 17, 1982," *Justica U.S. Law*, http://law.justia.com/cases/federal/appellate-courts/F2/685/1227/301573/.

8. Howell Melton Oral History, 16.

9. Radelet, Bedau, and Putnam, *In Spite of Innocence*, 318; and "Killer Brothers Win Death Stay," *Daytona Beach Morning Journal*, July 19, 1983.

10. "Federal Judge Grants Stays of Execution for 2 Half-Brothers," *Miami Herald*, July 19, 1983.

11. Ibid.; and "Witness Recants at Hearing for 2 Death Row Inmates," *Miami Herald*, July 20, 1984.

12. William Fox, "Lawyers for Jent, Miller Win a Round," *St. Petersburg Times*, February 13, 1987.

13. Ibid.; Dave Von Drehle, "Judge Indicates He May Order New Trials for Half Brothers on Death Row 8 Years," *Miami Herald*, November 3, 1987; Milo Geyelin, "Judge Hints at New Trials," *St. Petersburg Times*, November 3, 1987; and "Judge Orders New Trials for 2 Death Row Inmates," *Fort Lauderdale Sun-Sentinel*, November 4, 1987.

14. Milo Geyelin, "Judge Lambasts Prosecutors in Miller-Jent Case," *St. Petersburg Times*, November 14, 1987.

15. Richard Danielson, "Judge Sets New Trial Dates in Pasco Murder Case, *St. Petersburg Times*, December 9, 1987.

16. Milo Geyelin and Richard Danielson, "Miller, Jent Freed after Pleading Guilty, but in News Conference, Half Brothers Proclaim Their Innocence," *St. Petersburg Times*, January 16, 1988.

17. Sydney Freedman, "We'd Rather Have Died than Stay in That Place for Something We Didn't Do," *St. Petersburg Times*, July 4, 1999.

18. J. Craig Crawford, "Sharp Often Does the Unexpected, Judge in Bundy Case Makes no Apology for His Courtroom Style," *Orlando Sentinel*, December 18, 1987; see also Larry King, "Bundy Was Competant—Judge's Ruling Moves Convicted Killer Closer to Death," *St. Petersburg Times*, December 18, 1987; and J. Craig Crawford, "Livid Judge Broadsides Bundy Case," *Orlando Sentinel*, December 18, 1987.

19. Crawford, "Livid Judge."

20. Donna O'Neal and Roger Roy, "Buenoano Faces Execution Today, Lawyers for 'Black Widow' Will Try for a Reprieve," *Orlando Sentinel*, June 21, 1990; "Execution Delayed on Issue of Chair," *Miami Herald*, June 22, 1990; Bob Levenson, "U.S. Judge's Order Spares Buenoano," *Orlando Sentinel*, June 22, 1990; "Woman Called 'Black Widow' Wins New Sentencing Trial," *Tampa Tribune*, June 12, 1992; and Jim Leusner, "'Black Widow' Killer Seeks to Overturn Death Sentence," *Orlando Sentinel*, January 5, 1994.

21. Denham, *"Rogue's Paradise,"* 210.

22. "Endangered Species Act of 1973," Digest of Federal Resource Laws of Interest to the U.S. Fish and Wildlife Service, http://www.fws.gov/laws/lawsdigest/esact.html.

23. "Judge Orders Dumping on Reefs Halted," *Miami Herald*, December 28, 1982; see also "Silt Dumping Set to Resume Near Tampa Bay," *Miami Herald*, February 21, 1984.

24. "Fisherman Gets 6 Months for Turtle Catch," *Miami Herald*, October 3, 1986.

25. "Gator Scheme Traps Hunters—2 Are Fined $10,000 Each," *Orlando Sentinel*, October 18, 1988.

26. Tim Smart, "Lawyers Wrangle over Damages in Skyway Collapse," *Miami Herald*, July 4, 1982.

27. Patti Bridges, "A Year Later—Everyone Is Suing Someone," *St. Petersburg Independent*, May 7, 1981.

28. "Judge: Pilot Whose Ship Hit Bridge Was in the Wrong," *Gainesville Sun*, April 29, 1982; see also "Board Clears Lerro of Wrongdoing," *St. Petersburg Times*, December 24, 1980; Smart, "Lawyers Wrangle"; and Jane Meinhardt, "Skyway Bridge Collapse Five Years Ago Left Legacies of Change," *St. Petersburg Evening Independent*, May 4, 1985.

29. "Judge Rules Astronauts Widow Cannot Sue U.S.," *Fort Lauderdale Sun-Sentinel*, February 27, 1988.

30. Lender, *"This Honorable Court,"* 240.

31. "Summaries of Significant Court Decisions with Opinions Written by Judge Susan Harrell Black," MDFA; and Hoffman and Robel, "Federal Court Supervision of State Criminal Justice Administration," 154, 156–58. See also Shitama, "A Pioneer in Prison Reform"; and Sheppard, "Early Jail and Prison Conditions," 4–8.

32. Sheppard, "Early Jail and Prison Conditions," 5–6. Sheppard's client was Franklin Miller, who had filed a petition in the federal court against the county because of the circumstances of his confinement.

33. Susan Harrell Black Oral History, 49–50.

34. Ibid.

35. *Celestino v. Singletary*, 147 F.R.D. 258 (M.D. FL 1993).

36. "Jacksonville Gets 12 Days to Find Way to Cut Jail Population, *Miami Herald*, September 9, 1988.

37. "Federal Court Ends Oversight of Jail," *St. Petersburg Times*, May 20, 1994. See also "Judge Orders Jacksonville to Hire Monitor to Study Jails," *Fort Lauderdale Sun-Sentinel*, April 2, 1989.

38. Orfield, *Public School Desegregation*, 5, 6, 8.

39. Ellen Moses, "Loophole Fosters White Flight from Schools," *Bradenton Herald*, January 21, 1991; M. C. Poertner, "Racial Balance an Elusive Goal in Orange County Schools," *Orlando Sentinel*, April 7, 1986; Craig Crawford, "Battle for Integration Stretched over Years," *Orlando Sentinel*, April 8, 1986; Wilkinson, *From Brown to Bakke,* 216–49; Patterson, *Brown v. Board of Education*, 174–75, 178–81, 186; and Chemerinsky, "Segregation and Resegregation," 29–47.

40. Tyler Ward, "Board Nominates Desegregation Experts," *Ocala Star-Banner*, April 21, 1983; Tyler Ward, "Judge Approves Marion Desegregation Plan," *Ocala Star-Banner*, December 28, 1983; and Tyler Ward, "School Board, Federal Officials Agree on Desegregation Plan," *Ocala Star-Banner*, November 30, 1983.

41. T. Roe Oldt, "Board Disapproves Desegregation Plans," *Lakeland Ledger*, November 13, 1975.

42. Nancy Stohs, "Judge Orders Aug. 29 Busing," *Lakeland Ledger*, August 9, 1977. See also Terri Wood, "Schools Face Forced Busing for Racial Balance," *Lakeland Ledger*, July 31, 1977; and Hodges Oral History, 57.

43. L. A. Maxwell, "6 Elementary Schools Exceed Limit on Blacks," *Tampa Tribune*, November 4, 1990.

44. L. A. Maxwell, "Desegregation Plan Unveiled," *Tampa Tribune*, November 17, 1990; L. A. Maxwell, "66% Black Enrollment Sought for New School," *Tampa Tribune*, March 20, 1991; L. A. Maxwell, "Parents Unhappy with Desegregation Plan," October 10, 1991; Beth Foshee, "Talks to Be Kept out of Public Eye," *Tampa Tribune*, February 19, 1992; L. A. Maxwell, "Racial Plan Wins Court OK," *Tampa Tribune*, July 10, 1992; and L. A. Maxwell, "Judge Oks Plan for Bartow Schools," *Tampa Tribune*, August 18, 1992.

45. Dan Fagin, "Judge Lifts Ban on AIDs Kids: Desoto County School Board Ordered to Admit 3 Brothers," *Sarasota Herald-Tribune*, August 6, 1987.

46. "Family in AIDS Case Quits Florida Town after House Burns," *New York Times*, August 30, 1987.

47. "Eliana: Test Case for Education," *St. Petersburg Times*, August 11, 1988.

48. "AIDS Girl's Mom Resists Ruling," *Miami Herald*, August 22, 1988.

49. Karen Dukes, "Eliana Goes to School for the First Time," *St. Petersburg Times*, April 28, 1989. See also Jennifer L. Stevenson, "Student with AIDS Not Alone in Fight," *St. Petersburg Times*, August 29, 1988; Leslie Brody, "Girl 7, with AIDS Leaves Hospital," *St. Petersburg Times*, December 9, 1988.

50. Elizabeth Kovachevich Oral History, 15–17.

51. "Electoral System Discriminatory, U.S. Judge Rules," *Miami Herald*, February 25, 1983.

52. Christopher Boyd, "How Blacks Beat the Election System in Fort Myers," *Miami Herald*, May 1, 1983.

53. "Apopka Gets Costly ($346,599) Lesson," *Miami Herald*, May 17, 1983.

54. Ramsey Campbell, "Blacks Taking Long, Painful Road to True Equality, Justice," *Orlando Sentinel*, July 1, 1993. See also Bill Bond, "Taxpayers Now Footing the Bill for Bad Judgment 13 Years Ago," *Orlando Sentinel*, June 16, 1985.

55. "Judge Halts Set-Aside Programs," *Fort Lauderdale Sun-Sentinel*, April 8, 1989; "Jacksonville Revives Minority Set-Asides," *St. Petersburg Times*, March 7, 1990; and "Court Throws Out Ruling against Set-Asides," *Miami Herald*, February 6, 1992.

56. "Shipyards' Pinups Calendars Are Coming Down," *St. Petersburg Times*, April 30, 1991.

57. Tamar Lewin, "Nude Pictures Are Ruled Sexual Harassment," *New York Times*, January 23, 1991.

58. Howell Melton Oral History, 21.

59. Price, "You've Come a Long Way, Baby," 261.

60. John H. Moore Oral History, 32.

61. *Arline v. Nassau County Public Schools*, 772 F.2d 759, http://openjurist.org/772/f2d/759/arline-v-school-board-of-nassau-county; "Teacher Wins Her Job Back," *Miami Herald*, August 3, 1988. See also Flemming, "'Otherwise Qualified.'"

62. Tomsich, "Summary of Some of Judge William Castagna's Court Cases," Historical Files, MDFA; and *David L. Picou, Plaintiff-Appellant, v. Jim Gillum, Sheriff of Pasco County and James T. Russell, State Attorney, Defendants-Appellees*, 874 F.2d 1519 (11th Cir. 1989), http://www.leagle.com/decision/19892393874F2d1519_12174.

Chapter 11. New Judges, New Challenges, 1988–1992

1. "More Federal Judges Needed to Ease Case Load, Graham Says," *Orlando Sentinel*, May 28, 1991.

2. Michael Blumfield, "Judges Get Sympathy but No Help," *Orlando Sentinel*, November 26, 1989.

3. J. Craig Crawford, "Drug Cases Inflating the Courts Judge Sharp Doesn't See Much Progress for Decline," *Orlando Sentinel*, December 15, 1991.

4. Simpson, quoted in Lyles, *Gatekeepers*, 162.

5. Brian Edwards, "Federal Courthouse Swamped with Record Criminal Caseload," *Tampa Tribune*, December 28, 1992.

6. Ibid.; and Bruce Vielmetti, "Defender's Work Has Its Rewards," *St. Petersburg Times*, June 17, 1991.

7. Karla Spaulding Oral History.

8. Blumfield, "Judges Get Sympathy but No Help."

9. Bush, quoted in Lyles, *Gatekeepers*, 155.

10. Bob Graham interview with the author, April 30, 2012.

11. "District Judge Returns Home after Brain Surgery," *St. Petersburg Times*, March 2, 1989.

12. Craig Basse and Bruce Vielmetti, "George C. Carr, Chief Judge of Florida's Middle District," *St. Petersburg Times*, January 27, 1990. See also "Carr Becomes Chief Judge," *St. Petersburg Times*, October 28, 1989.

13. "Portrait Ceremony Memorializing Honorable George C. Carr," Tampa, April 27, 1990, 758 F. Supp. LXXXI.

14. Bruce Vielmetti, "Magistrate to Step Down, Plans to Hit the Road," *St. Petersburg Times*, April 9, 1990; and "Federal Judge in Florida Plans February Retirement," *Orlando Sentinel*, December 14, 1990.

15. Bruce Vielmetti, "Hillsborough Judge Picked to Replace U.S. Magistrate," *St. Petersburg Times*, May 7, 1990.

16. Ibid.; and Larry Dougherty, "U.S. Attorney Dims Spotlight on His Job," *St. Petersburg Times*, June 23, 1997.

17. Lyles, *Gatekeepers*, 18; and Carp and Rowland, *Politics and Judgment in Federal District Courts*, 53.

18. Jim Leusner, "Orlando Competes for Judge to Help Ease Its Caseload," *Orlando Sentinel*, October 31, 1990.

19. Tom Brennan, "Tampa, Orlando Awarded New Federal Judgeships," *Tampa Tribune*, December 15, 1990.

20. Tom Brennan, "Federal Judges Try to Stay Afloat until Relief Arrives," *Tampa Tribune*, May 12, 1991.

21. Tom Brennan, "Heavy Caseload in Federal Courts Limits Civil Trials," *Tampa Tribune*, January 17, 1991.

22. Kovachevich, quoted in Orval Jackson, "Judge Blasts Lawyers for Not Pushing for More Federal Jurists," *Tampa Tribune*, April 12, 1991.

23. Brennan, "Federal Judges Try to Stay Afloat."

24. Tom Brennan, "Longtime Federal Judge to Relocate to Jacksonville," *Tampa Tribune*, March 6, 1991.

25. Brennan, "Federal Judges Try to Stay Afloat."

26. Harvey E. Schlesinger Oral History, 17–19.

27. Ibid.

28. Tom Brennan, "2 Judges Confirmed for Middle District," *Tampa Tribune*, June 29, 1991; Jessie-Lynne Kerr, "U.S. Judge Honored with Portrait: Ralph Nimmons Died Two Years Ago; Ceremony Marked His 67th Birthday," *Florida Times-Union*, September 15, 2005; Allison Thompson, "Colleagues Welcome Return of Judge to City Where He Began," *Florida Times-Union*, 1997; and Jessie-Lynn Kerr, "Nimmons, Federal Judge, Dies at 65 Longtime Jurist also Served in State Courts," *Florida Times-Union*, November 25, 2003.

29. Bruce Vielmetti, "Nominee for Judge Lauded," *St. Petersburg Times*, May 27, 1991.

30. Ibid.; see also Bruce Vielmetti, "New Judge Has Had Dirt under His Fingernails," *St. Petersburg Times*, May 25, 1992.

31. Lynch, "Hon. Anne Conway"; Mike Oliver, "Orlando Lawyer Picked for Federal Judgeship," *Orlando Sentinel*, July 24, 1991; Jim Leusner, "Trail of Honors Leads to Judge's Seat," *Orlando Sentinel*, January 11, 1992; Bruce Vielmetti, "Judge Wins Her Dream Job Early," *St. Petersburg Times*, January 13, 1992; and "Follow-up: Anne Conway," *Orlando Sentinel*, January 3, 1993.

32. Vielmetti, "New Federal Judge Has Had Dirt"; see also "Hillsborough," *Tampa Tribune*, May 28, 1992.

33. Bruce Vielmetti, "A Favorite Heads North," *St. Petersburg Times*, March 30, 1992.

34. Edwards, quoted it Vielmetti, "Judges Are Packing Boxes in Tampa."

35. "Welcome Judges," *St. Petersburg Times*, March 18, 1992; and Jeff Testerman, "Pinellas Snubbed in Push for U.S. Court," *St. Petersburg Times*, April 3, 1992.

36. Jeff Testerman, "New Courthouse? Just Sign Here," *St. Petersburg Times*, April 25, 1992.

37. Kevin Shinkle, "Courthouse in St. Pete Hot Topic," *Tampa Tribune*, April 28, 1992.

38. Jeff Testerman, "Justice Is too Far Away," *St. Petersburg Times*, April 28, 1992.

39. David Sommer, "New Courthouse to Tower Over Tampa," *Tampa Tribune*, July 28, 1993.

40. Jim Leusner, "U.S. Mix-up Blocks Court Renovation," *Orlando Sentinel*, August 1, 1991.

41. "Florida Judge Confirmed for U.S. Appeals Court," *St. Petersburg Times*, August 12, 1992.

42. "Federal Judge Finds Higher Post Bittersweet," *Orlando Sentinel*, August 31, 1992; see also Susan Black Oral History; and Joe Wilhelm, "U.S. Judge Celebrated for 30 Years of Service and Advancement of Women in Law," *Jacksonville Financial News & Daily Record*, July 12, 2010.

43. "Judge Leaves His Mark—and Name—on the Court," *Orlando Sentinel*, October 24, 1992; Jim Leusner, "U.S. Building's New Name Is Judge's," *Orlando Sentinel*, June 3, 1993; and Jim Leusner, "Prosecutors, Defenders Give Judges Good Grades—Survey Ranks Baker 1st," *Orlando Sentinel*, July 28, 1995.

44. Administrative Office of the U.S. Courts, *Justices and Judges of the United States Courts*, 921.

45. Ibid., 762; and Jim Leusner, "Newest Federal Judges Get Top Grades from Lawyers," *Orlando Sentinel*, December 20, 1993.

46. Brian Edwards, "Federal Courthouse Swamped with Record Caseload," *Tampa Tribune*, December 28, 1992.

47. Ibid.; Bruce Vielmetti, "Judicial Shuffling in the Cards," *St. Petersburg Times*, January 27, 1992.

48. Doug Nurse, "Polk Men Face Federal Carjacking Charges," *Tampa Tribune*, December 18, 1992; Henry Pierson Curtis, "3 Polk Men Convicted in Nation's First Trial of Fatal Carjacking," *Orlando Sentinel*, February 26, 1993; and Doug Nurse, "Judge Sentences 3 Carjackers to Life—The Jurist Blasts the First Men Convicted under the New Federal Law," *Tampa Tribune*, April 27, 1993.

49. O'Bryant, "Crime Control."

50. Landers, "Prosecutorial Limits," 65.

51. Bruce Vielmetti, "Actions Saddle U.S. Marshal with Criticisms," *St. Petersburg Times*, October 16, 1989; and Bruce Vielmetti, "8-Year U.S. Marshal in Tampa Resigns," *St. Petersburg Times*, September 7, 1990.

52. "Operation Gunsmoke Nets 30 Local Arrests," *St. Petersburg Times*, May 1, 1992; and Bill Duryea, "Bay Area Has 3 of 5 Marshal Candidates," *St. Petersburg Times*, July 1, 1993.

53. Phil Davis, "Ex-Sheriff Wonders What to Do during Retirement," *Ocala Star-Banner*, January 16, 1993; "Ideal Nominee for U.S. Marshal," *Ocala Star-Banner*, July 1, 1993; Bruce Vielmetti, "U.S. Marshal Nod Goes to Ex-Sheriff," *St. Petersburg Times*, November 9, 1993; and Jim Leusner, "Marshal Choice Upsets Finalists—Picking Moreland Called Political Ploy," *Orlando Sentinel*, November 15, 1993.

54. David Sommer, "Marshals Have Star Attraction," *Tampa Tribune*, December 3, 1994.

55. Bruce Vielmetti, "Outgoing U.S. Attorney Looks Back over His Tenure," *St. Petersburg Times*, June 18, 1993.

56. Richard Danielson," Genzman Says He'll Resign," *St. Petersburg Times*, March 24, 1993; Bruce Vielmetti, "Reno Names Interim U.S. Attorney for Tampa," St. Petersburg Times, June 16, 1993.

57. David Sommer, "Federal Court Caseload Heading toward Regional 'Meltdown,'" *Tampa Tribune*, February 20, 1993.

Chapter 12. The Court Expands and Confronts Antigovernment Activity, 1992–2000

1. Lyles, *Gatekeepers*, 169.

2. Ibid.

3. Ibid., 170–71.

4. Ibid., 174–75.

5. Quoted in ibid., 181.

6. Ibid., 177–78.

7. Bruce Vielmetti, "Many Have Called, but Only Two Will Be Chosen," *St. Petersburg Times*, April 12, 1993; Bruce Vielmetti, "Panel Screens Applicants for Tampa's Federal Bench," *St. Petersburg Times*, April 18, 1993; Jeff Stidham, "Graham Picks Finalists for Judicial Posts," *Tampa Tribune*, April 21, 1993; and Bruce Vielmetti, "2 Tapped for U.S. Bench in Tampa," *St. Petersburg Times*, July 21, 1993.

8. Kevin Graham, "Bucklew Leads, Others Follow," *St. Petersburg Times*, April 26, 2008; and "Bucklew Sworn in as Federal Judge," *Tampa Tribune*, February 8, 1994.

9. Judge Henry Adams interview with the author, May 23, 2011; see also Stuart, "Judge Henry Lee Adams," 31–32.

10. Jessie-Lynne Kerr, "After 31 Years on the Bench, Jacksonville Jurist Takes Senior Status," *Jacksonville Times-Union*, April 7, 2010; and Stuart, "Judge Henry Lee Adams," 28.

11. Judge Henry Adams interview with the author, May 23, 2011.

12. William Yelverton, "Defense Lawyer Will Become Magistrate," *Tampa Tribune*, September 23, 1993; Administrative Office of the U.S. Courts, *Justices and Judges of the United States Courts*, 868, 892.

13. Bruce Vielmetti, "Tampa Bay Law Firm Gets National Exposure," *St. Petersburg Times*, December 13, 1993.

14. Karl Vick and Bruce Vielmetti, "Historic Choice for U.S. Attorney?" *St. Petersburg Times*, August 10, 1993.

15. "Larry Colleton Nominated for U.S. Attorney's Post," *Orlando Sentinel*, November 21, 1993.

16. Bruce Vielmetti, "A Different Kind of U.S. Attorney," *St. Petersburg Times*, February 14, 1994.

17. Ibid.

18. Bruce Vielmetti, "U.S. Attorney Lists His Priorities," *St. Petersburg Times*, March 2, 1994; see also Bruce Vielmetti, "U.S. Attorney Candidate Explores Role," *St. Petersburg Times*, October 11, 1993.

19. Bruce Vielmetti, "A Top Federal Attorney Quits," *St. Petersburg Times*, February 25, 1994; Bruce Vielmetti, "New U.S. Attorney Has More Changes up His Sleeve," *St. Petersburg Times*, February 28, 1994; and Douglas Frazier Oral History 14–15.

20. Mary Anne Lewis, "U.S. Attorney Videotaped in Confrontation with TV Reporter," *Tampa Tribune*, May 8, 1994; and Bruce Vielmetti, "'I Never Got to Ask the Question,'" *St. Petersburg Times*, May 10, 1994.

21. "Lawyers Battle in Porno Scandal—Prosecutor Denies Favoritism in Case," *Ocala Star-Banner*, April 15, 1994.

22. Harvey E. Schlesinger interview with author, May 24, 2010.

23. David Sommer, "Prosecutor's Woes Rooted in Duval," *Tampa Tribune*, May 15, 1994.

24. Jim Leusner, "Plot Aimed at Colleton Suspected—Probe to See if Judge was Misled," *Orlando Sentinel*, May 22, 1994.

25. Lewis, "U.S. Attorney Videotaped"; Bruce Viemetti, "A Turbulent Tenure for U.S. Attorney," *St. Petersburg Times*, May 23, 1994; and Jim Leusner, "U.S. Drops Review of Duo Who Talked About Colleton," *Orlando Sentinel*, May 30, 1994.

26. David Sommer, "Prosecutor Gets Leave of Absence," *Tampa Tribune*, May 11, 1994; Jim Leusner, "U.S. Attorney to Take Leave While Scuffle Investigated," *Orlando Sentinel*, May 11, 1994; and Bruce Vielmetti, "Colleton Charges Called Unlikely," *St. Petersburg Times*, May 12, 1994.

27. David Sommer, "U.S. Attorney Sworn in on Interim Basis," *Tampa Tribune*, May 13, 1994.

28. Jim Leusner, "Attorney Colleton's Future on the Line," *Orlando Sentinel*, May 15, 1994.

29. Brian Edwards and David Sommer, "Acting Federal Prosecutor Reassigns Colleton's Top Aides," *Tampa Tribune*, May 25, 1994.

30. Mark Johnson and David Sommer, "White House to Determine Colleton's Fate," *Tampa Tribune*, July 22, 1994.

31. Jim Leusner, 'Colleton Ouster Try Blasted as 'Witch Hunt,'" *Orlando Sentinel*, July 21, 1994.

32. Bruce Vielmetti and David Dahl, "Colleton Gets a New Job," *St. Petersburg Times*, July 30, 1994.

33. Bill Duryea, "No Challenge Expected to U.S. Attorney Choice," *St. Petersburg Times*, September 14, 1994.

34. "A Choice for Unity and Justice," *St. Petersburg Times*, September 17, 1994.

35. Jim Leusner, "Lawyer Answer's Washington's Call," *Orlando Sentinel*, November 6, 1994.

36. Bruce Vielmetti, "U.S. Attorney Makes Change," *St. Petersburg Times*, March 20, 1995.

37. David Sommer, "UF Faculty Member Named Prosecutor," *Tampa Tribune*, March 22, 1995.

38. Bruce Vielmetti, "In Court, Comings and Goings Are Fast and Furious," *St. Petersburg Times*, August 14, 1995; and Jim Leusner, "Federal Court Clerk Post Filled," *Orlando Sentinel*, November 17, 1995.

39. William Terrell Hodges Oral History, 72–74, 87–88.

40. David Sommer, "Federal Caseload Still Hefty," *Tampa Tribune*, June 11, 1996.

41. Jeff Stidham, "U.S. Attorney: Office Accomplished 'More with Less,'" *Tampa Tribune*, November 27, 1996.

42. Bruce Vielmetti, "As Chief Judge, She Fills Tall Orders," *St. Petersburg Times*, January 22, 1996.

43. "On Hold—As Much of the Federal Government Comes to a Halt—Some Expect the Shutdown to Last Through the Week," *Tampa Tribune*, November 15, 1995.

44. David Sommer, "Federal Courts in Tampa Brace for Layoffs," *Tampa Tribune*, December 31, 1995.

45. Bruce Vielmetti, "As Chief Judge, She Fills Tall Orders, *St. Petersburg Times*, January 22, 1996.

46. "Officials Claim Notes Show White-Supremacy Plot," *Orlando Sentinel*, January 27, 1991; and Potok, "C-4 and the Confederacy."

47. Jim Leusner, "Anti-Government Militias Are Strong in Florida," *Orlando Sentinel*, April 26, 1995.

48. Jim Leusner, "Tax Protester Vanishes before Court Date," *Orlando Sentinel*, January 31, 1996.

49. Jim Leusner, "IRS Gets Last Word in Fight with Tax Protester McEwan," *Orlando Sentinel*, November 26, 1997.

50. Jim Leusner, "2 Years for Tax Protester," *Orlando Sentinel*, March 26, 1998; and Jim Leusner, "Tax Protester Says 'Patriots' Are Profiteers," *Orlando Sentinel*, March 29, 1998.

51. Pat Leisner, "Militia Leader Sentenced to 5 Years in Terror Plot," *Fort Lauderdale Sun-Sentinel*, July 29, 2000.

52. Sarah Hundley, "Judge Gives Terrorist 5 Years," *Tampa Tribune*, July 29, 2000.

53. Leisner, "Militia Leader Sentenced."

54. Brian Edwards, "State Inmate Indicted in Death Threats Made to U.S. District

Judge," *Tampa Tribune*, August 26, 1993; and Bruce Vielmetti, "2 Held in Plot to Kill Judge," *St. Petersburg Times*, March 17, 1994.

55. Jacqueline Soteropoulos, "Threats Target Federal Judges," *Tampa Tribune*, May 25, 1997.

56. Debbie Salamone, "Orlando Man Found Guilty of Threatening to Shoot, Kill Bill Clinton," *Orlando Sentinel*, May 28, 1994; and Jim Leusner, "Threats against Clinton Bring 5-Year Sentence," *Orlando Sentinel*, August 4, 1994.

57. Jeff Stidham, "Judge Throws out Lawsuit against Florida Bar," *Tampa Tribune*, June 12, 1993.

58. "State News—Freemen Stir up Florida Fracas," *Naples Daily News*, April 15, 1996.

59. Ibid.

60. Larry Dougherty, "Jury for Threat Case to Remain a Secret," *St. Petersburg Times*, May 6, 1997; Larry Dougherty, "Man Who Chided System Convicted," *St. Petersburg Times*, August 14, 1997; and Soteropoulous, "Threats Target Federal Judges."

61. Pat Leisner, "Defendant Accuses Judge of Treason," *Florida Times-Union*, June 6, 1997.

62. "Anti-Government Group Is Found Guilty in Tampa," *Orlando Sentinel*, August 14, 1997.

63. Dougherty, "Man Who Chided System Convicted."

64. "Anti-Government Group Is Found Guilty."

65. Twila Decker, "Witness: Accident Averted Race War—Bomb Maker Targeted Blacks, Cellmate Says," *Orlando Sentinel*, October 21, 1997.

66. Jim Leusner, "3 Charged in Orlando Bomb Plot—Agents: Suspects Wanted Blasts as Diversions," *Orlando Sentinel*, May 8, 1998; and Mike McIntire, "Danbury Bank Robbery Linked to Neo-Nazis," *Hartford Courant*, May 12, 1998.

67. Susan Clary, "Final Bank Robbery Plotters Sentenced to 78 Months in Prison," *Orlando Sentinel*, February 27, 1999.

Chapter 13. Bankruptcy in the Middle District, 1984–2000

1. Leonard Gilbert Oral History, 4, LCCFH.

2. Alexander Paskay Oral History, 34–35.

3. Ibid., 37–38.

4. McCarthy and Treacy, eds. *History of the Administrative Office*, 171–72; George, "From Orphan to Maturity," 1491–1501; and Geib and Kite, *Federal Justice in Indiana*, 223–25.

5. Robin Foster, "Bearing the Blow of Failure: Individuals, Companies Swarm Bankruptcy Court," *Orlando Sentinel*, November 4, 1985.

6. Tim Gray, "Bankruptcy Filings Keep Climbing at Torrid Pace," *St. Petersburg Times*, November 17, 1996.

7. Kenneth Michael, "Orlando Lacks Its Own Judge Despite Load," *Orlando Sentinel*, May 19, 1985.

8. McCarthy and Treacy, *History of the Administrative Office*, 171–72.

9. Ibid.; and George, "From Orphan to Maturity," 1494–97.

10. George Proctor Oral History, 13–14.

11. Alexander Paskay Oral History, 30.

12. Philip Morgan, "Prisoners of Debt Find Home in Court," *Tampa Tribune*, January 5, 1992.

13. D. Amos, "Judge Curbs Lawyers' 'Feast,'" *St. Petersburg Times*, October 17, 1990. See also Paskay Oral History, 49.

14. Mary Jo Melone, "Judge Left Speechless by Praise," *St. Petersburg Times*, June 24, 1988.

15. Gary White, "Federal Judge from Lake Wales Dies at 69," *Lakeland Ledger*, December 19, 2009; and Paul M. Glenn, "Remarks at the Annual Dinner of the Tampa Bay Bankruptcy Bar Association Honoring the Honorable Thomas E. Baynes, Jr. upon His Retirement," June 8, 2005, MDFA.

16. "Lionel Silberman Has Been Named the First Bankruptcy Judge in Orlando," *Orlando Sentinel*, August 14, 1988; Prakash Gandhi, "Bankruptcy Judge Dies Suddenly," *Orlando Sentinel*, December 26, 1988; and "In Memoriam, Honorable Lionel H. Silberman," MDFA.

17. "Lawyer Gets Bankruptcy Appointment," *St. Petersburg Times*, August 15, 1989; and "C. Timothy Corcoran III," *Orlando Sentinel*, June 18, 1990.

18. John F. Sugg, "10,000 Bankruptcy to Be Filed in Tampa Court," *Tampa Tribune*, October 12, 1990.

19. Oral Jackson, "Bankruptcy Backlog Mounting," September 2, 1990.

20. Susan Taylor Martin, "No Relief Likely for Bankruptcy Judges," *St. Petersburg Times*, November 7, 1990.

21. Alexander L. Paskay, "Bankruptcy Court Bending under Weighty Caseload," *Tampa Tribune*, February 24, 1991.

22. B. Stengle, "Relief Still Way Off for Frazzled Bankruptcy Judges," *St. Petersburg Times*, November 7, 1991.

23. Chris Roush, "House Adds Bankruptcy Court Judges," *Tampa Tribune*, August 14, 1992.

24. Alexander Paskay Oral History, 76.

25. Bernice Stengle, "This Judge Is the Baron of Bankruptcy," *St. Petersburg Times*, April 25, 1993.

26. Mickie Anderson, "Bankruptcy Trustee Collapses in Court, Dies," *Tampa Tribune*, January 6, 1993.

27. Alexander Paskay Oral History, 28.

28. Susan Taylor Martin, "Debtors May Find 'Paradise' Lost," *St. Petersburg Times*, March 1, 1991.

29. Dave Szymanski, "More Agree that Bankruptcy System Must Be Fixed," *Tampa Tribune*, June 8, 1993.

30. Suzy Hagstrom, "Couple Get a Rude Awakening," *Orlando Sentinel*, September 6, 1993.

31. *Jacksonville Business Journal*, March 5–11, 1993.

32. John Finotti, "Bankruptcy Court Help on Way," *Jacksonville Times-Union*, November 6, 1993.

33. Karen S. Jennemann to George L. Proctor, March 10, 1993, Proctor Papers, box 1, fo. 1, MDFA; and Dave Szymanski, "2 New Judges Added to Tampa Bankruptcy Court," *Tampa Tribune*, December 8, 1993.

34. Jerry A. Funk interview with the author, May 25, 2011; and *Court Connection: Bi-Monthly Newsletter for the Clerk's Office for the U.S. Bankruptcy Court, Middle District of Florida* 12, November 15, 1993.

35. Jerry A. Funk interview with the author, May 25, 2011; and *Court Connection: Bi-Monthly Newsletter for the Clerk's Office for the U.S. Bankruptcy Court, Middle District of Florida* 12, November 15, 1993.

36. Jerry A. Funk interview with the author, May 25, 2011; and *Court Connection: Bi-Monthly Newsletter for the Clerk's Office for the U.S. Bankruptcy Court, Middle District of Florida* 12, November 15, 1993.

37. Administrative Office of the U.S. Courts, *Justices and Judges of the United States Courts*, 633.

38. Leonard Gilbert Oral History, 12. See also Bernice Stengle, "Trial Ordered on Asbestos-Suit Liability," *St. Petersburg Times*, August 27, 1992; and Kevin Shinkle, "Landmark Legal Decision on Walter Industries Delayed," *Tampa Tribune*, September 9, 1992.

39. Stengle, "Trial Ordered on Asbestos-Suit Liability."

40. Dave Szymanski, "Walter Corporate Veil Trial Begins," *Tampa Tribune*, December 14, 1993.

41. "Kudos from the Boss of Bankruptcy Court," *Tampa Tribune*, December 20, 1993.

42. Dave Szymanski, "Walter Escapes Asbestos Suit," *Tampa Tribune*, April 19, 1994.

43. Dave Szymanski, "Walter Creditors Unite behind Plan," *Tampa Tribune*, May 20, 1994.

44. Sarah Cohen, "Judge Urges Walter Settlement," *Tampa Tribune*, October 20, 1994.

45. Alexander Paskay Oral History, 27–28.

46. Ibid.; Sarah Cohen, "Walter Parties Agree to End Its Chapter 11," *Tampa Tribune*, October 21, 1994; and Sarah Cohen, "Walter Creditors OK Deal," *Tampa Tribune*, November 23, 1994.

47. Alexander Paskay Oral History, 77.

48. Alexander Paskay Oral History, 27–28; see also Jean Gruss, "Walter Industries Emerges from Chapter 11 Protection," *Tampa Tribune*, March 18, 1995.

49. Alexander Paskay Oral History, 77.

50. Jerome R. Stockfisch, "Ruling May Insulate Celotex from Litigation," *Tampa Tribune*, December 7, 1996; and Jerome R. Stockfisch," Judge Oks Celotex Plan to Reorganize," *Tampa Tribune*, March 21, 1997.

51. Glenn, "Remarks at the Annual Dinner."

52. Alexander Paskay Oral History, 72–73. See also "Lykes Ships Protected," *St. Petersburg Times*, October 13, 1995.

53. Steve Huettel, "Lykes Bros. Division Won't Face Chapter 7," *Tampa Tribune*, May 9, 1996. See also Teresa Burney, "Judge Rejects Motion on Lykes," *St. Petersburg Times*, May 10, 1996.

54. Jerome R. Stockfisch, "Lykes Gets out of Shipping Industry," *Tampa Tribune*, April 3, 1997.

55. Jerome R. Stockfisch, "Bankruptcy 'Dean' to Step Down," *Tampa Tribune*, March 20, 1999.

56. Paskay's first book, *Handbook for Trustees and Receivers*, appeared in 1968. Revised editions appeared in 1972, 1973, and 1978. *A Supplement to 1978 Handbook for Trustees and*

Receivers in Bankruptcy appeared in 1979. In 1996 Paksay published *Creditors' Rights*. Full revisions of that work came out in 1998, 2002, and 2006.

57. Rex Henderson, "Bankruptcy Court Goes High Tech," *Tampa Tribune*, July 15, 1997.

Chapter 14. First Amendment, Abortion Rights, Employment Discrimination, and School Desegregation Litigation Runs Its Course, 1992–2000

1. Murphy, "To Pray or Not to Pray."

2. "Judge Halts School Bible Readings," *Miami Herald*, October 4, 1990.

3. "Board Debates Appeal of Bible-Reading Ban," *Miami Herald*, October 6, 1990; and "School Board to Drop Fight for Bible Stories," *Miami Herald*, January 26, 1991.

4. "Student Prayer Upheld," *Miami Herald*, June 6, 1993.

5. "Court Okays Prayer at Graduation," *St. Petersburg Times*, May 11, 1994.

6. Monica Richardson, "Ruling Expected Today on Graduation Prayers," *Florida Times-Union*, May 28, 1998. See also Ron Word, "Judge Hears Arguments on Student Prayer at Graduation," *Fort Lauderdale Sun-Sentinel*, May 28, 1998; "Graduates May Pray in Messages," *Orlando Sentinel*, May 29, 1998.

7. Laura Diamond, "School Board Appeals Ruling on Prayer Policy," *Jacksonville Times-Union*, June 2, 1999. See also Derek L. Kinner and Laura Diamond, "Graduation Messages' Illegal," *Jacksonville Times-Union*, May 13, 1999.

8. Mauro, "High Court Turns away Question"; and Staver, "Legal Memorandum on Graduation Prayers."

9. "Parental Consent: A History," *Miami Herald*, March 12, 1989.

10. "Judge Halts Abortion Consent Law," *Miami Herald*, October 7, 1988.

11. Ibid.

12. Ibid.

13. "Governor Decries 'Liberal' Ruling," *Miami Herald*, October 12, 1988.

14. "Parental Consent: A History," *Miami Herald*, March 12, 1989; and "Abortion Consent Law Reinstated," *Palm Beach Post*, February 14, 1989.

15. "Freedom of Access to Clinic Entrances Act of 1994," S. 636, http://www.gpo.gov/fdsys/pkg/BILLS-103s636enr/pdf/BILLS-103s636enr.pdf.

16. Ana Puga and Guy McCarthy, "Marshals to Guard Clinics-Reno Assigns Officers after Recent Violence," *Ocala Star-Banner*, August 2, 1994.

17. Sherri M. Owens, "Doctor to City: Let's End Fight," *Orlando Sentinel*, April 20, 1996.

18. Sherri M. Owens, "Doctor in Orlando Can Do 2nd-Trimester Abortions—A Federal Judge Issued a Ruling to Permit the Procedures," *Orlando Sentinel*, April 19, 1996; and Sherri Owens, "City Oks $325,000 For Doctor," *Orlando Sentinel*, May 21, 1996.

19. Bridget Hall, "A Federal Judge Has Dismissed the Abortion Clinic's Lawsuit against Local Law Enforcement and Anti-Abortion Protesters," *Ocala Star-Banner*, December 23, 1999.

20. Rick Cundiff, "A Federal Judge Has Ruled That the Extortion Trial of Abortion Provider James Scott Pendergraft Will Be Held in Ocala," *Ocala Star-Banner*, August 24, 2000; and Rick Cundiff, "With Abortion Rights Supporters Picketing outside the Courthouse and Abortion Opponents Picketing His Clinic Two Blocks Away, the Federal Extortion Trial of Dr. James Scott Pendergraft IV Began Tuesday," *Ocala Star-Banner*, January 3, 2001.

21. Rick Cundiff, "Jurors in the Federal Extortion Trial . . . Deliberated Nearly Seven Hours," *Ocala Star-Banner*, February 1, 2001. See also Frank Stanford, "Defender: Physician Is Being Persecuted," *Orlando Sentinel*, January 31, 2001.

22. Frank Stanford, "Verdict Won't Close Clinics, Doctor Vows," *Orlando Sentinel*, February 2, 2001.

23. Ibid.; Henry Pierson Curtis and Amy Rippel, "Conviction of Florida Doctor Is Overturned," *Orlando Sentinel*, July 17, 2002; and "Doctor Admits to Deception for Associate," *Orlando Sentinel*," June 10, 2004.

24. David Sommer, "Sex Discrimination Suit Targets Albertsons," *Tampa Tribune*, April 6, 1996.

25. Mark Albright, "Judge to Review Winn-Dixie Suit Deal," *St. Petersburg Times*, July 27, 1999.

26. Simon Barker-Benefield, "Details, but Few Answers Plaintiffs, Winn-Dixie Won't Discuss Settlement," *Florida Times-Union*, July 20, 1999.

27. Lara Wozniak, "Federal Agency Joins Suit Accusing Publix of Sex Bias," *St. Petersburg Times*, November 29, 1995.

28. Ibid.; and Lara Wozniak, "EEOC Allowed to Join Publix Suit," *St. Petersburg Times*, February 2, 1996.

29. Mark Albright, "Publix Takes Aim at Union's Role in Suit," *St. Petersburg Times*, January 9, 1996.

30. Lara Wozniak, "Publix Sex Bias Suit May Be Biggest," *St. Petersburg Times*, March 13, 1996.

31. Mickie Valente, "Everyone Won Something in Publix Ruling," *St. Petersburg Times,* March 13, 1996.

32. Mark Albright and Lara Wozniak, "Employees Rally for Publix," *St. Petersburg Times*, January 27, 1996.

33. Brad Kuhn, "Sex-Bias Suit against Publix A Class Action," *Orlando Sentinel*, March 13, 1996.

34. Lynn N. Duke, "Publix Request Denied: Bias Suit to Continue," *Lakeland Ledger*, November 20, 1996.

35. Lynn N. Duke, "Publix Settles Case for $81.5 Million," *Lakeland Ledger*, January 25, 1997.

36. Ibid. See also Mark Albright, "Bias Suits Settled for $85-Million," *St. Petersburg Times*, January 25, 1997.

37. Mark Albright, "Settlement with Publix Approved," *St. Petersburg Times*, May 24, 1997.

38. Henry Lee Adams Oral History, 26.

39. Mark Albright, "Church Backs Suit against Publix," *St. Petersburg Times*, April 4, 1997.

40. Jacqueline Soteropoulos, "Judge Will Look Familiar to Publix Lawyers," *Tampa Tribune*, April 4, 1997.

41. Mark Albright, "Magistrate: Publix Racial Bias Case Suit Should Widen," *St. Petersburg Times*, June 17, 1998.

42. Mark Albright, "Publix Settles Race Bias Dispute," *St. Petersburg Times*, December 20, 2000.

43. Caren Burneister, "Former Workers File Suit against Florida Power," *Ocala Star-Banner*, February 16, 1996; Barry Flynn, "Age-Bias Case Will Go to High Court," *Orlando Sentinel*, December 4, 2001; and Louis Hau, "Florida Power Settles Age Bias Cases," *St. Petersburg Times*, November 22, 2002.

44. Jeff Kunerth, "Has Reality of School Integration Matched Promise?" *Orlando Sentinel*, March 2, 2008.

45. Orfield and Eaton, *Dismantling Desegregation*, xxiii. See also "Orange County De-segregation Timeline," *Orlando Sentinel*, February 27, 2008.

46. Orfield and Eaton, *Dismantling Desegregation*, xxiii.

47. "Orange County Desegregation Time Line," *Orlando Sentinel*, February 27, 2008.

48. Frankenberg, Lee, and Orfield, *A Multiracial Society*, 5–6.

49. Stephen Hegarty, "Busing Case Barred from State Court," *St. Petersburg Times*, March 5, 1993. See also Stephen Hegarty, "Busing Case Official Back in State Court," *St. Petersburg Times*, July 15, 1992.

50. B. C. Manion, "Parents Speak out Against Busing," *Tampa Tribune*, August 5, 1993. See also B. C. Manion, "Judge Kills Hope to Put Busing Asunder," *Tampa Tribune*, August 17, 1993.

51. Stephen Hegarty, "Busing again the Legal Issue," *St. Petersburg Times*, November 23, 1994.

52. Tom Scherberger, "A Federal Case Made in the Classroom," *St. Petersburg Times*, June 11, 1995.

53. Ibid.; Hegarty, "Busing again the Legal Issue"; Stephen Hegarty and Bill Duryea, "Desegregation Case Referred to Mediation," *St. Petersburg Times*, November 24, 1994; and Stephen Hegarty, "Order May Allow Racial Imbalance in Schools," *St. Petersburg Times*, June 27, 1995.

54. Stephen Hegarty, "Judge's Move Could Lead to Busing's End," *St. Petersburg Times*, November 21, 1995.

55. "Schools Win Race Decision," *Florida Times-Union*, August 28, 1997.

56. Larry Dougherty, "Judge's Order Outlines What Ails Desegregation," *St. Petersburg Times*, October 28, 1998.

57. Marilyn Brown, "Ruling Stumps School Officials," *Tampa Tribune*, October 28, 1998.

58. Linda Chion-Kenney, "Judge Scolds Board over Integration," *St. Petersburg Times*, December 5, 1998.

59. Ibid.

60. See also Sarah Schweitzer, "NAACP Seeks Specific Courts in First Meeting with Schools," *St. Petersburg Times*, February 11, 1999; and Linda Chion-Kenney, "Duval County Desegregation Plan," *St. Petersburg Times*, June 13, 1999.

61. Marilyn Brown, "We Have Choice," *Tampa Tribune*, March 20, 2001.

62. "Ending Forced Busing," *Tampa Tribune*, March 20, 2001.

63. See also "Hillsborough Schools Pass Supreme Court Test," *Tampa Tribune*, October 3, 2001.

64. "Tampa—Education Mumbo Jumbo," *Tampa Tribune*, May 30, 1998.

65. Shelby Oppel, "Pressure Builds on Post-Busing Planners," *St. Petersburg Times*, November 28, 1999; "As Court Steps Aside, Pinellas Schools Face a New Challenge," *St.*

Petersburg Times, August 13, 2000; Thomas C. Tobin, "Looking Back on a 32-Year Journey—End of the Road for Pinellas Busing," *St. Petersburg Times*, May 21, 2003; and "Timeline: Racial Integration in Pinellas and Hillsborough Schools," *St. Petersburg Times*, June 29, 2007.

66. Eileen Kelley, "Court Rewards Lee's Desegregation Efforts," *Naples Daily News*, August 27, 1996.

67. Thomas Nord, "Mediation Ordered Parties to Meet on Desegregation," *Florida Times-Union*, January 13, 1996; Mary McDonald, "35-Year Battle Ending? 'Judge's Judge' Gets Desegregation Trial," *Florida Times-Union*, August 17, 1997; and Jim Saunders, "Duval School Talks Constructive," *Jacksonville Florida-Times Union*, January 30, 1996.

68. Stephanie Desmon, "Face to Face on Desegregation School Board, NAACP Poised for Mediation." *Florida Times-Union*, January 28, 1996.

69. Jim Saunders, "School Plan Gains Quiet Acceptance," *Florida Times-Union*, March 15, 1996.

70. Jim Saunders, "Back to the Table, School Board Wants to Soften Language in Deal," *Florida Times-Union*, March 20, 1996; and Jim Saunders, "Desegregation Plan Alteration Blasts NAACP Lawyer Says Changes Unacceptable," *Florida Times-Union*, March 21, 1996.

71. Jim Saunders, "Plan May Save School Deal," *Florida Times-Union*, March 22, 1996.

72. Jim Saunders and Beau Halton, "NAACP: Plan Needs Teeth Stronger Language Sought," *Florida Times-Union*, April 18, 1996; Jim Saunders, "NAACP, Board Near an Impasse," *Florida Times-Union*, April 25, 1996; Jim Saunders, "End in Sight for NAACP, Board," *Florida Times-Union*, May 5, 1996; Jim Saunders, "School Agreement Still Possible, Jacksonville NAACP Vote Wasn't Fatal, Attorney Says," *Florida Times-Union,* May 22, 1996; and Jim Saunders, "School, NAACP Meeting, Desegregation Plan Subject of Lawyers Talks in D. C.," *Florida Times-Union*, August 6, 1996.

73. Stephanie Desmon, "Judge to Rule," *Florida Times-Union*, April 10, 1997.

74. Jim Saunders, "School Board Set on Going to Court for 'Unitary' Ruling," *Florida Times-Union*, September 29, 1996; and Stephanie Desmon, "NAACP: School Board 'Utterly Failed,'" *Florida Times-Union*, November 6, 1996.

75. Mary MacDonald, "School Desegregation Trial Begins," *Florida Times-Union*, August 19, 1997.

76. Mary MacDonald, "Schools, the NACCP Open Trial," *Florida Times-Union,* August 19, 1997.

77. Mary MacDonald, "Natural Integration at Issue," *Florida Times-Union*, August 21, 1997.

78. Beau Halton, "Federal Judge Declares Duval Schools Integrated, Ruling Ends 39 Years of Legal Battles," *Florida Times-Union*, May 28, 1999.

79. Ibid.

80. Ronald L. Littlepage, "NAACP Shouldn't Appeal Court Ruling," *Florida Times-Union*, June 10, 1999.

81. Laura Diamond, "NAACP Appealing School Case," *Florida Times-Union*, June 25, 1999; Laura Diamond, "No Budging in NAACP Appeal of School Suit Court May Schedule Hearing in February," *Florida Times-Union*, November 11, 1999.

82. Monica Bryant, "School District Wants Desegregation Order Lifted," *Ocala Star-Banner*, August 17, 2005.

83. Joe Callahan, "U.S. District Judge Lifts Marion's 28-Year Desegregation," *Ocala Star-Banner*, January 16, 2007.

84. Leslie Postal, "Judge Ends 1960s Schools-Desegregation Case," *Orlando Sentinel*, August 3, 2010.

85. Jeff Kunerth, "Has Reality of School Integration Matched Its Lofty Promise?" *Orlando Sentinel*, March 2, 2008.

86. Ibid.; see also *Evelyn R. Ellis, et al. v. Board of Public Instruction of Orange County, Florida.*

Chapter 15. Drugs, Outlaws, Fraud, Pollution, Endangered Species, and a Baby Named Sabrina

1. Jim Leusner, "Judge's Dismissal of MBI Drug Case Overturned," *Orlando Sentinel*, September 2, 1992.

2. Ibid.

3. Bruce Vielmetti, "Federal Action Taken against Deadbeat Parents," *St. Petersburg Times*, March 10, 1996.

4. Rehnquist, "1998 Year-End Report."

5. Ibid.; see also Sarah Huntley, "U.S. Judges Bristle as Federal Laws Rise," *Tampa Tribune*, March 14, 1999.

6. Alliniece Taylor, "Drug-Trafficker Faces Prison Time 'Miami Boys' Member," *Florida Times-Union*, November 6, 1999; and "Miami Boys Gang Leader Gets Life," *Miami Herald*, February 2, 2000.

7. Jim Leusner, "Drug Arrests Seize 15 Suspects," *Orlando Sentinel*, November 20, 1996

8. Ibid.

9. Jim Leusner, "Suspect Admits He Led Drug Ring," *Orlando Sentinel*, July 29, 1997.

10. Andrew Lyons, "Crack Kingpin Faces Life in Prison," *Daytona Beach News-Journal*, December 18, 1998; see also Andrew Lyons, "Alleged Area Drug Trafficker Is No Longer an Untouchable," *Daytona Beach News-Journal*, October 24, 1998; and Andrew Lyons, "Crack Kingpin Gets Life in Prison," *Daytona Beach News-Journal*, March 25, 1999.

11. Jacqueline Soteropoulos, "Criminal Pockets Emptied by Feds," *Tampa Tribune*, September 15, 1997.

12. "Five Convicted on Prostitution Ring Charges," *St Petersburg Times*, December 23, 1981; and "3 Outlaws Draw Jail Sentences," *Miami Herald*, August 13, 1982.

13. "13 Outlaws Convicted," *Miami Herald*, April 2, 1983.

14. "Former Outlaw Members Sentenced to Prison," *Miami Herald*, July 2, 1983.

15. Vickie Chachere, "Outlaw Motorcycle Gang Leaders to Begin Murder Trial," *Lakeland Ledger*, August 18, 2003.

16. Bruce Vielmetti, "Outlaws Go on Trial in Tampa," *St. Petersburg Times*, April 17, 1995.

17. David Sommer, "Shackles In, Gum Chewing Out, at Upcoming Outlaws Trial," *Tampa Tribune*, April 15, 1995.

18. Vielmetti, "Outlaws Go on Trial in Tampa."

19. David Sommer, "Trial Opens with Look into Outlaws' Bloody History," *Tampa Tribune*, April 25, 1995.

20. Bruce Vielmetti, "Humor Livens Up Jurors' Daunting Deliberations," *St. Petersburg*

Times, August 17, 1995; David Sommer, "13 Outlaws Face Lengthy Prison Terms," *Tampa Tribune*, August 30, 1995; and Bruce Vielmetti, "Some Outlaws Found Guilty; Two Acquitted," *St. Petersburg Times*, August 30, 1995.

21. David Sommer, "Outlaw Jurors Blast Feds," *Tampa Tribune*, August 31, 1995.

22. David Sommer, "Judge Erred in Outlaws Trial, Jurors Say," *Tampa Tribune*, December 19, 1995.

23. Katherine Shaver, "Federal Indictments Zero in on Bikers," *St. Petersburg Times*, November 14, 1996.

24. Ibid.; Jim Leusner, "Bikers Hit with More Charges," *Orlando Sentinel*, November 14, 1996; and Larry Dougherty, "Former Outlaw President Cuts a Deal," *St. Petersburg Times*, April 24, 1997.

25. "Broward Biker Is Convicted, Verdict Ends Outlaws' 30-Year Reign of Terror," *Miami Herald*, November 22, 1997.

26. Paula Christian, "Gang Defectors Get Lightened Terms," *Tampa Tribune*, September 1, 2001. See also Paula Christian, "Security Strict for Outlaw Leader's Trial," *Tampa Tribune*, February 21, 2001; Paula Christian, "Prosecutors Begin Biker Trial Case," *Tampa Tribune*, March 21, 2001; Paula Christian, "Gang Leader Will Be Outlaw behind Bars," *Tampa Tribune*, July 28, 2001.

27. Vickie Chachere, "Outlaw Motorcycle Gang Leaders."

28. Vickie Chachere, "Bike Gang Leader Faces 10 to Life," *Miami Herald*, October 1, 2003; and Vickie Chachere, "Ex-Leader of Biker Gang Sentenced," *Miami Herald*, January 31, 2004.

29. Mike Stobbe, "Trial Date Set in Columbia/HCA Case," *Tampa Tribune*, April 16, 1999; and "4 Hospital Executives Face Medicare Fraud Charges," *Orlando Sentinel*, May 1, 1999.

30. Jason Hall, "Jury Selected in Columbia Case," *Sarasota Herald-Tribune*, May 4, 1999.

31. Sarah Huntley, "Jurors Must Sift through Complex Topic," *Tampa Tribune*, May 17, 1999.

32. Sarah Huntley, "Tapes of Phone Calls Complicate HCA Trial," *Tampa Tribune*, June 8, 1999; and Karen L. Shaw, "Columbia Fraud Mistrial Denied," *Stuart News*, June 9, 1999.

33. Sarah Huntley and Mike Stobbe, "HCA Verdicts Split," *Tampa Tribune*, July 3, 1999.

34. Paula Christian, "HCA Officials' Convictions Overturned," *Tampa Tribune*, March 26, 2002.

35. Ibid.

36. Ibid.; and "Largest Health Care Fraud Case in U.S. History Settled HCA Investigation Nets Record of $1.7 Billion Total," Department of Justice News Release, June 23, 2003, http://www.justice.gov/opa/pr/2003/June/03_civ_386.htm.

37. Jim Leusner, "Grand Jury: McCorkle Sold Empty Promises," *Orlando Sentinel*, March 7, 1998.

38. Jim Leusner, "Hosts of Infomercials Sent to Jail," *Orlando Sentinel*, March 11, 1998; and Jim Leusner, "Jury Chosen, McCorkle Case Goes to Trial," *Orlando Sentinel*, September 3, 1998.

39. Jim Leusner, "McCorkle Attorneys Put Agents on Trial," *Orlando Sentinel*, September 11, 1998; and Jim Leusner, "McCorkle's Defense Team Gets Scolding from Judge," *Orlando Sentinel*, September 18, 1998.

40. Jim Leusner, "McCorkle's Attorneys Wrap up Their Case," *Orlando Sentinel*, October 29, 1998; Jim Leusner, "Prosecutor: McCorkle Plan Adds up to Fraud," *Orlando Sentinel*, November 3, 1998; Jim Leusner, "McCorkle Guilty—Then He Collapses," *Orlando Sentinel*, November 5, 1998; and Jim Leusner, "McCorkles Lose Their Possessions," *Orlando Sentinel*, November 6, 1998.

41. Jim Leusner, "McCorkle, Wife Get 24-Year Sentences," *Orlando Sentinel*, January 26, 1999.

42. Jim Leusner, "Bailey Is in Hot Water over $2 Million," *Orlando Sentinel*, March 23, 1999. See also Jim Leusner, "Bailey Must Pay $2 Million by May 3, *Orlando Sentinel*, April 2, 1999.

43. Jim Leusner, "F. Lee Bailey May Be Forced to Return $2 Million," *Orlando Sentinel*, January 15, 2000. See also Jim Leusner, "Bailey's Hearing Delayed," *Orlando Sentinel*, June 1, 1999; "F. Lee Bailey May Owe $2 Million in Fees," *Orlando Sentinel*, July 1, 2000.

44. S. Clary, "U.S. Judge Finds Bailey in Contempt," *Orlando Sentinel*, August 18, 2000.

45. Mike Schneider, "Jury Tells F. Lee Bailey to Hand over $5 Million," *Miami Herald*, March 28, 2003.

46. David Sommer, "Federal Probe Targets Lyons," *Tampa Tribune*, August 22, 1997; Larry Dougherty and Craig Pittman, "Feds Join Investigation of Pastor," *St. Petersburg Times*, August 22, 1997; and Jacqueline Soteropoulas and Jeff Stidham, "Testifying about Lyons," *Tampa Tribune*, December 12, 1997.

47. Dougherty and Pittman, "Feds Join Investigation."

48. "The Lyons Saga," *Tampa Tribune*, February 16, 1998.

49. Monica Davey, David Barstow, and Larry Dougherty, "Feds Indict Lyons, Women," *St. Petersburg Times*, July 3, 1998.

50. Larry Dougherty, David Barstow, and William R. Levesque, "Lyons Admits List of Wrongs," *St. Petersburg Times*, March 18, 1999.

51. Ibid. See also William R. Levesque and Larry Dougherty, "Lyons Discussing Plea Deal on Federal Charges," *St. Petersburg Times*, March 12, 1999.

52. Peter E. Howard, "Lyons Draws Light Sentence," *Tampa Tribune*, June 19, 1999.

53. "Captain Admits Dumping at Sea, First Pollution Case of Its Kind," *Miami Herald*, April 23, 1997.

54. Ibid.; and Jacqueline Soteropoulas, "Legal Bite Added to Earth Day," *Tampa Tribune*, April 23, 1997.

55. "Captain Admits Dumping at Sea"; and Larry Dougherty, "U.S. Attorney Accents Environmental Cases," *St. Petersburg Times*, April 23, 1997.

56. Jacqueline Soteropoulos, "Prosecutor Sets up Environmental Fund," *Tampa Tribune*, January 7, 1998.

57. Tom Palmer, "Company to Pay Highest Environmental Fine in Polk," *Lakeland Ledger*, November 13, 1998; Sarah Huntley, "Mulberry Firm Can't Pay Pollution Fine," *Tampa Tribune*, June 3, 2000; and Tom Palmer, "Largest Pollution Case Hits Dead End," *Lakeland Ledger*, November 8, 2001.

58. "Industrial Polluter Gets 13 Years in Prison," *Miami Herald*, August 17, 1999.

59. Ibid.

60. Ace Atkins, "Taxpayers Likely to Pay Costs of Cleanup," *Tampa Tribune*, January 22, 2000.

61. Blake Fontenay, "Battle Lines Forming over Sea Turtles," *Orlando Sentinel*, July 22, 1995.

62. Blake Fontenay, "U.S. Judge to Hear Beach Driving Case," *Orlando Sentinel*, July 8, 1995.

63. Cory Lancaster, "Turtles Crushed on Road," *Orlando Sentinel*, July 25, 1995.

64. Blake Fontenay, "Driving Banned in Turtles' Territory," *Orlando Sentinel*, August 2, 1995.

65. Blake Fontenay, "Volusia Orders Beach Driving Ban," *Orlando Sentinel*, August 4, 1995.

66. Blake Fontenay, "Judge Delays Trial on Beach Driving," *Orlando Sentinel*, March 2, 1996.

67. Blake Fontenay, "Judge: Volusia Doing OK for Turtles," *Orlando Sentinel*, May 9, 1996.

68. Derek Catron, "Sea Turtle Activists Get Court Victory," *Orlando Sentinel*, August 5, 1998.

69. Derek Catron, "Odds May Be against Volusia's Appeal on Turtles," *Orlando Sentinel*, January 19, 1999; and Derek Catron, "High Court Won't Hear Turtle Lawsuit." *Orlando Sentinel*, April 20, 1999.

70. Derek Catron, "A Dark Walk on the Beach Ends Sea Turtle Suit," *Orlando Sentinel*, June 14, 2000. See also Derek Catron, "Judge: County Doing all It Can for Turtles," *Orlando Sentinel*, May 19, 2000.

71. Marty Rosen, "Infant Disappears from Her Crib," *St. Petersburg Times*, November 25, 1997.

72. Ibid.

73. Ibid.; and Pat Leisner, "FBI Joins Search for Missing Baby," *Miami Herald*, November 26, 1997.

74. Marty Rosen, "Parents of Missing Infant Hire Lawyer," *St. Petersburg Times*, November 27, 1997.

75. Darlene McCormick, "Aisenbergs Avoid Talking to Grand Jury," *Tampa Tribune*, February 5, 1998.

76. Ibid.; Marty Rosen, "Aisenbergs Appear Briefly at Grand Jury," *St. Petersburg Times*, February 12, 1998; and Marty Rosen, "Aisenbergs are 'Subjects' of Grand Jury," *St. Petersburg Times*," February 14, 1998.

77. Daniel Ruth, "Gadzooks! Who Caused that Leak?" *Tampa Tribune*, February 17, 1998; and John Martin, "Events in the Disappearance of Sabrina Aisenberg," *St. Petersburg Times*, September 10, 1999.

78. Richard Danielson, "Search Persists: Family to Move," *St. Petersburg Times*, May 4, 1999.

79. Sarah Huntley, "Baby Sabrina's Parents Indicted, A Seven Count Federal Indictment Accuses the Aisenbergs of Lying about the Disappearance of Their Daughter," *Tampa Tribune*, September 10, 1999.

80. Ibid.

81. Ibid.

82. Ibid.; and Larry Dougherty, Sue Carlton, and Richard Danielson, "Aisenbergs Arrested," *St. Petersburg Times*, September 10, 1999.

83. Michael Fechter, "Aisenberg Case Lawyers Scolded, Told Not to Expect Leniency," *Tampa Tribune*, May 24, 2000.

84. Sarah Huntley, "Judge to Rule on Clarity of Aisenberg Tapes," *Tampa Tribune*, July 18, 2000.

85. Paula Christian, "Aisenberg Recordings 'Largely Inaudible,'" *Tampa Tribune*, November 14, 2000.

86. Paula Christian, "Filings Defend Aisenberg Tapes," *Tampa Tribune*, November 23, 2000.

87. Paula Christian, "Aisenberg Detectives 'Reckless,'" *Tampa Tribune*, February 15, 2001. See also "Judge, Expert Wrangle over Tapes' Quality," *Fort Lauderdale Sun-Sentinel*, December 20, 2000.

88. Paula Christian, "Aisenberg Indictment Scrutinized," *Tampa Tribune*, February 17, 2001; and Paula Christian, "Sabrina Case Collapses," *Tampa Tribune*, February 22, 2001.

89. Graham Brink, "Questions Swirl Aisenberg Case," *St. Petersburg Times*, February 16, 2001.

90. Graham Brink, "Judge Weighs Sum Due to Aisenbergs," *St. Petersburg Times*, October 26, 2002. See also Michael Fechter, "U.S.: Aisenberg Fee Claim Illegal," *Tampa Tribune*, October 23, 2002.

91. Graham Brink, "Aisenberg Bill for Feds: $2.9-Million," *St. Petersburg Times*, February 1, 2003.

92. Ibid.; and Elaine Silvestrini, "Government Gets Breather to Mull Aisenberg Ruling," *Tampa Tribune*, February 6, 2003.

93. Graham Brink, "Judge Orders Release of Aisenberg Transcripts, *St. Petersburg Times*, May 6, 2003; and "Aisenberg Case Justifies Criticism of Government Power," *Tampa Tribune*, May 9, 2003.

94. Elaine Silvestrini, "Government to Appeal Aisenberg Case Ruling," *Tampa Tribune*, February 15, 2003.

95. Elaine Silvestrini, "Aisenbergs' Prosecutors Immune, Judge Rules," *Tampa Tribune*, July 21, 2004.

Chapter 16. "It's a Tidal Wave . . . and I'm Not Kidding about It!"

1. Jacqueline Soteropoulos, "Federal Judges Seek Help," *Tampa Tribune*, December 30, 1996.

2. Ibid.

3. "Testimony Focuses on Judicial Improvements, Judgeships, and Arbitration," *Third Branch*, November 1, 1997. See also Jacqueline Soteropoulos, "Chief Judge Lobbies Congress Again for Caseload Relief," *Tampa Tribune*, May 16, 1997.

4. Mauldin, "Hon. Gerald Bard Tjoflat," 24–28; see also Charlie Patton, "Corrigan Family Making Its Mark," *Florida Times-Union*, February 12, 2007.

5. Pedro Ruz Gutierrrez and Jim Leusner, "Well-Regarded, 'Vibrant' Judge Dies Awaiting Surgery," *Orlando Sentinel*, May 4, 2007; "Magistrate Shares U.S. Legalities: Algeria Learns of Our Love of Judicial Independence," *Orlando Sentinel*, December 12, 2002; and Administrative Office of the U.S. Courts, *Justices and Judges of the United States Courts*, 822.

6. Jim Leusner, "New Orlando Magistrate to Be Picked This Week," *Orlando Sentinel*, July 21, 1997.

7. Karla Spaulding Oral History, 20.

8. Larry Dougherty and Rob Nelson, "Woman Chosen as Magistrate," *St. Petersburg Times*, December 16, 1997.

9. Ibid.; Lara Wozniak, "Professor Teaches What She Practiced," *St. Petersburg Times*, September 30, 1996; and "Mary Scriven," *Tampa Tribune*, January 18, 1992.

10. Larry Dougherty, "Judges to Help Relieve Tampa's Caseload," *St. Petersburg Times*, August 29, 1997; Jacqueline Soteropoulos, "Court Tackles Trial Backlog," *Tampa Tribune*, August 29, 1997; and Allison Thompson, "Colleagues Welcome Return of Judge to City Where He Began," *Florida Times-Union*, March 30, 1997.

11. Jim Leusner, "'Wake-up Call' for Lawyers on Federal-Judge Shortage," *Orlando Sentinel*, March 19, 1998.

12. Larry Dougherty, "Tampa Federal Courts' Caseload Drops with Threat," *St. Petersburg Times*, April 29, 1998.

13. "An Overwhelming Caseload Tests Florida Court," *Third Branch*, August 1, 1999.

14. *Congressional Record*, vol. 143, no. 131, S10051–52, Friday, September 26, 1997, http://www.gpo.gov/fdsys/pkg/CREC-1997-09-26/html/CREC-1997-09-26-pt1-PgS10050.htm.

15. Ibid.

16. Bruce Vielmetti, "Judge Oversees Tampa's New Federal Courthouse," *St. Petersburg Times*, August 23, 1996; and Dougherty, "Judges to Help Relieve Tampa's Civil Caseload."

17. Bob Graham and Connie Mack, "Crushing Load of Cases Await Their Turn," *Tampa Tribune*, December 12, 1997.

18. Steve Otto, "A Lazzara Comes Home," *Tampa Tribune*, October 17, 2004; "Richard A. Lazzara," in *Justices and Judges of the United States Courts*, by Administrative Office of the U.S. Courts, 315; and "Lazzara Deserves Appointment," *Tampa Tribune*, January 7, 1997.

19. Karen Redmond, "Oversight Hearing Shows Increasing Workload Is Straining Resources of Federal Judiciary," *Third Branch*, June 11, 1998.

20. John Dunbar, "Federal Court District Cited as Neediest," *Florida Times-Union*, March 18, 1999.

21. Carl Hulse, "Federal Judge in Florida Pleads for Help on Bench," *Lakeland Ledger*, March 27, 1999.

22. Charlie Whitehead, "New Federal Courthouse Up and Running," *Naples Daily News*, March 23, 1998; and Erinn Hutkin, "New Federal Courthouse Officially Opens," *Naples Daily News*, August 15, 1998.

23. Charlie Whitehead, "Panel Pushing for Full-Time Federal Judge in Fort Myers," *Naples Daily News*, November 18, 1998. See also "Judicial Woes in Fort Myers Point up Problem," *St. Petersburg Times*, January 5, 1998; Eric Pace, "Lee P. Gagliardi, 80, Nixon Aide' Judge," *New York Times*, November 5, 1998; and Mary Kelli Bridges, "District Judge Will Step Down Next Month," *Naples Daily News*, December 6, 1999.

24. Jeff Stidham, "Ben Krentzman, Judge, Dies at 84," *Tampa Tribune*, March 31, 1998.

25. Terry Smiljanich interview with the author, April 26, 2012.

26. Derek L. Kinner, "U.S. Judge Is Retiring," *Florida Times-Union*, April 16, 1999.

27. "A Rare and Deserving U.S. Judge," *Tampa Tribune*, April 30, 1999.

28. Administrative Office of the United States Courts, *Reports of the Proceedings of the Judicial Conference of the United States, 1999*, 43–44.

29. "Opportunity and Challenge: An Interview with Judge Wm. Terrell Hodges," *Third Branch*, July 1, 1999.

30. Jim Leusner, "Controversial Judge Sharp with Cut Back," *Orlando Sentinel*, August 24, 1999.

31. Sarah Huntley, "Top Tampa Prosecutor in Line for Judgeship," *Tampa Tribune*, April 10, 1999.

32. "The Strong Case for Charles Wilson," *Tampa Tribune*, April 15, 1999.

33. Jacqueline Soteropoulos, "Politics Jam 11th Circuit Nomination," *Tampa Tribune*, June 14, 1999.

34. Jacqueline Soteropoulos, "Senate Panel Interviews Wilson for Federal Judgeship," *Tampa Tribune*, July 14, 1999. See also Sarah Huntley, "Wilson's Dream as Clerk Fulfilled," *Tampa Tribune*, August 1, 1999.

35. Susan Clary, "Nomination of Woman Is Milestone," *Orlando Sentinel*, August 11, 1999. See also Derek L. Kinner, "U.S. Attorney Candidate No Jacksonville Newcomer," *Jacksonville Florida-Times Union*, August 12, 1999.

36. Jacqueline Soteropoulos, "Circuit Judge Nominated for Federal Post," *Tampa Tribune*, October 21, 1999; and Catherine Hollingsworth, "State's Middle District Gets Funds for Judges," *Lakeland Ledger*, October 22, 1999.

37. Jacqueline Soteropoulos, "Circuit Judge Nominated," *Tampa Tribune*, October 21, 1999.

38. Ibid.; Bill Adair, "Young Brings Home More Bacon," *St. Petersburg Times*, October 21, 1999; Catherine Hollingsworth, "State's Middle District Gets Funds for Judges," *Lakeland Ledger*, October 22, 1999; "James D. Wittemore," Judge Biography File, FJC; and Gary Sprott, "Judge Gets Federal Recommendation," *Tampa Tribune*, July 29, 1999.

39. Jim Leusner, "Admirers Celebrate Judge's Career," *Orlando Sentinel*, February 19, 2000.

40. Jennifer Maddox, "Tampa Judge Interviewed for Federal Bench," *Naples Daily News*, February 23, 2000.

41. Confirmation Hearings on Federal Appointments, Hearings before the Committee on the Judiciary, 106th Congress, 2nd sess., February 22, March 23, April 27, and May 10, 2000, part 2, no. J-106-33, S. Hrg. 106–399, pt. 2, 194–97.

42. Sarah Hundley, "2 Federal Judgeships Confirmed," *Tampa Tribune*, May 25, 2000; and Molly Justice, "Daytona Beach Judge Approved for Orlando Federal District Court," *Daytona Beach News-Journal*, May 26, 2000.

43. Katherine Rizzo, "Logjam on Confirmations Broken, Conservative Nominee for Elections Panel Is Key," *Miami Herald*, May 25, 2000.

44. "John Antoon," Judge Biography File, FJC; Hundley, "2 Federal Judgeships Confirmed"; "Justice, Daytona Beach Judge Approved for Orlando Federal District Court"; Lynne Bumpus-Hooper, "Lawyers Rate Antoon the Best," *Orlando Sentinel*, May 24, 1988; and "Brevard's Antoon to Fill Appeals Court Opening," *Orlando Sentinel*, June 20, 1995.

45. Carl Hulse, "Panel Sends Names to Mack and Graham," *Lakeland Ledger*, March 1, 2000; and Gary Sprott, "Clinton Fills Bench Slot in Florida's Middle District," *Tampa Tribune*, June 9, 2000.

46. Bill Rufty, "For Judges, Senators Buck System: To Help the Middle District, Graham and Mack Ignore Protocol," *Lakeland Ledger*, July 3, 2000.

47. Confirmation Hearings on Federal Appointments, Hearings before the Committee on the Judiciary, 106th Congress, 2nd sess., July 12, 2000, part 3, no. J-106-33, S. Hrg. 106–399, pt. 3, 611–16; and Sarah Huntley, "3 Federal Judges Confirmed for Florida," *Tampa Tribune*, July 22, 2000.

48. Huntley, "3 Federal Judges Confirmed for Florida."

49. Mike Oliver, "High-Profile Lawyer Has Low Profile," *Orlando Sentinel*, February 22, 1993. See also Moran, "Hon. Gregory A. Presnell," 42–43; and Gregory Presnell interview with the author, May 15, 2012.

50. Karie Partington, "One of Three New Judges to Be Assigned to Fort Myers," *Naples Daily News*, July 22, 2000. See also Mary Kelli Bridges, "Fort Myers: First Full-Time Federal Judge," *Naples Daily News*, July 28, 2000; and "Fort Myers First Full-Time U.S. District Judge Sworn into Office," *Naples Daily News*, July 29, 2000.

51. Mary Kelli Bridges, "Judge Named to Fill Fort Myers Vacancy," *Naples Daily News*, November 8, 1999. See also Bruce Vielmetti, "Reno Names Interim U.S. Attorney for Tampa," *St. Petersburg Times*, June 16, 1993.

52. Suevon Lee, "Jones Move Leaves Vacancy," *Ocala Star-Banner*, September 27, 2010.

53. Jim Schoettler and Bruce I. Friedland, "Bipartisan Effort Earns Judgeships," *Florida Times-Union*, August 29, 2000. See also Chris Hand, "Graham and Mack Restore Faith in Bipartisanship," *Orlando Sentinel*, October 8, 2000.

54. Russomanno, "Florida's Winning Team."

55. Elizabeth Kovachevich Oral History, 33.

Chapter 17. Into the New Century, 2000–2004

1. Brands, *America since 1945*, 296–98.

2. Molly Justice, "Manual Recount Can't Be Discounted, "*Daytona Beach News-Journal*, November 15, 2000; see also Greene, *Understanding the 2000 Election*, 76–78. See also Pleasants, *Hanging Chads*.

3. *Touchston, Shepperd et al. v. McDermott and McFall* (2000), http://www.floridasupremecourt.org/pub_info/election/EleventhCircuitB.pdf.

4. Paula Christian, "Tampa Courtrooms Close: Security Tightens after Attack," *Tampa Tribune*, September 12, 2001.

5. Bush, quoted in Brands, *America since 1945*, 305.

6. Julie Kay, "Florida Republicans Look to Put Stamp on Judiciary with Picks to Panels," *Miami Daily Business Review*, April 9, 2001; and Cory Reiss, "Judicial Fight May Be in Store; Florida Senators Will Soon Get a Look at Selections of a GOP Committee," *Lakeland Ledger*, July 8, 2001.

7. David Karp, "Faded Grandeur Holds New Promise," *St. Petersburg Times*, September 25, 2003.

8. Linda Chion-Kenney, "Buzzards' Judgment: It's Home," *St. Petersburg Times*, December 24, 1998. See also "Leaky Glass Ceiling Latest Glitch at New Courthouse," *St. Petersburg Times*, May 29, 1998.

9. David Pedreira, "A Shock for the Flock," *St. Petersburg Times*, October 27, 1999.

10. Shannon Colavecchio-Van Sickler, "Courthouse Maintains Costly Ways," *St.*

Petersburg Times, April 4, 2006; and Kevin Graham and Drew Harwell, "Courthouse Sickens Nelson," *St. Petersburg Times*, February 17, 2009.

11. Mary Bridges, "Federal Courthouse: Building's 'Illness' May be Passed on to Employees," *Naples Daily News*, August 24, 2001; and "Health Concerns Prompt Examination: Middle District of FL," *Third Branch*, September 2001.

12. Jim Schoettler, "Judges Seek Ruling on Courthouse," *Florida Times-Union*, December 4, 2001.

13. Sean Holton, "Money Comes through for U.S. Courthouse," *Orlando Sentinel*, October 3, 1996; Jim Leusner and Sherri Owens, "New Land War Starts over Site for Courthouse," *Orlando Sentinel*, March 18, 1998; and Jim Leusner, "'Wake-Up Call' for Lawyers on Federal-Judge," *Orlando Sentinel*, March 19, 1998.

14. Susan Clary, "Anger over Courthouse Won't Die," *Orlando Sentinel*, February 2, 2001. See also Roger Roy and Gwyneth K. Shaw, "Judges Object to Designs for Federal Courthouses," *Orlando Sentinel*, October 4, 2000.

15. Susan Clary, "Courthouse Verdict: Wow!" *Orlando Sentinel*, August 11, 2001.

16. David Damron, "Courthouse Wins over Its Critics," *Orlando Sentinel*, August 23, 2001.

17. Henry Pierson Curtis, "Structurally Unsound: Federal Courthouse Cracks," *Orlando Sentinel*, February 14, 2002.

18. Pedro Ruz Gutierrez, "Judge Trades in Robe for an Apron," *Orlando Sentinel*, June 17, 2005. See also David Damron, "House Moves Orlando's New Federal Courthouse a Step Closer to Reality," *Orlando Sentinel*, February 14, 2003; Henry Pierson Curtis, "Officials Launch New Courthouse," *Orlando Sentinel*, April 6, 2004.

19. Jim Leusner, "Judges' New Home Sparkles," *Orlando Sentinel*, August 27, 2007.

20. Jim Leusner, "6 Stories of Service to Justice," *Orlando Sentinel*, September 22, 2007.

21. Jim Schoettler, "A Lawyer, a Leader and a Public Servant Federal Prosecutor Combines Compassion with Love of Country, the Law," *Florida Times-Union*, July 24, 2000.

22. "Clouds over U.S. Attorney's Office," *Tampa Tribune*, December 27, 1999; Richard Danielson, "Bar Seeks Two-Year Suspension for Prosecutor," *St. Petersburg Times*, December 31, 1999; and Pat Leisner, "Drug Case Dropped Due to 'Moral Tarnish,'" *Miami Herald*, February 27, 2000.

23. Gary Sprott, "Panel Selects 3 Finalists for U.S. Attorney," *Tampa Tribune*, June 27, 2001.

24. Jim Schoettler and Paul Pinkham, "Jacksonville Man Appears Pick for U.S. Attorney," *Florida Times-Union*, October 19, 2001.

25. Henry Curtis, "U.S. Attorney Nomination Is Latest Twist in Road to Success," *Orlando Sentinel*, March 5, 2002.

26. Derek L. Kinner, "Prosecutor of Convictions," *Florida Times-Union*, December 26, 1998.

27. Paula Christian, "U.S. Attorney Makes Shifts in Management System," *Tampa Tribune*, May 3, 2002. See also Curtis, "U.S. Attorney Nomination Is Latest Twist in Road to Success"; Jim Schoettler, "U.S. Attorney's Office Has Jacksonville Flavor, Perez Sworn In, Klindt to be his First Assistant," *Florida Times-Union*, March 19, 2002; and Michael Fechter, "Ashcroft to Talk Terror in Tampa," *Tampa Tribune*, November 20, 2002.

28. Graham Brink, "Marshal Candidates Line up, out of the Spotlight," *St. Petersburg*

Times, May 13, 2001; "Former Citrus Sheriff Finalist for U.S. Marshal," *St. Petersburg Times*, January 15, 2002; Lucy Morgan, "U.S. Marshal Finalists Win Support," *St. Petersburg Times*, January 21, 2002; and Lucy Morgan, "Graham Removes Blockade on Marshals, Judge Approvals," *St. Petersburg Times*, March 13, 2003.

29. Jim Schoettler, "Judge Denies New Delay in Waldon Case," *Florida Times-Union*, March 12, 2002; Jim Schoettler, "Waldon Defense Requests Assailed Prosecutors Say They Have No Merit," *Florida Times-Union*, September 11, 2002; and Jim Schoettler, "The U.S. against the Cop Karl Walden, a Former Jacksonville Officer, Faces Trial in a 1998 Slaying and other Crimes," *Florida Times-Union*, September 29, 2002.

30. Jim Schoettler, "Ex-cop Says Peer Admitted Slaying Defense to Highlight Conflicts in Testimony," *Florida Times-Union*, October 16, 2002.

31. Jim Schoettler, "Witness Recounts Safar's Slaying Plot Went Insane, McLaughlin Says," *Florida Times-Union*, October 18, 2002.

32. Jim Schoettler, "Waldon Guilty on 14 Counts, Former Cop Could Face Death Penalty, Jury Returns on Tuesday for Sentencing Phase," *Florida Times-Union*, November 7, 2002; Jim Schoettler, "Waldon Avoids Death Penalty, Cop Killer Headed for Life in Prison," *Florida Times-Union*, November 14, 2002.

33. Jim Schoettler, "5 Sentenced in Crime Spree with Former Cop, Judge Grants Leniency for Help," *Florida Times-Union*, January 22, 2003; "Ashcroft Honors Prosecutor," *Orlando Sentinel*, November 15, 2003; and Jim Schoettler, "Waldon Prosecutor Wins Prestigious Honor," *Florida Times-Union*, November 15, 2003.

34. Brigid O'Malley, "Edison Found Guilty of Extortion Charges: The Jury Acquitted Edison of One Count of Conspiring of Distribute Cocaine," *Naples Daily News*, February 1, 2001. See also Brigid O'Malley, "Tearful Edison Gets 14-Year Sentence," *Naples Daily News*, May 3, 2001.

35. Pedro Ruz Gutierrez, "Former Housing Authority Accountant Gets Prison," *Orlando Sentinel*, January 22, 2005.

36. Elaine Silvestrini, "Ryan Testifies LaBrake Traded Bids for Favors," *Tampa Tribune*, November 11, 2004.

37. Brad Smith, "Sentenced," *Tampa Tribune*, February 26, 2005.

38. Ibid. See also Silvestrini, "Ryan Testifies LaBrake Traded Bids"; and Elaine Silvestrini, "Jury Picked for LaBrake Trial," *Tampa Tribune*, November 2, 2004.

39. David Karp, "Judges Discuss Use of Cameras as Camera Rolls," *St. Petersburg Times*, September 29, 2001.

40. "Magistrate Nominated," *Orlando Sentinel*, May 24, 2002; "Corrigan Confirmed," *Florida Times-Union*, September 14, 2002; Charlie Patton, "Corrigan Family Making Its Mark," *Florida Times-Union*, February 12, 2007; and Nomination of Timothy J. Corrigan, of Florida, to Be United States District Judge for the Middle District of Florida, *Congressional Record-Senate*, September 12, 2002, S8510–15.

41. "Another Honor for Judge Hodges," *Tampa Tribune*, August 26, 2003.

42. Jessie-Lynne Kerr, "Nimmons, Federal Judge, Dies at 65, Longtime Jurist also Served in State Courts," *Florida Times-Union*, November 25, 2003.

43. Kristen Zambo, "Fort Myers Judge Believed to Have Heaviest Caseload," *Naples Daily News*, March 29, 2004.

44. Mary Kelli Bridges, "Fort Myers Begins Search for Second Magistrate," *Naples Daily News*, October 2, 2002.

45. Reginald Luster, "New Magistrates Sworn In," *Jacksonville News and Daily Record*, November 3, 2003.

46. U.S. Judicial Nominee from Tampa"; and "Judge Virginia M. Hernandez Covington," Judge Biography File, FJC

47. "Nomination of Virginia Maria Hernandez Covington to Be United States District Judge for the Middle District of Florida," *Congressional Record: Senate*, September 7, 2004, S8832–33, S8836.

48. Valerie Kalfrin, "Senate Confirms Tampa Native to Serve as U.S. District Judge," *Tampa Tribune*, September 9, 2004. See also Jason Geary, "Covington Becomes A Federal Judge," *Lakeland Ledger*, September 11, 2004.

49. Paul Pinkham, "Senate Oks Bush Choice for Judgeship," *Florida Times-Union*, September 9 2004.

50. Richard Lazzara Oral History, 26.

51. "Awards," *11th Circuit Historical News* 2 (December 2005).

Chapter 18. Contesting Sentencing Guidelines, the Patriot Act, Terrorism, and Cases Involving International Questions

1. Gregory Presnell interview with the author, May 15, 2012; Mike Oliver, "High Profile Lawyer Has Low Profile," *Orlando Sentinel*, February 22, 1993; see also Susan Clary, "Lawyers Have Their Say about Federal Judges," *Orlando Sentinel*, September 8, 2002.

2. Thomas W. Krause, "It's Hand to Hand Combat," *Tampa Tribune*, June 8, 2006; Pedro Ruz Gutierrez, "Who Needs Law School? Judge Resorts to Child's Play," *Orlando Sentinel*, June 8, 2006; Carrie Weimar, "Rock, Paper, Scissors, and Gavel Will Settle It," *St. Petersburg Times*, June 8, 2006; and Thomas W. Krause, "Judge Calls off Rock, Paper, Scissors Game," *Tampa Tribune*, June 28, 2006.

3. Weimar, "Rock, Paper, Scissors."

4. Moran, "Hon. Gregory A. Presnell," 43.

5. Gregory Presnell interview with the author, May 15, 2012.

6. *U.S. v. Hamilton*, No. 6:05-cr-157-Orl-31JGG (M.D. Fla. March 16, 2006). Presnell, quoted in "Judge Presnell on Crack/Powder Disparity," *Sentencing Law and Policy*, March 16, 2006, http://sentencing.typepad.com/sentencing_law_and_policy/2006/03/judge_presnell_.html.

7. K. Graham, "Nearly 1,500 Fla. Crack Offenders Eligible for Early Release," *St. Petersburg Times*, March 4, 2008.

8. Burke, *Becoming President*, 185–86.

9. Paul I. Perez, "USA Patriot Act Improves Efforts at Counter Terrorism," *St. Petersburg Times*, September 4, 2003. See rebuttals in *St. Petersburg Times*, September 9, 2003. See also Henry Pierson Curtis, "USA Patriot Act Is Defended, Derided at Law School Debate," *Orlando Sentinel*, March 31, 2004; Paul Perez, "Patriot Act Protects Civil Liberties While Defending Our Nation," *St. Petersburg Times*, June 4, 2005; and Paul Perez, "In Defense of the Patriot Act," *Tampa Tribune*, February 5, 2006.

10. Pedro Ruz Gutierrez, "Judges Debate Patriot Act Use," *Orlando Sentinel*, March 12, 2006.

11. Henry Pierson Curtis, "Judges Unafraid to Side with Accused over Cops," *Orlando Sentinel*, May 9, 2004.

12. Henry Pierson Curtis, "Debate over Tape Sparks Courtroom Heat," *Orlando Sentinel*, April 10, 2002; Henry Pierson Curtis, "Old Recordings a Factor in Judge's Decision to Overturn Conviction," *Orlando Sentinel*, May 24, 2002; Henry Pierson Curtis, "Judge Orders Release of Accused Drug Dealer," *Orlando Sentinel*, June 26, 2002; "Drug Suspect's Release Denied," *Orlando Sentinel*, July 2, 2002; Henry Pierson Curtis, "Judges OK Drug Conviction," *Orlando Sentinel*, November 22, 2002; and Gregory Presnell Oral History, 18.

13. Henry Pierson Curtis, "Federal Judges Blast Trial's Prosecution," *Orlando Sentinel*, January 17, 2004.

14. Henry Pierson Curtis, "U.S. Asks Judge to Toss Drug Conviction," *Orlando Sentinel*, May 19, 2004.

15. Henry Pierson Curtis, "Judge Tosses Brevard Man's Convictions," *Orlando Sentinel*, October 2, 2004.

16. Brad Heath and Kevin McCoy, "Prosecutors' Conduct Can Tip Justice Scales," *USA Today*, September 23, 2010; Scott Gunnerson, "Justice Department Agrees to Pay $140,000 to May Wrongly Jailed," *USA Today*, March 15, 2012; and Gregory Presnell Oral History, 18–19.

17. Buddy Jaudon, "Key Developments," *Tampa Tribune*, February 21, 2003; and Michael Fechter, "Citizenship Denied for USF Professor," *Tampa Tribune*, October 3, 1996.

18. Jaudon, "Key Developments"; Ben Feller, "Al-Arian to Get Hearing in Federal Court," *Tampa Tribune*, November 20, 2002; Graham Brink, "Judge to Decide Next Step for Al-Arian Case," *St. Petersburg Times*, December 13, 2002; Rachel La Corte, "USF Suit against Professor Rejected," *Orlando Sentinel*, December 17, 2002; and Steve Cavendish et al. "Building a Case: Ties to Terror," *St. Petersburg Times*, February 21, 2003.

19. Phil Long and Gail Epstein Nieves, "Professor Named in Terror Plot," *Miami Herald*, February 21, 2003.

20. Elaine Silvestrini, "Al-Arian Wins Bail Hearing Delay," *Tampa Tribune*, February 26, 2003.

21. Graham Brink and Brady Dennis, "Judge Denies Bail to Al-Arian," *St. Petersburg Times*, April 11, 2003.

22. Elaine Silvestrini, "Money Spells Defense," *Tampa Tribune*, March 20, 2003.

23. William March, "Al-Arian Trial Postponed from January Until April," *Tampa Tribune*, November 13, 2004; and Elaine Silvestrini, "Al-Arian Jury Pool Cut from 46 to 35," *Tampa Tribune*, May 17, 2005.

24. Elaine Silvestrini and Michael Fechter, "Both Sides Bring up Jihad," *Tampa Tribune*, June 7, 2005.

25. Pedro Guttierez, "Professor's Case Shows Role of Feds after Sept. 11," *Orlando Sentinel*, November 14, 2005.

26. Pedro Ruz Gutierez, "Al-Arian Acquitted on 8 Terror Counts—Trial Tests Power of Patriot Act After 9/11," *Orlando Sentinel*, December 7, 2005.

27. Pedro Ruz Gutierez, "Al-Arian's Fate Remains up in the Air—Though Not Convicted on Terror Charges, He May Be Deported—or Retried," *Orlando Sentinel*, December 8, 2005.

28. Elaine Silvestrini, "Al-Arian—Admits Role—in Jihad," *Tampa Tribune*, April 18, 2006.

29. Meg Laughlin, "Judge Sentences Al-Arian to Limit," *St. Petersburg Times*, May 2, 2006.

30. Pedro Ruz Gutierrez, "Al-Arian Receives Maximum Sentence, during Sentencing Hearing, Judge Assails Fired Professor as a 'Master Manipulator,'" *Orlando Sentinel*, May 2, 2006.

31. Ibid.

32. Chris W. Colby, "Former Naples Resident Receives Prison Sentence for Posing as FBI Agent to Steal from Immigrants," *Naples Daily News*, May 21, 2003.

33. Henry Pierson Curtis, "Maali Loses Early Round," *Orlando Sentinel*, August 11, 2004.

34. Ibid.; and Pedro Ruz Gutierrez, "Judge: Maali Charged Fairly," *Orlando Sentinel*, September 30, 2004.

35. Pedro Ruz Gutierrez, "I-Drive's Maali Dies of Cancer," *Orlando Sentinel*, January 23, 2004

36. Ibid.; and Pedro Ruz Gutierrez, "Maali Associates Get Prison Time in Fraud Case," *Orlando Sentinel*, September 3, 2005.

37. "Florida's Slave Laborers," *St. Petersburg Times*, July 24, 2005; and Wan J. Kim and Paul Perez, "Justice Marshaling Resources against Human Trafficking," *Tampa Tribune*, August 6, 2006.

38. Kati Bexley, Marcia Lane, and Madelyn Troyanek, "Feds Bust East Palatka Labor Camp," *St. Augustine Record*, June 6, 2005; "More Charges against Palatka Area Farm Labor Contender," *St. Augustine Record*, July 16, 2005; "Evans Pleads Guilty to Conspiracy," *Florida Times-Union*, July 13, 2006; Matt Galnor, "Camp Owner Found Guilty," *Florida Times-Union*, August 26, 2006; and "East Palatka Labor Camp Owner's Wife Sentenced," *St. Augustine Record*, February 9, 2007.

39. Christine Stapleton and John Lanitigua, "Growers Housing for Migrant Workers Illegal, Judge Rules," *Palm Beach Post*, May 18, 2007; and J. Lantigua, "Ag-Mart Ordered to Pay $500,000," *Palm Beach Post*, September 27, 2007.

40. Charles Seabrook, "Illegal Animal Trade Lucrative for Smugglers," *Palm Beach Post*, December 21, 2003.

41. Henry Pierson Curtis, "Engineer Sentenced in Fake-Money Case," *Orlando Sentinel*, October 15, 2003.

42. Larry Dougherty, "Ruling Strips Man of Citizenship," *St. Petersburg Times*, August 18, 1998. See also Sarah Huntley, "After 57 Years, Nazi Chase Lives on in U.S.," *Tampa Tribune*, August 23, 1998.

43. Carrie Weimar, "Serb's Case Ends in Mistrial," *St. Petersburg Times*, June 12, 2007; "Federal Charges against Serb Dropped," *St. Petersburg Times*, September 27, 2007; and Luis Perez, "Former St. Petersburg Resident Accused of War Crimes in Bosnia Is Deported," *Tampa Bay Times*, January 16, 2011.

44. Brian Baxter, "Covington Helps Spain Sink Salvage Claims in Shipwreck Suit," *American Lawyer*, June 8, 2009.

45. Ibid.; and Mitch Stacy, "Confidentiality Sought in Treasure Case," *Key West Citizen*, November 27, 2007.

46. Mitch Stacy, "Explorers Told to Give Loot to Spain—But Judge's Decision Likely Not Final Word," *Fort Lauderdale Sun-Sentinel*, June 6, 2009; see also "Odyssey Marine Exploration Opposes Black Swan Decision," *Sarasota Gulf Coast Business Review*, June 26, 2009.

47. James Thorner, "Judge Rules against Odyssey," *St. Petersburg Times*, December 24, 2009.

48. *U.S. v. Christopher J. Benbow*, (11th Cir. 2008); and Jenifer Liberto, "International Drug Sting Lands 4 in County Jail," *St. Petersburg Times*, July 15, 2005.

49. "Man Sentenced after Trying to Peddle Radioactive Materials," *Florida Times-Union*, February 3, 2007; and Elaine Silvestrini, "British National Gets Prison Term in 'Dirty Bomb' Case," *Tampa Tribune*, April 24, 2009. For the details of this interesting international case, see Thomas, *Secret Wars*.

50. Paula Christian, "Captain of Decoy Boat Guilty on Drug Charges," *Tampa Tribune*, April 20, 2002.

Chapter 19. Constitutional Questions of the Twenty-First-Century Court

1. Jon Steinman, "Attorney: Rave Rules Right to Dance," *Orlando Sentinel*, September 7, 2001; see also "Rave Ordinance Stands," *Orlando Sentinel*, September 19, 2001.

2. "Battle Plan against Nude Clubs Must Include Proof of Harm," *Tampa Tribune*, February 2, 2006; see also John Bozzo, "Daytona Beach Struggles with Nude Dancing," *Daytona Beach News-Journal*, February 13, 2005.

3. Pedro Ruz Gutierrez, "Dancers Get More Artistic Freedom," *Orlando Sentinel*, April 5, 2007.

4. Jeffrey C. Billman, "Features," *Orlando Sentinel*, April 5, 2007.

5. Jeff Brumley, "Cross off Starke's Water Tower: A Federal Judge Rules the Lighted Christian Symbol Endorses Religion," *Florida Times-Union*, March 23, 2007.

6. Lise Fisher, "Judge Rules Starke Must Keep Cross off Water Tower," *Gainesville Sun*, March 22, 2007.

7. Chad Smith, "Judge Rules against District," *St. Augustine Record*, April 16, 2009.

8. Jenna Deopere, "Attorney to Refile School Uniform Suit," *Lakeland Ledger*, January 16, 2001; and Jenna Deopere, "Judge Refuses to Drop Lawsuit," *Lakeland Ledger*, April 8, 2001.

9. Jenna Deopere, "Judge Hears School Uniform Case," *Lakeland Ledger*, July 18, 2001.

10. Deborah Alberto, "Magistrate Finds School Uniforms Legal," *Tampa Tribune*, August 14, 2001.

11. Ibid.

12. Richard Peacock, "Judge Kills School Dress Code Lawsuit, *Lakeland Ledger*, November 19, 2002.

13. Carrie Weimar, "Judge to Bucs: No More Fan Patdowns," *St. Petersburg Times*, July 29, 2006.

14. Carrie Weimar, "Got Bucs Tickets? Get a Free Patdown," *St. Petersburg Times*, June 27, 2007.

15. Robbyn Mitchell, "Wand Searches Now Required For Fans at Tampa Bay Buccaneers Games," *Tampa Bay Times*, August 17, 2012.

16. Mark Pino, "Federal Lawsuit Could Delay Osceola Elections," *Orlando Sentinel*,

June 21, 2006; see also Mark Pino, "Judge Postpones Osceola Elections," *Orlando Sentinel*, June 27, 2006.

17. Mark Pino, "Osceola Leaders Reject Hispanic-Voting Ruling," *Orlando Sentinel*, June 28, 2006.

18. Mark Pino, "Voting Trial in Osceola Postponed 2 Months," *Orlando Sentinel*, July 8, 2006; and "Get on with It—Our Position: Osceola Has No More Reason to Stall," *Orlando Sentinel*, September 23, 2006.

19. Mark Pino and Daphne Sashin, "Judge Wants New Osceola Voting Plan in 5 Weeks," *Orlando Sentinel*, October 19, 2006.

20. Mark Pino, "Federal Judge Will Decide Merits of Osceola Vote Plan," *Orlando Sentinel*, December 7, 2006; Mark Pino, "Judge Ponders Osceola Case," *Orlando Sentinel*, December 8, 2006; and Mark Pino, "Changes Engulf Us," *Orlando Sentinel*, December 31, 2006.

21. David Sommer, "Fate of Comatose Wife in Federal Judge's Hands," *Tampa Tribune*, April 20, 2001; and David Sommer, "Judge Grants Parents 3 Days to Appeal Daughter's Right-to-Die Case," *Tampa Tribune*, April 21, 2001.

22. Graham Brink, "Schiavo's Parents Rebuffed By Judge," *St. Petersburg Times*, September 3, 2003; "Hearing Set in Feed-Tube Case," *Orlando Sentinel*, September 24, 2003; and "Short Life, Long Fight," *Tampa Tribune*, April 1, 2005.

23. David Sommer, "Governor Backs Bid to Wean Schiavo from Feeding Tube," *Tampa Tribune*, October 8, 2003. See also Sean Mussenden and Maya Bell, "Disabled Woman Will Get Guardian, Feeding Tube Reinserted, Schiavo Returns to Hospice," *Orlando Sentinel*, October 23, 2003.

24. David Sommer, "Judge Won't Rule on Schiavo," *Tampa Tribune*, October 11, 2003.

25. Mussenden and Bell, "Disabled Woman Will Get Guardian."

26. "Short Life, Long Fight."

27. Phil Long, Cara Buckley, and Martin Merzer, "Tube Stays out as Judge Deliberates," *Miami Herald*, March 22, 2005.

28. "Short Life, Long Fight"; Noah Bierman, "Judge's Style Is by the Book," *Miami Herald*, March 22, 2005; and David G. Savage, "Judge Faces Dilemma," *Orlando Sentinel*, March 22, 2005.

29. Noah Beirman and Scott Hiassen, "Schindlers' Court Fight Complicated," *Miami Herald*, March 23, 2005.

30. Alessandro Rizzo, "Removing Schiavo's Tube 'Capital Punishment,'" *Miami Herald*, March 23, 2005.

31. Jesse J. Holland, "Not all Leaders Agree with Law," *Miami Herald*, March 23, 2005.

32. Wes Smith and Sean Mussenden, "New Ruling Sparks Appeal," *Fort Lauderdale Sun-Sentinel*, March 23, 2005.

33. Phil Long, Erika Bolstad, Martin Merzer, "Schiavo in 'Death Process,'" *Miami Herald*, March 25, 2005.

34. Steve Bousquet, "Judicial Comments Sets Crist Apart," *St. Petersburg Times*, July 31, 2005.

35. Curt Anderson, "Ashcroft Urges Tallying of Judge's Lenient Sentences," *Orlando Sentinel*, August 8, 2003.

36. Justin George and Colleen Jenkins, "U.S. Attorney Resigns for New Job," *St. Petersburg Times*, March 14, 2007.

37. Ibid.

38. Mark K. Matthews and Pedro Ruz Gutierrez, "Nelson Seeks Inquiry of Prosecutor's Exit—U.S. Attorney Denies Connection to Dismissals," *Fort Lauderdale South Florida Sun-Sentinel*, March 27, 2007.

39. Pedro Ruz Gutierrez, "Orlando Native to be Area's Top U.S. Prosecutor," *Orlando Sentinel*, March 28, 2007.

40. Elaine Silvestrini, "Acting U.S. Attorney Picked for District," *Tampa Tribune*, March 28, 2007.

41. Jim Leusner, "Attorney Post Has Few Takers," *Orlando Sentinel*, May 30, 2007.

42. Ibid.

43. Carrie Weimar, "Small Field Applies for Job of U.S. Attorney," *St. Petersburg Times*, June 18, 2007.

44. Billy House, "Acting U.S. Attorney's Term Ending," *Tampa Tribune*, October 23, 2007; see also Paul Pinkham, "Revolving Door for Federal Prosecutor Continues, Democrats Say White House Is Stalling on U.S. Attorney Vacancies," *Florida Times-Union*, October 26, 2007.

45. David Ball, "The Court's Ace on the Mound: Hundreds Welcome Jacksonville's Newest Federal Judge to the Bench," *Jacksonville Financial News and Daily Record*, April 14, 2008.

46. Elaine Silvestrini and Billy House, "Veteran Prosecutor Named Interim U.S. Attorney, *Tampa Tribune*, October 27, 2007. See also Kevin Graham, "White House Taps New Interim U.S. Attorney," *St. Petersburg Times*, October 27, 2007.

47. Kevin Graham, "Albritton Chosen for U.S. Attorney," *St. Petersburg Times*, July 16, 2008.

48. William March, "Tampa Man Picked for U.S. Attorney," *Tampa Tribune*, July 16, 2008.

49. Marcia Morales Howard, Judge Biography Files, FJC; "Maria Morales Howard to Be United States District Judge for the Middle District of Florida, February 15, 2007," *Congressional Record—Senate*, S1986–88; and *Florida Times-Union*, February 21, 2007.

50. Elaine Silvestrini, "36 Step up for 2 Open Federal Judgeships," *Tampa Tribune*, November 12, 2007.

51. Mike Brassfield, "Magistrate Picked for Judgeship," *St. Petersburg Times*, July 11, 2008.

52. Billy House, "Senate Committee Quizzes Scriven for U.S. Judge Post," *Tampa Tribune*, September 10, 2008; "Nomination of Mary Stenson Scriven," September 26, 2008, *Congressional Record—Senate*, S9592–93; and Billy House, "Senate Approves Scriven for U.S. District Judgeship," *Tampa Tribune*, September 26, 2008.

53. Pedro Ruz Gutierrez and Jim Leusner, "Well-Regarded, 'Vibrant Judge Dies Awaiting Surgery," *Orlando Sentinel*, May 4, 2007; and Jim Leusner, "Veteran Civil-Trial Lawyer Takes Post," *Orlando Sentinel*, July 12, 2008.

54. Paul Pinkham, "Courthouse to Have Late Judge's Name," *Florida Times-Union*, May 18, 2004

55. Wilhelm, "Courthouse Named after Civil Rights 'Pioneer,'" *Jacksonville News and Daily Record*, August 12, 2008.

56. Kay, "New Chief Judge to Start."

57. *Tyne v. Time Warner*, 204 F. Supp. 2d 1338 (M.D. Fla. 2002).

58. Lynch, "Hon. Anne Conway," 24–28.

Chapter 20. Income Tax Evasion, Medicare Fraud, Organized Crime, Environmental Disputes, and Bankruptcy

1. Mabel Perez, "Snipes Wanted for Tax Fraud," *Ocala Star-Banner*, October 18, 2006.

2. Mabel Perez, "Snipes's Tax Trial Will Be Held in Ocala," *Ocala Star-Banner*, September 9, 2007.

3. Rick Cundiff, "Snipes Trial: Attorneys Debate Part Actor Played," *Ocala Star-Banner*, January 17, 2008.

4. Ibid.

5. Rick Cundiff, "Snipes' Ex-Advisors Testify in Tax Evasion Trial," *Ocala Star-Banner*, January 18, 2008. See also Joe Van Hoose, "All-White Jury Seated for Snipes," *Ocala Star-Banner*, January 16, 2008.

6. Stephen Hudak, "3 Years in Slammer for Wesley Snipes," *Orlando Sentinel*, April 25, 2008

7. Ibid.; and Suevon Lee, "Judge to Snipes: It's Prison Time," *Gainesville Sun*, November 19, 2010.

8. Mike Saewitz, "M. D. Charged, but Practices On," *Sarasota Herald-Tribune*, May 19, 2005.

9. Susan Taylor Martin, "Dermatologist Barred from Surgery," *St. Petersburg Times*, June 16, 2005.

10. Mike Saewitz, "Records: Doctor Had Surgery Quota; Michael Rosin Told Employees He Needed to Make $10,000 a Day," *Sarasota Herald Tribune*, May 6, 2005; and Mike Saewitz, "Friends See a Totally Different Michael Rosin," *Sarasota Herald Tribune*, June 16, 2005.

11. Todd Ruger, "Rosin Guilty of Defrauding Medicare," *Sarasota Herald-Tribune*, March 4, 2006; and Todd Ruger, "Dr. Rosin Sentenced to 22 Years," *Sarasota Herald-Tribune*, October 5, 2006.

12. *U.S. v. Michael A. Rosin* (11th Cir. 2008).

13. Dana Willhoit, "Doctor's Sentencing Rescheduled," *Lakeland Ledger*, May 12, 2007.

14. Ibid.; and Dana Willhoit, "Doctor Faces Years in Jail for Fraud," *Lakeland Ledger*, June 1, 2007.

15. Carrie Weimar, "Throwback: Tampa Mob Trial," *St. Petersburg Times*, October 16, 2006.

16. Lenny Savino, "Defendant Keeps Attorney with Gambino Family Ties," *Tampa Tribune*, May 26, 2006; and Carrie Weimar, "Accused in Mob Plot, Man to Help Prosecutors," *St. Petersburg Times*, September 27, 2006.

17. Colleen Jenkins, "Mob Trial Defendant to Represent Self," *St. Petersburg Times*, October 17, 2006; Elaine Silvestrini, "Mob Suspect Hands Case to Lawyer," *Tampa Tribune*, October 20, 2006; and Carrie Weimar, "Racketeering, Extortion Trial Close to Jury Phase," *St. Petersburg Times*, November 21, 2006.

18. Elaine Silvestrini, "Persistent Jury Convicts 4," *Tampa Tribune*, November 30, 2006. See also Carrie Weimar, "All 4 Guilty in Mob Trial," *St. Petersburg Times*, November 30, 2006.

19. Carrie Weimar, "Trucchio Receives Life Sentence," *St. Petersburg Times*, March 3, 2007; Carrie Weimar, "Mobster Avoids a Long Term," *St. Petersburg Times*, March 28, 2007; and Thomas W. Krause, "Scaglione—Gets 5 Years," *Tampa Tribune*, March 28, 2007.

20. Kevin Graham, "Tampa Loses Gotti Case to New York," *St. Petersburg Times*, December 3, 2008.

21. "Defensive Linemen in Black Robes," *St. Petersburg Times*, November 27, 2005.

22. Greg Martin, "Judge Halts Mosaic Mine," *Port Charlotte Sun*, July 3, 2010. See also Craig Pittman, "Phosphate Mine Expansion Halted," *St. Petersburg Times*, July 2, 2010; and Kevin Bouffard, "Mosaic Warns Layoffs," *Lakeland Ledger*, July 13, 2010.

23. Martin, "Judge Halts Mosaic Mine."

24. Greg Martin, "Judge Suggests Mediation in Mine Lawsuit," *Port Charlotte Sun*, July 25, 2010; and Kate Spinner, "Mosaic Reaches Settlement over Fort Meade Mine," *Sarasota Herald-Tribune*, February 21, 2012.

25. Curtis Morgan, "Judge's Endangered Species Ruling Aids Builders," *Miami Herald*, July 13, 2007. See also Phil Davis, "Judge: Complete Review of Endangered Species," *Fort Lauderdale Sun-Sentinel*, July 13, 2007.

26. Jay Stapleton, "News-Journal Directors Fired, *Daytona Beach News-Journal*, April 30, 2009; and Etan Horowitz and Ludmilla Lelis, "Newspaper CEO Brings Art Dream to Life," *Orlando Sentinel*, January 27, 2006.

27. Horowitz and Lelis, "Newspaper CEO Brings Arts Dream to Life."

28. Ibid.; and Etan Horowitz, "*News-Journal* Feud Is Now up to Judge to Decide," *Orlando Sentinel*, December 16, 2005.

29. Horowitz and Lelis, "Newspaper CEO Brings Arts Dream to Life"; and Etan Horowitz, "*News-Journal* Feud Is Now up to Judge to Decide," *Orlando Sentinel*, December 16, 2005.

30. Jay Stapleton, "Judge to N-J: Pay Installments," *Daytona Beach News-Journal*, September 28, 2006.

31. Jay Stapleton, "Court Upholds N-J Value," *Daytona Beach News-Journal*, December 22, 2007; Ludmilla Lelis, "News-Journal Gets Reprieve," *Orlando Sentinel*, April 22, 2008; Jay Stapleton, "Receiver in Charge of News-Journal," *Daytona Beach News-Journal*, April 29, 2009; and Stapleton, "News-Journal Directors Fired."

32. Ludmilla Lelis, "Judge Approves $20M Deal for News-Journal," *Orlando Sentinel*, March 24, 2010. See also Ludmilla Lelis, "Judge to Rule Soon on News-Journal Sale," *Orlando Sentinel*, February 2, 2010; Jim Witters, "Judge Appoints Appraisers in News-Journal Sale," *Daytona Beach News-Journal*, February 23, 2010.

33. Jay Stapleton, "N-J Sales Assets to be Distributed," *Daytona Beach News-Journal*, August 18, 2010.

34. "Chief Judge Paul M. Glenn Receives Prestigious Patton Award," *11th Circuit Historical News* 4 (Summer 2007).

35. Paul, M. Glenn, "Remarks at the Tampa Bay Bankruptcy Bar Association Honoring the Hon. Thomas E. Baynes, Jr.," June 8, 2005, fo. "Contributions," Historical Committee Files, MDFA.

36. Gary White, "Federal Judge from Lake Wales Dies at 69," *Lakeland Ledger*, December 19, 2009.

37. Helen Huntley, "Ready for Her Next Big Chapter," *St. Petersburg Times*, August 20, 2005. See also "Bankruptcy Judge McEwan Receives Pro Bono Service Award," *11th Circuit Historical News* 5 (Fall 2008).

38. Huntley, "Ready for Her Next Big Chapter"; and Joe Rauch, "Bankruptcy Court Braces for Big Case," *Jacksonville Business Journal*, April 18, 2005.

39. Alexander Paskay Oral History, 39–40.

40. Ibid.; and "Court Appoints Judge," *Tampa Bay Business Journal*, August 2, 2005.

41. Alexander Paskay Oral History, 41–42. See also "A Brief History of Bankruptcy," BankruptcyData.com, http://www.bankruptcydata.com/Ch11History.htm.

42. Joe Rauch, "Judge Moves Winn-Dixie Bankruptcy to Jacksonville," *Jacksonville Business Journal*, April 12, 2005; Rauch, "Bankruptcy Court Braces for Big Case"; Ron Word, "Winn-Dixie Submits Reorganization Plan," *Lakeland Ledger*, June 30, 2006; and "Winn-Dixie Bankruptcy Advances, *New York Times*, August 5, 2006.

43. "Delano Appointed Tampa's Newest U.S. Bankruptcy Judge," *11th Circuit Historical News* 5 (Summer 2008): 8.

44. Karen Brune Mathis, "It's a Record: Bankruptcies End 2010 Near 67,000: Middle District of Florida Filings up 8 Percent," *Jacksonville Financial News and Daily Record*, January 7, 2011.

45. Jeff Harrington, "Backlog of Bankruptcy Cases Persists," *Tampa Bay Times*, November 24, 2012.

46. Karen Jennemann to Bankruptcy Bench, April 27, 2012, Historical Committee Files, MDFA.

47. Richard Mullins, "Federal Bankruptcy Judge Alexander L. Paskay Dies," *Tampa Tribune*, April 28, 2012.

48. Glenn, "Eulogy in Memory and Honor of Alexander L. Paskay," 1, 5–6.

49. Ibid.

Chapter 21. Closing Arguments and Taking Stock

1. Tindall and Shi, *America: Narrative History*, 1126–33; and Brands, *America since 1945*, 326–28.

2. Tindall and Shi, *America: Narrative History*, 1134.

3. Ibid., 1135–37.

4. Kevin Graham, "Bucklew Leads, Others Follow," *St. Petersburg Times*, April 26, 2008.

5. Tom Brennan, "Obama Nominates Hillsborough Judge for Federal Court," *Tampa Tribune*, June 27, 2009.

6. Ibid.; Orval Jackson, "Honeywell, Gomez Seek Judgeship," *Tampa Tribune*, September 1, 1994; and David Karp, "Defeat Became Blessing for Judge," *St. Petersburg Times*, February 11, 2002.

7. Nichole Hutcheson, "Dreaming to the Top," *St. Petersburg Times*, January 30, 2010.

8. Jessie-Lynne Kerr, "After 31 Years, Jurist Takes Senior Status," *Florida Times-Union*, April 7, 2010.

9. Roy Dalton, Judge Biography File, FJC; and Foglesong, *Immigrant Prince*, 97–98, 185–88.

10. Joe Wilhelm, "Jacksonville Native Returns as Federal Judge," *Jacksonville Financial News and Daily Record*, May 31, 2011.

11. Elaine Silvestrini, "Federal Prosecutor Appointed as U.S. Magistrate Judge," *Tampa Tribune*, August 6, 2009.

12. "Judicial Snapshot: The Honorable Joel Toomey," *Jacksonville Financial News and Daily Record*, April 25, 2011.

13. Elaine Silvestrini, "Federal Prosecutor Sworn in on Lunch Break," *Tampa Tribune*, October 6, 2010. See also Robbyn Mitchell, "11 Apply for U. S Attorney Position," *St. Petersburg Times*, June 11, 2009.

14. "Jurist from St. Petersburg, Russia, Visit St. Petersburg and Tampa, Florida, on Library of Congress–based 'Open World Program,'" Open World Leadership Center, November 18, 2002, http://openworld.gov/press/print.php?id=21&lang=1.

15. Ibid.; and Graham Brink, "Justice, U.S. Style—Russians Witness Trial," *St. Petersburg Times*, November 19, 2002.

16. "Russian Judges Visit Orlando through Open World Program," Open World Leadership Center, October 25, 2004 http://openworld.gov/press/print.php?id=60&lang=1.

17. Joe Wilhelm, "Open World Program," *Jacksonville Financial News and Daily Record*, April 4, 2011.

18. "Sister Court in Slovenia," *Third Branch*, November 2010.

19. Williamson and Case, "Report on a Proposed Bankruptcy Law for Afghanistan."

20. Gregory Presnell interview with the author, December 12, 2012; and "Third Amended and Restated Guidelines and Plans for Administration of Non-Appropriated Funds," Middle District of Florida, rev. December 7, 2009, http://www.flmd.uscourts.gov/Forms/General/Plan-BarAdmissionFees12-09.pdf.

21. Elizabeth Warren to Tomlyn Wright, December 13, 2012, e-mail, copy in the author's possession; and "The Bench and Bar Fund Committee Members," and "The Historical Committee Members," in Darlene Knapp to James M. Denham, June 24, 2013, e-mail, copy in the author's possession.

22. Buhler and Elligett, "Openings of Jacksonville, Tampa Middle District Historical Exhibits," 10–11.

23. Elaine Silvestrini, "History Goes on Display at U.S. Courthouse," *Tampa Tribune*, June 14, 2010.

24. Amy Pavuk, "Exhibit Gives History of Orlando Federal-Court System," *Orlando Sentinel*, October 19, 2011.

Bibliography

Primary Sources

ARCHIVAL MATERIALS

Alexander Paskay Papers, MDFA
Bryan Simpson Papers, PKYL
Chesterfield Smith Papers, PKYL
Federal Courthouse File, FJC
George Proctor Papers, MDFA
Historical Committee Files, MDFA
"Important/Significant Decisions Judge [William Terrell] Hodges Ruled On," MDFA
Judge Biography File, FJC
McCarthy, Andrew, Taylor Ford, and Jules Cohen, "Summaries of Significant Court Decisions with Opinions Written by Judge Joseph Hatchett," May 24, 2006, MDFA
Records of Department of Justice, RG 60, NARA
Records of the District Courts of the United States, Middle District of Florida, RG 21, NARA-MG
Records of the Public Buildings Service, RG 121, NARA-CP
Records of the United States Attorney, Middle District of Florida, RG 118, NARA-MG
Senate Committee on Judiciary Files, Records of the United States Senate, RG 46, NARA
Senate Nomination Files, Records of the United States Senate, RG 46, NARA
"Significant Cases: Judge [Alexander] Paskay, Bankruptcy Court," MDFA
"Summaries of Significant Court Decisions with Opinions Written by Judge Susan Black," MDFA
Tomsich, Raequel. "Summaries of Cases of Judge William J. Castagna," MDFA
William Terrell Hodges Photo Collection, MDFA

ORAL HISTORIES

Adams, Henry, August 30, 2010, SPOHP
Black, Susan, June 26, 2007, SPOHP
Bucklew, Susan, March 30, 2012, SPOHP
Castagna, William J. September 26, 2006, SPOHP
Ellsworth, William, February 25, 27, March 5, 2004, LCCFH
Frazier, Douglas, February 25, 2012, LCCFH
Game, Paul, June 27, 2007, SPOHP

Gilbert, Leonard, December 18, 2012, LCCFH
Hatchett, Joseph, August 10, 2006, SPOHP
Hodges, William Terrell, July 10, 2006, SPOHP
———. May 29, 2012, LCCFH
Kovachevich, Elizabeth, August 26, 2010, SPOHP
Krentzman, Isaac Benjamin, 1987, SPOHP
Lazzara, Richard, March 30, 2012, SPOHP
Lundy, Roy, April 3, 2004, LCCFH
Melton, Howell W., May 15, 2004, SPOHP
Moore, John H., II, July 16, 2006, SPOHP
Paskay, Alexander, August 3, 2006, SPOHP
Presnell, Gregory March 23, 2012, SPOHP
Proctor, George L., October 18, 2002, SPOHP
Salcines, E. J., July 26, August 3, 2010, LCCFH
Schlesinger, Harvey E. November 28, 2006, SPOHP
Sessums, Terrell, August 7, 2003, LCCFH
Sharp, G. Kendall Sharp, August 26, 2004, SPOHP
Simpson, Bryan Simpson, April 12, 1987, MDFA
Spaulding, Karla R., May 15, 2012, LCCFH
Swartz, George T. January 17, 2007, SPOHP
Tjoflat, Gerald, May 17, 2007, SPOHP
Waller, David, December 12, 2012, LCCFH
Warren, Dan, May 26, 2010, LCCFH
Young, George C., June 2003, SPOHP
———. August 4, 2011, LCCFH

INTERVIEWS WITH AUTHOR

Adams, Henry Lee, Jr., May 23, 2011
Black, Susan, May 23, 2011
Bucklew, Susan, October 13, 2010, December 18, 2012
Castagna, William J., October 13, 2010
Funk, Jerry A., May 25, 2011
Graham, Bob, March 30, 2012
Greenewalt, Herman, October 18, 2012
Hudson, Chuck, February 7, 2012
Jenkins, Elizabeth, October 13, 2010, February 3, 2012
Marshall, Alysia, October 13, 2010
Melton, Howell W., May 27, 2011
Merryday, Steven S., October 14, 2010
Moody, James S., Jr., October 13, 2010
Pavese, Frank, February 26, 2013
Pizzo, Mark, October 13, 2010
Presnell, Gregory A., May 15, 2012, December 13, 2012
Schlesinger, Harvey E., May 24, 2011
Sharp, G. Kendall, July 28, 2010
Smiljanich, Terry, April 26, 2012

Smoot, Tom, February 26, 2013
Tjoflat, Gerald, May 27, 2011
Williamson, Michael G., December 18, 2012
Wilson, Thomas, October 14, 2010

MISCELLANEOUS PRIMARY SOURCES

Administrative Office of the U.S. Courts. *Justices and Judges of the United States Courts*, Washington, D.C.: U.S. Government Printing Office, 1999.
———. *Report of the Proceedings of the Judicial Conference of the United States, March 13–14, 1961*. Washington, D.C.: U.S. Government Printing Office, 1962.
———. *Reports of the Proceedings of the Judicial Conference of the United States, 1999*. Washington, D.C.: Administrative Office of the United States Courts, 1999.
Bogart, Joseph I. "History of Federal Courts of Florida," January 19, 1981. Possession of Hon. William Terrell Hodges, Copy in the author's possession.
Federal Court Management Statistics, Washington: Administrative Office of the United States Courts, (1962–2013)
Federal Judicial Center, *Guide to Research in Federal Judicial History*, 2010.
McCarthy, Cathy A., and Tara Treacy, eds. *Sixty Years of Service to the Federal Judiciary: The History of the Administrative Office of the United States*. Washington, D.C.: Administrative Office of the U.S. Courts, 2000.
"Memo of Mr. Ted Mack to Barbara Wood," 1977, Possession of Hon. William Terrell Hodges, Copy in the author's possession.
"Proceedings Attendant upon Induction of Hon. Bryan Simpson as United State District Judge, for the Southern District of Florida at Jacksonville, Florida," October 6, 1950.

Secondary Sources

Adams, James Ring, and Douglas Franz. *A Full Service Bank: How BCCI Stole Billions Around the World*. New York: Simon and Schuster, 1992.
Alexander, Roberta Sue. *"A Place of Recourse: A History of the U.S. District Court for the Southern District of Ohio, 1803–2003*. Athens: Ohio University Press, 2005.
Ambrose, Stephen E. *Nixon: The Triumph of a Politician, 1962–1972*. New York: Simon and Schuster, 1989.
Askew, Reubin O'D. "The Law Demands, and Rightly So." *University of Florida Law Review* 24 (Winter 1972): 203–6.
Barrow, Deborah J., and Thomas G. Walker. *A Court Divided: The Fifth Circuit Court of Appeals and the Politics of Judicial Reform*. New Haven, Conn.: Yale University Press, 1988.
Bartley, Abel A. "From Old South to New South, Or Was It? Jacksonville and the Modern Civil Rights Movement in Florida," in *Old South, New South or Down South?: Florida and the Modern Civil Rights Movement*, ed. Irvin D. S. Winsboro, 48–67. Morgantown: West Virginia University Press, 2009.
Bass, Jack. *Taming the Storm: The Life and Times of Judge Frank M. Johnson, Jr. and the South's Fight Over Civil Rights*. New York: Doubleday, 1993.
Beale, Sara Sun. "Federalizing Crime: Assessing the Impact on the Federal Courts." *Annals of the American Academy of Political and Social Science* 543 (January 1996): 39–51.
Beaty, Jonathon, and S. C. Gwynne. *The Outlaw Bank: A Wild Ride into the Secret Heart of BCCI*. New York: Random House, 1993.

Belknap, Michael R. *Federal Law and Southern Order: Racial Violence and Constitutional Conflict in the Post-Brown South.* Athens: University of Georgia Press, 1987.

Block, Alan A., ed. *The Organized Criminal Activities of the Bank of Credit and Commerce International: Essays and Documentation.* Dordrecht, Netherlands: Kluwer Academic Publishers, 2001.

Blum, Brian A. "Bankruptcy." In *Oxford Companion to American Law*, ed. Kermit L. Hall, 54–55. New York: Oxford University Press, 2002.

Bodenhamer, David J. *Fair Trial: Rights of the Accused in American History.* New York: Oxford University Press, 1992.

Bourne, Peter G. *Jimmy Carter: A Comprehensive Biography from Plains to Post Presidency.* New York: Scribner, 1997.

Branch, Taylor. *Pillar of Fire: America in the King Years, 1963–1965.* New York: Simon and Schuster, 1998.

Brands, H. W. *America since 1945.* Upper Saddle River, N.J.: Pearson Education, 2012.

Brinkley, Alan. "Great Society." In *A Readers Companion to American History*, ed. Eric Foner and John A. Garraty, 470–72. Boston: Houghton Mifflin, 1991.

Brown, Canter, Jr. *None Can Have Richer Memories: Polk County Florida, 1940–2000.* Tampa: University of Tampa Press, 2005.

Buck, Morison. "Edward Francis Boardman: Judge Gregarious the First (1912–1990)." Digital Collection—Florida Studies Center Publications. Paper 2474. January 2000. http://scholarcommons.usf.edu/flstud_pub/2474.

———. "George W. Whitehurst: Panoramic Jurist Extraordinaire, 1891–1974." (1998). Digital Collection—Florida Studies Center Publications. Paper 2501. http://scholarcommons.usf.edu/flstud_pub/2501.

———. "Joseph P. Lieb: Gentleman, Gentle, Judge, 1901–1971." (1990). Digital Collection—Florida Studies Center Publications. Paper 2456. http://scholarcommons.usf.edu/flstud_pub/2456.

———. "William J. Barker: Real Life Judge Hardy, 1886–1968," (1990). Digital Collection—Florida Studies Center Publications. Paper 2465. http://scholarcommons.usf.edu/flstud_pub/2465.

Buhler, Phillip A., and Raymond T. Elligett. "Openings of Jacksonville, Tampa Middle District Historical Exhibits Are Fruits of a Long-Range Plan." *11th Circuit Historical News* 7 (Summer 2010): 10–11.

Burke, John P. *Becoming President: The Bush Transition, 2000–2003.* Boulder, Colo.: Lynne Rienner, 2004.

Byers, Andy J. *The Imperfect Spy: The Inside Story of a Convicted Spy.* St. Petersburg, Fla.: Vandamere Press, 2005.

Calhoun, Frederick S. *The Lawmen: United States Marshals and Their Deputies, 1789–1989.* Washington, D.C.: Smithsonian Institution Press, 1989.

Carp, Robert A. "United States Courts." In *Oxford Companion to American Law*, ed. Kermit L. Hall. New York: Oxford University Press, 2002.

Carp, Robert A., and C. K. Rowland. *Politics and Judgment in Federal District Courts.* Lawrence: University of Kansas Press, 1996.

Carp, Robert A., and Ronald Stidham. *The Federal Courts.* Washington, D.C.: *Congressional Quarterly*, 1985.

Carter, Dan T. *The Politics of Rage: George Wallace, Conservatism, and the Transformation of American Politics.* New York: Simon and Schuster, 1995.

Chemerinsky, Erwin. "The Segregation and Resegregation of American Public Education: the Court's Role." In *School Re-segregation: Must the South Turn Back?*, ed. John Charles Boger and Gary Orfield, 29–47. Chapel Hill: University of North Carolina Press, 2005.

Clark, David S. "Adjudication to Administration: A Statistical Analysis of Federal District Courts in the Twentieth Century." *Southern California Law Review* 55 (November 1981): 69–152.

Clark, James C. *Red Pepper and Gorgeous George: Claude Pepper's Defeat in the 1950 Democratic Primary.* Gainesville: University Press of Florida, 2011.

Colburn, David R. *Racial Change and Community Crisis: St. Augustine, Florida, 1877–1980.* New York: Columbia University Press, 1985.

Colburn, David R., and Lance deHaven-Smith. *Government in the Sunshine: Florida Since Statehood.* Gainesville: University Press of Florida, 1999.

Colburn, David R., and Richard K. Scher. *Florida's Gubernatorial Politics in the Twentieth Century.* Gainesville: University of Florida Press, 1980.

Cooper, William J., and Thomas E. Terrill. *The American South: A History.* Lanham, Md.: Rowman and Littlefield, 2009.

Couch, Harvey C. *A History of the Fifth Circuit, 1891–1981.* Washington, D.C.: Bicentennial Committee of the Judicial Conference of the United States, 1984.

Crew, B. Keith. "The Death and Resurrection of Capital Punishment." In *Historic U.S. Court Cases, 1690–1990*, ed. John W. Johnson, 44–49. New York: Garland, 1992.

Days, Drew S., III. "The Other Desegregation Story: Eradicating the Dual School System in Hillsborough County, Florida." 61 *Fordham Law Review* 33 (October 1992).

Deitche, Scott M. *Cigar City Mafia: A Complete History of the Tampa Underworld.* Fort Lee, N.J.: Barricade, 2004.

Denham, James M. "Creating the United States District Court for the Middle District of Florida." *Florida Historical Quarterly* 92 (Fall 2013): 183–204.

———. *"A Rogue's Paradise": Crime and Punishment in Antebellum Florida, 1821–1861.* Tuscaloosa: University of Alabama Press, 1997.

DeVault, John A. "'Counsel, You Are Dangerously Close to Violating Rule 13!'" *Florida Bar Journal* 69, no. 9 (October 1995): 8.

Due, Tananarive, and Patricia Stephens Due. *Freedom in the Family: A Mother-Daughter Memoir of the Fight for Civil Rights.* New York: Ballantine Books, 2003.

Dyckman, Martin A. *Floridian of His Century: The Courage of Governor LeRoy Collins.* Gainesville: University Press of Florida, 2006.

———. *A Most Disorderly Court: Scandal and Reform in the Florida Judiciary.* Gainesville: University Press of Florida, 2008.

———. *Reubin O'D. Askew and the Golden Age of Florida Politics.* Gainesville: University Press of Florida, 2011.

Elligett, Raymond T. "Judge William Castagna: 30 Years on the Federal Bench," *HCBA Lawyer*, June 2009, 24–29.

Finkleman, Paul. "Earl Warren." In *The Oxford Companion to American Law*, ed. Kermit L. Hall, 827–28. New York: Oxford University Press, 2002.

Flemming, Patrick. "'Otherwise Qualified': The Rehabilitation Act of 1973 and the Origin of the Direct Threat Defense." *Florida Historical Quarterly* 92 (Fall 2013).

Foglesong, Richard E. *Immigrant Prince: Mel Martinez and the American Dream.* Gainesville: University Press of Florida. 2011.

Foner, Eric, and John A. Garraty, eds. *A Reader's Companion to American History.* Boston: Houghton Mifflin, 1991.

Frankenberg, Erica, Chungmei Lee, and Gary Orfield, eds. *A Multiracial Society with Segregated Schools: Are We Losing the Dream?* Cambridge, Mass.: Civil Rights Project, Harvard University, 2003.

Friedman, Lawrence M. *American Law in the Twentieth Century.* New Haven, Conn.: Yale University Press, 2002.

Friedman, Leon. "The Federal Courts of the South: Judge Bryan Simpson and His Reluctant Brethren," in *Southern Justice*, ed. Leon Friedman, 187–213. New York: Random House, 1965.

Gannon, Michael, ed. *The New History of Florida.* Gainesville: University Press of Florida, 1996.

Garrow, David J. *Bearing the Cross: Martin Luther King Jr. and the Southern Christian Leadership Conference.* New York: Random House, 1986.

———, ed. *St. Augustine, Florida, 1963–1964.* Brooklyn, N.Y.: Carlson Publishing, 1989.

Geib, George W., and Donald B. Kite. *Federal Justice in Indiana: The History of the United States District Court for the Southern District of Indiana.* Indianapolis: Indiana Historical Society, 2007.

George, Lloyd D. "From Orphan to Maturity: The Development of the Bankruptcy System during Ralph Mecham's Tenure as Director of the Administrative Office of the United States Courts." *American University Law Review* 44 (June 1995): 1491–1501.

"A Giant in the Field of Bankruptcy Law, a Scholar, a Mentor, a Wise Human Being: Remembrances of Judge Alexander Paskay." *11th Circuit History News* 9 (Summer 2012): 6–12.

Glenn, Paul. "Eulogy in Memory and Honor of Alexander L. Paskay, November 5, 1922–April 27, 2012." *11th Circuit Historical News* 9 (Summer 2012): 1, 5–6.

Goldman, Sheldon. *Picking Federal Judges: Lower Court Selection from Roosevelt through Reagan.* New Haven, Conn.: Yale University Press, 1997.

Goulden, Joseph G. *The Bench Warmers: The Private World of the Powerful Federal Judges.* New York: Weybright and Talley, 1974.

Gragido, Will, and John Pirc. *Cybercrime and Espionage: An Analysis of Subversive Multi-Vector Threats.* Burlington, MA: Elsevier Inc., 2011.

Graham, Hugh Davis. *The Civil Rights Era: Origins and Development of a National Policy.* New York: Oxford University Press, 1990.

Green, Robert P., Jr. "The School Busing Case." In *Historic U.S. Court Cases, 1690–1990: An Encyclopedia*, ed. John W. Johnson. New York: Garland, 1992.

Greene, Abner. *Understanding the 2000 Election: A Guide to the Legal Battles That Decided the Presidency.* New York: New York University Press, 2001.

Gugliotta, Guy, and Jeff Leen. *Kings of Cocaine: Inside the Medellín Cartel: An Astounding True Story of Murder, Money, and International Corruption.* New York: Simon and Schuster, 1989.

Haldeman, H. R. *The Haldeman Diaries: Inside the Nixon White House*. New York: Putnam, 1994.

Hall, Kermit L., ed. *The Oxford Companion to the American Law*. New York: Oxford University Press, 2002.

———. *The Magic Mirror: Law in American History*. New York: Oxford University Press, 1989.

Hall, Kermit L., and Eric W. Rise, *From Local Courts to National Tribunals: Federal District Courts of Florida, 1821–1990*. Brooklyn, N.Y.: Carlson Publishing, 1991.

Hodges, William Terrell, David L. Edwards, and Susan H. Walsh. "The Middle District of Florida." *Florida Bar Journal* 63 (December 1989): 19–22.

———. "Segregation and Integration in the Middle District of Florida, 1962–2012." Paper presented at 50th Anniversary of the Creation of the Middle District of Florida Academic Symposium, Orlando, Florida, October 26, 2012.

Hoffman, Joseph L., and Lauren K. Robel, "Federal Court Supervision of State Criminal Justice Administration." *Annals of the American Academy of Political Science and Social Science* 543 (January 1996): 154–66.

Hough, Marie T., Bernadette Grabb, and Nancy Woolfolk. *The American Bench: Judges of the Nation*, 5th ed. Sacramento: Foster-Long, Inc. 1989.

Houston, Benjamin. "Voice of the Exploited Majority: Claude Kirk and the 1970 Manatee County Forced Busing Incident." *Florida Historical Quarterly* 83 (Winter 2005): 258–86.

Jackson, Donald Dale. *Judges*. New York: Atheneum, 1974.

Johnson, David R. *American Law Enforcement: A History*. Arlington Heights, Ill.: Forum Press, 1981.

Johnson, Herbert A., and Nancy Travis Wolfe. *History of Criminal Justice*, 2nd ed. Cincinnati: Anderson Publishing, 1996.

Johnson, John W. *Historic U.S. Court Cases, 1690–1990: An Encyclopedia*. New York: Garland, 1992.

Johnson, Malcolm B. *I Declare: A Collection of Editorial Commentaries*. Tallahassee: *Tallahassee Democrat*, 1983.

Jung, William F. "The Last Unlikely Hero: Gerald Bard Tjoflat and the Jacksonville Desegregation Crisis—35 Years Later." *The Federal Lawyer*, July 2006, 30–34.

Kallina, Edmund F., Jr. *Claude Kirk and the Politics of Confrontation*. Gainesville: University Press of Florida, 1993.

Karl, Frederick B. *The 57 Club: My Four Decades in Florida Politics*. Gainesville: University Press of Florida, 2010.

Kay, Julie. "New Chief Judge to Start for Middle District of Florida." *National Law Journal*, August 22, 2008.

Kelly, Robert J. "Organized Crime." In *Oxford Companion to American Law*, ed. Kermit L. Hall, 593–94. New York: Oxford University Press, 2002.

Kunstler, William W. *Deep in My Heart*. New York: William Morrow, 1966.

Landers, Renee M. "Prosecutorial Limits on Overlapping Federal and State Jurisdiction." *Annals of the American Political and Social Science* 543 (January 1996): 64–71.

Larson, Lawrence H. *Federal Justice in Western Missouri: The Judges, the Cases, the Times*. Columbia: University of Missouri Press, 1994.

Lassiter, Mathew D. *The Silent Majority: Suburban Politics in the Sunbelt South*. Princeton, N.J.: Princeton University Press, 2007.

Lender, Mark Edward. *"This Honorable Court": The United States District Court for the District of New Jersey, 1789–2000*. New Brunswick, N.J.: Rutgers University Press, 2000.

Lyles, Kevin L. *The Gatekeepers: Federal District Courts in the Political Process*. Westport, Conn.: Praeger, 1997.

Lynch, S. Brendan. "Hon. Anne Conway: Chief U.S. District Judge, Middle District of Florida." *Federal Lawyer*, May 2009, 24–28.

Mack, Edward (Ted). "Some Recollections of Federal Courts in Tampa, 1940–1970," 1991. Unpublished paper in the author's possession.

Manley, Walter W., II, E. Canter Brown Jr., and Eric W. Rise. *The Supreme Court of Florida and Its Predecessor Courts, 1821–1917*. Gainesville: University Press of Florida, 1997.

Marion, Nancy E. *A History of Federal Crime Control Initiatives, 1960–1993*. Westport, Conn: Praeger, 1994.

Mauldin, Gregory B. "Hon. Gerald Bard Tjoflat: U.S. Circuit Judge, U.S. Court of Appeals for the Eleventh Circuit," *Federal Lawyer*, January 2010, 24–28.

Mauro, Tony. "High Court Turns away Question: Is Prayer at School Events Constitutional." *Freedom Forum*, December 11, 2001. http://www.freedomforum.org/templates/document.asp?documentID=15512.

McFeeley, Neil D. *The Appointment of Judges: The Johnson Presidency*. Austin: University of Texas Press, 1987.

McLain, Denny, and Mike Nahrstedt. *Strikeout: The Story of Denny McLain*. St. Louis: Sporting News Publishing Company, 1988.

Mohl, Raymond A., and Gary Mormino, "The Big Change in the Sunshine State: A Social History in Modern Florida," in *The New History of Florida*, ed. Michael Gannon, 418–46. Gainesville: University Press of Florida, 1996.

Moran, Marilyn G. "Hon. Gregory A. Presnell: U.S. District Judge, Middle District of Florida." *Federal Lawyer*, July 2005, 42–43.

Mormino, Gary R. *Land of Sunshine, State of Dreams: A Social History of Modern Florida*. Gainesville: University Press of Florida, 2005.

Morris, Allen, and Joan Perry Morris, comp. *The Florida Handbook, 2003–2004*. Tallahassee: Peninsular Publishing Company, 2003.

Murphy, Paul. "To Pray or Not to Pray: The Supreme Court Says No to Prayer in the Public Schools." In *Historic U.S. Court Cases, 1690–1990*, ed. John W. Johnson, 572–77. New York: Garland, 1992.

Nagle, Ilene. "Structuring Sentencing Discretion: The New Federal Sentencing Guidelines." *Journal of Criminal Law and Criminology* 80 (1990): 883–943.

Nimmer, Raymond T. "Bankruptcy: Business." In *Oxford Companion to American Law*, ed. Kermit L. Hall, 57–59. New York: Oxford University Press, 2002.

———. "Bankruptcy: Personal." In *Oxford Companion to American Law*, ed. Kermit L. Hall, 55–56. New York: Oxford University Press, 2002.

O'Bryant, JoAnne. "Crime Control: The Federal Response." *Congressional Research Service*, March 5, 2003.

Orfield, Gary. *Public School Desegregation in the United States, 1968–1980*. Washington, D.C.: Joint Center for Political Studies, 1983.

Orfield, Gary, and Susan E. Eaton, ed. *Dismantling Desegregation: The Quiet Reversal of Brown v. Board of Education.* New York: Free Press, 1996.

Orrick, Bentley, and Harry L. Crumpacker. *The Tampa Tribune: A Century of Journalism.* Tampa: University of Tampa Press, 1998.

Patterson, James T. *Brown v. Board of Education: A Civil Rights Milestone and Its Troubled Legacy.* New York: Oxford University Press, 2001.

———. "The Rise of Rights and Rights Consciousness in American Politics, 1930s–1970s," in *Contesting Democracy: Substance and Structure in American Political History, 1775–2000,* ed Byron E. Shafer and Anthony J. Badger, 201–23. Lawrence: University of Kansas Press, 2001.

Pleasants, Julian M. *Hanging Chads: The Inside Story of the 2000 Presidential Recount in Florida.* Gordonville, Va.: Palgrave, 2004.

Potok, Mark. "C-4 and the Confederacy." *Southern Poverty Law Center Intelligence Report,* no. 115 (Fall 2004). http://www.splcenter.org/get-informed/intelligence-report/browse-all-issues/2004/fall/scv-standoff/c-4-and-the-confederacy.

Powers, Ormund. *E. C.: Mr. Speaker, E. C. Rowell.* Webster, Fla.: The Honorable Board of Governors of the E. C. Rowell Public Library at Webster, Florida, 1977.

———. *Martin Anderson: Editor, Publisher, Galley Boy.* Chicago: Contemporary Books, 1996.

Price, Tara R. "You've Come a Long Way, Baby: Stripping Pornography from America's Workplaces." *Florida Historical Quarterly* 92, no. 2 (Fall 2013): 261–75.

Radelet, Michael, Hugo Adam Bedau, and Constance E. Putnam. *In Spite of Innocence: The Ordeal of 400 Americans Wrongly Convicted of Crimes Punishable by Death.* Boston: Northeastern University Press, 1992.

Read, Frank T., and Lucy S. McGough. *Let Them Be Judged: The Judicial Integration of the Deep South.* Metuchen, N.J: Scarecrow Press, 1978.

Reeves, Richard. *President Kennedy: Profile of Power.* New York: Simon and Schuster, 1993.

Rehnquist, William H. "The 1998 Year-End Report of the Federal Judiciary." *Third Branch,* January 1, 1999. http://www.uscourts.gov/News/TheThirdBranch/99-01-01/The_1998_Year-End_Report_of_the_Federal_Judiciary.aspx.

Reitz, Kevin R. "The Federal Role in Sentencing Law and Policy." *Annals of the American Academy of Political and Social Science* 543 (January 1996): 116–29.

Russomanno, Herman J. "Florida's Winning Team: U.S. Senators Graham and Mack Protecting Floridian's Right to Justice." *Florida Bar Journal* 75 (January 2001).

Sabbag, Robert. *Too Tough to Die: Down and Dangerous with the U.S. Marshals.* New York: Simon and Schuster, 1992.

Sanders, Randy. *Mighty Peculiar Elections: The New South Gubernatorial Campaigns of 1970 and the Changing Politics of Race.* Gainesville: University Press of Florida, 2002.

———. "Rasseling a Governor: Defiance, Desegregation, Claude Kirk, and the Politics of Nixon's Southern Strategy." *Florida Historical Quarterly* 80 (Winter 2002): 332–59.

Saunders, Robert W. *Bridging the Gap: Continuing the Florida NAACP Legacy of Harry T. Moore.* Tampa: University of Tampa Press, 2000.

Schnur, James A. "Desegregation of Public Schools in Pinellas County, Florida." 1991. Copy in University of South Florida Special Collections, Tampa, Florida.

Sheppard, William J. "Early Jail and Prison Conditions Litigation in the Middle District of

Florida." Paper presented at 50th Anniversary of the Creation of the Middle District of Florida Academic Symposium, Orlando, Florida, October 26, 2012.

Shitama, Mariko. "A Pioneer in Prison Reform: *Costello v. Wainwright* and Its Paradoxical Legacy in Florida Prisons." *Florida Historical Quarterly* 92, no. 2 (Fall 2013): 381–96.

Skene, Neil. "Reapportionment in Florida." In *The Florida Handbook, 2003–2004*, comp. Allen Morris and Joan Perry Morris, 178–82. Tallahassee: Peninsular Publishing Company, 2003.

Slate, Claudia. "Battle for St. Augustine: Public Record and Personal Reflection." *Florida Historical Quarterly* 84 (Spring 2006): 541–68.

Smith, Christopher E. "From U.S. Magistrates to U.S. Magistrate Judges: Developments Affecting the Federal District Courts' Lower Tier of Judicial Officers." *Judicature* 75 (December–January 1992): 210–14.

———. *United States Magistrates in the Federal Courts: Subordinate Judges*. Westport, Conn.: Praeger, 1990.

Staver, Mathew D. "Legal Memorandum on Graduation Prayers in Public Schools." *Liberty Counsel*, 2005–2007. http://www.lc.org/resources/memogradprayer.pdf.

Stuart, Devan. "Grit and Grace: Chief Judge Patricia Fawsett Goes Senior." *Orlando Lawyer Magazine*, July 2008, 15–19.

———. "He Ain't No Heavy: No Nonsense Judge Has a Soft Side—So Long as you Mind Your Ps." *Jacksonville Lawyer Magazine*, November 2008, 19–22.

———. "Judge Henry Lee Adams: Making Good, Making History." *Jacksonville Lawyer Magazine*, January 2007, 26–34.

Thomas, Gordon. *Secret Wars: One Hundred Years of British Intelligence Inside MI5 and MI6*. New York: Macmillan, 2010.

Thompson, Bailey H. "Orlando's Martin Anderson: Power Behind the Boom." *Florida Historical Quarterly* 79 (Spring 2001): 492–516.

Tindall, George Brown, and David Emory Shi. *America: A Narrative History*, brief 8th ed. New York: Norton, 2009.

Wainscott, Stephen H. "From the 'Political Thicket' to 'One Man, One Vote.'" In *Historic U.S. Court Cases, 1690–1990: An Encyclopedia*, ed. John W. Johnson, 124–32. New York: Garland, 1992.

Warren, Dan. *If It Takes All Summer: Martin Luther King, the KKK, and State's Rights in St. Augustine, 1964*. Tuscaloosa: University of Alabama Press, 2008.

Wilkinson, J. Harvie. *From Brown to Bakke: The Supreme Court and School Integration: 1954–1978*. New York: Oxford University Press, 1979.

Williamson, Michael, and Charles G. Case II. "Report on a Proposed Bankruptcy Law for Afghanistan: USAID Economic Growth and Governance Initiative," July 23, 2010. Copy in the author's possession.

Wilson, Steven Harmon. *The Rise of Judicial Management in the U. S. District Court, Southern District of Texas, 1955–2000*. Athens: University of Georgia Press, 2002.

Winsboro, Irvin D. S. "Brotherhood of Defiance: The State-Local Relationship of the Desegregation of the Lee County Public Schools, 1954–1969," in *Old South, New South or Down South?: Florida and the Modern Civil Rights Movement*, ed. Irvin D. S. Winsboro, 68–86. Morgantown: West Virginia University Press, 2009.

Index

James M. Denham is professor of history and the director of the Lawton M. Chiles Jr. Center for Florida History at Florida Southern College. Before coming to Lakeland in 1991, Denham held teaching appointments at Florida State University (FSU), Georgia Southern University, and Limestone College in South Carolina. A specialist in southern, Florida, and criminal justice and legal history, he is the author of *"A Rogue's Paradise": Crime and Punishment in Antebellum Florida, 1821–1861*; *Florida Sheriffs: A History, 1821–1945*, with William W. Rogers; *Cracker Times and Pioneer Lives: The Florida Reminiscences of George Gillette Keen and Sarah Pamela Williams*, with Canter Brown Jr.; and *Echoes from a Distant Frontier: The Brown Sisters' Correspondence in Antebellum Florida*, with Keith Huneycutt.

*　　*　　*

The University Press of Florida is the scholarly publishing agency for the State University System of Florida, comprising Florida A&M University, Florida Atlantic University, Florida Gulf Coast University, Florida International University, Florida State University, New College of Florida, University of Central Florida, University of Florida, University of North Florida, University of South Florida, and University of West Florida.